WAY

THE O━━━━━━━━━━IDE

WordPerfect®

Office 2002

THE OFFICIAL GUIDE

WordPerfect® IIIIIIII Office 2002

Alan
Neibauer

Osborne McGraw-Hill

Berkeley   New York   St. Louis   San Francisco
Auckland   Bogotá   Hamburg   London
Madrid   Mexico City   Milan   Montreal   New Delhi
Panama City   Paris   São Paulo
Singapore   Sydney   Tokyo   Toronto

Osborne/McGraw-Hill
2600 Tenth Street
Berkeley, California 94710
U.S.A.

For information on translations or book distributors outside the U.S.A., or to arrange bulk purchase discounts for sales promotions, premiums, or fund-raisers, please contact Osborne/McGraw-Hill at the above address.

WordPerfect® Office 2002: The Official Guide

34567890 DOC DOC 0198765432

ISBN 0-07-213249-3

Publisher: Brandon A. Nordin
Vice President and Associate Publisher: Scott Rogers
Acquisitions Editor: Megg Bonar
Acquisitions Coordinator: Alissa Larson
Technical Editor: Corel Corporation
Copy Editor: Alison de Grassi
Production and Editorial: Apollo Printing and Typesetting
Series Design: Mickey Galicia & Peter F. Hancik

This book was composed with Corel VENTURA™ Publisher.

Dedication

To Barbara, the one I love

About the Author...

Alan Neibauer is the best-selling author of Osborne's wildly successful *Corel WordPerfect Suite 8: The Official Guide*, as well as over 40 other computer book titles. A graduate of the Wharton School, University of Pennsylvania, Neibauer has worked as a high school and college teacher, and has been an enthusiastic user and respected expert on WordPerfect since version 4.2 in the days of DOS.

Contents At A Glance

Contents

xii WordPerfect Office 2002: The Official Guide

Foreword

With the availability of WordPerfect® Office 2002, Corel is delivering a high-performance, affordable office solution designed for maximum ease of use and packed with features that will help you get the job done. WordPerfect Office 2002 offers you the latest office software, graphics and Internet tools to help boost productivity, and gives you enhanced compatibility within the software suite as well as the latest Internet features. With leading-edge technology including new facets in the CorelCENTRAL™ groupware to allow users to collaborate across a local area network, and the addition of CorelCENTRAL™ Mail, the WordPerfect Office 2002 Suite offers exciting new features. Further, the cross-application compatibility with Microsoft® Visual Basic® for Applications allows current and future WordPerfect users to enjoy a familiar environment and remain technologically current and compatible.

WordPerfect Office 2002 provides an office suite that gives you multiple ways of getting a job done. Now you can focus more on attaining results instead of figuring out how to use your software. In fact, the *whole focus* of WordPerfect Office 2002 is on performance, compatibility, and value, so that you can make the most of your office software.

Just as WordPerfect Office 2002 provides a solution to enhance your productivity, so does this *Official Guide to WordPerfect Office 2002*. In your hands you hold a guide which was developed in conjunction with the WordPerfect Office 2002 team at Corel – a guide designed to help you make the most of your software tools. This book will show you how to quickly upgrade to the WordPerfect working environment with its familiar interface and increased power and more features.

Corel is excited about the new technologies now available with WordPerfect Office 2002, and we invite you to follow along in this CorelPRESS™ Official Guide. Author Alan Neibauer, along with the WordPerfect Product Team at Corel, spent many hours working on the accuracy and features of this book, and we think you'll appreciate our efforts.

The Official Guides to Corel software represent a giant step in the ability of Corel to disseminate information to our users with the help of Osborne/McGraw-Hill and the creation of the CorelPRESS series of books. Congratulations to the team at Osborne who have created this excellent book, and to the team at Corel who supported the creation of this book!

Derek J Burney
CEO and Chairman, Corel Corporation
Ottawa, Ontario
April 2001

Acknowledgments

In 1987 I wrote a book about an up-and-coming word processing program called WordPerfect, version 4.2. No one bothered distinguishing between DOS and Windows programs back then because Windows just wasn't around, and few of us even owned a mouse. WordPerfect ran nicely on a computer with just two floppy disks (the huge 5.25" ones) and was making a name for itself. After all, here was a program that didn't even need a hard disk, could work with a variety of printers, and would even underline without me typing special codes.

Since then, the world has seen some drastic changes and computer software has gone through several evolutions. Probably not even a handful of WordPerfect 4.2 users could have envisioned the power and versatility that would be before them on the screen with WordPerfect Office 2002.

What hasn't changed, however, is the resilient spirit of editors, proofreaders, designers, and others whose daily grind it is to publish books. They wait for no one, but march on steadfastly from one project to another, like a relay race without end.

The wonderful crew that made this book possible is well ahead of the pack. My thanks to everyone who worked on this project, especially acquisitions editor Megg Bonar, editorial assistant Alissa Larson, project editor Jan Benes, copy editor Alison de Grassi, and indexer Valerie Robbins. Thanks also to the team at Corel for taking time from their active development cycle to check the accuracy of this book.

Working alongside of me throughout this entire project has been a remarkable woman, my wife Barbara. She was always there with a helping hand, a kind word, a gentle nudge, and a captivating smile. We're working on our fourth decade as a couple, and I'm still looking forward to her surprises.

Introduction

WordPerfect Office 2002 is a remarkable suite of programs and utilities designed to create and polish documents and information of all types – on paper, on screen, as electronic mail and faxes, and for the world to see on the Internet. The standard edition of WordPerfect Office 20002 includes these powerful core programs:

- WordPerfect 10
- Quattro Pro 10
- Corel Presentations 10
- CorelCENTRAL 10

But the suite all includes:

- Thousand clipart images and graphics
- Hundreds of fonts
- Bitstream Font Navigator
- Adobe Acrobat Reader
- Net2Phone
- Quick View Plus

The Official Guide to WordPerfect® Office 2002 covers all of the suite's key features with enough detail and illustrations so you'll be using the software almost as fast as you can install it. As a Corel "Official Guide," every instruction in the book has been checked and approved by the experts at Corel Corporation, and just like the WordPerfect Office 2002 itself, this book packs quite a punch.

In the first two chapters you will learn to use the common elements that run through the suite's major applications—including the Corel Address Book, file management with QuickFinder, the Scrapbook for inserting clipart, and writing tools such as Spell Check, Thesaurus, Grammatik, the Dictionary, and QuickCorrect. You will learn to use Bitstream Font Navigator to manage fonts, how to create your own Adobe Acrobat PDF files to share with friends and colleagues, how to view all types of files using Quick View Plus, and how to make free phone calls and faxes using Net2Phone.

Because the suite is integrated with the Net, in Chapter 3 you will learn how to use WordPerfect Office 2002 applications to send e-mail and to create Web documents. In Chapter 4, you will learn how to use CorelCENTRAL to organize your schedule and address books, and to keep track of tasks. You'll also learn the exciting new features of CorelCENTRAL that let you share and collaborate with schedules over your local area network, and how to use CorelCENTRAL Mail for sending and receiving mail over the Internet.

Chapters 5 through 14 are all about WordPerfect 10 the powerhouse word processing program praised by millions of devoted users around the world. In Chapter 5 you will learn how to create, save, and print documents, as well as how to check your spelling as you type, insert and delete text, and change the view and magnification of text and graphics on the screen. Chapter 6 is all about editing documents, and teaches you how to perform tasks such as moving and copying text, finding and replacing text, inserting comments and bookmarks, working with multiple windows, and revising documents. Formatting characters, lines, and paragraphs is covered in Chapter 7. In Chapter 8 you will learn how to create professional-looking documents using templates and styles. Templates let you create completely formatted documents, such as newsletters, with a few clicks of the mouse.

In Chapter 9 you will learn how to format pages by changing margins and page size, set up pages for binding and printing on both sides, and print booklets, envelopes, and labels. Creating tables and working with columns are covered in Chapter 10. You will learn how to create and format tables, even adding formulas and functions to perform math, and how to create multiple-column documents. You'll also learn how to insert footnotes and endnotes, create an index and table of contents, build a table of authorities for legal references, and add cross-references.

If you want to customize Corel WordPerfect or create macros to save you from repeating keystrokes, then check out Chapter 11. There you will also learn how to create custom toolbars and menus, and how to assign key combinations to your favorite tasks.

Creating form documents is covered in Chapter 12, and you'll learn all about Corel WordPerfect's graphics features in Chapter 13, which includes sections about adding pictures and charts, formatting equations, and creating special effects with text. Finally, you will learn how to share information between applications in Chapter 14, so you won't have to retype any information to use it in another program.

Quattro Pro 10 is the focus of Chapters 15 through 22. This powerful program lets you create worksheets, graphs and maps, databases, and even slide shows. After learning what the program is all about in Chapter 15, you will learn how to create worksheets in Chapter 16, and Chapter 17 teaches you how to edit and format worksheet contents.

Chapter 18 explains how to work with blocks of information, use multiple windows, and manipulate entire notebooks. In Chapter 19 you'll learn how to work with formulas and functions. Adding maps, charts, and graphics to worksheets is discussed in Chapter 20. Using the map feature, for example, you can show a map of the United States, along with major highways, illustrating the geographic distribution of your company's sales or organization's membership.

In Chapter 21 you will learn how to use sophisticated but easy tools to analyze the information in your worksheet, and in Chapter 22 you'll learn how to create macros and share information with other applications.

Corel Presentations 10 is covered in Chapters 23 through 25. You will learn how to create slides of all types in Chapter 23, add eye-catching graphics in Chapter 24, and then build complete slide shows in Chapter 25. You'll even learn how to take your slide show on the road, and how to publish it to the Internet completed with framed pages.

Because this book is organized by WordPerfect Office 2002 application, you do not have to read it from cover to cover. You should read the first two chapters to get acquainted with the suite, but then you can jump ahead to the section or chapter you are most interested in. You can read the other sections later to learn how the remaining applications and features work, so you can take full advantage of the suite. You'll find easy-to-follow, step-by-step instructions and clear but complete details on the features that you'll want to use.

You'll also find some helpful elements along the way:

Look for these tips to learn how the features of the Suite applications are integrated.

 Here you'll find some additional bits of information about the topic being discussed.

 Look here for shortcuts or special techniques.

CAUTION *Keep an eye out for these warnings about potential problems.*

Integrate IT! *Here you'll learn how to share information among WordPerfect Office 2002 applications.*

Following chapters 5 through 25, you'll find a hands-on exercise, called Try It Out. These exercises take you through some of the key tasks covered in the chapter, so you get additional experience creating real-life documents, spreadsheets, and presentations.

WordPerfect Office 2002 is perfect for use in the office, classroom, home, or dorm. The more you use it, the more features you'll find, and you'll grow to love its ease and versatility. In fact, once you get CorelCENTRAL Mail up and running, use it to drop me a line describing what you like best about the suite. You can reach me at aneibauer@yahoo.com.

Part 1

Guide to WordPerfect Office 2002

Chapter 1

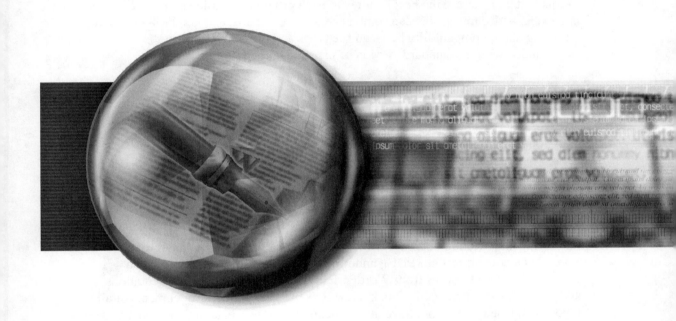

The WordPerfect
Office 2002 Suite

WordPerfect Office 2002 is a complete set of desktop applications and tools for creating, publishing, and distributing documents of all types. The applications are integrated to provide stand-alone and workgroup solutions and easy access to the Internet and online services.

Integration means the convenient flow from one application to another. It also means that you can use the best features of each program to build *compound documents*—documents that can combine text, tables, charts, and graphics—without worrying about compatibility between file types and program features.

Included with the standard version of the suite are these programs:

- WordPerfect 10
- Quattro Pro 10
- Corel Presentations 10
- CorelCENTRAL 10

You also get about 1000 fonts, Bitstream Font Navigator, Net2Phone for making PC to phone and PC to PC calls over the Internet, and thousands of clip art images. WordPerfect Office 2002 also includes Adobe Acrobat Reader for displaying and printing documents and online manuals in the popular Acrobat Portable Document format (PDF), and it includes Acrobat drivers that let you create your own PDF files from WordPerfect documents and Corel Presentations slide shows. Also included is Quick View Plus that lets you view documents of all types even when you do not have the application used to create the document installed on your system.

NOTE	*WordPerfect Office 2002 Professional includes Dragon NaturallySpeaking, powerful speech recognition software, Paradox 10 for database management, as well as other programs and utilities.*

To make WordPerfect Office 2002 easy to use, the main applications are installed directly on the Windows taskbar, and you can access them from the Start menu. Click on the Start button, and point to Programs and then WordPerfect Office 2002 to see the applications that you've installed and other options as shown in Figure 1-1. To start a WordPerfect Office 2002 application or accessory, just click on the program name in the Start menu, or use the Desktop Application Director (DAD).

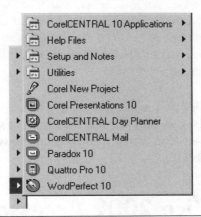

FIGURE 1-1   WordPerfect Office 2002 on the Start menu

 WordPerfect Office 2002 applications and utilities are designed to work together. So, for example, you can easily insert a Quattro Pro 10 worksheet into a Corel Presentations 10 slide and into a WordPerfect 10 document.

Desktop Application Director

A series of buttons to start the WordPerfect Office 2002 applications and special features has been placed within the Windows taskbar. This series is called the *Desktop Application Director* (DAD), shown in Figure 1-2. Click on the button to run the program you want.

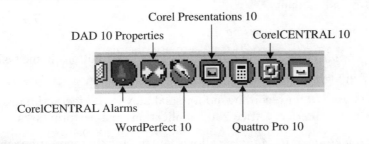

FIGURE 1-2   Desktop Application Director

If the DAD buttons do not appear on your Windows taskbar, you'll need to install the DAD from the WordPerfect Office 2002 CD.

 If the Quick Alarm button does not appear in the DAD bar you'll need to start Alarms from the Start menu.

You can also right-click on the buttons to launch one of the features from a menu, to exit (remove) the bar, or to display the Properties dialog box to remove specific items from the bar. You can also add any currently installed application to the DAD bar for easy access.

WordPerfect Office 2002 Accessories

In addition to the major applications and the Desktop Application Director, WordPerfect Office 2002 includes some useful accessories. To access them, click on the Start button, point to Programs and then WordPerfect Office 2002, and then point to Setup and Notes or Utilities to see a menu of additional items.

Utilities

The Utilities submenu contains these items:

- *Bitstream Font Navigator* for finding, installing, and organizing fonts.

- *CARM Organizer (Corel Applications Recovery Manager)* for tracking and reporting software problems.

- *Corel Web Server* opens a full-function Web server.

- *CorelCENTRAL Admin* for creating and managing CorelCENTRAL databases and accounts.

- *Corel Connector* for browsing the web.

- *Desktop Application Director 10* displays the DAD buttons in the taskbar if they are not already displayed.

- *PerfectScript 10* for recording, editing and playing PerfectScript macros that open WordPerfect Office 2002 applications and perform tasks.

- *Corel QuickFinder 10 Manager* allows you to quickly search frequently used files and folders.

- *Corel QuickFinder 10 Searcher* launches QuickFinder to locate a file or folder.

- *WordPerfect XML Project Designer* lets you create layouts for an XML document.

> **NOTE**   *Depending on your installation, you may also have other utilities and programs on your WordPerfect menus.*

Setup and Notes

The items in this menu help you find information or set up WordPerfect Office 2002 and its applications. The options are as follows:

- *Approved Service Bureau* lists the names, addresses, and telephone numbers of authorized trainers and service bureaus around the world.

- *Corel Registration* for registering your copy of WordPerfect Office over the Internet.

- *Corel Setup Program* lets you modify your installation by adding or deleting components.

- *Corel Uninstaller* removes the suite from your system.

- *Release Notes* displays last-minute information about the suite.

- *Technical Support Online* explains how to get customer support.

- *Training and Certification Resources* explains how to get professional assistance and training.

CorelCENTRAL Programs

Two of the most popular CorelCENTRAL programs – CorelCENTRAL Day Planner and CorelCENTRAL Mail — are listed on the WordPerfect menu along with other applications. Point to CorelCENTRAL 10 Applications to access these additional features:

- *CorelCENTRAL Address Book* lets you maintain an address book of contacts. You'll learn about the Address Book later in this chapter.

- *CorelCENTRAL Alarms* inserts an icon in the taskbar for setting reminders on the desktop.

- *CorelCENTRAL Calendar* lets you record and schedule your appointments and meetings.

- *CorelCENTRAL Cardfile* lets you create databases to track information.

- *CorelCENTRAL Day Planner* keeps track of current appointments and events.

- *CorelCENTRAL Mail* for sending and receiving e-mail over the Internet.

- *CorelCENTRAL Memos* lets you make notes to yourself for quick recall.

- *CorelCENTRAL Profile Manager* for organizing and maintaining e-mail accounts.

QuickFinder Searcher

Even with the Windows Explorer, finding the correct file on your hard disk can be a problem. The suite can help you, though, with QuickFinder Searcher. Not only is QuickFinder Searcher available in the Tools menu, it is also integrated into most WordPerfect Office 2002 file management dialog boxes (when enhanced dialogs are enabled). For example, when you open or save a document using Open and Save, you have full access to the QuickFinder Searcher system.

Since QuickFinder Searcher is a common utility found in all WordPerfect Office 2002 applications, we'll discuss it in Chapter 2. If the QuickFinder Searcher is not on your file management dialogs, click Tools > Settings in WordPerfect and Corel Presentations to enable it.

CorelCENTRAL Address Book

Use the *CorelCENTRAL Address Book* to store names, addresses, telephone numbers, e-mail addresses, and other useful information about the people you contact. You can also store information about organizations, grouping your contacts according to their company or other affiliation. The Address Book is fully integrated into WordPerfect Office 2002; you can access it directly from WordPerfect 10 when creating letters, envelopes, and labels. You should add your own information to the Address Book—for example, to use with WordPerfect 10 templates, so your name and address appear on fax cover pages and letters.

To open the address book, select CorelCENTRAL Address Book from the CorelCENTRAL 10 Applications menu.

If this is the first time you started the Address Book application, a dialog box appears asking if you want to open an existing address book or create a new one. Select to create a new address book and then click OK to display the options shown in Figure 1-3.

Choose Personal if you do not want other users of your computer to have access to the address book. Click Next. Enter the address book name and then click Finish. If a box appears asking if you want to create the directory, click Yes. The address book opens, as shown in Figure 1-4. You may have other items listed in the address book depending on your setup.

The CorelCENTRAL Address Book is more than just an address book. It is an application that lets you access a number of address books, which are listed in the pane on the left.

To see the listing within a book, click on it in the left pane. The addresses appear on the right. The options available for you when you add a person to an

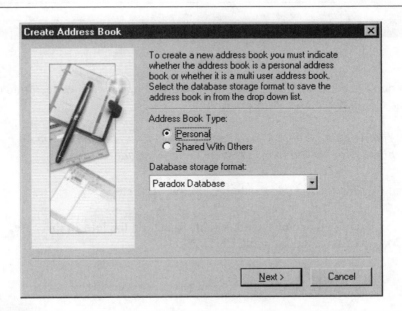

FIGURE 1-3   Select the type of address book

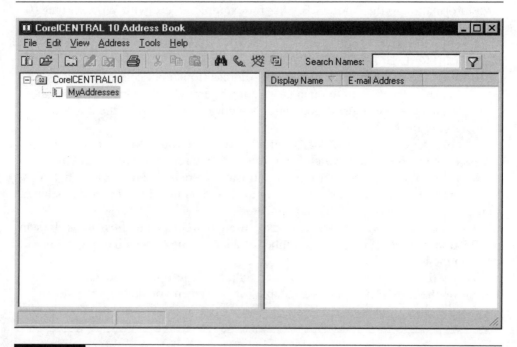

FIGURE 1-4   Typical CorelCENTRAL Address Book

address book depend on the type of book. In this chapter we'll concentrate on using the CorelCENTRAL Address Book.

> **NOTE** *You will not be able to add items to an address book that you do not have permission to add items to, such as network address books.*

To add a person to an address book, follow these steps:

1. Click on the name of the book in the panel on the left. In this case, MyAddresses under CorelCENTRAL 10.

 ←——— Create a new address entry

2. Click the Create a New Address Entry button on the toolbar, or select New from the Address menu. A dialog box appears with four options:

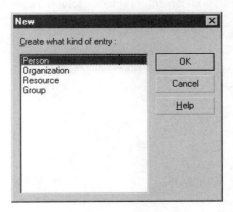

3. To add someone, click on Person and then on OK. You'll see the dialog box shown in Figure 1-5.

4. Enter information into the tabs of the dialog box, and then click on OK.

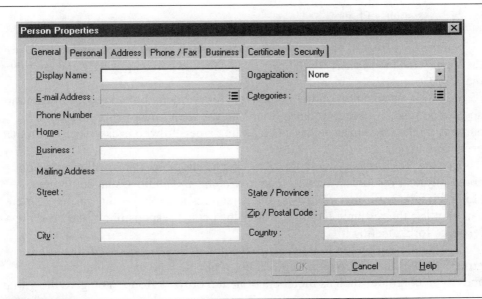

FIGURE 1-5   Adding a person to the address book

To enter an e-mail address, click on the icon on the right of the E-Mail Address text box. In the box that appears, enter the address, click Add and then OK.

On the Phone/Fax tab you can enter up to six telephone numbers in 12 categories:

- Home Phone 1

- Home Phone 2

- Business Phone 1

- Business Phone 2

- Other Phone

- Main Phone

- Home Fax

- Business Fax

- Cellular Phone

- Pager

- E-Mail

- Assistant's Phone

On the Security tab you can designate the listing as hidden or read-only. Use the Certificate tab to enter digital certificates for the person to verify and encrypt messages.

Use the Organization option in the New Entry dialog box to record information about a company or other organization. You can then select the organization's name from the Organization list when adding a person who is associated with that organization.

Use the Resource option in the New Entry dialog box to record information about physical resources, such as meeting rooms and audio-visual equipment, along with the name and address of the person responsible for that resource. You can later use the resource listing to notify the person responsible if you need the resource for a meeting

Use the Group option in the New Entry dialog box to create a distribution group. A distribution group is a collection of people who have an interest or activity in common, such as members of a club or workgroup. You give the group a name and then specify which persons from the address book are members of that group. You could then use the name of the group, for example, to send the same e-mail message to every member of the group by creating just one message.

Working with Address Books

You use the buttons on the Address Book toolbar to edit, delete, or print an address book entry:

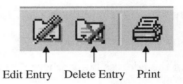

Edit Entry   Delete Entry   Print

TIP   *To make an Internet telephone call to a person, select their name and then click on the Net2Phone button on the toolbar.*

To create another address book, click the Create a New Address Book button on the toolbar, or select New from the File menu to see the types of address books that you can create:

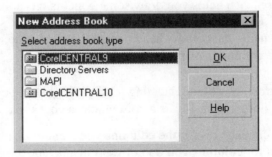

A MAPI address book contains listings from an address book using the Mail Application Programming Interface (MAPI) standard

Click on the type, and then click OK. Selecting to add a CorelCENTRAL 10 book displays the dialog box shown previously in Figure 1-3. Select to create either a personal or shared book, and then complete the process.

The new book will be listed under its type on the left panel. Click on the new address book to create entries for it.

Use Options on the File menu to delete and rename address books, import and export addresses, and to create a Web page (HTML document) from an address book.

When you have more than one book, you can copy and move addresses between them. To move a name from one to the other, use the Edit Cut and Edit Paste commands. Cut the name from one address book, and paste it in the other. To copy a name from one to the other, use the Edit Copy and Edit Paste commands.

1. Select the name or names in the address book.

2. Click the Cut or Copy buttons in the toolbar.

3. Click on the name of the address book where you are placing the items.

4. Click on the Paste button.

Sorting Addresses

Your addresses appear in the same order that you entered them. When you're scanning the book to find a particular contact, however, it would be easier if the addresses were sorted in some other order, such as by name or organization. Sorting the addresses also helps you draw some conclusions about your contacts, such as how many are in a particular organization or live in the same city.

You sort items using the column headings on the right pane, so the first step is to make certain the column is displayed.

1. Right-click on any column heading to display a list of possible columns. Each field that you can add as a column has a checkbox.

2. Enable the checkboxes for the columns you want to display. Disable the checkboxes for columns you do not want displayed.

3. Click OK.

To sort the list, click on the column heading for the field you want to sort on. Each time you click, you'll see a little triangle change from pointing downward indicating an ascending sort, and upward for a descending sort.

In addition to adding and removing columns, you can change the order of fields and adjust the width of columns.

To change the width of a column using the mouse, point to the line on the right of its column heading, and drag. To change the position of a column, drag its name to the left or the right.

Searching for Addresses

If you do not have many addresses in your book, you can locate one by scrolling the list. However, this becomes tedious as your address books grow. Rather than scrolling, you can use two techniques to locate an address—searching and filtering.

To search an address book, select the address book and then click on the Find button on the toolbar, or select Find from the Edit menu to see this dialog box:

In the Find box, type the first name of the person you are looking for, and then click Find Now. The box will enlarge, listing persons with that name. You can also use the Search name text box available in the toolbar to perform a quick filter on the display name field.

Using a Filter

Using the Find command displays persons with the same name in a separate box. You can also filter the address book to determine what addresses are shown in the book itself. A filter hides those items that don't meet the criteria that you create, displaying only those that do match.

A *filter* is a logical statement, such as "Zip Code Equals 94501." It includes a column name (Zip Code), an operator (Equals), and a condition (94501). The statement means "show only addresses that have the value 94501 in the Zip Code field." You can combine several statements in logical AND and OR operations for more exact searching, and you can even group the conditions for a precise selection.

To create a filter, follow these steps:

1. Select Filter from the View menu to see the dialog box shown in Figure 1-6.

2. Pull down the list in the first column, and choose the column you want to filter by.

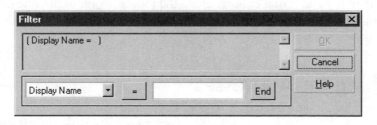

FIGURE 1-6   Using a filter to select addresses

3. Click on the operator button, shown with the equal sign (=) in Figure 1-6, and choose from these options:

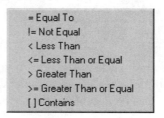

4. Enter the value in the last text box.

You can include wildcards in the condition, using the asterisk to represent any number of characters and the question mark for a single character. For example, to locate all persons whose last name begins with "G," use the equal operator and enter **G*** in the condition field. This tells the filter to locate all persons whose last name begins with the letter "G," regardless of how many characters are in the name.

To further narrow the search, you can create compound conditions. Start by clicking on the End button and choosing Insert Row from the shortcut menu. Another row of boxes appears, and the END button is now labeled AND:

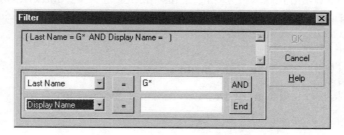

The AND operator matches persons who meet more than one condition. To create an OR condition, click on the AND button, and select OR. Use the OR operator to find persons who meet one or the other condition but not necessarily both. There will be a separate row for each condition. Use Insert Row and Delete Row as needed to add and remove statements. For example, Figure 1-7 shows a filter that locates all persons in California, as well as those whose last name begins with the letter "G."

> **TIP** *You can also create groups for even more complex conditions. Select New Group from the operator list to start a new group.*

When you close the dialog box, the filter is applied, listing just those records that match the conditions. To display all of the addresses without removing the filter, select Remove Filter from the View menu.

PerfectScript

PerfectScript is a macro creation tool that you can use from the Utilities menu. Using PerfectScript, you create a macro that opens one or more WordPerfect Suite applications and performs functions within them. It also gives you a common way to make a macro regardless of the application. PerfectScript does not replace the macro functions in the individual programs. Rather, it provides another layer of utility to access the applications from the DAD bar.

Creating macros from within applications is discussed in Chapters 11 and 22. To record a macro using PerfectScript follow these steps:

1. Select PerfectScript from the WordPerfect Office 2002 Utilities menu, to display the window shown in Figure 1-8.

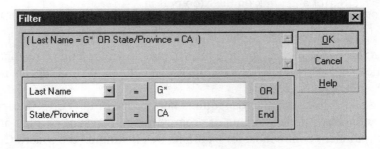

FIGURE 1-7   Sample filter

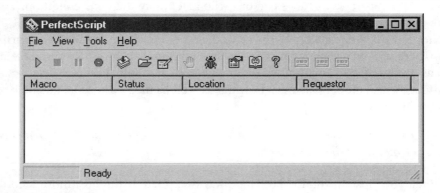

FIGURE 1-8 PerfectScript

2. Open the WordPerfect Office 2002 application that you want the macro to work with.

3. Click on the PerfectScript button in the Windows taskbar to switch to the PerfectScript window, and then click on the Record button or select Record from the File menu. The Record Macro box appears.

4. Type a macro name, and then click on Record.

5. Switch to the WordPerfect Office 2002 application. The application appears with its own record macro mode. With WordPerfect 10, for example, you'll see its macro feature bar on the screen.

6. Record the keystrokes or menu selections that you want in the macro.

7. Click on the Stop button in the application's macro toolbar, or switch to PerfectScript and click on the Stop button.

The four most recent PerfectScript macros you created or edited are listed in the PerfectScript File menu. To run a macro, pull down the File menu, and click on its name. The macro switches to or opens the application and repeats the keystrokes and menu selections.

Editing and debugging macros requires knowledge of the PerfectScript macro language and a basic understanding of programming. You can see a list of all PerfectScript macro commands, for example, by clicking on the Macro Command Browser button in the PerfectScript toolbar. You can also click on the Debug button on the toolbar to step through your macros command by command, and to look at the value of your variables. For more information on PerfectScript, search the WordPerfect, Quattro Pro or Corel Presentations online help files.

To edit macros, you must first select a macro editor. Choose Settings from the Tools menu, and click on the Edit tab. Enter the path and filename, choose the word processing program you want to edit the macro in, and then click on OK. You can now select Edit from the File menu and choose a macro to edit.

 TIP *Use the Dialog Editor option from the Tools menu to create custom dialog boxes for a macro. See Chapter 11 for more information on creating dialog boxes.*

Visual Basic for Applications

Macros that you record while running a WordPerfect Office 2002 application are created in the WordPerfect macro language. This language is compatible with macros created in previous versions of WordPerfect applications, so you should be able to use existing macros if you are upgrading to WordPerfect Office 2002.

Many other application programs use macros created in Visual Basic for Applications (VBA), a language popularized by Microsoft and used in Microsoft's and other companies' programs.

To make WordPerfect Office 2002 applications as compatible as possible with a wide variety of programs, you can now create and run VBA macros in WordPerfect, Quattro Pro, Corel Presentations, and CorelCENTRAL.

To create a macro in VBA from these applications, choose Visual Basic from the Tools menu, and select Visual Basic Editor. The VBA window appears as in Figure 1-9. You have to write VBA macros or insert commands yourself, a subject far beyond the scope of this book.

Bitstream Font Navigator

WordPerfect Office 2002 includes 1000 fonts, and you probably have other fonts already installed on your system. To help manage and organize your fonts, Corel has provided Bitstream Font Navigator.

To run the program, select Bitstream Font Navigator from the WordPerfect Office 2002 Utilities menu. The first time you run the program, you'll see the Font Navigator Wizard that lets you locate all of the fonts on your system. Click on Next to see a tree diagram of your system with checkboxes next to each drive.

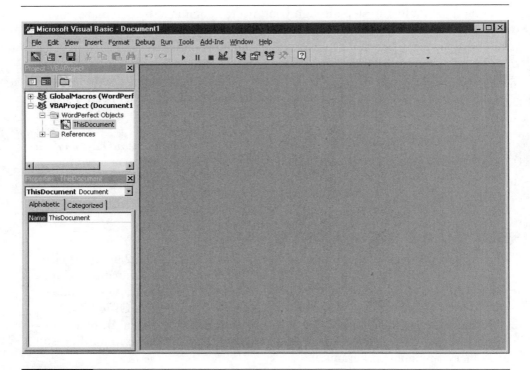

FIGURE 1-9   Visual Basic for Applications

Enable the checkboxes for the drives that contain your fonts, and then click on
Next and then Finish. The program searches your disk, creating a database of the
fonts, and then displays them as shown in Figure 1-10. To see what a font looks
like, click on it in either list. A sample of the font appears in the Font Sample panel.

Use the toolbar buttons and menu to work with the fonts. For example, the
toolbar contains these features:

- *Folder List*—Lets you navigate through your system, much like the
  Explorer. Pull down the list to select drives and folders.

- *Up One Level*—Moves to the next highest folder level.

- *View All Fonts*—Displays all of the fonts in your system.

- *View Fonts by Format*—Select to display all fonts, or just True Type or
  PostScript fonts.

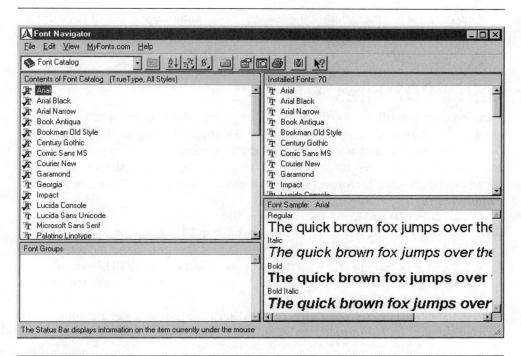

FIGURE 1-10   Bitstream Font Navigator

- *View Fonts by Style*—Select to display all fonts, or those categorized as decorative, monospaced, sans serif, script, serif, or symbol.

- *Create New Font Group*—Create a group in which to store similar fonts.

- *View Properties*—Select to see detailed information about the selected font.

- *Explore Font* —Displays the selected font in a window showing samples in various sizes and styles.

- *Print Font Sample*—Prints a sample of the selected font. You can choose a one- or two-line sample, a sample of the font family, or a chart of the characters in the font.

- *MyFonts.Com*—Lets you purchase additional fonts over the Internet.

- *Help*—Displays information about the item you click on.

The View menu offers additional features. For example, you can change the size and text that appears in the Font Sample panel, and the size of the panels within the windows.

Creating PDF Files

Included with WordPerfect Office 2002 is the Adobe Acrobat Reader. This is a program that lets you access fully formatted documents having the PDF (Portable Document Format) extension. Since the Adobe Acrobat Reader can also be downloaded free over the Internet, it is also a convenient way to share your documents with other persons who may not have WordPerfect Office 2002 themselves.

WordPerfect 10 and Corel Presentations 10 let you save your documents and slide shows as PDF files. Just select File | Publish to PDF to open the dialog box shown in Figure 1-11. By default, WordPerfect will save the file in the same directory as the document and with the same name but using the PDF extension. You can change the name and location, and choose to save only a selected part of the document to the PDF file.

Use the Objects tab of the dialog box to determine how fonts and graphics are converted into the PDF format. By default, for example, the fonts you selected are

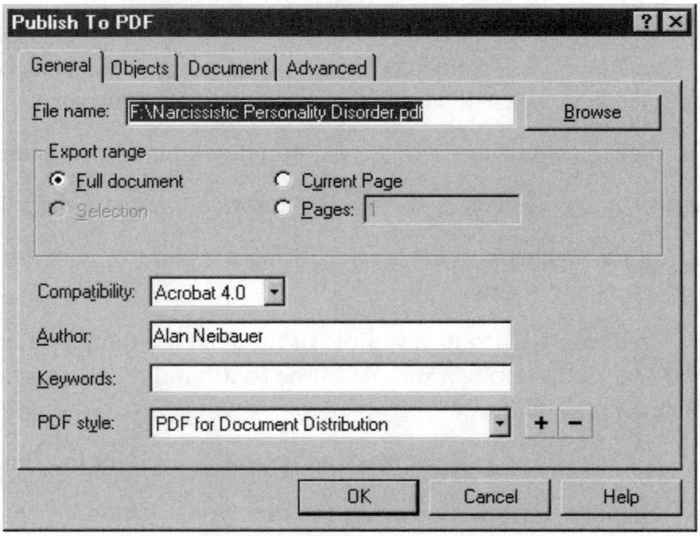

FIGURE 1-11   Creating a PDF file

embedded into the PDF file so the resulting document appears just as it does in WordPerfect. You can choose not to embed the fonts and other options on the Objects tab.

The Documents tab lets you choose to include bookmarks and hyperlinks with the PDF file, and to display just a single page, the full screen, or bookmarks when the file is opened.

The Advanced tab lets you optimize the file for viewing on the Internet, and lets you select a new location to store embedded files.

Using Quick View Plus

There are so many programs used to create documents of all types, that no one can possibly have them all. If someone e-mails you a document created with a program that you do not have on your computer, you may not be able to display it.

Quick View Plus allows you to look at and print documents created with over 200 different file formats, even if you do not have them installed on your computer. You can zoom in and out, find text, copy text and graphics for pasting into an application you do have installed, and convert graphics into Windows wallpaper.

Figure 1-12, for example, shows how the slides in a Microsoft PowerPoint presentation appear in Quick View Plus. The presentation was received as an e-mail on a computer in which Microsoft PowerPoint was not installed.

To display a file in Quick View Plus, right-click on it in Windows Explorer and select Quick View Plus from the Quickmenu. To print a file, right-click on it and select Quick Print from the Quickmenu. You can also select QuickView Plus from the Programs menu and choose View a File. Then locate the file you want to display or print and click Open.

To also view e-mail message attachments using Quick View Plus, right-click the mouse on the attachment and select Quick View Plus from the QuickMenu.

Making Internet Phone Calls

Net2Phone is a tool that lets you place telephone calls from your computer to another computer free of charge. It also lets you place telephone calls from your computer to a telephone anywhere in the world. You use your computer's microphone to talk and your speakers to hear, rather than an actual telephone.

FIGURE 1-12 Microsoft PowerPoint file in Quick View Plus

> **TIP** *You can also sign up to make International phone calls and obtain other telephone services for additional cost.*

When you start Net2Phone for the first time the Setup Wizard will take you through the process of setting up your microphone and speakers. It will then dial into the Internet and let you register with Net2Phone for your free calls. You'll be asked to enter an ID number, such as your phone number, and select a PIN that you'll need to enter each time you start the program.

Net2Phone appears at the bottom of your Windows desktop, as shown in Figure 1-13. To make a call to a regular telephone, select the PC2Phone option button, enter the number to call, and then click on the Call button. You'll hear the phone dialing and then ringing. Speak as you would when using a regular telephone, just expect some delay depending on the speed of your Internet connection.

You can also use Net2Phone to communicate directly with other Net2Phone users who are also online. Using the PC2PC feature, each user selects a virtual

FIGURE 1-13 Making an Internet phone call

nickname that is assigned to their computer. To contact a user directly, without going through their telephone, select the PC2PC option button, enter their virtual nickname and click Call. If the person is online and running Net2Phone, they will hear a ring and will be able to answer your call using their computer's microphone and speakers.

In addition to phone calls, Net2Phone includes a free fax service called Net2Fax. You can use Net2Fax to send faxes directly from your computer to any fax machine in the world. Faxes within the United States are free, but you'll have to pay for international faxes.

If you're working on a document, such as a letter or report in WordPerfect, select Print from the File menu to open the Print dialog box. Pull down the Name list on the Main tab of the dialog box and choose Net2Fax from the list. When you click Print, Net2Phone opens and displays the box shown here:

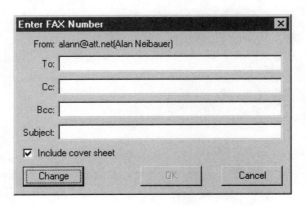

Click the Change button if you want to edit your return address. Enter the phone number of the recipient in the To box, and the phone numbers of any carbon and blind copy recipients, and then click OK. If a box asks for your PIN, enter it and click OK. Net2Fax will then transfer your document to its fax servers and send the fax to the recipient's machine. You will receive an e-mail confirming when the fax has been received.

| NOTE | *The fax number must include the country code (1 in the United States) and area code of the recipient.* |

To fax a document on your disk once Net2Phone is started, click the Net2Fax button in the Net2Fax window. Select the document to be faxed, and then continue the procedure to specify the recipients and transmit the document.

You can also place a Net2Phone call directly within CorelCENTRAL Address Book. Simply select an Address Book contact, right-click the mouse and select Net2Phone. The Net2Phone interface will start with the default telephone number of the contact in the number text box. Click Dial to connect to Net2Phone and make the call.

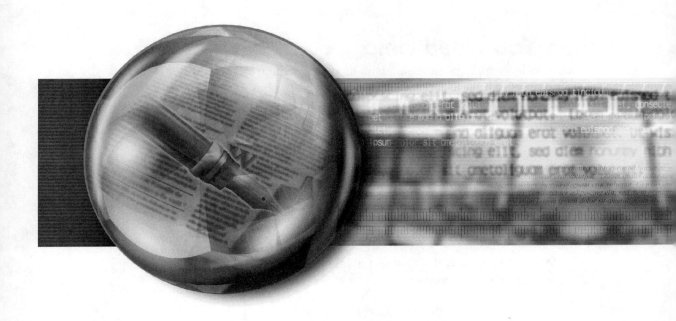

Chapter 2

Using Corel Tools and Utilities

27

The integration of WordPerfect Office 2002 components gives us the advantage of a common set of tools. Features such as Help and Spell Checker and processes such as file handling work the same way in WordPerfect 10, Quattro Pro 10, and Corel Presentations 10. Once you learn the basics of these features, you don't have to retrace your steps with every application. In this chapter, you'll learn how to use the tools that are common to the three major applications.

When You Need Help

All Windows applications come with an onscreen help system. Although each WordPerfect Office 2002 application and accessory has its own help information, the interface works the same in all of them.

To start Help from within an application, pull down the Help menu in the menu bar to see these options:

- *Help Topics*—Get Help by topic, search for keywords, and see interactive demonstrations.

- *PerfectExpert*—Displays a panel of interactive options.

- *Corel Connector*—Opens a Web browser to connect to the Internet.

- *Corel on the Web*—Connect online to Corel via the Internet by selecting one of these options:

Corel <u>W</u>eb Site
<u>F</u>onts Online
<u>P</u>rinting Info Online
<u>M</u>acros Online
<u>T</u>echnical Support
T<u>i</u>ps and Tricks
Training and <u>C</u>ertification

You may see some other options, depending on the application. These additional help choices will be discussed in later chapters.

You can also connect to Corel over the Internet by clicking on the Corel Web Site or Corel Connector buttons in the toolbar.

Help Topics

Help Topics is perhaps the most comprehensive way to find information. The Help Topics dialog box contains four pages: Contents, Index, Find, and Corel Knowledge Base. Each page gives you a different way to search the Help database for the information you want. If you have trouble finding what you need on one page, try another.

Contents Page

The Contents page works just like a table of contents in a book. You'll see a list of major topics, each with an icon of a book. Clicking on an icon opens the book to display other topic areas, with their own book icon, or specific help topics indicated by the Help icon. Continue opening books until you see a listing for the exact information you need, and then double-click on the topic to display a Help dialog box.

In some of the help systems you'll see a Showcase option, such as Showcase WordPerfect. Clicking on that option displays a help topic illustrating several samples of documents that can be created with the application. When one of the samples is selected, an enlarged version of it appears with triangles marking parts of the document for which help is available. Click on the sample that you are interested in, and then click on a triangle to read instructions on how to create that effect.

Index Page

The Index page works like an index at the back of a book. It is an alphabetical list of the keywords in all of the Help topics. Rather than manually scrolling through the list, however, type the first few characters of the subject you need help with to automatically scroll the list to that part of the index. If the exact topic isn't shown, type a few more characters of the topic or scroll the list manually using the scroll bar. When you see the topic, double-click on it.

Find Page

You can also locate a Help topic using the Find page. This makes available a database of all of the words in the Help system.

The first time you select Find in each application, you'll be given a choice of the type of database you want to create. Choose Minimize Database Size for a simple search of words and phrases as they appear in Help windows. Select Maximize Search Capabilities to be able to look up subjects with similar concepts. Choose Customize Search Capabilities to specify which Help files you want to search. You can later rebuild your database to choose another option.

Once the database is created, enter a word or phrase that you are looking for. Help displays two lists, as shown in Figure 2-1. One list shows matching words that the Help system found in the database, and the other shows Help topics containing those words. To narrow your search, click on each of the matching words to see which topics it has found. When you see the topic in the second list, double-click on it, or select it and then click on Display.

If you choose to maximize your search capabilities, each of the Help topics has a checkbox. To locate related information, click on the checkboxes for the topics you are interested in, and then click on the Find Similar button.

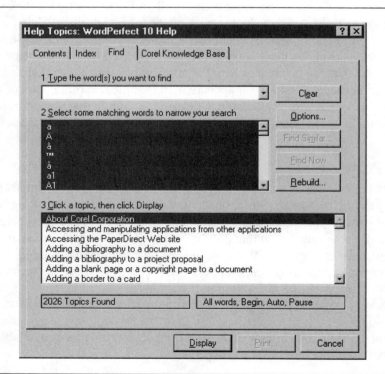

FIGURE 2-1   The Find page of the Help dialog box

The number of matching topics and the Help settings appear at the bottom of the Find dialog box. The default setting is All Words, Begin, Auto, Pause. Here's what they mean.

- *All Words* means that the Help topic must contain all of the words that you type in any order. If you type "landscape nut," for example, no topics will be listed because none contain both words.

- *Begin* means that Find looks for words that begin with the same characters that you typed.

- *Auto* means that Find starts searching for words after each of your keystrokes.

- *Pause* means that Find waits until you've stopped typing before it searches.

You can change these settings by clicking on Options to see the Find Options dialog box. There you can choose to match all or at least one of the words. If you selected Maximize the Search Capabilities, you can also choose to search for the words in the exact order you typed them and to display matching phrases.

The Show Words That option lets you find words that begin or end with, contain, or match those that you've typed.

In the Begin Searching section, choose to start the search only after you click the Find Now button, or immediately after each keystroke. The Files button lets you choose which Help files to search.

Corel Knowledge Base

The Corel Knowledge Base lets you read, print, and download documents that contain answers to many technical questions or problems. The Corel Knowledge Base is located at http://kb.corel.com/ on the Internet.

Help Windows

When you select a topic, a window appears onscreen with information about it. Two typical Help windows are shown in Figure 2-2.

On the left is an *overview* window that gives some general information about using endnotes and footnotes. Click on the How To button to see a list of related topics. This box also contains the Related Topics option that you can click to learn more.

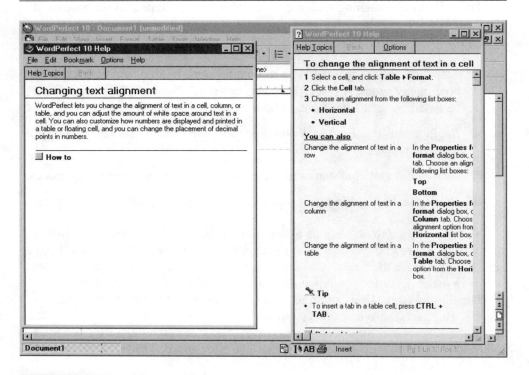

FIGURE 2-2   Help windows

You might also see words or phrases underlined with a series of dashes. These are called *jump terms* or *pop-up terms*. Click on the term to display a box with a definition or explanation. Click elsewhere in the Help window when you have finished.

Click on Help Topics in the Help window toolbar to return to the Help Topics dialog box. Click on Back, if it is not dimmed, to return to the previously displayed Help window. The Options menu lets you choose from these functions:

- *Keep Help on Top* controls how the Help window appears when you click on another window. You can choose to keep the Help window on top, displayed in the foreground, rather than moved into the background when you switch windows.

2

- *Display History Window* displays a list of all of the Help topics you have referred to during the current session.

- *Font* lets you choose the size of the text in the window. Options are Small, Normal, and Large.

- *Use System Colors* applies the same colors that you see in the application window to the Help system.

On the right of the illustration is a detailed Help window that explains how to create footnotes. The detailed window contains a series of steps to follow and a few notes and time-saving tips. Click on Options in the detailed window to display the options Keep Help on Top, Font, and Use System Colors, as well as these choices:

- *Annotate* lets you type a note, message, or reminder and "attach" it to the Help page. When you close the Annotate window, an icon of a paper clip appears next to the topic. Double-click on the icon to read or edit the note.

- *Copy* places a copy of the text in the Help window in the Clipboard. You can then paste the information into a program. Only the text in the window is copied, not any graphics.

- *Print Topic* prints the contents of the Help window.

Corel Web Site

The Corel Web Site button in the toolbar and the Corel on the Web option on the Help menu launches your Internet account, if you have one, to link to Corel Corporation's OfficeCommunity.com site (http://www.officecommunity.com).

| TIP | *You can also access Corel from the Corel Web Site button in an Open or Save dialog box. You'll learn more about this feature later.* |

You can get free downloads such as templates, macros, and clip art for your product. You can also access information on fonts, printing, macros, tips, training, and more.

Using PerfectExpert

PerfectExpert does more than just answer your questions. PerfectExpert is also a menu of options, which take you step by step through many Corel functions; it's a perfect aid for users new to the WordPerfect Office 2002 applications. To display PerfectExpert, select it from the Help menu. For example, Figure 2-3 shows the PerfectExpert that appears in WordPerfect 10. The PerfectExpert makes it easy to perform typical WordPerfect tasks by choosing options from the panel.

Use the buttons on the top of the PerfectExpert panel to navigate through its menus. The panel contains a series of buttons and a text box with some useful and/or interesting information. Clicking on a button may display additional options in the panel, open a dialog box, or perform some action in the application you have open. For example, clicking on the Set Up the Document button in WordPerfect 10

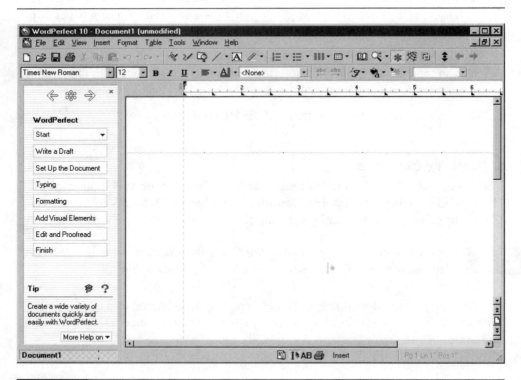

FIGURE 2-3   PerfectExpert

displays buttons for changing the margins, font, and justification; for adding page numbers and headers and footers; for turning on guidelines; and for changing the magnification of the display.

Quick Help

The Help system is comprehensive, but it often requires negotiating through a series of Help topics to find just what you are looking for. Several shortcuts for getting help bypass the Help menu.

Many dialog boxes have a Help button—click on it to go directly to the help system pages for that dialog box. If there is no Help button, press F1—the application displays a Help dialog box explaining that option. If a dialog box is not displayed, pressing F1 shows the Help Contents page.

To find out about a specific item in a dialog box, right-click on the option. Read the information that appears, and then click the mouse. You can also click on the What's This? button (with the question mark) in the box's title bar. The mouse changes to an arrow with a question mark. Point and click on the option you need help with.

You will also see a What's This? option on all QuickMenus. A QuickMenu appears when you right-click on an object. Choose the What's This? option to read a brief description of the selected object.

Managing Files

Windows offers several ways to locate files and folders. You can use the Explorer, the Find command from the Start menu in the taskbar, or just surf through your folders starting with the My Computer icon. WordPerfect Office 2002 incorporates its own file management capabilities directly in dialog boxes, such as Open, Insert File, Save As, and New, that let you access files. You can locate files based on their names through these dialog boxes, and you can index commonly used files and folders for even faster searches.

Figure 2-4 is an example of a file management dialog box, the Open File box from WordPerfect 10. If you don't see the menu bar on your dialog box, click the Toggle Menu On/Off button, the button on the far right of the Look In text box.

TIP *You can display the QuickFinder file management box by selecting Corel QuickFinder 10 Searcher from the WordPerfect Office 2002 Utilities menu.*

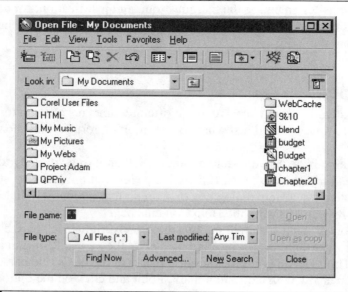

FIGURE 2-4 Corel WordPerfect's Open File dialog box

Browsing Through Folders

The dialog box lets you list files by the folder in which they are stored. First, select the folder that you want to look in. The current folder being displayed appears in the Look In list.

To move up one level at a time, click on the Up One Level icon next to the Look In list. For example, suppose you are viewing the Template folder in the path C:\Program Files\Corel\WordPerfect Office 2002\Template. The large list displays the folders and files within the Template folder. Here's what selecting Up One Level displays:

1st click	WordPerfect Office 2002 folder
2nd click	Corel folder
3rd click	Program Files folder
4th click	C: drive
5th click	My Computer, including all of your drives
6th click	Desktop

Rather than clicking, however, you can just pull down the Look In list and choose the disk drive that you want to search. For example, suppose you want to find a file on drive C, located in some entirely different path than the current folder.

1. Pull down the Look In list, and click on [C:]. All of the folders in the drive appear in the large list box, along with files on the drive's root directory.

2. In the large list box, double-click on the folder in which the file is stored. This displays all of the folders and files in that folder.

3. Continue opening folders in the same way until you see the file you are searching for.

> **TIP** *If you know the full path and name of the file you want to locate, you can just type it in the File Name box.*

Changing the Default Folder

Corel applications are set up to display a default folder when you first open a file management dialog box. This default is used each time you start the application, unless you change it using the application's Settings or Properties commands.

During a work session, however, the application remembers the last folder selected in the dialog box. So the next time you open the box in that session, the same folder appears. If you do not want the application to change the folder during a session, pull down the Edit menu and deselect the Change Default Folder option.

The Favorites Folder

Chances are you often use certain files and folders. Rather than search for them each time you want to access them, you can store a shortcut to each file in the Favorites folder. You can then open the Favorites folder and click on the folder or file that you want to open.

To add a file to the Favorites folder, click on it in the file list, and then click on the Favorites button in the toolbar and select Add Selected Items to Favorites. Use the same technique to add selected folders to your favorites list.

When you want to open the file or folder, select Go To Favorites in the Favorites menu. The folder will open, displaying the shortcuts. Click on the folder shortcut to open the folder, or click on the document shortcut to open the document.

 Once in Favorites, select Return From Favorites again to return to the previous folder.

Displaying Files

Once the correct folder is displayed, you'll need to display the files. You can do this in either the File Type list or the File Name text box.

The File Type list offers preset choices. Pull down the list, and select All Files (*.*) if you want to see every file in the folder. The other options depend on the application you are using. In WordPerfect 10, for example, you can choose to see templates, macros, text files, or other types of files used by WordPerfect. In Quattro Pro 10, you can select from a list of common spreadsheet program formats.

If none of the choices in the File Type list are appropriate, you can use a wildcard pattern in the File Name box. Use asterisks to represent any number of unknown characters. For example, typing **report*.*** and pressing ENTER lists only files starting with the letters "report," and with any extension. To list just files with the TXT extension, type ***.TXT**, and press ENTER.

 In the Open dialog box in WordPerfect 10, pull down the list at the end of the File Name text box to see a list of recently opened files.

Viewing Files

By using the buttons in the toolbar and the View menu, you can select how the folders and files are displayed in the list box. All of the options display an icon along with the filename. The shape of the icon indicates its type.

To select a view, select it from the View menu:

■ Select *Large Icons* to display each filename under a large icon that is easy to see.

■ Select *Small Icons* to display each filename to the right of the icon. When there are more files than can be displayed, a vertical scroll bar appears.

■ Select *List* to display each filename to the right of the icon, but with a horizontal scroll bar to scroll left and right.

■ Select *Details* view to display a list with four columns—the file icon and name, its size, type, and the date it was created or last modified.

■ Select *Thumbnails* (in Windows ME) to display graphic illustrations of the items in the folder.

Arranging Icons and Files

By default, all items are listed in alphabetical order by name, but with all folders first, and then the files. You can change the order of the files to arrange them by their size, type, or date. Pull down the View menu, point to Arrange Icons, and select the desired order. If you are displaying the files in the Details view, you can click on the column heading. Click on Type, for example, to sort the list by type in ascending order.

TIP	*Click on the heading in which the list is already sorted to change between ascending and descending order.*

In addition to the folder and file lists just described, you can display two other windows—Folder view and Preview. Here's how to use Folder view:

1. Click on the Folders button in the toolbar to display the complete structure of your system in a list on the left, with the folder and files on the right. Unlike the Look In list, Tree view lets you expand or collapse the folder structure. A small plus sign next to a Drive or Folder icon means that it contains an additional folder.

2. Click on the plus sign to expand the drive or folder so you'll be able to see the other folders contained within it. The icon will then be marked with a minus sign—click on it to collapse the display.

3. To see the contents of a drive or folder in the list on the right, click on the Drive or Folder icon itself.

The Preview button opens a viewer window in which the file management dialog box displays the contents of a selected text or graphic file. You can control how the file appears using the Preview option in the View menu. Pull down the View menu, point to Preview, and then select one of these options:

■ *No Preview* closes the preview window.

■ *Use Separate Window* displays the preview in a separate window, outside of the dialog box.

Working with Folders and Files

You can use the file management dialog boxes not only to display, open, and save files, but to delete, move, copy, and rename them as well. You can perform many of the same functions within the WordPerfect Office 2002 applicationas you can perform in Windows Explorer.

To delete a file or folder, for example, select it in either the tree diagram or file list, and then press the DEL key. A dialog box appears asking you to confirm that you want to delete the item into the Windows Recycle Bin. Click on Yes or No.

To rename a folder or file, use these steps:

1. Right-click on the folder, and select Rename from the QuickMenu. You can also click two separate times—not a double-click—on the name, or press F2. The name appears in reverse in a dotted box.

2. To delete the current name, press DEL, or start typing a new name.

3. To edit the name, press the LEFT ARROW or RIGHT ARROW key to remove the highlight, and then proceed with the edit.

You also can move or copy a file or folder to another location. When you move or copy a folder, all of the folders and files located within it move as well. To use drag and drop to move a folder, follow these steps:

1. Display the Folder view.

2. Expand the drive or folder so you can see the location where you want to insert the folder.

3. Display the icon for the folder you want to copy or move.

4. Click on the folder you want to move, and then drag it to the location in the tree diagram where you want to place it. The destination location becomes highlighted.

5. To move the folder, just release the mouse. To copy the folder, hold down the CTRL key and release the mouse.

To move or copy a file, use a similar technique:

1. Display the name of the file in the list box on the right.

2. Expand the tree diagram on the left to see the drive or folder where you want to insert the file.

3. Drag the file to the drive or folder and release the mouse. Hold down CTRL as you release the mouse to copy the file.

If you prefer not to use drag and drop, you can use the File menu. Follow these steps:

1. Select the folder or file you want to move.

2. Pull down the File menu. Select Move to Folder or Copy to Folder, depending on what you want to do. The application displays another Browse dialog box.

3. Select the destination location in the Browse box.

4. Click on the Move or Copy button at the bottom of the dialog box.

| TIP | *You can also use the Cut, Copy, and Paste options from the Edit menu or the QuickMenu.* |

Printing Files

You can print a file from the file management dialog boxes. To print a file, however, it must have an extension that is associated with an application already installed on your computer. For example, the extension WPD is associated with WordPerfect 10 and QPW with Quattro Pro 10. You can print a Quattro Pro 10 Notebook directly from the file management box because Windows associates the extension with the application.

To print a file, right-click on it in the file list, and then choose Print from the QuickMenu. You can also select Print from the File menu.

> | **TIP** | *The options in the QuickMenu depend on the type of file you click on. If you click on a sound file or a Corel Presentations 10 runtime slide show, for example, the menu includes the option Play Slide Show as well as Print.* |

QuickFinder

If you don't know where the file that you are looking for is located, you can spend a great deal of time surfing your disk. WordPerfect Office 2002 provides a faster alternative: QuickFinder.

With QuickFinder, you can locate files by their name or contents. For example, you could list all files that contain the word "budget," or just files with a certain extension.

Access QuickFinder in any file management dialog box, such as Save As and Open, or by selecting QuickFinder 10 Searcher from the WordPerfect Office 2002 Utilities menu.

To start a search, type a word or characters that you are looking for in the File Name box. You can use wildcards to help narrow the search. Then click on the Find Now button. Corel locates the files whose title or contents contain the word and displays them in the QuickFinder Search Results folder, along with their locations.

You can change the view and manipulate the files just as you can files in any folder. To start a new search, click on the New Search button, and then enter the new filename or pattern. Click on the Goto/From Search Results button to toggle between the current location and the QuickFinder Search Results.

Performing an Advanced Search

Searching for files by entering text in the File Name box is useful, but WordPerfect 10 looks for only one word or phrase. For even more search options based on the content, filename, or date of a document, click on the Advanced button in a file management box to see the dialog box shown in Figure 2-5.

> | **NOTE** | *The dialog box contains any search criteria already entered in the File Name box.* |

Move Item Up

Move Item Down

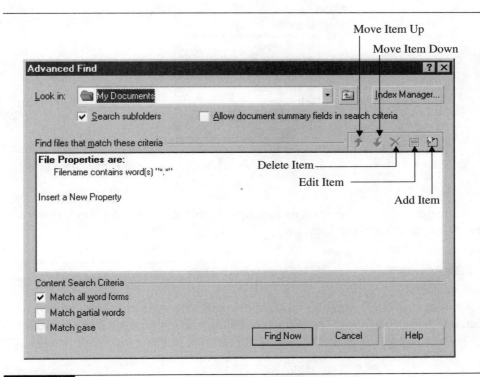

Delete Item

Edit Item

Add Item

FIGURE 2-5   The dialog box for performing an advanced search

To search for a file by its contents or name, double-click on the *Filename contains words* prompt to see these pull-down lists:

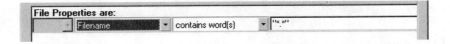

- To search for the same text in either the filename or contents of the document, pull down the first list, and choose Filename or Content. To locate a file by its date, choose Last Modified Date from the list.

- If you are searching based only on the filename, choose either *contains word(s)* or *does not contain word(s)* from the second list, depending on how you want to search. If you are searching for files based on their date, the second list contains options such as these:

■ Enter the text or the date you are searching for in the text box, then press ENTER.

To search for a file based on its contents, double-click on the prompt *Insert a New Property* to see these lists:

Choose And or Or from the first list, then pull down the third list, and choose from options such as those shown here (scrolling the list for even more choices):

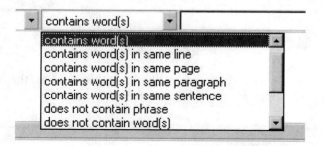

Enter the text you are searching for in the last text box, then press ENTER.

To enter additional search criteria, click on *Insert a New Property* again, and repeat the process. Use the buttons to the right of the Find Files That Match These Criteria box to organize your criteria—adding and deleting criteria, combining them into groups, and changing their positions.

Finally, select options from the checkboxes at the bottom of the dialog box, and click on Find Now.

Using QuickFinder Manager

When you perform a search for contents, QuickFinder has to look at every word in all of the files specified in the Look In box. If you are searching through many files, this may be a slow process.

To make QuickFinder quicker, you can create an index of the files that you search often. The index is an actual listing of every word in the files, so QuickFinder can locate contents by scanning through the index rather than the documents themselves.

To access QuickFinder Manager, select QuickFinder 10 Manager in the WordPerfect Office 2002 Utilities menu, or click on the Index Manager button in the Advanced Find dialog box. The QuickFinder Manager dialog box is shown in Figure 2-6. You can set up two types of indexes. A Standard Fast Search searches a single folder and all of its subfolders. A Custom Fast Search can include one or more folders, with or without their subfolders. Let's look at Standard Search first.

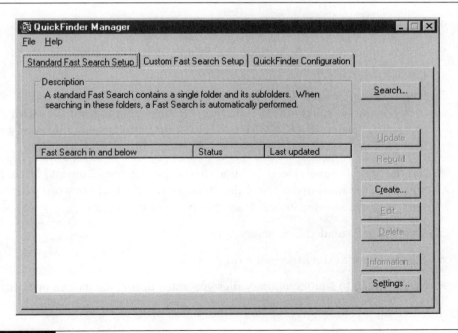

FIGURE 2-6   QuickFinder Manager

Creating a Standard Fast Search

If you want to create an index of the documents in a single folder, including its subfolders, display the Standard Fast Search Setup page of the QuickFinder Manager dialog box. Then create a search using these steps:

1. Click on Create to display the QuickFinder Standard Fast Search dialog box.

2. Specify the folders or path you want to include in the index.

3. Select the updating method. When you select automatic updating, QuickFinder Manager periodically—every time period that you specify—reindexes the files. This means that your searches will be more up to date, but the reindexing may occur when you are performing other tasks and may slow the system response. If you select manual updating, you have to tell QuickFinder Manager to update the index.

You can now specify options to customize the index. Follow these steps:

1. Click on the Options button to display the dialog box in Figure 2-7.

2. Choose an option in the Include For Search section to determine which parts of the documents to include in the index.

3. Choose options in the Other Settings section. By default, the search includes only document files—not graphic files and program files with extensions such as EXE, COM, and DLL—and it indexes numbers as well as words.

4. Set the Search Level. Drag the slider to choose between Low and High. As you drag, the label under the slider changes to reflect where word patterns must be located—sentence, paragraph, page, or document.

5. Choose an Extended Characters option.

6. Select where to store the index file.

7. Select where to store temporary files generated during the index's operations.

8. Click on OK to return to the previous dialog box.

9. Click on OK to begin the indexing.

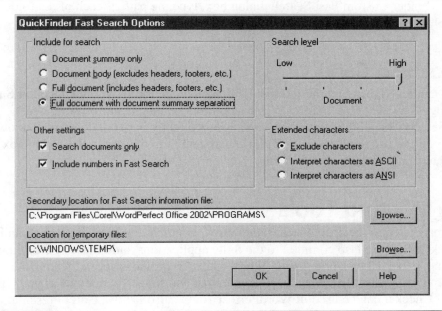

FIGURE 2-7   QuickFinder Fast Search Options dialog box

NOTE *Use the Settings button in QuickFinder Manager to set default options for all searches.*

Using a Standard Search is automatic. Just open QuickFinder and perform a search that includes the specified folder. QuickFinder automatically uses the index.

If you selected to manually update the index, you should perform an update after you change the files in the folder. To do so, display the QuickFinder Manager dialog box, click in the index you want to update, and then click on the Update button. Use the Rebuild button to reindex the files from the beginning.

TIP *Use the Edit button to change the specification of a search; click on Delete to remove a search; or click on Information to see details about the index.*

Creating a Custom Fast Search

Creating a Custom Fast Search is similar to a Standard Search, except you can select more than one folder, and you can choose not to index the subfolders. In the

QuickFinder Custom Fast Search dialog box, type the path of each of the folders, or select them from the browse list, and then click on Add.

Reaching Corel

You can reach Corel on the Internet while you are working with the Open or Save dialog box. Click on the Corel Web Site button to launch your browser and connect to Corel. The Corel Web site appears directly in the dialog box window, and you can use the Back, Forward, Reload, and Stop buttons in the dialog box toolbar to navigate around the site.

Using Writing Tools

Features such as the spell checker, thesaurus, grammar checker, dictionary, and QuickCorrect are also common to the Suite applications, although not every tool is available in each program. While WordPerfect 10 provides special features to automatically check your spelling and grammar and suggest synonyms as you type, Spell Checker can be used in WordPerfect 10, Quattro Pro 10, Corel Presentations 10, and CorelCENTRAL Mail 10. You access the writing tools from the program's Tools menu. In this section, you'll learn how to use these powerful tools.

Spell Checker, Thesaurus, Grammatik (the grammar-checking program), and Dictionary are listed in the tabs in the same dialog box, so you can easily switch between them.

Checking Spelling

The Spell Checker feature compares every word in a document with those in a built-in word list. If a word is not found in the list, it is reported as a possible misspelling. To start the spell checker, pull down the Tools menu, and click on Spell Checker. Some applications also have a Spell Checker button in the toolbar.

 In Corel Presentations, a text box must be selected before you can access Spell Checker, Thesaurus, and Grammatik.

Spell Checker starts comparing the words in the document, the slide, or the selected cells of a sheet with those in the dictionary. When it finds the first possible error, it displays the word and a list of alternative spellings, as shown in Figure 2-8.

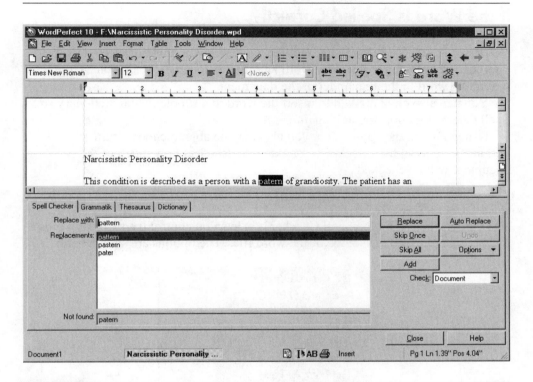

FIGURE 2-8   Spell Check dialog box

If the Word Is Spelled Incorrectly

If the word is spelled wrong, look for the correct spelling in the list. If it is there, double-click on it to replace the misspelled word. To retype the word correctly yourself, type the correct spelling in the Replace With text box, and then click on Replace. Click on Auto Replace to replace the same word with the corrected one throughout the entire document, and to create a QuickCorrect entry so the word will be corrected for you when you next type it.

If you are not sure of the correct spelling, try typing an alternate in the Replace With text box—as you type, Spell Check looks up and displays words in the Replacements list. If you just want to skip the word and correct it later, click on Skip Once.

If the Word Is Spelled Correctly

If the word is spelled correctly but is not in the word list, you have several choices. You can click on Skip Once to accept the word as it is in this instance—however, Spell Check will stop at the same word later in the document. Click on Skip All to ignore the word in the remainder of the document.

You can also click on Add to insert the word in a supplemental dictionary so Spell Check does not stop at it again.

Depending on the application, you also may be able to choose from other options. Pull down the Check list, for example, to select how much of the document will be checked.

Spelling Options

The Options button on the Spell Checker box lets you control the types of words that are checked and the source of the word file. The options are shown here:

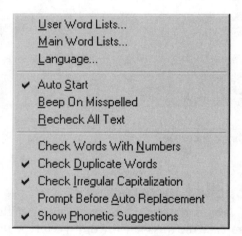

WordPerfect Spell-As-You-Go

WordPerfect 10 and CorelCENTRAL Mail automatically checks your spelling as you create your document or e-mail message using its Spell-As-You-Go feature, placing a wavy red line under words it cannot find in its dictionary, as shown here (the wavy line appears red on your screen):

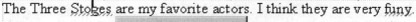

The Three Stoges are my favorite actors. I think they are very funy.

You can leave the wavy lines where they are and correct your errors later on, or you can fix them as you work. If you know the correct spelling, and the mistake was just a typo, you can press the BACKSPACE key to erase the mistake, and then type the word again.

You can also let WordPerfect 10 or CorelCENTRAL Mail 10 correct the word for you. Point to the word, and click the right mouse button to see the Spell-As-You-Go QuickMenu, shown here:

The Three Stokes are my favorite actors. I think they are very funy.

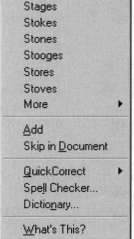

At the top of the menu are some suggested spellings. Just click on the correct word to insert it in place of your own. The word "More" means that WordPerfect has found more suggested spellings than can fit on the menu—point to "More" to see these other choices.

Here are the other options on the QuickMenu:

- *Add*—Select this option if the word is spelled correctly and you want to add it to WordPerfect's word list. The word will not be flagged with a wavy line again in any WordPerfect document.

- *Skip in Document*—Choose this if you want to ignore the word only in this document. It will be flagged in other documents, however.

- *QuickCorrect*—Pick this to create a QuickCorrect entry for the word.

- *Spell Checker*—Use this to start the Spell Check feature.

- *Dictionary*—Opens the dictionary.

 The QuickCorrect option only appears when WordPerfect 10 has suggested spellings.

You can turn off the Spell-As-You-Go feature if you don't like all of the wavy lines. Pull down the Tools menu, point to Proofread, and click on Off.

Using the Thesaurus

When you just can't think of the correct word, use the Thesaurus. It displays a list of synonyms for the word at the position of the insertion point. In WordPerfect 10, the Prompt-As-You-Go feature displays synonyms for words as you type. Here's how to use the Thesaurus:

1. Pull down the Tools menu, and click on Thesaurus to display the Thesaurus dialog box, as shown in Figure 2-9. The box lists alternate meanings of the selected word or the word nearest the insertion point. Each is indicated by its part of speech—a verb, noun, or adjective

2. Scroll the list of definitions, and click on the plus sign to the left of the one that best suits your meaning. The list expands to show synonyms plus options including Related Words, Is a Type of, Has Types, and Is a Part of.

NOTE *Use the Options button in the Thesaurus to set the possible options that will appear in addition to synonyms.*

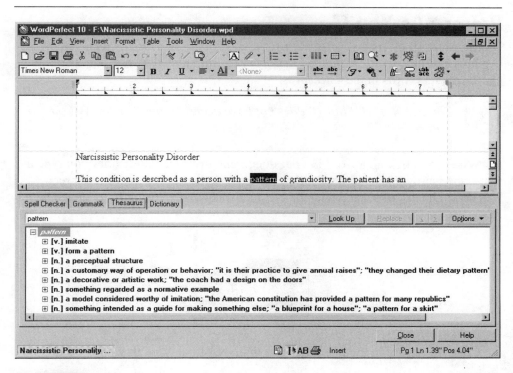

FIGURE 2-9 Thesaurus

3. Click on one of the synonyms to display a second column showing possible meanings. If you want to use the synonym you selected, click on Replace. If none of the suggested synonyms in the first list box seem appropriate, click on one that is the best possible, and then select a definition and synonym from the second list box. You can also choose one of the other options from the first box, such as Related Words, to see additional meanings and synonyms.

4. Each time you select a synonym, another list appears in the box to its right. Once three list boxes contain information, clicking on a word in the rightmost box causes them all to scroll toward the left. You can then use the buttons on the far right and left to scroll the boxes into view. Continue looking up words until you find one that you want to insert.

Prompt-As-You-Go

WordPerfect 10 offers a special feature called *Prompt-As-You-Go*. This option displays alternate words from the Dictionary for misspelled words, and displays synonyms for words in the Thesaurus.

 CorelCENTRAL Mail 10 does not have access to the Prompt-As-You-Go feature.

When you click on a word in your document, or immediately after you type a word, the word appears in the Prompt-As-You-Go box at the top of the screen. Pull down the list associated with the box to display alternate words, as shown here:

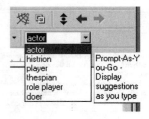

Click on a word in the list to insert it in place of the word in your document.

 When you misspell a word, a suggested spelling appears in the box. Move the insertion point back over the word, and then pull down the list to see suggested spellings. Suggested spellings also appear if you click on a word that Spell-As-You-Go has underlined.

Checking Your Grammar

Grammatik is a program that checks your grammar, looking for words, phrases, and sentence structure that don't agree with the program's grammatical rules.

 Quattro Pro 10 does not have access to Grammatik. WordPerfect 10 can check your grammar for you with Grammar-As-You-Go.

To start the program, pull down the Tools menu, and click on Grammatik. When it finds the first possible error, it displays it in a dialog box, such as the one shown in Figure 2-10.

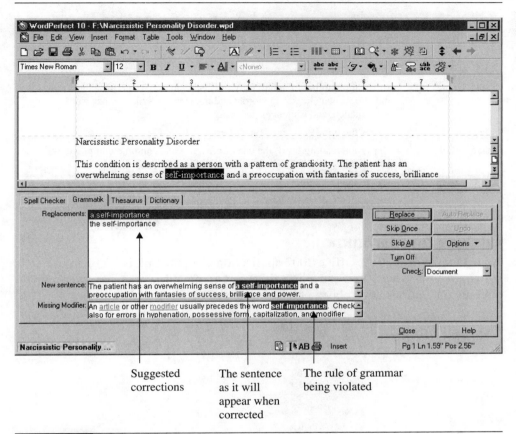

Suggested corrections

The sentence as it will appear when corrected

The rule of grammar being violated

FIGURE 2-10   Grammatik dialog box

If the suggested correction is acceptable, click on Replace. You can also click on Skip Once or Skip All to leave the text as it is and to continue to the next problem. If you want to ignore the grammatical rule that is being violated for the remainder of the process, click on the Turn Off button.

You can also evaluate your writing by clicking on the Options button and selecting Analysis to choose from the options shown in Table 2-1.

Option	Description
Parse Tree	Displays a tree diagram of the grammatical structure of your text, including the parts of speech
Parts of Speech	Displays its usage under each word
Basic Counts	Shows the number of syllables, words, sentences, paragraphs; short, long, and simple sentences; big words; and the average syllables per word, words per sentence, and sentences per paragraph
Flagged	Shows the number of each type of error detected
Readability	Shows the reading level, the use of passive voice, and the complexity of your document

TABLE 2-1   Grammatik options

Customizing Grammatik

As with all WordPerfect Office 2002 applications, Grammatik is set up to use certain default values. You can adjust the way Grammatik works, however, by clicking on Options to display a pull-down menu.

Use the Checking Styles feature, for example, to choose the range of grammatical rules that are checked during the process. You can select from 11 general types of documents or sets of rules, such as formal letters or technical documents. The style you select determines which grammatical rules are applied and how strictly your text must conform to them. You'll be given more latitude, for example, in informal letters than on student compositions.

The Options menu also lets you determine whether Grammatik also checks spelling, prompts you before performing an automatic replacement, and in Corel WordPerfect also allows you to check headers, footers, and footnotes.

Grammar-As-You-Go

WordPerfect 10 also includes Grammar-As-You-Go. With this feature turned on, you'll see wavy blue lines under possible grammatical errors. Right-click on the error to see the rule of grammar being violated and a suggested correction.

To turn this feature on or off, pull down the Tools menu, point to Proofread, and click on Grammar-As-You-Go.

Using the Dictionary

Corel WordPerfect 2002 includes a partial version of the Oxford University Press dictionary. (You can upgrade to the complete version by selecting Upgrade from the Dictionary's Options menu.)

To look up a word in the dictionary, click on it in the document and choose Dictionary from the Tools menu to open the dictionary shown in Figure 2-11.

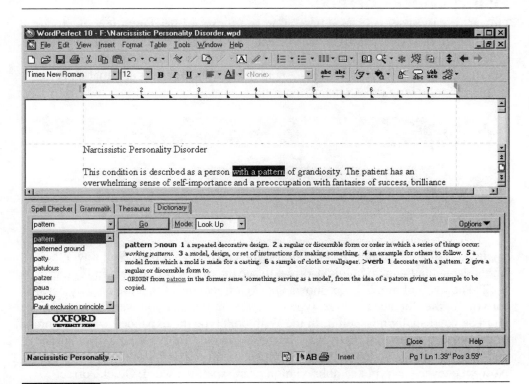

FIGURE 2-11   Dictionary

Find other words by scrolling the word list on the left. Instead of scrolling the list, however, you can search for a word. Pull down the Mode list and choose Search to clear the list of words. In the text box above the empty list, type the word you are looking for and press Enter.

Streamlining Your Work with QuickCorrect and Format-As-You-Go

It is easy to get spoiled using WordPerfect Office 2002. Not only does it check your spelling—even as you type in WordPerfect 10—but it can correct mistakes and insert special symbols and characters as you type. This magic is performed by two special features: QuickCorrect and Format-As-You-Go.

Using QuickCorrect

QuickCorrect can expand an abbreviation and fix your mistakes automatically as you type. In fact, QuickCorrect can correct over 125 common misspellings and typographic errors as you type. For example, if you type "adn," QuickCorrect automatically replaces it with "and." In addition, QuickCorrect automatically makes the following replacements for you:

Replace	With
(c	©
(c)	©
(r	®
--	—
1/2	½

In addition to the built-in corrections, you can add your own. Pull down the Tools menu, and click on QuickCorrect to see the dialog box shown in Figure 2-12. The two-column list box shows QuickCorrect entries that are already defined for you. In the Replace text box, type the abbreviation that you want to use or a word as you usually misspell it. In the With box, type the expanded word or phrase or the correct spelling of the word. Then click on Add Entry. Your abbreviation and/or correction is added to the list in alphabetical order. Close the dialog box. Now whenever you type the abbreviation or misspell the word, QuickCorrect expands or corrects it for you.

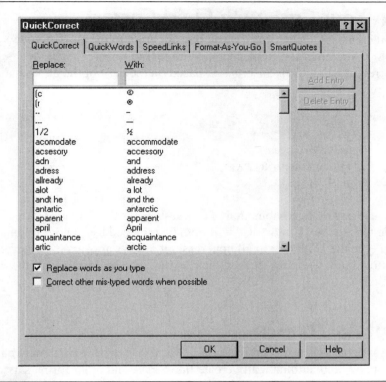

FIGURE 2-12   Creating QuickCorrect entries

> **TIP** *If you select text before opening the QuickCorrect box, the text appears in the With box—just enter the abbreviation for it.*

If you do not want QuickCorrect to replace words for you, deselect the Replace Words As You Type checkbox. You'll need to do this, for example, if you want to type (C) and not change it into the copyright symbol. To delete a QuickCorrect entry, select it in the list, and then click on Delete Entry.

> **TIP** *Select the Correct Other Mis-Typed Words When Possible option to have WordPerfect automatically correct other words when only one possible suggested replacement is in the dictionary.*

QuickCorrect entries are not case-sensitive. If you already have an abbreviation "pc," then creating one as "PC" replaces it.

Watch Your Case with QuickCorrect

When you create a QuickCorrect entry, pay attention to the case of your characters. If you enter the Replace and With text in lowercase characters, QuickCorrect automatically inserts text based on the case of the abbreviation, as shown here:

If You Type	QuickCorrect Inserts
tlc	tender loving care
TLC	TENDER LOVING CARE
Tlc	Tender loving care

If you use any other combination of cases, such as "tLC," QuickCorrect matches the first letter. So "tLC" and "tlC" will both be replaced by "tender loving care."

If you type the With text in all uppercase, it always appears uppercase. If you type it with an initial capital letter, QuickCorrect matches the case of the abbreviation.

Format-As-You-Go

Format-As-You-Go is a special feature of WordPerfect 10. This feature can adjust sentence spaces and automatically create lines, lists, and other formats as you type. If you forget to capitalize the first letter of the sentence, Format-As-You-Go does that also. It changes two spaces following a sentence to one space and corrects two irregular capitals (such as changing "WHen" to "When"). To access these features in Corel WordPerfect, select QuickCorrect from the Tools menu, and then click on the Format-As-You-Go tab to see the options shown in Figure 2-13.

The Sentence Corrections section determines the capitalization and spacing within a sentence. It capitalizes the first letter of a sentence, fixes two initial capitals, and replaces two spaces between words with one space.

The End of Sentence Corrections section determines the spacing between sentences. You can select to leave your sentences as you type them (none), or to replace a single space with two, or vice versa.

The Format-As-You-Go choices section determines the special formats WordPerfect 10 will apply as you type.

- *CapsFix* corrects improper capitalization and turns off the CAPS LOCK key if you type text after accidentally clicking on it.

2

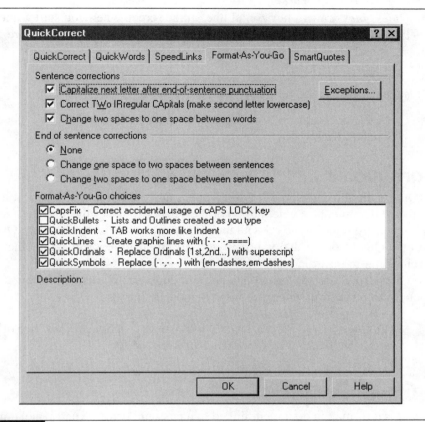

FIGURE 2-13   Format-As-You-Go settings

■ *QuickBullets* starts the automatic numbering or bulleted list feature. If you start a paragraph with a number or letter followed by a period and a tab, or a special character at the beginning of a line followed by an indent or tab, WordPerfect 10 continues numbering, lettering, or bulleting subsequent paragraphs.

■ *QuickIndent* lets you indent a paragraph from the left margin. If you press the TAB key at the beginning of any line but the first, WordPerfect 10 indents the entire paragraph.

- *QuickLines* draws a horizontal line on the screen when you start a line with three or more hyphens, or a double line when you type three or more equal signs and press ENTER.

- *QuickOrdinals* replaces the characters "st", "nd", and "rd" with superscripts behind numerals such as "1st", "2nd", and "3rd."

- *QuickSymbols* replaces two hyphens with an en dash and three hyphens with an em dash.

SmartQuotes

SmartQuotes are the curly types of apostrophes and quotation marks that you see in published documents. By default, WordPerfect 10 replaces the straight quotes that you enter from the keyboard with their curly equivalents. Use the SmartQuotes page of the QuickCorrect dialog box to turn off this feature, or select another curly quote character to insert in its place.

You can also choose to leave plain straight quotation marks that follow numbers, which is useful when you want to indicate inches.

 NOTE *In Chapter 6, you'll learn about QuickWords and SpeedLinks, two other time-saving features available in WordPerfect 10.*

Using Corel Projects

A *project* is a formatted document linked to a custom PerfectExpert panel—all you need to do is enter your own information. If you need to send a fax, for example, you can choose a fax cover page project. Need to create a budget in Quattro Pro 10? Select a budget project. Want to develop a presentation of your business plan? Select a business plan project.

You can access the projects in any of three ways:

- Clicking on the Corel New Project DAD button in the taskbar

- Selecting Corel New Project from the WordPerfect Office 2002 menu

- Selecting New from Project from the File menu in WordPerfect 10, Quattro Pro 10, and Corel Presentations 10.

In the dialog box that appears, click on the Create New tab to see the options as shown in Figure 2-14.

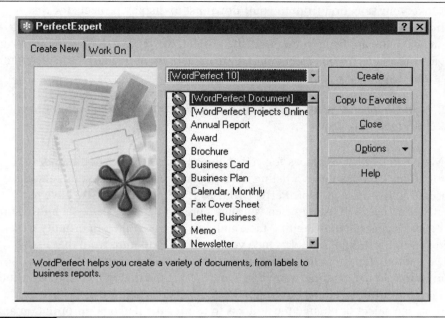

FIGURE 2-14 Projects to automate your work

If you display the box from within a WordPerfect Office 2002 application, you'll see projects for that application. Otherwise, pull down the list on the top of the box to select another application or to choose from groups of projects, as shown here.

Make your selection from the pull-down list to display projects for that application or list in the large list box. Double-click on the project you want to use. If you are in the application that uses the project, the project document opens and appears onscreen. If you select a project from another application, the program starts and displays the project. It's that easy.

NOTE   *In Chapter 8, you'll learn how to use WordPerfect 10 templates to automate your work.*

Many projects have places for your name, address, phone number, or other information. You designate a listing from the Address Book as your personal information listing, and WordPerfect 10 uses it for projects. If you have not yet selected your personal listing when you start a project that uses personal information, a dialog box appears reporting that fact, and you are given the opportunity to select a listing from the Address Book. Once you do so, information from that listing appears automatically in the project or in dialog boxes prompting you for information. In the example shown in Figure 2-15, the dialog box appears after clicking on Fill in Heading Info in the PerfectExpert panel for the Memo project.

You can select or change the address to use for the personal information at any time from within the PerfectExpert dialog box. Pull down the Options list and select Personal Information, then click OK in the box that appears to open the address book. Choose the listing containing your personal information and click Insert. The Open Address Book box appears. Click Cancel.

ClipArt and the Scrapbook

The three major WordPerfect Office 2002 applications share a common resource—the Scrapbook. The Scrapbook is a handy location to store clip art and other graphic files that you find useful in your publications. Access the Scrapbook by clicking on the ClipArt button in the application's toolbar to see the dialog box shown in Figure 2-16. Use the dialog box tabs to select to display clip art, photos, sounds, or movies.

The Scrapbook shows graphics, sounds, and movies stored on your computer's hard disk. To access additional graphics, click on the Internet button to launch your Web browser and connect to a site provided by Corel.

To use a graphic from the Scrapbook, drag and drop it into the document, or click on the graphic and then on the Insert button. You can also right-click on the

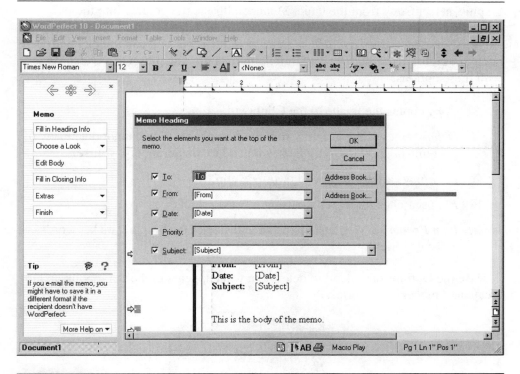

FIGURE 2-15 Using a project

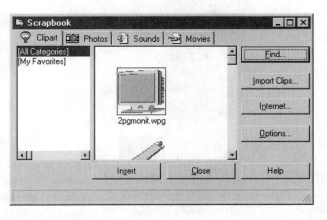

FIGURE 2-16 The Scrapbook

graphic, select Copy from the QuickMenu, and paste the graphic into the document.

The Scrapbook does not have a menu or toolbar, but you can interact with it using the right mouse button. Right-clicking on a graphic presents a QuickMenu with these options:

- *Copy* copies the image to the Clipboard.

- *Delete* removes the graphic from the Scrapbook. You cannot delete any of the built-in graphics, only those you add to the Scrapbook yourself.

- *Play* plays a selected sound or movie clip.

- *Find* searches for a graphic using a keyword that you specify.

- *Item Properties* displays the name and size of the graphic, its keywords, and categories.

Use the Options command to determine what appears in the Scrapbook and to create and manage categories:

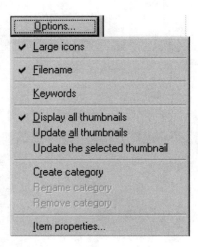

Categories provide a convenient way to organize graphics according to a theme. To create a category, click on the tab for the type of object you want to categorize—ClipArt, Photos, Sounds, or Movies. Then select Create Category from the Options menu, type its name in the box that appears, and then click OK. Use the Rename Category and Remove Category commands from the Options menu to manage your category list. Your categories will now be listed along the left of the appropriate tab in the Scrapbook.

To assign a graphic to a category, right-click on it, and choose Item Properties from the QuickMenu to open the Scrapbook Item Properties box, as shown in Figure 2-17. Enable the checkboxes for each of the categories you want to assign.

To list just the items in a category, click on the category name in the list. Click on All Categories to display every object.

To add other items that you have available on your disk to the Scrapbook, click on the Import Clips button. In the Insert File dialog box that appears, locate the graphic you want to add, and then click the Open button. The Scrapbook Item Properties box appears. Enter one or more keywords that you want to describe the graphic, and then click OK. The item automatically is placed in the appropriate tab of the Scrapbook—photographs are placed in the Photos page, video clips in the Movies page, and so forth.

NOTE   *To insert graphics other than those in the Scrapbook, select Graphics from the application's Insert menu, and choose From File.*

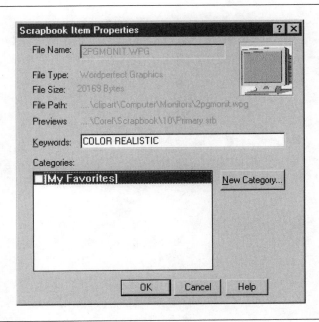

FIGURE 2-17   Scrapbook Item Properties

Chapter 3

WordPerfect Office 2002 and the Internet

The World Wide Web ("the Web" for short) is a graphic interface to the Internet, an informal network of computer systems around the world.

If you subscribe to an online service such as America Online, CompuServe, or Prodigy, then you have access to the Web and the Internet. You may have access to the Internet through your company's network, your school, or through any one of thousands of service providers around the world. The Web is one way that you can connect to and share information across the Internet. It's also the most popular method because of its graphic capabilities, which allow you to see pictures and hear sounds as you move easily to sites all over the planet.

When you connect to a site on the Web, you'll see a Web page. This is really just a special document that contains information, as well as hypertext links to other documents and the Web. A *hypertext link* (hyperlink) is a graphic or line of text that you can click on to move to another Web location.

For a document to be used as a Web page, however, it must be written using special formatting codes. These codes tell the *Web browser,* the program that lets you contact the Web, how to display the document on the screen, and what to do when you click on a hypertext link. These formats are known as *HTML* (Hypertext Markup Language), and the codes are called *HTML tags.* You can create a Web document using any word processing program by typing in the HTML tags. However, trying to visualize how a Web page will appear from just looking at the tags is difficult. Since the tags must use specific formats, it is all too easy to make a mistake and get a terrible mess when you view it on the Web page screen.

Luckily, WordPerfect Office 2002 lets you create Web pages without having to worry about HTML tags. You can just create your document, worksheet, or presentation as you normally would, then have WordPerfect Office create the Web page for you, as you will learn in this chapter.

But first, let's take a look at sending e-mail quickly through your WordPerfect Office 2002 applications.

 You can quickly connect to the Web and begin surfing by clicking on the Corel Connector button in WordPerfect Office 2002 applications.

Sending Email and Faxes

Sending your WordPerfect Office 2002 document as an e-mail message couldn't be any easier. When your document is ready to send, select File | Send To | Mail Recipient. With Corel Presentations 10, you'll be asked if you want to mail just the current slide or the entire presentation—make your choice, and then click OK. Your default e-mail application starts—just enter the address of the recipient and the subject, and then click on Send. In Chapter 4 you'll learn how to set CorelCENTRAL Mail as your default e-mail application.

To send the current document as a fax, choose File | Send To | Net2Fax to send the current document as a fax using the Net2Fax feature, or choose File | Send To | Fax to use another installed fax driver.

Web Pages in WordPerfect 10

Rather than type HTML tags, you can use WordPerfect 10 to create a Web page graphically—by selecting formats, styles, and page elements from the menus and toolbars.

Before actually saving your document as a Web page, you can preview how it will appear on the Internet. Select View | Preview in Browser to open your Web browser with the document displayed. Close the browser window to return to WordPerfect.

When you are satisfied with the look of your document, select File | Publish to HTML to open the dialog box shown in Figure 3-1.

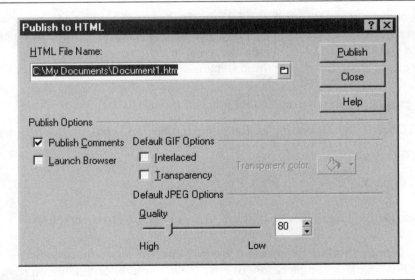

FIGURE 3-1 Publishing a Web page

Change the location and name of the page, as desired, choose from the other options in the dialog box, and click Publish. If you selected the Launch Brower option, the saved Web page will automatically be displayed in your Web browser.

| TIP | *To determine the format of a graphic, right-click on the graphic and choose HTML Properties. On the Publish tab of the box that appears, select either GIF or JPEG, and then click OK.* |

Creating Hyperlinks

Hyperlinks are really what make the Web so powerful. They let you move from site to site—surfing the Web by clicking on keywords or graphics. There are basically three ways to use hypertext links:

- To move to another location in the same document—up or down to another paragraph or page, for example.

- To move to another HTML document on your disk. Clicking on the link opens the HTML document and displays it in the browser or in Internet Publisher.

- To move to another Web site, anywhere in the world.

If you want to create a link to a location in the current Web page, you must first set a bookmark. A *bookmark* gives a name to a specific location or block of text. To go to that location, you use the name in the link.

To create a bookmark, use these steps:

1. Select the text or graphic that you want to use as the bookmark.

2. Click on the Hyperlink button in the toolbar, and click on Insert Bookmark.

3. Type the bookmark name.

4. Click on OK.

Once the bookmark is set, you have to create the link to it, as follows:

1. Type and format the text that you want to click on to move to the bookmark. It can be before or after the bookmark, depending on if you need to jump up or down.

2. Select the text, click on the Hyperlink button in the toolbar, and click on Create Link to display the Hyperlink Properties dialog box shown in Figure 3-2.

NOTE *CorelCENTRAL Mail also lets you add hyperlinks to e-mail messages.*

3

3. In the Bookmark text box, enter the bookmark name, or select it from the drop-down list.

You also can use the Hyperlink Properties dialog box to create links to other HTML documents on your disk, and to Web sites. To open another document as the link, enter its path and name in the Document text box, and click on the Document option button. To move to a bookmark in the document as soon as it opens, type the bookmark name in the Bookmark text box under the document name.

To jump to another site on the Web, type the desired site's Web address in the Document text box. If the Web page consists of frames, you can also indicate the frame to display. If you do not know the correct address, you can surf the Web to find it, using these steps:

1. Click in the Document text box.

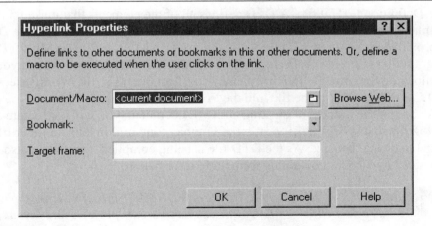

FIGURE 3-2 Creating a link

2. Click on the Browse Web button in the toolbar to launch your Web browser. WordPerfect 10 launches your Internet browser. As you surf the Web, the address of the Web page being displayed appears in the Document text box.

3. When you find the correct location, switch to the dialog box, and click on OK.

4. Exit your browser when you have finished browsing.

Working with XML Documents

The Extensible Markup Language is another way to create Web pages. While WordPerfect Office 2002 includes tools for using XML, this language requires some knowledge of its features and techniques. In this chapter, we'll summarize the procedures required to create an XML page. For additional information, refer to the WordPerfect Reference Center.

NOTE   *XML is actually a simplified version of the Standard Generalized Markup Language (SGML).*

Before you can create an XML document, you need to select or create an XML Project. The project contains information about the type of XML document, as well as a special WordPerfect 10 template that has been created from a Document Type Definition (DTD) file. A DTD defines all of the elements that make up the document and describes the relationships between elements. Several sample DTDs are provided in the \Program Files\Corel\WordPerfect Office 2002\XML\DTD and \Program Files\Corel\WordPerfect Office 2002\XML\Tutorial folders, and you can download others from the Internet. Once you select the DTD, the WordPerfect DTD Compiler converts the file into the WordPerfect 10 template.

As part of the process of creating an XML document, you will also create a Catalog file that specifies the location of graphic, font, multimedia, or other files needed to create the page. As the DTD file is being compiled, the system also generates Layout files containing formatting information.

NOTE   *Advanced users can run the WordPerfect XML Project Designer from the WordPerfect Office 2002 Utilities menu to create projects and layout files.*

WordPerfect 10 provides a number of XML templates that already include compiled DTD files. To use a template to start a new XML document, select File | New from Template. Choose XML from the list, and then double-click on the template you want to use.

If you want to create a new project and XML document, use these steps:

1. Start WordPerfect 10.

2. Choose File | New XML Document to open the Select or Create an XML Project dialog box. If the box contains the name of an existing project you want to use, select it, and click Select.

3. Click New to open the Select WordPerfect Category/Project dialog box.

4. In the Project text box, enter the Project name, and click Next to open the Select WordPerfect Template dialog box. The default template name is the same as the project. If you already have a template that was created from a DTD file, you can select it here and then skip the remaining procedures for selecting and compiling a DTD.

5. Click Next to open the Choose Template Creation Method dialog box, shown in Figure 3-3.

6. Click the Compile DTD and create layout option button.

7. Click Next to open the Compile DTD dialog box.

8. Click Compile DTD to open the WordPerfect DTD Compiler dialog box shown in Figure 3-4.

9. In the Input File Name box, enter or choose the path and name of the DTD.

10. Click Compile. After the process is completed, the Compile Status box reports that the template was written successfully.

11. Click OK.

12. Click Close to close the WordPerfect DTD Compiler dialog box. The Compile DTD dialog box reappears.

13. Click Next to display the Create Layout dialog box. In this box, you can also choose to run Project Designer to create layout files.

14. Click Next to open the Select Catalog File dialog box.

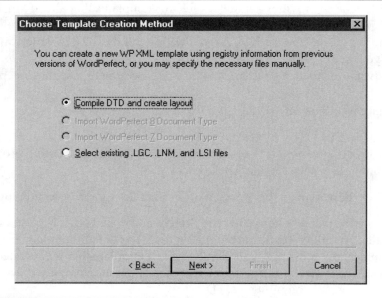

FIGURE 3-3   Choose Template Creation Method dialog box

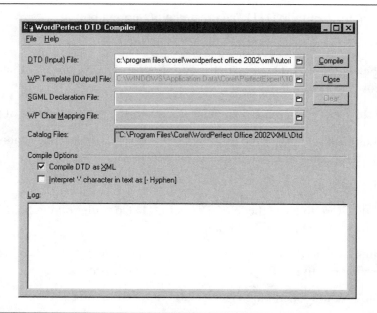

FIGURE 3-4   WordPerfect DTD Compiler dialog box

3

15. Type the name of a catalog file, and click Next to display the Project Summary box.

16. Click Finish. The Select or Create an XML Project dialog box appears, shown in Figure 3-5.

17. If the project is not shown in the Categories/Projects list, pull down the list and choose the category. Then click on the project in the Categories/Projects list, and then on Select.

The blank document window appears with two panes. Figure 3-6 shows WordPerfect 10 with a sample XML document. On the left is the XML Tree that shows the structure of the document. On the right are the text and XML codes of the document.

When you are done, you have to save the file. Select File | Save As, pull down the File Type list, and choose one of these formats:

- XML UTF-16 Big Endian
- XML UTF-16 Little Endian
- XML UTF-8

Enter the filename, and then click on Save to open the Save as XML dialog box, shown in Figure 3-7. Click OK to save the file.

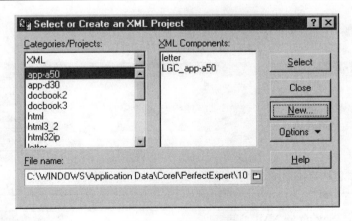

FIGURE 3-5   Select or Create an XML Project dialog box

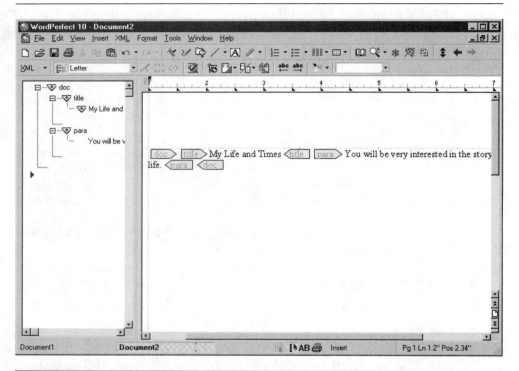

FIGURE 3-6 WordPerfect with a sample XML document

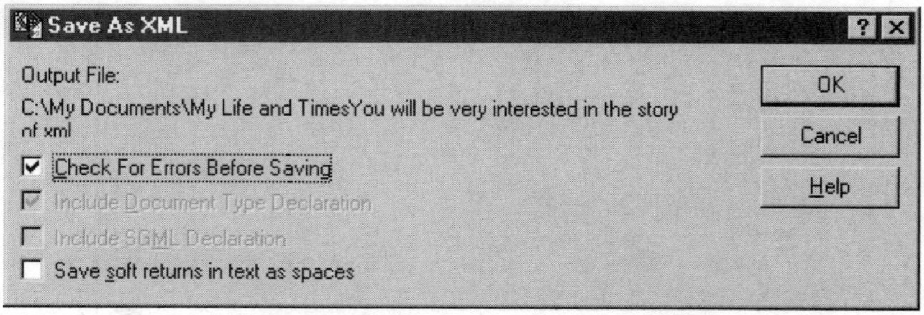

FIGURE 3-7 Saving an XML file

Publishing Your Corel Presentations Slide Show on the Web

With Corel Presentations 10, you can create several types of slide shows, depending on the options you select. Start by selecting Internet Publisher from the File menu or clicking on the Internet Publisher button on the property bar. (The button does not appear if an object or placeholder is selected on a slide.) If you haven't saved the presentation, you'll be prompted to do so. Once the presentation is saved, you'll see the dialog box shown in Figure 3-8. This is the first of a series of boxes in which you select options for creating a Web page.

You can either click Next to move from box to box, or click on one of the links on the left to go to a specific page.

In the second box, you can choose to create a new layout, select a default layout, or choose a layout that you already created and saved. In the third, you choose the graphic format— either GIF, JPEG, PNG, Show It!, or Flash. The Show It! format requires you to have a special add-in to see slide animations, but it can be downloaded free over the Internet. The Flash option requires a browser plug-in to see the slide show's animations and transitions.

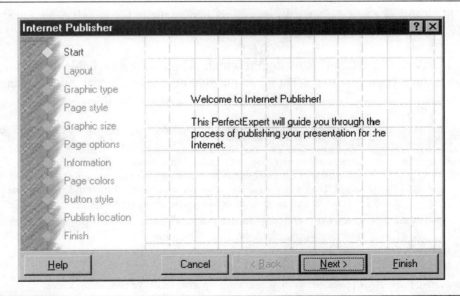

FIGURE 3-8 Creating a Web page from a Corel Presentation slide show

> **TIP** *Select an existing layout and click View Layout to see the layout's settings.*

The next box, shown in Figure 3-9, lets you choose a page style. The options shown depend on the graphic format you selected. If you choose GIF, JPEG, or PNG, the four default Web page organizations that you can create are listed in Table 3-1. Click on the style you want and then on Next. Only the browser frames and single page options are available if you choose Show It! Or Flash.

You can now choose the display size, the size of graphics, and the border style, if any, around slides.

Next you choose options for the page.

Here are some of the other options available:

■ *Title* inserts the title above each slide.

■ *Number* displays "Slide X of Y" at the bottom of each slide.

■ *Speaker Notes* displays speaker notes under each slide.

■ *Goto Bar* inserts a bar under each slide for changing slides.

■ *Self-Running Presentation* starts the show automatically.

■ *Table of Contents* lets you choose to display the index as text or graphic thumbnails of each slide.

The Goto Bar and Self-Running Presentation options are available only with frame pages. If you chose the Thumbnail layout, no options appear, but you can

Page Arrangement	Description
Browser Frames	Creates a Web page with two frames. The frame on the left contains a collapsible outline that serves as a table of contents listing links to your slides. The frame on the right contains your slides—each slide on separate pages—as well as navigation buttons for changing slides.
Multiple Pages	Creates one Web page for each slide. You can create a separate slide with a table of contents using the slide titles as links.
Single Page	Creates one long Web page containing all of the slides. You can include page numbers but not a table of contents.
Thumbnail Page	Creates one Web page containing thumbnail sketches of the slides.

TABLE 3-1   Web page layouts

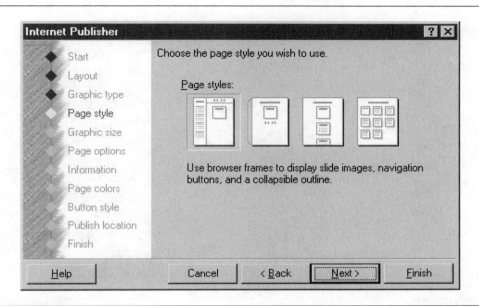

FIGURE 3-9   Select the page style

designate the thumbnail size. If you selected the Frame layout, you can also choose to display the table of contents as a text outlook or as slide thumbnails.

The next dialog box lets you enter your e-mail address and Web home page site. It includes a large text box in which you can enter other information, and you can choose to include a link viewers can click to download the entire show to their computer.

You can now choose to use the browser's colors or custom colors, and to include a background image.

In the next box, shown in Figure 3-10, you choose the style of button for the page. You then enter a Web page title and location to store the page. You can also click Advanced to set these options:

- Filename of the initial HTML file, index.html is the default.

- Extension for other HTML files, html is the default.

- If you want to save graphics in a subfolder (the default).

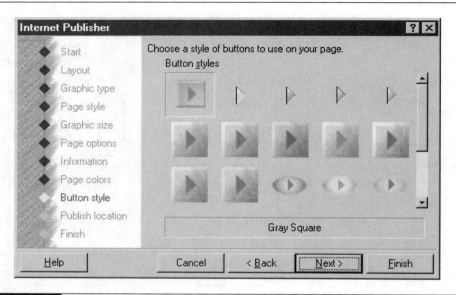

FIGURE 3-10   Select the button style

When you click Finish on the last page, you'll be asked if you want to create the destination folder if it does not yet exist, and then if you want to save your settings if you are creating a new layout:

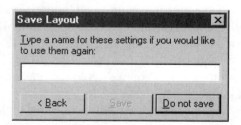

You can save the settings and then recall them when you start Internet Publisher again, or click on Do Not Save. You'll see an animation as your slides are converted into graphics, and you'll be asked if you want Internet Publisher to show you the resulting Web page. If you select Show Me, Internet Publisher launches your browser and begins the slide show.

The Web pages generated by Internet Publisher are stored in the location you specified. The default initial, or start page, is called INDEX.HTM. When you display this page in your browser, you'll see a list of slides and the link Start Here. Click on Start Here to begin displaying the slides. Figure 3-11 shows a Corel Presentations 10 slide show on a frame-based Web page.

If you select the Include Link to Download Original Presentation File, there is a button for downloading on the slide. When clicked, the slide show is downloaded to the viewer's computer so the viewer can then open the file in Corel Presentations.

Web Pages from Quattro Pro Spreadsheets

When you create a Web page from a Quattro Pro 10 spreadsheet, the rows and columns of the spreadsheet appear as a table in your Web browser. You can even

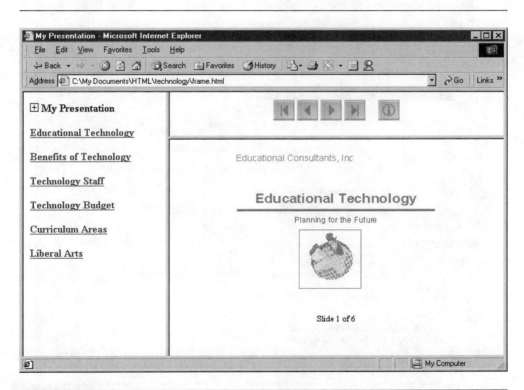

FIGURE 3-11   Corel Presentations slide show Web page

publish Quattro Pro charts so they appear as graphics. In fact, you have quite a few options for converting your spreadsheet to a Web page.

When you are ready to create the Web page, choose File | Publish to Internet to open the dialog box shown in Figure 3-12. You can choose an HTML or XML file, or to insert the tables and charts in an existing HTML file specified in the Save File box.

If the range of cells is incorrect, use Point mode to select the cells you want to publish. Use the Add and Delete buttons to insert or remove cell ranges and charts, and use the Move Up and Move Down buttons to change the order in which elements will appear on the Web page. You can also choose to display cells as either a table or plain text.

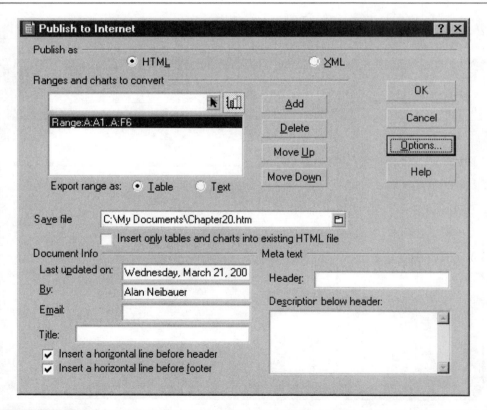

FIGURE 3-12 Creating a Web page from Quattro Pro

Use the remaining items in the Publish to Internet dialog box to set the page title and header and determine other aspects of the page.

NOTE   *Most options are not available if you select to publish an XML document.*

To further customize the Web page, click Options in the Publish to Internet dialog box to display the dialog box in Figure 3-13, then select from the options described here:

■ *Graphic Type*—Specifies the format of graphics created for the Web page.

■ *Layout Options*—Determines the number of pages created. You can create one single page with all of the information in one window, a page with multiple frames, or a series of pages.

■ *Color Settings*—Use the browser's default color scheme, or select colors for text, links, and the background.

When you have selected all of the appropriate options, click OK in the Publish to Internet dialog box to save the file. You can then open the file in your Web browser or upload it to your Web server.

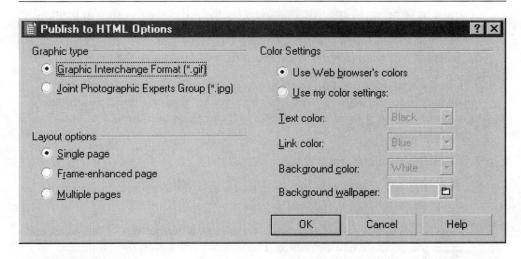

FIGURE 3-13   Publish to Internet Options

Publishing a CorelCENTRAL Address Book

CorelCENTRAL lets you publish an address book as an HTML file. This feature lets you share listings over the Internet or a company Intranet. It is useful, for example, to create a company or client directory. To publish an address book, just follow these steps from within CorelCENTRAL Address Book:

> **TIP** *You can use the Publish to HTML command from the File menu to also publish a CorelCENTRAL calendar and card file.*

1. To publish an entire address book, select the book in the left window. If any filter is applied to the book, choose View | Remove Filter. If you only want to publish selected records from an address book, select them in the list box on the right or use a filter that displays only the records you want to publish. You can also use a filter to display a subset of the records and then select specific records from the resulting list.

2. Choose File | Publish to HTML to open the dialog box shown in Figure 3-14.

3. Choose to create either a table or page layout. In a table layout, each record appears in a separate row with information in columns. In page layout, complete records are printed in order down the page.

4. Select the range of records. If you choose the Selected entries option, you must have selected specific records. Use the All entries option to print all of the records listed.

5. Select if you want to append the resulting records to an existing HTML file.

6. Choose the columns that you want to publish. By default, the columns displayed in the address book will be printed. You can select additional columns, even if they are not displayed, or remove columns that you do not want printed.

7. Click the Banner/Signature tab.

8. Enter the text of a banner headline that you want to appear on the top of the page.

9. Choose which elements you want to appear on the bottom of the page, and enter the necessary information. The options are a copyright date and name, the current date, a person or e-mail address to send comments to, and an e-mail address.

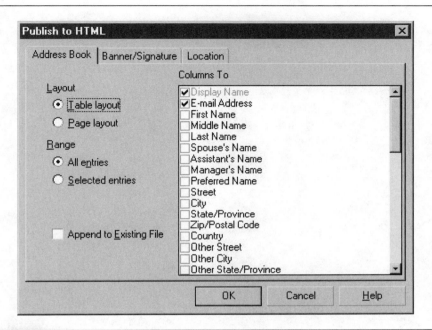

FIGURE 3-14　Publishing a CorelCENTRAL address book

10. Click the Location tab.

11. Choose the folder where you want the HTML file to be saved. The default is My Documents.

12. Enter the filename—just the prefix, Internet Publisher adds the HTML extension.

13. Choose if you want to be prompted before any existing files are replaced, the default.

14. Select if you want to view the HTML file after it is published (the default).

15. Click OK.

CorelCENTRAL creates the HTML file, and displays it in your browser window if you choose to view the file.

Chapter 4

Using
CorelCENTRAL 10

CorelCENTRAL 10 is a useful set of desktop tools—the same type of resources that you'd keep handy on your actual desk, such as a calendar and address book. In this chapter, you'll learn the basics of using CorelCENTRAL 10.

Introducing CorelCENTRAL 10

CorelCENTRAL 10 includes these features:

- An *e-mail* program for sending and receiving e-mail over the Internet.

- A *day planner* for quickly setting up and reviewing your appointments and tasks.

- A *calendar* for managing your appointments and tasks—with daily, weekly, or monthly views. You can also share your calendar on a network for managing group projects and activities in corporate environments.

- An *address book* for recording names and addresses.

- A *card file* for creating databases of all types.

- A *memo file* for recording notes and reminders.

- An *alarm* for setting an alarm clock.

Creating a Personal Calendar

CorelCENTRAL lets you work with two types of calendars—personal and shared. A personal calendar is designed just for you, containing a schedule of events and tasks that you have to perform.

A shared calendar is one which other users on your network can access. You can use a shared calendar to maintain a common schedule in an office or for a workgroup. For example, when working on a group project, a shared calendar allows all group members to check the schedule and set up meetings.

A shared calendar also lets you invite other users to an event, such as a meeting. When scheduling the event, you select which other users should be invited and have CorelCENTRAL automatically send them e-mail notifications. You use the CorelCENTRAL Admin feature to create a shared calendar. You'll learn more about that later in this chapter.

You can create a personal calendar at any time from within the CorelCENTRAL Calendar application. You'll also be able to create a personal calendar the first time you start CorelCENTRAL Day Planner or CorelCENTRAL Calendar. A dialog box appears asking if you want to open an existing shared or personal calendar or create a new personal calendar. Select the Create a Personal Calendar option button and click OK to see the Create Calendar dialog box, shown in Figure 4-1.

TIP *When you first start Day Planner or Calendar, you'll be asked if you want to automatically run Day Planner when you start your computer.*

4

Then follow these steps to create the calendar:

1. Enter a name for the Calendar

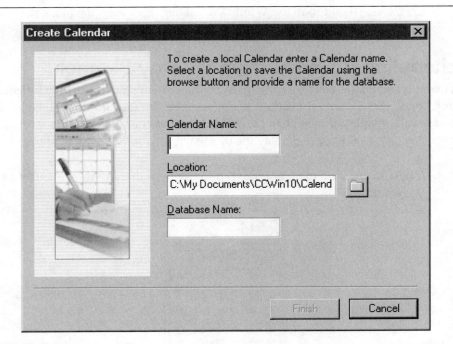

FIGURE 4-1 Creating a personal calendar

2. Select a location—the default is My Documents\CCWin10\Calendar

3. Enter a database name that will be used as the folder in which the calendar is stored.

4. Click Finish and then Yes if you are asked to create the folder.

Using the Day Planner

When you start your computer, the CorelCENTRAL 10 day planner, depending on your preferences, may automatically appear on the right edge of your screen, showing any events that you've planned for the day and tasks you have to perform, as shown in Figure 4-2. If the planner does not appear, select CorelCENTRAL Day Planner from the WordPerfect Office 2002 menu.

When you click anywhere else in the desktop, the planner seems to disappear. To restore the planner, just point to the far right of the screen, or click on the CorelCENTRAL 10 button in the Window's taskbar. This way, the planner is always ready.

Scheduling an Event from the Day Planner

An event is an appointment, meeting, party, or other item that you need to schedule. Many times, you'll want to schedule an appointment for the current day, which is automatically displayed when CorelCENTRAL 10 begins. To schedule an event for another day, you have to display the day using the following techniques.

1. Click on the calendar icon next to the date to display the calendar as shown here:

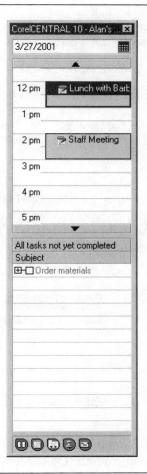

FIGURE 4-2   CorelCENTRAL day planner

2. Select the month that you want, or click on the arrows next to the year to change years.

3. Click on the date in the monthly calendar.

To add an appointment to the day planner, follow these steps:

1. Double-click on the time, scrolling if necessary, or right-click on the time and select Add Event from the QuickMenu.

2. Type a subject in the Subject box.

3. Choose a time from the Start list box.

4. Choose a duration from the Duration list box.

5. If you want to include comments about the event, type text in the Notes box.

6. If you want to assign an icon to the event—click the down arrow button next to the subject list box, and choose an icon.

7. Click OK.

The event appears in an accepted event colored box, representing the default one-hour duration. If you type more text than can fit into the event preview box, it does not appear but is saved with the event details in the Calendar. The event icon appears before the text, as shown here:

Here are some ways to work with events in the calendar:

■ Pause the mouse over the event to display a ScreenTip showing its complete information.

■ To delete an event, click on it and press the DELETE key, or right-click on it and choose Delete Event from the QuickMenu.

■ To edit the text of the event, click on its description, and then edit it as you would other text.

■ Drag and drop the event to change its starting time

■ Drag the top border of the selected event to change its start time, increasing its duration.

■ Drag the bottom border of the selected event to change its ending time, decreasing its duration.

Customizing Events

Each appointment can be associated with additional information, and you can
change an event's duration or make it a recurring event. Double-click on the
appointment, or right-click on it and choose Edit Event from the QuickMenu to
display the dialog box shown in Figure 4-3. If you want to assign an icon to the
event, click the down arrow button next to the subject list box, and choose an icon.

■ Change or set the date, start time, and duration of the event. To create a
multiple-day event, select the number of days from the duration list, or
enter the number of days followed by the letter "d", as in 6d.

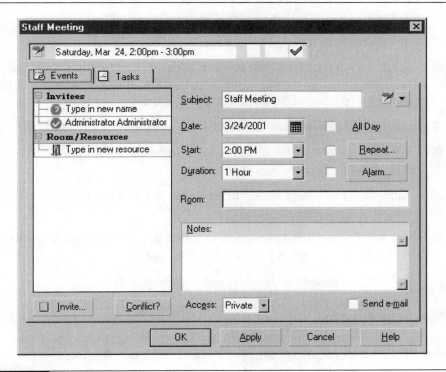

FIGURE 4-3   Editing event information

- Choose a category by clicking on the Categories button and choosing from these options:

- Change the date by clicking on the Mini-Calendar button next to the Date text box.

- Enter an optional location for the event.

- Enable the All Day checkbox to mark the event for the entire day. All day events are shown at the top of the time slots for each day—double-click on the event at the top of the time slot to edit the event.

- Enter any notes you want to make for the meeting.

- Pull down the Access list and choose either public or private to indicate the access level to the attendees of the event.

- Enable the Send e-mail button to send mail to those persons invited to the event, if this is a shared calendar.

- Click the Tasks tab and create any task that you want to associate with the event. You'll learn about tasks later in this chapter.

- Click OK to close the dialog box and save your changes.

Setting an Alarm

If you want to be reminded before the time of the event, right-click on it, and choose Alarm from the QuickMenu. (You can cancel the Alarm in the same way.) CorelCENTRAL 10 adds an Alarm icon next to the appointment text.

By default, CorelCENTRAL 10 sets an alarm to sound ten minutes before each event, as indicated by the Clock icon in the events list. A "snooze" option repeats the alarm every five minutes (or at a specified interval), until you turn off the alarm.

The alarm sounds a beep and displays a dialog box such as this:

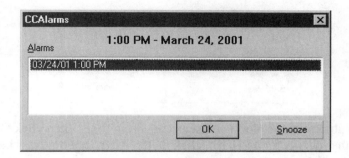

Click OK to dismiss the alarm, or click Snooze if you want to be reminded again in five minutes.

You can turn off the alarm, change its timing and snooze amount, and even change the sound that plays when the alarm goes off.

Double-click on the appointment, or right-click and choose Edit Event from the QuickMenu to open the Edit Event dialog box. Then click on Alarm to display these options:

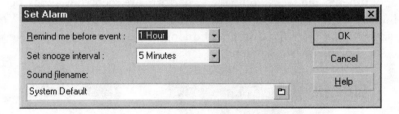

Use this dialog box to change the reminder time, the snooze time, and the name of the sound file that plays when the alarm goes off.

Using Quick Alarm

You can set an alarm to remind you of other events even without using CorelCENTRAL 10. WordPerfect Office 2002 normally installs a program called CorelCENTRAL 10 Alarm so you see it in the system tray on the end of the Windows taskbar, as seen here:

To set an alarm, click on the icon to display this dialog box:

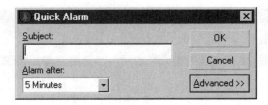

Enter a subject for the alarm and select an alarm time. Then click OK.

To set other details for an alarm, click on the Advanced button. The Quick Alarm box expands so you can set the date and time for the alarm, the snooze interval, and change the alarm sound.

If you need to edit the alarm information, right-click on the icon, and choose Edit Quick Alarm from the QuickMenu. A box appears listing all of the alarms that you've set. Select the one you want to change, and then click Edit to open the Quick Alarm dialog box. You can also choose to add a new alarm or delete an alarm.

Recurring Events

Many appointments and tasks you have to perform are recurring—they occur at regular intervals, such as every week or on the first day of every month. You can set a recurring event from the Edit Event dialog box by clicking on the Repeat button to see the options shown here:

Choose the tab that represents when and how often you want the event to occur:

■ *Weeks of Month* sets an event for the same day of the week each month, or for a certain number of months, such as on Monday of the first week of every month.

■ *Days of Month* sets an event the same day of the month or any number of months, such as the 15th of every other month.

■ *Weeks* sets an event the same day of every week or any number of weeks, such as every other Friday.

■ *Days* sets the event for every day or any number of days, as in every 15 days.

■ *Days of Month* sets the event for the same day of every month or number of months, such as the 15th of each month.

■ *Weeks of Year* sets the event for a day in a specific week of the year, as on Monday in the first week in February each year.

Next, enter or select from the mini-calendar the from and to dates for which to set the event—the default is one year. Choose options from the dialog box to set the recurring dates and click on OK. When you close the Edit Event dialog box, you'll see the recurring icon next to the event:

CorelCENTRAL 10 adds the event to each of the days determined by your selections.

Creating Links

A link lets you click on an event to perform one of these actions:

■ Display a memo from the Memo file

■ Display a card from the Card File

- Open a file or run an application
- Open a folder
- Send e-mail
- Jump to a Web site

To add a link, right-click on the field where you want to insert a link, point to Link To in the QuickMenu, and then choose the type of link:

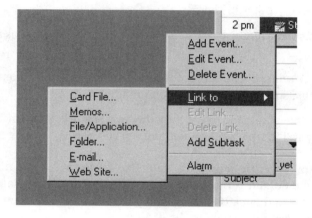

CorelCENTRAL 10 opens a dialog box in which you complete the link information. For example, if you choose to link the event to an e-mail, a dialog box appears in which you enter the e-mail address. This icon next to the event name indicates links:

When you click on the link icon, a box appears listing the links. Click on the link that you want to use. If you click on an e-mail link, CorelCENTRAL 10 opens your default e-mail program.

Using the Calendar

The day planner is useful but it only displays your schedule for one day at a time. To display a weekly or monthly calendar, to schedule appointments, and to keep track of special occasions, open the CorelCENTRAL 10 Calendar using the CorelCENTRAL Calendar option in the CorelCENTRAL 10 Applications menu. The calendar opens containing the toolbar and items shown in Figure 4-4.

You can create an event just as you learned to do for the day planner. Scroll the bar under the monthly calendar to change months. You can always return to the current date by clicking the View the Current Date button in the toolbar.

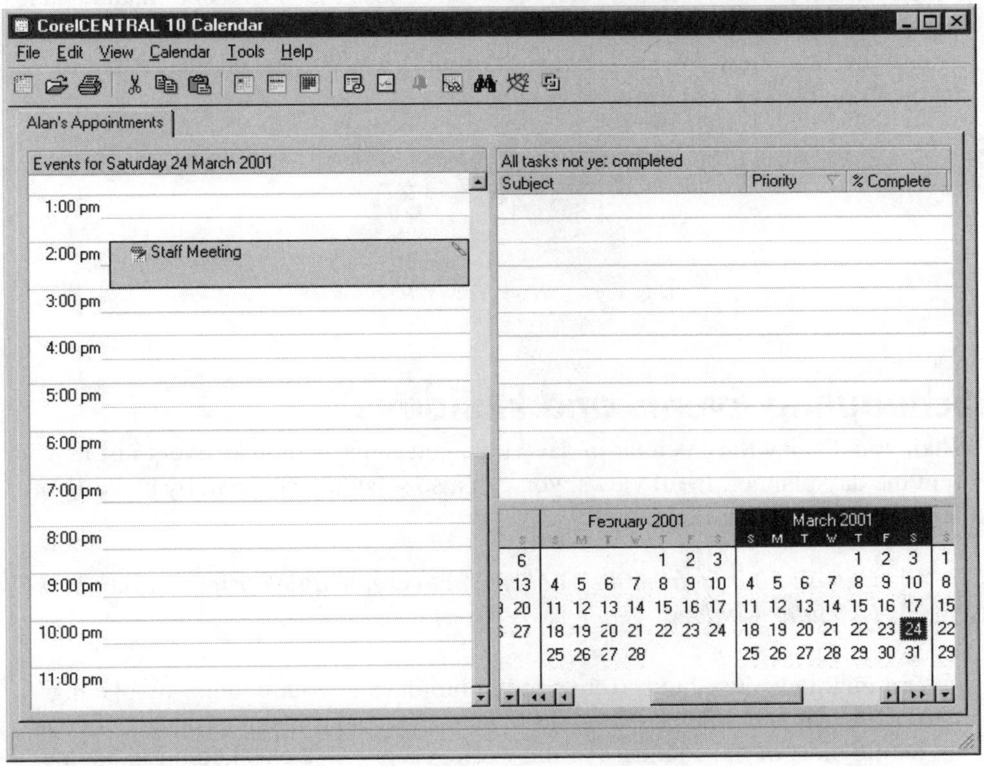

FIGURE 4-4   CorelCENTRAL Calendar

You can also choose Go to Today or Go to Specific Date from the Calendar menu. The Go to Specific Date option displays this dialog box:

Enter the date you want to go to or select it from the drop-down calendar next to the Pick a Date box. Alternatively, you can choose the Go To option and enter the number of days to advance, such as 30 days from the current day.

Use the Day View, Week View, and Month View buttons on the toolbar to change to daily, weekly, or monthly calendars:

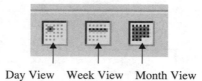

Day View   Week View   Month View

Scheduling Events and Holidays

When you display the calendar in day view, you can schedule an event just as you do in the day planner. In all views, you can also schedule an event by clicking on the New Event button in the toolbar.

 Choose Link To from the Tools menu to create a link from an event in the Calendar window.

You might also want to be reminded of holidays in your country by placing them on the calendar. Select Holidays from the Calendar menu to open a dialog box listing most of the countries of the world, each with a checkbox. Enable the checkbox representing the country whose holidays you want to place on the calendar.

NOTE   *Holidays displayed in the Events list are treated as all-day events.*

Using Task List

A task list contains reminders of things you have to do. You add items to the list so you can track your progress and establish priorities. Tasks can also be associated with events so you can schedule a meeting, for example, and create a list of tasks that you have to perform relating to it.

NOTE   *Tasks attached to calendar events will not appear in the Calendar Task list.*

You can create a task in either the day planner or the calendar.

1. Click on an empty line in the Task list. The Task list does not appear in the calendar in Month view.

2. Type a Task subject, and press ENTER.

3. Double-click on the Task icon to see the dialog box shown in Figure 4-5.

TIP   *You can also create a task by clicking on the New Task button in the calendar toolbar.*

1. Choose a category, such as business or personal, by clicking on the Categories button. To create a new category, type it in the Categories text box.

2. Change the start date, using the mini-calendars to select a date if needed.

3. Set a due date, if there is one.

4. Enter or select the percentage complete, if you've already performed some of the task.

5. Select a priority. The options are Highest, High, Normal, Low, and Lowest.

6. Enter the text of any notes.

7. If the task recurs, click on Repeat, and set the recurrence pattern.

8. Enter any notes you want recorded with the task.

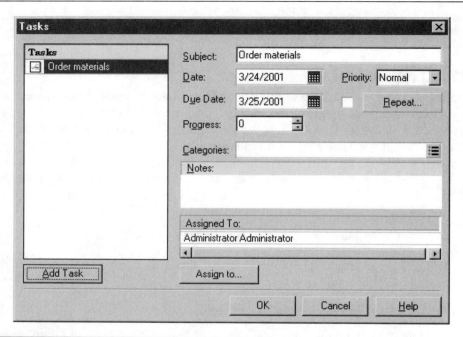

FIGURE 4-5   Edit Task dialog box

9. If you are using a shared calendar, you can assign the task to another user.

10. Click on OK. Your item will be added to the Task list.

> **TIP**   *You can add a link to a task just as you can to an event. Right-click on the task, point to Link To in the QuickMenu, and choose the type of link.*

You can mark your actions as completed when they are done and choose how you want them sorted in the Task list. When you complete an activity, click on the empty box to the left of the item in the Task list. CorelCENTRAL 10 places a check mark in the box and adds 100% to the % Complete column. You can also change the priority and percent complete by right-clicking on a task and choosing from this QuickMenu:

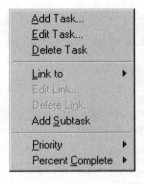

You can tell how the tasks are sorted by looking at the column heading. An up-pointing triangle next to the column name indicates that the tasks are sorted in ascending order by that column. A down-pointing arrow means the messages are sorted in descending order. To sort the tasks by another column, click that column heading. Each time you click the column heading, CorelCENTRAL 10 reverses the sort direction.

> **TIP**   *To add or remove columns from the Task list, right-click on any column heading, and choose the columns from the dialog box that appears.*

Filtering Tasks

As your Task list grows longer, you may not be interested in displaying every task at one time. You can filter tasks to display those that are not yet completed, just completed tasks, tasks in a specific category, or those within a specific time period. In fact, depending on your setup when you start CorelCENTRAL 10, tasks that have been completed may not even appear in the list.

Look at the bar above Subject heading in the Task list. The text in the bar shows which tasks are displayed, such as All Tasks or All Tasks Not Yet Completed.

Click on the bar to open the dialog box shown here:

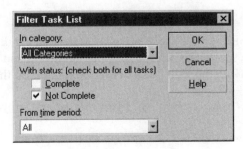

- Choose the category of tasks you want to display or All Categories.

- Select to show Complete tasks, Not Complete tasks, or both.

- Choose a time period from these options:

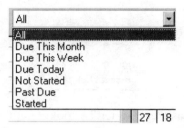

Subtasks

If you are working on a project that involves several tasks, you might not want to list each task as a separate item in the list. Instead, you can group the tasks so you can keep track of the overall project and control the flow of work from one task to the next.

You can construct a project by creating one or more subtasks in a hierarchical structure. You can create a subtask in either the Task list or the Edit Task dialog box.

To create a subtask from the Task list, right-click on the task, and choose Add Subtask from the QuickMenu. CorelCENTRAL 10 adds another task as a subtask, as shown next.

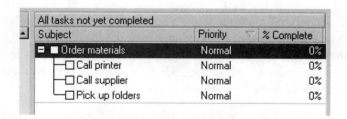

The minus sign indicates that the task has subtasks that are displayed. Click on the minus sign to hide the subtasks. Click on the plus sign to expand the subtasks again.

To create a subtask in the Edit Task dialog box, click on the Add Task button.

TIP *Use the Add Task button to add tasks to a calendar event.*

Printing a Calendar

You can print a calendar using standard Windows techniques. Click on the Print button in the toolbar, or select Print from the File menu to display this dialog box:

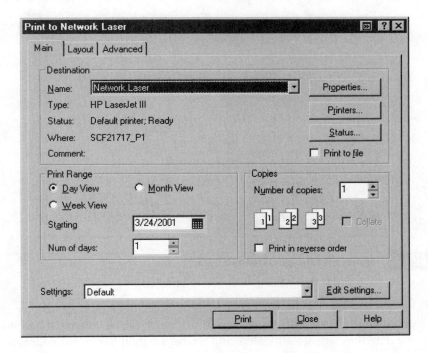

Choose to print a day, week, or month calendar, then enter the starting date and the number of days, weeks, or months. The default is the current day, week, or month depending on your selection in the Print section. Designate the number of copies to print, and then click on the Print button.

Publishing a Calendar to HTML Format

If you want to display your calendar on a Web site, you can publish to HTML format. Select File | Publish to HTML, then either Events or Tasks to see the dialog box shown in Figure 4-6.

■ On the Calendar page of the dialog box, which appears only if you selected to publish Events, choose the items you want to include, and then choose the range of days.

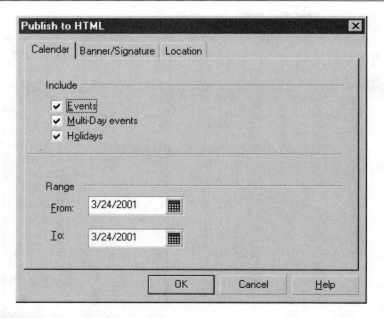

FIGURE 4-6   Publishing the calendar to HTML format

- On the Banner/Signature page, add the text for the banner across the page, and choose items for the signature block, such as the copyright and name, the date the page was updated, and a return e-mail name and address.

- On the Location page, specify where to store the HTML file and the filename prefix.

Click on OK to create the Web page.

Creating a Shared Calendar

When you want other network users to access a calendar, such as to plan group events, create and use a shared calendar. The person who creates the calendar and decides who can access it is called the administrator.

To create a shared calendar, select CorelCENTRAL Admin from the WordPerfect 2002 Utilities menu. The CorelCENTRAL Admin window is shown in Figure 4-7. Then follow these steps to create the calendar and assign it users on your network.

> **TIP**   *Use the Connect button on the toolbar to open an existing calendar database.*

1. Click the Create a New Database button on the toolbar or select New from the Database menu.

2. Select the format of the database—MS-SQL 7.0 Database or Paradox Database —and then click Next.

3. Specify the location and name of the database, and click Finish. Select a location on a network file server to provide full-time access to the calendar. If you place the calendar on a specific workstation, that computer must be turned on before other users can access it.

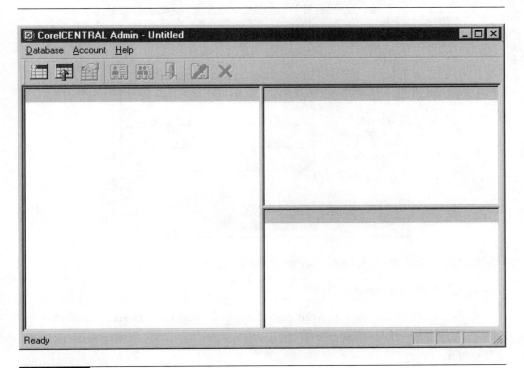

FIGURE 4-7   CorelCENTRAL Admin

4. Click Yes to create the folder. You'll now have to create accounts for users, groups, and resources. Each account you create essentially creates a separate calendar view for that account. By default, only the Administrator user is initially assigned to the calendar, as in Figure 4-8.

5. Click Administrator under User and then click on the Edit Account button.

6. In the box that appears, enter and then verify the password you want to use to access the account as the administrator. The default is Administrator.

Creating Database Accounts

The next step is to add user accounts to the Shared Calendar

1. Click the Add User button in the toolbar, or select New from the User menu and select User, to open this box:

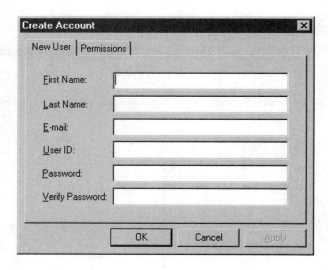

2. Complete the text boxes on the New User tab of the form.

3. Click the Permissions tab.

4. Select Normal User or Administrator. A Normal User is given read only access to the calendar database

5. Click OK.

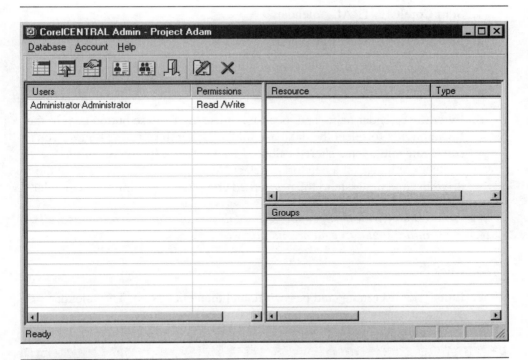

FIGURE 4-8   Calendar users

You can also create groups of users and add resources to the calendar. A group is a named collection of users. To create a group, click the New Group button in the toolbar, or select New from the User menu and select Group. Enter a group name and type, and then select the users who you want to be part of the group.

To add a resource, click on the New Resource button on the toolbar, or select New from the User menu and select Resource. In the box that appears, enter the resource name and description, select a type, enter a telephone number and click OK. Resources will be listed on the right of the Admin window.

> **TIP** *Click the Database Properties button on the toolbar to display the database name and location, and the number of users and resources.*

Opening a Shared Calendar

When you, or another user, want to open a shared calendar, follow these steps.

1. Start CorelCENTRAL Calendar.

2. Select Open from the File menu.

3. Select the Shared with Others option button.

4. Choose the format of the calendar you want to open and then click Next.

5. Enter the calendar name and location, or use the Browse button next to the Location box to select the database folder. Using the Browse button, you can locate and open a shared calendar on a network file server or on another computer on a network—select Network Neighborhood from the drive list and navigate to the networked computer containing the calendar.

 Your administrator will supply the database name and location, as well as your initial login user name and password.

6. Click Next.

7. Enter your user name and password, and then click Next. The calendar will open and appear as another tab in the Calendar window:

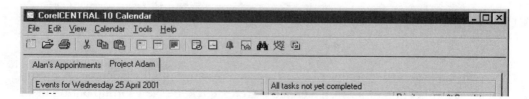

Once you open a shared calendar, you'll be prompted for your user ID and password whenever you start CorelCENTRAL Calendar. Each time you open the Calendar application, the shared calendar will appear. To close the shared calendar so it does not open automatically, select the calendar you want to close and from the File menu select Close.

Working With Agendas

An agenda is a view of a user's event schedule from the shared calendar. When you open your agenda, you see only those events to which you are invited. You can also open another person's agenda to see the events scheduled for them.

NOTE   *Only events are visible in the agenda, not tasks.*

NOTE   *The Delegate feature lets you allow other users to see all events and tasks within your calendar, and to have complete read and write access to your calendar. This is useful for an assistant or secretary.*

To open an agenda, select Open Agenda from the File menu, enter the user name and press Enter. The agenda appears as another tab in the window. Figure 4-9, for example, shows a private and shared calendar as well as two user agendas. Click on the tab for the calendar or agenda you want to display. To close an agenda, select Close from the File menu when the agenda is displayed.

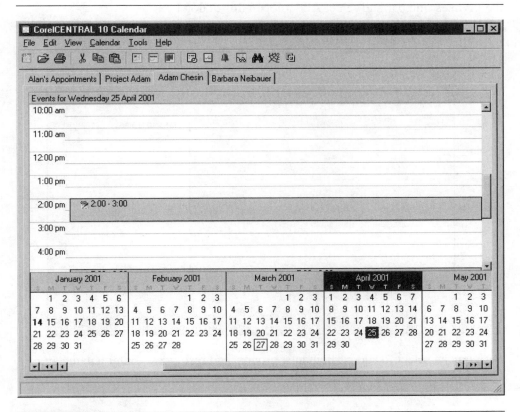

FIGURE 4-9   Private and shared calendars and user agendas.

Inviting Users to Events

When you create an event in a shared calendar, you can invite other users to attend. Invited users can then respond to the invitation so their attendance is indicated in the calendar event details. When you invite members to attend, their names appear in the Assign To list in the Event display window. You can only invite users who have been given access to the shared calendar.

To invite a person to the event, double-click on Type in New Name and then enter the name of a user of the shared calendar. CorelCENTRAL will locate users with names starting with the characters you type. If it cannot locate a user, the notation <No Matches Found> appears. If more than one match is found, the notation <Multiple Matches Found> appears—continue typing until the name of the user you want to invite appears.

You can also invite a user by clicking on the Invite button or right-clicking on the Invitees title bar and select Add to open this dialog box:

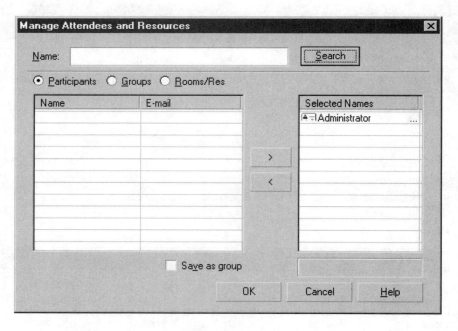

You can select to add participants, groups, and resources. Enter a name and press Enter. Click OK to close the dialog box when you are done.

| NOTE | *To remove an invited guest from the list, right-click and select Remove.* |

Sending E-Mail Invitations

You can automatically send e-mails to invited users notifying them of the event or of changes to the event. In the event window, enable the Send e-mail checkbox.

However, CorelCENTRAL must first be set up so that it knows the name of your outgoing e-mail server. To do so, select Preferences from the Edit menu to open the dialog box shown in Figure 4-10.

In this dialog box:

■ Select the colors to indicate accepted or declined event status.

■ Specify how often you want changes to be updated.

■ Enter the name of your outgoing e-mail server.

■ Add holidays.

■ Edit your password

■ Add a delegate.

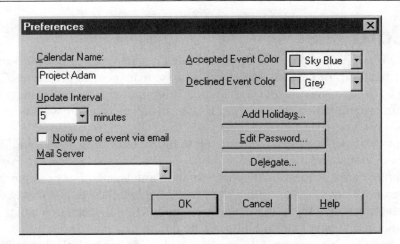

FIGURE 4-10   Setting Calendar Preferences

Responding to Invitations

Whether or not you send out e-mail notifications, invited users can indicate whether they plan to attend the event. When the user opens the event in the shared calendar, they will see these buttons on the bottom of the event window:

Clicking on one of the buttons updates the icons in the event window to indicate their response. When the event creator opens the event in the shared calendar, they will be able to see which users plan to attend, are unable to attend, or are still undecided.

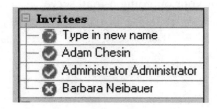

Using Card File

Card File is a mini database manager. Although it cannot perform the advanced database functions of Paradox and other database management programs, Card File can be used to store, display, and report information in much the same way as a database program. You can use Card File as an enhanced address book or to record almost any type of information.

Like a database, each card is divided into fields, but CorelCENTRAL 10 allows both global and local fields. A global field is one that appears in every card in a group of cards. A local field appears in individual cards. For example, suppose you have one client who has a Web site. You can add a field to just that client's card in the file containing a link to the Web site URL. All of the fields in a card file are indexed to help you find information quickly.

The cards can be organized into groups, and fields can be linked to other cards, to surf the Web, and even start applications.

There are two primary ways to use groups. If you have a large number of fields that you want to store, you can divide the fields into groups. The cards in a group are then related to the corresponding cards in other groups using a linked field. This is very much like creating related tables and using key fields in Corel Paradox 10 or another database management program. Another way to use groups is simply to divide the cards according to some common objects. You may, for example, group the cards for your wine collection into red, white, and sparkling. A card can be contained in more then one group. For example, you may have a group called "All Wines." Each wine in your collection will be in the All Wines group as well as the group for its type—red, white, or sparkling.

To display the card file shown in Figure 4-11, click the Card File icon in the Day Planner and choose CorelCENTRAL 10 Card File from the WordPerfect Office 2002 Utilities menu. CorelCENTRAL 10 includes a number of Card File

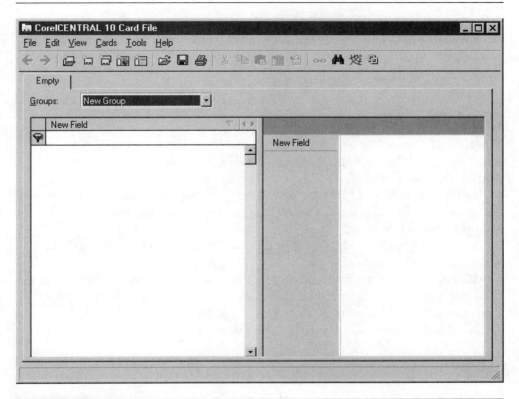

FIGURE 4-11   CorelCENTRAL Card File

templates to demonstrate how the file can be used. The Card File toolbar is shown here:

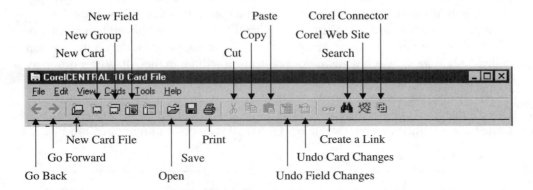

The power of CorelCENTRAL 10 Card File view is that you can create or customize card files, adding and deleting fields, creating links, and changing field properties.

Card File Window

You can have more than one card file open at a time. The names of the files are shown in tabs at the top of the Card File window. Click on the tab to display the cards in the file.

On the left of the Card File window is the Card list, which displays an index of the cards in the file. Use the arrows on the right of the column heads to scroll additional fields into view.

Above the Card list is the Group pull-down list. Pull down the list to select which group you want to display.

Click on a card in the list to display it in the Card Detail area on the right of the Card File window. You can also double-click a card in the Card list to display it in a separate window. To see more than one card at the same time, double-click on each card in the Card list, then arrange their windows.

NOTE *The card title is taken from the contents of the first global field.*

The left side of the Card Detail list is the field name column, with global and local fields separated by a horizontal line—global fields above the line, local fields below the line. To change the order of fields, just drag and drop the field to the new position in the field list. Dragging a global field below the horizontal line converts it into a local field, and vice versa. A field can be global (or local) in one group and local (or global) in another.

You can change the sizes of the panes by dragging the vertical line between them. Drag the line to the right of the field name column to change the size of columns in the Card Detail pane. Drag the line between column headings in the Card List pane to adjust the width of columns.

Working with Card Files

CorelCENTRAL 10 lets you use more than one card file. To create a new card file, click on the New Card File button, or select New from the File menu. In the New Card File dialog box, enter the name that will appear on the card file tab, and the filename and location in which to store the file on your disk. If you do not want to use the default name, enter a new one for both the tab and the filename. It is best to accept the default path, however.

Click on OK to create the card file and display it in the CorelCENTRAL 10 window. A new tab appears at the top of the window showing the name of the new file.

To delete a card file, choose Delete from the File menu. In the dialog box that appears, select the file you want to delete, and then click OK. Click Yes to the prompt that appears asking you to confirm the deletion.

> **TIP** *Use the Reorder Card Files options from the View menu to change the order of the card file tabs.*

To change the name of a card file, choose Rename from the File menu. In the dialog box that appears, type the name you want to give the file, and then click OK.

Adding Fields

The next step is to enter the fields that you want to use to store information. You don't have to enter all of the fields at one time. You can create some, enter information into them, and then add other fields later on.

If you want to insert a global field to a card, you can start with any card in the group. To create the first field, click on the New Field text in the Card Detail list, and type the field name. To insert additional fields, select New Global Field from the Cards menu, or click on the New Global Field button in the toolbar to insert the field, and type the field name in the text box that appears.

To add a local field to a specific card, display that card in the Card Detail pane. Click on the New Local Field button in the toolbar or select New Local Field from the Cards menu. You can also just click under the last local field and type the new field name.

To duplicate a current field, click on the field in the Card Detail pane, then choose Duplicate Field from the Cards menu, or right-click on the field and choose Duplicate Field from the QuickMenu. To delete a field, right-click on the field, then choose Delete Field from the QuickMenu. Deleting a global field removes it from all of the cards in its group.

Setting Field Properties

You can set properties for Card File fields to define their type and size and the way they are displayed. By default, all fields that you add are alphanumeric (they can contain text and numbers) and are displayed as text boxes. You can leave the fields blank or enter as much into a field as you want.

You can change a field's properties to help control the information entered into a card. Right-click on the field, and choose Field Properties from the QuickMenu to see the dialog box shown in Figure 4-12.

Pull down the Field Type list, and choose from these types:

- Alpha/Numeric
- Check Box
- Currency
- Date/Time
- E-mail address
- Internet URL
- Mailing address
- Numeric
- Radio Button
- Separator

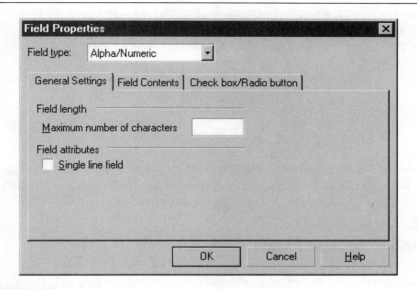

FIGURE 4-12   Field Properties

The dialog box has three pages: General Settings, Field Contents, and Check box/Radio button. Not all pages are available for every field type, and some options on a page may be dimmed for some field types.

■ In the General Settings page, enter the maximum number of characters allowed, and check the Single Line Field option to allow only one line of text in the field.

■ In the Field Contents page, enter the default text that you want to appear in the field.

■ In the Check box/Radio button page (which is available only for those types of fields), enter the information you want to appear next to each checkbox or radio button in the group (up to ten), and set the default status of each box or the selected radio button.

The type of field determines the characters that you can enter, the number of lines, and the way the field appears. After completing the Check box/Radio button page of the dialog box, for example, a Check Box field might appear like this:

Fields of the e-mail address and Internet URL types appear as links. The separator type creates a horizontal line across the field information column. Use the field type to divide fields into groups for easy reference.

Adding Comment Fields

Use a comment field to store additional information about the object. You add one or more comment fields to existing global or local fields and then decide if you want the comments to appear onscreen.

To add a comment field, right-click on the field you wish to add a comment to, then choose New Comment Field from the QuickMenu. The new field appears under the current field as shown here:

Type the name for the field, then click to its right, and enter the field information. When you're done, the field is displayed with a minus sign next to the field that contains the comment. The minus sign indicates that the field contains comments that are displayed—that the field is expanded, much like an outline in WordPerfect 10 or a folder in Windows Explorer. Click on the minus sign to collapse the field, hiding the comments—the icon changes to a plus sign. Click on the plus sign to redisplay the comment fields.

The comment field is added only to the current card, even if the field it is attached to is global. To delete a comment field, right-click on it, and choose Delete Comment from the QuickMenu.

4

Adding Information to Cards

To add information to a card, you have to show it in the Card Detail. First pull
down the Group list, and choose the group where the card is contained. Then,
scroll the Card list and click on the card's listing.

In the Card Detail, click where you want to enter data, and then type. Do not
press ENTER after the text, unless you want to add a new line of information in the
field, such as when entering a two-line address. To move to another field, click in
the field, or use the UP ARROW, DOWN ARROW, TAB, or SHIFT-TAB keys.

CorelCENTRAL 10 features QuickType. When you type, CorelCENTRAL 10
looks at the other cards in the file for information in the same field beginning with
the same characters. If it finds a match, it displays it in the field selected. To
accept the entry, just move to another field. To reject the QuickType suggestion,
just keep typing—CorelCENTRAL 10 will continue to look for matching entries
using the additional characters that you type. To edit the suggested QuickType
entry, press the LEFT ARROW or RIGHT ARROW keys, edit the entry, and then move
to another field.

| NOTE | *You can also click on a field to change its name. If you change the name of a global field, the name is changed for all cards in the group.* |

Adding Cards

To add a card, first pull down the Group list, and choose the group you want to
add the card to, then click on the New Card button in the toolbar. You can also
right-click in the Card list, and choose New Card from the QuickMenu. The new
card will contain all of the global fields from that group. Click in the Card Detail
area, and enter the information to the card.

To add a duplicate of a current card to the file, click on the card in the Card
list, then choose Duplicate Card from the Cards menu, or right-click and choose
Duplicate Card from the QuickMenu.

| TIP | *To delete a card, right-click on the card in the Card list, choose Delete Card from the QuickMenu. In the box that appears, choose to delete the card from the current group or from all groups, and click on OK. Select several cards by holding down the CTRL key as you click, or use the SHIFT key to choose a range of cards.* |

Searching for a Card

Rather than scrolling the list to find a card, you can search for it or create a filter. Searching for a card scrolls the list to display a card that matches the text that you enter. Filtering the list temporarily hides all of the cards that do not contain the text that you type. You can perform both operations by entering the text you are looking for in the search boxes—the empty boxes under the field names in the Card list.

Start by selecting either the search or filter operation. When the icon next to the first search box appears as shown here, the list will be filtered.

Click on the icon to change it to the image shown here when you want to perform a search.

Next, enter the text you are searching for, or filtering by, in the empty search box under the field name that contains the text. CorelCENTRAL 10 scrolls or filters the list as you type. You can also use the > and < operators, although CorelCENTRAL 10 treats the > operator as "equal to or greater than" and the < operator as "equal to or less than."

> **NOTE** *To remove a filter, display all of the cards again and delete the text in the search boxes.*

Enter text in more than one search box to locate cards based on more than one field. CorelCENTRAL 10 treats the condition as an And operation, displaying cards that contain all of the search text.

With filters, you can also use operators within the search box to perform AND and OR operations. Use the plus sign character (+) to perform an Or operation and the ampersand character (&) to perform an And operation.

Sorting Cards

The order of the cards depends on their order in the Card list. The name of the field in which the cards are sorted contains a triangle icon:

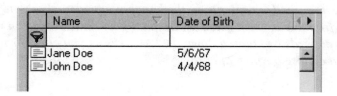

The direction of the triangle indicates the direction of the sort. The cards are in ascending order when the triangle is pointing down and descending when the triangle is pointing up. Click on the field name that you want to sort by—click it again to toggle between sort directions.

Adding Links

You can add links to a field just as you learned for events.

As an example, look at the card shown in Figure 4-13. The card contains a link in the Spouse field. When the user clicks on the link, CorelCENTRAL 10 opens the card for Jane Doe, the spouse of the person in the current card. Jane's card also contains a link back to her spouse. There is also a link to a Word document contain the person's employment record. Click on the plus sign before the link to display its source, as shown here, or click on the link to open the file:

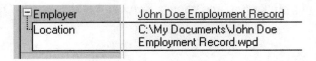

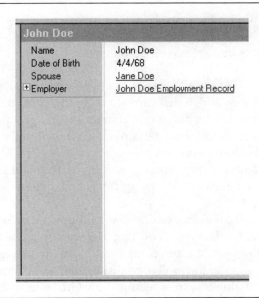

FIGURE 4-13   Card with links

To add a link, click on the field where you want to insert a link, click on the Create a Link button in the toolbar, and choose the type of link. You can also select Link To from the Tools menu.

If you choose to link the field to another card, a dialog box appears with a duplicate of the Card list. Select the card you want to link the field with, then click on OK.

When you add a link that displays another card, CorelCENTRAL 10 adds to that card a return link as a local field. This lets you jump to the card by clicking on the link, then return to the original card by clicking on the local field that CorelCENTRAL 10 inserted.

A link is shown as underlined and in the same color as the title bar. Links to other cards or to the address book are shown as information in the field itself. Links of all other types, such as to an application or to a Web site, are added as comment fields.

To edit a link, right-click on it, and choose Edit Link from the QuickMenu. To delete a link, right-click on it, and choose Remove Field from the QuickMenu.

Working with Groups

As you know, there are two reasons to create groups:

- To divide the Card file into logical groups of fields
- To divide cards into groups based on type

CorelCENTRAL 10 lets you create as many groups as you want. You can also delete and rename groups and assign cards to more than one group.

For example, a typical card file might contain several groups. Each group contains a set of related fields, with the cards to be linked to the appropriate card in the basic personal information group.

You can create a new empty group to which you then add fields, or you can base a new group on an existing one, using fields and optional information from one or more of its cards.

To base the new group on an existing one, pull down the Group list, and choose the group. Next, select any cards that you want to place in that group. Don't bother selecting cards if you want to place them all in the new group. Then click on the New Group button in the toolbar to display the New Group dialog box. You can also display this dialog box by selecting New Group from the Cards menu, or right-clicking on the Card list and selecting New Group from the QuickMenu.

Enter the name for the new group, then choose an option from the Contents section:

■ *Empty* creates a new group with no information from the current group, even if they are selected.

■ *Include selected cards* adds the selected cards along with their fields to the new group.

■ *Include all cards from [current group]* adds all of the cards to the new group.

■ *Include fields from [current group]* adds all of the global fields from the current group to the new group.

When you include existing cards in the new group, the cards are not actually duplicated but are synchronized in both groups. If you make changes to a card in one group, the changes are displayed when viewing the same card in other groups.

To delete or rename a group, pull down the Group list, and select the group. Right-click on the Card list, and then choose Delete Group or Rename Group from the QuickMenu. Deleting a group removes all the cards in the group but does not remove duplicated cards in other groups.

To move or copy a card between groups, right-click on it in the Card list, then choose Cut or Copy from the QuickMenu. Open the destination group, right-click in the Card list, and choose Paste. When you cut the card, it is removed from the original group and added to the destination group.

CorelCENTRAL 10 Memos

Use CorelCENTRAL 10 Memos to record messages and notes. Click on the Memos button under the Day Planner, or select CorelCENTRAL 10 Memos from the WordPerfect Office 2002 Utilities menu. The CorelCENTRAL 10 Memos window is shown in Figure 4-14.

Click on the New Memo button on the toolbar, or choose New from the File menu. A Memo icon appears in the box on the left, and the Type In The Memo text box on the right changes color. Click in the right box, type the text of your memo, and then click elsewhere. To read the text of a memo, click to its left.

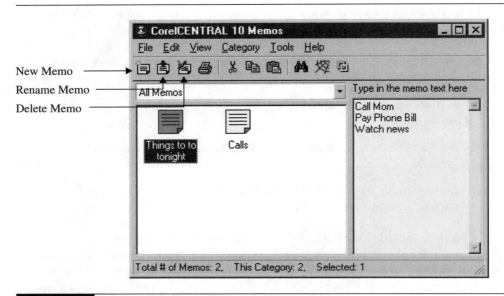

New Memo

Rename Memo

Delete Memo

FIGURE 4-14 CorelCENTRAL Memos

Using CorelCENTRAL Mail

In addition to serving as a calendar and task manager, CorelCENTRAL offers a full service e-mail program. Using CorelCENTRAL Mail, you can send and receive e-mail over the Internet through any ISP or e-mail provider that uses the POP or IMAP4 e-mail protocols.

CorelCENTRAL Mail works in the same way as other e-mail programs such as Microsoft Outlook Mail, Netscape Communicator, and Eudora. So if you've used any e-mail program that organizes messages in folders, you'll have no problem using CorelCENTRAL Mail.

To start the program, select CorelCENTRAL Mail from the WordPerfect Office 2002 menu.

 You may be asked if you want to make CorelCENTRAL Mail the default mail client. Select Yes or No depending if you want to use Mail for all of your e-mail applications.

Creating Your Mail Profile

The first time you run CorelCENTRAL Mail, you'll have to create a mail profile using the CorelCENTRAL Mail Profile Expert. A profile contains information about your e-mail account and mail server. You can have more than one e-mail account as part of a profile; if, for example, you want to work with your ISP mail and Yahoo e-mail at the same time. You can also have a separate profile for each member of the family to keep your e-mails separate. You'll learn how to work with multiple profiles and accounts later in this chapter.

The CorelCENTRAL Mail Profile Expert helps you create your first profile and e-mail account. You can later add additional e-mail accounts and profiles from within CorelCENTRAL Mail.

In the first CorelCENTRAL Mail Profile Expert box, enter a profile name (your name will appear by default) and then click Next. You will then be given three options for setting up a mail account:

- Compact Expert
- Detailed Expert
- Manual

The Compact Expert option takes you though creating a mail account but skips some settings that you may have to adjust manually from within Profile Manager. The Manual method lets you create a mail account using a series of dialog boxes in Profile Manager. In this chapter, we'll use the Detailed Expert option as an example. Just follow these steps.

1. Select the Detailed Expert option button and then click Next.

2. Enter your full name and e-mail address, and click Next.

3. Enter your mailbox name and password, and click Next. The mailbox name is often the first part of your e-mail address—to the left of the @ sign.

4. Select the type of e-mail account you have—either IMAP4 or POP3—and if you want to designate a different mail server to send mail if your ISP provides you with both an incoming and outgoing server name. Then click Next.

5. Enter the incoming server, and a separate outgoing server if required by your mail provider, and then click Next.

6. Choose how you connect—through a modem or over the network—and then click Next.

7. If you connect over a modem, now select the setting from those in Window's Dialup Connection and then click Next. You can also click the New button and create a new account.

8. You are now asked to specify the location where your mail files are stored. Click Change if you do not want to use the default location. Click Next to continue.

9. Enter an optional password if you want to protect the profile, and then click Next.

   CorelCENTRAL Mail lets you digitally sign and encrypt mail messages. To use these features, you need to have a digital ID. While other e-mail programs require that you apply for and download a digital ID, CorelCENTRAL generates its own ID for you through the Mail Profile Expert box that now appears. CorelCENTRAL also lets you import an existing signed digital ID.

10. Type the words **random generation** in the Mail Profile Expert box and then click Next.

11. Select to encrypt and sign all messages by default, if you want to, and then click Next. You'll see a summary of your profile. If any of the information or settings are incorrect, click the Back button and make the necessary changes.

12. Click Finish to open Profile Manager. You use Profile Manager to change the properties or delete profiles or create new ones. You can also select which profile to use as the default and if you want to bypass the CorelCENTRAL log-on process when you start the mail program. The log-on process allows you to select which profile to use for the mail session.

13. Click Close to display the Mail login box.

This same box will appear each time you start CorelCENTRAL Mail unless you selected to bypass log-on. Select the profile you want to use from list and then click OK.

TIP *To edit a profile, open Profile Manager by selecting it in the Mail Logon box, or by choosing Tools | Options | Current Profile Options from within CorelCENTRAL Mail. You can also select CorelCENTRAL Profile Manager from the CorelCENTRAL 10 Applications menu.*

The CorelCENTRAL Mail window is shown in Figure 4-15. The list of folders is shown on the left, the contents of the selected folder on the right. Your mail messages are stored in your mailbox folders—Inbox, Outbox, Drafts, Sent Items, and Trash.

The Local Folders section, which you can expand by clicking on the plus sign to its left, contains a set of similar folders. You use those folders to store messages that you may be sharing among multiple accounts in the profile. If you have an IMAP4 mail server, which stores messages on the server, you can drag the message from an account folder to one of the Local Folders to store the message on your computer, removing it from the mail server. You can also right-click on the message, choose Copy To (which leaves the message on the server) or Move To (which deletes the message from the server) from the QuickMenu and select the folder where you want to place the message:

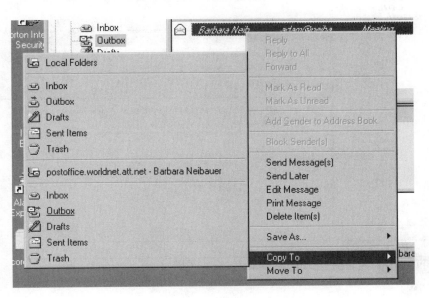

Click the Get/Send button to check for new mail and to send any mail you have in your Outbox. You can also pull down the Get/Send list and select to just send or receive mail.

Composing E-mail

To quickly compose and send an e-mail message, click on the New button to open the window shown in Figure 4-16.

Enter the text of the subject and the email address of the recipient. You can click on the To and CC buttons to select recipients from the CorelCENTRAL address book. Use the Attach button to browse for and select files you want to

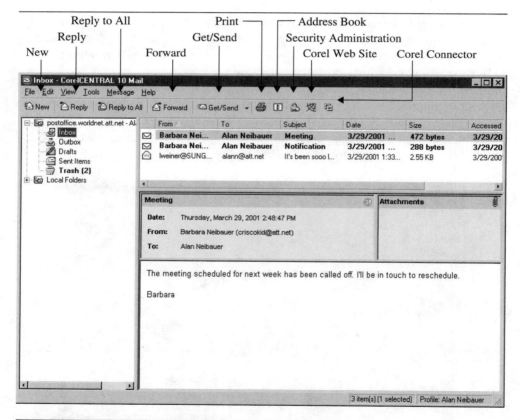

FIGURE 4-15   CorelCENTRAL Mail

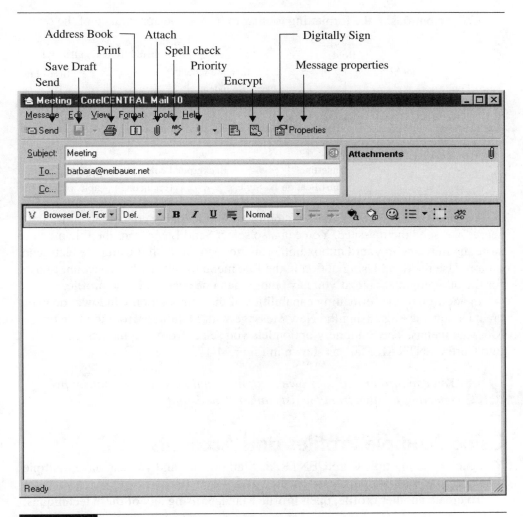

FIGURE 4-16 Mail composition window

include with the e-mail. Attachments will be indicated in the attachments section, as shown here:

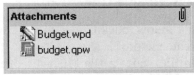

Use the buttons in the formatting toolbar to format the appearance of the text:

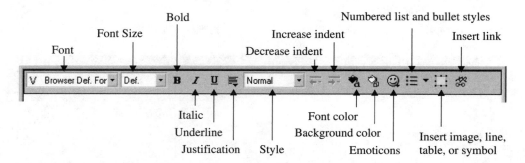

To send your mail, click the Send button to immediately connect to your mail server and send the message. You can also select Send Later from the File menu to store the message in your Outbox until you are ready to mail it using the Get/Send button. Use the Send Using option in the File menu to select which account to use for the outgoing message, if you have more than one account in the profile.

In addition to the formatting capabilities of the composition window, you can create a new message using the New Message with Stationery from the File or Message menus. The Stationery option lets you select from graphic designs built into CorelCENTRAL Mail, as shown in Figure 4-17.

 You can also create your own stationary options and access them by selecting Custom from the list, rather than default.

Using Multiple Profiles and Accounts

You can create multiple CorelCENTRAL Mail profiles and you can have multiple mail accounts within a profile.

To create another profile, open Profile Manager using any of these techniques:

- Select CorelCENTRAL Profile Manager from the CorelCENTRAL 10 Applications menu.
- Select Profile Manager from the Mail Login box
- Select Tools | Options | Profile Manager.

In the Profile Manager window, click Create to start the CorelCENTRAL Mail Profile Expert and then create the profile.

If you have to edit a profile, start Profile Manager, click on the name of the profile you want to edit, and then click the Properties button to open the dialog box shown in Figure 4-18.

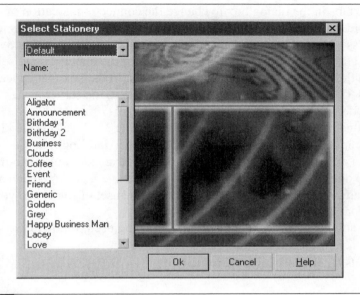

FIGURE 4-17   Using stationery designs

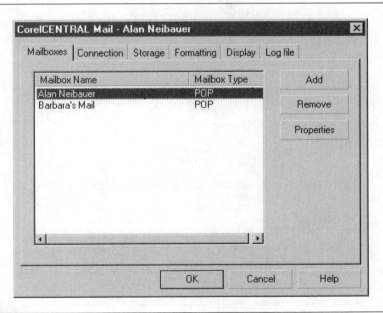

FIGURE 4-18   Working with a profile

Use the tabs in the dialog box to change the connection, location of the mailbox folders, default format of new messages and replies, the fonts used to display messages, and to create one or more log files recording the activities of CorelCENTRAL Mail. To change the properties of the mail account, select the account on the Mailboxes tab and click Properties. In the box that appears, shown in Figure 4-19, set the specifics of the e-mail account, the server names, and choose the default security settings.

To change profiles without exiting and restarting Mail, select File | Logon again and click Yes to display the CorelCENTRAL Mail Login box.

You can only use one profile at a time, but you can add multiple e-mail accounts to one profile. You can then send and receive mail from each account without changing profiles. Each account has its own set of folders so you can keep messages for each separate.

To add another mail account to the profile being used, follow these steps:

1. Tools | Options | Current Profile Options.

FIGURE 4-19   Setting account properties

2. Click Mailboxes tab.

3. Click Add.

4. On Mailbox tab, enter the account nickname, the account name and the e-mail address.

5. On Server tab, enter the incoming and outgoing mail servers.

6. Click OK twice.

Both accounts are listed in the window as shown here:

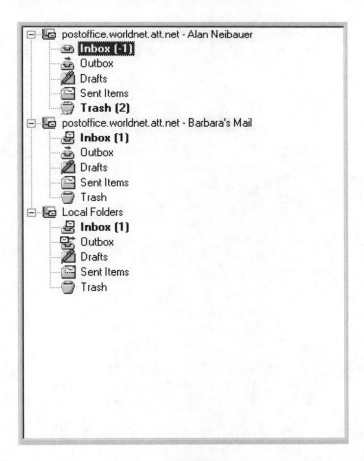

To compose an e-mail, click on any folder under the account you want to use and then click New. If you select the wrong account, you can choose from the message composition window by selecting Send Using from the File menu and then choosing the account.

To send and receive mail, click on any of the folders under the account and then use the Get/Send button.

| TIP | *Use local folders to store messages that relate to both accounts.* |

Part 2

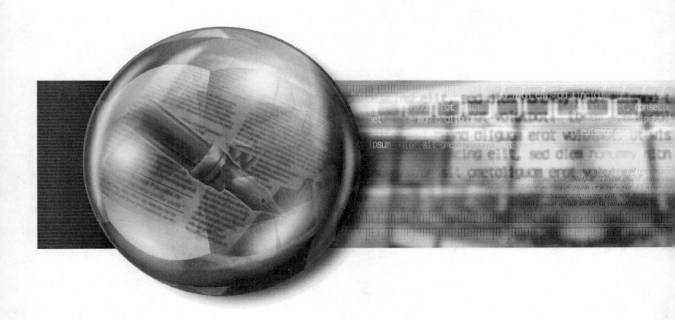

WordPerfect 10

Chapter 5

Creating Documents with WordPerfect 10

141

WordPerfect 10 is the flagship of the Office suite for a very good reason. It is known around the world as an outstanding word processing program, with millions of dedicated users. WordPerfect Office 2002 is the next generation of this legacy, bringing new, powerful, and timesaving features to this landmark program.

Starting WordPerfect 10

To start WordPerfect 10, click on the Start button, point to Programs, then WordPerfect Office 2002, and click on WordPerfect 10. You'll see the screen shown in Figure 5-1.

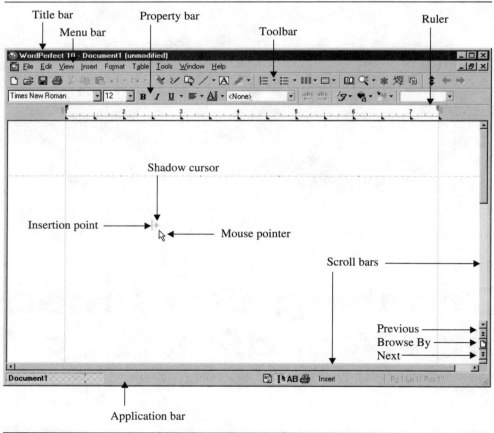

FIGURE 5-1   The WordPerfect screen

At the top of the screen are the title bar, menu bar, toolbar, and property bar. WordPerfect gives the name "Document1" to the first document window during the session, "Document 2" to the second, and so on. The word "unmodified" in the title bar means that you have not changed the document since it was started or opened. It disappears as soon as you start typing to indicate that you must save your work if you want to use it again. When you do save your document, the name you give it appears on the title bar.

> **NOTE**   *If the ruler does not appear on your screen, select Ruler from the View menu to display it.*

The property bar has pull-down lists and buttons for performing common functions, such as changing the type size or centering text on the screen. The items on the property bar may change, depending on the task you are performing. You'll learn each of the functions of the toolbar and property bar throughout this book.

The blank area under the property bar is the typing area where your document appears. The dotted lines around the typing area are the margin guidelines. They not only show you where your page margins are, but you can drag them to change the margins. The blinking vertical line is the insertion point where characters appear as you type. Next to the mouse pointer is the *shadow cursor*. This shows where characters are inserted when you click the mouse and the alignment that has been applied to the text. You'll also see the horizontal and vertical scroll bars. Use the vertical scroll bar to scroll lines up and down, the horizontal scroll bar to scroll right and left.

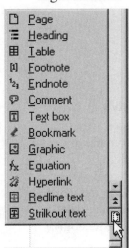

At the bottom of the vertical scroll bar are the Previous, Browse By, and Next buttons. You use the Previous and Next buttons to move forward or backward through a document. The icon on the Browse By button determines where the insertion points moves. By default, for example, Browse By is set as Page, so clicking on the Next button displays the next page. When you click on the Browse By button, you'll see a list of the options available.

For instance, to locate the next footnote in the document, click on Browse By and then on Footnote, and then click on the Next button.

Finally, at the bottom of the screen, just above the Windows taskbar, is the *application bar*. This bar shows the names of the documents that you have open and gives you information about WordPerfect 10 and your position in the current document. You can use the application bar to move and copy information between documents without having both documents displayed onscreen at the same time.

What you don't yet see on the screen are four helpful, timesaving features: QuickTips, QuickMenus, QuickStatus boxes, and SpeedLinks.

A *QuickTip* is a small box with a brief description that appears when you point with the mouse to a button on the toolbar, property bar, or application bar. If you're not sure what a button does, point to it, and read the QuickTip, as shown here:

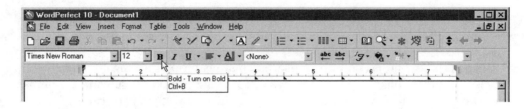

A *QuickMenu* is a list of items that appears when you right-click on an object. Which menu items are displayed depends on where the mouse is pointing. It is usually faster to display and use the QuickMenu than it is to perform the same functions with the menu bar or toolbar, since you don't have to slide the mouse to the top of the screen. Every QuickMenu has the What's This? option. Click on it to read about the object you are pointing to.

QuickStatus boxes appear when you change the position of tabs, and the sizes of margins, columns, and table cells, showing their exact dimensions. As you drag the mouse, watch the QuickStatus box—release the mouse button when the dimension is what you want.

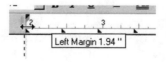

SpeedLinks are words that have been associated with sites on the World Wide Web. Corel has defined a number of SpeedLinks for you. SpeedLinks start with the @ symbol. If you type @Corel, for example, WordPerfect 10 automatically displays the word in color and underlined, indicating it is a SpeedLink to http://www.corel.com. When you point to the link, the mouse appears as a pointing hand, and a QuickStatus box shows the actual address. Click on the word to launch your Web browser, and connect to http://www.corel.com. In fact, when you type anything in the format www.xxxx.xxx (such as www.MyWebSite.com), or name@mail.xxx (such as alann@att.net), WordPerfect 10 automatically converts it to a SpeedLink.

From time to time, WordPerfect 10 also displays other small icons in the left margin indicating that some object has been inserted or that a special format has been applied. When you change tab stops, for example, an icon appears showing that new tab stops are in effect. If more than one icon should appear, WordPerfect displays a special icon showing that multiple formats exist in that paragraph. Click on that icon to see the icons for the individual objects. This icon, for example, indicates a comment, and a sound file:

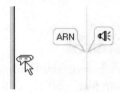

Typing a Document

You type a document in WordPerfect 10 just as you would in any other word processing program, and almost the same as on a typewriter. The letter and number keys insert exactly what you see on the keys; just remember to press SHIFT to get uppercase letters and the punctuation marks shown on the top part of the key. Press the CAPS LOCK key, or click on the CAPS LOCK button (the section labeled AB) on the application bar to type uppercase letters without holding down the SHIFT key. You can use the keypad to enter numbers, but you must first press the NUMLOCK key—otherwise, you will move the insertion point.

> **TIP** *Remember to use the PerfectExpert to help you create and format documents of all types.*

Press the BACKSPACE key to erase your mistakes. Each time you press BACKSPACE, WordPerfect deletes a character to the left of the insertion point. Indent the first line of a paragraph by pressing the TAB key, and press the ENTER key to insert a blank line or to end a paragraph. Do not press ENTER, however, when the insertion point reaches the right margin; just keep on typing. WordPerfect 10 senses when the word you're typing cannot fit on the line and automatically moves it to the next.

Remember, if you see wavy lines under text then the spelling or grammar may be incorrect. Refer to Chapter 2 to learn about Spell-As-You-Go, Grammar-As-You-Go, and Prompt-As-You-Go.

When your typing reaches the bottom of the screen, just continue. The text at the top scrolls up and out of view, but it is not deleted. You can always scroll the screen back to see it.

And don't worry about where the page ends—just keep on typing. WordPerfect automatically ends the page when it is full, and starts a new one. If you want to end a page before WordPerfect 10 does, press CTRL-ENTER.

Using the Shadow Cursor

WordPerfect 10 lets you type anywhere in the typing area. As you move the mouse in the white space of the typing window, you'll see the shadow cursor moving with it. The shadow cursor may appear to jump on the screen, and not move as smoothly as the mouse pointer, because it always aligns with the nearest tab stop position. (The default tab stops are set every half-inch.) When you click the mouse, the insertion point appears at the shadow cursor position.

You can click anywhere in the document, even in the middle of the page, and start typing. For example, you do not need to press ENTER to insert blank lines into a document, or press the TAB key to indent a line. Just point to the location where you want to type, and then click.

Along with the shadow cursor is an arrow indicating the alignment of the text. When the arrow points to the right, the text will be left-aligned at the tab stop position, with characters moving to the right as you type.

If you point the mouse at the exact middle of the screen, the shadow cursor appears with a two-pointed arrow. Click when the two-headed arrow appears to type text centered between the margins. As you type, characters move alternately to the left and right.

If you point at the far right margin, the arrow points to the left. Click there to right-align the text, so it shifts to the left as you type.

If you do not want to use the shadow cursor, select View | Shadow Cursor or click on the Shadow Cursor button on the application bar. Restore the shadow cursor using the same techniques.

Hard Versus Soft

When WordPerfect 10 moves the insertion point to the start of a new line, it is called a *soft return.* When it ends one page and starts another, it is called a *soft page break.* When you press ENTER to end a line, it's a *hard return.* When you press CTL-ENTER to end a page, it's a *hard page break.*

Why bother with hard versus soft? As you insert, delete, and format text within a document, WordPerfect 10 can automatically adjust the other text on the page. When you add text to a paragraph, for example, the other text in the paragraph and on the page moves over and down to make room. When you delete text, it may move text up from the next page, always ending pages when they become full.

If you pressed ENTER to end each line at the right margin, as you do with a typewriter, then each line would be considered a separate paragraph. Text would not flow neatly to adjust to your changes. Likewise, if you press CTRL-ENTER to end a page, a new page always starts at that location, even if you delete some text from the page before.

You cannot delete a soft page break; it adjusts automatically as you work. You can delete a hard page break by pressing DEL or BACKSPACE.

 Never end a page of continuous text by pressing ENTER, *until WordPerfect inserts a soft page break. If you later insert or delete text, the extra blank lines end up where you don't want them.*

Inserting and Deleting Text

If you don't catch a mistake until you are past it, you don't have to press BACKSPACE to delete all of the text back to that point. Instead, move the insertion point, and then make your changes to the text. To do this, move the mouse, and point to the area where you want to insert or delete characters.

You can also use the keyboard to move the insertion point by pressing the arrow keys. Press HOME to quickly move to the start of a line, and END to move to the end of the line.

Before trying to insert text, look at the application bar. If it says "Insert," you are in Insert mode. As you type, existing text moves over and down as necessary to make room. You can switch out of Insert mode by pressing the INS key, or by clicking on Insert in the status bar. This display changes to Typeover— now each character that you type replaces an existing one.

To delete text, press the BACKSPACE key to delete characters to the left of the insertion point, and DEL to delete characters to the right.

As you move about the document, you'll be clicking at locations where you want to insert or delete text. Each place you click is called an *editing position*. You can move to the previous editing position, and then back again by clicking on these buttons on the WordPerfect 10 toolbar:

Previous editing position ⟶  ⟵ Next editing position

Scrolling the Screen

How do you move the insertion point to a place in the document that has already disappeared off the screen? The answer is *scrolling*. Scrolling means to bring into view text that has disappeared off the top or bottom, or the left or right, of the document window. You can scroll in several ways.

The simplest way to scroll the window is to use the arrow keys. When the insertion point is at the top line of the document window, pressing UP ARROW scrolls a new line into view—if there are any. When the insertion point is on the last line in the window, pressing DOWN ARROW scrolls a new line into view— again, if there are any.

If you have to move a great distance through a long document, however, using the arrow keys is certainly not efficient. Instead, use the vertical scroll bar on the right of the screen to scroll up and down. Use the horizontal scroll bar at the bottom of the window to scroll left and right.

To scroll through your document line by line, just as you would by pressing the arrow key, click on the up or down triangles on the ends of the scroll bar. To scroll screen by screen, click above or below the scroll box—the box within the bar.

Each time you click, WordPerfect scrolls the window about the same number of lines that you can see. You can also drag the scroll box to scroll to a relative position in the document. If you drag the box to the middle of the scroll bar, WordPerfect 10 displays page five of a nine-page document, for example.

The screen can scroll automatically, while you just sit back and relax. Clicking on AutoScroll in the toolbar changes the mouse point and scroll bar so they appear like this:

When you move the mouse up or down in the window, the text starts to scroll in that direction. The more you move the mouse toward the top or bottom of the screen, the faster it scrolls. Move the mouse toward the center of the screen to scroll slowly. You can stop moving the mouse, and let the screen continue to scroll as you read. Click the mouse anywhere to turn off AutoScroll.

To move page by page through a document, click on the Previous Page and Next Page buttons on the bottom of the scroll bar. Remember, you can change the action of the Previous and Next buttons by clicking on Browse By and selecting from the list that appears. The icon on the Browse By button indicates its setting, and a QuickTip reports its name when you point to it. The QuickTips for the Previous and Next buttons also indicate the action, such as Previous Graphic or Next Footnote.

Keep in mind a very important point: scrolling with the scroll bars does not move the insertion point, it only changes the part of the document being displayed on the screen. You'll notice that the position indicators in the status bar do not change as you scroll, so if you don't click first, the screen scrolls back to its previous location when you begin typing or press an arrow key. To insert or delete text in the displayed area, you must first click where you want to type.

To go to the start of a specific page, click on the position indicator on the status bar to see the Go To dialog box, shown in Figure 5-2. Type the number of the page you want to move to, and then click on Go To.

You can also select to move by choosing any of the other options in the Go to what list, then clicking on Previous, Next, First, or Last. If you've already entered footnotes and endnotes, for example, you can select to move from note to note as

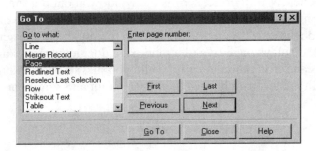

FIGURE 5-2   Go To dialog box

well. In some cases, like with pages and lines, you can specify an exact page or line to go to. With tables, you can specify the table number as well as the cell within the table.

To scroll the screen and move the insertion point with the keyboard, use these shortcuts when NUMLOCK is on:

Press	To Move
PGUP	Up one screen
PGDN	Down one screen
CTRL-HOME	To the start of the document
CTRL-END	To the end of the document
ALT-PGUP	To the previous page

Selecting Text

When you want to perform a WordPerfect 10 function on more than one character or word at a time, you need to select them. You can select text using either the mouse or the keyboard. Selected text appears highlighted—light letters over a dark background.

NOTE   *When you select text, the property bar changes. The Symbols button and Prompt-As-You-Go list are replaced by four new buttons: Block Protect, New Comment, QuickWords, and Hyperlink. You use Block Protect to keep a section of text from being divided into two pages. You'll learn how to use the other buttons in later chapters.*

It is easy to select text by dragging the mouse. Here's how:

1. Move the mouse so it is at one end of the text that you want to select. It can be at either end, in front of the first character or following the last character.

2. Press and hold down the left mouse button. Make sure the pointer that appears looks like an I-beam. If the pointer is an arrow, you'll draw a box to hold clip art or another object, as you'll learn in Chapter 13.

3. Keep the button down as you drag the mouse, until the pointer is at the other end of the text. Drag straight across the line, not up or down, unless you want to select more than one line of text.

4. When you reach the end of the text, release the mouse button. The selected text appears highlighted. Click the mouse to deselect the text, removing the highlighting.

TIP	*The Reselect Last Selection option in the Go To dialog box automatically moves to and highlights the last text selected.*

WordPerfect 10 uses QuickSelect, an intelligent selection system. If you start dragging in the center of a word, the program selects the entire word and the word next to it when you get to the next one. Something similar occurs when you drag the mouse up or down. When you drag to the line above, WordPerfect 10 automatically selects everything to the left of the original line and to the right of the new line. If you drag down to the next line, WordPerfect 10 selects everything to the right of the original and to the left of the next line.

As long as you do not release the mouse button, you can drag as much or as little text as you want. If you drag too far to the right, for example, just keep the mouse button down, and drag back toward the left.

If you want to delete text quickly, select it with the mouse, and then press the DEL or BACKSPACE key. You can also point to the selected text, click the right mouse button, and choose Cut or Delete from the QuickMenu that appears when you right-click on selected text.

CAUTION	*Before going any further, here's a word of warning. Selected text is deleted if you press any number, letter, punctuation, the* SPACEBAR, *or the* ENTER *key. WordPerfect 10 uses this technique to make it easy to replace characters with something else. If you do not want to replace text, make certain that no text is selected before you start typing.*

Just as there are many ways to scroll the screen and move the insertion point, there are many ways to select text. Double-click to select a word, click three times to select the sentence, or click four times to select the entire paragraph.

If you double-click on a word and then delete it, WordPerfect 10 also deletes the space following the word. WordPerfect 10 figures that if you want to delete the word, you don't want to leave an extra space between the words that remain.

If you want to select a portion of text without dragging, use the SHIFT key. Place the insertion point at one end of the text, hold down the SHIFT key, and then click at the other end of the text.

You can also select text by clicking on the left margin. When you place the mouse pointer in the left margin, the pointer is shaped like an arrow. Click the left mouse button once to select the sentence of text to the right of the pointer; click twice to select the entire paragraph. If you hold down the mouse button and drag in the left margin, you can select multiple sentences.

TIP	*Right-click in the left margin to see a QuickMenu with the options Select Sentence, Select Paragraph, Select Page, and Select All. Choose the text you want to select.*

You can also select text using the Edit menu. Point to Select on the menu, and choose to select by a specific section, sentence, paragraph, page, or entire document. The Section option displays a dialog box in which you can select a range of pages, chapters, volumes, or secondary pages.

NOTE	*Chapters, volumes, and secondary pages are special features that you set with the page numbering command that you'll learn about in Chapter 9.*

If you want to select text using the keyboard, remember these two important keys: F8 and SHIFT. To simulate dragging, press the F8 or hold down the SHIFT key. Now text is selected as you move the insertion point using the arrow keys or other key combinations, and even by clicking the mouse. For example, if you press F8 and then RIGHT ARROW, text is selected as the insertion point passes over it. To stop selecting text, press the F8 key again, or release the SHIFT key.

Using Undo and Redo

It would be nice if we never made mistakes, but unfortunately, life just isn't that perfect. It is all too easy to delete characters you really want, or type characters and then change your mind about them. Because WordPerfect 10 knows we are not always perfect, it gives us a quick and easy way to correct our mistakes using the Undo and Redo commands.

The Undo command reverses changes that you make in your document. Delete a paragraph by mistake? Use Undo to return it to the document. Type a sentence and then change your mind? Use Undo to remove it from the document. There are two ways to use Undo—from the Edit menu or using these toolbar buttons:

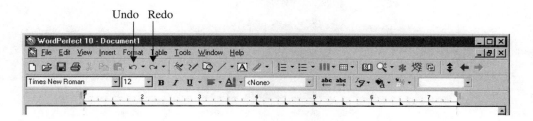

CAUTION *Not every action that you perform can be undone. For example, you cannot undo saving or printing your document.*

To reverse the change you just made to the document, pull down the Edit menu, and click on Undo, or click on the Undo button in the toolbar. WordPerfect 10 reverses the last action you took—whether it's restoring deleted text or undoing your last typing. WordPerfect 10 "remembers" the last ten actions that you performed, even when you save and close the document. Once you undo the very last action, WordPerfect 10 is prepared to undo the one before that; just click on Undo again, or select it from the Edit menu.

You can also undo more than one action at a time, or see the type of action that will be undone. Rather than clicking on the Undo button, pull down the list next to the button to see a list of the last ten actions that can be reversed, the most recent on top:

Clicking on the item at the top of the list will undo it, remove it from the list, and move the remaining items up. Clicking on an item not on top undoes every action from there to the top. In fact, when you point to an item in the list, it and all of the items above it become highlighted and the number of actions to be undone will be shown:

WordPerfect 10 remembers not only the action you took, but also the ones you undo. So if you undo something and then change your mind, you can redo it using any of these techniques:

- Pull down the Edit menu, and click on Redo.

- Click on the Redo button on the toolbar to redo the last action.

- Pull down the Redo list and select a number of items to redo

Undo/Redo History

If you do make a lot of changes to your document, you can forget which action will be undone or redone when you click on the button. To see a list of your last actions, and to increase the number of actions that WordPerfect remembers, choose Undo/Redo History from the Edit menu. You'll see a dialog box like the one shown in Figure 5-3.

Your last actions are listed with the most recent on top. To undo or redo the last action you took, just click on Undo or Redo. To reverse more than one action at a time, click elsewhere on the list. You cannot, however, delete a specific action other than the one that is listed on top. If you click on the third in the list, for example, WordPerfect 10 automatically selects all of the actions above it as well. So to undo your last five actions, click on the fifth item in the list and then on Undo.

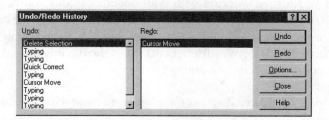

FIGURE 5-3   Undo/Redo History

To change the number of items that WordPerfect 10 remembers, click on Options in the dialog box. You can tell WordPerfect 10 to remember up to 300 actions, and to remember or forget them when you save the document.

Saving a Document

You should get in the habit of saving your documents, even if you think you may not need them again. You might not find a typo or other mistake in a printed copy until a later time. If you didn't save your document, you'd have to type it all over again. To save a document, follow these steps:

1. Click on the Save button in the toolbar, or choose Save As from the File menu to display the Save As dialog box.

   WordPerfect 10 will suggest a filename using the first line of text, up to 65 characters.

2. If you do not want to accept the suggested file name, enter a new name in the File Name box. You do not have to type the WPD extension—WordPerfect will add it for you.

3. If you do not want to store the document in the default folder, use the Save In list to choose the location.

4. Click on Save.

NOTE   *By default, WordPerfect 10 saves documents with the WPD extension in the My Documents folder.*

When you've finished working with your document, look for the word "Unmodified" in the title bar. If it is not there, it means that you've changed the document since you last saved it, and you must save the document again. When you click on Save this time, WordPerfect 10 saves the document immediately without first opening the Save As dialog box.

 Remember, use Save As from the File menu to save the document with a new name.

 In Chapter 14, you'll learn how to save your documents so you can share them with other programs.

Closing a Document

When you have finished working with your document, clear it from the screen by closing it. Click on the Close box on the right of the menu bar, or choose Close from the File menu. If you did not save your document since last changing it, a dialog box is displayed, asking if you want to save it now—select Yes or No.

If you are only working with one document at a time, a new blank one appears when you close it. If you have more than one document open, closing one document displays another open document.

Printing Documents

To print your document using all of the default printing settings, click on the Print button in the toolbar. To choose printing options, follow these steps:

1. Click on the Print button in the application bar, or choose Print from the File menu to display the Print dialog box shown in Figure 5-4.

2. Choose options, such as the print range and number of copies to be printed.

3. Click on Print.

In the Print Range section of the dialog box, you can choose to print the entire document, the current page, or specific pages. To print multiple pages, click on the Pages option button, then in the box that follows it, specify the pages to print. Use a hyphen to represent a range of pages, as in "1-6", and a comma to separate

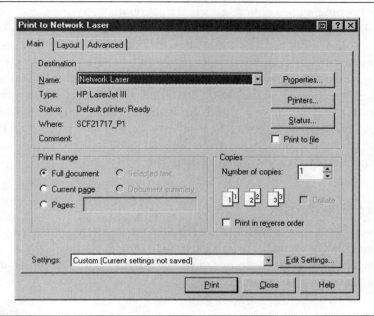

FIGURE 5-4   Print dialog box

individual pages "4, 6, 9". To print from one page to the end of the document, end with a hyphen, such as "10-". Begin with a hyphen to print from the first page to a specific page, as in "-5".

To print more than one copy of the document, set the Number of Copies option. If you are printing more than one copy, select how they are collated. Choose Collate when you want each complete set of the document to print separately. When Collate is not selected, WordPerfect prints multiple copies of the individual pages.

The Selected Text option is dimmed when no text is selected. The Document Summary option is dimmed when no summary is attached to the document.

Use the Print in Reverse Order box to print from the last page to the first. This is useful for some laser printers that eject pages face up, and the pages would otherwise be in reverse order.

Click on Status to see a list of the documents you printed during the current session, along with the time and date you sent them to the printer and when they began to print.

If your document does not print accurately, you may have selected the wrong printer. Pull down the Name list, and choose your printer. Click on Properties, and check the settings being used for the printer. If your printer is not listed, click on the Printers button, click on Add Printer to start the Windows Add Printer Wizard, and follow the directions on the screen.

Use the Advanced tab of the dialog box to print chapters and volumes, depending on how you laid out your document, and to select the options shown in Figure 5-5. The Document on Disk option, for example, lets you print a document that you do not have open. Choose from the Advanced options section depending on your printer and the type of output you desire.

Scaling Printouts

WordPerfect 10 offers a special feature that lets you customize the size of your printed document. You can enlarge a page, for example, so it fills up to one hundred pages to use as a poster, or reduce the size to print *thumbnails* of multiple pages on one sheet of paper.

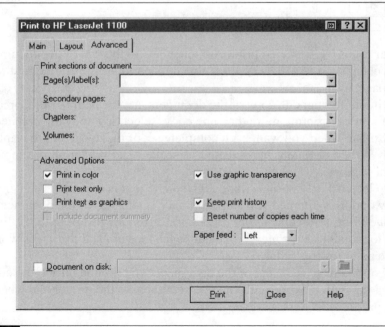

FIGURE 5-5   Advanced printing options

In the Print dialog box, click on the Layout Preview icon on the right of the title bar (just to the left of the Help icon), so the dialog box appears as in Figure 5-6 showing the effects of your changes. Select options from the Position and Size section to determine the layout of the final printout.

NOTE *You'll learn about the Two-sided printing part of this dialog box in Chapter 9.*

Use the Fit to output page option and the Output Page button to specify another paper size. You'll learn more about selecting page sizes in Chapter 9

Use the Scale/Tiling option to enlarge or reduce the printed image. You can set the size in inches, as a percentage of the current page, or by the number of pages you want the image to fill. For example, to reduce the page to a smaller size, decrease the settings in the Size boxes (which represent the length and the width) or in the Scale boxes. Increase the settings to enlarge the image. If the Maintain Aspect Ratio option is enabled, the overall image will always be in the same proportions as the original. Turn off the Maintain Aspect Ratio box if you want to set a specific length and width by inches or by its scale.

As you increase the size of the image, the # of tiles setting will show how many pages the resulting image will fill. If you want to set the number of pages

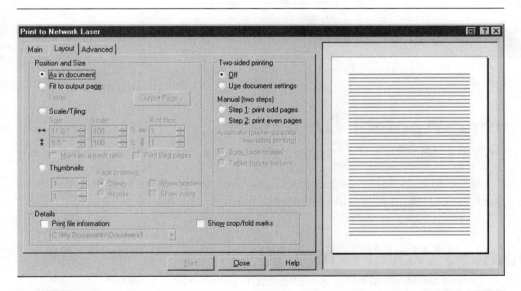

FIGURE 5-6 Scaling printouts

yourself, enable the Print tiled pages box, and then enter the number of pages horizontally and vertically. You can specify up to ten pages in either direction, for a maximum enlargement filling 100 pages.

Use the Thumbnail option to select the number of pages to print on each sheet of paper, up to 100. You can also select the order pages will print (either across or down the sheet), choose to show the page borders, or number pages (called an index) below each thumbnail. The layout to print six pages on each sheet, in down page ordering, with borders and indexing, for example, looks like this:

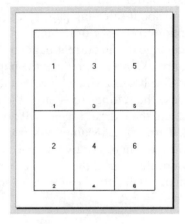

 Select Print File Information to print the document's path and name at the bottom of the page, and select Show crop/fold marks to indicate where a document should be folded or cut.

Starting Another Document

 To start a new document when you're still working with another, click on the New Blank Document button.

If you already have one document open, it moves to the background. You'll learn how to use multiple document windows in Chapter 6.

Quitting WordPerfect 10

When you are finished using WordPerfect 10, choose Exit from the File menu, or click on the Close box on the right of the WordPerfect title bar. If you made any changes to the document since you last saved it, a dialog box is displayed, asking if you want to save the document before closing. Select Yes to save the document, No not to save it, or Cancel to remain in WordPerfect 10.

Opening Existing Documents

To edit an existing document that is not already on the screen, you must first open it. When you open a document, WordPerfect 10 recalls it from the disk and displays it in a document window. Opening a document does not remove it from the disk; it just places a copy of it in your computer's memory. If you already have a document on the screen when you open another, WordPerfect 10 opens a new window for the new document. This window appears in the foreground, showing the document you just opened. The other document window moves into the background. The names of both documents appear in the application bar. See Chapter 6 for more information on working with multiple documents.

Because you often work on a document in more than one session, WordPerfect 10 gives you two ways to easily reopen the last documents that you worked on. Once a document is open, you can edit, print, or just read it.

Pull down the File menu. At the bottom of the menu, WordPerfect lists up to the last nine documents that you've opened or saved. Click on the name of the document you want to open.

Using the File Open Dialog Box

To open a document not listed in the File menu, you can either click on the Open tool in the toolbar or select Open from the File menu. The Open dialog box appears. WordPerfect 10 lists files in the My Documents directory. Double-click on the document you want to open, or highlight its name and then click on Open. Use the navigation tools in the dialog box to find files in other folders and disks.

If you make changes to a document, you must save it again to record the changes to the disk. Click on the Save button in the standard toolbar, or select Save from the File menu. WordPerfect saves the document without displaying the Save dialog box. If you want to change its name or folder, select Save As from the File menu.

Integrate IT! *In Chapter 14, you'll learn how to open documents created with other programs.*

Changing the Document View

When you start WordPerfect 10, it is in Page view. This means that you'll see your document as it will appear when you print it. The margin guidelines show the size of your margins, and you'll see headers, footers, page numbers, graphics, and other elements of your layout.

| TIP | *WordPerfect also provides a Print Preview mode to see exactly how your document will appear when printed. We'll look at this mode in Chapter 9.* |

While Page view shows how your document will look when printed, it has some disadvantages, so WordPerfect gives you two other views in which you can work on your document: Draft and Two Page. To change the view, pull down the View menu, and choose the view you want.

In Draft view, you'll see fonts, graphics, and the left and right margin guidelines, but not headers, footers, page numbers, and the top and bottom page guidelines. It lets you see more lines on the screen than Page view, while still showing most elements of your layout.

Two Page view displays two complete pages onscreen at one time, a useful preview of side-by-side pages. You can still edit and format text in Two Page view, but the text will probably be too small to read.

If you want to see how your document would look as a Web page, choose View | Preview in Browser.

Changing the Display Magnification

By default, WordPerfect 10 displays your document about the same size it will be when printed. Changing to Two Page view reduces the size of the document to two complete pages. If you are in Draft or Page view, you can adjust the magnification as you wish. If you have trouble reading small characters, you can enlarge the display. For example, set magnification at 200% to display your document at twice the printed size. You can also reduce magnification to display more text on the screen than normal, and you can display a full page or more at one time! Changing magnification does not actually change the font size, just how it appears onscreen.

| TIP | *You can edit and format your document no matter what magnification you select. And you can change to any view regardless of the magnification.* |

There are two ways to change magnification: with the toolbar and the View menu.

From the toolbar, use the Zoom button to reduce or enlarge the image by clicking with the mouse or by selecting a specific setting. Click on the Zoom button, for example, to change the mouse to a magnification lens icon. Then click the document with the left mouse button to enlarge, or the right mouse button to reduce. Click on the Zoom button again to turn off this feature.

To select a specific size, pull down the menu to the right of the Zoom button and select from these options:

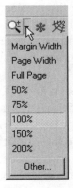

The Margin Width option sets the magnification so that the lines of text fill the width of the window. Choose Page Width so the full width of the page, including margins, fills the screen. Choose Other to set a custom magnification.

If you prefer selecting options from a dialog box, select Zoom from the View menu, or Other from the Zoom list in the toolbar, make your choice in the box that is displayed, and then click OK.

Displaying Guidelines and Toolbars

You have several ways to change what appears on the screen. If you want to see as much text as possible, you can remove the toolbar, property bar, and application bar from the screen. Here's how:

1. Pull down the View menu, and click on Toolbars. A dialog box appears with checkboxes for the optional toolbars and the property bar.

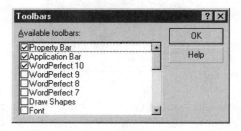

2. Select the bars you want to display; deselect the items you do not want to display.

3. Click on OK.

To remove all of the bars at one time, select Hide Bars from the View menu, and then click on OK in the dialog box that appears. WordPerfect removes everything—the menu, scroll bars, ruler, property bar, application bar, and toolbars — except the Windows taskbar. Redisplay all of the bars by pressing ESC or ALT-V H.

You can also turn the guidelines on and off. Select Guidelines from the View menu, and then select the view guidelines for tables, margins, columns, and headers and footers. The dialog box also lets you turn off the capability to drag guidelines with the mouse to change their position.

To quickly show symbols indicating spaces, carriage returns, tabs, centered text, indentations, flush right alignment, and some other formats, choose Show ¶ from the View menu. Select the option again to turn off the display.

  In Chapter 7, you will learn how to reveal all of the format codes, and in Chapter 11, you will learn how to further customize the look of WordPerfect.

Working with Toolbars

WordPerfect 10 comes with over 20 different toolbars. Most contain a set of common buttons, such as Save and Print, as well as buttons for performing special functions. To display a different toolbar, point the mouse on the toolbar already on the screen, and then click the right mouse button. You'll see the QuickMenu listing some of the toolbars that WordPerfect 10 makes available, shown in Figure 5-7. The check mark next to a toolbar name means that the toolbar is being displayed. Click on the name of another toolbar to display it.

> **NOTE**   *To choose from all of the available toolbars, select View | Toolbars, or choose More from the Toolbar QuickMenu.*

Moving a toolbar is as easy as dragging. Point the mouse to the blank area to the right of the toolbar, or to one of the vertical lines separating buttons into groups, so the pointer appears as a four-pointer arrow. Hold down the mouse button, and then drag the mouse. As you drag, a gray box representing the toolbar moves along with the pointer. Release the mouse button when the box is where you want the toolbar to appear.

If you drag the toolbar somewhere above the text area, or to the bottom of the screen above the status bar, the buttons on the toolbar appear in one row, just like the default layout. If you drag the toolbar to the far left or right of the screen, the

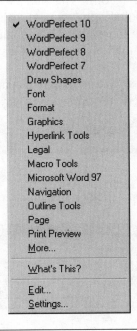

FIGURE 5-7   Select the toolbar to display

buttons are in one column. If you drag the toolbar into the typing area, however, the toolbar appears as a small *floating* window, complete with a title bar and control box. You can change the size and shape of the window by dragging one of its borders, just as you can change the size and shape of any window in Windows. Click on the control box to turn off the toolbar. To turn it back on, you'll need to display the Toolbar QuickMenu and select the name of the toolbar.

 In Chapter 11, you'll learn more about customizing toolbars, menus, and property bars.

Digitally Signing Documents

If you anticipate sending your WordPerfect document over the Internet as an email attachment, you may want to add a digital signature. A digital signature is embedded into the document as a verification that it came from you.

To use the signature feature, however, you must first obtain a digital certificate. You can obtain digital certificates over the Internet from companies such as VeriSign (www.verisign.com), Thawte (www.thawte.com), TrustWise (www.trustwise.com), and GlobalSign (www.globalsign.net). By following the instructions that you'll find on the website, you obtain and download a digital certificate and install it into e-mail programs such as Outlook Express to digitally sign your e-mail.

If you installed the digital signature feature as part of your Corel WordPerfect setup, you'll see an icon for it on the application bar:

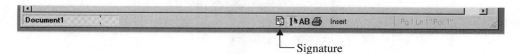

— Signature

To digitally sign a document, click on the icon to open the Sign Document box:

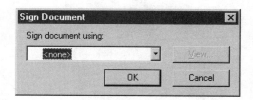

Pull down the list, select the digital signature that you want to use, and the click OK. The application bar icon now changes to this, indicating that the document is digitally signed:

5

NOTE   *You can also sign a document by selecting File | Signature | Sign Document.*

To display information about your digital certificate, click on the icon again to open the Digital Signature dialog box. A summary of the certificate appears in the dialog box, and you can click on the View Certificate button to display additional information.

To remove a digital signature from the document, select File | Signature | Sign Document to open the Sign Document box. Pull down the list of certificates, choose <none>, and then click OK.

Try It Out

You learned a lot in this chapter, so take some time to try out your new WordPerfect skills.

1. Start WordPerfect.

2. Move the mouse to the center at the top of the typing area so the shadow cursor indicates centering, and click.

3. Type **The History of Tae Kwon Do** and then press ENTER twice – once to end the line and a second time to insert a blank line. Notice that the line you typed is centered, but the insertion point is now at the far left, ready for a new paragraph. You'll also see wavy line under the word Tae, indicating that the word is not in WordPerfect's spelling checker.

4. Press Tab and type the next paragraph (including its misspellings), and then press ENTER.

   The history of Korea must always include the subject of Tae Kwon Do. The country, on a tiny penninsula, was instruemental in creating a martial art that is now practiced throughout the entire world. The art, started in the Shaolin Temple, was known as Chaun Fa.

5. Now in the same way, type the next two paragraphs:

   A Buddhist monk named Bodhidharma organized what is considered the first formal system of self-defense in 525 AD. While modern day Tae Kwon Do can trace some its style to Chaun Fa, its history goes back to pre-Christian times. Ruins of the Koguryo dynasty from 37 BC were discovered in Korea with figures positioned in Tae Kwon Do-like poses.

   It is not surprising that ancient Koreans practiced a martial art. In those early days, before the Korean nation was formed, the peninsula was divided into three warring kingdoms — Koguryo, Silla, and Paikche. Silla finally prevailed, and in 668 AD the three kingdoms united under Silla. It was during that period that the martial art known as Tae Kyon developed.

6. Point to the word Tae in the title and click the right mouse button.

7. Because the word is spelled correctly, select Skip in document. WordPerfect removes the wavy line from every occurrence of the word in the text.

8. Point to the word penninsula in the first paragraph and click the right mouse button.

9. Click on the correct spelling of the work — peninsula.

10. Now by yourself, use Spell-As-You-Go to correct the spelling of the word instrumental.

11. The remaining words with wavy lines are spelled correctly, so use Spell-As-You-Go to tell WordPerfect to skip them in the document.

12. Now add the next two paragraphs to the document and use Spell-As-You-Go to correct any spelling mistakes:

Silla was overthrown in 935 and became the kingdom of Koryo. Over the years, however, interest in martial arts declined, especially in the Yi dynasty that was founded in 1392. Buddhism was replaced by Confucianism, and a new national spirit turned interest away from the martial arts.

It was a period in which scholars, primarily Confucian scholars, gained great respect and control. The scholars convinced the political structure of the need to promote cultural activities, and to develop public works, museums, and art. Pacifistic by nature, the scholars drew public money away from the military.

13. Place the insertion point at the end of the first sentence you just typed, ending with *the kingdom of Kyryo.* Use the arrow keys to place the insertion point so it is just before the closing period of the sentence. Look down at the application bar and make sure that the word Insert appears after the printer icon. If the word Typeover appears, press the INS key.

14. Type a comma and then enter the follow text to insert it: **from which the name Korea is derived**. The sentence should appear as:

    Silla was overthrown in 935 and became the kingdom of Koryo, from which the name Korea is derived.

15. Drag over the entire last sentence of the document and press the DEL key.

16. Click Undo to restore your deletion.

17. Save the document with the name The History of Tae Kwon Do. Use either the Save button on the toolbar or the File I Save command.

18. Print a copy of the document. Experiment with some of the printing features, trying to reduce and enlarge the document using the Scale/Tiling options on the Layout tab of the Print dialog box.

19. Close the document so a new blank document appears.

20. Reopen the document using the list at the bottom of the File menu. The document appears as shown in Figure 5-8.

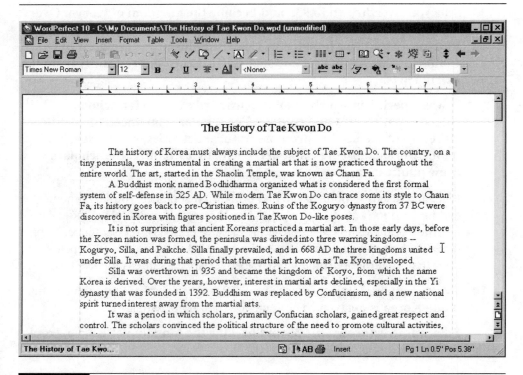

FIGURE 5-8 Completed sample document

Chapter 6

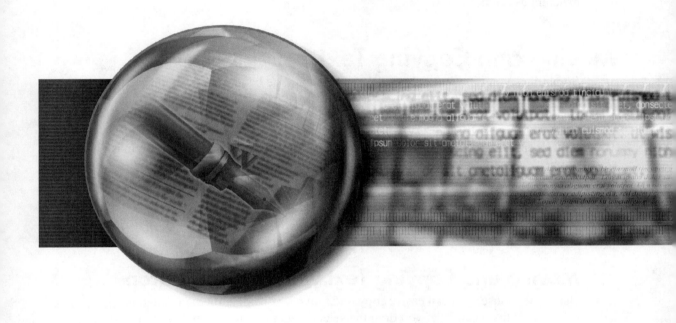

Editing Documents

171

Y ou already know how to edit documents by inserting and deleting text. However, sometimes you have to make major changes, such as moving text from one location to another, or changing a word or phrase that appears several times in the document.

In this chapter, you will learn editing techniques to make your work time as efficient as possible.

Moving and Copying Text

Sometimes you type text only to discover it would be better in a different location in your document. One of the great advantages of WordPerfect 10 is that you can easily move text from one place to another. You can even make a duplicate copy of text in another location. When you *move* text, you delete it from one place in your document and insert it into another location. When you *copy* text, you make a duplicate of selected text and place the copy in another location—the text in the original location is not affected.

 In Chapter 13, you will learn how to share WordPerfect 10 text with other applications.

Moving and Copying Text with Drag and Drop

Using the mouse, you can easily copy and move text using a method called *drag and drop*. This means that you drag the selected text to where you want to insert it, and then release the mouse button to drop it into place.

NOTE *Later in this chapter you will learn how to drag and drop text between open documents using the application bar.*

Use the mouse to select the text you wish to move, and then point anywhere in the selected area. Press and hold down the mouse button, and then drag the mouse to where you want to insert the text. As you drag the mouse, a small box and the insertion point accompany the pointer:

This is being moved to here

Release the mouse button when the dotted insertion point is where you want the text to appear.

If you want to *copy* text rather than move it, press and hold down the CTRL key while you press and hold down the mouse button. When you hold down CTRL, a plus sign appears with the pointer, confirming that you are making a copy of the text:

This is copied to here

| NOTE | *You do not have to hold down the* CTRL *key while you are dragging, only when you release the mouse button.* |

You can use drag and drop to move or copy text anywhere in the document, even in areas that have scrolled off the screen. When you drag the pointer past the top or bottom of the window, the screen scrolls automatically.

If you change your mind about moving the text while you are dragging, just move the pointer back to the selected text, and release the button. If you've already dropped the text and then change your mind, use the Undo command from the Edit menu, or click on the Undo button in the toolbar.

Dragging with the Right Mouse Button

If you drag selected text by pressing the *right* mouse button instead of the left, you'll be able to make some decisions about the effects of drag and drop. When you release the mouse button, you'll see these options:

- Move Here
- Copy Here
- Move Here without Font/Attributes
- Copy Here without Font/Attributes
- Cancel

You can then choose to either move or copy the text—without worrying about the CTRL key—and insert the text without its formats. Normally when you insert text, it retains the formats it had in its original position. If you choose to insert it without its fonts and attributes, the text takes on the same formats of the text where you insert it.

Moving and Copying Text Through the Clipboard

The *Clipboard* is an area in the computer's memory where Windows temporarily stores information. You can place text on the Clipboard and later take it from the Clipboard to insert elsewhere. When you move text using the Clipboard, it's called *cut and paste*—you cut the text from one location and paste it elsewhere. When you copy text with the Clipboard, it's called *copy and paste*—you make a copy of the text and then paste it elsewhere.

 To move text using cut and paste, first select the text you want to move. Then cut the text to the Clipboard by clicking on the Cut button in the toolbar. The selected text is now on the Clipboard. You can also cut text to the Clipboard by using one of these techniques:

- Select Cut from the Edit menu.

- Press CTRL-X.

- Select Cut from the QuickMenu that appears when you click the right mouse button on the selected text.

 Next, place the insertion point where you want to insert the text. Then paste it into the document by clicking on the Paste button. Word inserts whatever is on the Clipboard into the document. You can also paste the contents of the Clipboard using one of these techniques:

- Select Paste from the Edit menu.

- Press CTRL-V to insert the text with its fonts and attributes.

- Press CTRL-SHIFT-V to insert the text without its fonts and attributes.

- Select Paste or Paste without Font/Attributes from the QuickMenu that appears when you right-click.

 The Paste option is dimmed in the Shortcut menu when no text is on the Clipboard.

To *copy* text rather than move it, follow the same steps as described previously, but click on the Copy button. You can also select Copy from the Edit menu, press CTRL-C, or select Copy from the QuickMenu.

Normally, Windows can store only one thing at a time on the Clipboard. So think about the consequences. If you cut some text in preparation for moving it, and then absent-mindedly cut or copy something else, the text you want to move is erased from the Clipboard. Click on the Undo button twice to restore both cut portions of text, and then start over. If you do want to add text to what is already on the Clipboard, select the text, and then choose Append from the Edit menu.

The contents of the Clipboard remain there until you cut or copy something else, or until you exit Windows. This means that you can insert the same text over and over again in your document, as long as you do not cut or copy something else. To insert the Clipboard contents in multiple locations, just position the insertion point, and select Paste at each spot.

Inserting with QuickWords

In Chapter 2, you learned how to use QuickCorrect to quickly insert text or expand abbreviations. QuickCorrect is useful because sometimes you find yourself writing the same word or phase over and over again. You may repeat it several times in one document, or use the same phrase in a number of documents that you write. It's not difficult if you have to repeat a small word several times. But imagine having to repeat a complex scientific or medical term, or the full name of some company or government agency. Sure, you could copy the word and then paste it where you want it. But then the word would be deleted from the Clipboard if you had to cut or copy something else.

While QuickCorrect is handy, however, it does have two drawbacks. First, QuickCorrect always inserts text in the same format as the text it is expanding. Suppose you create a QuickCorrect entry by selecting a boldfaced underlined phrase. When QuickCorrect later inserts the phrase for you, it takes on the current format.

Second, QuickCorrect is always automatic. Suppose you create a QuickCorrect entry to replace the state abbreviation "CA" with "California." Just imagine your chemistry teacher's response when every reference to calcium (which is abbreviated "CA") in your report is printed as "California" instead. You can turn off QuickCorrect, but then it wouldn't make any of the corrections for you.

You can solve both of these problems by using QuickWords. With QuickWords you have the option of inserting any amount of text, formatted or plain, automatically or manually. Use QuickWords when you frequently use a word, phrase, or even a long section of text in a specific format, but you do not want it to be replaced automatically. You can then insert a word, phrase, or entire section of text by typing the abbreviation. You can use QuickWords to insert your name, address, and your telephone number, for standard closings, or for anything that you want to insert easily and quickly.

To create a QuickWord, first type, format, and select the text you want to assign to an abbreviation, and then click on the QuickWords button in the property bar (it only appears when text is selected), or choose QuickWords from the Tools menu. Try it now by typing your full name in a new document window. Select your name, and then choose QuickWords from the Tools menu to display the dialog box shown in Figure 6-1, listing any QuickWords that you've already created.

In the Abbreviated form box, type your initials—the abbreviation you want to represent your name.

Notice the checkbox labeled "Expand QuickWords when you type them." When this box is checked, WordPerfect 10 expands your QuickWords just as it does QuickCorrect entries. If you deselect this box, you cannot expand the QuickWords entry when you type it.

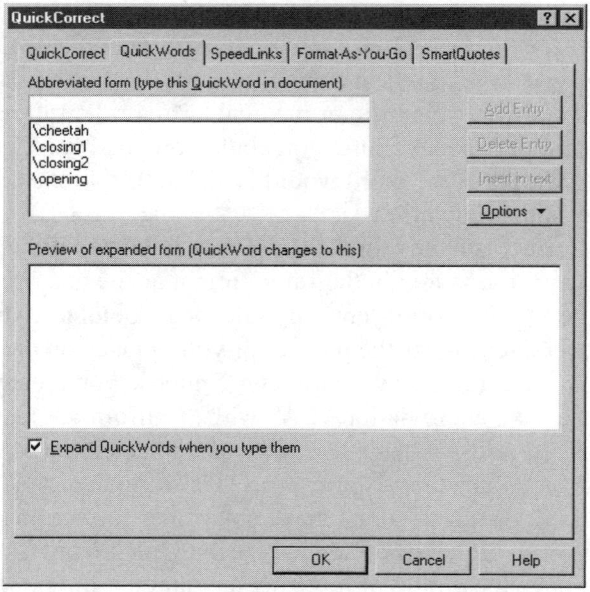

FIGURE 6-1   QuickWords

Click Add Entry to add the abbreviation to the list, and close the dialog box.

If you set QuickWords to expand words as you type them, it automatically expands the abbreviation when you press ENTER, the SPACEBAR, or TAB, just as QuickCorrect does. If you deselected the checkbox, when you want to enter the word, type the abbreviation for it, and press CTRL-SHIFT-A. WordPerfect 10 replaces the abbreviation with the complete word or phrase. If you did not deselect the box, QuickWords expands it automatically.

> **NOTE** *QuickWords names are not case-sensitive.*

If you forget which abbreviations you used, or you want to delete one, select QuickWords from the Tools menu, and choose the abbreviation. The full text appears in the Preview panel. To add the word to the document, click on Insert in text.

> **NOTE** *Refer to Chapter 2 to refresh your memory about QuickCorrect and Format-As-You-Go.*

QuickWords Options

By default, WordPerfect 10 inserts the expanded QuickWord in the same format in which it was created. This is the Expand as Text With Formatting setting. If you want to insert QuickWords in the current format, pull down the Options list, and choose Expand as Plain Text.

When you select an abbreviation in the list, you can also choose the Rename Entry and Replace Entry options. Rename Entry lets you change the abbreviation that you want to enter to expand the item. The Replace Entry command lets you change the expanded text that is associated with an abbreviation. Here's how to replace an entry:

1. Select the new text you want the abbreviation to represent.

2. Select QuickWords from the Tools menu.

3. Click the abbreviation you want to change.

4. Pull down Options, and choose Replace Entry.

5. Click Yes in the dialog box that appears.

6. Click OK to close the QuickWords dialog box.

Inserting SpeedLinks

A SpeedLink is a word or phrase that WordPerfect 10 automatically converts into a hyperlink to a site on the World Wide Web. When you click on a hyperlink, Windows starts your Web browser, makes the connection, and opens the site named in the link.

To see the SpeedLinks already defined, select either QuickCorrect or QuickWords from the Tools menu, and then click on the SpeedLinks tab to see the dialog box in Figure 6-2.

The list shows the SpeedLink words, along with the Web sites they are linked to. You can insert the link into your document by choosing it in the list and then clicking on the Insert Entry button. You can also simply type the SpeedLink word into the document, starting with the @ symbol. If you type @yahoo, for example, SpeedLinks converts the word into a link to http://www.yahoo.com. When you point to the link, the mouse pointer appears as a pointing hand, and a QuickStatus box appears showing you the Web address. Click on the link to make the connection.

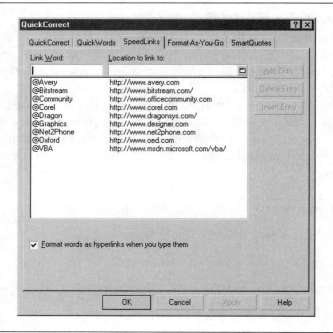

FIGURE 6-2   SpeedLinks

You can also add your own SpeedLink words and Web sites. In the appropriate text boxes in the SpeedLinks tab, type the link word and the location to link it to, and then click on Add Entry.

> **TIP** *WordPerfect 10 converts any text in the format, www.something.something, into a SpeedLink.*

Inserting the Date and Time

You probably add the date to letters, memos, and faxes. You might even add the time to faxes, logs, journals, messages, and other documents when the time of distribution or printing is important. Rather than manually typing the date or time, have WordPerfect 10 do it for you.

You can enter the date and time in two ways—as text or as a code. When you have WordPerfect 10 insert the date or time as *text*, it is entered as a series of characters, just as if you had typed it yourself. You can edit or delete individual characters, just as you can edit any text that you've typed.

When you have WordPerfect 10 insert the date or time as a *code*, however, the date or time is displayed on the screen, but WordPerfect 10 has actually entered a code. The date or time changes to the current date or time whenever you open or print the document. You can't edit the date or time.

> **TIP** *Press* CTRL-D *to insert the date as text, or* SHIFT-CTRL-D *to insert it as code.*

To insert the date or time, select Date/Time from the Insert menu to see this dialog box:

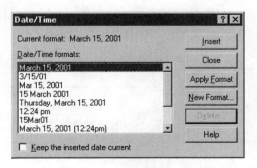

Scroll the Date/Time formats list, and click on the format for the date or time you want to insert. To insert the date or time as a code, check the Keep the Inserted Date Current checkbox. Finally, click on Insert to add the date to the document.

Changing Date Formats

Once you enter the date as text, you have to edit it yourself or reinsert it if you want to use a different format. If you change your mind about the format of a date code, however, you can have WordPerfect 10 change it for you.

Place the insertion point just before the date, and then display the Date/Time dialog box. Choose the new format that you want and click on the Apply Format button. WordPerfect 10 automatically reformats dates entered as codes that follow the insertion point.

Custom Date Formats

If none of the formats suits your taste, you can create your own. Click on New Format in the Date/Time dialog box to see the options shown in Figure 6-3.

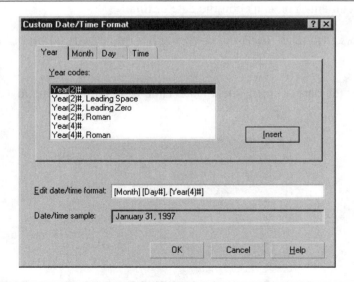

FIGURE 6-3   Creating custom date formats

The currently used format appears in the Edit date/time format text box, shown as a series of codes. A sample date in that format is displayed. To change a format, you must enter codes that represent the year, month, day, and time. All of the possible codes are shown in the list boxes in the four pages of the dialog box. Select a code from the list, and then click on Insert to add it to the Edit date/time format text box. A preview of how the format displays a date appears in the Date/time sample box.

Inserting Other Useful Objects

In addition to inserting the date, you can insert the name of the file and other items into a document. These may not be used as often as the date, but they are handy when you need them, even in headers, footers, and captions. Pull down the Insert menu, and point to Other to access these options:

- *Filename* inserts the name of the current document. Nothing appears if you have not named it yet—the default Document1 name, for example, will not be inserted.

- *Path and Filename* inserts the complete path as well as the name. The path is the location of the folder in which the document is stored, starting from the root directory of the disk drive.

- *Counter* inserts codes to consecutively number figures, tables, and other objects.

- *BarCode* inserts a POSTNET bar code. A dialog box appears for you to enter the ZIP code.

Inserting Comments

A *comment* is an annotation, a note, reminder, or reference that you want to place in the document but not print along with it. It is a handy way to record reminders to yourself, and explanations to others who may be reading or editing your document. To insert a comment, pull down the Insert menu, and point to Comment to see the options Create, Edit, and Convert to Text.

To convert existing text into a comment, select the text, and then click on the New Comment button in the Selected Text property bar. The text is removed from the document and inserted into the comment.

Click on Create to display the Comment window, shown in Figure 6-4. Now type the text that you want in the comment, or click on the property bar buttons to add your initials, name, date, or time, or to move to other comments in the document. When you've finished writing the comment, click on the Close icon in the property bar.

NOTE   *WordPerfect 10 display your initials or name only if they are defined as part of the WordPerfect 10 environment.*

You'll see your initials in a small box in the margin, or you'll see a Comment icon if your initials are not in the environment:

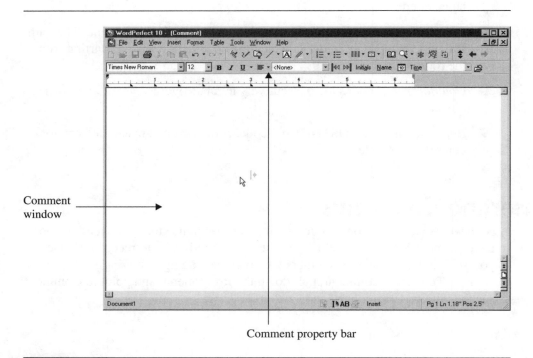

Comment window

Comment property bar

FIGURE 6-4   Comment window

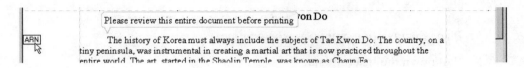

To read a comment, click on it with the mouse. The comment appears as a balloon near the text.

There are two different comment QuickMenus. The menu that appears when you right-click on the Comment icon has these options:

- Cut
- Copy
- Delete
- What's This?
- Information
- Edit

The QuickMenu that appears when you right-click on the displayed comment has these options:

- Convert to Text
- Delete
- What's This?
- Information
- Edit

The Information option displays a dialog box showing the name, initials, and user color of the person who created the comment, and the date the comment was inserted into the document.

To edit a comment in its own window, double-click on the icon, or display the QuickMenu and click on Edit. Edit it as you wish, and then click on Close.

To print a comment, open it in the Edit window, and click on the Print button in the toolbar.

To convert a comment to regular text so it appears normally in your document, use the following steps:

1. Place the insertion point after the comment.

2. Pull down the Insert menu.

3. Point to Comment.

4. Click on Convert to Text.

You can also click on the comment to display it, and then right-click on the displayed comment, and select Convert to Text.

To delete a comment, right-click on it, and select Delete from the QuickMenu.

Setting Bookmarks

A *bookmark* marks your place in the document. Like a bookmark in a book, it allows you to quickly return to a specific location. You can add any number of bookmarks in a document, giving each a name, so you can return to a specific location later on. You can also create a QuickMark, which lets you return to a position with two clicks of the mouse, and you can set up WordPerfect 10 to automatically set a QuickMark at the last position of the insertion point when you save the document.

To create a bookmark, place the insertion point where you want the bookmark to be set. WordPerfect 10 associates the bookmark with the location of that insertion point. If you want the bookmark to be linked to text, select the text before creating the bookmark. Then pull down the Tools menu, and click on Bookmark to display the dialog box in Figure 6-5. Click on Create. In the box that appears, type a name for the bookmark, and click on OK.

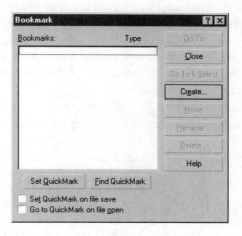

FIGURE 6-5   Bookmark dialog box

TIP   *When text is selected, set a bookmark by clicking the Hyperlink button in the property bar and selecting Insert Bookmark.*

To return to a bookmark position, select Bookmark from the Tools menu, click on the bookmark name in the list, and then click on Go To. If the bookmark is associated with selected text, click on Go To & Select. WordPerfect 10 moves to the text and selects it.

NOTE   *Use the Go To Bookmarks button on the Navigation toolbar to create a bookmark or to open the Bookmark dialog box.*

You can also set one QuickMark in a document. This is a bookmark that you do not have to name. Use these steps:

1. Place the insertion point at the position you want to mark—or select the text.

2. Display the Bookmark dialog box.

3. Click on Set QuickMark button.

4. To return to that position, select Find QuickMark from the dialog box.

One of the best uses for a QuickMark is to set your place when you save the document, so you can start where you left off when you next open the document. To have WordPerfect 10 do this automatically, select the two checkboxes at the bottom of the Bookmark dialog box. One box sets the QuickMark when you save the document, while the other sets WordPerfect 10 to move to the bookmark position when you open the document.

Other options in the dialog box let you delete, rename, and move a bookmark. Moving a bookmark associates an existing bookmark with a new location or selected text.

We'll look at inserting sounds and other items in later chapters.

Finding and Replacing Text

The Find and Replace command can be a real time-saver. Suppose you're looking for a specific reference in your document, but you're not sure exactly where it is. Instead of scanning through the entire document, with a chance that you'll miss it, let WordPerfect 10 locate the text for you. The Replace part of the command can even replace text that it locates, so you can quickly correct an error in several locations, or change one word to another in every place it is used.

You can also find a word by example. Let's look at that option first.

Using QuickFind

QuickFind lets you place the insertion point in a word that's already in the document, then quickly move to the next or previous occurrence of the same word.

 To use QuickFind to locate the first occurrence of a word, just type the word at the start of the document, and then use the QuickFind Next command.

Here's how to use this feature.

1. Click anywhere in the word onscreen that you want to locate. To locate an entire phrase, first select the phrase.

2. Click on the QuickFind Next button on the property bar (or press ALT-CTRL-N).

WordPerfect 10 locates and highlights the next occurrence of the word or phrase. You can now edit, delete, or format the word as you want. Click the button again to find the next occurrence, or click the QuickFind Previous button (or press ALT-CTRL-P) to locate words toward the start of the document.

Finding Text

Both the Find and the Replace functions are in the same dialog box (Figure 6-6), displayed when you select Find and Replace from the Edit menu.

The Find command scans your document for the first occurrence of the word or phrase that you specify. After it finds the word or phrase, you can repeat the command to find the next occurrence, and so on, until your entire document has been searched. This is similar to using QuickFind, except you can also specify formats in order to find text that's in a specific font, size, or style.

WordPerfect 10 starts looking for text at the current location of the insertion point. If you want to make sure that the entire document is searched, move to the start of the document. Pull down the Edit menu, and select Find and Replace to display the dialog box. In the Find text box, type the characters you want to locate. WordPerfect 10 saves your last ten search phrases. To select one, pull down the list on the right of the Find text box, and click on the word you want to locate.

 If you performed a QuickFind, the searched text appears in the Find text box of the Find and Replace dialog box.

Then click on Find Next. WordPerfect 10 selects the next occurrence of the text following the insertion point. To locate text above the insertion point, click on

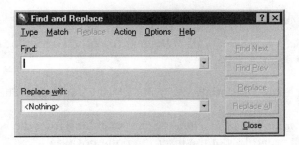

FIGURE 6-6   Find and Replace

Find Prev. The Find dialog box remains on the screen so you can find the next occurrence by clicking on Find Next again. If the text is not found, a dialog box with the message "Not Found" is displayed. Select OK, or press ENTER to remove the message, leaving the insertion point in its original position.

WordPerfect 10 locates the characters you search for even if they are part of another word. Searching for the word "love," for example, selects the characters in the word "lovely." You can customize how WordPerfect 10 locates text by using the Find and Replace menu bar.

The Match menu, for example, determines what is considered a match. The options are:

- *Whole Word* locates just whole words that match the text you are looking for. If you are looking for "love," it does not match with "lovely."

- *Case* matches only characters in the same case. By default, searches are not case-sensitive, so looking for *love* locates *LOVE*.

- *Font* lets you choose a specific font, so you can look for a word only if it is in Times Roman, for example.

- *Codes* lets you search for a formatting code, or a specific format of text. Use it, for example, to locate any text that is centered, or a specific centered word.

The Action menu determines what happens when WordPerfect 10 locates a match. The options in the menu are:

- *Select Match* highlights the located text.

- *Position Before* places the insertion point before the text.

- *Position After* places the insertion point after the text.

- *Extend Selection* selects all of the text from the current location of the insertion point.

The Options menu determines the way the search operates. The options are:

- *Begin Find at Top of Document* starts searching from the beginning of the document regardless of the insertion point position.

- *Wrap at Beg./End of Document* continues at the beginning of the document when WordPerfect 10 reaches the end and you did not start at the beginning. If you search using Find Previous, WordPerfect 10 wraps to the end when it reaches the start.

- *Limit Find Within Selection* searches only the currently selected portion of text.

- *Include Headers, Footers, etc. In Find* searches for the text in headers, footers, and all document elements, even those not displayed.

- *Limit Number of Changes* makes only a specific number of replacements that you specify, when using the Replace All command.

The Type menu determines what WordPerfect 10 looks for. The default setting is Text. You can also select Word Forms and Specific Codes. If you want to locate all forms of a word, such as "drink," "drank," and "drunk," pull down the Type option, and click on Word Forms. Type one form of the verb, and then click on Find Next. For example, searching for "sing" with this option selected locates "sing," "sang," and "sung." The Specific Code option lets you search for a code that has specific settings, such as a certain indentation or margin.

Replacing Text Automatically

Making a mistake is only human, but making the same mistake more than once is downright annoying. Have you ever typed a document only to discover that you've made the same mistake several times? The Replace part of Find and Replace searches your document to find text automatically and replace it with something else. You can use it not only to correct errors, but also to recycle documents. Perhaps you created a sales proposal that mentions a person's name in several places. You may be able to modify the proposal for another prospect by changing just one or two words several times. You can have WordPerfect 10 scan the entire document, automatically replacing "Mr. Smith" with "Mrs. Jones." It just takes a few keystrokes.

To replace text automatically, use these steps:

1. Move the insertion point to the location where you want the replacements to begin.

2. Choose Find and Replace from the Edit menu.

3. In the Find box, enter the text that you want to replace.

4. In the Replace With box, enter the text that you want to insert. When you click in the Replace With box, the notation <Nothing> disappears.

CAUTION *Selecting Replace or Replace All when <Nothing> is in the Replace With box deletes the located text.*

The Replace operation first locates the text that you want to replace, so you should select options from the menus to specify how you want the Find part of the operation to proceed. In fact, the options and the Find text are the same as you selected in the last Find operation. If you want to replace the text only when it appears as a whole word, for example, pull down the Match list, and select Whole Word. The Match list is selectable only when you are in the Find text box.

When you are in the Replace With text box, you can pull down the Replace list to select these options:

- *Case* toggles case-sensitive replacing on and off.

- *Font* replaces text formatted a specific way.

- *Codes* lets you choose a code to insert.

Confirming Replacements

You might not want to replace every occurrence of the text in the document. For example, suppose you refer to the titles of two persons in your document. You call Mrs. Jones the "President," and you refer to Mr. Smith as "Vice President." After completing the letter, you learn that Mrs. Jones's correct title is "Chairperson." Should you use Replace All to change every occurrence of President to Chairperson? Not really. If you do, you would change Mr. Smith's title to "Vice Chairperson."

When you do not want to replace every occurrence of the text, use the Find Next and Replace buttons. Click on Find Next to locate and select the next occurrence of the text following the insertion point. (Use Find Previous to locate text above the insertion point.) To replace the selected text, click on Replace. WordPerfect 10 makes the replacement and then automatically locates and selects the next occurrence. If you want to leave the text as it is and locate the next occurrence, click on Find Next again.

Automatic Replacements

If you feel confident that you want to replace every occurrence of the text, click on the Replace All button. WordPerfect 10 scans the document making the replacements for you. Use this option with caution. Remember, the default Find and Replace settings ignore case and locate characters even if they are part of another word. With these settings, replacing every occurrence of the text could unintentionally change parts of other words. Changing "his" to "her" would also change "history" to "hertory" and "Buddhism" to "Buddherm."

To safeguard against these types of errors, either confirm each replacement, or use the Match Case and Match Whole Words options.

Finding and Replacing Formats and Codes

Sometimes you want to find information that you cannot type into the Find What box. For example, suppose you want to find a word, but only when it is in italic format. You must tell WordPerfect 10 not only what text to locate, but also its format.

In the Find text box, enter the text that you want to find. Then, pull down the Match list, and click on Font to display the dialog box shown in Figure 6-7. To search for text in a certain font and style, pull down the Font list, choose the font, and then select the style in the Font style list. To search for text in a specific point size, choose the size in the Point size list. In the Attributes section, choose any other font formats that must be applied to the text.

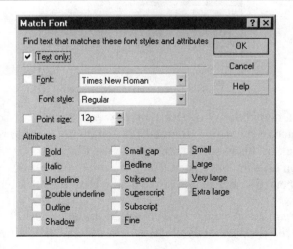

Finding and replacing a font

To later search for text without considering its format, click on Text Only.

When you replace the text, it will appear in the same font as that replaced. To apply other formats to the replaced text, click on the Replace With box, pull down the Replace menu, and click on Font. Select the formats that you want applied to the new text. The dialog box shows the formats you are locating and replacing, as follows:

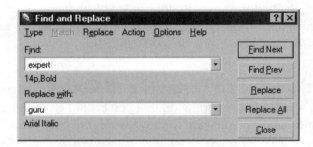

To find just a code, such as a tab or paragraph mark, click on the Find text box, pull down the Match menu, and click on Codes to see this dialog box:

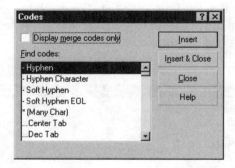

Scroll the list, and choose the code that you want to locate. (Codes that cannot be inserted in place of others are dimmed.) If you do not want to replace the code with another, click on Insert to add the code to the Find text box, and close the dialog box. If you do want to replace the code with another, click on the Replace With text box. Then choose the code in the dialog box, and click on Insert & Close.

 If you are not sure which code to select, use the Reveal Codes feature to see how the code is named for the format you want to find or replace.

Other codes have specific settings. For example, if you choose to replace a Margins code, you have to designate the margin settings. In either the Find or Replace With box, pull down the Type menu, and click on Specific Codes. In the box that appears, select the code you want to find or replace, and then click on OK. A dialog box appears in which you can select or set the exact value.

Replacing All Word Forms

The Word Forms feature locates and replaces all forms of a word. For example, suppose you typed "He was going to run to the store, but he already ran ten miles." You now realize that you want the sentence to read "He was going to walk to the store, but he already walked ten miles." To make the changes, use these steps:

1. Select Find and Replace from the Edit menu.

2. Type **run** in the Find text box.

3. Pull down the Type menu, and click on Word Forms. If the word in the Find box cannot be found in WordPerfect 10's dictionary, a warning box appears. Click on OK to clear the warning box, and enter another word or turn off Word Forms.

4. In the Replace With box, type **walk**.

5. Click on Replace All. WordPerfect 10 highlights the word "run" in the sentence and displays this dialog box asking which form of the replacement word you want to insert:

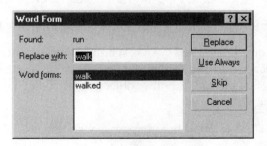

6. Click on Replace to use the suggested "walk." WordPerfect 10 makes the change, then automatically changes the word "ran" later in the sentence with the word "walked" and displays a message that two occurrences have been changed.

7. Click OK and then close the Find and Replace dialog box.

 The Use Always button in the Word Form dialog box automatically uses the same selection for all replacements. The Skip option leaves the work unchanged.

Replacing Text Using Variables

Sometimes you know in advance that there are words or phrases that you may be replacing in a document. Suppose, for example, that you're typing a memo announcing a meeting, but you're not quite sure if the time and date will be changing. There is a chance that each date and time you mention in the memo might change. You might also want to type the memo once and use it each week or month for regular meetings, just changing the date and time.

Rather than searching through the document to manually change the time and date, you can insert each as a variable. You can then instantly change each occurrence of the date and time by changing the text associated with the variable.

First, define the variables that you want to use in the document. Follow these steps, for example, to create variables called Meeting Time and Meeting Date.

1. Select Insert | Variable.

2. In the Variables dialog box, click Create to open the Variables Editor shown in Figure 6-8.

3. In the Variable text box, type the variable name: **Meeting Time**.

4. In the Description text box, enter **Time of the monthly progress meeting**.

5. In the Contents box, type **10 AM**. While in the Contents box, you can use the menu bar to edit and format the text. You can use the Insert menu to add graphics, symbols, and other objects; and you can use the Tools menu to access the writing tools.

6. Click OK. The Variables box reappears with your variable listed, as shown in Figure 6-9.

7. Now follow the same procedure to create a variable called Meeting Date, with the current date as its contents.

8. Close the Variables dialog box.

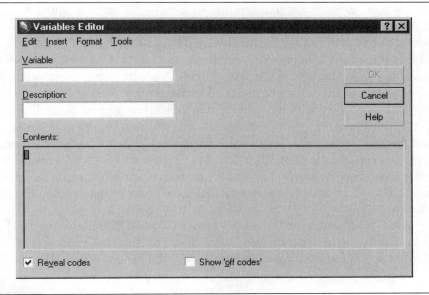

FIGURE 6-8 Defining a variable in the Variable Editor

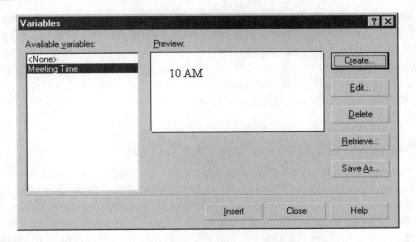

FIGURE 6-9 List of defined variables

Now whenever you want to insert the contents of the variable into a document, select Insert | Variable, click on the name of the variable and click Insert.

When you need to change the text inserted by a variable, select Insert | Variable, click on the name of the variable and click Edit. Change the text in the Contents box and click OK. When you close the Variables box, every occurrence of the variable you edited will have the updated contents.

Variables are saved with the document in which you created them. If you want to use the same variables with other documents, you can save them in a separate file and then retrieve them when needed. From the Variables dialog box containing the variables you want to save, click Save As. Enter a name for the variable file and click OK. When you want to use the variables in another document, open the Variables dialog box and click Retrieve. Enter the name of the variable file and click Open.

Use the Browse button in the Save Variables To and Retrieve Variables From boxes to specify the location of the variable file. The default location is Windows\Application Data\Corel\PerfectExpert\10\Custom WP Templates.

Using Multiple Documents and Windows

WordPerfect 10 lets you have more than one document open at the same time, so you can move and copy text between documents as easily as you can within a document. For example, suppose you are on a tight deadline and you are trying to complete an important report. You realize that you need to refer to a letter that you wrote last month. With WordPerfect 10, there's no need to rummage through your file cabinets. Just open the letter in its own window on the WordPerfect 10 screen so you can refer to it as you work on your report.

Because the names of all documents appear in the application bar, you can tell at a glance which documents are open, switch between them with a click, and even drag and drop text from one document to another.

Arranging Windows on the Screen

When you open a second document, it appears in the foreground, and its name is added to the application bar. The first document is moved into the background behind the new document window. To switch from one document to the other, just click on the document's name in the application bar. You can also pull down the Window menu to see a list of the documents, and click on the one you want to display.

It is much easier to work with multiple documents when you can see them on the screen. To arrange windows on the screen, pull down the Window menu. Select Cascade to display all open windows overlapped, as shown in Figure 6-10. Select Tile Top to Bottom to display each window stacked vertically, one above the other. Choose Tile Side to Side to arrange the windows horizontally, next to each other. To edit or format the text in a window, click in it to make it active. The active window contains scroll bars and the ruler when it is turned on. Inactive windows do not have rulers, and their title bars are dimmed.

When you want to display a window full-screen, click on its Maximize button. To close a window, click on its Close button. The active window is the one affected by options you select in the menu bar and toolbar. If you click on the Print button, for example, only the document in the active window is printed.

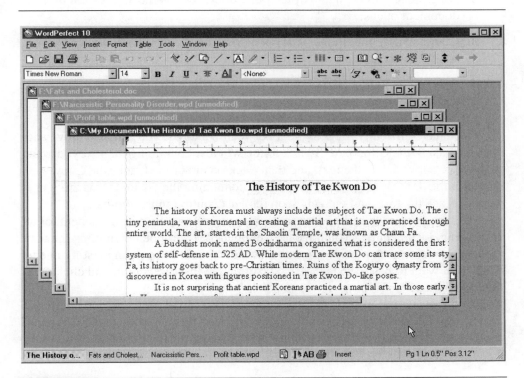

FIGURE 6-10   Cascaded windows

Moving Text Between Documents

You can move and copy text from one open document to another whether or not they are displayed at the same time. Because of the application bar, you can drag and drop text between documents even when both are not displayed at the same time.

To drag and drop text from one displayed window to another, select the text, point to it with the mouse, hold down the mouse button, and drag the selected text to the other window. When you release the mouse button, the window to which you dragged the text is active. Remember to hold down the CTRL key if you want to copy the text rather than move it.

To drag and drop text to a document in the background, use this technique.

1. Select the text that you want to move.

2. Drag the text to the name of the other document on the application bar. The document opens.

3. Continue dragging in the now-open document to the location where you want to place the text.

4. Release the mouse. Remember, hold down the CTRL key when you release the mouse to copy the text rather than move it.

If you have difficulty dragging text between windows, you can also move and copy text using the Clipboard. Switch to the window containing the text you want to move or copy. Select the text, and then click on either the Cut or the Copy button in the toolbar. Switch to the window containing the document where you want to place the text, and then click on the Paste button in the toolbar.

You can also use the Clipboard to copy or move text to a new document, or to an existing document that you have not yet opened. After you cut or copy the text to the Clipboard, click on New to start a new document or open an existing one to which you want to paste the text. Then position the insertion point, and click on the Paste button.

Once you cut or copy text to the Clipboard, you can close the document that it came from. The document does not have to be open for you to paste the Clipboard contents elsewhere. If you forget what you've placed in the Clipboard, open a new document, and click on Paste to display the contents of the Clipboard.

Inserting a File into a Document

Use drop and drag, or the Clipboard, to move or copy text from one document to another. You don't really even have to open a document if you want to copy all of it into another document.

To insert one entire document into the open document, place the insertion point where you want to insert the contents, and then select File from the Insert menu. WordPerfect 10 displays the Insert File dialog box, which is similar to the Open dialog box. Select the document that you want to insert, and then click on OK. WordPerfect 10 inserts the document using the page layout setting of the active document. You can now edit the inserted text, just as if it were originally part of the document.

Changing the Case of Characters

Did you type a title and then decide it would be better all uppercase? Pretty annoying, isn't it? Rather than retype everything, quickly change the case of existing characters using the Edit menu. To change the case of text, start by selecting the text, and then point to Convert Case in the Edit menu. Click on UPPERCASE, lowercase, or Initial Capitals. The Initial Capitals option, by the way, changes the first letter of every word to capital except articles, prepositions, and certain other words when they do not start or end the sentence.

Repeating Actions

Sometimes you want to repeat an action a specific number of times in succession. For example, suppose you want to insert a row of 78 asterisks across the screen, or paste 10 copies of the contents of the Clipboard. The Repeat Next Action option from the Edit menu lets you repeat one action the number of times you specify. It repeats a single keystroke, cursor movement, or a selection from the toolbar or power bar that is activated by a single click of the mouse.

When you want to repeat a keystroke, pull down the Edit menu, and select Repeat Next Action to display this dialog box:

By default, your next keystroke after closing the box is performed eight times. To repeat it a different number of times, enter the number in the text box. If you want that number to be the new default, click on the Use as Default button. Then click on OK, and enter the keystroke or use the command that you want to repeat, such as typing an asterisk or clicking on the Paste button.

Highlighting Text

You've no doubt seen, or used, those transparent highlighting pens. When you want to mark an important word or phrase in a textbook, for example, you draw over it with a colored highlighting pen. This emphasizes the text, so you can quickly find it when scanning over the pages. You can use the WordPerfect 10 Highlight tool to do the same thing. You can even choose a color and print the highlight with the document.

To highlight text, select it, and then click on the Highlight tool in the toolbar. You can also click on the Highlight tool first, before selecting text, so the mouse pointer changes to the same icon that is on the face of the button. Then drag over the text you want to highlight. When you release the mouse button, the text is covered with the highlighting color. The Highlight function remains on after you release the mouse button, however, so you can continue highlighting other text. This way you can scan through a document, highlighting text as you find it. To stop highlighting, click on the Highlight tool again.

WordPerfect 10 gives you several ways to remove highlighting from text. To quickly do so, click anywhere in a section of the highlighted area, and click on the Highlight tool. If you want to remove the color from just part of a highlighted section, such as one word in a highlighted sentence, select the text first and then click on the Highlight tool, or click the Highlight tool and drag over the text. You can also select the text, and then pull down the Tools menu, point to Highlight, and click on Remove.

By default, the highlight color is yellow. To select another color, pull down the list next to the Highlight button on the toolbar, and select a color from the palette that appears. The color you choose will now be used as the default when you click on the Highlight tool—until you select another color—and is indicated by the color on the Highlight tool itself.

You can also select a color by pointing to Highlight on the Tools menu and clicking on Color to see this dialog box:

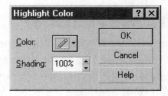

Click on the box containing the color sample to display a palette of 42 colors. Click on the color you want to use. You can also choose a shading for various degrees of the selected color. Choosing 50%, for example, prints the color at half of its intensity.

For even more choices, click on the More button at the bottom of the color palette to see the dialog box shown in Figure 6-11. Use this box to create custom colors by mixing red, green, and blue. If you pull down the Color Model list, you can also choose HLS to mix by hue, lightness, and saturation, or choose CYMK to mix cyan, yellow, magenta, and black.

When you print your document, what you see is what you get. If you have a color printer, the highlight prints in the same color it is on the screen. If you have a monochrome printer, highlights print in shades of gray. To hide the highlighting so

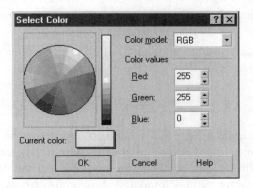

FIGURE 6-11   Color Palette

it does not appear onscreen or when printed, pull down the Tools menu, point to Highlight, and click on Print/Show Highlighting. Use the same options to later redisplay the highlight.

Tracking Document Revisions

If you are working on a document with other authors, or editors, you can keep track of revisions. You'll be able to see at a glance the text that someone else added or thinks should be deleted. The changes each person makes are shown in a different color, so you can tell who made the changes. You can then go through the document, quickly moving to each edited section, and accept or reject individual edits, or all that appear.

How you use this feature depends on whether you are the author or a reviewer.

Reviewing a Document

If you are reviewing a document written by someone else, pull down the File menu, point to Document, and click on Review. A dialog box appears with two choices: Reviewer and Author. It also lets you decide if you want to indicate lines of edited text with a marker. You can specify the marking character (the default is >) and choose to place the marker at the right or left margin, or on alternating margins.

Click on Reviewer to display the Reviewer pane at the top of the document, as shown in Figure 6-12.

| NOTE | *If you have not yet entered your name or initials into the WordPerfect 10 environment, a dialog box appears that gives you the opportunity to do so.* |

First, choose the color that you want your editing to appear in. Click on the Set Color button, and choose a color from the palette that appears. (The palette also has a More button that you can click on to mix your own personal colors.) The name and colors used by other reviewers, if any, are listed in the Other User Colors box.

Now edit the document. Text that you insert appears in the selected color. Text that you delete changes to the color and appears with a strikeout line.

Click on the Switch Color mode button on the lower left of the Reviewer pane to temporarily remove text you deleted and show your inserted text in the normal

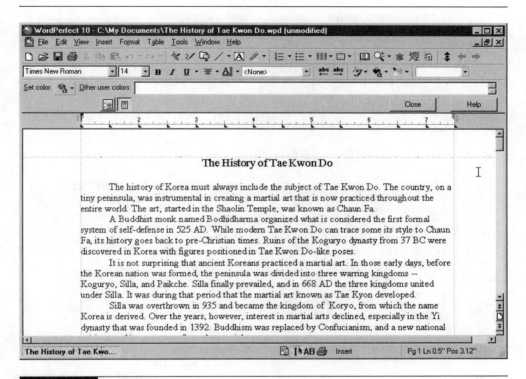

FIGURE 6-12   Reviewer options

text color. Use the Switch Color Mode button to switch between displaying inserted text in the reviewer color or the normal text color.

When you have finished reviewing, click on the Close button in the Reviewer pane. WordPerfect 10 displays all of the text in the normal color

Reviewing Changes as the Author

When reviewers send back the document to you, the author, you'll want to review the changes and decide which ones should be made. Pull down the File menu, point to Document, click on Review, and then click on Author. The Author pane appears as shown in Figure 6-13, with the first change in the document highlighted.

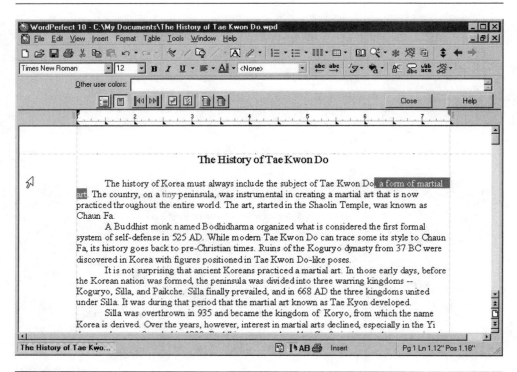

FIGURE 6-13 Reviewing as the author

Use the review buttons in the pane to look at the changes and decide which should be saved or deleted.

- *Display annotations in normal text color* temporarily hides deleted text and shows all text in the normal color.

- *Go to next annotation* moves to and highlights the next change.

- *Go to previous annotation* moves to and highlights the previous annotation.

- *Insert Current Annotation* accepts the highlighted change, either removing deleted text or changing inserted characters into regular text.

- *Insert All Annotations* accepts all of the changes to the document.

■ *Delete Current Annotation* rejects the highlighted change, replacing text that was marked for deletion, or deleting text that was added.

■ *Delete All Annotations* rejects all of the changes that were made.

NOTE   *The options in the Review pane do not affect text marked separately by the Redline or Strikeout font attributes discussed in Chapter 7.*

6

Try It Out

This chapter covered a lot of ground, so take some time to try out some of your new WordPerfect skills.

1. Open the document The History of Tae Kwon Do.

2. Drag the mouse to select this sentence in the first paragraph:

   The art, started in the Shaolin Temple, was known as Chaun Fa.

3. Point to the selected text, and while holding down the mouse button, drag the mouse so it is pointing at the end of the first sentence in the next paragraph.

4. Release the mouse button to move the selected text to its new position. If you dropped the text in the wrong position, select it and move it again. Also make sure that there is a space between the sentence you inserted and the sentence that follows it—insert a space if needed.

   Now, let's copy the words Tae Kwon Do from one location to another so it replaces text.

5. Drag over the words Tae Kwon Do anywhere in the document and then click the Copy button on the toolbar.

6. Double-click on the word its before history (its history) in the second paragraph.

7. Click the Paste button. The selected text is deleted and replaced with the text that you pasted in its position.

8. Add **'s** to the end of Tae Kwon Do that you just inserted so it reads Tae Kwon Do's.

We'll be using the phrase Tae Kwon Do several tines through this document so let's add it to the QuickWords list.

9. Drag over the words Tae Kwon Do anywhere in the document.

10. Select Tools | QuickWords.

11. In the Abbreviation from box, type **tkd** and click Add Entry. Now whenever you want to enter Tae Kwon Do, just type tkd.

12. Add the following sentence to the end of the last paragraph, watching WordPerfect expand the abbreviation tkd to Tae Kwon Do:

    However, tkd would still be a powerful art for the Korean people.

13. Add the text shown in Figure 6-14 to the end of the document.

Now, let's use the Find and Replace dialog box to italicize each occurrence of Tae Kwon Do in the document.

When an army of over 250,000 Japanese invaded Korea in 1592, the country was not prepared to defend itself. Throughout the next centuries, Korea faced other invasions. Yet, the spirit of the Korean people prevailed. Many of the Koreans who fled their homeland carried Tae Kyon to other countries. There, the martial art was refined. After the war, when Korea was liberated, interest in the native martial art increased and in 1955 the name Tae Kwon Do was formally accepted.

One thing that distinguishes Tae Kwon Do is that is has always been practiced in the defense of civilization and in protection of the weak.

The art of Tae Kwon Do owes its flavor to the rich history of Korea and Korean martial arts. More than a self-defense system, Tae Kwon Do lives up to the ideals and spirit of Admiral Yi Sun-sin, the brave soldier who epitomizes the saying Never Retreat in Battle.

FIGURE 6-14   Add this text to your document

14. Move the insertion point to the start of the document.

15. Select Edit | Find and Replace.

16. Type Tae Kwon Do in the Find box.

17. Type Tae Kwon Do in the Replace with box.

18. Select Replace | Font.

19. In the Attributes section of the Replace Font dialog box, click the Italic checkbox and then click OK.

20. Click Replace All and then OK to the message reporting the number of replacements that have been made.

21. Close the Find and Replace dialog box.

22. Select the words Tae Kwon Do in the title of the document and click the Italic button in the Property Bar. This deletes the italic format.

    We want to save the document but with a different name. This will leave the original document named History of Tae Kwon Do on your disk unchanged.

22. Select File | Save As, type **Tae Kwon Do** as the file name and click Save.

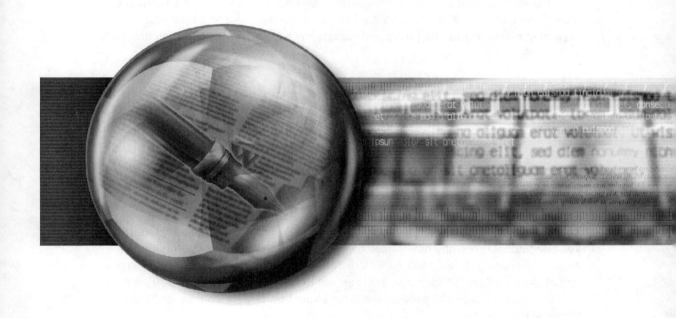

Chapter 7

Formatting Text

W hen you edit a document, you change its content. When you format a document, you change its appearance. As with editing, you can format text as you type it or any time after; you don't have to worry about the format when you're struggling to find the right words. In this chapter you will learn how to format characters, lines, and paragraphs.

Character formatting affects the shape, size, and appearance of characters. Use these formats to make your document visually appealing and to emphasize important points. Formatting lines and paragraphs adjusts their position on the page.

Working with WordPerfect 10 Codes

Before learning how to format, you should have a basic understanding of WordPerfect 10's codes. Every format that you apply to text, including noncharacter keys such as TAB and ENTER, is inserted as an invisible code into the document. The codes tell WordPerfect 10 when to turn formats on and off, insert a tab, end a paragraph, end a page, and perform every other WordPerfect 10 function. Knowing that all formats insert codes into the document will help you later understand how formats affect text.

As long as you have no problems inserting and deleting text and formatting your document, you may never need to worry about the codes. But sometimes, especially when you just can't seem to format the text the way you want, it pays to reveal the codes on the screen so you can see exactly what's happening. You may find that you accidentally pressed the wrong function key, or applied and then forgot about a format.

You reveal the codes in a separate window at the bottom of the screen. The quickest way to reveal codes is to drag the Reveal Codes line, the small rectangle at the bottom of the vertical scroll bar. As you drag the line up, a bar appears across the screen showing the size of the Reveal Codes window. When you release the mouse button, you'll see a window that shows your text, as well as symbols that represent the codes, as shown in Figure 7-1.

The insertion point is seen as a red rectangle, while codes appear in boxes. Hard carriage returns (created by pressing the ENTER key) are represented by HRt, soft carriage returns (added by word wrap) are shown as SRt, tabs are Left Tab, and spaces are diamonds.

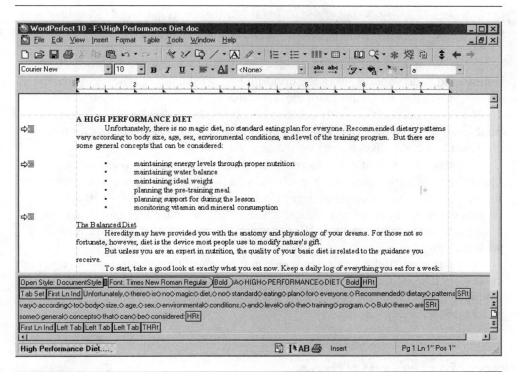

FIGURE 7-1   Reveal Codes

Codes that format text surround the characters that they affect. The shape of the box indicates if it is an On code or an Off code, as you can see in these bold codes:

Open Style: DocumentStyle | Font: Times New Roman 〉Bold 〉A◇HIGH◇PERFORMANCE◇DIET〈 Bold | HRt |

Other codes appear abbreviated when the insertion point is not immediately to their left. For example, the Tab Set code indicates that you've made a change in the tab stops. If you place the insertion point just before the code, it is expanded to show the full tab settings:

| Tab Set: (Rel)-0.75"L, -0.5"L, +0.75"L, +1"L, +1.5"L, +2"L, +2.5"L, +3"L, +3.5"L, +4"L, +4.5"L, +5"L, +5.5"L, +6"L, ... | Left Tab |

> **TIP** *You can also reveal codes by pressing* ALT-F3, *or selecting Reveal Codes from the View menu.*

If you want, you can leave the codes revealed as you continue writing. To remove the code window, drag the dividing line off the top or bottom of the screen, select Reveal Codes from the View menu, or press ALT-F3 again.

If a code is associated with a dialog box, open the dialog box by double-clicking on the code. For example, double-clicking on a character format code, such as bold, displays the Font dialog box.

Not all codes appear at the location in the text where you applied them. A code that affects the entire page, such as changing a page size, is placed near the start of the page, before any codes that only affect paragraphs. WordPerfect 10 also deletes duplicate or redundant codes. If you select one page size and then change your mind, and choose another, WordPerfect 10 replaces the first Page Size code with the other.

You can view, delete, and edit codes in the Reveal Codes window. To delete a code from the document, and thus remove its format, drag it off of the Reveal Codes window. You can also delete a code by pressing DEL or BACKSPACE, as you would delete other characters.

Character Formatting

You can apply literally thousands of combinations of formats to your document. You can access all of these formats using the Format command from the menu bar. Some of the most common formats used in documents are also provided as buttons on the property bar.

Real Time Preview

Many of the formats that you can apply from the property bar are contained in lists, such as Font and Font Size.

When you point to a choice on one of these lists, any text that will be affected by your selection changes to show how it would appear if you make that choice. (You may have to pause the mouse pointer over a choice on a list until the change takes effect.) Continue pointing to other items on the list until the text appears how you'd like it.

This real time preview works for the Font, Font Size, Alignment, and Font Color lists, as well as Drop Caps and Underline.

Applying Bold, Italic, and Underline Formatting

Three of the most popular character formats are bold, italic, and underlining, by themselves or in combination. These are quick and easy to apply because buttons for them are on the property bar, as shown here:

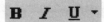

Shortcut key combinations for the three most used character formats are CTRL-B *for bold,* CTRL-I *for italic, and* CTRL-U *for underlining.*

To format text as you type it, just click on the appropriate button, and then type. You can also pull down the list next to the Underline button and choose the type of underline you want to apply:

Try it now using the following example:

1. Type **Your bill is**, and then press the SPACEBAR.

2. Click on the Underline button in the property bar, and then type **seriously overdue**. WordPerfect 10 underlines the words and the spaces between them as you type.

3. Now turn off underlining by clicking on the Underline button again. This stops the formatting and changes the button so it no longer appears pressed down. This type of action is called a *toggle,* named after a toggle switch that turns a light on and off.

> **TIP** *Not all property buttons act as toggles.*

4. Press the SPACEBAR, type **and we will be forced to take**, and then press the SPACEBAR again.

5. Click first on the Bold button and then on the Italic button in the property bar. To use a combination of the formats, click on each button that you want to apply.

6. Type **legal action**, and then click on the Bold and Italic buttons again. You can click the buttons in any order.

7. Type a period, and then press ENTER. Your sentence should look like the one shown next.

Your bill is <u>seriously overdue</u> and we will be forced to take *legal action*.

To format text that you've already typed, first select the text, and then click on the button of your choice. You can format a single word by clicking anywhere in the word and then choosing the button from the toolbar—you do not have to select the word first.

If you format characters by mistake, or just change your mind, select the text. The formats applied appear as depressed buttons. Click on the button representing the format you want to remove.

> **NOTE** *The format buttons do not appear pressed down when you select text that is not formatted. For example, if you select a word that is bold along with a word that's not formatted, the Bold button does not appear pressed down. When you click on a format button, it is applied to all of the selected text—it does not remove the format from text already in that style.*

Selecting Fonts and Sizes from the Property Bar

The property bar contains drop-down lists for selecting the font and size of characters. You can set the font and the size of text as you type it, or you can change the font and size of text—even a single character—by selecting it first. To change the font and size of a single word, however, just place the insertion point in the word before selecting the formats.

The Font box on the property bar displays the font being used at the location of the insertion point. To select another font, pull down the list to display the fonts that are installed on your system. When you point to a font on the list, a sample of it appears enlarged under the property bar, and any text that will be affected by the choice appears in the font:

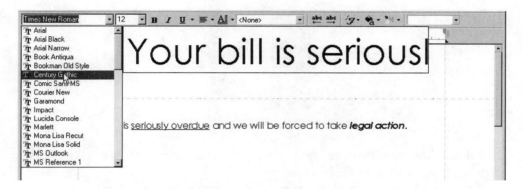

The fonts are listed in alphabetical order. However, after you start using WordPerfect 10 to select fonts, you'll see several fonts at the beginning of the list, separated from the rest by a line. These are the fonts that you've used recently. WordPerfect 10 places them first to make it easy for you to select the fonts that you use most often. To select a font, click on its name in the list.

If you select text first, your choice affects only that text. Otherwise, it affects all text from the position of the insertion point to the end of the document. Its effect ends, however, when you choose another font, and it does not change text to which you have already applied another font.

This is an important concept that affects many formatting commands, so make sure you understand it before going on. Let's say that you typed an entire document with the default font that WordPerfect 10 uses automatically. If you then move the insertion point to the start of the document and choose a font, all of the text in the document changes to that font.

Now, suppose again, that you typed an entire document in the default font. You then selected the third paragraph and chose a font from the property bar. Only that text is affected. But now you move to the start of the document and choose a font. This time, your selection affects every paragraph except the third one because it has a font already applied to it on its own.

You change the size of text using the Font Size list in the property bar. It affects text just like the Font command.

Font Color

With color inkjet printers becoming increasingly popular and affordable, it's nice to know that WordPerfect 10 has made it easy to change the color of text. Click the Font Color button in the property bar to display a palette of colors, as shown here:

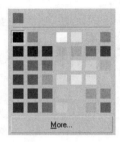

Click on the color that you want to apply to the selected text, or to all the text starting at the location of the insertion point.

To mix a custom color, click on the More button in the palette to see the dialog box shown here:

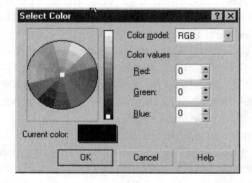

You can select a color model (RGB, HLS, or CMYK), enter amounts of the colors shown, or click in the color wheel and intensity bar to select a custom color. Click on Select when you've finished.

NOTE *If you do not have a color printer, WordPerfect 10 prints colors in corresponding shades of gray.*

Using QuickFonts

As you use WordPerfect 10, you'll find combinations of fonts, sizes, styles, and colors that you'll want to use often. To reselect one of the last ten combinations you used, pull down the QuickFonts list in the property bar, as shown here:

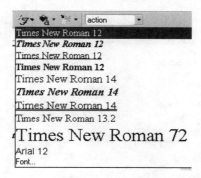

Each item in the QuickFonts list includes the combination of typeface, font size, font colors, and attributes. Choosing an item from the list applies to all of the formats. For example, if you click on an item that says Arial 18, and that appears underlined and bold, all four attributes are applied to selected text, or to the text that you are about to type.

Use the QuickFonts list to format selected text, or the word in which the insertion point is placed. QuickFonts does not affect any other text on the page.

> **TIP** *The Font option at the bottom of the QuickFonts list displays the Font dialog box.*

Formatting with the Font Properties Dialog Box

The formatting options in the property bar offer only a sampling of WordPerfect 10's formats. For a full range of choices, display the Font Properties dialog box shown in Figure 7-2. Display the box using any of these methods:

- Select Font from the Format menu.

- Right-click on the text window, and select Font from the QuickMenu.

- Pull down the QuickFonts list, and click on Font.

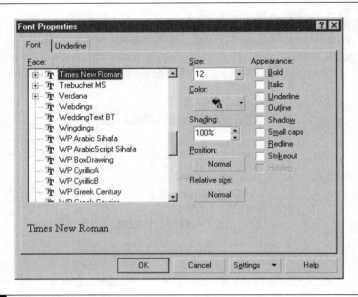

FIGURE 7-2   Font dialog box

Make your choices from the dialog box, watching the preview area to see their effects, and then click on OK to apply the settings to your text.

You can select a font, size, and appearance. When you close the dialog box, the font and size you select are shown in the font and size boxes in the toolbar. The appearance options you select are reflected in the look of the Bold and Italic buttons in the toolbar. If you choose the Bold appearance option, for example, the Bold button in the toolbar appears pressed down. You can later change the font, size, and appearance using either the toolbar or the dialog box.

Here are some other options in the dialog box:

- Select a Position option to create superscripts and subscripts.

- Pick a color and shading for the text. If you do not have a color printer, WordPerfect 10 substitutes a corresponding shade of gray.

- Use the Settings button to select the default font for the current document or for all new WordPerfect 10 documents.

NOTE *The Edit Font Mapping command in the Settings list lets you change what appears when you modify font attributes and sizes. For example, you can use one set of attributes on the screen, and another when printed. You can also specify the font to use when you select one that is not available.*

Selecting a Relative Font Size

When you choose a font size using the property bar or the Size list in the Font dialog box, you are selecting a specific point size. Sometimes, however, you may want to format text in relation to the text around it. You might want a headline, for example, to be twice the size of the text in the paragraph, or a portion of legalese fine print to be half the size.

To format text in a relative size, follow these steps:

1. Select the text you want to format.

2. Open the Font Properties dialog box.

3. Pull down the Relative size button in the Font Properties dialog box to see the choices Fine, Small, Normal, Large, Very Large, or Extra Large.

4. Click on OK.

Each of the relative size choices are defined as a percentage of the current font:

Option	Percentage of Current Font
Fine	60
Small	80
Normal	100
Large	120
Very Large	150
Extra Large	200

If you are using the default 12-point font, for example, choosing Small formats text in 9.6 points, while Extra Large is 24 points. If you were using a 10-point text font, then Small would be 8.1 points and Extra Large would be 20 points.

Using Hidden Text

The Hidden Text feature lets you enter text that you selectively either hide or reveal, print or not print. Use it to create notes to yourself that you may want to print in draft copies for your review, but not on the final copy for distribution.

If the Hidden Appearance option is grayed in the Font Properties dialog box, the display of hidden text is turned off. To turn it on, select Hidden Text from the View menu.

When you select Hidden Appearance, just enter text as you would normally. When you want to hide it, so it does not appear onscreen or print with the document, deselect Hidden Text from the View menu.

Using Redline and Strikeout

In Chapter 6, you learned how to add, reject, or accept reviewers' comments. Text that a reviewer inserts appears in a different color than other text, and text that is deleted appears with strikeout.

You can also mark inserted and deleted text using the Redline and Strikeout Appearance options in the Font Properties dialog box. Strikeout text to show that you'd like to delete it, and redline text that you'd like to add. Redline text appears in a different color than other text; strikeout text has lines through it. You have to apply these formats yourself; WordPerfect 10 does not automatically do it for you as you edit. Either select the text first and then choose the Redline or Strikeout Appearance, or choose the format first and then type the text.

To accept or reject the changes, pull down the File menu, point to Document, and click on Remove Markings for four options:

- *Remove Redline Markings and Strikeout Text* removes the color from redlined text and deletes the strikeout text from the document.

- *Remove Strikeout Text Only* deletes strikeout text but leaves the redline color on inserted text.

- *Remove Document Compare Deletions Only* deletes text that was struck out using the Compare command from the File Document menu. This command compares the document on the screen with one on the disk, marking differences.

- *Remove All Document Compare Markings* deletes all marks inserted by the Compare command.

The Redline Method option on the Document menu allows you to indicate redlined text with a marker in the margin. You can choose to place a vertical line either in the left, right, or alternating margins next to redlined text, and you can change the marker to some other character.

Selecting Underline Options

The Underline page of the Font Properties dialog box, shown in Figure 7-3, lets you customize how text is underlined. You can select what gets underlined and the shape and color of the line. The default setting places the underline under the text and spaces between words, and in the same color as the text. You can choose to underline just the words or the spaces inserted when you press TAB, a different line style, and you can pick a color other than that used for the text.

Selecting an underline line style other than the first (which represents no line) turns on underlining, if it is not already turned on. Your choice also becomes the new default style that is applied when you click on the Underline button in the property bar, or choose Underline in the Font Properties dialog box.

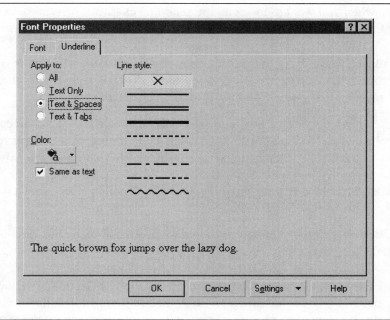

FIGURE 7-3   Underline options

To restore the default setting, display the Font Properties dialog box, Underline page, choose the single line style, and turn on the Same as Text checkbox. Close the dialog box. If you are not ready to underline text, click the Underline button on the property bar to turn off underlining.

Using Special Characters and Symbols

Most fonts contain symbols and accented characters in addition to the characters shown on your keyboard. These characters and symbols are useful when you are composing scientific or technical documents, or writing in a language other than English or in British English—an American might, for example, need to enter the British currency symbol when writing to a business in England. WordPerfect 10 lets you access these characters, as well as hundreds of other foreign language, mathematical, and scientific characters and graphic symbols.

To select from a basic set of commonly used characters, click the Symbols button on the property bar. Select the character that you want to insert into your document.

To access all of the symbols that WordPerfect makes available, use this procedure when you want to insert an international character or symbol in your document:

1. Select Symbol from the Insert menu, or click the Symbols button on the property bar and select More, to see the dialog box shown in Figure 7-4. You can also choose Symbols from the QuickMenu.

2. Pull down the Set list box, and select the character set. The characters are collected in 15 character sets. The characters in that set are displayed in the Symbols box. The character sets are ASCII, Multinational, Phonetic, Box Drawing, Typographic Symbols, Iconic Symbols, Math/Scientific, Math/Scientific Extended, Greek, Hebrew, Cyrillic, Japanese, Current Font Symbols, Arabic, and Arabic Script.

3. Click on the character that you want to insert, and then click on the Insert and Close buttons.

WordPerfect 10 inserts the character at the position of the insertion point, in a size that matches the surrounding text. So if you are typing a headline in 24 points, for example, the special character appears in 24 points. If the character is one that appears on the keyboard, WordPerfect 10 also matches the current font.

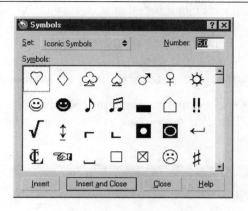

FIGURE 7-4   Inserting special characters

7

If you want to insert a number of characters, leave the dialog box on the screen, and move back and forth between your document and the dialog box. Drag the dialog box out of the way, and then double-click on the character you want to insert, or choose the character and then click on Insert. WordPerfect 10 inserts the characters but leaves the dialog box open so you can insert additional characters. Click in the document window to position the insertion point where you want to insert another character—even to add or edit text if you want—and then click back in the dialog box when you want to insert a different character.

The sets are numbered from 0 to 14, and each character is numbered within the set. You'll notice that when you click on a character, its set and character numbers appear in the Number box, such as 7,2 to represent the second character in set seven. If you know the set and number, you can enter them in the Number box yourself. When you type the character number, the set appears in the dialog box with the character selected.

NOTE   *Remember that QuickCorrect automatically inserts some special characters for you, such as the copyright and registered symbols.*

Duplicating Formats with QuickFormat

With all of the format options that WordPerfect 10 makes available, there are certainly a large number of possible combinations. If you've gone to the trouble of selecting a combination that you like for one section of text, you do not have to make the selections all over again for other text. Just apply the same combination using QuickFormat.

When you want to copy a format, use these steps:

1. Place the insertion point in the text that uses that format.

2. Click on the QuickFormat button in the toolbar to see a dialog box with four options. The table options are available only when the insertion point is in a table.

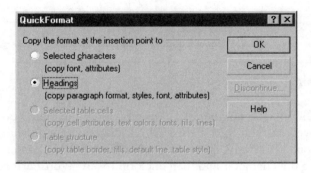

You can also choose QuickFormat from the Format menu or from the QuickMenu.

3. Choose the Selected Characters option in the dialog box if you only want to copy the font and character formats of the text. Select the Headings option in the dialog box if you want to copy all of the formats, including the font, line, and paragraph formats.

4. Click on OK. The shape of the mouse pointer will change to a paint roller.

5. Drag over the text that you want to apply the format to. When you release the mouse button after selecting the text, WordPerfect 10 applies the formats. It leaves QuickFormat on, however, so you can apply the same formats to other sections of text.

6. To turn off the feature, click on the QuickFormat button again.

Formatting Lines and Paragraphs

When you want to add some style and flair to your document, apply *line* or *paragraph* formats. These formats affect the alignment of text on the page. Probably the first two formats that you'll want to learn are centering text between the margins and changing the line spacing. Again, WordPerfect 10 offers much more. As with character formats, you can format paragraphs as you type them or any time afterward.

There are several ways to apply formats. You can use the property bar, the menu bar, or the QuickMenu.

Using the QuickMenu

Before discussing the formats that you can apply, take a look at the QuickMenu that appears when you right-click in the typing area (when no text is selected):

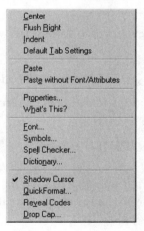

> **NOTE** *The QuickMenu shown here does not appear if you right-click on a word that Spell-As-You-Go has marked as a possible error.*

You'll learn how these options work as the formats are discussed, but here's a summary of the QuickMenu options:

- *Center* lets you center text, either between the margins or at the location of a tab stop.

- *Flush Right* aligns text along the right margin.

- *Indent* lets you indent a paragraph from the left margin.
- *Default Tab Settings* restores the default tab stops, deleting custom tabs that you created.
- *Paste* inserts the contents of the Clipboard.
- *Paste without Font/Attributes* inserts the contents of the Clipboard in the same fonts and attributes as surrounding text.
- *Properties* displays summary information and the word, sentence, and character count for the current document.
- *What's This?* displays a brief explanation about the area your cursor is in.
- *Font* opens the Font dialog box.
- *Symbols* displays the WordPerfect 10 Characters dialog box.
- *Spell Checker* starts the spell checker.
- *Dictionary* starts the dictionary.
- *Shadow Cursor* toggles on and off the shadow cursor.
- *QuickFormat* toggles on and off the QuickFormat feature.
- *Reveal Codes* displays or hides the reveal codes area.
- *Drop Cap* displays options for inserting a drop capital.

Changing Line Spacing

The line spacing command affects text in the same way as changing a font. If you select text first, the line spacing is applied only to that text. If you did not select text, it affects all of the text from the location of the insertion point, up to any text that has another line spacing applied to it.

To change the line spacing, choose Line from the Format menu, and then click on Spacing. In the dialog box that appears, type the line spacing number, or click on the up or down pointers to increment or decrement the setting in intervals of one-tenth line with each click. Click on OK to return to the document.

Aligning Text Between the Margins

Probably the first paragraph format you'll want to use is centering. You may need to center your address on a letterhead or a title on a report. WordPerfect 10 provides six options for aligning text between the margins.

- With *Left alignment,* lines of text align evenly at the left margins, with an uneven right margin.

- *Center alignment* centers the text between the left and right margins, with uneven left and right margins.

- *Flush Right alignment* creates even right margins, with an uneven left margin.

- *Flush Right with Dot Leaders* inserts periods in the blank space to the left of right-aligned text.

- *Full* adds spaces to the lines of text, except lines ending with hard carriage returns when you press ENTER, so they are aligned evenly on both the left and right. This option does not affect the last line of a paragraph.

- *All* extends every line between the margins, including the last line of paragraphs, titles, and other single-line paragraphs.

You can select alignment options using the property bar and menu bar, but there are two general ways to do so: line formatting and justification.

Line formatting affects individual lines or paragraphs. If you turn on the format and type text, the format ends when you press the ENTER key. If you place the insertion point in existing text and select a line format, only the current paragraph is affected. Text following the current paragraph is not changed.

The *justification* commands, on the other hand, insert codes that affect all of the text starting in the paragraph where the insertion point is located—up to the first other justification code. If you are typing new text, the format remains on when you press the ENTER key. So if you use the line center command to center text, the insertion point returns to the left margin when you press ENTER. If you use the justification center command, the insertion point moves to the center of the screen when you press ENTER. You have to choose another justification command when you no longer want centered text.

| NOTE | *If you select text first, both methods affect only the selected text* |

If you apply a justification format to text, you cannot change its format with a line formatting command. You can only change it by applying another justification. The justification commands take precedence over line formatting. If you already applied a line format to text, applying a justification format changes it. A line format command, however, does not affect justified text.

| TIP | *WordPerfect 10 displays an instant preview when you point to an item in the alignment list in the property bar.* |

Centering Text

To center a single paragraph or selected text, choose Center from the QuickMenu, or pull down the Format menu, point to Line, and click on Center. To center existing text, however, make sure you first place the insertion point at the start of the line or paragraph. If you start with the insertion point within the text, only text in the paragraph following the insertion will be centered.

> **TIP** *To center a new line of text using the shadow cursor, point to the middle of the page so the cursor includes a two-directional arrow, and then click.*

To turn on centering for all text from the insertion point to the next justification code, or for all selected text, pull down the Justification button in the property bar, and click on Center. You can also pull down the Format menu, point to Justification, and click on Center. To turn off centering, pull down the Justification list and choose Left, or choose Left from the Format Justification menu.

Aligning Text on the Right

To align a single paragraph or selected text so it is flush with the right margin, select Flush Right from the QuickMenu, or pull down the Format menu, point to Line, and click on Flush Right. To align text on the right and insert periods in the blank space before the text, select Flush Right with Dot Leaders from the Format Line menu. Start with the insertion point at the start of the line to format all of the text.

> **TIP** *To right-align a new line of text using the shadow cursor, point to the right margin of the page so the cursor includes a left-pointing arrow, and then click.*

To turn on the Flush Right format for all text from the insertion point to the next justification code, or all selected text, pull down the Justification button in the property bar and select Right. You can also pull down the Format menu, point to Justification, and click on Right.

Justifying Text

To justify text on the left and right, pull down the Justification button in the property bar, and select Full or All. You can also select Full or All from the Format Justification menu. Remember, All justifies every line of text, even those ending with a hard carriage return. This can result in some strange effects by spacing out words in the last line to reach the right margin.

Enhancing Text with Borders

When you want to draw attention to a paragraph or section of text, enclose it in a border, or fill in the background with a color, shading, or pattern. It's an easy way to add a little pizzazz to a document without going all the way to graphics.

To add a border to a single paragraph, place the insertion point anywhere in it. To enhance more than one paragraph, follow these steps:

1. Select all of the paragraphs you want to enhance.

2. Pull down the Format menu, point to Paragraph, and click on Border/Fill to see the dialog box in Figure 7-5. The box has four pages.

On the Border page, choose the color and style of lines to surround the text. You can also choose to place the border around all of the remaining paragraphs in the document by deselecting the Apply Border to Current Paragraph Only checkbox.

7

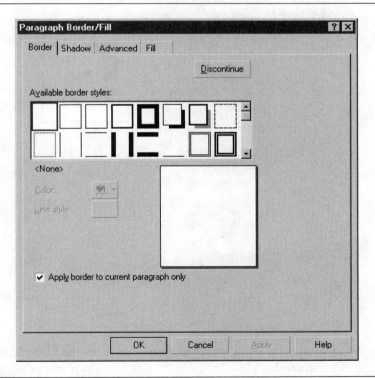

FIGURE 7-5   Paragraph Border/Fill dialog box

You can select Advanced and Shadow options only if you choose a border. You can add a fill without a border.

On the Fill page, you select a color or pattern to print in the background behind the text. If you select a pattern rather than a solid color, you can also choose a background and foreground color for two-tone patterns.

On the Advanced page, you can customize your selected border and fill patterns. You can adjust the distance between the border lines and text, and adjust the pattern of the fill color. Experiment with the options to discover how they work.

On the Shadow page, create a shadow effect by choosing the direction and depth of the shadow, and the shadow color. You can even use scroll bars to graphically adjust the position of the shadow. Use the scroll bar on the right to move the shadow up and down; the scroll bar on the bottom to move the shadow left and right:

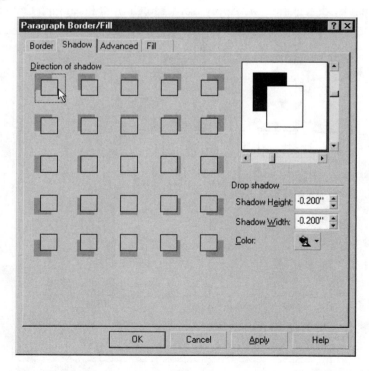

If you just want to draw a line on the screen, remember the QuickLines feature of QuickCorrect Format-As-You-Go. Type four or more hyphens or equal signs, and then press ENTER. WordPerfect 10 draws a single or double line across the page.

Adding a Drop Capital

A drop capital is a large initial letter at the beginning of a paragraph. To create a drop capital, place the insertion point anywhere in the paragraph, then right click and choose Drop Cap from the QuickMenu or choose Format | Paragraph | Drop Cap. WordPerfect opens the dialog box shown in Figure 7-6.

In the Format tab of the dialog box, select the style of the drop capital, its height in lines, and any number of lines that you want to lower the regular text of the paragraph below the top of the drop capital character.

In the Font tab of the dialog box, choose the font, color, shading, and style of the character. By default, WordPerfect uses the character's current font and color.

In the Options tab of the dialog box you can customize your drop capital by selecting from these options:

- Select number of characters to drop, or the entire first word.

- Wrap the text around the character; adjust for diacritical marks and descenders.

- Set the position of the character within the margin or the text.

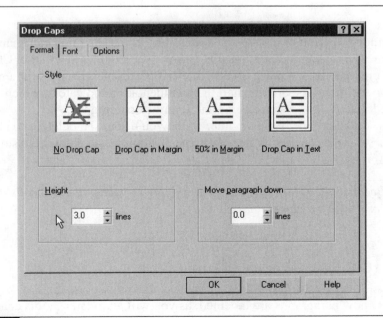

Adding a drop capital

Introducing the Ruler

You'll usually want to change margins, set tabs, or indent paragraphs by specific amounts. You can set all of these formats using dialog boxes, where you can enter the measurements in inches, millimeters, or other units of measurement. If you want to use the mouse to create these formats, it helps if you first display the ruler. In fact, to set tabs and indent paragraphs by dragging the mouse, you must display the ruler. The ruler is an onscreen object that indicates the positions of tabs, margins, and indentations, just as if you actually held a ruler against the screen.

To display the ruler, pull down the View menu, and click on Ruler. The WordPerfect 10 ruler, shown here, has three parts.

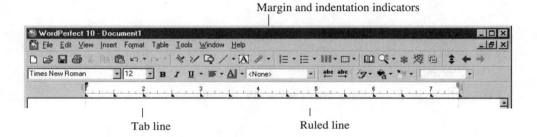

Margin and indentation indicators

Tab line   Ruled line

The middle section of the ruler is a ruled line in inches. (You can change the units of measure using the Settings dialog box that you'll learn about in Chapter 10.) Use the ruled line to place objects in exact positions in your document.

Above the ruled line are the margin and indentation indicators, which you use to set the left and right page margins and to indent paragraphs.

Below the ruled line is the tab line, which you use to set, delete, and change tab stops. The triangles on the tab line show the position of the default tab stops, set every half inch.

 Because the ruler represents the spacing of your page, it scrolls as you scroll your document horizontally.

Setting Tabs

Tab stops not only control the distance moved when you press the TAB key, but they affect how paragraphs are indented, as you will learn later in this chapter.

You can use the mouse to quickly set and delete tab stops on the ruler, or you can work with tabs using a dialog box. WordPerfect 10 lets you set eight types of tab stops, as shown in Figure 7-7. The default left tab aligns a column along the left. Characters that you type shift normally to the right of the tab stop. A right tab aligns characters on the right. As you type, your text shifts toward the left of the tab stop. Use a center tab to center text at the tab stop. As you type, text shifts alternately to the left and to the right. Use a decimal tab to align a column of numbers on the decimal point. As you type, the characters shift toward the left until you type the decimal point. Decimal values then shift to the right. You can insert dot leaders with all tab types.

To set a tab, simply click in the tab line of the ruler, just below the desired position in the ruled line. To set a tab at the 1.75-inch position, for example, click as shown at the arrow here:

7

![WordPerfect 10 application window showing menu bar, toolbar, and ruler with a cursor arrow pointing to the tab area below the ruled line.]

NOTE *You must click in the tab area, below the actual ruled line but above the document area.*

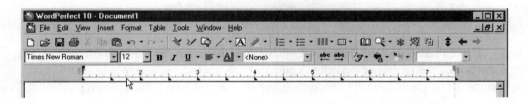

LEFT	CENTER	RIGHT	DECIMAL
One	One	One	1.00
Two	Two	Two	22.00
Three	Three	Three	333.00
. . . . . One	One	One	1.00
. . . . . Two	Two	Two	22.00
. . . . . Three	Three	Three	333.00

FIGURE 7-7   Tab types

Left-aligned tabs are set by default. To choose another type of tab stop, right-click on the tab line to see the QuickMenu shown here:

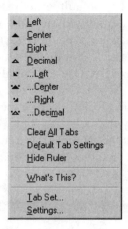

You can also display this menu by clicking the left mouse button on the tab indicator on the far left of the ruler. You won't see this indicator, however, unless you reduce the magnification. The reduction required depends on your screen resolution.

Click on the tab type that you want to set, with or without dot leaders. The shape of the button changes to illustrate the type of tab that you set:

Left

Center

Right

Decimal

Left (left tab with leaders)

Center (center tab with leaders)

Right (right tab with leaders)

Decimal (decimal tab with leaders)

You can also move and delete tabs using the mouse and the ruler. To delete a tab stop, use these steps:

1. Point to its marker in the ruler.

2. Drag the mouse down into the typing area.

To move a tab stop to a different position, drag its indicator to a new position on the ruler. As you drag the tab indicator, a dotted line appears down the screen showing where text will align, and a QuickStatus box shows the distance from the edge of the page. To delete all of the tab stops, right-click on the tab line, and select Clear All Tabs—click on Default Tab Settings to reset to WordPerfect 10's default tabs every half-inch.

Be careful when setting, deleting, or moving tabs. If you do not have any text selected, your changes affect all text that does not have its own tab formats. If you just delete the tab stop at the half-inch position, for example, the indentations of the subsequent text shift to the next tab on the right.

When you press TAB, you are inserting a tab code into the document. The code tells WordPerfect 10 to move the insertion point to the next tab stop position on the right. If you delete the tab stop where the text was aligned, it automatically moves to the next tab stop. If you insert a tab stop prior to that position, the text shifts to that new tab stop.

NOTE	*When you click to the right of the left margin with the shadow cursor, WordPerfect 10 inserts a series of tab codes between the left margin and the position where you clicked.*

To change the tab stops for just a portion of the document, select the text first. Then the tab stop changes will only affect the selected text. If you later change tabs elsewhere in a document, all text except the selected text will be affected.

Using the Tab Bar

When you change the tab stops in a paragraph, WordPerfect 10 displays the Tab icon in the margin, as shown here:

⇨≣   Heredity may have provided you with the anatomy and physiology of your dreams. For those not so fortunate, however, diet is the device most people use to modify nature's gift.

The icon indicates where the code that affects tab stops was inserted. If you click on the icon with the left mouse button, WordPerfect 10 displays a tab bar just above the paragraph showing the tabs applied to the text:

You can use the tab bar to add, delete, or change tab stops in the text, just as you can by using the ruler. To remove the tab bar from the display, click elsewhere in the document.

If you select text and change the tabs, WordPerfect 10 inserts a Tab icon in the margin of the edited text, as well as at the start of the next paragraph. This shows that different tab settings apply at those locations. What happens if you change tabs within a section that has already had a different set of tabs applied?

WordPerfect 10 displays a special icon showing that multiple formats exist in that paragraph, such as the end of one tab setting and the start of another. When you click on the icon, you'll see two or more icons representing the different tab settings. Click on each of the icons to show the tab bar for the format.

Setting Tabs with the Dialog Box

The Tab Set dialog box, shown in Figure 7-8, gives you even greater control over tab stops, although it may not be as easy to use as clicking the mouse. To adjust tabs, right-click on the ruler, and select Tab Set from the QuickMenu, or pull down the Format menu, point on Line, and click on Tab Set.

To set a tab, pull down the Tab Type list, and choose a tab type. Enter the location of the tab in the Tab Position text box, and then click on the Set button. To delete a tab, type its location in the Tab Position box, and click on the Clear button. Click on Clear All to delete all of the tabs. If you want to restore all of WordPerfect 10's default tab stops, click on Default.

The Repeat Every checkbox lets you enter a series of evenly spaced tabs. Select the Repeat Every checkbox, and then enter the spacing in the text box. Type **.75**, for example, to set tabs every three-fourths of an inch across the ruler.

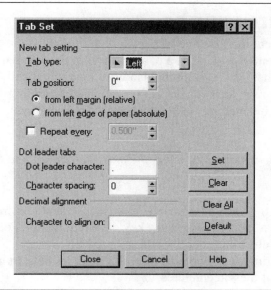

FIGURE 7-8   Setting tabs

You can also change the character that is used as the dot leader, the number of spaces between each character, and the character used for decimal alignment.

Relative versus Absolute Tab

When you type a position setting for a tab, WordPerfect 10 sets it relative to the left margin. A tab set at 1.25, for example, is 1.25 inches from the left margin, or 2.25 inches from the left edge of the paper using the default one-inch margin.

Because the tab is relative, it remains at that distance from the margin even if you change the left margin setting. So if you change the margin to 1.5 inches, the tab stop still is 1.25 inches from it, but now 2.75 inches from the edge of the page.

If you want a tab stop to remain at a fixed position, regardless of the margins, click on the From Left Edge Of Paper (Absolute) option in the Tab Set dialog box. Now, changing the left margin does not affect the position of tab stops from the edge of the paper. They are set at a distance from the edge of the paper, rather than the margin.

Indenting Paragraphs

If you want to indent the first line of a paragraph, just press the TAB key. But you might want to indent every line of a paragraph from the left margin, or from both the right and left margins. You might also want to automatically indent the first line of every paragraph to save yourself the trouble of pressing TAB. You can control paragraph indentations using the ruler, the QuickMenu, or the Paragraph dialog box.

NOTE *You can also indent text using the margin settings. See Chapter 8 for more information on this method.*

WordPerfect 10 gives you a variety of ways to indent text from the left. The quickest ways are to either press the F7 key or pull down the Format menu, point to Paragraph, and click on Indent.

To indent existing text, place the insertion point at the start of the paragraph, and then use any of these techniques:

- Press F7.

- Right-click at the start of the paragraph, and choose Indent from the QuickMenu.

- Pull down the Format menu, point to Paragraph, and choose Indent, or choose Double Indent to indent from both margins.

Each time you use an Indent command, the paragraph is indented another tab stop position to the right.

NOTE *If you use the Indent command when the insertion point is not at the start of the paragraph, WordPerfect 10 shifts the following text to the next tab stop and creates the hanging indentation at that position.*

To indent new text as you type it, use the Indent command to move the insertion point where you want the paragraph to start, and then type. Each line of the paragraph will begin at the tab stop position. When you press ENTER after the paragraph, WordPerfect 10 ends the indentation and moves the insertion point back to the left margin.

You can also indent text from the left with a dialog box. Pull down the Format menu, point to Paragraph, and then click on Format to see this dialog box:

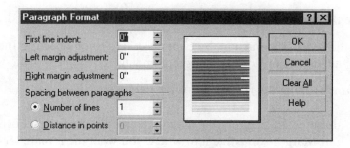

Enter the amount of left indentation in the Left Margin Adjustment box, and the amount of right indentation in the Right Margin Adjustment box. To automatically indent the first line of every paragraph, so you do not have to press TAB, enter a setting in the First Line Indent option.

Use the Spacing Between Paragraphs option to automatically add space between paragraphs, in either line increments or points. For example, if you want to double-space between single-spaced paragraphs, set the option at 2.

Hanging Indentations

You can also create a hanging indentation, where the first line extends to the left of the remainder of the paragraph. There are two general uses for hanging indentation, as shown here:

VLDL   Very Low Density Lipoprotein – The largest of the lipoproteins, these contain mostly triglycerides and are about 10 percent protein. They are usually not reported in typical lipid profiles because they only transport through the bloodstream from 5 to 12 percent of the cholesterol. Too many VLDL's make the plasma appear cloudy.

Low Density Lipoprotein – Commonly called the "bad cholesterol", these tend to promote deposits of plaque in the arteries. They are made up of about 50% cholesterol and carry from 60% to 70% of your total cholesterol through the bloodstream. Your LDL level should be less than 130 mg/dl. Your diet should be aimed at lowering LDL's.

In one case, some text stands by itself to the left of the paragraph. In the other, the text is continuous. To create a hanging indentation with continuous text that you've already typed, move the insertion point to the beginning of the paragraph, and then choose Hanging Indent from the Format Paragraph menu. To type a hanging indented paragraph, select Hanging Indent before you start typing.

Creating a hanging indentation with text that stands by itself is just as easy:

1. Type the text that you want to stand by itself.

2. Use the Indent command—by either pressing F7 or selecting Indent from the QuickMenu or Format Paragraph menu.

3. Continue typing the remainder of the paragraph.

You can also create a hanging indentation using the Paragraph Format dialog box. Set the Left Margin Adjustment to where you want the remainder of the paragraph to be, and enter a negative distance for the First Line Indent.

Indenting with the Ruler

You can also create indentations—from the left, from the right, for the first line, and hanging—using the ruler. To indent text from the right, drag the Right Margin Adjust marker, which is the small object at the right end of the ruler, to the position at which you want to indent the text.

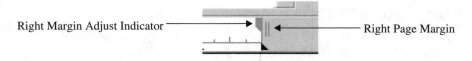

Right Margin Adjust Indicator ⸻ Right Page Margin

To indent text from the left, use the left section of the ruler. There are actually two separate indentation controls.

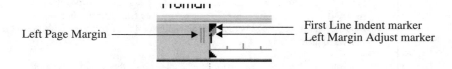

Left Page Margin ⸻ First Line Indent marker
Left Margin Adjust marker

The First Line Indent marker controls the position of the first line of every paragraph. To indent just the first line of the paragraph, drag the top darker triangle on the left side of the ruler.

To indent every line of a paragraph on the left, drag the Left Margin Adjust marker, the bottom triangle on the left of the ruler, to the right.

When you drag the Left Margin Adjust marker, the First Line Indent marker also moves in order to always remain at the same relative distance. If you want to set both, set the left margin adjust first and then the first line indentation. So if you want to create a hanging indentation, first set the left indentation where you want remaining lines to appear, and then drag the First Line Indent marker to the hanging position of the first line.

Creating Lists

Another way to enhance text is to format it as a list. A list makes it easy to read a series of related items and helps to organize your points. The two types of lists are bulleted and numbered. A bulleted list has a small graphic object, such as a circle or diamond, at the start of each paragraph. A numbered list looks like an outline, with numbers or letters.

When you begin a list, WordPerfect 10 automatically turns on the outlining feature and displays the Outline property bar. First, I'll discuss how to create the lists and then explain about outlining.

7

Using the Toolbar

The toolbar provides two buttons to help you create lists and outlines:

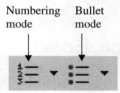

To begin a numbered list, click the Numbering button to apply the style shown on the button, or pull down the list next to the button and select the type of numbering you want from these options:

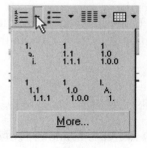

> **NOTE** *Turning on bullets or numbering displays the Outlining property bar that you'll learn about later in this chapter.*

WordPerfect 10 automatically numbers paragraphs like an outline, using indentations to correspond to outline levels, and creating a hanging indentation when text wraps to the next line. To stop numbering, press ENTER after the last line and then BACKSPACE to delete the last number inserted.

To create a bulleted list, click on the Bullets button or pull down the list next to the button and choose from these options:

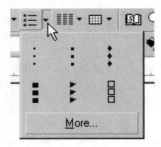

The symbol you select is inserted at the start of each line. Press ENTER and then BACKSPACE to stop inserting bullets.

Using Format-As-You-Go

The QuickBullets feature of QuickCorrect Format-As-You-Go senses when you are starting a list and takes over from there. First, make sure that the feature is turned on by following these steps:

1. Select Tools | QuickCorrect.

2. Click the Format-As-You-Go tab.

3. If a checkmark does not appear in the QuickBullets checkbox in the Format-As-You-Go options section, click in the box to select it.

4. Click OK.

Now to create a list, follow these steps:

1. Type an asterisk or a lowercase **o**, and press TAB. When you press TAB, WordPerfect 10 changes the character you typed to a bullet.

2. Type the first paragraph, and then press ENTER. When you press ENTER, WordPerfect 10 inserts another bullet on the next line.

3. Continue typing the items for the list.

4. Press ENTER after the final item and then BACKSPACE to delete the bullet.

In addition to the small bullet, you can insert other bullet characters by using these keys:

To Use This Bullet	Start With This Character
▸	>
♦	^
★	+
•	o
●	O
—	-

You can number lists in the same way with the QuickBullets feature using these steps:

1. Type the first number, letter, or Roman numeral.

2. Type a period, and press TAB.

3. Type the paragraph—WordPerfect 10 creates a hanging indentation when text wraps to the next line.

4. Press ENTER, and WordPerfect 10 inserts the next highest number or letter in the series and indents the insertion point at the indented position of the line above.

5. Press ENTER and BACKSPACE to stop numbering.

Bullets and Numbering Dialog Box

For more bullet and list options, use the Bullets and Numbering dialog box—either before typing the list or to format existing paragraphs. Select Outline/Bullets & Numbering from the Insert menu, or click on More from the Numbering or Bullets button on the toolbar, to display the dialog box shown in Figure 7-9.

The Options list lets you choose the template in which to save the format. You'll learn about these options in Chapter 8. The Text tab of the dialog box lets you create custom list formats to use for standard types of text, such as headings, quotations, and definitions.

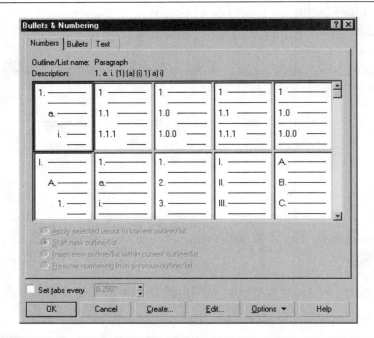

FIGURE 7-9   Outline/Bullets & Numbering

If you already have a list in the document before the insertion point, you can choose to apply the selected format to it, start a new outline, insert an outline in the current one, or resume numbering where you left off.

You can choose or edit the standard numbering and bullet formats, or create your own. When you choose to create or edit a style, you'll see a dialog box like the one shown in Figure 7-10. If you are editing a format, its name and other specifics are listed in the box.

In the Type of Numbered List section, choose a single list for just numbering or bulleting paragraphs, or a multiple-level list for an outline.

In the Number Set list, choose the type of numbering. You can choose standard outline numbering, legal numbering, bullets, and user-defined to create your own. Then, for up to nine levels, indicate the following:

- Any text that you want to appear before the number
- The number, letter, or bullet to use for the level
- The style to apply to the text

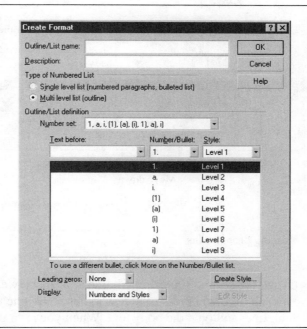

FIGURE 7-10   Creating or editing a bullet/list style

Outlining

When your cursor is in a list, WordPerfect 10 displays the property bar shown in Figure 7-11, with the new buttons labeled. Use the buttons on the bar to create your outline.

You can press TAB or click on the Demote button to move to the next lowest outline level (such as from I to A and from A to 1). Press SHIFT-TAB or click on the Promote button to move to the next highest.

To display icons indicating outline levels and body text, click the Show Icons button on the Outline property bar. Use the Set Paragraph Number button to change the outline level and number, and the Modify button to create a custom outline in the Create Format dialog box.

Body Text

Body text is text that is not numbered as part of the outline, but appears between outline entries. To type body text, press ENTER twice at the end of an outline entry.

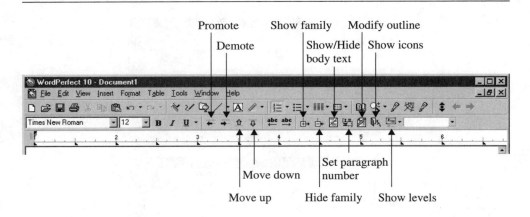

FIGURE 7-11   Outlining property bar

When you press ENTER the second time, a blank line appears between the two outline levels. Now each time you press ENTER, another blank line is inserted. Move up to the blank line, and type the body text. When you're in the body text line, by the way, the Outline property bar is replaced by the standard property bar.

> **NOTE**   *To continue adding to the outline, move the insertion point down to the numbered lines and begin typing.*

If you just want to view the outline itself, with the narrative of body text, click on the Show/Hide Body Text button in the Outline property bar. WordPerfect 10 removes the body text from display. Click on the button again to redisplay the body text.

Moving Outline Families

The arrangement of outlines in families make them easier to work with. An *outline family* consists of a heading at any level and all of the subheadings and text under it. You can move outline families by clicking on these buttons:

Move up ──────►  ◄────── Move down

To move just an individual line in the outline, click anywhere in it, and then click on Move Up or Move Down. WordPerfect 10 moves the text and renumbers the outline levels depending on where you insert the line. Moving just the line does not affect any sublevels that may have been under it.

To move an entire family, select the family, and then click on the Move Up or Move Down button. To select the family, point to anywhere in the heading line, and drag to the end of the section you want to move.

 When you select a family, make sure the Outline property bar is still visible. If the standard property bar is displayed, select the family again, making sure that the start and end of the selection are within outline levels.

7

Collapsing and Expanding Outlines

 One of the advantages of working with an outline is that it lets you visualize the organization of topics and subtopics. You can see at a glance how subjects are related. When you have a long outline, however, headings may be too far apart to show the structure. To solve this problem, you can collapse and expand outline families.

 When you collapse a family, you hide its sublevels, displaying just the heading that you select. To collapse a family, click in the heading, and then click on the Hide Family button in the Outline property bar. To collapse more than one family, select them first.

To expand the family, click on the Show Family button.

 To collapse the entire outline to a specific level, pull down the Show Outlines Levels list in the property bar, and select the lowest level to display.

Hyphenating Text

When you justify text on both the left and right, WordPerfect 10 inserts extra space to fill out the line, but sometimes the extra space is just too obvious. You can hyphenate text to reduce these extra spaces. Hyphenation divides some words between lines, adding enough characters at the right to avoid large blank spaces between words. You can have WordPerfect 10 hyphenate automatically as you type, or you can have it hyphenate a selection of existing text. To turn on Hyphenation, pull down the Tools menu, point to Language, and click on Hyphenation to display the dialog box shown in Figure 7-12. Click on Turn Hyphenation On, and then click OK.

WordPerfect 10 automatically inserts a hyphen based on certain rules. If its rules cannot be applied to the end of a line, you'll see a dialog box such as this:

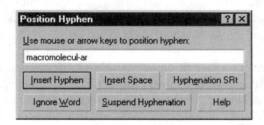

Press the RIGHT ARROW or LEFT ARROW to place the hyphen where you want it to appear, and then click on the Insert Hyphen button. You can also choose to insert a space at that location or a Hyphenation SRt code—a position where WordPerfect 10 divides a word without a hyphen character.

You can always hyphenate words yourself, but don't just press the hyphen key. Pressing the hyphen key actually inserts a hyphen code that should only be used for hyphenated words such as "mother-in-law." If the word must be divided between lines, WordPerfect 10 uses one of the hyphen positions. If you later add or delete text, the hyphen may be moved to another line so it always appears between the words. If you press the hyphen key to simply hyphenate a word, later editing may move the hyphen to another line, separating the word incorrectly with a hyphen character.

If you want to hyphenate a word only when it must be divided between lines, press CTRL-SHIFT- (the CTRL, then the SHIFT and hyphen keys together) to enter a soft hyphen code. The hyphen appears only when WordPerfect 10 must divide the word between lines.

FIGURE 7-12   Hyphenating text

If you want to hyphenate a word or other text, but do not want to divide it between lines, press CTRL- (the CTRL and the hyphen keys together). Use this for minus signs in formulas or for hyphens in phone numbers that you do not want divided.

Inserting Other Codes

Other hyphenation styles are available, along with other special formatting codes. To access these, pull down the Format Line menu, and click on Other Codes to display the Other Codes dialog box, shown in Figure 7-13. The Other Codes dialog box includes some useful features. You may not need them often, but it pays to be prepared just in case.

A *hard tab* is a tab code that moves the insertion point to the next tab stop position on the right, just like pressing the TAB key. But unlike a tab inserted with the TAB key, a hard tab is not affected if you change the tab type. Use this type of code, for example, to set a different tab type without affecting other lines. If you set a hard center tab at two inches, for example, the tab indicator does not change, but text at that location—for that line only—will be centered. The Other Codes dialog box lets you enter left, right, center, and decimal hard tabs, with and without dot leaders.

The dialog box also includes the Hard Space and the End Centering/Alignment codes. Use a hard space when you want to put a space between words, but don't

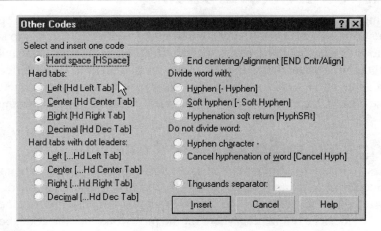

FIGURE 7-13   Inserting Other Codes

want them ever divided between lines. WordPerfect 10 treats the hard space as a real character and will not wrap the two words at that point.

The End Centering/Alignment code stops the current centering or alignment. For example, suppose you want to type text so the first character starts at the exact center of the screen. Start by centering the insertion point with the Center command, and then select the End Centering/Alignment code from the dialog box. Your text now moves to the right as you type, rather than being centered.

The dialog box contains these five options:

- *Hyphen [- Hyphen]* lets WordPerfect 10 divide the word between lines at the hyphen position.

- *Soft Hyphen* displays the hyphen only if the word is wrapped at that location.

- *Hyphenation Soft Return* divides a word at that location without displaying a hyphen character.

- *Hyphen Character* prevents WordPerfect 10 from dividing the word between lines.

- *Cancel Hyphenation of Word* moves the word to the next line, rather than hyphenating it.

Changing Character Spacing

The spacing of characters and lines is set by the font, font size, and line spacing commands. But sometimes you may want to make minor adjustments to spacing to fit text into a certain space or create a special effect. Book and magazine publishers do this all the time when they compose pages for publication. WordPerfect 10 gives you some of the same capabilities in the Typesetting options in the Format menu. Use these commands when your document requires precise spacing.

Printing Text in Specific Positions

Sometimes you need to print text in an exact position on the page. When filling in a preprinted form, for example, a word or phrase must appear on a line or in a box already printed on the paper. To specify an exact position, use the Advance command. It doesn't even matter where on the page you enter the code, because the text prints at the designated location regardless of where it appears on the screen.

Select Advance from the Typesetting menu to see the dialog box shown in Figure 7-14. You can set a horizontal or vertical position relative to either the current location of the insertion point or the edges of the paper. To set an exact position on the paper, set it relative to the left edge and the top edge of the page. Use positions relative to the insertion point to create custom subscripts or superscripts.

When you do set a position relative to the top of the page, WordPerfect 10 places the baseline of the text at that location so characters appear above it. This means that if you set a position two inches from the top of the page, the bottom of the text will be two inches from the top. If you want the top of the text to be two inches from the top, deselect the Text Above Position checkbox.

Overstriking Characters

When you overstrike, you print two or more characters in the same position. Use this command to create special effects, such as slashed zeros or combinations such as those shown here:

Select Overstrike from the Format Typesetting menu to see the following dialog box. Type the characters that you want to superimpose. To change the style

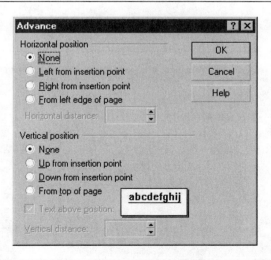

FIGURE 7-14   Advance dialog box

or relative size of the characters, click on the Codes button and select a style or size from the list. Click on OK to see the characters onscreen.

Spacing Between Words and Characters

To customize the spacing between characters and words, select Word/Letter Spacing from the Format Typesetting menu to see the dialog box shown in Figure 7-15.

Use the Word Spacing options to set the spacing between words. Normal is the spacing determined by the font; Optimal is WordPerfect 10's default spacing. To change the spacing, select Percent of Optimal, and enter a percentage of the default spacing. Use values less than 100 to reduce the spacing between words, and over 100 to increase the spacing. Print a specific number of characters per inch by entering the number in the Set Pitch text box.

The Word Spacing Justification Limits options control the spacing between words in fully justified text. Use the Compressed To and Expanded To settings to control the minimum and maximum amount that words can be spaced as a percentage. For example, by default, WordPerfect 10 only reduces the spacing between words to as little as 60 percent or increases it by as much as 400 percent.

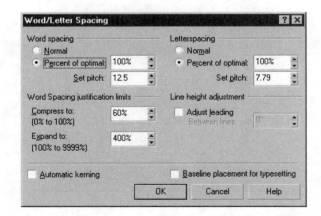

FIGURE 7-15   Word/Letter Spacing

If your justified text appears packed too close, increase the Compressed To setting. If words appear spaced too far apart, reduce the Expanded To setting.

The Letterspacing options control the spacing between letters. Change the spacing if fonts appear too tight or too loose.

Kerning

Kerning is the process of moving together certain pairs of characters that have opposite slants, such as *A* and *V*, to create a smoother appearance with less space between them. To have WordPerfect 10 automatically kern a default set of letter combinations, check the Automatic Kerning option in the Word/Letter Spacing dialog box.

To control the spacing between two characters, place the insertion point between them, and select Manual Kerning from the Format Typesetting menu to see the dialog box shown next. Click on the UP and DOWN arrows at the Add/Remove Space text box to adjust the space between the characters. The character adjusts onscreen as you change the setting so you can see the results before closing the dialog box.

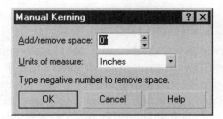

Adjusting Line Spacing

The Line Spacing command is just one way to control the spacing and position of lines. You can create special effects and customize line spacing in a variety of ways.

The distance between lines of text in a paragraph is determined by the size and style of the fonts. WordPerfect 10 automatically spaces lines based on the font settings. To increase or decrease the spacing, select Height from the Format Line menu, click on the Fixed option button, and enter a specific line height in the text box. This sets the baseline-to-baseline distance at a specific size regardless of the font size.

You can also adjust line height in the Word/Letter Spacing dialog box. Click on the Adjust Leading box in the dialog box, and then enter any extra spacing you want, in points, between lines in the Between Lines text box. If you enter "6p," for example, WordPerfect 10 adds an additional 6 points between lines. Enter a negative number to bring your lines closer together.

Setting the Baseline

The *baseline* is the imaginary line on which characters sit. The position of the first baseline on the page is determined by the size of the top margin and the font. For example, if you are using a 12-point font, and the default one-inch (72-point) margin, the first baseline is 84 points from the top of the page. The position of the first baseline affects the location of other text, such as where characters appear using Advance up and down commands.

To set a specific location for the first baseline, display the Word/Letter Spacing dialog box, and click on Baseline Placement for Typesetting. This tells WordPerfect 10 to position the first baseline at the top margin, so it is in the same position on every page regardless of the font or font size being used.

Giving Printer Commands

WordPerfect 10 and Windows should be able to take advantage of all of your printer's special features. If your printer has a feature that is not supported, however, you can still use it by entering printer codes. These are special commands that turn on and off printer features, such as condensed or other types of printing. Your printer's manual should include a complete list of commands.

Select Printer Command from the Format Typesetting menu to see the Printer Command dialog box. Enter the codes between angle brackets, as in "<18>". The Escape character is "<27>". You can also specify a file that you want downloaded to the printer.

If you have an old-fashioned daisy wheel printer, you can also pause it to change print wheels or the ribbon color. To pause the printer, place the insertion point where you want to make the change, display the Printer Command dialog box, and click in the Pause Printer checkbox.

Controlling Widows and Orphans

You know that as you type, WordPerfect 10 divides your document into pages. As one page becomes full, WordPerfect 10 adds a soft page break and begins a new page. Sometimes, however, WordPerfect 10 may divide text in a way that creates widow or orphan lines. A *widow* is the first line of a paragraph that appears by itself at the bottom of a page. An *orphan* is the last line of a paragraph that appears by itself on the top of a page. With WordPerfect 10, you can avoid these undesirable situations and control how text is divided between pages.

To avoid widows and orphans, pull down the Format menu, and select Keep Text Together to see the dialog box in Figure 7-16. Click in the checkbox in the Widow/Orphan section to prevent the first and last lines of paragraphs from being divided between pages.

Widow and orphan control, however, affects just one line of a paragraph. It does not, for example, move a two-line widow to the next page, nor does it prevent a title or subtitle from appearing at the bottom of the page, with the first paragraph relating to that title starting on the next. If you want to keep a section of text on the same page—such as a title with the first paragraph that follows it—select the text, display the Keep Text Together dialog box, and then click on the box in the Block Protect section. WordPerfect 10 keeps all of the selected text on the same page.

7

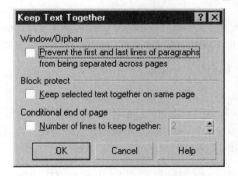

FIGURE 7-16 Keep Text Together

> **TIP**   *You can keep text together by selecting it and then choosing Block Protect from the QuickMenu.*

If you just want to keep together a specific number of lines at the end of a paragraph, place the insertion point in the last line of the paragraph, and display the Keep Text Together dialog box. Click in the checkbox in the Conditional End of Page section, and then enter the number of lines that you want to keep together in the text box.

Try It Out

After reading this chapter, you can create some eye-catching documents. Remember, you can apply formats to text as you type it or at any time afterward by first selecting the text and then applying the format.

Let's take our practice document and add some formats.

1. Open the document Tae Kwon Do.

2. Select the heading at the top of the document. Either drag over it with the mouse, or point to the margin next to the heading and click.

3. Pull down the list next to the Font Size box on the property bar and click on 14.

4. While the text is still selected, pull down the list next to the Underline button in the property bar and select the double underline – the second option in the list.

5. Place the insertion point at the start of the first paragraph.

6. Click the Justification button on the property bar to see the options and select Full.

7. Right-click anywhere in the first paragraph and select Drop Cap from the QuickMenu.

8. Click the Drop Cap in Margin style and click OK.

The History of Tae Kwon Do

The history of Korea must always include the subject of *Tae Kwon Do*. The country, on a tiny peninsula, was instrumental in creating a martial art that is now practiced throughout the entire world.

9. Select Format | Paragraph | Format.

10. Enter 2 in the Number of Lines box in the Spacing Between Paragraphs section and click OK.

11. Click anywhere in the fifth paragraph, the one starting with *It was a period*.

12. Select Format | Paragraph | Border\Fill

13. Click the second border style – the one to the right of the blank space and then click OK.

14. Select that entire paragraph by clicking twice in the left margin next to it.

15. Drag the Right Margin Adjust of the ruler to the left until the QuickStatus box shows that it is over one inch – Right Margin Adjust 1".

16. Drag the left Margin Adjust of the ruler to the right until the QuickStatus box shows Left Margin Adjust 1".

Silla was overthrown in 935 and became the kingdom of Koryo, from which the name Korea is derived. Over the years, however, interest in martial arts declined, especially in the Yi dynasty that was founded in 1392. Buddhism was replaced by Confucianism, and a new national spirit turned interest away from the martial arts.

It was a period in which scholars, primarily Confucian scholars, gained great respect and control. The scholars convinced the political structure of the need to promote cultural activities, and to develop public works, museums, and art. Pacifistic by nature, the scholars drew public money away from the military. However, *Tae Kwon Do* would still be a powerful art for the Korean people.

17. Add the following line as a new paragraph to the end of the text, using the abbreviation tdk to take advantage of the stored QuickWord:

    The history of Korea and Tae Kwon Do can be summarized by these important dates:

18. Press Enter twice.

19. Select Format | Line | Tab Set.

20. Click Clear All and then Close.

21. Click at the 2" position on the tab line to set a left tab.

22. Right-click at the 6.5" position on the ruler and select ...Right.

23. Press Tab and type **57 BC**.

24. Press Tab and type **Silla dynasty was founded**.

25. Press Enter, and in the same way, complete the table shown here:

57 BC	Silla dynasty is founded
313 AD	Korea drives out Chinese invaders
425 AD	Buddhism established in Korea
918 AD	The Koguryo dynasty is founded
1259 AD	Mongol armies conquer Korea

26. Save the document.

Chapter 8

Working with Styles and Templates

There are many ways to make your documents look good. Formatting characters, lines, and paragraphs is just the start. If you don't want to spend a great deal of time with formatting, but still want your documents to look great, then use a few of WordPerfect 10's special helpers. In this chapter, you'll learn about two powerful ways to create terrific-looking documents.

Using templates, you can start with a completely formatted document and then just add your own text. And with styles, you can apply sets of formats with a single click of the mouse.

Styles

When you apply a style, such as Heading 1, to text, you are applying a combination of formats at one time, such as a font, font size, and character style. With one selection, you can apply several formats, because they are combined into one option, or style.

A *style* is just a collection of formats that you can apply to text. Remember QuickFormat? With QuickFormat you apply the formats in one paragraph of text to another paragraph. A style is a place to store the formats before you apply them. You can store many different styles and then apply them to text whenever you want.

Styles provide two benefits: consistency and flexibility. By defining a set of formats in a style, you can easily apply the formats to similar portions of text. Using a headline style, for example, ensures that all headlines use the same format. It is easier than having to individually apply multiple formats.

However, one of the greatest benefits of styles is their ability to change text. If you edit a style, all of the text formatted by it changes automatically. For example, suppose you type a long document with 20 subtitles formatted the same way. If you want to change the format of the headings, you'd need to individually reformat each of them. If you used a style to format the subtitles, however, you could simply edit the style to the desired format. All 20 subtitles would change immediately to the new style.

WordPerfect 10 comes with a set of styles ready for you to use. The styles are really provided because they are used by certain WordPerfect 10 functions, such as outlining and table of contents. To apply a WordPerfect 10 style, pull down the Style list in the property bar, and click on the style you want to apply.

Creating Styles-by-Example

If you decide that you want to use combinations of formats other than those provided in WordPerfect 10's built-in styles, then create your own. You can create a style by selecting formats in a special dialog box, or by copying the formats from existing text. Copying the formats is called *styles-by-example*.

The easiest way to create a style is by example, using QuickStyle. Here's how to use QuickStyle:

1. Format text using the options that you want to save in a style.

2. Place the insertion point in the text, pull down the Style list in the property bar, and click on QuickStyle to display this dialog box:

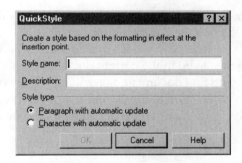

3. Type a name for the style in the Style Name text box, and enter a brief description of it in the Description box.

4. Select whether you want the style to be for a paragraph or a character. With a paragraph style, you can later apply it to the entire paragraph in which the insertion point is placed, without selecting the paragraph first. With a character style, you must select the text before applying the style, or apply the style and then type the text.

5. Click on OK. The name you gave the style appears on the property bar.

6. To apply the same style to other text, pull down the Style list, and click on the style name.

NOTE *The notation "with automatic update" in the QuickStyle dialog box means that WordPerfect 10 will change the style if you later change the format applied to text using the style.*

Defining Styles

Styles that you create are saved with the document. So whenever you open the document, the styles are available in the Style list of the property bar. To make your styles available for all documents, you have two options:

■ Add the styles to the default template, the file WordPerfect 10 uses for all new documents.

■ Save the styles in a separate file, and then recall them when you need them.

In this chapter, you'll learn about both options.

To create a style, select Styles from the Format menu. You'll see the Styles dialog box in Figure 8-1.

The box lists the built-in WordPerfect 10 styles. To apply a style from this list, click on the style and then on the Apply button.

Before creating a new style, you should decide where you want the style saved. By default, new styles are saved in the current document. This means it is available for use only with that document, not with any other ones. You can choose, however, to save the style in the default template. The default template contains styles, formats, and other items that can be used with every document. To

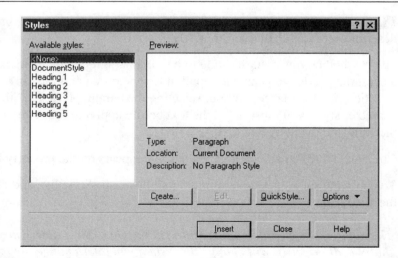

FIGURE 8-1   Creating a style

choose the location, pull down the Options list in the Styles dialog box, and select Settings to see this dialog box:

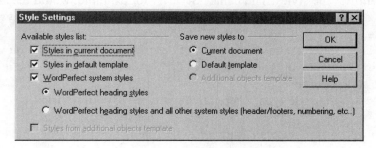

Click the Default Template option button in the Save New Styles To section, and then click OK. Other options in the dialog box let you choose which styles are displayed in the Styles dialog box.

Then to create a new style, click on Create to see the Styles Editor dialog box in Figure 8-2.

8

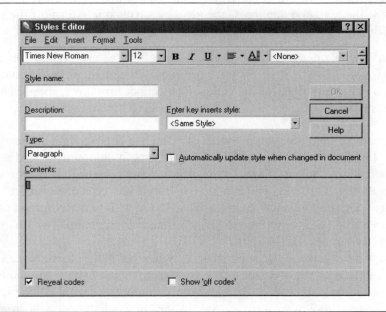

FIGURE 8-2   Styles Editor

In the Style Name box, type a name up to 12 characters. This is the name that will be shown in the Style list of the property bar, so make it something that clearly identifies the styles. The name "Style1," for example, would mean nothing to you several months from now, but "ReportTitle" clearly explains why you created the style.

In the Description text box, type a brief description of the style. You will see this description when you select a style in the Styles dialog box, so use it to further clarify the style's purpose.

Next, select the style type. There are three types to choose from:

- *Paragraph*—Create a Paragraph style when you want to be able to apply it to a section of text that ends with a carriage return. You do not have to select the text first, just place the insertion point, and select the style. WordPerfect 10 inserts the Style On code at the beginning of the paragraph and inserts the Style Off code at the carriage return. If you do not select text first, but choose the style, and then type, WordPerfect 10 turns off the style when you press ENTER.

- *Character*—Use the Character style type for words or phrases that do not necessarily end with a carriage return. To use this type of style, turn it on, type the text, and then press the RIGHT ARROW key to turn off the style. You can also apply the style to selected text.

- *Document open*—An open style does not have an end. When you apply this type of style, it stays on for the entire document, or until you override it by entering other format codes. You cannot turn it off; simply change the formats.

For Character and Paragraph styles, you can also choose what happens when you press the ENTER key with the Enter Key Inserts Style option. With Paragraph styles, for example, select <Same Style> if you want to leave the style on when you press ENTER. This way, you can turn on a style and type one or more consecutive paragraphs in the same formats. The style is actually turned off when you press ENTER, but is reapplied to the next line automatically. To turn off the style, you have to use the Style list.

If you want to turn off the style when you press ENTER, select <None>. This way you can turn on the style for a title, for example, and have it automatically turn off when you press ENTER. In addition to <Same Style> and <None>, you will be able to choose any of your own custom styles in this list, once you create some (so you can have some other styles turned on when you press ENTER).

You can also select an action on the ENTER key with Character styles. Remember, to turn off a Character style, press the RIGHT ARROW key. If the Enter Key Inserts Style option is set at <Same Style>, then pressing ENTER when a Character style is on has no effect—it does not even move to the next line. If you want to use the ENTER key to move the insertion point to the next line and repeat the same style, set Enter Key Inserts Style to <None>.

Enter the formats and any text you want to insert, in the Contents box. Click in the box, use the property bar or the menu bar in the Styles Editor to select format options, and type any text to be included with the style. To enter a hard return code, so your style performs a carriage return, press ENTER. To enter a page break, press CTRL-ENTER.

> **CAUTION**   *Before typing any text or pressing* ENTER *to be included in the style, make sure the blinking insertion point is in the large contents box.*

There are three other options in the dialog box:

- *Automatically Update Style When Changed in Document* lets you edit the style directly in the document. When you want to change the style, simply select some text that is formatted by it, and change the format. The style itself changes, as does other text formatted by it. To edit a style otherwise, you have to edit it in the Styles Editor.

- Use the *Show 'Off Codes'* option to display off codes for corresponding on codes. Normally, only the on codes are shown, such as to turn on bold or underlining. When you turn off the style, the formats in it are also turned off. But if you want to confirm it, select this option, and then apply the same format to insert the off code.

- Turn off *Reveal Codes* when you do not want to see the codes for the style in the Contents box.

As an example, let's create several styles. We will start with a memorandum heading, a style that will include text and formats:

1. Select Styles from the Format menu, and then click on Create to display the Styles Editor.

2. Type **Memorandum** in the Style Name text box, and then type **Starts a Legal Memo** in the Description box. This is going to be a Document open style because it sets the format for the entire document.

3. Pull down the Type list box, select Document (open), and then click in the Contents box.

4. We will start by selecting the legal-sized paper. Pull down the Format menu in the Styles Editor, point to Page, and click on Page Setup.

5. On the Page Setup tab, choose Legal 8.5" x 14" in the list box, and then click on OK. WordPerfect 10 adds the code to select that paper size in the Contents box.

6. Pull down the Font list in the Styles Editor property bar, and choose the Arial font. You can also select Font from the Format menu, and use the Font dialog box.

7. Pull down the Size list in the property bar, and choose 24 points.

8. Click on the Bold button in the property bar.

9. Click on the Justification button in the property bar, and click on Center in the list that appears.

10. Type **Memorandum**, the text you want to appear when you apply the style, and then press ENTER to enter a carriage return.

11. Using the property bar or Font dialog box, choose Times New Roman in 12 point, and deselect the Bold attribute.

12. Press ENTER two more times; then select Left from the Justification list in the property bar.

13. Select OK to accept the style and return to the Styles dialog box.

NOTE	*If the Styles dialog box does not appear after creating a new style, reopen it to continue.*

Now let's create a character and a Paragraph style. We'll use one to format headings, such as To, From, and Subject, and the other for a paragraph indentation format. Follow these steps:

1. Click on Create, and type **MemoHeading** in the Style Name text box.

2. Type **Memorandum headings** in the Description text box.

3. Pull down the Type list, and select Character. This example uses a Character style so it can be turned off to allow other text to be typed on the same line using a different font.

4. Pull down the Enter Key Inserts Style list box, and select <None>.

5. Click in the Contents box.

6. Use the property bar or Font dialog box to select Arial, 14 point.

7. Select OK.

Now, define an indented Paragraph style.

1. Select Create.

2. Type **DoubleIndent** in the Style Name box.

3. Type **Text indented on both sides** in the Description text box.

4. Pull down the Type list, and select Paragraph.

5. Select <None> in the Enter Key Inserts Style list.

6. Turn on the option Automatically Update When Changed in Document.

7. Click in the Contents box.

8. Select Paragraph from the Format menu in the Styles Editor property bar, and click on Double Indent.

9. Select OK.

Saving Styles

If you now save the document, the style is saved along with it or the default template based on your selection in the Settings dialog box. If you chose to save the styles just in the current document, you can still make them available for other documents by saving them to a separate file that can be retrieved when needed.

Still in the Styles dialog box, pull down the Options list, and select Save As. Use the box that appears to name the styles. You can also choose to save just your own custom styles, the built-in system styles, or both. Type **MemoStyles**, and then click on OK. Close the Styles dialog box and then the document.

Retrieving and Using Styles

When you want to create a memo using the styles, you have to retrieve the styles from the disk, as follows:

- Pull down the Format menu, and click on Styles.

- Click on Options, and choose Retrieve.

- In the dialog box that appears, type **MemoStyles**, and then click on OK. A message appears asking if you want to overwrite any existing styles with the same name in the file you are retrieving.

- Click on Yes.

Your custom styles are now listed in the dialog box, and they will be in the Style list of the property bar. We'll use the property bar for our styles, so close the dialog box.

1. Pull down the Style list in the property bar, and click on Memorandum. WordPerfect 10 changes the paper size and displays the memorandum heading on the screen. Now let's enter the headings, as follows.

2. Pull down the Style list, and click on MemoHeading.

3. Type **TO:**, and then press the RIGHT ARROW key to turn off the style.

4. Press TAB twice, and type the recipient's name—pick someone you know.

5. Press ENTER.

Now in the same way, complete the headings as shown here:

Memorandum

TO: Allison Wing
FROM: Jerry Beebe
SUBJECT: Ratings

When you have finished, press ENTER twice. Now turn on the indented Paragraph style. Pull down the Style list in the property bar, and select DoubleIndent. Now type the following text, and press ENTER.

We should get together to discuss the ratings. Management is happy that we went to number 1 and this would be a good time to demand a raise!

When you press ENTER, WordPerfect 10 turns off the style and returns to the default paragraph format.

You can also apply a style to existing text. To apply a Paragraph style, place the insertion point anywhere in the paragraph, or select multiple paragraphs, and then choose the style from the property bar or Styles dialog box. To apply a character style, select the text first. For a Document style, place the insertion point where you want the format to start.

If you created a Paragraph style that does not turn off when you press ENTER, you have to turn off the style yourself. Display the Styles dialog box, and double-click on <None> in the list of styles.

Changing Styles

Styles are so powerful because they not only format text, but they also can change the format. For example, suppose we want to change the style of the memo headings. Since they are all formatted with the same style, we just need to edit the style.

1. Pull down the Format menu, and click on Styles.

2. Click on the MemoHeading style in the list, and click on Edit to display the Styles Editor.

3. Click in the Contents box.

4. Click on the Bold button in the property bar to insert the bold code.

5. Select OK, and then click on Close to return to the document.

All of the headings formatted with the style are now bold.

Now let's see how to edit a style that's been created for automatic updating:

1. Select the entire indented paragraph, and click on the Italic button in the toolbar. The DoubleIndent style has now been changed.

2. To confirm this, move the insertion point after the paragraph, pull down the Style list, and click on the DoubleIndent style.

3. Type some text. It will be indented and italic, conforming to the changed style. If you were to display the style in the Styles Editor, you would see the italic code in the Contents box.

Deleting Styles

To delete one of your custom styles, use these steps:

1. Display the Style dialog box, and click on one of your styles.

2. Press DELETE. A dialog box appears listing your custom styles with the options Including Formatting Codes and Leave Formatting Codes in Document.

3. Click on the style that you want to delete. You can use the CTRL or SHIFT keys to select more than one style in the list.

4. Select Leave Formatting Codes in Document to delete the style from the list and remove the codes that it has already applied to text. This deletes the code but does not change the format of any text in the document.

5. Select Including Formatting Codes to delete the style and remove its formats from the document.

6. Click OK.

Creating Templates

As you learned in Chapter 2, projects are documents that contain standard information and formats. Corel supplies a number of useful projects, but you may have your own special formats that you want to apply. Does your office use a standard format for faxes, memos, or letters? If so, you can create templates for those documents so you won't have to enter and format the standard text. *Templates* are similar to projects, but they do not have PerfectExpert tasks linked to them. Like projects, however, templates can be interactive, prompting you for information to insert or taking it automatically from the CorelCENTRAL Address Book.

Why use a template, and not just a regular document that contains the "boilerplate" text? If you open a regular document and insert information into it, clicking the Save button replaces the original file. The document now contains more than just boilerplate text, so the next person who uses it must delete the inserted information. If you use a template, the original file remains on disk unchanged. In addition, you can use a template to build dialog boxes prompting for information, and even to insert items directly from the Address Book.

To create a template, use these steps:

1. Select New From Project from the File menu, and click on the Create New tab.

2. Pull down the Options list, and select Create WP Template. WordPerfect 10 opens a template property bar. In this window, enter any boilerplate text and formats that you want in every copy of the document.

> **TIP**   *If the formatting property bar no longer appears, right-click on the toolbar, and select Font from the list. You can later turn off the extra toolbar the same way.*

3. Type and format the document, leaving empty spaces in the document to be filled in with template prompts that will be built later.

4. When you've finished, click on the Save button in the toolbar to display the Save Template dialog box.

5. Type a brief description in the Description box.

6. Enter the name for the template in the Template Name box.

7. Select an option from the Template Group list. Using other techniques, you can create groups in which to store your templates.

8. Click on OK. WordPerfect 10 stores templates in a subfolder with the group name in the \Windows\Application Data\Corel\PerfectExpert\10\Custom WP Templates-folder with the WPT extension.

9. Click on the Close button in the template property bar.

To use the template, select it just as you would one of WordPerfect 10's templates. Select New from the File menu, select the group you added the template to, and then double-click on the template name.

Customizing Templates

The template feature bar gives you the tools you need to further customize your templates.

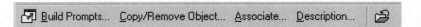

Use the Insert File button on the far left of the feature bar, for example, to insert the contents of a document into the template. This is useful if you've already created a document that contains the boilerplate text and formats that you want the template to contain. Click on Insert File, and choose the document in the dialog box that appears. Once the document is inserted, delete any text that you do not want in the generic template.

Building Prompts

The Build Prompts button lets you create a dialog box that prompts for information, just like those provided in WordPerfect 10's own templates. It may take a few minutes to create the dialog box, but it helps to ensure that important information is not overlooked when the template is used.

A template can actually use three types of information:

■ *Personal information* will be inserted automatically from the listing you designate in the Address Book. Once you select your personal listing, WordPerfect 10 inserts it in templates without any further prompts. You can always change the information by editing it in the Address Book or by selecting a new Address Book listing.

■ *Prompted information* must be entered into text boxes when you use the template. The Template Information dialog box contains prompts and text boxes for you to enter. Use these types of prompts for information that will change with each use of the template.

■ *Address information* is retrieved from another listing in the Address Book, such as the recipient of a fax or an e-mail. When you use the template, click on the Address Book icon, and select a listing from the book. WordPerfect 10 inserts information from a listing into the appropriate prompts in the dialog box and then into the document.

8

To create prompts, click on the Build Prompts button in the feature bar to display the Prompt Builder dialog box shown here:

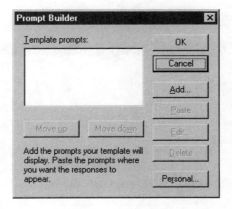

Use the Add button to define a prompt, including its name and any information you want inserted from an Address Book. By linking a prompt with an address book, you can select an address and have WordPerfect automatically insert information into the document. If you do not link a prompt with an address book, you'll be prompted to enter the information into the document when you use the template.

After defining the prompts, you add codes into the document showing where the prompted information will be inserted. Figure 8-3 shows how your custom prompts would appear when you use the template.

Click on the Address Book icon next to Recipient Information to select the listing for the recipient. The information from that listing appears in the appropriate sections of the dialog box. Enter the date of the last order in the corresponding text box. This is then inserted into the document, along with the Address Book fields, when you click on OK.

We'll take you through the steps of creating prompts in the Try It Out section at the end of this chapter.

For more advanced template designers, a template can also include custom styles, macros, abbreviations, toolbars, menu bars, and keyboards. You can design a special toolbar, for example, and have it open when the template is being used.

Editing the Default Template

You can change the settings used by the default template by changing styles. All of the default values are stored in styles in the default template. To change a

| Template Information | ? ☒ |

Personal information: ▢ Alan Neibauer

Recipient information: ▢
Name of Recipient :
Address of Recipient :
City :
State :
Zip :
First Name :
Date of Last Order :

OK
Cancel
Next Field
Help

FIGURE 8-3   Using a custom template

default setting, you have to change the style in the template. You can do this from within any document, without opening the template itself.

Select Styles from the Format menu. Pull down the Options list, and select Settings to display the Style Settings dialog box. Click on the Default Template option button in the Save New Styles To section.

WordPerfect 10 lists only a set of basic styles in the Style list box. There are actually styles for every format that can be applied by built-in WordPerfect 10 features. To see these styles, click on the option button labeled "WordPerfect Heading Styles and All Other System Styles" in the Available Styles List section. Then click on OK to see all of the styles. To change a default setting, just edit the corresponding style. Edit the style named "DocumentStyle," for example, to change the default font, paragraph, page size, and margin formats.

To return a style to its original format, select the style in the list, pull down the Options menu, and click on Reset.

Try It Out

Templates and prompts make it easy to create personalized documents of all types. As an example, let's create a new template and build a series of prompts to build the dialog box shown previously in Figure 8-3.

1. Select New From Project from the File menu, and click on the Create New tab.

2. Pull down the Options list, and select Create WP Template.

3. Type and format the document shown in Figure 8-4.

4. When you've finished, click on the Save button in the toolbar to display the Save Template dialog box.

5. Type a brief description in the Description box.

6. Enter the name for the template, **Credit Notice**, in the Template Name box.

7. Click on Business Forms in the Template Group list.

8. Click on OK.

3500 Winchester Avenue
Longport, NJ 08403

November 16, 2002

Dear :

We regret to inform you that because you have not placed an order since we will no longer be able to extend you credit. Please call if you want to reinstate your account.

Sincerely,

FIGURE 8-4 Creating a template

Now let's add the prompts to the Credit Notice template you just created, using the following steps:

1. Click on the Build Prompts button in the feature bar to display the Prompt Builder dialog box.

   We'll start by entering codes that will insert the recipient's name and address from a list you select in the Address Book.

2. Click on Add in the Prompt Builder dialog box to display the Add Template Prompt dialog box.

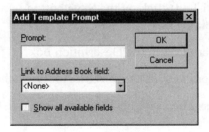

3. In the Prompt text box, type **Name of Recipient**, the prompt that you want to appear in the Template Information dialog box.

4. Pull down the Link to Address Book Field list. This displays a list of fields in the Address Book.

5. Scroll the list and click on Display Name and then on OK. When you use the template, WordPerfect 10 inserts the name from a listing you will select into this prompt in the dialog box, and then into the template.

6. Click on Add in the Prompt Builder dialog box.

7. Type **Address of Recipient**.

8. Pull down the Link to Address Book Field list.

9. Click on Street and then on OK.

10. Now using the same techniques, add fields for the recipient's city, state, ZIP code, and first name.

Next, add a field to prompt for information that you need to enter into the document:

1. Click on the Add button in the Prompt Builder dialog box.

2. Type **Date of Last Order**, and click on OK.

The prompts will appear in the Prompt Builder dialog box. When you use the template, the prompts will be listed in the Template Information dialog box in the order shown in the list. Use the Move Up and Move Down buttons to reposition a prompt by selecting the prompt you want to move and then clicking on the appropriate button.

Finally, you have to add codes into the document showing where the prompted information will be inserted. Drag the Prompt Builder dialog box out of the way, so you can see the inside address section of the letter. You can move back and forth between the document and the dialog box to insert codes. Follow these steps:

1. Place the insertion point in the second blank line under the date. If the insertion point is not at the left margin, pull down the Align Text button in the property bar, and click on Left.

2. Click on Name of Recipient in the Prompt Builder box.

3. Click on the Paste button in the Prompt Builder dialog box. The prompt appears as "[Name of Recipient]" in the template.

4. Place the insertion point in the blank line under the prompt you just added, inserting a blank line as needed.

5. Click on Address of Recipient in the Prompt Builder dialog box, and then on Paste.

6. In the same way, add the prompts for the city, state, ZIP code, recipient's first name, and the date of last order so they appear as shown in Figure 8-5. The last step is to add your name from the Personal Information listing in the Address Book.

7. Move the insertion point four lines under "Sincerely" in the document.

8. Click on Personal in the Prompt Builder dialog box to see the Personal Fields box.

9. Click on Display Name in the list and then on the Paste button in the dialog box. The notation "<Display Name>" appears in your template.

10. Click on Close to return to the Prompt Builder dialog box, and then click on OK.

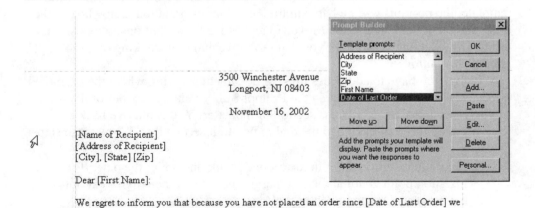

FIGURE 8-5   Prompts for template

When you use the new template, WordPerfect 10 will display the dialog box shown in Figure 8-3. Click on the Address Book icon next to Recipient Information, and then double-click on the listing for the recipient. The information from that listing appears in the appropriate sections of the dialog box. Type the date of the last order in the corresponding text box, and then click on OK. WordPerfect 10 will insert the information from the dialog box and your name from your personal listing into the document.

8

Chapter 9

Formatting Pages

P age formats affect the look of the entire page and even the entire document. They include setting the margins, changing page size, dividing the page into sections, and even printing labels and envelopes. In this chapter, you'll learn how to apply these and other page formats to enhance your documents. Remember, you can also use the Corel PerfectExpert to apply formats of all types.

> **TIP**   *You can access many formats from the Format Page toolbar. Right-click on a toolbar, and then select Format Page from the QuickMenu to display it.*

Entering Measurements

When you set margins, page sizes, indentations, and other settings in WordPerfect 10, you can type a measurement directly in a text box. WordPerfect 10 is set to use a certain unit of measurement. This means that if you just type a number in a text box, WordPerfect 10 assumes it is that set unit. So if your system is set to use inches, when you type **2** and move to another text box, WordPerfect 10 adds the inch marks and displays it as 2".

As you will learn in Chapter 11, however, the program can be set to use other units of measurement: millimeters, centimeters, points, and 1200ths of an inch. If your system is set for millimeters, for instance, and you do not type a unit following a number, WordPerfect 10 assumes it is in millimeters and will add the characters "mm" after the number.

You can always designate the unit following the number, using " or "i" for inches, "c" for centimeters, "mm" for millimeters, "p" for points, and "w" for 1200ths of an inch. Even if you designate the unit, however, WordPerfect 10 will always convert the amount to whatever unit your system is set for. So if your system is set to accept inches, and you type **50mm**, WordPerfect 10 converts it to 1.97".

In this and other chapters in this book, measurements are illustrated using inches expressed as decimal fractions. Just remember that you can use another unit of measurement instead.

Changing Margins

The top, bottom, left, and right margins determine how much text you can fit on a page. The left and right margins determine the length of the lines; the top and bottom margins determine the number of lines that fit on the page. All of the margins are set at one inch by default.

In most other word processing programs, the margins affect the entire page, if not the entire document. WordPerfect 10 is more flexible. When you change margins, WordPerfect 10 inserts a code at the beginning of the paragraph at the insertion point. The change affects only text starting at that location, up to the next margin code. This means that you can use the left margin to indent the entire page, or just individual or selected paragraphs. The margin command can serve as another way to indent text.

The advantage of using the margin command is that it is not canceled when you press ENTER, as are indentations. You can also see the spacing onscreen because the margin guidelines show you the reset position, as shown in Figure 9-1. Indentations, on the other hand, only affect the current paragraph.

The quickest way to change the page margins is to use the guidelines or the margin indicators in the ruler. To use the guidelines for the top and bottom margins, you must be in Page or Two-Page view; otherwise, those guidelines do not appear on the screen.

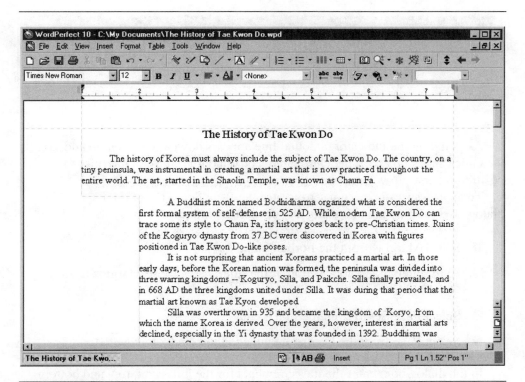

FIGURE 9-1 Margins are indicated by guidelines

The margin guidelines are the dotted lines around the page. If the guidelines are not displayed, use these steps:

1. Select Guidelines from the View menu.

2. Check the Margins option in the dialog box that appears. Also, make sure that the option Drag to Move Guidelines is turned on.

3. Click on OK.

When you point to a margin guideline, the mouse pointer is shaped like a two-headed arrow. As you drag a guideline, WordPerfect 10 displays a QuickStatus box showing the margin position. Release the mouse when the margin is where you want it.

You can also set the margins using the ruler—drag the left or right margin indicators to the desired position:

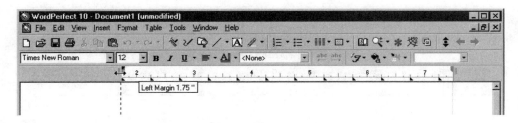

As you drag the indicator, a dotted line appears down the screen, in addition to the QuickStatus box. Use the QuickStatus box and markings on the ruler to position the margin where desired.

To enter a specific margin setting, use the Page Setup tab of the Page Setup dialog box. Display the box using any of these techniques:

■ Select Margins from the Format menu.

■ Right-click on the top section of the ruler, and choose Margins from the QuickMenu.

■ Select Page Setup from the File menu.

■ Select Page from the Format menu, and then click on Page Setup.

In the dialog box, enter the measurements for the left, right, top, and bottom margins. To make all of the margins the same size, enter the measure for any of the margins, then click on the Equal button in the dialog box. Click on the Minimum button to quickly set all of the margins to the smallest allowed by your printer. Click on OK to close the dialog box.

Formatting Pages for Books

Pages that are destined to be bound—if only in a three-ring binder—present some additional formatting opportunities. In most cases, the binding takes up some of the space on each page. In a ring binder, for example, some space is taken up by the punched holes. This space is called the *binding width* or *printing offset*. You have to decide which side of the page the printing offset is to be located, and the amount of the offset. How you lay out a page for binding depends on whether you are printing one side or both sides of the page, but it's all done using the Layout page of the Page Setup dialog box, shown in Figure 9-2.

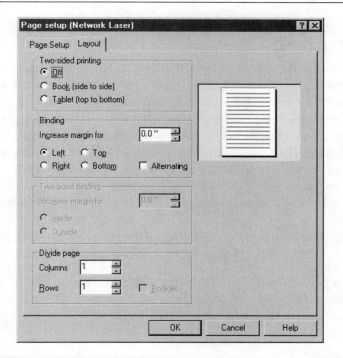

FIGURE 9-2   Layout options

Binding Single-Sided Pages

To set the printing offset when you are binding one-sided pages, display the Layout page of the Page Setup dialog box—File | Page Setup | Layout. Then follow these steps:

1. Make sure the Off option button is selected in the Two-Sided Printing section of the dialog box.

2. In the Binding section of the dialog box, choose the edge of the paper to which you want the extra space added: Left, Right, Top, or Bottom.

3. Enter the amount of the printing offset in the text box. If you are binding pages as a booklet, for example, choose the Left edge. If you want to turn over the pages like a flip chart, choose the Top edge.

4. Turn on the Alternating checkbox if you want the edge to alternate between odd and even pages.

Duplex Printing

You can save a lot of money on paper, binding, and mailing costs by *duplex printing*—printing on both sides of the paper. The more expensive duplex printers have this capability built in by printing on both sides of the paper at the same time.

Most of us probably do not have duplex printers; ours can only print on one side at a time. You can still print on both sides of the paper, but you have to use the two-step manual process. With this method, WordPerfect 10 first prints all the odd-numbered pages. You then reinsert the pages, and WordPerfect 10 prints the even-numbered pages on the other side of the sheets.

To use the two-step manual method of duplex printing, do the following:

1. Set up the pages for any extra binding area as you learned in Binding Single-Sided Pages. Choose the Alternating option in the Binding section.

2. When you are ready to print the document, select File | Print, and click on the Layout tab and look at the Two-sided Printing options.

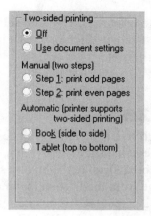

3. Click on the Step 1: Print odd pages button.

4. Click on Print. WordPerfect 10 prints just the odd-numbered pages.

Now comes the critical step. You have to reinsert the same pages so they will be printed on the blank side, and so the top of the pages are in the proper position. It may take you a few tries to get it just right.

1. Display the Layout tab of the Print dialog box again, and click on the Step 2: Print even pages option.

2. Click on Print to complete the document.

If you're lucky enough to have a duplex printer, then you don't have to manually feed in the pages. With duplex printers, there are two ways to print on both sides.

Display the Layout page of the Page Setup dialog box. In the Two-Sided Printing section of the dialog box, select how you plan to turn over the pages: either as a Book or Tablet. Then in the Two-sided binding section of the dialog box, select either Inside or Outside, and then enter the amount of the printing offset. When you are ready to print the document, choose Use Document Settings in the Layout tab of the Print dialog box.

■ Set up the pages for any extra binding area as you learned in Binding Single-Sided Pages. Choose the Alternating option in the Binding section.

When you are ready to print the document, select File | Print, and click on the Layout tab. Choose either Book or Tablet in the Two-sided section of the page and then click Print.

Changing Page Size

WordPerfect 10's default page size is 8 1/2 x 11 inches. To use a different page size, such as legal paper or personal stationery, you have to display the Page Setup tab of the Page Setup dialog box. Display the box by selecting Page Setup from the File menu, or choose Page from the Format menu and then Page Setup. The page size options are shown in Figure 9-3. The dialog box lists the standard forms — the most commonly used page sizes that WordPerfect 10 has set for your printer. To display all of the possible page sizes for your printer, click the Display Printer/Standard Forms button.

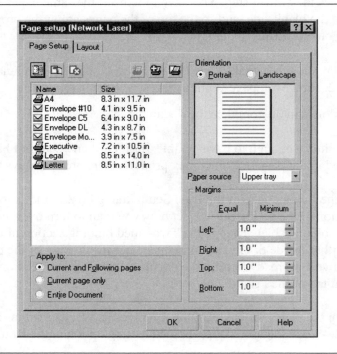

FIGURE 9-3   Changing the page size

To see the orientation of a page size, click on the page size in the list, then see which orientation option button is selected. In *landscape* orientation, your lines print across the wider dimension of the page, which is useful for wide tables and graphics. In *portrait* orientation, your lines of text print across the narrow dimension of the page. Select the orientation desired.

> **NOTE** *Some page sizes are available in only one orientation.*

You can also choose the source of the paper. Many printers have several input areas or paper trays. You may use one tray to hold letter-sized paper, another for envelopes or legal paper.

Choosing a page size inserts a code at the beginning of the page at the insertion point. It affects every page from that point to the end of the document or until another page size code appears. To use the same page size for an entire document, place the insertion point at the start of the document before selecting a page size. You can also override the codes on following pages by choosing the Current and Following pages, the Current Page Only, or the Entire Document options in the Apply To section of the box. For example, follow these steps to change to landscape orientation on 8 1/2 x 14-inch paper:

1. Place the insertion point at the start of the existing document, or start a new document.

2. Pull down the File menu, and click on Page Setup.

3. Click on the Page Setup tab if it is not already displayed.

4. Click on Legal 8.5 in x 14.0 in in the list of page sizes.

5. Click on the Landscape option button.

6. Click on OK.

> **NOTE** *Changing the page size does not affect the margins. If you choose a small-sized paper, make certain the default margins are still suitable.*

If you want different sizes of margins on various pages of your document, just go to the top of the page you want to change and make your settings. Choose Current Page Only in the Apply To section.

For example, suppose you want to use letterhead paper for the first page of a document but blank paper for all following pages. You'll need to set up your document in this way:

At the top of the first page, open the Page Setup dialog box and set the top margin large enough to accommodate the pre-printed letterhead. In the Paper Source list, choose the location where you will insert the letterhead paper. For example, choose Single Sheet if you want to insert the page in your printer's manual input slot. It doesn't matter what you select in the Apply To section because you'll be inserting a new page code at the start of the second page.

At the start of the second page, open the Page Setup dialog box and set the top margin to one inch. Change the Paper Source setting to Auto Select or the bin in which your blank paper is stored.

Custom Page Sizes

The page sizes available in WordPerfect 10 should be appropriate for most situations. If you need to use a paper size that is not already defined, you can create your own. Get a sample of the paper, and carefully measure its length and width. Decide if you want to print in portrait or landscape orientation, and then follow these steps:

1. Pull down the File menu, and click on Page Setup.

2. Click on the Page Setup tab, if it is not already shown.

3. Click the Add a new form button, the leftmost button above the page size list, to see the dialog box in Figure 9-4.

4. In the Name text box, type a descriptive name for the paper. Include the word "landscape" if you plan to set it up for landscape orientation. This isn't necessary, but it serves as a reminder to help you select the correct paper size later on.

5. Choose a type from the Type list. This also is not critical, but it will help you identify the paper later on.

6. Scroll the Size list, and click on User Defined Size. To see additional page size options, click on All Printers in the Show Page Size For section at the bottom of the dialog box.

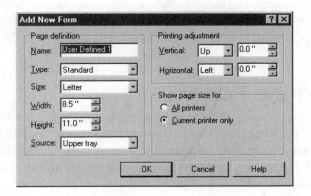

FIGURE 9-4 Add New Form dialog box

7. Enter the width of the page in the Width text box, and enter the height in the Height box.

8. Pull down the Source list, and choose where you feed the paper. The options in the list are determined by your printer. With laser printers, for example, you can usually choose from Paper Bin and Single Sheet. Select Single Sheet if you plan to insert the sheets yourself in the manual input tray.

9. Select OK to return to the Page Setup dialog box.

Your custom page size should print correctly. However, in a few rare cases, the first line of text may not print in the expected location. Something about your printer or paper may cause the first line of text to print at some location other than the top margin, or the left edge of lines to not align with the left margin. If this occurs, you have to set the Vertical and Horizontal settings in the Printing Adjustment section of the Add New Form dialog box.

The setting in the Vertical option determines the distance of the first line of text from the top edge of the page. You can choose to move the first line up or down, and you can designate the distance to move it. So if your text always prints 1/8 inch too high, choose Up, and enter **.125**. The Horizontal setting adjusts the distance of the left margin from the left edge of the page. Choose Left or Right, and enter the measurement to move the text.

If you've already created the page size, click on the page size in the Page Setup tab of the dialog box, then click the Edit form button. To delete a page size, select it in the list and click the Delete form button. If you delete a built-in page size by mistake, click the Regenerate Standard Forms button or the Regenerate Printer Forms button, depending on the type of form that you deleted.

Subdividing the Page

There are occasions when you want to print small documents, such as tickets, announcements, or envelope stuffers. These documents are usually too small to feed through your printer. One solution is to print one on each regular-sized sheet and then cut off and throw away the waste. A more economical choice is to print several of the items on one sheet of paper and then cut them apart.

If the paper size you want is close to some even portion of a page, such as one-half, one-quarter, or one-sixth of a sheet, then you can subdivide the page. This creates more than one logical page on the physical sheet. WordPerfect 10 treats each logical page as a separate sheet of paper for page numbering, headers and footers, and other page elements. When you press CTRL-ENTER with a subdivided page, for example, WordPerfect 10 inserts a page break. However, WordPerfect 10 moves the insertion point to the next logical page on the sheet and starts a new sheet only when all of the logical pages have been used on the physical page.

To subdivide a page, specify the number of rows and columns you want the page divided into. You do not have to worry about specifying their exact width and height.

To subdivide a page, display the Layout page of the Page Setup dialog box. Set the number of columns and rows of logical pages in the Divide Page section

Click on OK. Your screen will appear as in Figure 9-5, with the logical page size shown. When you press CTRL-ENTER to end one logical page and start the next one, WordPerfect 10 displays a new logical page on the screen, in the position it will print on the page. You can also press ALT-PGDN or ALT-PGUP to move to the next or previous logical page.

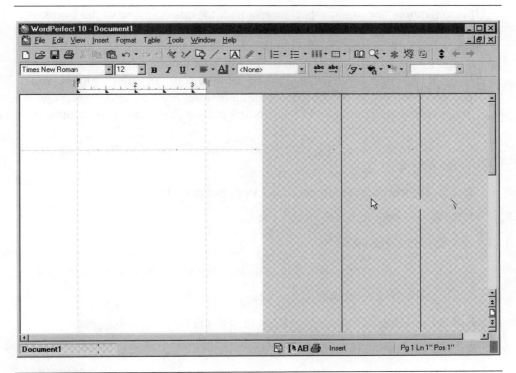

FIGURE 9-5   Subdivided page

As with changing page size, subdividing the page does not automatically change the margins. If you create a small logical page, the default one-inch margins may be too large. If you are in Page view, you'll be able to see right away the actual area in which you can enter text on the page, and whether you have to change the margins.

Printing Booklets

One of the best examples of using a subdivided page is printing booklets. Picture a booklet as a document with two logical pages on each side of a sheet of paper, printed in landscape orientation. You print on both sides of the page, and then fold the sheet in half for four pages on each sheet. Creating a booklet requires a landscape orientation and a subdivided page.

It also requires one other important element, the correct order of the pages. If you just typed the pages of a four-page booklet in the order 1-2-3-4, the pages would not be in the correct order when printed. Depending on how you folded the sheet, either page 2 or 4 would be on the cover, with pages 1 and 2, or 3 and 4 on the inside. Rather than try to arrange the pages in the correct order yourself, you can turn on WordPerfect 10's booklet printing feature. Start by selecting a page size in landscape orientation and then subdividing the page into two columns.

1. If you already typed the text, move the insertion point to the start of the document.

2. Display the Page Setup tab of the Page Setup dialog box.

3. Choose Letter in the page size list.

4. Click on Landscape.

5. Set all of the margins to 0.5 inch to accommodate the smaller paper size.

6. Click on the Layout tab.

7. Set the number of columns to 2 in the Divide Page section.

8. Select the Booklet check box.

9. Click OK.

10. Click on Print to print the document.

WordPerfect 10 organizes the pages in the correct order, and then prints the first sides of all of the pages. It then displays a message telling you to reinsert the paper to print on the other side. Insert the pages so the blank side will be printed on, in the correct position, and then click on OK in the message box. Fold the pages in half, and you have a booklet.

 If the document does not print correctly, print it manually using the Duplex Printing method described previously.

If you have a duplex printer, you can print both sides at the same time using the Document Settings option.

Title Pages

A title page usually contains text that is centered both horizontally and vertically on the page. Following the title page is the first page of the document. You could create the title page manually by pressing ENTER until the text appears to be centered. However, all of these extra carriage returns could be a problem if you later insert or delete text. So rather than center the page manually, let WordPerfect 10 do it for you.

To center the text vertically on the page, use these steps:

1. Select Page from the Format menu, and click on Center to display the Center Page(s) dialog box.

2. Select Current Page to center only the page at the insertion point, or Current and Subsequent Pages to center all of the pages.

3. Click on OK.

To also center the text between the left and right margins, use the line center or justification center formats.

If you want to later remove the centering, display the Center Page(s) dialog box, and click on No Centering.

Enclosing the Page in a Border

In Chapter 7, you learned how to use the Border/Fill command to enclose text in a border and to add a shaded background. You can also enclose the entire page in a border and even select from decorative borders of graphic and fancy lines.

To add a page border, place the insertion point in the page, select Page from the Format menu, and click Border/Fill to display the dialog box shown in Figure 9-6. There are two general border types, Fancy and Line. Fancy borders use graphic images and clip art, while Line borders use one or more straight lines of various thickness and shades.

If you select the Line type, you'll display the same options that were available for paragraph borders, but the border will surround the whole page. You can also choose to apply the border to just the current page, the default value.

TIP *Deselect the Apply Border to Current Page Only checkbox to apply the border to all of the pages in the document.*

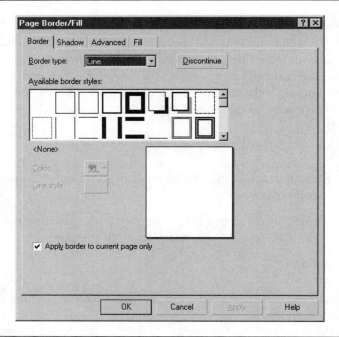

FIGURE 9-6 Adding a page border

Some of the Fancy styles are quite decorative, and many are in color if you have a color printer. When you select a style, a sample of it appears in the preview area, and the name of the file storing the graphic is shown under the list box.

Use the Fill, Advanced, and Shadow pages of the dialog box to add a fill color or pattern, or a drop shadow. The Fill and Advanced page of the dialog box is not available for Fancy borders.

Decorating Pages with Watermarks

A *watermark* is a graphic image or text that appears in the background of the page. It prints in a light shade of gray, so you can see it and still read the text in the foreground. Watermarks are useful to display your company logo or even an advertisement or other message, such as the word "Draft" or "Confidential."

You can have up to two watermarks on one page. WordPerfect 10 automatically inserts the watermark on all subsequent pages, but you can discontinue it when you no longer want the watermark to appear. You can also change the watermark at any time, so every page could have two different watermarks.

Integrate It! You can create a drawing in Corel Presentations and open it as an image to use as a watermark in WordPerfect 10.

Watermarks appear onscreen only in Page and Two-Page views, so change to one of these views before starting these steps:

1. Choose Watermark from the Insert menu. (In Page view, you can also right-click in the top or bottom margin area and select Watermark from the QuickMenu.) A dialog box appears where you can select either Watermark A or Watermark B, the two watermarks for the page. Choose either of these, and then click on Create. WordPerfect 10 changes to a full-page display and shows the special property bar, as in Figure 9-7.

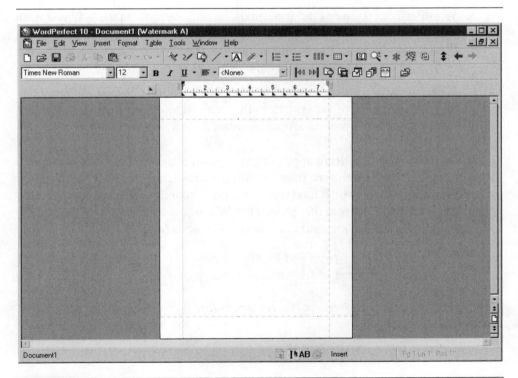

FIGURE 9-7   Creating a watermark

2. If you want the watermark to be text, move the insertion point to where you want the text to appear. You can just click in the spot using the shadow cursor, or choose to center it in the page as you learned for creating a title page. If you do use the center page option in this view, only the watermark will be affected, not the regular text on the page.

> **NOTE** *You'll learn how to add graphics to the watermark in Chapter 13.*

3. To use an existing document as the watermark, click on the Insert File button in the property bar, and choose the document file from the dialog box that appears.

4. WordPerfect 10 watermarks appear in a 25 percent shade—that is, 25 percent of the density of a solid color. To make the watermark either lighter or darker, click on the Watermark Shading button in the property bar, and then enter a percentage.

5. WordPerfect 10 repeats the watermark on all subsequent pages. If you want a watermark to repeat on just odd or even pages, click on the Watermark Placement button on the property bar, and choose Odd Pages, Even Pages, or Every Page from the box that appears.

6. When the watermark appears as you want it, click on Close in the property bar. To add a second watermark to the same page, repeat the procedure but choose the other watermark option, either A or B.

To stop the watermark from appearing on a page, place the insertion point on the page, and choose Watermark from the Insert menu. Click on the watermark you want to stop, either A or B, and then click on Discontinue. To use a different watermark on the page, repeat this procedure. When you create a new watermark for a page, it replaces the one continued from a previous page.

You can use the Next and Previous buttons on the watermark feature bar to display the watermarks on other pages.

> **TIP** *Use the Edit button in the Watermark dialog box to change the watermark.*

Using Headers and Footers

Pages of a long document can easily get separated. They can get out of order or be misplaced, or one page may get stuck in the copying machine and never make it into the document at all. Headers and footers help to identify the pages of your document, as well as the document itself, and they can even create pleasing visual effects that grab and hold the reader's attention. A *header* is text or a graphic that prints at the top of every page. A *footer* is text or a graphic that prints at the bottom of every page. Two common uses of a header or footer are to number pages and to repeat the document's title on each page.

You create headers and footers in much the same way as a watermark. Each page can have up to two headers and two footers, and you can repeat them on every page, or just on odd or just on even pages. You can discontinue headers or footers when you want, or change headers or footers so each page can have different ones.

To create a header or footer, follow these instructions:

1. Place the insertion point on the first page you want to contain the header or footer.

2. Choose Header/Footer from the Insert menu. (In Page view, you can also right-click in the top or bottom margin area and select Header/Footer from the QuickMenu.)

3. Select Header A, or Header B to insert a header, or Footer A or Footer B to insert a footer, and click on Create to see the property bar shown here:

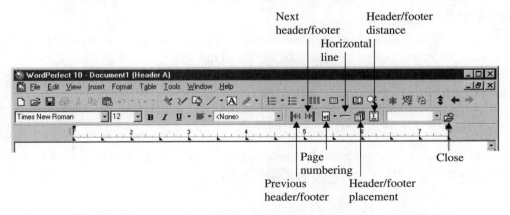

4. Enter the text of the header or footer, using the property bar or menus to format it.

5. Click on the Horizontal Line button to insert a horizontal line across the page.

6. Use the Header/Footer Placement button to select even pages, odd pages, or every page. If you are using two headers or two footers on the same page, however, coordinate them so they do not overlap.

7. By default, WordPerfect 10 leaves 0.17 inch, about one line, between the document text and the header and footer. To change the distance, click on the Header/Footer Distance button, and enter the measurement in the box that appears.

8. To number pages in a header or footer, place the insertion point where you want the number to appear, pull down the Page Numbering button in the property bar, and click on Page Number. You can also select Total Pages to display the number of pages, such as "Page 1 of 5."

9. To align text on the right of the header, select Flush Right from the Format | Line menu.

10. Click on the Close button in the property bar to return to the document.

 Remember, you can use the Insert Date/Time command to display the date or time in the header, or Insert Other to include the filename.

Page Numbers

You can also number pages without using a header or footer. The Page Numbers command actually gives you great flexibility in numbering, since you can choose the number style and position, and you can even number using chapters and volumes. You can number every page of your document consecutively, use sections to start with page 1 at the beginning of every chapter, or use Roman numerals for a table of contents and index.

 If you use page numbers, headers, and footers at the same time, make sure the numbers do not overlap.

Select Page from the Format menu, and then click on Numbering to see the dialog box shown in Figure 9-8.

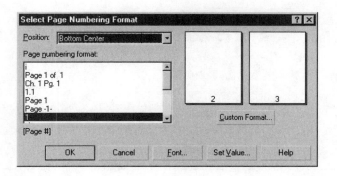

FIGURE 9-8   Adding page numbers

Pull down the Position list box, and select a position. The options are no page numbering; top left, top center, and top right; top outside alternating and top inside alternating; bottom left, bottom center, and bottom right; and bottom outside alternating and bottom inside alternating. Your choice is reflected in the preview area.

Next, select a format. By default, an Arabic page number appears by itself, but you can choose other options:

- Change to letters or Roman numerals

- Include the word "Page"

- Include the total number of pages, as in "Page 1 of 10"

The page number will appear in the default document font. To change the font, size, or character style, click on the Font button, and make your selections from the dialog box that appears.

You can also change the page number itself. For example, suppose you created a long report in a number of documents. You already printed the first document, with the pages numbered 1 through 10. Before printing the second document, you need to change the page number of the first page to 11, so its pages will be numbered consecutively from there.

To change the number, click on the Set Value button to see the dialog box shown in Figure 9-9. Enter the number you want for the page in the Set Page Number box, or optionally change the chapter, volume, or secondary page numbers. You always set the number using Arabic numbers, regardless of the

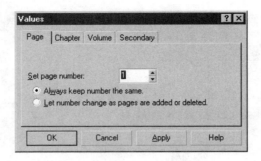

FIGURE 9-9 Setting the page number

number format. Enter **5**, for example, if you are using Roman numerals and want to number the page as V.

To set a new page number without placing the number on the page, select No Page Numbering from the Position list.

If you want to add your own text to a page number, then click on the Custom Format button in the Select Page Numbering Position dialog box. A dialog box is displayed with a text box labeled "Custom page numbering format," with the code [Page #] that represents the number. Add your text, such as "Senate Report, Page [Page #]".

To insert the page number once at the location of the insertion point in the document, select the format in the Custom Page Numbering box and click Insert in format.

Suppressing Page Elements

Many documents do not include headers, footers, or page numbers on title pages or cover letters. You may also want to turn off one of these elements on a specific page of the document. If you choose the Discontinue option for a header, footer, or watermark, however, it turns the feature off for all subsequent pages as well.

To suppress one of the elements from appearing on a page, choose Page from the Format menu, and then click on Suppress to see the Suppress dialog box shown next. Select the checkboxes for the items that you do not want to appear on the current page, or click on All to suppress all of them. If your page numbering is included in a header or footer, you can suppress the header or footer but number the page anyway by checking the Print Page Number at Bottom Center on Current Page option.

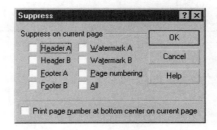

Delaying Codes

Normally, the page formats take effect on the page where you insert them. Using the Delay Codes command, you can specify that they take effect on another page. For example, suppose you plan to use letterhead paper for the first page and legal paper for the remaining pages. Rather than trying to remember to change page sizes when you start the second page, you can enter the legal size code at the beginning of the document and delay it one page.

Here's how you would format the pages that way:

1. Go to the start of a document that uses letter-sized paper.

2. Select Page from the Format menu, and click on Delay Codes. A dialog box appears asking how many pages you want the codes to be delayed.

3. Click on OK to accept the default setting of one page. You'll see the Define Delay Codes window with a feature bar and reveal codes area, as shown in Figure 9-10. You use the buttons in the feature bar to select the codes you want to delay. Notice you can delay when an inserted image appears and delay page size codes, headers and footers, and watermarks.

4. Click the Page Size button to display the Page Size tab of the Page Setup dialog box.

5. Pull down the Name list, and select Legal.

6. Click on OK to close the dialog box. The Paper Sz/Typ codes appear in the reveal codes area.

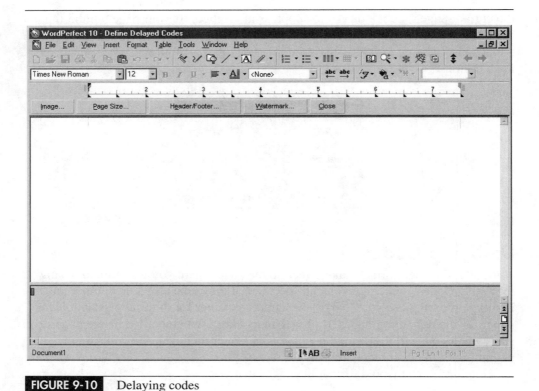

FIGURE 9-10   Delaying codes

7. Click on Close.

The second page of the document will now be formatted as legal size.

> **TIP** *Double-click on a code in the reveal codes area to display a dialog box for editing the code.*

Numbering Lines

Legal documents, such as contracts, pleadings, and depositions, often have line numbers down the left margin—so may printed copies of computer programs and macros. The numbers make it easy to reference a specific line in the document. If you did not have WordPerfect 10, you could try to type the numbers yourself, but fortunately, WordPerfect 10 can number lines automatically for you.

When you want to number lines, use these steps:

1. Select Line from the Format menu, and click on Numbering to see the dialog box in Figure 9-11.

2. Check the Turn Line Numbering On box to start line numbering.

3. Specify the numbering method or style, what number to begin counting from, the first line you want numbered, and the intervals of numbers. As you select options, the effects are displayed in the preview area.

4. By default, the numbers appear 0.6 inch from the left edge of the paper. You can adjust this measurement or set a distance relative to the margin.

5. You can specify whether to restart numbering on every page, count blank lines, or insert numbers when using columns.

6. Click on the Font button to change the font, size, and style of the numbers.

7. Click on OK.

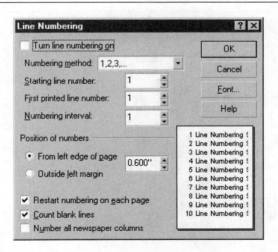

FIGURE 9-11   Line numbering

Making Text Fit

You can adjust the margins, fonts, and font size to fit text into fewer or more pages. If one or two lines of text spill over into a page, for example, you can try a slightly smaller top or bottom margin for the entire document. You can also have WordPerfect 10 try to make the text fit for you. To fit a selected portion of text into an area, select the text first. Otherwise, WordPerfect 10 adjusts the entire document. Then follow these steps:

1. Click on the Make It Fit option from the Format menu to see the dialog box shown in Figure 9-12.

2. Specify the number of pages that you want the text to fit in.

3. Select the items that WordPerfect 10 can modify to adjust the text. By default, for example, WordPerfect 10 changes only the font size and line spacing. If you want WordPerfect 10 to adjust only the margins, deselect the Font Size and Line Spacing boxes, and select the margins that you want WordPerfect 10 to adjust.

4. Click on Make It Fit to adjust the text.

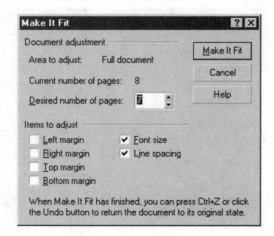

FIGURE 9-12   Making text fit in a specific space

The number of pages you set must be within 50 percent of the document's current size.

If you want to make just a certain portion of the document fit in a specific space, select that portion before opening the Make It Fit dialog box. The top margin and bottom margin options will be dimmed in the dialog box, but you'll still be able to adjust the left and right margins, font size, and line spacing.

Hyperlinks

You learned in Chapter 3 to create hyperlinks for Web pages. You can use the same handy tools in any document to move quickly from one location to another. Start by creating a bookmark at the location where you want to jump. You can use the Bookmark option from the Tools menu, or select the text, click on the Hyperlink button in the Property bar, and click on Insert Bookmark.

Once the bookmark is set, move to the location that you want to use as the link. Type, format, and select the text you want to use as the link, click on the Hyperlink button in the Property bar, and choose Create Link to display the dialog box shown next:

Hyperlink Properties	? ×
Define links to other documents or bookmarks in this or other documents. Or, define a macro to be executed when the user clicks on the link.	

Document/Macro: `<current document>`   Browse Web...

Bookmark:

Target frame:

OK   Cancel   Help

Select the bookmark in the current document that you want to jump to, or choose another document to open. You can also click on Browse Web to launch your Web browser and select a Web site to jump to.

Click on the link to move to the bookmark, open the document, or jump to the Web site.

Formatting and Printing Envelopes

An envelope is just another page size, but formatting and printing envelopes can often be intimidating. WordPerfect 10 makes it easy, however, because it provides a built-in envelope feature that not only selects the correct page size, but can also automatically insert the return address, mailing address, and POSTNET bar code for you.

Some printers have an alternate input tray, or a switch or knob, that allows you to feed envelopes and other types of paper straight through the printer to avoid wrinkling. The glue on some envelopes may become sticky when fed through a laser printer—open the flap immediately after the envelope is printed.

Envelope Page Size

To use the envelope feature, you must define an envelope page size. Chances are there is one for your printer, but check ahead of time, anyway. Select Page Setup from the File menu. In the list on the Page Setup tab of the dialog box, look for the item Envelope #10 4.1 in x 9.5 in—the standard business envelope for letter-sized paper.

If it is not listed, create the page size as explained earlier in this chapter. Use a width of 4.13" and a height of 9.5", and then select the envelope type. If you have a laser or inkjet printer, choose landscape orientation. Unless you have an envelope feeder, choose Envelope Manual as the paper source.

If Envelope Manual is not an option, choose Single Sheet.

Creating an Envelope

You can format and print just an envelope or print an envelope for a letter or other document already on the screen. Here is all you have to do, for example, to create an envelope for a letter:

1. Select the recipient's address. If you just need to print a quick envelope by itself, start with a blank document screen.

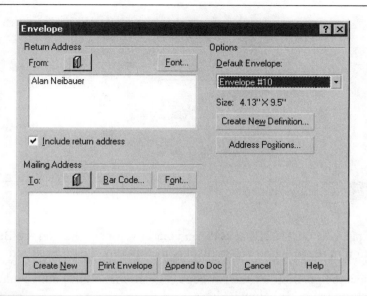

FIGURE 9-13 Creating an envelope

2. Choose Envelope from the Format menu to open the dialog box shown in Figure 9-13. (If you have not yet specified your personal information as part of the template feature, you will be prompter to at this point.)

3. If you selected the inside address of a letter, it automatically appears in the mailing addresses section. Otherwise, click in the section and type the address. You can also click on the Address Book button in the Mailing Address section button in the property bar and select Address Book to choose an address from the CorelCENTRAL address book.

4. To include your return address on the envelope, enter it in the return address section. You can also click on the Address Book button in the Return Address Book to choose an address from the CorelCENTRAL address book. Deselect the Include Return Address check box if you do not want it printed on the envelope

5. Pull down the Default Envelope list and choose the envelope size. Use the Create New Definition button if your envelope size is not shown.

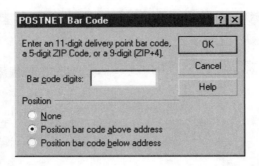

FIGURE 9-14 Creating a bar code

6. To print a POSTNET bar code on your envelopes, click on the Bar Code button in the property bar to display the options shown in Figure 9-14.

7. Select the position for the bar code—Position bar code above address, or Position bar code below address.

8. Enter the ZIP code in the Bar Code Digits box and click OK.

9. Now select one of these options:

   ■ Create New – inserts the envelope into a new document

   ■ Print Envelope – prints the envelope immediately

   ■ Append to Doc – adds the envelope to the end of the current document

10. If you selected either Create New or Append to Doc, you'll see your envelope on screen, as shown in Figure 9-15. The page has two address sections: the return address in the upper-left corner and the mailing address. The property bar now includes these buttons:

    ■ Return Address lets you select an address from the address book, or choose to print no return address on the envelope.

    ■ Mailing Address lets you choose the recipient's address.

    ■ Bar Code lets you add a POSTNET bar code.

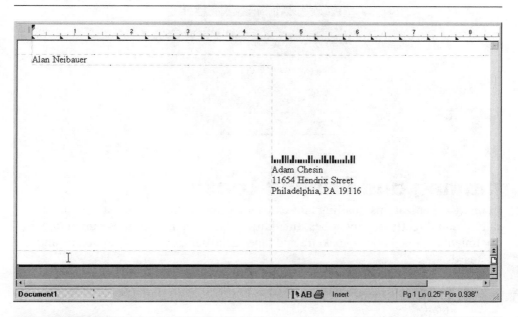

9

FIGURE 9-15   Envelope document

- Envelope Positions lets you adjust the position of the return and mailing addresses.

- Envelope Size lets you select another define envelope size or create a new one.

- Print Current Envelope prints the envelope as it appears.

Changing the Position of Addresses

WordPerfect 10 prints the return and mailing addresses at the customary positions for the size envelope you selected. You can adjust the position if it is incorrect, or if you just want to change it. Click on the Address Positions button in the Envelope dialog box to see the Envelope Positions dialog box shown next. Then adjust the From Left and From Top settings in the Return Address Position and Mailing Address Position sections:

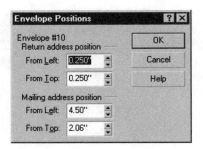

Formatting and Printing Labels

In many organizations, mailing addresses are printed almost exclusively on labels rather than directly on envelopes. In addition, labels can be used for any number of documents: name badges, diskette and tape identifiers, even business cards and postcards.

In Chapter 12 you will create a data file for labels and learn how to sort labels.

It is easy to format and print labels because WordPerfect 10 includes page definitions for the most popular sizes of labels made by major label companies, such as Avery. If you have labels from another manufacturer, you can probably find a compatible Avery number. You can also define your own label size when you cannot find a match.

You should work with labels in Page view so you can see the arrangement of labels on the page.

To format labels, use these steps:

1. Choose Labels from the Format menu to see the dialog box shown in Figure 9-16. WordPerfect 10 classifies labels as either Laser Printed, which come on individual sheets of paper, or Tractor-fed, which are continuous pages for use with dot-matrix printers. The Labels list shows all of the predefined labels, but you can click on either Laser Printed or Tractor-fed to display just that category.

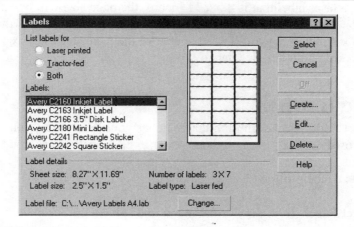

FIGURE 9-16 Formatting labels

2. Scroll the Labels list, and click on the label that matches yours. The specifications for the label are shown in the Label Details section, and its layout appears in the preview area. If none of the specifications match your labels, try another selection from the list.

3. When you find the correct label, click on Select.

NOTE *WordPerfect includes a number of label definition files, each containing labels from popular manufacturers. To select another file, click Change and choose the file from the list that appears.*

If you are in Page view, you'll see one label on the screen. Some of the label definitions do not include margins, so you should set margins yourself to avoid printing in unprintable areas. Type the address or other information you want on the label, and then press CTRL-ENTER. WordPerfect 10 displays the next blank label in the same layout as on the page. WordPerfect 10 completes each row of labels before starting another row. In Draft view, labels always appear one below the other, separated with page break lines.

If you want to stop using the label format in the document, select Labels from the Format menu, and then click Off in the Labels dialog box. WordPerfect 10 adds enough blank labels to fill out the current page and then starts a new page. The page will be the same size as the label carrier sheet that you turned off. If you're using a laser label that is 8.5 x 11 inches, the page size will be 8.5 x 11 inches. If you are using what's referred to as a "half-size label sheet," the page size will be 4.25 x 5 inches, so you'll need to change the page size to 8.5 x 11 inches to continue working on letter-size paper.

Defining a Label

If you cannot find a label definition that matches your label stock, you can easily create your own definition. It will then appear in the Labels list so you can select it when needed.

To create a label, follow these steps:

1. Select Labels from the Format menu to display the Labels dialog box. If there is a label close in specifications to the label you are using, select it on the list. This will serve as the starting point for your own label, and you won't have to enter the elements matching the specifications. If you have a half-sheet laser label, for example, select another half-sheet label from the list. At least that way you won't have to enter the page sizes.

2. Click on the Create button to see the dialog box shown in Figure 9-17. Start by entering the Label Description. This will be the name that appears in the Labels list, so make sure it describes the label.

> TIP *Labels are listed alphabetically, so to list a particular label at the top, start the description with a number.*

3. Make sure the size shown under Label Sheet Size is correct. If not, click on the Change button, which is dimmed until you enter a description, to display the Edit Page Size dialog box. Specify the sheet size and orientation, just as you did when creating a page size, and then click on OK.

4. Select the Label Type. This determines if the label will be listed with Laser Printed labels, Tractor-fed labels, or both.

5. Finally, enter the measurements that describe the label. Remember, you can enter measurements in inches, points, millimeters, centimeters, or even 1200ths of an inch.

WordPerfect 10 changes the preview of the label as soon as you enter a measurement, assuming the default is inches. So if you type **5** in the width box, for

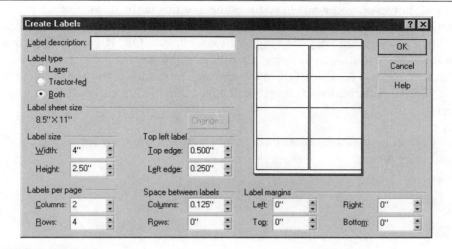

FIGURE 9-17 Creating a label definition

example, the preview label widens to show five inches. Once you enter "p" or "m," the size adjusts to the actual measurement, so don't panic if your 50 millimeter labels start to appear wider than the page.

Try to be as accurate as possible with the measurements—you might even find them on the label box.

In the Label Size section, enter the width and height of the labels themselves, not including any space between labels or any margins between the labels and the edge of the carrier sheet. In the Labels Per Page section, specify the number of labels in each column and in each row. The product of those two numbers should equal the total number of labels on the page.

The Top Left Label section determines the exact position of the first label on the page. This tells WordPerfect 10 where the first line of text can be and sets up the spacing for the remainder of the labels. If this measurement is not correct, then all of the labels will be off. In the Top Edge box, enter the distance from the top of the page to the top of the first label. In the Left Edge box, enter the distance from the left edge of the page to the left edge of the label.

In the Space Between Labels section, enter any spacing between the rows and columns of labels. These are usually small measurements, so try to be precise.

The Label Margins section determines the margin areas within the label. Imagine it as the page margins for each individual label. The margins for most of WordPerfect 10's defined labels are set at zero. If you set a margin when defining the label, however, you won't have to set the margins in the document after selecting the label.

When you've completed the specifications, click on OK. If your settings create an impossible layout, such as more labels than will fit on the page, a dialog box appears telling you so. Click OK in the message box, and correct the problem. Once your label definition is complete, it appears in the Labels list for you to select.

> **NOTE** *You can define as many custom labels as you want, giving each its own name.*

Try It Out

Now it is time to try out your WordPerfect page formatting skills. In this section, we'll create a folded card like you'd use for an invitation or greeting. We'll use a letter-sized sheet, folded in half, so in two-page view, the document will appear as shown in Figure 9-18.

1. Select Page Setup from the File menu.

2. Set all of the margins to .5 inches. The smaller margins are more appropriate for the eventual "page size" of 8.5 by 5.5 inches.

3. Click on the Layout tab.

4. Set the Rows to 2 in the Divide Page section.

5. Click OK.

6. The cover of the greeting is actually on the bottom half of the first side, so press CTRL+ENTER to go to the bottom half of that page.

7. Select Format | Page | Center.

8. Select Current Page and click OK.

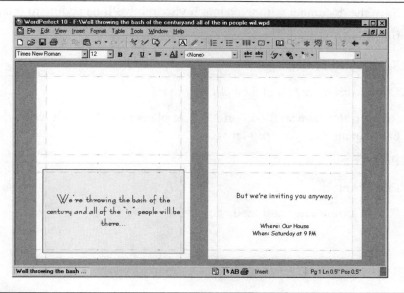

FIGURE 9-18   Invitation using a divided page

9. Select Center from the Justification list on the Property Bar.

10. Enter the following:

    We're throwing the bash of the century and all of the "in" people will be there...

11. Select the text and choose a font and a font size that you like.

12. Select Format | Page | Border/Fill.

13. Select a border option and click OK.

14. Make sure the insertion point is at the end of the text on the page and press CTRL+ENTER twice.

15. Change the font size to 22, press Enter three times and enter:

    But we're inviting you anyway.

    Place: Our House

    When: Saturday at 9 PM

16. Save the document with the name Invitation; we'll be adding to it later.

17. Press CTRL+HOME to go to the start of the document.

18. Select File | Print

19. Click Current Page and then click Print

20. Reinsert the page so it will print on the blank side. You'll have to experiment with your printer.

21. Press PGDN twice

22. File | Print

23. Click Current Page and then click Print

Chapter 10

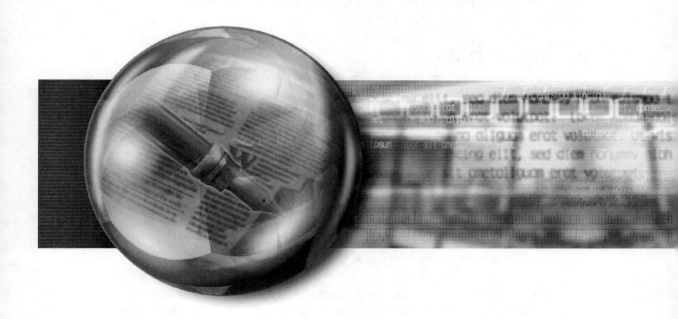

Using Tables, Columns, and Other Formats

319

Numbers and text sometimes look best when they are neatly arranged in columns. Numbers formatted into a table are easy to read and can show relationships and trends that cannot easily be expressed in text. Text formatted in columns makes newsletters look professional and can enhance almost any document. In this chapter, you will learn how to create tables and columns, as well as insert footnotes and endnotes into a document. You'll also learn how to create an index, table of contents, table of authorities, and cross-references.

Creating Tables

A table lets you enter text in neatly arranged rows and columns, just as you would in Quattro Pro 10. By adding a table to your WordPerfect 10 document, you can display columns of numbers to maximize their impact. You can create a table by left-clicking and dragging the mouse or by selecting from a dialog box.

 If you've already created a table as a Quattro Pro worksheet, don't duplicate your efforts. You can share the worksheet with a WordPerfect 10 document.

Building a Table

To create the table with the mouse, use the following steps:

1. Click and hold down the mouse button on the Table QuickCreate icon on the toolbar. A miniature grid appears representing the rows and columns of a table.

2. Hold down the mouse button, and drag down and to the right. As you drag, you select squares in the grid; the number of rows and columns is indicated at the top of the grid.

3. Drag the mouse until you select the number of rows and columns that you want in the table, and then release the mouse button.

Use this method to create a table with seven rows and five columns. WordPerfect 10 inserts a blank table with grid lines and displays a special Table property bar, as shown in Figure 10-1.

TIP   *You can add or delete rows and columns at any time.*

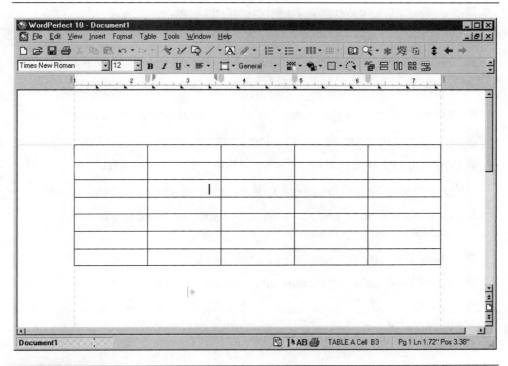

FIGURE 10-1   Table inserted into a WordPerfect document

The table extends from the left to the right margin, with equal-sized columns. As with a spreadsheet program, each cell in the table is referenced by its row and column numbers; for example, the upper-left cell is A1. The ruler, if it is displayed, shows the width of the cells, and the status bar shows the cell in which the insertion point is placed.

The Table property bar contains the first standard six buttons, as well as these features:

TIP   *The Table toolbar appears only when the insertion point is located in the table.*

■ *Vertical Alignment* lets you select the alignment of text in the cell in relation to the top and bottom lines. Use the Justification button as usual for left-to-right alignment.

- *Number Format* controls the way numbers appear.

- *Cell Fill* lets you add a fill pattern to cells.

- *Table Cell Foreground Fill Color* selects the fill color for the pattern.

- *Change Outside Lines* lets you customize the lines around the table cells.

- *Rotate Cell* rotates the contents of the cell 90-degrees counterclockwise.

- *QuickJoin* displays a tool for joining several cells into one larger cell.

- *QuickSplit Row* displays a tool for splitting a cell into two rows.

- *QuickSplit Column* displays a tool for splitting a cell into two columns.

- *QuickSplit Colums and Rows* displays a tool for splitting a cell into multiple rows and columns

- *Insert Row* inserts a row at the current location.

- *Select Table* selects the entire table, column, or row.

- *Formula Toolbar* displays an input bar and feature bar below the ruler. Use the input bar and feature bar to perform spreadsheet-like calculations on the cell contents.

- *QuickSum* computes and displays the total of the values in the table cells.

Depending on your screen resolution, you may have to scroll the property bar to display the tools on the far right of the table property bars. If a scroll bar does not appear on the far right of the property bar, follow these steps to display the scrollbar so you can access all of the buttons:

1. Select Settings from the Tools menu.

2. Click Customize.

3. Click on the Property Bars tab and click the Options button.

4. Select the Show scroll bar check box and click OK.

5. Click Close twice.

Creating Tables Using Other Methods

The largest table you can create with the mouse is 32 columns by 45 rows. To create a table with up to 64 columns and 32,767 rows, select Create from the Table menu to display the dialog box you see next. Enter the number of columns and rows desired in the appropriate text boxes, and then click on Create.

You can also use the Shadow Cursor to create a table. Click the mouse in any white space on the screen (where the shadow cursor appears), and then drag to form a box the width that you want the table. When you release the mouse, you'll see the options shown here. Click on Table to see the Create Table dialog box; then choose the number of columns and rows. The columns are sized to fit within the box, but the height automatically adjusts to fit in the rows you selected.

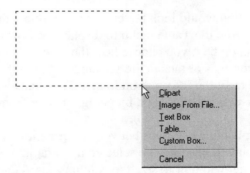

Another method is to select the Drag to Create a new table option in the Create Table dialog box. Specify the numbers of rows and columns that you would like to have in your table, select the Drag to Create a new table option and click OK.

Now drag the mouse to create your table. Again, the columns are sized to fit within the box, but the height automatically adjusts to fit in the rows you selected.

A table that you create using the Shadow Cursor or the Drag to Create feature is treated as a graphic object. You can change its size and position by dragging, just as you can for other graphic objects. You'll learn more about graphic objects in Chapter 13.

> **TIP** *Select the Drag to create checkbox in the Create Table dialog box to use Drag to Create for all tables. With this option, you'll need to Drag to Create the table whenever you use the Create Table dialog box or the Table button in the toolbar. The Drag to Create function stays on as long as the checkbox is marked.*

Converting Between Tables and Text

If you've already typed information in columns separated by tabs, you can automatically convert the text into a table. For example, suppose you had typed this text before reading this chapter:

Joan	President	$35.987	
Jane	Vice President		$31,998
Paul	Secretary	$21,500	
Ringo	Treasurer	$18,750	

Since the information would look better as a table, select the text, and then choose Create Table from the Table menu to display the Convert Text to Table dialog box. In this dialog box, you choose how the new table columns are to be created, such as by commas or tabs in the selected text, and if columns should be equal-width or sized to fit the information in them You can also choose to create a table based on a user-defined character, by paragraphs, or from a merge data file or parallel columns.

Because the sample table uses tabs between information in each line, you'd use the tabs option, which will probably be selected by default. You can also choose to create columns of equal width or to size the columns based on their contents. Finally, make sure that the number of columns shown in the dialog box is correct, and then click OK.

> **NOTE** *See Chapter 12 for more information about merging and merge data files.*

Entering Information into Tables

After you create the table, you are ready to enter text into it. To enter text, place the insertion point in a cell and type. You can place the insertion point by clicking in the cell, or by pressing TAB, SHIFT-TAB, or the arrow keys. If you type more text than can fit in a cell, WordPerfect 10 automatically wraps the text and increases the row height. It does not widen the cell automatically.

 Do not press ENTER *to move out of a cell. When you press* ENTER, *the height of the current cell increases by one line. To delete the extra line, press* BACKSPACE.

Make sure the insertion point is in the first cell in the second row, and type **Chesin**. By default, everything you type in a cell—text and numbers—is left-aligned. Press the DOWN ARROW to reach the next cell in the column, and then complete the table as shown:

Wing	67584	56544	34545	75423
Beebe	56300	67544	45634	78000
Cohen	43457	45763	46900	68500
Rocco	67643	56544	47500	54654
Total				
Average				

TIP *Use the property bar, toolbar, and Format menu to format text in cells just as you format any text in the document.*

Selecting Cells

To format a cell, row, or column, you do not necessarily have to select it first. But if you want to cut or copy an entire column or row, you must select it. To select a cell, point to its top border so the mouse appears as an up-pointing arrow, or point to the left border so the mouse appears as a left-pointing arrow.

■ Click once to select the cell.

■ Click twice to select the row (if you are pointing to the left) or the column (if you are pointing up).

■ Click three times to select the entire table.

To select multiple cells, rows, or columns, select one first and then drag the mouse.

You can select a row, column, or the entire table using the Select Table list in the Table property bar.

When cells are selected, the property bar changes. The property bar displayed when you have a cell, row, or column selected includes the first standard six buttons as well as these:

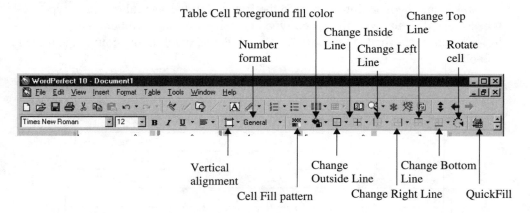

There are three other buttons that, depending on your screen resolution, you may have to scroll the property bar to display:

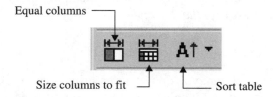

The following property bar is displayed when you select the entire table:

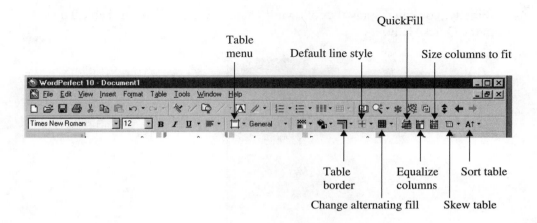

Working with Tables

WordPerfect 10 provides a number of special ways to work with tables in addition to the Table property bar. Most of these options are in the property bar, and more are also in the Table menu. You'll also find most of the options in the QuickMenu that appears when you right-click in a table:

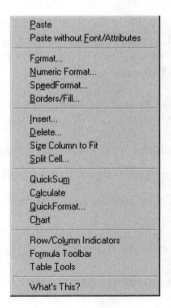

Finally, you can display the following Table Tools by choosing Table Tools from the QuickMenu:

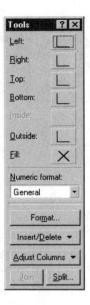

All these methods offer access to most table functions. You can perform a given function using any of several techniques. For example, the Size Column to Fit option adjusts the width of a column to the widest entry. You can perform this function using any of these techniques:

- When cells are selected, click on the Size Column to Fit button in the property bar.

- Select Size Column to Fit from the Table menu.

- Right-click and select Size Column to Fit from the QuickMenu.

- Display the Table Tools, pull down the Adjust Columns list, and click on Size Column to Fit.

As you work with tables, you'll find which method you prefer.

TIP *To make it easier to identify rows and columns, select Row/Column Indicators from the QuickMenu or Table menu. WordPerfect 10 displays the column letters below the property bar, and the row numbers at the left of the screen.*

Saving Time with QuickFill

In many cases, a row or column of labels or values is a *series,* such as the days of the week, months of the year, or four quarters. When you need to enter a series of incrementing values such as these, you only need to type the first element of the series yourself. The QuickFill command will do the rest. Here's how to use it:

1. Enter the first element of the series into its cell—type **Qtr 1** in cell B1.

2. Select the cell and drag to select the other cells in the row or column that you want to fill. In this case, drag over cells B1 to E1.

3. Click on the QuickFill button in the Table property bar, or select QuickFill from the Table menu or QuickMenu.

WordPerfect 10 completes the series for you, inserting "Qtr 2," "Qtr 3," and "Qtr 4" in the other selected cells.

If WordPerfect 10 does not recognize the series, it repeats the first value in the remaining cells. In this case, try entering the first two members of the series yourself, and then select both and drag across the row or down the column before using QuickFill. WordPerfect 10 completes a series of Roman numerals if you start with "I," for example, but it does not enter consecutive Arabic numbers or letters based on one initial value. To number cells "1," "2," "3," "4," and so on, you must enter the first two values. To insert a series of years, enter the first two years, and then use QuickFill.

Moving and Copying Cells

All of the same techniques that you know for moving and copying text can also be applied to tables. You can move cells using drag and drop or the Clipboard.

To move or copy the contents and format of a cell, select it by clicking on a cell border. To move or copy just the contents of a cell but not the formats applied to it, click in the cell and drag so the text within it is selected. Do not click on the cell border.

When you move or copy cells, you insert the contents and formats of the cells into another location. If you move or copy an entire row or column, however, other rows or columns shift over or down to make room. The row or column that you paste does not replace the one where you paste or drop it; so copying an entire row, for instance, actually inserts another row into the table.

10

To move a cell, row, or column by drag and drop, select what you want to move, and drag it to the new location. To copy the selection rather than move it, hold down the CTRL key when you release the mouse button.

You can also move and copy cells, rows, and columns using the Clipboard with the Cut, Copy, and Paste commands. When you select cells and choose Cut or Copy, however, you'll see the Cut or Copy Table dialog box shown next. Select to cut or copy just the selected cells (Selection), or the entire row or column of the selected cells. Click on OK, move the insertion point to where you want to insert the cells, and select Paste.

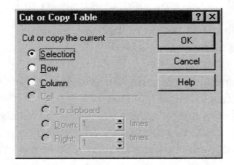

You can also use the Cut or Copy Table dialog box to copy a single selected cell into any number of consecutive cells in the row or column. Click on the Cell option in the Cut or Copy Table dialog box. The default option is Clipboard, indicating that the cell will be placed into the Clipboard for pasting elsewhere. To copy the cell down to cells in the column, click on the Down option, and then enter the number of cells you want to paste it to in the Times box. To copy the cell across the row, click on the Right option, and enter the number of cells.

Sorting Tables

If you do not like the order of information in your table, you can have WordPerfect 10 sort rows for you, rather than moving individual rows. You can perform a numeric, alphabetic, or date sort in either ascending or descending order.

The sort is performed using the values in the current column. Select the rows that you want to sort, or select the entire column to sort the entire table. Then click on the Sort Table button in the property bar (you may have to scroll the property bar to display the button) to see the following options and make your choice:

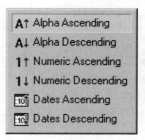

   The Sort Table option is available only in the property bar and only when cells are selected.

Changing Cell Width and Height

WordPerfect 10 gives you complete control over the size of rows, columns, and cells.

You can change the width of a column in several ways. If you point to a vertical grid line in the table, the pointer changes to a two-headed arrow. Point to and drag a line between two cells to change the width of the cells on either side. As you drag, a QuickStatus box shows the dimensions of the cells. If you drag the leftmost or rightmost grid line, only the cell next to it is affected.

You can also adjust columns with the ruler using the markers in the Indentation and Margin area:

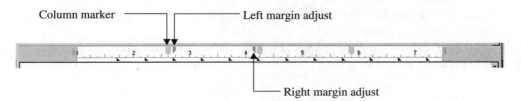

Drag a column marker to change the width of the cells on both sides. Drag the left or right margin indicator to adjust the width of the end cells. When the insertion point is in a table, dragging the margin indicators does not change the page margins, just the column width.

The left and right margin adjust markers represent the indentation of text within the column in which the insertion point is placed. Drag these markers to change the indentation of text within the cell.

Adjusting Column Width Automatically

Rather than dragging column indicators to change column width, you can have WordPerfect 10 automatically adjust the column for you. To adjust the column so it is as wide as the widest entry in it, right-click in any cell in the column, and then choose Size Column to Fit in the QuickMenu. You can also choose Size Column to Fit from the Table menu in the property bar or from the Adjust Columns list in the Table Tools.

To make a column just wide enough for a specific entry, first select the cell containing that entry, and then use the Size Column to Fit command—using the button on the property bar, or selecting the command from the QuickMenu, Table menu, or Table Tools. (You may have to scroll the property bar to display the button.) If any cells contain wider entries, however, their text will be wrapped onto two or more lines, increasing the height of their row.

 The Equalize Columns command makes selected columns the same size, equally dividing the existing space occupied by the columns. Choose the command from the property bar, Table menu, or QuickMenu when you select cells in the columns you want to equalize.

Splitting and Joining Cells

You can also change the size and shape of cells by splitting and joining. *Splitting* divides a cell into two rows or columns. *Joining* combines selected cells into one large cell. You can split and join cells by using the mouse, or by selecting the cells first and choosing a command.

To join cells by using the mouse, click on the QuickJoin Cells button in the Table property bar—the mouse pointer appears as shown here:

45634
46900
47500

Now select the cells that you want to combine. WordPerfect 10 leaves the tool on so you can join other cells. To turn off the function, click on the QuickJoin Cells button again.

You can also join cells by selecting them first, and then choosing Join Cells from the QuickMenu, or then choosing Join from the Table menu and clicking on Cell. Any contents in the cells will also be combined, with a tab separating information from side-by-side cells and a carriage return separating cells that were in the same column.

 To split a cell into two rows, click on the QuickSplit Row button in the property bar. The mouse pointer appears as shown in the next illustration, and a horizontal line appears in the cell you point to. Point to the cell you want to split into two rows and click. Click on the button again to turn it off.

| 45634 |
| 46900 |
| 47500 |
| |

 To split a cell into two columns, click on the QuickSplit Column button in the property bar. The mouse pointer appears as shown here, along with a QuickStatus box showing the size of the column. Click where you want the cell divided; then click on the button again to turn it off.

45634	78000
46900	0.663 " 0.638 "
47500	54654

When using either the QuickSplit Row or QuickSplit Column tool, hold down the ALT key to switch to the other—from the QuickSplit Row to the QuickSplit Column tool, for example. Hold down the SHIFT key to switch to the QuickJoin tool.

 To split cells into multiple rows or columns, click on the QuickSplit Columns and Rows button in the property bar. The mouse pointer appears as shown here, along with a QuickStatus box showing the size of the column and row. Click where you want the cell divided; then click on the button again to turn it off.

10

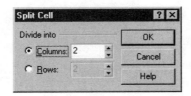

You can also use the Split Cells command to split cells into rows or columns. Right-click in the cell that you want to split, and then choose Split Cell from the QuickMenu to see the Split Cell dialog box:

Choose if you want to split the cell into rows or columns, enter the number of cells you want to create, and then click on OK.

NOTE *The Join and Split commands are available in the Table Tools.*

Changing Grid Lines

The grid lines in a table help to separate cells, and they make it easier to keep track of rows and columns. To give your table a more polished look, you can customize grid lines and even add color backgrounds and patterns to the cells. Of course, grid lines and background fills are for more than just good looks; they can call attention to parts of the table and make it easier to read.

You can add grid lines and fills using the property bar, QuickMenu, Table menu, or Table Tools. You can format a single cell without selecting it, or a cell or cells after you select them.

Using The Properties Dialog Box   To format the lines around a single cell, click in the cell; otherwise, select the cells you want to format. To customize the lines or fill of the entire table, you can be anywhere in the table. Choose Borders/Fill from the QuickMenu or Table menu to see the dialog box shown in Figure 10-2.

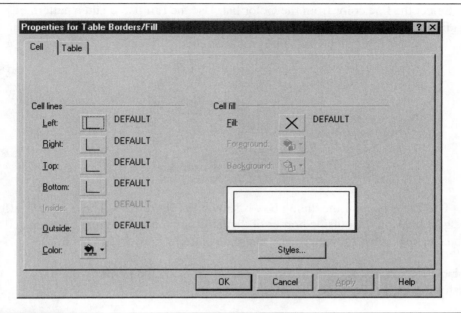

FIGURE 10-2   Properties for Table Border/Fill dialog box

The options on the Cell tab let you select the type and color of lines around the cell, and its fill color and pattern. The lists in the Cell Lines section let you select from 32 types of lines for the left, right, top, and bottom of the cell, as shown here:

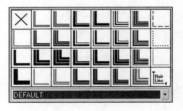

You can either click on one of the displayed options, or pull down the list and select one by name.

Choosing an option from the Outside list adds the selected pattern to all four lines. If you selected a block of cells, however, the Outside option only affects the border around the selected area, and you can choose an Inside line pattern to appear on the grid lines between the cells, without affecting the border.

Select the line color from the Color list. Use the Fill list to add a pattern or shading to the cell, from the following options. If you choose a fill pattern, you can also select foreground and background colors.

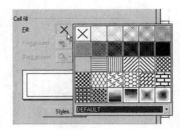

The Table page of the dialog box is shown in Figure 10-3. These options affect the grid lines on the outside border of the table and the default line between cells. You can also add a fill pattern and alternate patterns in rows and columns.

Using The Property Bar   You can also use buttons on the property bar to customize the borders and fills of selected cells.

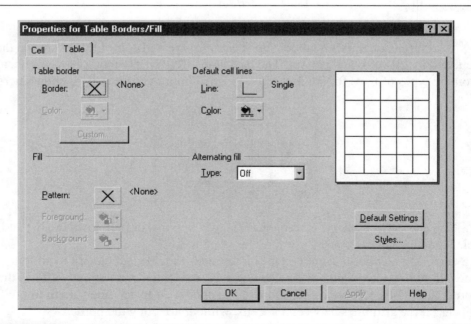

FIGURE 10-3   Customizing all table lines

If cells are not selected, use the Outside Lines, Cell Fill, and Foreground Color buttons. If cells are selected, pull down the Left Line, Right Line, Top Line, Bottom Line, Inside Lines, Outside Lines, Cell Fill, and Foreground Color lists, and choose the line and fill type desired.

If you selected the entire table, choose options from the Table Border, Line Style, Cell Fill, Foreground Color, and Alternating Fill buttons.

> **TIP** *Border and fill options are available in the Table Tools.*

Changing Table Size

You may create a table, only to realize later that you want to change the size. When this happens, you'll need to insert or delete rows or columns.

Inserting Rows and Columns

If you need to insert only an additional row at the end of the table, place the insertion point in the last cell of the last row, and press TAB. WordPerfect 10 inserts a blank row and places the insertion point in the first cell of the new row.

To insert a new row above the current row, click on the Insert Row button in the toolbar. You can also insert a row using shortcut key combinations. Press ALT-INS to insert a row above the insertion point, or press ALT-SHIFT-INS to insert a row below the insertion point.

To insert several rows at one time or to insert new columns, use the Insert command. Start by placing the insertion point in the row or column that you want to insert a new row or column before or after. Then select Insert from the Table menu, or right-click on the cell and select Insert from the QuickMenu, to see the dialog box in Figure 10-4. Here's how to use the dialog box.

> **TIP** *The Insert and Delete commands are available in the Table Tools.*

1. Click on either Columns or Rows to choose what you want to insert.

2. Enter the number of rows or columns desired.

3. Choose either Before or After the row or column.

10

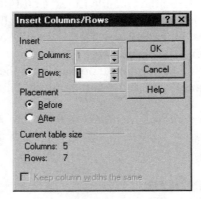

FIGURE 10-4   Inserting rows and columns

4. If you are inserting columns, choose Keep Column Widths Same if you want to insert the columns in the same width as existing ones.

5. Click on OK.

Deleting Rows, Columns, and Cells

It's as easy to delete rows, columns, and cells as it is to insert them. To delete the current row, press ALT-DEL. This deletes the row at the insertion point. To delete any number of rows or columns, place the insertion point in the first row or column you want to delete, and then choose Delete from the Table menu to see the dialog box in Figure 10-5. Delete rows or columns using these steps:

1. Click on either Columns or Rows to choose what you want to delete.

2. Enter the number of rows or columns you want to delete.

3. Choose if you want to delete Cell Contents Only or Formulas Only. Choosing Formulas Only deletes any formulas in the cell by leaving the results of the formulas as text.

4. Click on OK.

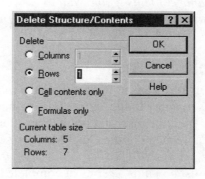

FIGURE 10-5   Deleting rows and columns

Splitting and Joining Tables

One other way to change table size is to split a table into two or join two tables.
You can only split and join tables at rows, not columns.

To split a table, start by placing the insertion point in the row where you want
to start the new table, and then choose Split from the Table menu and click on
Table.

To combine tables, click on the bottom row of the first table, choose Join from
the Table menu, and then click on Tables. To join tables, they must have the same
number of columns, and there must be no blank lines between the tables.

Deleting Tables

You can delete a table by selecting it and then pressing DEL. WordPerfect 10
displays the following dialog box. Make your choice from the dialog box, and
click on OK.

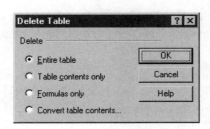

10

Select Convert table contents if you want to convert the table into text or into a merge data file.

Selecting a Table Format

Rather than using a variety of means to format the parts of a table, you can choose a complete set of formats to apply to the entire table at one time by use of the SpeedFormat command. With the insertion point in any cell of the table, select SpeedFormat from the Table menu or the QuickMenu to see the dialog box in Figure 10-6.

The Available Styles list contains a series of complete table formats. Click on each format, and see how it affects the sample table in the preview panel area. Choosing the Fancy Shading format, for instance, changes our sample table to this:

	Qtr1	*Qtr2*	*Qtr3*	*Qtr4*
Wing	67584	56544	34545	75423
Beebe	56300	67544	45634	78000
Cohen	43457	45763	46900	68500
Rocco	67643	56544	47500	54654
Total				
Average				

Now take a look at some of the options in the dialog box:

- The Apply Style on a Cell by Cell Basis checkbox automatically applies the same formats to rows or columns that you later add to the table. Deselect this checkbox if you want to add unformatted rows or columns.

- The Clear Current Table Settings Before Applying checkbox removes all of the table's original formats so none of them are retained when you apply a selected style.

- The Use as Default button applies the selected formats to all new tables that you create. Select the style, click on Initial Style, and then click on Yes in the message box that appears.

When you find a format that you want for your table, click on Apply.

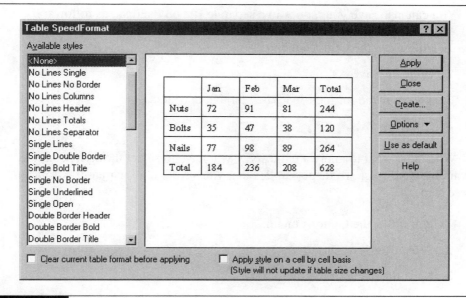

FIGURE 10-6   Selecting a table format

Creating Your Own Styles

If you don't like any of the built-in table styles, you can create your own. This way you can quickly reapply the same formats to another table. First, use all of WordPerfect 10's formatting features to format the table the way you want to. You'll learn more about formatting tables soon. Then follow these steps:

1. Use any of the techniques you learned previously to display the Table SpeedFormat dialog box.

2. Decide where you want to save your styles. Pull down the Options button menu, and click on Setup to see the Table Style Settings dialog box.

3. You can save your styles in the current document or in the default template. Click on your choice and then on OK.

4. Click on the Create button.

5. In the dialog box that appears, type a name for the style and then click on OK. Your style is now listed in the Available Styles list and shown at the top of the list, along with the most recently used style.

You can also save your styles in a separate file on the disk, as follows:

1. Pull down the Options menu.

2. Click on Save As.

3. Type a name for the file in the box that appears.

4. Click on OK.

When you want to apply a table style, you have to select the style from the Available Styles list. To display styles that you saved in a separate file, follow these steps:

1. Pull down the Options menu.

2. Select Retrieve.

3. Type the name of the file.

4. Click on OK.

To list styles in either the document or the default template, pull down the Options button menu, click on Setup, and make your choice from the dialog box.

You can also use the Options menu to delete or rename one of your custom styles. You cannot delete or rename WordPerfect 10's built-in styles.

Applying Table Formats

You can always format the text in cells using the options in the property bar and format menus. Selecting text in a cell and clicking on the Bold button, for example, formats the text in boldface. To adjust the width of columns, you can always use the mouse to drag the column border, or you can use the column indicator in the ruler.

You have greater control over formats, however, if you use the Format command to display the dialog box shown in Figure 10-7. Display the dialog box using any of these techniques:

■ Select Format from the Table menu.

■ Right-click and select Format from the QuickMenu.

■ Click on Format in the Table Tools.

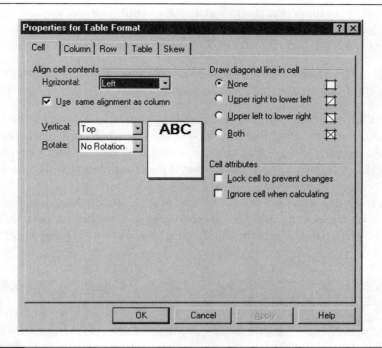

FIGURE 10-7   Properties for Table Format dialog box

The pages in this dialog box let you format cells, rows, columns, or the entire table. The default page displayed depends on what is selected in the table. If you select a row before displaying the dialog box, for example, the Row page is opened. Let's look at each of the pages and the options they offer.

Applying Cell Formats

These options affect the current cell or the group of selected cells.

Use the Horizontal list to align the text in the cell on the left, right, center, or on the decimal point, or use Full or All justification. When you choose an option, the check mark is cleared from the Use Same Alignment as Column box. Select the box if you want the cell to use the default alignment or the alignment that you've assigned to the entire column.

NOTE   *Selecting an alignment is the same as choosing an option from the Justification list in the power bar.*

The options in the Vertical and Rotate boxes control where the text appears vertically in the cell, and its rotation. You can select a vertical position of top, center, or bottom, and you can rotate the text in 90-degree increments—90, 180, and 270 degrees.

> **TIP** *Quickly rotate text in a cell in 90-degree increments by clicking on the Rotate Cell button in the Table property bar.*

In the Cell Attributes section, decide if you want to lock the cell so it cannot be edited and if you want to ignore the value in the cell when performing math operations. Ignoring the cell during math is useful when you have a numeric label, such as a year, and you want to ensure that it is not accidentally used to calculate a total or average value.

The Draw Diagonal Line in Cell section is a nice touch. Diagonal lines are often used to indicate cells that should be ignored because they have no value or significance. Figure 10-8 shows the alignment and diagonal line options applied to cells.

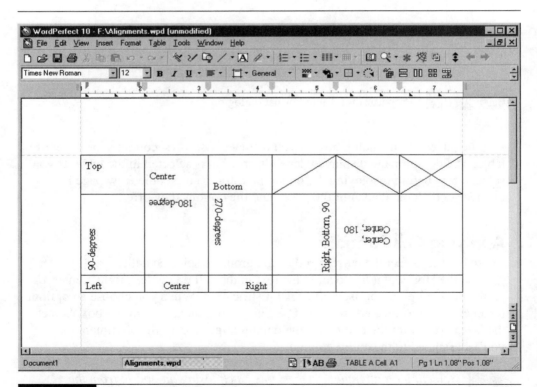

FIGURE 10-8 Alignment and diagonal options

Formatting Columns

The Column page of the Properties for Table Format dialog box is shown in Figure 10-9. Your selections affect the entire column that the insertion point is in—the column itself does not have to be selected.

Use the Horizontal section to assign an alignment to every cell in the column. It does not affect any cell that you've already applied an alignment to using the property bar or the Cell page of the dialog box. If you select Decimal Align justification, you should also select one of the options in the Decimal Alignment section. These determine the position of the decimal point in the cell, and thus where the numbers align. To position the decimal point a number of characters from the right, choose Digits after Decimal, and enter a number in the corresponding box. To position the decimal point at set distances, choose Position From Right, and enter a measurement in the text box.

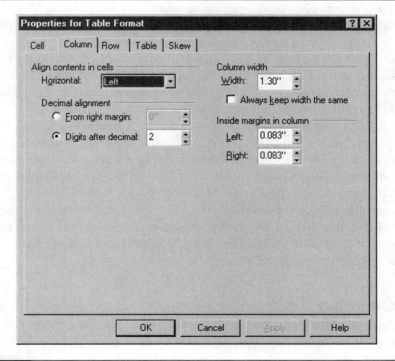

FIGURE 10-9   Column format options

The Inside Margins are the space WordPerfect 10 leaves on the right and left of text. The margins determine how much text fits in the cell before WordPerfect 10 wraps the text to the next line.

Use the Column Width box to set the width of the column to a specific measurement. Use this if you have trouble getting the width to an exact amount by dragging. If you select the Always Keep Width the Same box, WordPerfect 10 does not change the width of the column as you change the width of other columns in the table.

You can also apply justification formats using the property bar. Try that now. Select cells B1 through E1, pull down the Justification list in the power bar, and click on Center.

Formatting Rows

The options in the Row page of the Properties for Table Format dialog box, shown in Figure 10-10, affect the entire row. As with columns, you do not have to select the row first; simply click in any cell in the row.

By default, WordPerfect 10 is set to accept multiple lines in a cell—either lines that are word wrapped or those created when you press ENTER. If you carefully designed a table to fit a certain space, however, wrapped lines widen the row height and the spacing of the table on the page. If you select Single Line in this dialog box, you can enter only one line of information—WordPerfect 10 just stops accepting keystrokes when the cell is filled.

Also use this dialog box to create a header row. A header is a row or rows that repeat on every page when your table spans a page break. If you have a row of labels at the start of the table, for example, you might want it to repeat so the reader can identify the columns on the next page. Select the row, display the Row page of the Format dialog box, and click on the Header Row checkbox.

You can also allow a row to span a page break. If the row contains more than one line of text, this divides the row between pages. Deselect this option to keep the entire row on the same page. The dialog box also lets you set the row height and width to a specific measurement.

Formatting the Table

The Table page of the Properties for Table Format dialog box applies formats to the entire table. Some of these options are the same as those you can set for columns, but they apply to all of the cells. For example, you can select a default

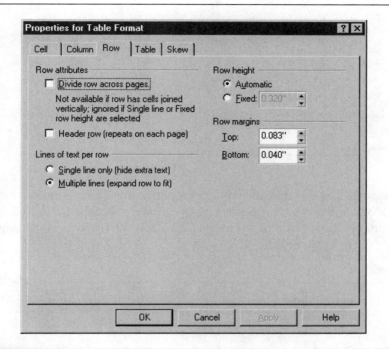

FIGURE 10-10   Row format options

justification, set the number of decimal digits and distance from the right cell border, and enter default column margins and width.

In addition, you can determine the position of the entire table between the margins, and you can change the table size by specifying the number of rows and columns.

You can also disable all of the cell locks so you can enter and edit information, and you can control whether you can insert rows automatically when you press TAB in the last cell of the table.

Creating a Skewed Table

A skewed table gives the impression of three dimensions by positioning the first row, and the first or last column, at an angle from the rest of the table, as follows:

	Qtr1	Qtr2	Qtr3	Qtr4
Wing	67584	56544	34545	75423
Beebe	56300	67544	45634	78000
Cohen	43457	45763	46900	68500
Rocco	67643	56544	47500	54654
Total				
Average				

To create a skewed table, display the Properties for Table Format dialog box, then click on the Skew tab to see the options shown in Figure 10-11. Select an option from the Skew Settings list to see the effects on the table in the sample pane, then click Apply or OK.

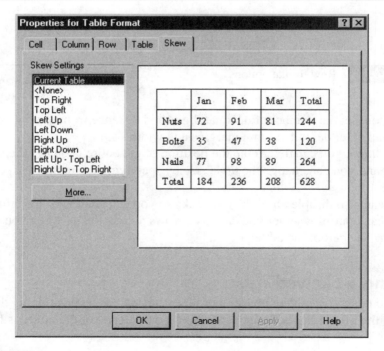

FIGURE 10-11 Skew options

When the entire table is selected, you can also skew a table by clicking on the Skew Table button in the property bar.

To customize the design of the skew, click on More in the dialog box to see these options:

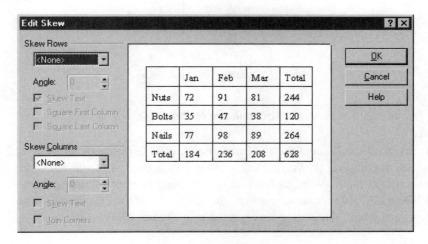

You can choose whether or not to skew the top row, and the angle of the skew. You can also select not to skew the text in the row, and to square off the line coming up from the first or last column. In the Skew Columns section, choose which column to skew, the angle, and whether or not to skew the text as well.

 By combining skewed rows and columns with cell shading, you can create some dramatic and eye-catching effects.

Changing the Numeric Format

As you insert numbers and perform math operations, you may want to customize the way numbers appear. You can, for example, display values as currency, with dollar signs and with commas separating thousands, or you can control the number of decimal places that appear. To change the format of numbers in a single cell, pull down the Number Format list in the Table property bar, and choose an option from those shown next:

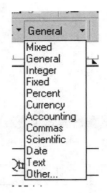

TIP   *The number formats are available in the Table Tools.*

For even more choices, use the Properties for Table Numeric Format dialog box where you can set the format for a group of selected cells, entire columns, or the entire table. Display the dialog box by choosing Numeric Format from the QuickMenu or Table menu, or by selecting Other from the Number Format button in the property bar. The dialog box is shown in Figure 10-12.

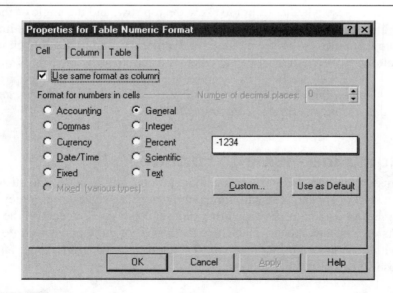

FIGURE 10-12   Change the numeric format

Choose if you want to apply the format to the selected cells, columns, or to the entire table, and then select one of the numeric formats. An example of this follows:

1. Select cells B2 through E7.

2. Right-click on the cells, and choose Numeric Format from the QuickMenu.

3. Click on the Currency format, and then click on OK. All of the amounts will include dollar signs and two decimal places. The cells should still be selected, so align them on the decimal point.

4. Right-click on the cells, and select Format from the QuickMenu.

5. Pull down the Horizontal list, and click on Decimal Align.

6. Click on OK.

If you want a special format, create your own. Click on the Custom button, and set the options in the Customize Number Type dialog box.

TIP   *You can also assign the type as the default initial style for all tables.*

10

Performing Calculations in Tables

A WordPerfect 10 table has many of the same characteristics as a spreadsheet. Information is presented in rows and columns, and each cell is referenced by its row and column position. And as with a spreadsheet, you can perform calculations on the numbers in your table. For example, you can display the sum of values in a row or column, compute averages, and insert formulas that reference cells and other values.

The quickest calculation you can make is to total the values in rows or columns using the QuickSum feature. You place the insertion point in the empty cell below the ones you want to total, and then click on QuickSum in the property bar. (You can also select QuickSum from the Table menu or from the QuickMenu.) Do that now:

1. Place the insertion point in cell B6.

2. Click QuickSum in the property bar. You may have to scroll the property bar to display this button.

QuickSum totals the values of the numeric values above the cell and displays the results in the current cell along with a formula marker:

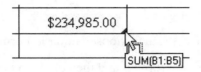

The marker indicates which cells in your table contain formulas that will be recalculated when other cells change values.

QuickSum totals numbers up to the first blank cell or a cell that contains text. If you have a column label that is a year, such as 1997, Quick Sum may mistakenly include that in the total. If you have a column label such as that, or want to total numbers when blank cells are in the column, select the cells you want to total first, including the blank cell where you want to insert the total—then use the QuickSum command.

You can also use QuickSum to total the values in a row. Click in the blank cell after the last number in the row, and then select QuickSum. If you have values in both the row and column surrounding the cell, however, first select the cells containing the values you want to add.

Using the Formula Bar

QuickSum is useful, but it only totals. When you want to add, subtract, multiply, divide, and perform other types of math operations, you must enter a formula. With WordPerfect 10, you enter formulas in a special formula bar. Display the following bar by clicking on the Formula Bar button in the Table property bar, or by selecting Formula Toolbar from the Table menu or the QuickMenu.

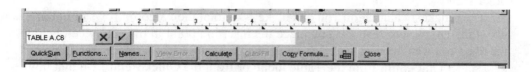

NOTE   *The formula toolbar appears automatically when you click in a cell containing a formula.*

Here's how to use it. Click in the cell where you want to insert a formula, and then click in the formula bar. The cell's coordinates are in the text box on the left. Type the formula in the next text box, and then click on the checkmark in the formula bar to accept the entry, or click on the "X" to cancel the formula. If a formula starts with a cell reference, begin it with a plus sign, as in **+B3-B4**.

You create a formula with a mathematical operation using the plus sign (+) to perform addition, the hyphen (-) for subtraction, the asterisk (*) for multiplication, and the forward slash (/) for division. Your formula can contain numbers and cell references. For example, to calculate a 6 percent sales tax on the value in cell A6, use the formula +A6*.06. When you accept the entry, WordPerfect 10 inserts a plus sign in front of the operation.

> **TIP** *Use parentheses to control the order and precedence of operations, such as (100+100+100)/3.*

Rather than typing the cell reference into the formula bar, you can insert it by clicking. When you are ready to add the reference to the formula, make sure the insertion point is in the formula bar, and then click on the cell that you want to reference. Drag over cells to insert a reference to their range.

The other options in the formula bar help you work on tables and perform math:

- *QuickSum* performs the same function as clicking on QuickSum in the Table toolbar.

- *Functions* displays a dialog box of functions that perform operations.

- *Names* lets you name cells and select names to insert in formulas.

- *View Error* displays a description of an error in the cell.

- *Calculate* recalculates the values of formulas and functions.

- *QuickFill* completes a series of entries, just like the QuickFill button in the Table toolbar.

- *Copy Formula* lets you copy a formula from a cell down or across to the cells.

- *Row/Column Indicators* toggles the display of column letters and row numbers.

- *Close* closes the formula bar.

Copying Formulas

In many tables, you use a similar formula in several adjacent cells. Instead of repeating your keystrokes to retype a similar formula, you can copy one formula into other cells. When you copy a formula, it is copied in a relative way. This means that the cell references in the formula are adjusted for the cell in which the formula appears.

The easiest way to copy a formula is to drag the formula marker. Here's how it works.

1. Point to the formula marker in cell B6. You'll see a QuickStatus box showing the formula within the cell.

2. Hold down the mouse button and drag across the row to cell E6.

When you release the mouse, WordPerfect 10 copies the formula, but adjusts the cell references. Each copy of the formula computes the total of the cells above it in the column.

You can also use the Copy Formula button to copy the contents of a cell down or across cells. It displays the following dialog box:

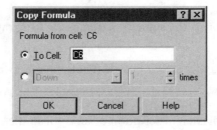

1. Select if you want to copy the formula to a specific cell, or choose to copy it up, down, or to the right or left, and the number of times.

2. Then click OK to copy the formula.

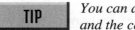 *You can also copy formulas using the QuickFill button. Select the formula and the cell you want to copy it to, and click on QuickFill.*

Working with Functions

The QuickSum button actually inserts a function into the cell. A *function* is a shortcut because it performs a math operation that may have taken an entire series of operations or even a number of formulas. For example, the QuickSum command might insert a formula that looks like SUM(A1:A20). This tells WordPerfect 10 to total the values in the cells from A1 to A20 in a much faster way than the formula A1+A2+A3 . . . , and so on.

WordPerfect 10 comes with over 100 functions that perform all types of operations. To see the functions, and to insert one into the formula bar, click on the Functions button in the formula bar to see the dialog box in Figure 10-13.

By default, all of the functions are available in the Functions list. You can also pull down the List Functions list and choose to see only functions in these categories:

- Mathematical
- Date
- Financial
- Logical
- Miscellaneous
- String

10

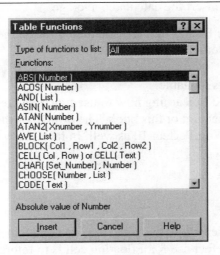

FIGURE 10-13   Corel WordPerfect's table functions

To insert a function into the formula bar, click on it in the Functions list, and then click on the Insert button.

Most functions require one or more arguments. An *argument* is a value or cell reference that follows the name of the function in parentheses. For example, in the @SUM function, the argument is the range of cells that you want to total. This function needs just one argument, the range of cells that contains the values to average. Many other functions require several arguments, which are separated from each other by commas.

When you insert a function into the formula bar, you'll see its name and a list of its arguments. The first argument is highlighted, so all you have to do is click on or drag over the range of cells that you want to insert into the argument. After you insert the reference, double-click on the next argument, if it has one, and then click on or drag over the cell references for it. Continue the process until all of the arguments are complete.

Let's use a function now to calculate the average for each quarter in the table:

1. Click in cell B7.

2. Click on the Functions button.

3. Click on AVE(List) and then on Insert. The function appears in the formula bar with the word "List" selected.

4. Drag over cells B2 through B5, and then click on the checkmark in the formula bar to insert the calculated average.

5. Drag over cells B7 through E7, and then click on the QuickFill button to copy the function.

Figure 10-14 shows the table.

If you are interested in learning how to use functions, read Chapter 19 in Part III, the Quattro Pro 9 section of this book. The principles that you'll learn about in that chapter apply to WordPerfect 10 as well. In fact, many of the functions are similar if not identical.

Floating Cells

A floating cell is a table cell that you insert in text and which can contain a calculated value. A perfect use for a floating cell is to reference the calculated value in a table.

	Qtr1	Qtr2	Qtr3	Qtr4
Wing	$67,584.00	$56,544.00	$34,545.00	$75,423.00
Beebe	$56,300.00	$57,544.00	$45,634.00	$78,000.00
Cohen	$43,457.00	$45,763.00	$46,900.00	$68,500.00
Rocco	$67,643.00	$56,544.00	$47,500.00	$54,654.00
Total	$234,985.00	$226,397.00	$174,582.00	$276,581.00
Average	$58,746.00	$56,598.75	$43,644.75	$69,144.25

FIGURE 10-14   The average added to row 7

For example, suppose you have the table shown previously in Figure 10-14 in a document. You'd like to include a line in the text that references the total figure for Quarter 4 that is shown in cell E6, as in

So as you can see, the total for the fourth quarter is $276,581.00.

10

If you just type the value into the text, you'd have to edit it if you later change any of the values in column E. While the value in the table will recalculate automatically, the number you typed in the text would not. The solution is to create a floating cell in the text using these steps:

1. Move the insertion point below the table and type **So as you can see, the total for the fourth quarter is**.

2. Enter a space at the end of the line.

3. Select Table | Create.

4. Click on the Floating Cell option and click Create. WordPerfect displays the Formula bar.

5. Click in the formula bar and then click cell E6 in the table. WordPerfect inserts a reference to that cell: TABLE A.E6.

6. Click the checkmark in the formula bar.

7. Right-click on the inserted value and select Numeric Format from the QuickMenu.

8. Select Currency and then click OK.

Now if you later change any of the values that would recalculate cell E6, the value in the floating cell in the text would change as well.

Creating Columns

Tables are fine for displaying numbers in columns, but you can format text in columns just as easily. Newsletters, reports, and other published documents are attractive in columns where text flows from one column to the next. WordPerfect 10 makes it easy to create columns. In fact, you can type your text first, and then apply the column formats to see how it appears, or you can turn on columns before you type.

Creating Newspaper Columns

Newspaper columns are just as you see in the newspaper—columns of text flow from one column right to the next on the page. When you fill the column on the far right of the page, the text moves to the left column on the next page. The text adjusts, moving from column to column, as you insert or delete text above it.

When you create columns, you actually insert a column code into the document. Like a justification code, the column code affects all text from the paragraph in which the insertion point is placed to the end of the document, or until the next column code. This means that you can mix single-column and multiple-column text on the same page, and you can even mix the number of columns on the same page, such as some two-column and three-column text on the same page.

When you want to format text in columns, follow these steps:

1. Place the insertion point where you want the columns to begin.

2. Click on the Columns button on the toolbar.

3. Select the number of columns desired, from 2 to 5.

WordPerfect 10 displays dotted boxes on the screen representing the width of the columns and the spacing between them, as in Figure 10-15. "Col" appears in the general status area of the Application bar, followed by the number of the column in which the insertion point is placed. If the ruler is displayed, it indicates the width of each column, with the space between the columns.

TIP   *If you do not see the dotted lines, select Guidelines from the View menu, click on Column in the dialog box that appears, and then click on OK.*

If you selected columns in existing text, the text appears in the column format. Otherwise, type your text starting in the leftmost column. As you type, the text flows from column to column and from page to page, repeating the column format on each page.

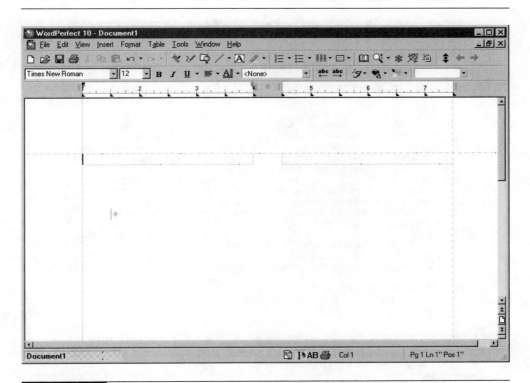

FIGURE 10-15   The width and spacing between columns shows on the screen

If you want to end a column before the text flows, press CTRL-ENTER, or select Column Break from the Column list in the toolbar. What occurs when you press CTRL-ENTER depends on where the insertion point is placed, and how previous columns were ended. If you press CTRL-ENTER in a column that's not the rightmost one, WordPerfect 10 ends the current column and moves the insertion point into the column to its right.

What about pressing CTRL-ENTER in the rightmost column? If your previous columns were ended by WordPerfect 10 flowing the text, then WordPerfect 10 will insert a page break and begin the left column on the next page. However, if you've ended all of the previous columns by pressing CTRL-ENTER, pressing CTRL-ENTER in the rightmost column ends it and starts a new column group, as shown in Figure 10-16. The group will have the same number of columns and will start under the longest column in the previous group.

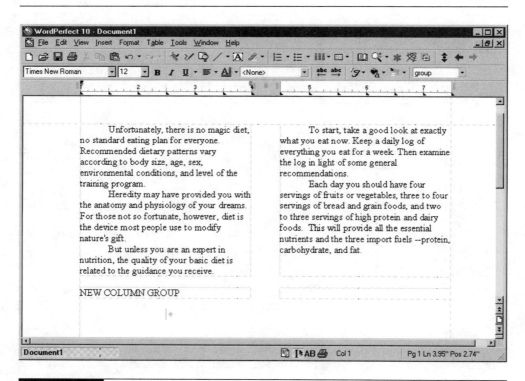

FIGURE 10-16   A new column group

You can now continue typing, or change the number of columns in the group by selecting another option in the Columns button of the toolbar. To type single-column text, for example, pull down the Columns button in the power bar, and select Columns Off. You can also select Columns from the Format menu and click on Discontinue. To change the number of columns on the page, simply place the insertion point at the start of the group, and choose an option from the Columns button on the toolbar.

> **NOTE** *If you want the columns in a group to be the same length, see "Defining Columns" later in this chapter.*

Changing the Column Width

Columns that you create using the toolbar are always the same width, a half-inch apart, and spaced to fill the page width. You sometimes may want to design a newsletter or other document that has uneven columns. To change the column width, use either the column guidelines or the ruler.

The dotted lines on either side of a column are its guidelines. To change the width of a column, drag its guidelines. Dragging the leftmost guidelines on the page really changes the left margin, but the left column adjusts in width accordingly. Dragging the rightmost column guideline changes only the column width, not the right page margin.

When you drag any other column guidelines, you change the width of the column and of the spacing between the columns. As you drag a guideline, a QuickStatus box shows the resulting column and spacing width.

If you want to maintain the same spacing between columns and just change the column width itself, point in the space between columns and drag. Only the space moves as you drag, changing the columns on both sides of it.

As an alternative to dragging the guidelines, you can change the column or spacing width using the ruler. The ruler contains individual sections with left and right margin indicators that represent the left and right edges of the column. The section for the column that has the insertion point also has left and right indentation indicators, and a first line indent marker.

Change column width and the spacing between columns by dragging the right or left column margin indicators. Change only the column width by dragging a gray area that represents the space between two columns.

Placing a Border Between Columns

To insert a vertical line between columns, click anywhere in the columns, select Columns from the Format menu, and click on Border/Fill. The Border/Fill dialog box is the same one that you've used to place a border around paragraphs. To add a border between the columns, however, click on the option that the arrow is pointing to in the following illustration:

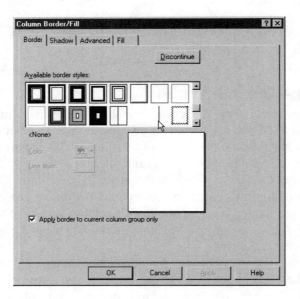

Defining Columns

If you want to create columns of specific sizes without dragging, or a column group in which all of the columns are the same length, then you have to define the columns. Select Format from the Column list in the toolbar, or select Columns from the Format menu to display the dialog box shown in Figure 10-17.

Enter the number of columns you want to create in the Number of Columns text box. When you move to another section of the dialog box, WordPerfect 10 calculates the width of the columns and displays their measurements in the Column Widths text boxes, along with 0.5 inch spacing between them. To customize the column widths or spacing, enter a measurement, or click the up or down arrows to change the widths. The preview graphic of the page will illustrate the resulting columns.

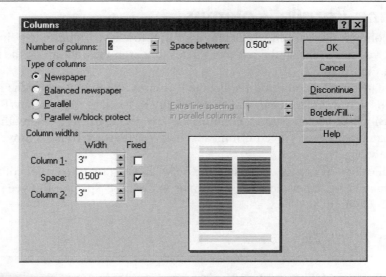

FIGURE 10-17   Defining columns

10

As you increase or decrease the width of one column, WordPerfect 10 automatically adjusts the width of the other columns to fit the columns between the margins. If you want a column to remain exactly as you set it, regardless of how you change the other columns, select the column's Fixed checkbox.

You can also change the width of the spaces between columns. To set them all to the same width in one step, enter the width in the Spacing Between box.

Balancing Columns

If you want all of the columns in a group to be the same length, click on the Balanced Newspaper button in the Type of Columns section. As you type, WordPerfect 10 shifts text back and forth between the columns to keep them the same length.

You can also apply the Balanced Newspaper format to existing columns. Use this, for example, if you complete a document and the last column on the page is not full. However, if you ended a column other than the one on the right by pressing CTRL-ENTER, WordPerfect 10 uses that position to end the column group. It divides all of the text above the position of the column break into balanced columns, and start a new column group with the text after the column break position.

Creating Parallel Columns

Parallel columns are ones in which text does not flow from column to column. In this case, you have text on the left that relates to text in the column on the right, as shown in Figure 10-18.

To create parallel columns, display the Columns dialog box, enter the number of columns you want to create, and click on either Parallel or Parallel W/Block Protect. Block-protected parallel columns are always kept next to each other. They do not span a page break, even if it means that WordPerfect 10 must move them all to a new page.

WordPerfect 10 inserts one blank line between each set of parallel columns. To change this setting, enter the number of lines in the Line Spacing Between Rows in Parallel Columns text box.

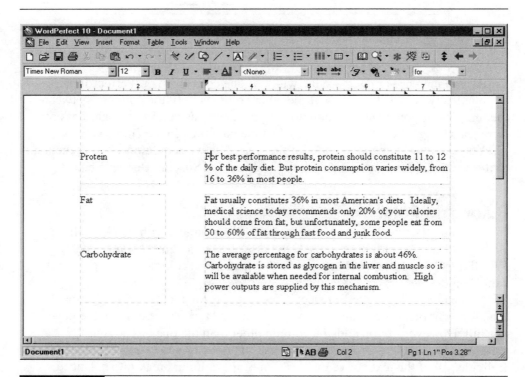

FIGURE 10-18   Parallel columns

With parallel columns, you enter text in sets. First, type the text in a column on the left. Then press CTRL-ENTER, and type the text in a column to its right. When you press CTRL-ENTER in the rightmost column, WordPerfect 10 starts a new column group. It only inserts a page break when there is not enough room for another set of parallel columns on the page.

Working With Footnotes and Endnotes

Before programs such as WordPerfect 10 came along, typing footnotes could be a laborious task because you had to judge just how much space to reserve at the bottom of the page. If you inserted or deleted text, the footnote reference could move to another page, forcing you to move the note as well. You could only hope that there would be enough space for the footnote on the new page. Well, WordPerfect 10 takes away this worry by automatically adjusting your text so footnotes always appear on the same page as their reference numbers. You can insert or delete text—even insert and delete footnotes—and WordPerfect 10 takes care of the rest.

Inserting Footnotes

To type a footnote, place the insertion point where you want the reference number or mark to appear, and then select Footnote/Endnote from the Insert menu to display the dialog box shown in Figure 10-19. The footnote number is set automatically.

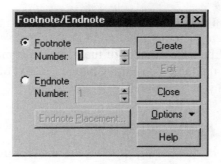

FIGURE 10-19   The Footnote and Endnote dialog box

When you click on Create, WordPerfect 10 inserts the reference number in the text. If you are in Draft view, WordPerfect 10 opens a separate window for the note with the property bar shown here. If you are in Page view, WordPerfect moves to the bottom of the page displaying the footnote separator and reference number.

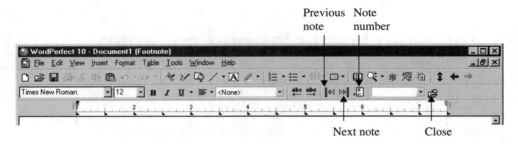

Type the text of the footnote, then click Close in the property bar. As you enter footnotes, WordPerfect 10 numbers them consecutively. If you insert a new note in the text, or delete an existing note, WordPerfect 10 automatically renumbers those following the insertion point.

To move or copy a footnote, select its reference number in the text, then use either drag and drop or the Clipboard to move or copy the note to the new location. Remember, hold down CTRL while you drag and drop to make a copy of the note. WordPerfect 10 automatically renumbers the notes. To delete a note, select its reference number and press DELETE.

Editing Footnotes

To edit a note, you must display it. If you are in Page view, just scroll to the bottom of the page where the note appears. In Draft view, select Footnote/Endnote from the Insert menu. Enter the number of the note you want to edit in the Footnote Number box, then click on Edit. Change the text of the note as you would any other text in your document.

Setting Footnote Options

To change the position or numbering method, use the Options button in the Footnote/Endnote dialog box. The options are:

- *Set Number* lets you designate a number out of sequence or increase or decrease from the previous number by one.

- *Separator* lets you choose the position, length, and style of line between the text and the footnotes.

- *Advanced* lets you position footnotes either at the bottom of the page or end of the document, change the type of reference numbers, and determine how long notes are continued on the next page.

Inserting Endnotes

Endnotes are references that appear at the end of the document rather than on the same page as their reference number. You insert an endnote in much the same way as a footnote, except that you select Endnote in the Footnote/Endnote dialog box.

To customize endnotes, select Options from the Footnotes/Endnotes dialog box, and then click on Set Number or Advanced. The Advanced options are similar to those for footnotes, except that endnotes are always at the end of the document.

Creating a Table of Contents

A table of contents appears near the beginning of a document, showing readers the organization of topics and subtopics. WordPerfect 10 can automatically create a table of contents for you from titles and subtitles formatted in the heading styles.

To prepare a document so that WordPerfect 10 can generate the table of contents, just type your document using heading styles from the Style list for titles and subtitles.

If you want to mark other text to use for the table, you have to mark it, designating the level. Select Reference from the Tools menu, and click on Table of Contents to see the following feature bar:

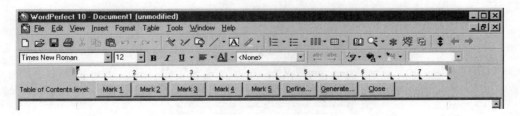

Select the text to use for a heading, then click on the appropriate Mark button.

You should then create a page to hold the table of contents at the beginning of the document. Move the insertion point to the start of the document, and press CTRL-ENTER to insert a blank page. Place the insertion point at the start of the new page, and use the Numbering option from the Format Page menu to insert the page number. Select lowercase Roman numerals.

Next, move the insertion point to the first page of text. Select Reveal Codes from the View menu, and make sure the insertion point is immediately after the hard page code, and before any other text or codes on the page. Then use the Numbering option from the Format Page menu to change the numbering format to Arabic. Click on Set Value, and change the starting number of the page to 1.

Generating the Table of Contents

When you've entered all of the headings to use for the table, or marked entries, you are ready to generate the table of contents.

Move the insertion point to the start of the blank page you created to hold the table. If the table of contents feature bar is not displayed, choose Reference from the Tools menu, and click on Table of Contents. Click on Define to see the dialog box in Figure 10-20, then follow these steps to generate the table:

1. Set the number of levels.

2. Choose a style for each level.

3. Click OK.

WordPerfect 10 inserts this message into the document:

<<<Table of Contents will generate here>>>

Finally, click on Generate to see this dialog box:

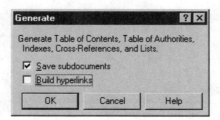

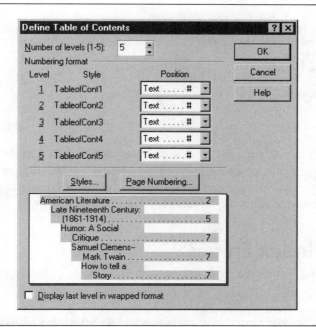

FIGURE 10-20   Defining a table of contents format

If you turn on Build Hyperlinks, each page number in the table become a link. Click on the link to move to the page. Click OK to insert the table of contents.

If you add, edit, or delete text so the pagination or headings change, you must update the table. Click anywhere in the table, and then select Generate from the feature bar again.

Creating an Index

An index usually appears at the end of your document, listing the page numbers of topics, or key words or phrases, in alphabetical order. When a topic—or main entry—can be divided into more than one subtopic, the index contains subentries. For example, here is a section of an index containing two main entries:

10

To create an index, you first have to indicate each location in the text that you want to reference, and the word or phrase to use as the main entry or subentry. You can use a word or phrase that is actually in the text, or a word or phrase that is not in the text but describes the reference.

Marking Index Entries

Start by selecting Reference from the Tools menu, and clicking on Index to see this feature bar:

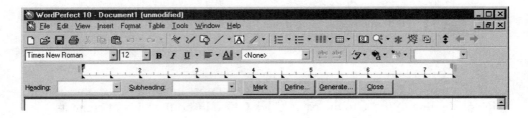

To mark a specific word or phrase to use in the index, select it first, then click in the heading box on the feature bar. WordPerfect 10 inserts the selected word in the box. Otherwise, just type the phrase in the Heading box that you want to use for the index for that location in the document. Repeat the same step to mark a subheading to be associated with the heading. Then click on Mark.

Generating the Index

When you've marked all of the entries for the index, move the insertion point to where you want the index to appear—usually at the end of the document. Click on Define in the Index feature bar to see this dialog box:

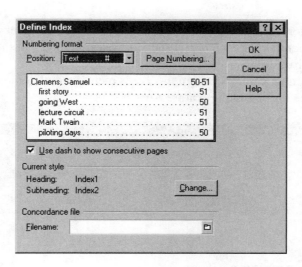

Select the number position, then click OK. Finally, click Generate, choose if you want to create hyperlinks, and then click on OK.

> **TIP** *If you add, edit, or delete text you should update the index. Click anywhere in the index, and then select Generate from the feature bar again.*

10

Using a Concordance File

Rather than scan through your entire document to mark index entries, you can have WordPerfect 10 do it for you by using a *concordance file*. The file is simply a document listing the words or phrases—in the exact case—that you want WordPerfect 10 to include in the index.

Create the concordance file, and save it on your disk. Then, mark any words or phrases in the document you want to index that you may not have included in the concordance. WordPerfect 10 uses both when it generates the index.

In the Define Index dialog box, enter the name of the concordance file in the Filename box, click on OK, and then generate the index.

Creating a Table of Authorities

A table of authorities is similar to an index, but it lists all of the legal citations in a document and the pages that refer to each citation. Each citation is associated with two entries, a short form and a long form. The long form is the complete legal reference; the short form is an abbreviation that you'll use for later reference. You also designate sections for each entry, such as Cases, Statutes, Regulations, and Constitutional Provisions.

Start by selecting Reference from the Tools menu, and clicking on Table of Authorities to see the following feature bar:

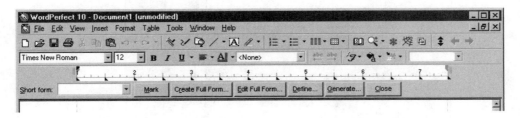

Defining Sections

The first step is to define the sections, or categories, of your citations. Click Define in the feature bar to open the Define Table of Authorities dialog box, then click Create to see these options:

Enter the section name, choose its format from the Position list, and then click OK. The section name appears in the Define Table of Authorities box. Repeat the process for each section, and then close the Define Table of Authorities dialog box.

Marking Citations

The first time you mark a citation, you designate how you want the full form to appear and give it a short form name. You then mark every other occurrence of the citation using the short form.

Select the long form text, then click on the Create Full Form button:

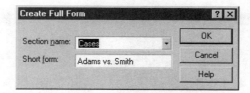

Enter or choose the section name, edit, as necessary, the short form name, and then click OK.

WordPerfect 10 opens a separate window showing the selected full form text. Edit the text so it is exactly how you want it to appear in the table, then click on Close in the feature bar.

When you want to mark the next occurrences of the same citation, click where you want to mark, then select the short form name from the Short form list in the feature bar. Then click on Mark.

Generating the Table

Finally, you have to designate the order of sections in the table and define each section.

Enter one of the section headings where you want the table to appear. Click on Define, choose the section from the list, and click on Insert. This tells WordPerfect 10 to insert the citations for that section at this location.

Repeat the procedure for each section, and then click on Generate to generate the table.

Creating Lists

If you insert a number of figures, statistical tables, equations, or other elements in your document, you should consider creating one or more reference lists. A reference list looks just like a table of authorities, but references any type of item you want. It can even reference words or phrases that you want to list along with their page numbers.

To create a list, you define its name, and then mark the locations in the text to include in it.

Start by selecting Reference from the Tools menu, and clicking on List to see the feature bar shown here:

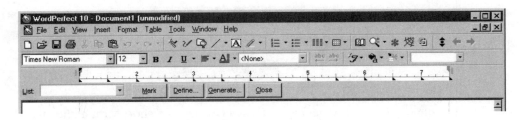

The first step is to define a list. It is almost identical to defining a section for a table of authorities. Click Define in the feature bar to open the Define List dialog box, then click on Create. Type the list name, choose a format, then click on OK. Define each list in the same way, then close the Define List dialog box.

To mark an item for the list, select the text to include, pull down the List list in the feature bar, choose the list, then click on Mark.

Type a heading for the list where you want it to appear in your document. Click on Define, choose the name from the list, and click on Insert. This tells WordPerfect 10 to insert the items marked for that list at this location.

Repeat the procedure for each section, and then click on Generate to create the list.

Creating Cross-References

A cross-reference refers the reader to the location of a heading, bookmark, footnote, endnote, equation, figure, or table. For example, you can refer the reader to a section titled "Computers" using the reference "Please see the section Computers on page 23." Or if you make changes to a paragraph on page 20, you can insert a bookmark in that paragraph and use a cross-reference such as "See my additions on page 20."

Start by selecting Reference from the Tools menu, and clicking on Cross-Reference to see the feature bar shown here:

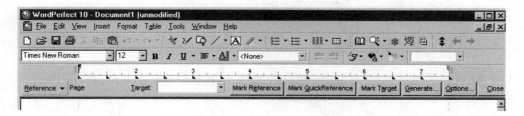

To create a cross-reference, follow these steps:

1. Place the insertion point where you want the cross-reference to appear in the document. Type any text that you want to appear with the reference, such as "Please refer to."

2. Select the type of item you want to reference in the Reference Type list, such as page, chapter, and footnote.

3. Type a target name in the Target box, then click on Mark Reference. A question mark will appear in the reference until you generate it.

4. Move to the location where you want the reference to refer to, and click on Mark Target.

5. Repeat the same procedure for each cross-reference. To reference a target already marked, just select its name from the Target list.

6. To generate the references, click Generate.

Using Quick References

Once you mark references by giving them target names, you can quickly add cross-references to them that include text, such as *page 10* and *number 4 footnote*. By default, each QuickReference type except counter is set to display the type, as in *page 1*, *chapter 5*, and *footnote 4*. You can use the default text or specify other text to appear before and after the reference.

To use the default text to create a QuickReference, just follow these steps:

1. Click in the document where you want the cross-reference to appear.

2. Pull down the Target list and choose the target that you want to reference.

3. Click Mark QuickReference.

4. Repeat the same procedure for each cross-reference.

5. Click Generate.

To change the text that automatically appears before and after a QuickReference, click the Options button on the Cross Reference feature bar. In the dialog box that appears, select the type of reference, enter the text that you want to precede and follow the reference and click OK.

Try It Out

For this chapter, we're going to work on two projects: a table and a columnar document. For the table, we'll enter information, perform some math, and add formats. To create a columnar document we'll reformat some existing text—to save you a little typing. Save both documents when you're done because we'll use them again in later chapters.

We'll start by creating the table shown in Figure 10-21.

1. Use the Tables button in the toolbar to create a table that has six columns and four rows.

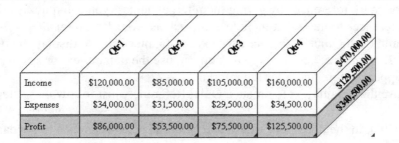

	Qtr1	Qtr2	Qtr3	Qtr4	
Income	$120,000.00	$85,000.00	$105,000.00	$160,000.00	$470,000.00
Expenses	$34,000.00	$31,500.00	$29,500.00	$34,500.00	$129,500.00
Profit	$86,000.00	$53,500.00	$75,500.00	$125,500.00	$340,500.00

FIGURE 10-21 Table for our exercise

2. Enter the information into the table, shown here.

	Qtr1	Qtr2	Qtr3	Qtr4	Total
Income	120000	85000	105000	160000	
Expenses	34000	31500	29500	34500	
Profit					

3. Right-click on the table and select Formula toolbar.

4. Click in cell B4 and, in the formula bar, enter the formula **+B2-B3**.

5. Drag across cells B4 to F4, and click the QuickFill button in the Table property bar.

6. Click in cell F2, and click the QuickSum button in the Formula Bar.

7. Drag across cells B3 to F3, and then click in cell F3, and click the QuickSum button.

	Qtr1	Qtr2	Qtr3	Qtr4	Total
Income	120000	85000	105000	160000	470000
Expenses	34000	31500	29500	34500	129500
Profit	86000	53500	75500	125500	340500

8. Select cells B2 to F4.

9. Pull down the Numeric Format list and select Currency.

10. Pull down the Justification list and select Right.

11. Select cells B1 to F1.

12. Pull down the Justification list and select Center.

13. Right-click in the table and select SpeedFormat from the QuickMenu.

14. Scroll the Available Styles list and select Skewed Right Up Top Right.

15. Click Apply and then Close.

16. Select row 3, pull down the Bottom Border button and select one of the double-line styles.

17. Select row 4, pull down the Cell Fill button and choose one of the light shades or colors.

18. Save the table with the name Profit Table.

Now, let's tackle a columnar document.

1. Open the document Tae Kwon Do.

2. Place the insertion point at the start of the first paragraph of text.

3. Pull down the Column button in the toolbar and select 2 Columns.

4. Click in the paragraph that is surrounded in a text box.

5. Select Format | Paragraph | Border/Fill.

6. Select the no border option (the blank space on the far top left of the Available Border Styles list) and click OK.

7. Select Format | Paragraph | Format.

8. Set the left and right margin adjustments to 0.

9. Click OK.

10. Select all of the text below the headline.

11. Select Format | Paragraph | Format.

12. Set the Number of Lines option to 1, and click OK.

Finally, look at the way the tabbed text appears at the end of the document:

```
⇨≡                    5    7           B    C
                      Silla dynasty is founded
                      3    1    3          A    D
                      Korea  drives  out  Chinese
      invaders

                      4    2    5          A    D
                      Buddhism established in Korea
                      9    1    8          A    D
                      The    Koguryo    dynasty    is
      founded

                      1    2    5    9         A    D
                      Mongol armies conquer Korea
```

The tabs and spacing that we set when we originally typed the document are no longer appropriate. We'll convert that text into a table and adjust the spacing.

13. Select all of the tabbed text.

14. Select Convert from the Table menu.

15. Specify 2 as the number of columns and click OK. (If there is an extra blank column at the start of the table, delete that column now.)

16. Adjust the right margin of the table so it is at the right margin of the column.

17. Finally, select the heading of the document, above the columns, and choose 32 from the Font Size list.

18. Using the Save As command in the File menu, save the document with the name Tae Kwon Do Columns.

The final document will appear as shown in Figure 10-22.

10

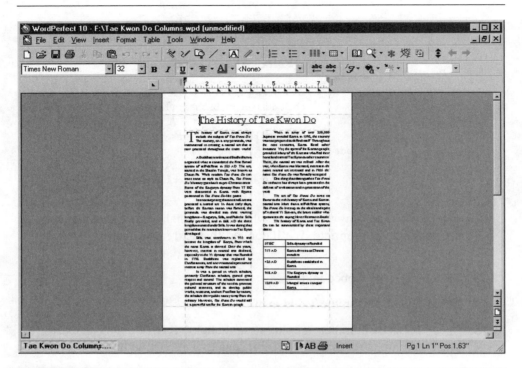

FIGURE 10-22 Complete columnar document with table

Chapter 11

Customizing WordPerfect 10

Y ou probably have personalized your desk and office to suit yourself. You've spread out your pictures and desk accessories and arranged things for the way you like to work. Your office probably looks different from other offices, because we all have our own tastes and ways of working. You can customize WordPerfect the same way, adjusting how things look and work to suit your own work habits.

You learned in earlier chapters how to change WordPerfect's default document settings. These settings determine how your documents will appear if you don't bother changing any formats.

For example, in Chapter 8, you learned how to change the default template and system styles. In Chapter 7, you learned how to select a new initial font, and in Chapter 10, you found out how to select an initial format for tables.

In this chapter you'll learn how to customize the way WordPerfect works.

Saving Printer Settings

Let's start with something that has everyday use: printer settings. When you display the Print dialog box to print a document, you have to select options, such as the number of copies, printer resolution, and so on. If you find yourself changing the same settings frequently, then consider saving the settings.

1. Click on the Print button to display the Print dialog box.

2. Set the printer options the way you want them. The text in the Settings box changes to Custom (Current settings not saved).

3. Click on the Edit Settings button at the bottom of the Main tab of the Print dialog box, point to open the Named Settings dialog box, shown in Figure 11-1. The box lists the categories of print settings that you can save. Disable the checkboxes next to the categories you do not want to save; enable the checkboxes next to the categories that you want to save. You can also click on the plus sign next to a checkbox to display and select the specific settings in that category.

4. Type a name for the saved settings in the Name for Current Settings box. Leave the name box set at Default if you want to use these settings for every document.

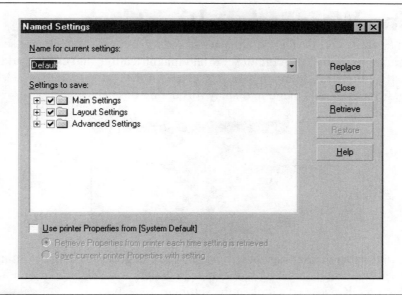

FIGURE 11-1   Saving printer settings

5. Select the Use Printer Properties from [System Default] option if you also want to save the printer's properties. The properties include such items as the paper type, resolution, and other settings unique to your printer.

6. Click Add.

7. Click Close.

The setting name that you entered is now included in the Settings drop-down list. To later use the specifications, just select its name in the list.

> **NOTE**   *You can also apply the settings by clicking on the setting name in the Named Settings dialog box and clicking on Retrieve.*

If you want to return to WordPerfect's default printer settings, pull down the Settings list, point to Application Default, and click on Restore.

Changing WordPerfect 10 Settings

All of the other WordPerfect defaults are stored as settings. You edit the settings, for example, to change the default view and magnification, and even to add your own custom toolbars and menu bars. To set any of the settings, start by selecting Settings from the Tools menu to display this dialog box:

The options in the Settings box represent the categories of default settings. To change settings, click on the icon to display a dialog box, select your options, and then click on OK. Now let's look at the settings.

Display Settings

The Display Settings dialog box, shown in Figure 11-2, controls the default appearance of the WordPerfect document window. The box contains several pages, each dedicated to a classification of options.

Document Page

The Document page of the dialog box controls which WordPerfect elements are displayed on the screen. In the Show section, you can choose to display text and dialog boxes using the Windows color settings rather than WordPerfect's, and you can choose to display or hide these elements:

- Table grid lines
- Table formula indicators
- Margin icons
- Graphics
- Hidden text

FIGURE 11-2   Display settings

- RealTime Preview
- Windows system colors

Use the options in the Shadow Cursor section to determine the color and shape of the shadow cursor, when it appears, and where the cursor aligns when you click. By default, the shadow cursor appears only when you're pointing in a blank white space, but you can choose to have it appear only when you're in text, or both. The Snap To options determine where the actual cursor appears when you click. If you select Margins, for example, you can only click to place the cursor at the left or right margin, or in the center of the page. You can also choose to have the cursor snap to tab stops (the default), indentation positions, or any character (spaces) position.

In the Scroll Bars section you can deselect the Vertical or Horizontal checkboxes if you do not want the scroll bars to appear on the screen. Use the Browse By Position option to determine where the Browse By button appears in the scroll bar: Bottom Only, Top Only, or Bottom and Top.

Use the Measurement section to set the units of measurement in dialog boxes and in the application bar and ruler. Use the Units of Measure list to determine the default unit accepted in dialog boxes, such as when changing margins and creating a page size. Your choices are inches (" or i); centimeters (c); millimeters (mm); points (p); and units of 1200ths of an inch (w), formerly known as "WordPerfect units." Use the Application Bar/Ruler display list, which offers the same options, to determine the way measurements are displayed on the ruler and in the position section of the application bar. In this case, for example, the ruler appears marked in points:

Symbols Page

When you click on the Show ¶ command in the View menu, WordPerfect displays symbols for many characters and codes that normally do not appear, such as spaces, tabs, and carriage returns. You can choose which characters appear in this page of the dialog box. Deselect the checkbox for any items that you do not want to appear.

Reveal Codes Page

The options in this page of the dialog box, shown in Figure 11-3, let you change the appearance of the Reveal Codes window.

You can choose to use the default system colors or select a custom text and background color. Click on the Font button to select the font and size that you want the text to appear in the window—the default is 10.5-point MS Sans Serif. Make the font smaller, for example, if you want to see more lines of codes in the Reveal Codes window without taking up additional space on the screen. Your choices in the Format section determine the appearance of the text and the default size of the window:

■ *Wrap Lines at Window* divides codes between lines if they do not fit on the line. With this option deselected, the code may scroll off the right edge of the window.

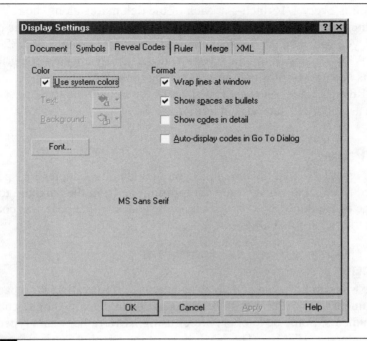

FIGURE 11-3   Reveal Codes Page

11

■ *Show Spaces as Bullets* uses bullet characters to represent where you've pressed the SPACEBAR in a document. Deselect this option to show spaces as blank spaces.

■ *Show Codes in Detail* displays the full details of all codes. With this option off, many codes are shown abbreviated and are only shown in detail when you place the insertion point immediately to the left of a code.

■ *Auto-display codes in Go To Dialog* will display the Reveal Codes pane when you find a successful match when looking for a WordPerfect code from the Go To dialog box.

Ruler Page

There are only two options in this page of the dialog box.

Tabs Snap to Ruler Grid forces tabs that you set to appear at the nearest grid point on the ruler. When the unit of measurement is inches, for example, the ruler has grid points every 1/16-inch—at each of the tick marks along the ruler. In addition, there are also grid points in between the tick marks. With this option turned off, you can set a tab between the grid lines, for example, at 1/32-inch intervals. With this option on, the tab stop automatically appears at a grid point, so every tab is at some 1/16th-inch multiple along the ruler.

Show Ruler Guides controls the display of the dotted line that appears down the screen as you move tabs and margin markers.

Merge Page

When you create a merge document, as you will learn in Chapter 12, special codes are inserted to indicate where you want information from the database to appear. In this page of the dialog box, you set how the codes will appear—as codes, as graphic markers, or not at all.

XML Page

Extensible Markup Language (XML) is a language for creating Web pages and other documents. WordPerfect allows users to create, open, validate, and save XML documents. Some developers prefer using XML rather than Hypertext Markup Language (HTML). The XML page of the Display Settings box lets you determine how the codes appear in the document and in the Reveal Codes pane.

Environment Settings

The environment settings, shown in Figure 11-4, determine some basic ways that WordPerfect performs.

General Page

The User Information section determines what appears on the summary page and in comments you create. Enter the name you want in the summary page, the initials you want to appear with comments, and the color you want to indicate your comments.

The Activate Hypertext Links option determines if hypertext links are on or off. When this option is selected, clicking on a hypertext or Web link moves to the bookmark or Web page. If you are working in a document with Web page links and don't want to launch your browser accidentally, deselect this option.

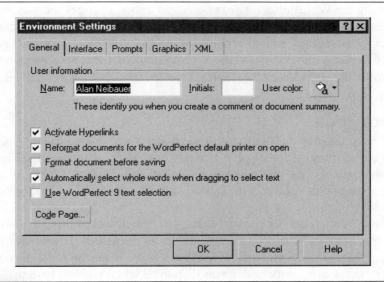

FIGURE 11-4   Environment Settings

WordPerfect documents contain font and other codes that correspond to the features of your printer. If you open a document that was created for another printer, the codes will not match those of yours. To avoid any printing problems, WordPerfect reformats the document when you open it to match the printer currently being used. You'll know this is happening because you'll see a message on the screen reporting that the process is taking place. Here's the rub: if you save the document and later open it on the computer using the other printer, WordPerfect will have to reformat it again. In some cases, the reformatting back and forth may change spacing or other formats, so you can turn off this feature by deselecting the Reformat Documents for the WordPerfect Default Printer on Open checkbox.

Select the Format Document Before Saving checkbox (formerly the Slow Save option) if you want WordPerfect to completely format documents before it saves them.

The Automatically Select Whole Words When Dragging to Select Text option controls how WordPerfect selects words when you drag the mouse. With this option turned on, WordPerfect selects the entire word when you drag over the space before or after it. Turn this option off if you want to select parts of a word, and the space before or after, without selecting the entire word.

Choosing the WordPerfect 9 Text Selection option changes the way words are selected as you drag. In WordPerfect 9, for example, if you quadruple-click, you will select the paragraph and all of the hard returns after it until the next paragraph. When you deselect this option (to use WordPerfect 10's text selection), only the hard return at the end of the paragraph is selected.

Interface Page

In the Items to Display on Menus section, choose what you want to appear in menus. You can turn off the display of recently used documents in the File menu and choose to display the shortcut key combinations in menus or the QuickTips that appear when you point to a menu item, a toolbar button, or other button or screen object.

The Save Workspace section can save you a great deal of time. The *workspace* is the arrangement of your document windows on the screen. If you save the workspace, the next time you start WordPerfect, you'll see the same documents, in the same window arrangement that was displayed when you last exited WordPerfect. You can choose to always save the workspace when you exit WordPerfect, to never save the workspace, or to display a prompt asking if you want to save the workspace when you exit. Prompt on Exit is a good compromise, since it gives you the choice. This way, you can determine if you want to return to the same window arrangement the next time you start.

Use the Interface Language list to choose the language you are using—chances are you'll have only one choice.

Prompts Page

Use the Prompt section to control when WordPerfect prompts you to select a hyphenation point and how it operates when you delete codes and table formulas. Pull down the On Hyphenation list, and choose if you want WordPerfect to always or never prompt you to select a hyphenation point, or just to display a prompt when a suitable automatic hyphenation is not available. You can also choose if you want WordPerfect to stop the insertion point when pressing BACKSPACE or DEL would erase a hidden code, or to display a message asking you to confirm if you are about to delete a formula in a table cell.

In the Beep On section you tell WordPerfect when to beep at you—when an error occurs, when an automatic hyphenation is suggested, or when a find command cannot locate the text.

Graphics Page

When you want to use a graphic in a document, as you'll see in Chapter 13, you insert it, and then change its position and size to fit in your document. The Graphics page gives you the option of using the mouse to first drag a box where you want the graphic to appear and then selecting the graphic.

This page also lets you select between two equation editors or choose to display a prompt asking which one you want to use each time you begin an equation.

XML Page

The options on this page offer three settings for working with XML documents:

- Import HTML documents using the XML component

- Prompt for the file type when importing XML/SMGL documents

- Insert omitted tags required by DTD during SGML import

> **NOTE** *DTD stands for Document Type Definition, and SGML stands for Standard Generalized Markup Language*

Files Settings

The Files Settings dialog box, shown in Figure 11-5, determines where documents, templates, graphics, and other files used by WordPerfect are stored on your disk. Each page of the dialog box sets the location of one type of file.

> **TIP** *Click on View All for a summary of all file locations.*

Use the options in the Document page of the dialog box, for example, to determine the default format, directory, and extension of your documents, and to automatically save documents. In the Default Document Folder text box, enter the folder where you want your documents to be saved. When you display the Open and Save dialog boxes, the files in that directory will automatically appear. You can also designate another default document extension or choose not to use a default extension at all.

By default, WordPerfect performs a timed backup of your document every ten minutes. As you work, WordPerfect saves the document to a temporary file, so if

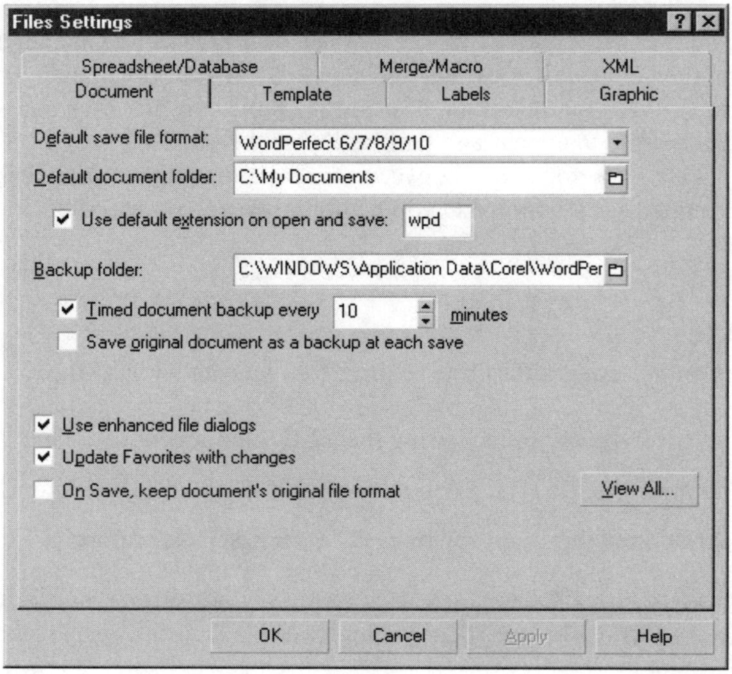

FIGURE 11-5 Files Settings dialog box

your computer goes haywire and you have to reboot, you'll have the opportunity of opening the temporary file to retrieve your work. This option is turned on when the Timed Document Backup checkbox is selected. The number of minutes between backups is specified in the corresponding text box. The backup files are stored in the location specified in the Backup Folder box. You can turn off this feature by deselecting the checkbox, or change the folder or number of minutes between backups.

You can also choose to create an original document backup. With this option on, WordPerfect saves a copy of the current version of the document with the same name but using the extension BK!. This file will not contain any of the editing or formatting that you performed since you last saved the document. If you change your mind about all of the last changes you made, open the BK! file.

The Update Favorites with Changes setting changes the shortcuts in the Favorites folder to the directories that you select in this dialog box.

Deselect the Use Enhanced File Dialogs checkbox if you do not want to access all of the features of WordPerfect's Open and Save file dialog boxes. You will still be able to open and save files, but the toolbar, find, and search options will not be available. Disable this option if using the enhanced boxes creates problems on your system.

When you open a file that is not in WordPerfect's format and then save it, you'll be asked if you want to save it in WordPerfect format. Turn on the On Save Keep Document's Original File Format checkbox if you want to automatically save documents in their original format.

Summary Settings

A summary sheet contains statistical information about your document and reference information about who created it, when it was modified, and what the document is all about, including a descriptive name. You can see the document's summary sheet by selecting Properties from the File menu.

In the Summary page, enter the information requested. You can also click on the Setup button to choose additional text boxes to add to the summary. The Options lists in the Summary page let you print or delete the summary, save it as its own document, or extract information from the document into the Subject text box. If you select Extract Information from Document, WordPerfect looks for a line starting with the characters "RE:" and inserts any text following the characters into the Subject text box.

In the Summary Settings dialog box, you can set WordPerfect to display the Summary page when you save and exit a document, so you can enter information into it. You can also choose these options:

- On open, use the descriptive name as the new filename

- When saving a new document, use the long filename as the descriptive name

In addition, you can enter a default descriptive type that initially appears in all Summary pages, and enter subject search text other than "RE:". For example, if your office uses "Subject:", enter it in place of "RE:". Then when you click on Extract in the Options list of the Summary box, WordPerfect will insert the text following "Subject:" in the Subject text box.

Convert Settings

When you open graphic files or documents created by other word processing programs, WordPerfect converts them into a format that it understands. The Convert Settings option controls how this process is performed in two pages, Compatibility and Convert.

In the Compatibility page, you select the format that you will be converting from, such as Microsoft Word, and how specific conversion options are handled. You can choose, for example, to allow graphic boxes in the nonprintable margins of the page.

The Convert page of the dialog box contains options for dealing with text files and graphic objects.

The Delimiters section of the Convert page controls how ASCII-delimited text files are converted. This file is usually created by a database or spreadsheet program—each row of the spreadsheet or database record is a document line. You use this section of the dialog box to determine the character that separates database fields or spreadsheet cells, and the character or code that separates rows or records.

The Characters section designates any special characters that surround database fields or information from a spreadsheet cell. The default is the quotation mark. You can also designate characters that you want WordPerfect to remove—strip—from the information when it is converted.

The Windows Metafile options control how graphic files are converted. The Metafile format (using the WMF extension) is a common format that Windows applications use for graphic objects. By default, WordPerfect opens a Metafile graphic and inserts it into the document but leaves it in its original format. You can also choose to convert the file into WordPerfect's own WPG format or to save the file in both formats. Choose the WPG option if you want to use the document with earlier versions of WordPerfect.

The Options button in the Convert Settings dialog box lets you set other conversion settings. The options are as follows:

- *Code Pages* lets you select sets of characters that will be used to convert characters in a document. In most cases, for example, the letter "A" in the original document will be displayed as the letter "A" on the screen. Depending on the system and the font that you used to create the file, some characters in the document may not have equivalents in WordPerfect. The Code Pages option lets you select character sets to use when converting documents.

■ *Document* lets you select the language, units of measurement, underline style, margins, and page size for converted documents.

■ *WP 4.2 Fonts* lets you designate the fonts that you used with documents created with WordPerfect 4.2 for DOS so Windows fonts can be substituted for them.

■ *DCA/DisplayWrite Fonts* lets you designate the fonts you used for DCA- and DisplayWrite-formatted documents.

Application Bar Settings

When you want to change the items that appear on the application bar, click the Application Bar icon in the Settings dialog box to display the options shown in Figure 11-6.

> **TIP**   *You can also customize the application bar by right-clicking on it and choosing Settings from the QuickMenu.*

11

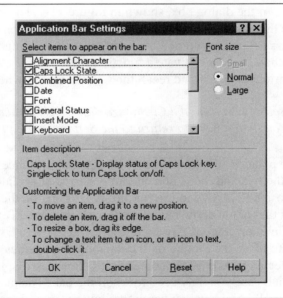

FIGURE 11-6   Changing the items on the application bar

Click on the checkboxes for the items that you want to add or remove from the application bar, and select a font size—either small, normal, or large. You can also remove an item from the bar by dragging it off, and you can change an item's position by dragging it within the bar.

The default bar is a mix of icons and text. The Shadow Cursor, Caps Lock, and Printers items are icons; Insert and the position indicators are text.

> **TIP** *Click on Default to return to the default WordPerfect application bar.*

Customization Settings

You can customize toolbars, property bars, menus, and keyboard layouts using different tabs of the Customize dialog box. Access the dialog box from Customize in the Settings box, or by right-clicking on a toolbar or property bar and choosing Settings from the QuickMenu. The options are similar in each.

Toolbar Settings

The Toolbars page of the dialog box, shown in Figure 11-7, lets you create and edit toolbars. Use this feature to add buttons for features that you use often or to create new toolbars for custom combinations of tools. By adding frequently used functions to a toolbar, you can activate a function with a single click of the mouse. You can create various toolbars and recall them to the screen when needed.

> **TIP** *You can select tabs from the Customize dialog box to customize the other objects. You do not have to return to the Settings dialog box.*

To change the position of a toolbar, as well as the appearance of its tools, click on the toolbar in the list, and then click on Options to see the dialog box shown in Figure 11-8. Choose a Font Size to use for the style of text on the button face, and select if you want the tool to show the name of the command (Text), an icon representing the function (Picture), or both (Picture and Text). Use the Toolbar Location options to place the toolbar on the top, bottom, or sides of the screen, or to display it as a rectangular palette. You can also choose to display the button in a larger size (in which case you may need to scroll the bar to display some buttons) and to include a scroll bar when there are more buttons than fit across the screen, or to display the buttons in more than one line. Click on OK to return to the Toolbars page.

FIGURE 11-7   Customize dialog box for toolbars

11

To add or delete a button from a toolbar, select it in the Available Toolbars list, and click on Edit. The toolbar appears onscreen along with the Toolbar Editor, shown in Figure 11-9. To create a new toolbar, click on Create, type the name for

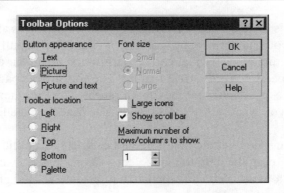

FIGURE 11-8   Changing the position and appearance of the toolbar

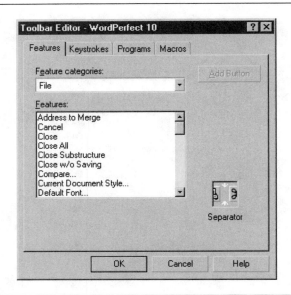

FIGURE 11-9 Toolbar Editor

the bar in the box that appears, and click on OK. The Toolbar Editor appears with a blank toolbar on the screen.

> **TIP** *You can also edit the current toolbar by right-clicking on it and choosing Edit from the QuickMenu. Choose Customize from the QuickMenu to open the Customize dialog box.*

The first step is to select the type of item you want to add as a tool. A *feature* is a command that you can perform by selecting an item from a pull-down menu. You select the feature category that corresponds to the menu bar commands and then choose the specific WordPerfect feature. The Keystrokes page lets you enter a series of keystrokes that you want the tool to repeat. The Programs page lets you select a program you want the tool to execute. The Macros page lets you assign a macro to the tool.

To add a feature, double-click on it in the Features list, or click on it and then on Add Button, or drag the item to the toolbar—WordPerfect inserts a button for the feature in the toolbar. You can organize buttons into related groups by adding extra space between them. Drag the Separator icon to the bar where you want to add space between buttons.

To remove a tool from the toolbar and change its position, use the Toolbar
Editor. Remove a tool by dragging it off the bar; change its position by dragging it
to another location on the bar. When you're satisfied with the toolbar, click on OK.

You can always edit it by selecting it in the Available Toolbars list and
clicking on Edit. You can also use the Customize dialog box to delete, rename, and
copy a toolbar.

*When working in your document, you can remove an icon or change its
position by pressing and holding the ALT key and clicking and dragging
the icon off the toolbar or to its preferred location.*

Editing Toolbar Buttons   To customize the toolbar even more, you can change the
icon on a tool or the text that appears on it, and edit the text of the QuickTip that
appears when you point to the button. To do this, however, you must be in the
Toolbar Editor. In the Toolbars page of the Customize dialog box, click on the
toolbar that contains the tool you want to change, and then click on the Edit
button. Next, point to the tool that you want to change in the toolbar, right-click
the mouse, and select Customize from the menu that appears. WordPerfect
displays the Customize Button dialog box:

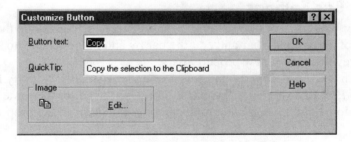

Enter any text that you want to appear on the tool in the Button Text box, and
enter the text for the tool's QuickTip. To change the icon on the tool, click on the
Edit button to see the Image Editor shown in Figure 11-10. In the box that
displays the enlarged icon, click with the left or right mouse button to add one
pixel of color. Choose the color by clicking the left or right mouse button on the
color in the Colors section. In the Drawing mode section, select Single Pixel or
Fill Whole Area to select the action of the click. Single Pixel inserts one pixel; Fill
Whole Area inserts the color in all consecutive cells where you click. You can
also draw in the small graphic of the button in the lower-right corner. Select Undo
to cancel your last change, or click on Clear to erase the entire icon to start from a
blank button.

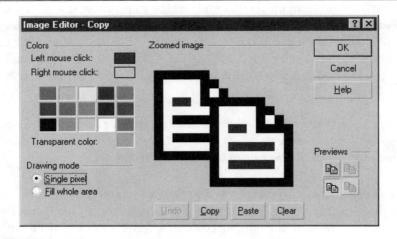

FIGURE 11-10   Image Editor

Property Bar Settings

The Property Bars page of the Customize dialog box lets you change the appearance of the property bar and edit the bar by adding new items to it. You cannot, however, create a new property bar.

To add an item to a property bar, select it in the Available Property Bars list, and click on Edit to display the Toolbar Editor. Use the editor the same way as you learned previously for customizing toolbars, but drag items to the property bar instead.

 You can also edit the current property bar by right-clicking on it and choosing Edit from the QuickMenu.

Menu Bar Settings

Just as you can edit and create toolbars, you can also edit and create menu bars and pull-down menus. Select the Menus tab in the Customize Settings box to see the following options:

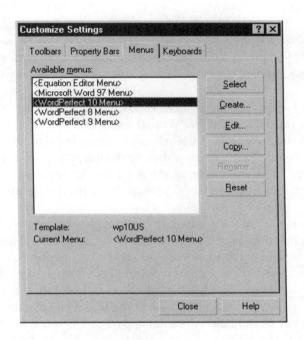

You can display any of the five built-in menu bars or create your own. You cannot edit one of the built-in bars, but you can create new menu bars by adding menus and items to an existing one. Start by clicking on the built-in bar that you want to use for the base, and then click on the Create button. Type a name for the bar in the box that appears, and then click on OK.

You'll see the Menu Editor, which is exactly like the Toolbar Editor but with icons labeled "Menu" and "Separator." To add features to the menu that you can perform with a single click, double-click on the Menu icon. To create a new menu, drag the Menu icon to the menu bar. When the item labeled "Menu" appears, double-click on it to display a dialog box where you give it a name and a description that appears when you point to it. Use an ampersand to designate the underlined selection letter—for example, "&Special" becomes "Special."

To add an item to a menu, drag the item to the menu you want to insert it in, continue pulling down the menu, and place the item in the desired position. You can also double-click on the program feature to place it in the menu bar and drag it to the menu. To delete an item or a menu, drag it off the menu bar.

Drag the Separator icon to add a separator line between items in the menu.

11

Keyboard Settings

You're in luck if you prefer using keyboard combinations to perform commands. You can use the Keyboard Shortcuts dialog box to create your own shortcut key combinations.

Click on the Keyboards tab on the Customize Settings dialog box to see a list of six built-in keyboard layouts: WPWin 10 Keyboard, WPWin 9 Keyboard, WPWin 8 Keyboard, WPDOS 6.1 Keyboard, Equation Editor Keyboard, and MS Word 2000 Keyboard. To create your own keyboard, select the one that you want to use for the base, click on Create, type a name for the keyboard, and click on OK. WordPerfect then displays the Keyboard Shortcuts dialog box that is shown in Figure 11-11.

In the list on the left, click on the key combination that you wish to assign to a feature, key combination, program, or macro. To assign the new item to it, select it in the appropriate page in the section on the right of the dialog box, and then click on Assign Feature to Key. The item you selected is assigned to the key combination, replacing any that had already been assigned to it. For each key combination in the list, you can also deselect the Shortcut Key Appears on Menu checkbox so the key combination does not appear on the related pull-down menu.

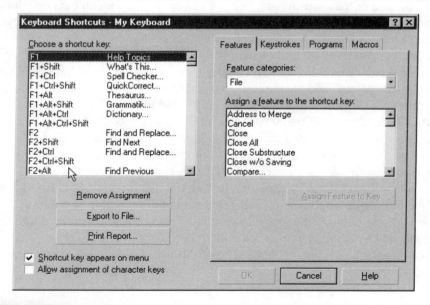

FIGURE 11-11   The Keyboard Shortcuts dialog box

If you click on Allow Assignment of Character Keys, the list on the left changes to contain all of the regular character keystrokes. You can then assign a feature or other keystroke to it.

Even those of us with the best memories may have difficulty remembering all of the keyboard assignments. As a guide, you can choose to save a list of the assignments in a file or print out a copy of them. Click Export to File to save the assignments in a format that you can open into a spreadsheet program or word processor (called a Comma Separated Values, or CSV) file. Use the Print Report button for a hardcopy reference.

> **TIP** *To remove a shortcut key function from a key combination, click on it in the list, and click on the Remove Assignment button.*

Creating Macros

> **TIP** *If you are an advanced user, select Tools | Macros | Visual Basic Editor to create macros in Visual Basic for Applications (VBA).*

One other way to customize WordPerfect is to add your own commands through macros. A *macro* is a series of keystroke, menu, property bar, and toolbar selections that you can store on your disk or in a template. You can then repeat all of the keystrokes and commands by just "playing" the macro at some other time. You can use a macro to insert formatted text, to apply a set of commonly used formats, or to perform any action that you can save time by repeating.

The easiest way to create a macro is to record it. You just enter the keystrokes, or perform any other function, and WordPerfect records them.

> **TIP** *You can also create a macro using the PerfectScript accessory from the taskbar.*

You can record macros in two locations: in a file on your disk or in a template. Storing the macro on the disk means that you can later access it no matter what document or template you are using. You can also copy the macro on to a floppy disk and use it on another computer that's running WordPerfect for Windows. If you store the macro in a template, you still may have two choices. If you are using a template other than the default, you can choose to store the macro with either the default template or the one being used with the document. Saving the macro in the default template makes it available with every document using that template.

11

To record a macro, pull down the Tools menu, and select either Macro or Template Macro, depending on where you want to save it.

Storing Macros on the Disk

To save the macro on the disk, point to Macro, and then click on Record in the menu that appears. WordPerfect displays a dialog box where you select the folder in which to store the macro and enter the macro name. By default, macros are stored in the \Windows\Application Data\Corel\PerfectScript\10\WordPerfect folder and use the WCM extension. It's best to use the default folder so you'll be able to easily access your macros in the default location. Type a name for the macro, and then click on Record.

Saving Macros in a Template

To save your macro in a template, pull down the Tools menu, point to Template Macro, and then click on Record. In the dialog box that appears, type a name for the macro.

Your macro is only available to documents using the template where it is stored. If you started the document using the default template, then the macro is available to all new documents that use the default template. If you started the document with another template, the macro is saved there. To store the macro in the default template, click on Location to see this dialog box:

Choose the template where you want to store the macro. To use your choice as the default for all template macros, click on the Use As Default checkbox. Click on OK to return to the Record Template Macro dialog box. Now click on Record to start recording your macro.

Recording Macros

Once you select Record, WordPerfect displays the macro bar shown here and starts recording your keystrokes.

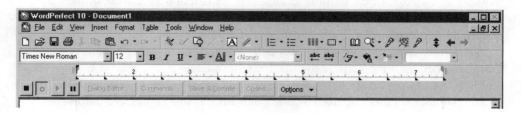

When you are recording a macro, you can only use the mouse to select menu, toolbar, property bar, and dialog box options. You cannot use it to select text and to position the insertion point—use keystrokes for that. Perform all of the functions that you want to record, and then click on the Stop button in the macro bar.

Playing Macros

To play a macro, pull down the Tools menu, and select either Macro or Template Macro, depending on where the macro is stored.

If the macro is stored on the disk, the Play Macro dialog box lists macros in the default directory. Double-click on the macro name, or type the name, and click on Play.

If the macro is stored in a template, the Play Template Macro dialog box appears. Double-click on the macro name, or select it, and click on Play. If the macro isn't listed, click on Location, and then choose the template where the macro is stored. Click on OK, and then select it in the Play box.

Assigning Macros to Menus, Toolbars, or the Property Bar

Earlier in this chapter, you learned how to customize WordPerfect by adding items to the menu bar, toolbar, or property bar. In each case, the Toolbar Editor dialog box used to add items also contained a Macros page (see Figure 11-9 earlier in this chapter).

To add a macro to the bar, select either Add Template Macro or Add Macro, depending on where the macro is stored. Double-click on the macro to insert it into the menu, toolbar, or property bar.

Editing Macros

If you make a mistake when recording a macro, you can record it again. You can also edit the macro to change or add commands. Editing and writing macros requires knowledge of the command language and an understanding of the principles of computer programming. (For more information about the macro command language, refer to the WordPerfect Help system.)

To edit a macro, pull down the Tools menu, and select either Macro or Template, depending on where the macro is stored, and then click on Edit. In the dialog box that appears, double-click on the macro you want to edit, or select it, and then click on Edit. The macro commands appear in a separate window, numbered, along with the macro bar, as shown in Figure 11-12.

All of the commands are listed in WordPerfect's macro language. This is an extensive programming language that can be used to write complete applications built around WordPerfect for Windows.

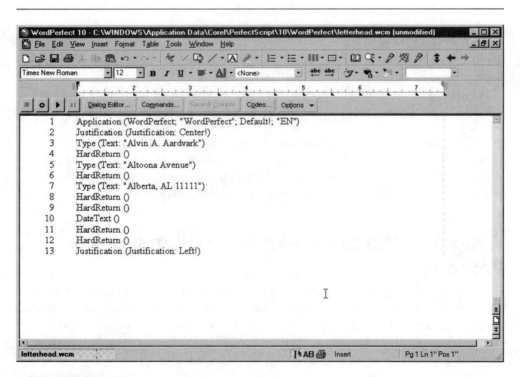

FIGURE 11-12   Editing a macro

The first line of the macro identifies the program and default language that it uses. The remainder of the macro performs the reported instructions. For example, the Type command inserts text into the document using the syntax Type(Text: "*insert this text*"). Pressing ENTER when recording the macro inserts the HardReturn() command.

If you want to change the text that a macro generates, just edit any of the text within the quotation marks in the Type command. To insert new text, you have to insert a new Type command, following the proper syntax. If you want the macro to perform a carriage return, type the HardReturn() command; pressing ENTER in the macro itself does not perform a carriage return when you play the macro. Remember that when you play the macro, WordPerfect follows the macro commands exactly. So if you enter commands in the wrong order, or don't use the proper syntax for a command, your macro will not operate correctly.

Rather than type commands into the macro, it is more efficient to add them by recording. Place the insertion point in the macro where you want the new commands to appear, and then click on the Record button in the macro bar. WordPerfect opens a new blank window with another macro bar. Type the text or perform the functions that you want to add to the macro, and then click on the Stop button. WordPerfect switches back to the macro window, with your newly recorded commands inserted. Click on the Save & Compile button in the macro bar, and then close the window.

Command Inserter

WordPerfect 10's macro language is a sophisticated programming language with hundreds of commands. You can learn about the commands using the online help system and the Reference Center documents that come with the WordPerfect Office 2002 CD. You can quickly insert macro commands by clicking on the Commands button in the macro bar to display the dialog box shown in Figure 11-13.

In the Command Type box, select the type of command you want to insert. By default, the box lists all WordPerfect commands. (If WordPerfect does not appear in the Command Type box, pull down the list and select WordPerfect to record a WordPerfect function.) Select the command in the Commands list box. If you select a command that includes parameters, the parameters appear in the Parameters list box. Select the parameter you want to set. If the parameter has optional items, an additional Enumerators list box appears, and you can select a value from the list. In the Command Edit text box, you can edit the macro command. When you are ready to insert the command, select Insert.

11

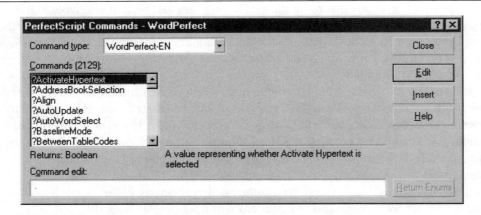

FIGURE 11-13   Selecting a macro command

Other Macro Features

You might find the other options in the macro bar useful. Both of these options are for advanced macro writers. The Codes button displays lists of search, merge, date, and other codes that you can insert into the macro.

The Options button lets you change how the macro is saved. If you are editing a template macro and want to save it on the disk, for example, click on Options, and select Save as Macro. You can also choose Save as Template Macro to store a disk macro on the template. You can use the other options to remove the macro bar and close the macro.

Dialog Editor

Dialog Editor displays a dialog box for creating dialog boxes for your macros. While creating a dialog box is easy using the editor, taking advantage of the box in your macro requires extensive knowledge of the WordPerfect macro language. You can get additional information on the macro language using the WordPerfect Help menu and on the Corel Web site, http://www.corel.com.

The general procedure, however, is to click on Dialog Editor to see the dialog box shown next. The box lists all of the dialog boxes that have been created and stored for use with the current macro.

To create a new dialog box, select New from the File menu. The notation "NewDialog" appears highlighted in the list. Replace "NewDialog" with a name that you want to use for the box you are creating. Then, double-click on the icon next to the name to display the Corel PerfectScript Dialog Editor and a blank dialog box as shown in Figure 11-14.

Use the buttons and commands in the Dialog Editor to add items to the dialog box. For example, click on the icon of an OK button in the Dialog Editor toolbar, then click in the dialog box where you want to place a push button to serve as an OK, a Close, or a Cancel button. You can add all of the objects that you've seen in Corel WordPerfect's own dialog boxes. You can move and resize the objects by dragging, and you can set their properties by right-clicking on the item and choosing Properties from the QuickMenu. Use that technique, for example, to designate the button as OK, Close, or Cancel, to add items to a list box, or to change the default name of an option button or checkbox.

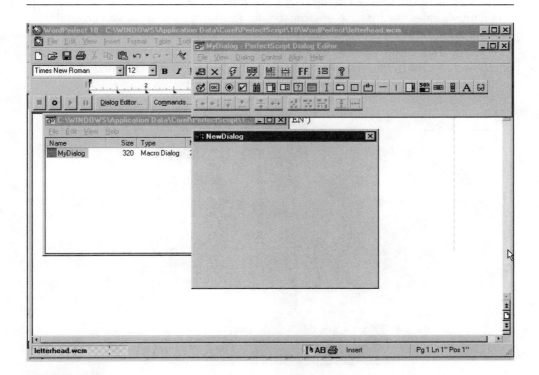

FIGURE 11-14   Corel PerfectScript Dialog Editor

To see how the dialog box will actually appear in your macro, click on the Test the Dialog button in the Dialog Editor toolbar, as shown in the margin. Figure 11-15, for example, shows a custom dialog box with option buttons, a text box, push buttons, and a list box. To return to editing, press ESC, or click on a push button that you've added.

By setting the properties of items in the box, you can create a macro that displays text and performs operations. For example, the option button labeled Credit has been associated with the variable Credit, while the list box as been assigned the variable Customer. A command in the macro Type(Customer), for example, will then insert the name of the person selected in the list box.

When you've finished, select Save from the Dialog Editor File menu, and then choose Close from the File menu to return to the list of dialog boxes. Finally, select Close from the File menu to return to the macro.

When you want to use the dialog box in your macro, insert the DialogShow command using the syntax DialogShow("*boxname*";"WordPerfect"). The dialog box name is case-sensitive, so you must enter the name exactly as you created it. The macro in Figure 11-16, for instance, uses the dialog box shown in Figure 11-15. The dialog box was named MyDialog in place of NewDialog, and that name was used in the macro. Note that you must use the name assigned in the box in the Dialog Editor, not the title displayed on the box itself.

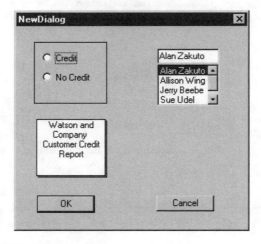

FIGURE 11-15   Custom dialog box

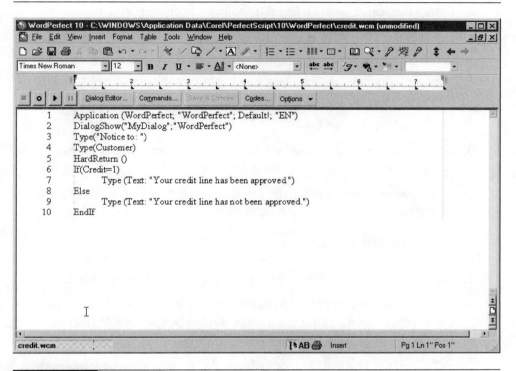

```
1      Application (WordPerfect; "WordPerfect"; Default!; "EN")
2      DialogShow("MyDialog";"WordPerfect")
3      Type("Notice to: ")
4      Type(Customer)
5      HardReturn ()
6      If(Credit=1)
7             Type (Text: "Your credit line has been approved.")
8      Else
9             Type (Text: "Your credit line has not been approved.")
10     EndIf
```

FIGURE 11-16   Macro using custom dialog box

Try It Out

As an example of customizing WordPerfect, let's create your own personal toolbar that contains a combination of features and macros. We'll start by creating macros that insert your letterhead and closing into a letter. We'll then add those macros, along with some other items, to a custom toolbar.

1. Select Tools | Macro | Record.

2. Type **letterhead** as the macro name, and then click Record.

3. Pull down the Justification list in the property bar and select Center.

4. Enter your name, address, and telephone number, and press Enter twice.

5. Select Insert | Date/Time, click Keep this date current, and then click Insert.

6. Press Enter twice and then choose Left from the Justification list in the Property Bar.

7. Click the Stop Record button.

8. Now in the same way, create a macro called **closing** that inserts your standard letter closing, including your name.

9. When you are done creating the macro, close the current document without saving it.

Now let's create the toolbar.

1. Right-click on the toolbar and select Settings from the QuickMenu.

2. Click Create, type My Own Bar as the toolbar name, and click OK to open the Toolbar Editor. You'll see a blank toolbar below WordPerfect's standard toolbar. That's your custom toolbar.

3. Pull down the Feature Categories list in the Toolbar tab and select Format.

4. Drag the 1.5 Line Spacing command from the Features list to the far left of the blank toolbar.

5. Scroll the Features list until you see several Center commands.

6. Add the commands Center Page and Center Text to the toolbar.

7. Click on the Macros tab of the Toolbar Editor, then click the Add Macro button.

8. Click on the Letterhead macro, and then click Select. A box appears asking if you want to save the macro with the full path.

9. Select No. An icon for the macro appears on the toolbar. When you point to the icon, the name of the macro will appear in the QuickTip. If you selected Yes, the complete path and name would appear.

10. In the same way, add the Closing macro to the toolbar.

Both macros have the same icon on the toolbar, as shown in the complete bar:

1. Right-click on the first macro icon and choose Customize from the QuickMenu to open the Customize Button dialog box.

2. Click Edit to open the Image Editor.

3. Use your best skills to create a custom icon and then click OK twice.

4. In the same way, customize the icon for the closing macro. Here's my own very rough example of icons:

When you want your toolbar to appear on the screen, just right-click on the standard toolbar and click My Own Toolbar in the QuickMenu. Remove the toolbar from the screen in the same way.

11

Chapter 12

Creating Form Letters and Labels

Although form letters may have a bad reputation, they are one of the best features of WordPerfect 10. A *form letter* is merely a document that you want to send to more than one person. Each copy of the letter has the same format, and perhaps much of the text, in common. You just need to change some of the text, even if it's only the address and salutation, to customize the letter for each recipient. With WordPerfect 10 you can create form documents of all types—not just form letters. You can merge envelopes and labels, and even create any document that merges information from a database.

Understanding Form Documents

To create a form letter or other document, you actually need two things: a *data file* and a *form document*. The data file is like an electronic index card file. Every card, called a *record*, contains all the information you need about each object in your data file—a person or inventory item, for example. If your data file contains stored information about people—clients, members, patients, friends, enemies— then it may have their first and last names, address, city, state, and ZIP code. If your data file is about an inventory item or products, it may contain the product's name, amount you have in inventory, price, and the name of the vendor who sells it to you. Each of these items is called a *field*.

The form document contains the standard text that you want to include in each copy of the final merged documents. In every place in the document where you want some item from the data file, you insert a code giving the name of the field that you want inserted at that position. So instead of writing a letter and actually typing the recipient's name, for example, you insert a field code for the first name and last name.

> | TIP | *You can use the Address Book, just as it is, as the data file.*

Once you have finished these two parts, the data file and form document, you merge them. WordPerfect 10 automatically inserts the information from the data file into the appropriate locations in the letter. For example, WordPerfect 10 inserts the information from the first record in the data file into the appropriate locations in the first copy of the document. It then inserts the information from the second record in the data file into the second copy of the document, repeating the process until all of the records have been used.

You can create the data file and document in any order. For example, you can write the form document and then complete the data file. Before merging the two parts, however, you have to tell WordPerfect 10 which data file to use for the merge operation. You can also create the data file first and then complete the document. This way, you can link the data file with the form document from the start. In fact, once you create the data file, you can use it any time for form documents—letters, envelopes, labels, or any other documents that include the merge codes associated with the data file.

Creating a Data File

With WordPerfect 10, the data file can take either of two forms. It can appear as a table, with each row in the table a record with the fields in the columns, or as a merge file, with records and fields separated by special codes. In either case, the data file works the same way. Because of the number of steps involved in creating a data file, it would be useful to go through the process together this first time. If you want to use your Address Book as the data file, skip ahead to the section "Associating a Data File."

> TIP   *You can use a Quattro Pro worksheet or a Paradox database as your data file.*

1. Pull down the Tools menu, and select Merge to display the dialog box shown in Figure 12-1.

2. Click on the Data Source button. You'll see the types of existing files that you can use for a source of your merge data, including the Address Book option to use records from the Corel Address Book.

3. Select Create Data File to open the Create Data File box. You'll use this dialog box to enter the names of the fields.

4. Click on Format Records in a Table. This creates a data file in a table format, so you can later work with it using all of WordPerfect 10's table commands.

5. In the Name a Field box, type **Last Name**, and then press ENTER. WordPerfect 10 adds the field name to the list.

6. Type **First Name**, and then press ENTER to insert the next field.

12

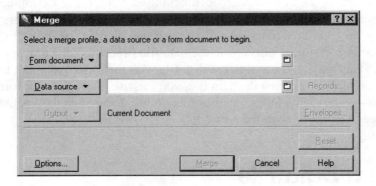

FIGURE 12-1 Merge dialog box

7. Now in the same way, add the fields Address1, Address2, City, State, Zip, Greeting, Last Order Date, Amount Due, and Credit.

8. Select OK to display the Quick Data Entry dialog box shown in Figure 12-2. The Quick Data Entry box makes it easy to enter information into the

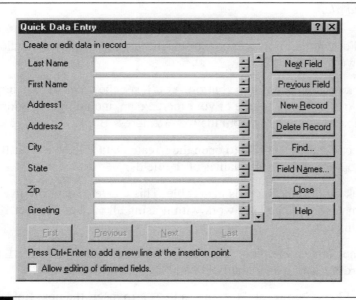

FIGURE 12-2 Quick Data Entry dialog box

data file, as well as to edit and find records. The insertion point will be in the text box for the first field.

9. Type **Chesin**, and then press ENTER. WordPerfect 10 moves the insertion point to the next field. Now fill in the rest of the fields in the following list, pressing ENTER after each. To enter text that appears on two lines within a field, press CTRL-ENTER.

> Chesin
> Adam
> 877 West Avenue
> Suite 302
> Camden
> NJ
> 08765
> Adam
> 11/1/01
> 500
> 1000

10. When you press ENTER after typing the entry for the Credit field, WordPerfect 10 adds the record to the data file, clears all of the text boxes, and places the insertion point in the first text box to start a new record. Enter the next record using this information, noting that the field Address2 is left blank:

> Schneider
> Joshua
> 767 Fifth Avenue
>
> New York
> NY
> 20918
> Mr. Schneider
> 10/11/01
> 467
> 1000

12

11. When you have entered the last field in this record, click on the Close button. WordPerfect 10 displays a dialog box asking if you want to save the database.

12. Click on Yes.

13. Type **Clients**, and then click on Save. WordPerfect 10 saves merge data files with the DAT extension.

You'll see the data file in the background behind the Merge dialog box. For now, click Cancel to close the Merge box.

Data File Window

The data file appears onscreen as a table, with the field names in the first row, the Table Property bar, and the Merge feature bar, as in Figure 12-3. The Row and Column buttons let you insert or delete rows and columns. You can use the Merge Codes button to display special codes that perform operations with the merge file.

> TIP *Right-click on the Merge feature bar to display other feature bars available in WordPerfect 10.*

The Merge button displays a dialog box where you can merge the data file with the form document. Click on Go To Form to display the open form document, if any, that is associated with the data file. The options let you sort and print the database, and control how the codes appear onscreen.

Use the Quick Entry button to return to the Quick Data Entry dialog box for inserting and editing records. The box shows the information from the record in which the insertion point is placed. Here's how to use the Quick Data Entry dialog box:

■ Edit the information for that record, or click on the New Record button to enter a new record.

■ To display a record in the box, click on the buttons along the bottom of the box—First, Previous, Next, and Last.

■ To search for a specific record, click on Find to display the Find Text dialog box, type the information you are looking for, and then click on Find Next. WordPerfect 10 displays the first record containing that

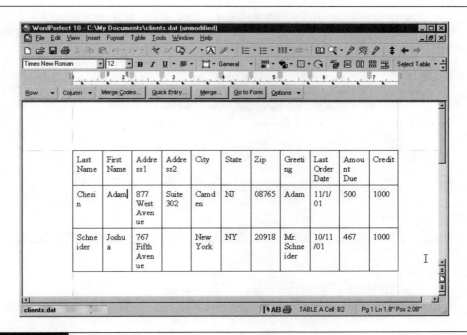

FIGURE 12-3   Data file as a table in Merge window

information. Continue clicking on Find Next to locate additional records with that information.

■ To add or edit the field names, click on the Field Names button.

Using Merge Files

Using a table to organize a data file has one disadvantage. If you have more fields than can be displayed across the screen, you can't see an entire record at one time. You'll have to scroll the screen back and forth to display fields. As an alternative, you can create the data file using merge codes, as shown in Figure 12-4.

At the start of the data file is a list of the field names. Each field of information ends with an ENDFIELD code, and each record ends with an ENDRECORD code followed by a page break. To create a data file in this format, do not select the Place Data in a Table checkbox when you create the data file. WordPerfect 10 still prompts you to enter the field names, and it displays the Quick Data Entry dialog box for entering records. The Merge window will also be the same, except the

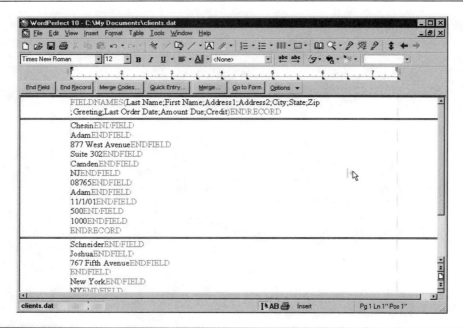

Row and Column buttons in the feature bar will be replaced by ENDFIELD and ENDRECORD buttons. Use these buttons to enter new records without returning to the Quick Data Entry dialog box. Click on ENDFIELD after you type information for a field, and then click on ENDRECORD at the end of the record.

Using Field Numbers Instead of Names

You can create a database in which each field is associated with a field number rather than a field name. In our sample database, for example, field 1 is the last name, field 2 is the first name, and so on.

If you do not want to use names, select OK in the Create Data File dialog box without entering any field names. A dialog box asks for the number of fields in each record. Enter the number of fields, and then select OK. The Quick Data Entry dialog box appears with each text box numbered.

Writing the Form Letter

You write, format, and edit a form document using the same techniques you use in any WordPerfect 10 document. However, when you come to a place where you want to insert information from the data file, you'll enter a field code.

You can use the fields in any order—they do not have to be in the order they are in the data file—and you can use a field as many times as you want, to repeat the information in the same document.

Associating a Data File

To access the field names when writing the form document, however, you need to associate the data file with the form document. By creating this association, you can later merge the documents without selecting the data file name. WordPerfect 10 keeps track of the association, so it knows what data file to use during the merge process.

You do not have to associate a form document with a data file when you create it, because you can always associate it later. You can even change the data file associated with a form document—as long as the data file contains the same field names.

You can start a form letter directly from the new data file or at any time after. Now that the data file is on the screen, here's how:

1. Click on Go To Form in the Merge feature bar. A dialog box appears reporting that the file is not associated with a form letter.

2. Click on Create to start a new form letter. (Use the Select button to associate the data file with an existing form letter.)

If you closed the data file after you created it, you can start a form letter and associate it with the data file. Here's how to do so:

1. Select Merge from the Tools menu.

2. Click on the Form Document button. The options let you select an existing file on your disk, use the current document, use the contents of the clipboard, and create a new document.

12

You can later change the associated data file by selecting its type from the Data Source menu and then specifying an existing file.

3. Select Create Form Document to open this dialog box:

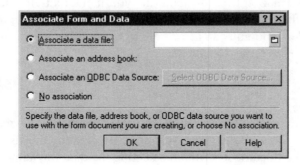

4. Click on the folder icon, locate the data file that you want to use for the form letter, and click Select. Notice you can also choose to associate an address book or ODBC data file with the form letter, or to create the form letter and associate it at a later time. To associate the form document with the Address Book, click on the Associate an Address Book option button, and then select the address book to use from the dialog box that appears.

5. Click OK and then click Cancel to close the Merge dialog box if it reappears. WordPerfect 10 displays a blank document with a Merge feature bar:

Here are the functions of the feature bar buttons:

■ *Insert Field* displays a dialog box of fields in the associated data file or Address Book. Double-click on the field that represents the information you want to insert in the document at the location of the insertion point.

■ *Insert Merge Codes* lets you insert the date or an interactive keyboard code, and displays a list of merge codes that you can use in your form document. Use these merge codes to create more sophisticated merge operations.

■ *Merge* displays the Merge dialog box to begin the merge operation.

- *Go To Data* displays the associated data file or Address Book so you can add or edit information. To return to the document from the data file, click on the Go To Form button.

- *Options* lets you determine how the merge codes appear onscreen.

Inserting Fields and Text

Now that the letter is associated with the data file, you can access its fields. Follow these steps to create the form document.

1. Click on the Insert Field button to display the Insert Field Name or Number dialog box:

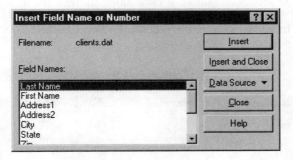

2. Double-click on the First Name field. WordPerfect 10 displays the code FIELD(First Name) in the document, indicating that the contents of that field will be placed into the form letter when it is merged. You'll notice that the dialog box stays on the screen so you can enter other field codes.

3. Press the SPACEBAR to insert a space after the code, and then double-click on the Last Name field. Press ENTER to move to the next line in the document.

4. Double-click on the Address1 field, and then press ENTER.

5. Double-click on Address2, and press ENTER to move to the next line. You want to place the next three fields on the same line—City, State, and Zip.

6. Double-click on City.

7. Type a comma, press the SPACEBAR, and insert the State field.

12

8. Press the SPACEBAR twice, insert the Zip field, and then press ENTER. So far the address looks like this:

```
FIELD(First Name) FIELD(Last Name)
FIELD(Address1)
FIELD(Address2)
FIELD(City), FIELD(State) FIELD(Zip )
```

9. Now press ENTER again, type **Dear**, and then press the SPACEBAR.

10. Insert the Greeting field, type a colon, and press ENTER twice.

11. Complete the form letter as shown in Figure 12-5, entering the fields in the appropriate locations and your own name in the closing.

12. Save the letter with the name **Accounts**. WordPerfect 10 saves form documents with the FRM extension.

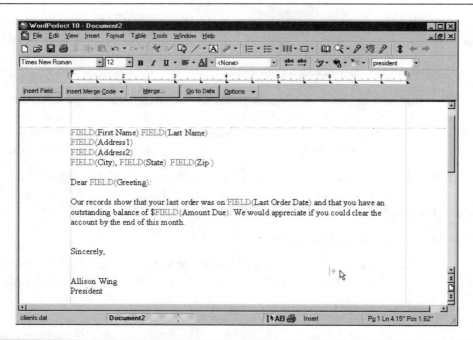

FIGURE 12-5   Completing the form letter

To change or create another association, open the form document, and click on the Insert Field button. In the Insert Field or Number dialog box, click on Data Source, and choose the data file or Address Book.

Merging Form Documents

With the form document and data file complete, you can merge them at any time. If you start from a blank screen, start a merge by selecting Merge from the Tools. You then have to enter the name of the form document and select its associated data file or Address Book.

It is easier if you open the form letter first. Whenever you open the form document, it automatically appears with the Merge toolbar, and it is linked with the associated data file. Once you open the form letter, merge it using these steps:

1. Click on the Merge button in the toolbar to display the Merge dialog box. Because the document is already associated with the data file, the name of the data file appears in the dialog box

2. Click on Output and select where you want to output the letters. The Output setting determines where the merge is performed. When set at New Document, WordPerfect 10 performs the merge, creating one large document containing all of the form letters. Each of the letters are separated by a page break. You can now edit the documents, print them, or save them together as a new document.

3. To print the form documents as they are merged, select Printer in the Output list. Other Output options let you insert the merged documents into the current document, save them directly to a file on the disk, or e-mail the merged documents.

4. Click on Merge to start the merge.

Printing Envelopes for Form Letters

When you are merging form letters, you might want to merge their envelopes at the same time. You could use the Envelopes option in the Format menu. This way, each envelope appears after its corresponding letter. If you don't have an envelope feeder, however, you'd have to stand or sit by the printer inserting an envelope into the manual tray after each letter prints.

A better method is to use the Envelopes command from the Merge dialog box. Using this procedure, the envelopes are inserted in a group after all of the letters. This also has the advantage that you can store the arrangement of field codes for various envelopes, and then simply retrieve the arrangement that you want to use for the set of envelopes. Use these steps to create envelopes:

1. Open the form document that contains the letter or other mailing.

2. Click on the Merge button in the toolbar to display the Perform Merge dialog box.

3. Click on the Envelopes button to display the Envelope window shown in Figure 12-6. In the mailing addresses section, design the layout of the fields for the mailing address, just as you did when creating the inside address for the form document.

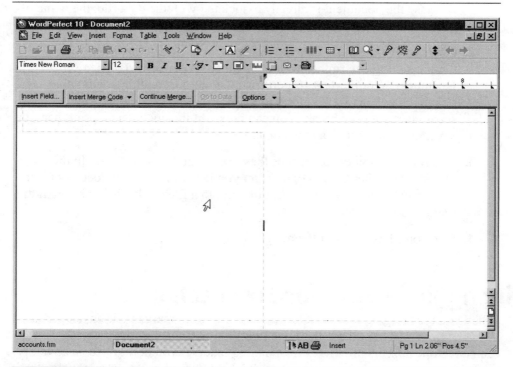

FIGURE 12-6   Creating a merge envelope

4. Click on the Insert Field button to display a list of the fields in the associated data file.

5. Insert and arrange the fields just as you learned for the form document.

6. To add a bar code, click the Insert Merge Code button and select More to see the Insert Merge Codes dialog box:

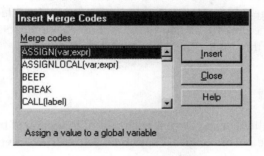

7. Scroll the list, and select POSTNET(string).

8. Click Insert, and then Close. The code is inserted as POSTNET() with the insertion point between the parentheses.

9. With the insertion point where it is presently located, click on the Zip code field in the Insert Field Name or Number dialog box. (Click Insert Field if the box is not still open.)

10. Click Insert and Close. The code appears as: POSTNET(FIELD(Zip)).

11. Click Continue Merge, and then perform the merge.

Merging to Labels

You can merge data onto mailing labels as easily as envelopes. You can get started in two ways:

■ Create a new form document, as explained earlier, and then use the Labels options from the Format menu to select the label form.

■ Starting from a blank document window, select the label form. Choose Merge from the Tools menu, pull down the Form Document list and select

12

Current Document. In the dialog box that appears, click on Use File In Active Window, and then click on OK. Enter the name of the data file, or select a page from the Address Book.

Once the form document is on the screen, use the Insert Field button to add the merge codes for the addresses, just as you created the address for the form document. Use the Merge Codes dialog box to print a POSTNET code on the label.

When you merge this form document, the labels will be filled in with the information from the data file. Perform the merge to a new document, then insert the label stock into the printer, and print the labels.

Merging Lists

When you create letters or envelopes, each record is separated by a page break. Labels print on special label paper. There may be times when you want to use the merge feature to create a list, such as an inventory of your clients or club members. In these cases, you will want the records to appear after each other, not on separate pages.

To do this, start by creating a form document, arranging the field codes as you want the list to appear. To create a columnar list, for example, you might arrange the codes like this, followed by pressing ENTER:

FIELD(First Name) FIELD(Last Name) FIELD(Amount Due)

Before merging the document, however, you have to tell WordPerfect 10 not to insert a page break after each record. To do so, click Merge in the Merge feature bar, and then click on Options to see the dialog box shown in Figure 12-7.

The choices in this dialog box let you print more than one copy of each merge document and control how blank fields are handled. By default, for example, WordPerfect 10 does not print a blank line in an address if there is no information in one of the fields, such as Address2. If you want, you can pull down the If Field Is Empty in Data Source option and choose to leave the blank line in place. You can also use this dialog box to control how merge codes appear during interactive merges.

To create a list, however, deselect the Separate Each Merged Document with a Page Break checkbox, and then click on OK. Now when you perform the merge, the records will be neatly arranged in rows.

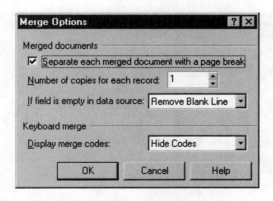

FIGURE 12-7   Perform Merge Options dialog box

Selecting Merge Records

Sometimes you won't want to merge all of the records, just selected ones, in a data file with a form document. You might want to send a mailing, for example, to clients who owe you money or who are located in a certain community. Rather than merging all of the records and throwing away the letters you do not want, you can select records before performing the merge.

To select records, use this procedure:

1. Open the form document.

2. Click on the Merge button in the feature bar, and then click on the Records button in the Merge dialog box. WordPerfect 10 displays the Select Records dialog box shown in Figure 12-8.

3. Select records using either the Specify Conditions or Mark Records option.

   ■ *Specify Conditions* lets you enter search criteria based on the content of the fields. Use this option if you have a large data file and want to select records that have a field value in common. You should also use this option if you want to merge a specific range of records, such as the first ten or the last five.

12

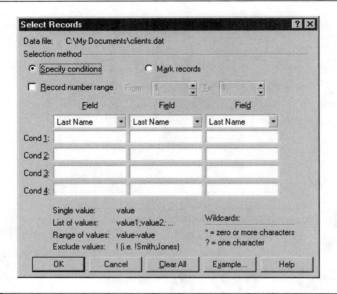

FIGURE 12-8 Selecting records

- *Mark Records* lets you click on the records that you want to merge. Use this option if your database is relatively small, or if you want to select records that may not have a common field value.

Let's look at both methods in more detail.

Specifying Conditions

When you want to merge a selected range of records, or records based on a field value—such as all clients in California—use the Specify Conditions options.

To merge a range of records, select the Record Number Range checkbox, and then enter the beginning record number in the From box and the ending record number in the To box. The record number corresponds to the table row of the record in the data file.

If you want to limit the records to those meeting a certain condition, create a filter. A *filter* tells WordPerfect 10 to use only the records that meet certain conditions for the merge operation, ignoring those that do not meet the conditions. The records not used during the merge remain in the data file—they are just ignored, not deleted.

You can select records based on up to three fields. Starting with the column on the left, pull down the list, and choose a field that you want to use for a condition.

You can specify up to four selection criteria, each on one to three fields. In the first row, enter the values or conditions that a record has to meet. For example, to merge the records of clients who are in New Jersey, select State for the first field, and enter **NJ** in the column under State. To further specify which clients are selected, use up to two additional fields. When you have more than one condition in a row, WordPerfect 10 treats them as AND conditions, which means that the record must meet all of the specifications to be selected. For example, to merge records for New Jersey clients who owe over $500, add the Amount Due field to the second column, and type **>500** as the condition under it. The conditions will appear as shown here.

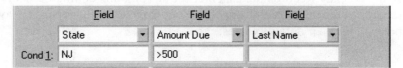

	Field	Field	Field
	State	Amount Due	Last Name
Cond 1:	NJ	>500	

Conditions in the other rows of the dialog box—Cond 2, Cond 3, and Cond 4—are treated as OR operations. This condition, for example, displays all New Jersey clients who owe more than $500, as well as all California clients no matter how much they owe, as shown here.

	Field	Field	Field
	State	Amount Due	Last Name
Cond 1:	NJ	>500	
Cond 2:	CA		

When you want to select records based on a specific value, just type the value in the condition box. You can also use > (more than) and < (less than) operators to meet conditions above and below a value.

If you have a list of possible matching values, enter them in the same condition, separated by semicolons, rather than on separate rows in the dialog box. For instance, enter **PA;NJ** under the State field to match clients in either Pennsylvania or New Jersey. You can also choose records in a range of values using a hyphen, as in 200-1000 for clients with a value from 200 to 1000 in the field. To exclude a specific value, precede it with an exclamation point. For example, to list clients in every state but California, enter **!CA** in the State field.

Finally, you can use the * and ? wildcard characters to represent, respectively, any number of characters and a single character. Entering **N*** in the Last Name field, for example, selects all clients whose last names begin with the letter "N." Entering **8450?** under the Zip code field selects clients whose ZIP codes start with the numbers "8450."

Marking Records

To pick the records you want to use, click on the Mark Records option. The dialog box changes as shown in Figure 12-9, listing all of the records in the data file with checkboxes. Then follow these steps:

1. In the Display Records boxes, enter the starting and ending numbers of the records you want to pick from. To select from all of the records, leave the boxes with their default values.

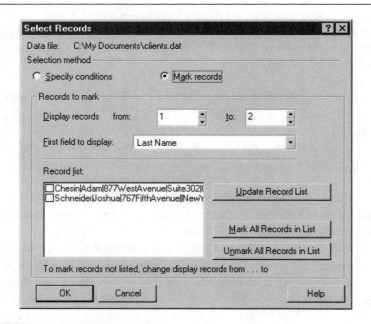

FIGURE 12-9   Marking records to select

2. In the First Field to Display list, select the field that you want to use to select records. For example, if you want to pick records based on the state of residence, pull down the list, and click on the State field.

3. Click on the Update Record List. WordPerfect 10 displays the records in the Record List.

4. Click on the checkboxes for the records that you want to merge.

5. Click on OK when you have finished, and perform the merge.

Customizing a Merge with Fields

The Insert Merge Code button in the Merge feature bar gives you great flexibility in controlling the merge process. You can use the merge codes, for example, to automate operations in much the same way that you can use macros. In fact, you can even run a macro directly from a merge file.

As an example of using merge codes, the next section illustrates several useful codes, starting with an interactive merge that lets you enter information into the merged document.

Interactive Merges

In most cases, your data file should have all of the variable information that you need to personalize the form document. But suppose it doesn't? Suppose you want to enter a personal salutation for a letter using a client's first name or nickname. To enter information into the form letter when it is being merged, you need to use the Keyboard code. This displays a dialog box asking for the user to enter information.

Place the insertion point in the form letter where you want to enter the information, click on Insert Merge Code and select Keyboard. In the dialog box that appears, type the text that will ask you for the information to be entered, and then click on OK.

When you merge the documents, WordPerfect 10 pauses and displays the Keyboard Merge box shown in Figure 12-10, and a special feature bar. The bar contains these items:

■ *Next Record* shows the data in the next record to be processed by the merge.

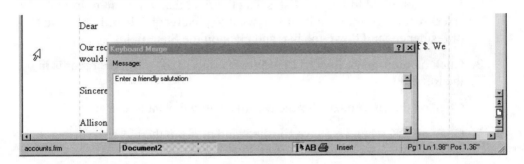

Keyboard Merge dialog box

- *Continue* inserts the text you enter into the document and continues the merge. Click Continue without entering text if you do not want to insert information into the current document.

- *Skip Next Record* continues the merge without inserting any information in the next documents.

- *Quit* continues the merge but ignores all remaining merge codes.

- *Stop* ends the merge at the current document.

Type the text that you want to insert into the document, and then click on Continue in the feature bar. WordPerfect 10 pauses at the same location for every letter.

Before clicking Continue, you can decide if you want to enter information into the next record or skip it. Look in the Next Record box and decide if you want to add interactive text into the record indicated. If you do not, click Skip Next Record to see its information in the Next Record box. When you want to insert information into the next record, click Continue to display the form document for that record.

Performing Calculations

In addition to typing information as the merge progresses, you can also perform calculations. For example, suppose you want to send a letter telling clients how much money remains in their credit line. You have the fields Credit and Amount

Due, so you must subtract them to calculate the difference. To perform this function, you need two commands: Assign and Variable. To insert a merge command into the document, click the Insert Merge Codes button in the Merge feature bar and select More to display the Insert Merge Code dialog box, and then double-click on the command you want to enter. In some cases, a dialog box will appear where you can enter a parameter for the command.

The Assign command uses the following syntax:

Assign(variable; value or expression)

Double-click on the command in the Insert Merge Code box to see this dialog box:

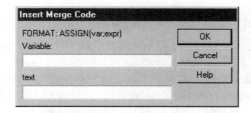

Type **Net** in the Variable text box, and then click on OK. Because the expression uses field codes, you have to enter them using the Insert Field button. The Assign(net;) code will appear in the document. Move the insertion point to the left of the closing parenthesis, and then click on Insert Field. Double-click on the Credit field, press the hyphen key, and then double-click on the Amount Due field. The final command will appear as Assign(net; Field(Credit)–Field(Amount Due)).

Now when you want to insert the amount in the merged document, use the Variable command. Display the Insert Merge Code box, and double-click on the Variable code near the bottom of the list. Type **Net** in the dialog box that appears, and click on OK. The code will appear as Variable(Net).

TIP *You can perform more complex math operations and create complete automated applications by combining merge codes with macro commands, but this is beyond the scope of this book.*

There are two drawbacks to this method. First, merge commands only work with integers—whole numbers. That's why whole numbers were used in the sample data file. Second, if you place the Assign command in a line by itself in the form document, it generates an extra carriage return, resulting in a blank line.

12

WordPerfect 10 performs the calculation to compute the amount, but it inserts the carriage return that ends the line. To avoid this problem, write the line like this, inserting the Comment command with the Insert Merge Codes dialog box but with the closing parenthesis on the next line:

Assign(net; Field(Credit)–Field(Amount Due))Comment(
)

Start the document on the same line as the closing parenthesis. The Comment command tells WordPerfect 10 to ignore any text or codes that follow it, so it ignores the carriage return.

Sorting Database Records

Your form document will be merged with the data file in the same order as the records appear in the file. In some instances, however, you may want to merge the file in some other order, such as by ZIP code to take advantage of bulk mailing.

To sort a database, display the database file, using Go To Data if the form document is displayed. Click on Sort in the Options menu of the Merge feature bar, or select Sort from the Tools menu. This displays the dialog box shown in Figure 12-11. The box offers a number of predefined sorts, such as the first cell in a table or the first characters in a merge file. It also lets you designate the input file (the data that you are sorting) and the output file where you want to place the document. Leaving both set at Current Document actually changes the order of the records in the table.

To create your own sort to use any other merge field, click on New to display the dialog box shown in Figure 12-12. Type a name for the sort in the Sort Description text box.

You use this dialog box to sort records in a data file, as well as lines, paragraphs, parallel columns, and table rows in a document. Our data file appears in the form of a table, so we want to select the Table Row option in the Sort By section. You would use the Merge Record option button if your data file used merge codes.

WordPerfect 10 sorts the information based on one to nine key fields. A *key* represents a field to sort on, or a word or line within the field. Each key can be sorted in either alphanumeric or numeric order, depending on its contents.

To sort the table by the Amount Due field, pull down the Type list, and select Numeric. Then choose if you want to sort your records in ascending or descending

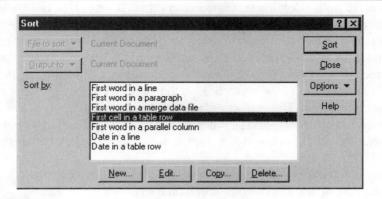

FIGURE 12-11   Predefined sort options

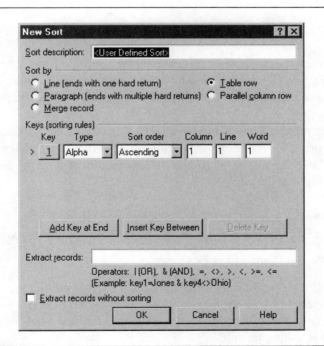

FIGURE 12-12   Defining a sort

12

order. Enter **10** in the Column text box because the Amount Due field is in the tenth column. Leave the Line and Word options set at 1.

You can also enter a criterion to select records, so the function sorts and selects at the same time. If you click on the Extract Records Without Sorting checkbox, WordPerfect 10 selects records that meet the condition without sorting them.

To add another key to the sort, click on the Add Key at End button, and then enter its specifications. The new key is added after the existing ones. Since the sort is performed in key order—giving precedence to key one, then key two, and so on—you can also click on Insert Key Between to add a new key before the current one.

When you have finished defining the keys, click on OK. Your sort is now listed in the Sort dialog box. Double-click on it to perform the sort.

Try It Out

You already created a data file in this chapter for a sample form letter. Once you have a data file, you can easily use it for all types of form documents. In this section, we'll use the same file for labels and use a more advanced merge code, the IF command.

The IF command allows you to be selective, placing text in a document or performing some other function, depending on the value of a field or a calculated amount. We'll use the command to place a special message on the envelope of clients with a high credit rating.

1. Open the document Clients.Dat that you created in this chapter. Because this is a merge database, the merge feature bar is automatically displayed.

2. Click Go To Form and click Create.

3. Select Envelope from the Format menu. If this is the first time you used the Envelope feature or a template, you'll be directed to select your personal listing from the address book. Just close the address book when it appears to skip selecting an entry.

4. Pull down the Default Envelope list and select Envelope #10.

5. Click Append to Doc. The layout of an envelope appears onscreen with the insertion point in the address section.

6. Now insert the codes for the address as you did for the form letter in the chapter. Use the Insert Field button to create the address and leave the Insert Field Name or Number box on the screen when done.

7. Move the insertion point to the line under the last line of the address.

8. Click Insert Merge Code and select More. You will have two boxes on the screen: the Insert Field Name or Number box for adding merge fields, and the Insert Merge Codes box for inserting codes. If one obscures the other, drag it out of the way so both can be seen.

9. Insert the POSTNET(string) code and the Zip field as you learned in the chapter, so the field appears as POSTNET(FIELD(Zip)).

10. Leave a blank line below the POSTNET code.

11. Scroll the Merge Codes list, select IF(exp) and click Insert. The Insert Merge Code box appears in which you can enter an expression.

12. Leave it blank for now and click OK. The code IF() appears with the insertion point between the parentheses.

13. In the Insert Field Name or Number box, select the Credit field, click Insert, and Close.

14. Type **> 500**.

15. Press the End key to move the insertion point to the end of the line.

16. In the Insert Merge Codes box, select INSERT(text) and click Insert.

17. Type **Special Offer for Good Customers** and click OK.

18. In the Insert Merge Codes box, select ENDIF and click Insert. The final command looks like this:

```
FIELD(Last Name) FIELD(First Name)
FIELD(Address1)
FIELD(Address2)
FIELD(City), FIELD(State) FIELD(Zip )
POSTNET(FIELD(Zip ))

IF(FIELD(Credit)>500)INSERT(Special Offer for Good Customers)
ENDIF
```

12

19. Close the Insert Merge Codes box.

20. Click Merge in the feature bar, and then click Merge to perform the operation.

The IF code tells WordPerfect to perform a function if an expression is true. In this case, the merge prints the words **Special Offer for Good Customers** only when the value of the Credit field is over $500.

Chapter 13

Working with Graphics

All of the formatting techniques that you've learned so far go a long way toward making a professional-looking document. But sometimes nothing does it better than graphics. WordPerfect 10 has a full range of graphics features that let you add clip art, charts, special text effects, horizontal and vertical lines, custom drawings, and even scientific equations to your documents.

Picture Basics

Inserting a picture into your document is one of the easiest ways to add pizzazz to a document. In Chapter 2, you learned how to add a graphic from the Scrapbook. Click on the ClipArt button in the toolbar to display the Scrapbook, select the graphic, then drag and drop it into the document. You can also insert other graphic files just as easily, by following these steps:

1. Place the insertion point where you want the graphic to appear.

2. Pull down the Insert menu, point to Graphics, and click on From File to display the Insert Image dialog box. This box lists graphic files in the Program Files\Corel\WordPerfect Office 2002\Graphics. To access images in other folders, use the Look In list and the directory/file listing. Click on the Up One Level button, for example, to select folders containing backgrounds, borders, pictures, and textures.

3. To see what a graphic looks like before inserting it, click on the Toggle Preview On/Off button in the dialog box's toolbar.

 Some of the graphics are words or phrases, such as "Secret," "Confidential," and "Do Not Duplicate." Others are dividers that you can use between paragraphs or at the top or bottom of the page.

4. Double-click on the name of the file you want to insert, or click on it and then on the Insert button.

The graphic appears in the document with the upper-left corner at the position of the insertion point, along with the Graphic property bar, as shown in Figure 13-1. The image is surrounded by small black boxes, called *handles,* showing that it is selected. To deselect the graphic, click elsewhere on the page.

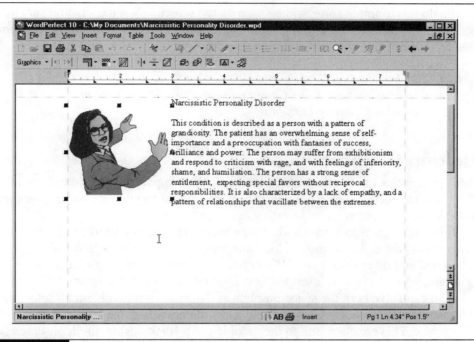

FIGURE 13-1   Graphic inserted into a document

Integrate IT!   *If you have a graphics-intensive layout, you can create the graphics in Corel Presentations and then import your text from WordPerfect 10.*

WordPerfect 10 Suite comes with more than 10,000 graphic files, many of which are not copied onto your computer but kept on the CD.

Using Drag to Create

You can always change the size and position of a graphic after you insert it. As an alternative, you can draw a box the size and in the position you want the graphic and then insert the image into the box. This is a good technique if you've already typed and formatted your document, and you know exactly where you want the image to appear.

13

To do this, point at some white space on the screen to see the shadow cursor, then drag the mouse. When you release the mouse, choose ClipArt or Image from File from the Shortcut menu, and then select the graphic.

 You can change WordPerfect 10's setting to let you Drag to Create all new graphic boxes. See Chapter 11 for more information on using the Graphics Environment settings.

Linking Graphic Files

Adding graphics to your documents increases their impact, but it also enlarges them. Graphics can take up a lot of disk space, and when you insert a graphic into a document, you are actually inserting the entire graphic file.

Inserting a graphic has one other drawback. Suppose you used a drawing program to create your company logo and then inserted the logo into your letterhead and other documents. If you later changed the logo with the drawing program, you'd have to reinsert the new logo into all of the documents.

You can solve both the space problem and the new logo problem by selecting the Image on Disk checkbox when you select the graphic in the Insert Image dialog box. This creates a link to the graphic on the disk, displaying it onscreen but not inserting the entire file into the document. If you later edit the drawing and save it to a file with the same name, the edited version will be retrieved automatically when you open the document in WordPerfect 10.

 If you copy your document to a floppy disk to transfer it to another computer, remember to copy the graphic file as well. When you use the Image on Disk option, the graphic file must always be available when you open the document.

Using Graphics in Headers, Footers, and Watermarks

You can insert a graphic directly into the document. But if you want the graphic to appear on every page, you can insert it into a header, footer, or watermark.

Small graphics and decorative dividers are useful in headers and footers. Create or edit the header or footer, as explained in Chapter 9, and then insert the graphic into the header or footer area.

Some graphics are especially effective when used in a watermark. Displaying "DO NOT COPY" in large letters across a page, for example, certainly gets your point across. It cannot be cut out or ignored, and makes it perfectly clear that copies are not endorsed.

To insert a graphic in a watermark, create or edit the watermark as you learned in Chapter 9, then use the ClipArt button on the toolbar to select and insert art from the Scrapbook, or use the Image button to select a graphic on your disk. You can insert several graphics as watermarks to create a special effect. In this chapter you will learn how to edit the graphic in the watermark window.

Changing the Position of Graphics

Once you insert a graphic, you can move it to any other position on the page— even to areas below the last text on the page. Use these steps:

1. If the graphic is not selected—that is, the handles do not appear around it—click on it.

2. Point inside the graphic, not on any of the handles, so the pointer appears as a four-headed arrow.

3. Dragging the mouse will drag a copy of the image, allowing you to place it in the desired location.

4. When the graphic is where you want to place it, release the mouse button.

Changing the Size of Graphics

You use the handles around the graphic to change its size.

- Drag a corner handle to change its height and width at the same time.

- Drag the center handle on the top or bottom to change its height.

- Drag the center handle on the left or right to change its width.

> **TIP** *You will learn later how to adjust the settings for a graphic to determine if dragging a corner handle maintains the current height-width ratio.*

13

Customizing the Graphic Box

WordPerfect 10 gives you a variety of ways to customize graphic images. First, understand that when you insert a graphic, you are really inserting two elements into the document—a graphic box and the graphic inside the box. By selecting ClipArt from the Graphics option in the Insert menu, you are telling WordPerfect 10 to insert a box using the Image Box style. You are then telling WordPerfect 10 what graphic to place inside the box. We'll look at the issue of box styles later; for now, let's consider ways to edit the box, as well as the image inside the box.

When you edit the graphic box, you are changing the container in which the graphic is placed. Dragging the box, or changing its size, for example, does not affect the image itself. These are the other ways you can edit the box:

- Add or change the border line around the box.

- Insert a fill color or pattern.

- Set the way text wraps around the box and the contour of the graphic.

- Set the position of the box in the document.

- Edit the box style.

- Add a caption.

- Modify the position of the contents within the box.

- Change the box size.

WordPerfect 10 provides a number of special ways to work with a graphic. The property bar that appears when you select a graphic includes these tools:

- *Graphics Menu* provides a complete list of graphic options, some of which are not found in the property bar.

- *Previous Box* selects the graphic box preceding the current one.

- *Next Box* selects the next graphic box in the document.

- *Border Style* determines the type of border line around the graphic.

- *Box Fill* determines the fill pattern and color within the box.

- *Caption* inserts a caption and numbers the graphic.

- *Flip Left/Right* flips a graphic from side to side.

- *Flip Top/Bottom* flips a graphic from top to bottom.

- *Image Tools* displays tools for changing the appearance of the graphic.

- *Object Forward One* moves the selected graphic in front of another that may be blocking it.

- *Object Back One* moves the graphic behind another.

- *Align and Distribute* adjusts the spacing of objects in relation to each other and to the page or margins.

- *Wrap* determines how text flows around the graphic.

- *Hyperlink* converts the graphic into a link.

Many of these same options, and more, are also available in the Graphics pull-down menu at the far left of the property bar:

13

And you can choose them from the QuickMenu:

In addition, you can customize the box in which the graphic is contained by right-clicking on the graphic and choosing Edit Box from the QuickMenu to display these options:

Since many graphic functions are in all of these items, you can perform them using various techniques. For example, to determine the type of line around the graphic, you need to display the border options. You can display these options using any of these techniques:

- Click on the Border Style button in the property bar.

- Select Border/Fill from the Graphics pull-down menu on the property bar.

- Right-click, and select Border/Fill from the QuickMenu.

- Display the Edit Box options and click on the Border button.

As you work with graphics, you'll find which method you prefer.

Changing the Borders and Fills

Each of WordPerfect 10's graphic box styles includes a default border and fill style. Image boxes have no border and no fill. Adding a border to the image is similar to adding borders around paragraphs and pages, except that the Fancy borders are not available.

To add a border, click the Border Style button in the property bar, and select the border you want from the choices that appear. To add a fill pattern, click the Box Fill button, and make a selection.

In addition, you can select from the Border/Fill dialog box. Display the box by choosing Border/Fill from the Graphics pull-down menu or QuickMenu. WordPerfect 10 displays the familiar Border/Fill dialog box with the Border, Shadow, Advanced, and Fill pages. Select options from the box, just as you learned for adding borders around paragraphs.

When you select a fill pattern, you can also select foreground and background colors. Picture a pattern of vertical lines. The foreground color determines the color of the lines; the background color fills in between the lines.

Wrapping Text Around Graphics

Wrap refers to the way text flows around a graphic. The default setting for an image box is called *Square Both Sides*. This means that text will appear on all sides of the image—if there is room for it between the margins—up to the rectangular shape of the image box.

You can select other wrap methods from either the options that appear when you click the Wrap button in the property bar or from the dialog box that appears when you choose Wrap from the QuickMenu. Figure 13-2 shows the dialog box (the Wrap button offers the same options displayed differently).

Choose In Front of Text if you want the graphic to be superimposed over the text, so the text behind it does not appear. Choose Behind Text if you want the graphic to appear in the background, or to create special effects by combining text and graphics. Choose Neither Side if you want the graphic to appear with no text on its left or right. Select Square and then a Wrap Text Around option to let text wrap but stop the text at the box borders. Select Contour and then a wrap option to allow you to wrap text but only up to the contour of the graphic.

Setting the Graphic Position

When you insert a graphic, WordPerfect 10 *anchors* it to the page. This means that the graphic is inserted in a specific location on the page, and inserting or deleting text above it will not change the position.

You can also anchor a picture to a paragraph or character. A *paragraph anchor* means that the box moves up or down with the paragraph as you insert or delete text above it. A *character anchor* means that the box is treated just like any other character in the line, and it moves with the line as you insert or delete text before it. Use a paragraph or character anchor when the text refers to the graphic and you want the graphic to be on the same page as its reference. Use a *page anchor* when you want the graphic to remain in the same position on the page regardless of the text.

To change the type of anchor, select Position from the QuickMenu or from the Graphics pull-down menu to see the dialog box shown in Figure 13-3. Pull down

FIGURE 13-2   Wrapping options in the Wrap Text dialog box

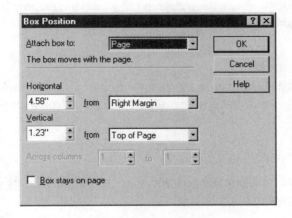

FIGURE 13-3   Position options for graphics

the Attach Box To list, and select Page, Paragraph, or Character. You can also select a horizontal and vertical position relative to the page margins, to the edges of the pages, or to the center of the page. If the graphic is within columns, you can also choose the relative position between columns. When you are working with a three-column newsletter, for example, you can choose to center the box across the first two columns. Select Column in the Vertical position list, and then enter **1** and **2** in the column text boxes.

TIP   *To keep the box on the page, however, you must select Page in the Attach Box To list, and select the Box Stays on Page checkbox.*

When you select a paragraph or character anchor, the image is anchored at its current location. If you later drag the image to another location, the anchor changes as well. WordPerfect 10 displays a paragraph anchor graphically as you drag:

13

Narcissistic Personality Disorder

This grandi import brillia and inferio of respon patter

condition is described as a person with a pattern of osity. The patient has an overwhelming sense of self-ance and a preoccupation with fantasies of success, nce and power. The person may suffer from exhibitionism respond to criticism with rage, and with feelings of rity, shame, and humiliation. The person has a strong sense entitlement, expecting special favors without reciprocal sibilities. It is also characterized by a lack of empathy, and a n of relationships that vacillate between the extremes.

The Push-pin icon shows the paragraph to which the graphic is linked. Release the mouse when the icon is at the desired paragraph.

Aligning Objects

The Align and Distribute feature sets the position of a single graphic on the page, or the relative alignment and spacing of two or more selected graphic objects. Here's how to use it.

1. Select the first object.

2. Hold down the Shift key and select any additional objects you want to align in relation to the others.

3. Click on the Align and Distribute button on the Graphic property bar, or right-click on one of the graphics and choose Align and Distribute from the QuickMenu. WordPerfect opens the Align and Distribute dialog box shown in Figure 13-4.

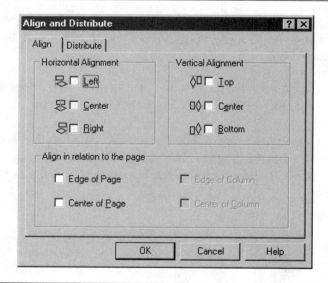

FIGURE 13-4   Aligning and distributing objects

4. Use the Horizontal Alignment section to align the objects in relation to their left or right sides or center. Use the Vertical Alignment section to align the objects in relation in relation to their top, bottom, or center. For example, to place two objects directly centered on each other, click both Center text boxes.

5. Choose Edge of Paper to position the objects in relation to the sides of the sheet, or choose Center of Page to position the objects in relation to the center of the sheet. To place a single selected object in the exact center of the page, for example, choose both center options and the Center of Page checkbox.

NOTE *The Edge of Column and Center of Column options are available only when you are working with graphics in placed in columnar documents.*

6. The options in the Distribute page of the dialog box let you space out the selected objects horizontally or vertically in relation to the page.

7. When you click OK, a message appears reporting that aligning the objects may change their anchor positions. Click OK to make the change.

Inserting a Caption

You can also add a caption that numbers the graphic and includes a descriptive word or phrase, just like the captions used with the figures in this book. Numbering graphics makes it easy to refer to them in the text. To add a caption to a graphic, follow these steps:

1. Click on the Caption tool in the property bar. WordPerfect 10 inserts the word "Figure," along with a figure number. Each image that you insert is associated with a number, even if you do not add a caption. The first image box in the document is Figure 1, the second is Figure 2, and so on, based on their positions in the document.

2. WordPerfect 10 leaves the insertion point to the right of the label, so you can type the descriptive text, as shown here:

13

Figure 1

3. When you have finished, click elsewhere on the page.

The position of the caption and its label (such as "Figure") are determined by the graphic box style. The default style for image boxes places the caption on the left below the graphic, outside any border around the graphic and using the label "Figure."

To change the position and orientation of the caption or its text, select Caption from the QuickMenu on the Graphics pull-down menu to open the Box Caption dialog box.

TIP *To edit the text of the caption, click on the Edit button in the dialog box.*

The Caption Position option determines the position of the caption in relation to the graphic box. You can select the side of the box and whether the caption is inside or outside of it. Pull down the Position list to choose if the caption is at the top, center, or bottom of the selected side. You can also enter a specific location using an absolute measurement, or a percentage offset, such as 25 percent from the left edge.

Use the Rotate Caption option to rotate the text. If you position the caption on the left side of the box, for example, you might want to rotate it 90 degrees so the characters print in landscape orientation up the edge:

The Auto Width option in the Caption Width section lets WordPerfect 10 wrap the caption as necessary based on the amount of text, the size of the box, and the caption's position. Sometimes, however, this may result in too much blank space around the caption, taking up needless room on the page. As an alternative you can designate a fixed width, but no wider than the box if the caption is on the bottom, or no taller if it is on the side. You can also set the width as a percentage of the box size, between 1 and 100 percent.

The Caption Numbering Method and Style options let you change the counter used to number the graphic.

Setting Content Options

The graphic box style also affects the position of the graphic within the box and the type of contents in the box. When you select ClipArt from the Graphics option in the Insert menu, WordPerfect 10 assumes you want to insert a graphic image and creates a box the default size for the graphic image. The Content option in the QuickMenu and Graphics pull-down menu gives you some control over these default settings. Click on Content to see the Box Content dialog box.

Keep in mind that the graphic and the box in which the graphic appears are two separate objects. This dialog box is designed to let you change what is in the box and its position.

The name of the graphic file you inserted appears in the Filename text box. If you want to replace the graphic with another, enter the new name in the box, or use the List button to select the file. The Content Type list lets you choose the type of content. It is set at Image or Image on Disk, based on how you inserted the graphic. You can also select Empty, Text, or Equation from the Content Type list. Selecting any of these, however, deletes the graphic from the box because it will no longer be considered an image box. You use the Content Type list mainly when you are creating a custom box style and you need to specify the type of contents that it will hold, or to switch to an Image on Disk.

If you inserted a graphic in a format other than WordPerfect 10's own WPG format, the Image on Disk option in the Content list has a nice side effect. Remember, Image on Disk creates a link to the graphic file. If you select Image on Disk after inserting a graphic, a dialog box appears asking where you want to save the graphic. You can then choose to save the graphic as a WPG file, converting it to WordPerfect 10's own format.

The Content Position options in the dialog box determine the position of the image within the graphic box. They do not affect the position of the box on the page. The default settings center the image horizontally and vertically, but you can

13

change the vertical position to the left or right, and the horizontal position to the top or bottom.

You won't see the effect of your changes immediately because, by default, the box size is the same as the graphic. This is because the Preserve Image Width/Height Ratio checkbox may not be selected. As you change the size of the graphic box by dragging a handle, the graphic changes as well. If you check this box, however, WordPerfect 10 will always maintain the original proportions of the image inside the box. If you enlarge the box in a different proportion, the box will become larger than the graphic, and you can then adjust the position of the graphic within the larger box.

You can select options from the Rotates Text Counterclockwise section only when you are using a text box.

Setting the Box Size

Trying to adjust a graphic to an exact size by dragging can be difficult, especially if you do not have a steady hand. To use measurements to change the graphic box size, select Size from the QuickMenu or Graphics pull-down menu to open the Box Size dialog box.

Use the Set options in the Width and Height sections to enter a specific size. Use the Full options in the Width section to automatically extend the box fully between the margins or the full width of the columns. Choose Full in the Height section to extend the box to the top and bottom margins and to anchor the graphic to the page.

Choose Maintain Proportions in either section to automatically adjust the width or height when you change the other size to maintain the picture's original proportions.

Changing the Image Settings

So far, all of the editing techniques have modified the box in which the graphic is placed. You can also edit the graphic itself. Editing the graphic changes the appearance of the image without affecting the box in which it is placed.

There are actually two ways that you can edit the graphic: you can edit its appearance without changing the actual design, or you can modify the design—the shape and elements that make up the graphic.

For example, the options to flip the graphic left/right and top/bottom are on the property bar. Flipping left/right (horizontally) is useful for some graphics that appear to be pointing in a certain direction. Flipping top/bottom (vertically) is useful for designs that do not contain text or other recognizable people, places, or things. For instance, if you use a divider graphic along the top of the page, insert the same graphic along the bottom, and then flip the graphic horizontally, the graphics appear to be framing the page. Use the same technique with graphics down the left and right edges of the page, but flip one horizontally.

To customize the graphic's appearance even further, click on the Image Tools button in the property bar or QuickMenu to display the palette of tools shown in Figure 13-5. Now take a quick look at each of these tools. How well you use them depends on your own design and artistic abilities.

Rotating Graphics

The Rotate tool lets you rotate the image within the box without rotating the box itself. Here's how it works:

1. Click on Rotate to display four corner handles around the graphic.

2. Drag one of the handles to rotate the image.

3. Click on the Rotate tool when you've finished.

FIGURE 13-5   Image tools

You can also drag the handle in the center of the graphic to change the focus point of the rotation.

Because you are only rotating the image within the box, some of it may now extend beyond the borders of the box and will no longer appear. Don't worry if part of the image seems to be missing, as shown here. The complete image is still in the document, so it will be displayed if you rotate the image back or enlarge the box size. For more precise control over rotation, use the Image Settings options that will be discussed later in this chapter.

Moving the Image

The Move tool lets you change the position of the image within the box. Follow these steps:

1. Click on the Move tool.

2. Point to the graphic, and drag the image.

You can drag the image so some parts of it scroll out of the box, but again, the parts that scroll are not lost—you can later move the image so they appear again.

Mirror Imaging

The Flip buttons let you flip the image horizontally or vertically, just like the Flip buttons in the property bar.

Enlarging the Image

By default, the image box is the same size as the graphic. Changing the size of the box also changes the size of the image within it. You use the Zoom tool to change the size of just the image within the box. Clicking on the Zoom tool displays these three options.

Use the Magnifier icon when you want to enlarge a selected portion of the graphic so it fills the image box. Follow these steps:

1. Click on the Magnifier icon—the pointer appears as a magnifying lens and a crosshair.

2. Drag the mouse to select a rectangular portion of the graphic.

3. When you release the mouse, that portion is enlarged to fill the image box.

Use the up and down arrows to enlarge or reduce the entire image. Here's how:

1. Click on the Arrows icon in the Zoom list. WordPerfect 10 displays a vertical scroll bar next to the graphic.

2. Scroll the bar up to reduce the size of the graphic.

3. Scroll the bar down to enlarge the graphic.

To return the graphic to its original size, click on the 1:1 icon.

TIP   *Click on Reset Attributes to return the image to its original state.*

13

Changing the Black and White Threshold

You can convert a color graphic or one that contains shades of gray to black and white. This is useful if you want to create some special effect, if you want to print in black and white on a color printer, or if your monochrome printer does not output gray shades correctly. When you do convert a color to black and white, the color threshold determines which shades of gray are converted to white and which to black. The lower the threshold, the darker the image, since more of the gray shades will be over the threshold and will be converted to black.

If you click on the B/W Threshold button, you'll see a palette representing different threshold levels. Click on the one that you want to use to convert the graphic to black and white.

Changing the Contrast

Contrast is the range of shades between light and dark areas of a color image. To change the contrast, click on the Contrast button, and then select a setting from the palette that appears.

Setting the Brightness

Brightness determines the overall saturation of colors in a graphic or the brightness of a black and white image. To change the brightness, click on the Brightness button, and then select a setting from the palette that appears.

Choosing a Fill Style

The Fill tool controls the transparency of the image. By default, the images are set at the normal fill. This means that areas of the graphic appear in the color or gray shade in which the graphic was designed. The Fill tool offers these options:

The option on the left is the default normal style.

The middle option removes the fill displaying the graphic as an outline, so the paper's color or any background text can be seen.

The option on the right inserts an opaque white as the fill pattern.

 Fill patterns affect graphics with the WPG extension but not BMP graphic files.

Inverting Colors

When you *invert* an image, you change it to its complementary colors. With a noncolor image this has the effect of displaying it as a photographic negative. To invert the color, click on the Invert Colors button.

Specifying Attributes

Many of the image settings interact with each other, so changing one has an effect that requires you to change another. You may also want to set the brightness, size, or other attribute to a specific setting. To enter settings and to change all of the attributes from one location, click on the Edit Attributes button to see the dialog box in Figure 13-6.

When you click on the attribute you want to change in the top section of the dialog box, the settings that you can make or choose from are shown in the bottom of the box. Select each of the categories that you want to adjust in turn, and then make your choices. The preview of the graphic shows how your choices will affect the picture.

The Print Parameters button displays a dialog box where you can adjust how graphics are printed. The options available in the dialog box depend on your printer, but you may be able to set a dithering method and source, and a halftone option.

Dithering is the process of mixing printed dots to simulate colors or shades of gray. You can choose a method to determine how the dot pattern is created, and choose the source—whether dithering is created by your printer or by WordPerfect 10. The halftone options determine the number of lines of dots per inch and their angle.

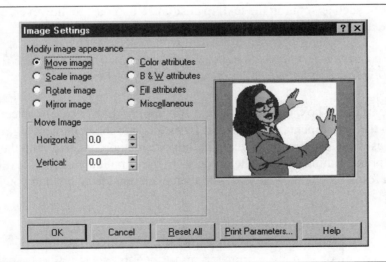

FIGURE 13-6   Changing the image settings

Resetting Attributes

WordPerfect 10 always stores the original settings of the graphic with the document. If you want to restore the graphic to these settings, click on the Reset Attributes button. You can also select Reset All in the Image Settings dialog box.

Editing the Graphic

Changing the image settings affects the way the graphic appears without actually changing the graphic design. To change the graphic itself, you need a set of drawing tools. WordPerfect 10 provides these tools in a special window that accesses the drawing features of Corel Presentations, the graphic presentation segment of WordPerfect Office 2002.

To display the graphic in that window, double-click on it, or select Edit Contents from the Image Tools box. Use the tools to draw objects over the graphic and to edit the lines and objects that make up the graphic itself.

Creating Text Boxes

In Chapter 7 you learned how to insert a border around text. The border isn't a graphic box because you cannot drag it within the document or use any of the image tools, such as rotating the text, to customize it. You can, however, create a graphic text box.

> TIP *To create a text box with existing text, select the text, and then click on the Text Box tool, or select Text Box from the Insert menu.*

To create a text box, click on the Text Box tool in the toolbar, or select Text Box from the Insert menu. WordPerfect 10 inserts into the document a graphic box 3.25 inches wide and one line high, with thin outside borders, and with the insertion point within the box. The borders are the default styles for a text box. Type and format the text in the box, and then click outside of it when you have finished:

> The physical and psychological training has practically eliminated minor health problems such as colds.

| TIP | *To insert a text box of some other size, use drag-to-create. Drag the shadow cursor to form the box, and then choose Text Box from the QuickMenu.* |

You can drag a text box within the document, and you can change its size. Though you cannot use the image tools with a text box, you can use the property bar and QuickMenu to customize it. Use the Contents box, for example, to rotate the text counterclockwise 90, 180, or 270 degrees.

Using TextArt

WordPerfect 10's TextArt application lets you create headlines, banners, logos, and other graphics from text. Instead of using plain text in a text box, you can select a shape that you want the text to appear in, choose a fill pattern and shadow, and even rotate or stretch the text for a special effect.

| TIP | *If you want to create an effect with text you've already typed, select the text, choose Graphics from the Insert menu, and click on TextArt.* |

To create an effect with text, follow these steps:

1. Choose Graphics from the Insert menu, and click on TextArt to open the window shown in Figure 13-7. If the TextArt Gallery appears instead, choose one of the sample designs shown and then click OK to open the window.

2. In the Type Here box, type the text that you want to use for the logo, headline, or other effect.

3. Click on one of the options shown in the Shapes box to choose the shape for the text, or click on More to see all of the available patterns.

4. Use the Font, Font Style, Justification, and Smoothness buttons to create the effect that you want. For example, since diagonal lines can sometimes

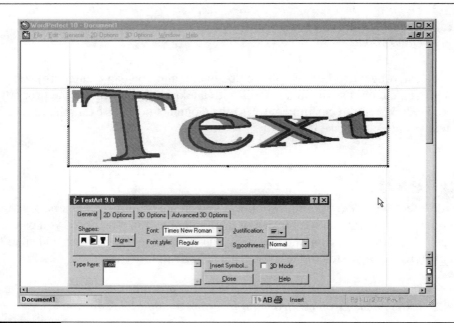

FIGURE 13-7 TextArt window

have a jagged or stepped look, select Normal, High, or Very High from the Smoothness list.

5. Use the Insert Symbol button to add a special character that is not available on the keyboard.

6. Click on 3D Mode to create text art with a more realistic 3-D look.

7. If you are creating a 2-D image, click on the 2D Options tab to see the page shown in Figure 13-8.

8. Use the Pattern button to choose a pattern and color for the fill.

9. Use the Shadow button to choose a shadow position and color.

10. Use the Outline button to choose a line thickness and color to surround the characters.

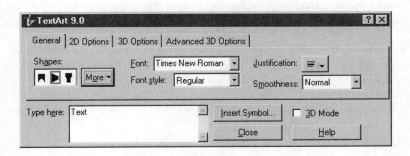

FIGURE 13-8   TextArt 2D Options page

11. To rotate the text, click on the Rotation button to display four handles. Drag one of the corner handles to rotate the text as desired, and then click on Rotation again. To use measurements to rotate the text, double-click on the Rotation button, and then enter the measurement in the dialog box that appears.

12. Select a color from the Text Color list.

13. Choose a style from the Preset list.

14. If you selected 3D mode, click on the 3D Options tab to see the page shown in Figure 13-9.

13

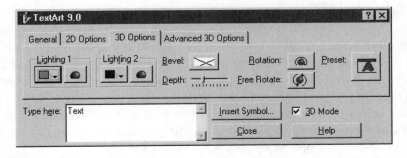

FIGURE 13-9   TextArt 3D Options page

15. Select options from the Lighting 1, Lighting 2, Bevel, and other lists to customize the 3-D effect.

16. For even more control over 3-D TextArt, click on the Advanced 3D Options tab. In this page, you can select textures for the front and back, and bevels of the image, as well as set the resolution quality in dots per inch.

17. Click on Close to insert the graphic into the document.

You can change the size and position of the box, and add borders and fill, just as you learned how to do for graphics. To edit or change the format of the text, double-click on the box to redisplay it in the TextArt window.

 You can also use TextArt in Quattro Pro and Corel Presentations.

Graphic Box Styles

Graphic box styles have been mentioned a number of times in this chapter. When you select Text Box from the Insert menu, or ClipArt from the Insert Graphics menu, you are actually selecting a box style. The style tells WordPerfect 10 the contents you want to place in the box, its default border and fill styles, and the caption position and label. There are really 14 different box styles, as shown in Table 13-1.

To change the style applied to an existing box, follow these steps:

1. Right-click on the box, and choose Style from the QuickMenu.

2. Select the style you want to apply from the Box Styles list.

These styles can hold three types of information—a graphic image, text, or an equation—and each box style can store any of the types. For example, you can insert text in a Figure box or a piece of clip art in a Text box. So if you want to insert a graphic in a box with thin borders all around, you can use a Text box style. The styles help you organize and coordinate your graphics. Choosing ClipArt, Text, or Equation gives you a place to start. But you can create any type of box using the Custom Box option, by following these steps:

1. Drag to create the box, and choose Custom Box from the QuickMenu. You can also select Graphics from the Insert menu and click on Custom Box.

Style	Description
Image	No borders, page anchor, top-right corner at the insertion point, 1.5 inches wide, auto height
Text Box	Thin outside border lines, paragraph anchor at the right border, 3.25 inches wide, auto height
Equation	No borders, paragraph anchor, full size between the margins, auto height
Figure Box	Thin outside border lines, paragraph anchor at the right border, 3.25 inches wide, auto height
Table	No border, paragraph anchor at the right margin, 3.25 inches wide, auto height
User	No borders, paragraph anchor at the right border, 3.25 inches wide, auto height
Button	Borders and fill to appear as a button, character anchor at the position of the insertion point on the baseline, 1 inch wide, auto height
Watermark	No borders, page anchor, full-page size
Inline Equation	No borders, character anchor at the position of the insertion point on the baseline, auto width, auto height
OLE 2.0	No borders, page anchor, top-right corner at the insertion point, 1.5 inches wide, auto height
Inline Text	No borders, character anchor at the position of the insertion point on the baseline, auto width, auto height
Draw Object	No borders, page anchor, top-right corner at the insertion point, 1 inch wide, 1 inch high
Draw Object Text	No borders, page anchor, top-right corner at the insertion point, 1 inch wide, auto height
Sticky Note Text	No borders, yellow fill color, page anchor, top-right corner at the insertion point, 1 inch wide, auto height

TABLE 13-1   Box styles

13

2. From the Custom Box dialog box that appears, choose the style of box that you want.

3. Click on OK.

Use the Contents dialog box to determine what goes in the box—an image, image on disk, text, or equation.

You can also create a custom box type:

1. Display the Custom Box dialog box.

2. Click on Styles and then on Create.

3. In the dialog box that appears, enter a name for the type.

4. Specify the borders, fill, contents, and other specifics.

5. Click on OK, and then close the Box Style dialog box.

Your new type will appear on the Custom Box list.

Graphic Styles

In addition to boxes, WordPerfect 10 includes graphic styles for borders, lines, and fill patterns. You can edit these styles or create your own to apply custom styles to these graphic elements.

Select Graphics Styles from the Format menu to see this dialog box:

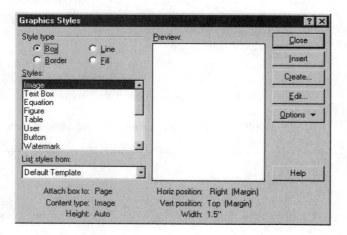

Choose the type of style you want to edit; the current styles in the Styles list will be displayed. Then click on Create to design your own style, or choose a style from the list, and click on Edit to customize it. The dialog box that appears depends on the style type you selected. If you choose to create a fill style, for example, you'll see options for choosing the pattern, foreground, and background colors. If you choose to create a Gradient fill in the dialog box, you'll see the options in Figure 13-10. Enter a name for your style, select options from the box until the sample appears the way you want it, and then click on OK.

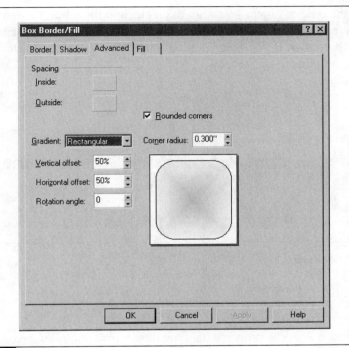

FIGURE 13-10   Creating a gradient fill pattern

Drawing Custom Graphics

You can access the Corel Presentations drawing tools at any time to create your own graphics. Click on the Draw Picture button in the toolbar to display the Corel Presentations window with a blank graphic box. Use the drawing tools and menu options to create your drawing. For example, select Organization Chart from the Insert menu to add an organization chart to your document. When you're done with the drawing, click outside the box to return to WordPerfect 10. Edit the drawing just as you learned in this chapter.

If you just want to draw geometric shapes and freehand sketches, right-click on any toolbar, and choose Draw Shapes from the menu to see the toolbar shown next:

Choose the type of object you want to create, and then drag the mouse to form the object. When you release the mouse, the object will be selected, and you'll see a special property bar. If you create a filled object, such as a rectangle or oval, the property bar contains these features:

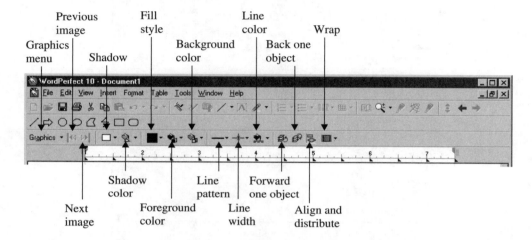

If you draw a line, the property bar contains Arrow Start and Arrow End lists to add an arrowhead to the line.

Use the tools on the property bar to customize the object.

Creating Shapes

If you'd rather not try to draw freehand, you can create many common shapes by selecting them from the toolbar or in a dialog box.

To use the toolbar, click on the Draw Shapes button and select a shape from the menu:

The mouse point appears like a crosshairs—hold down the mouse button, and drag to create the selected shape in the size desired. When you release the mouse, the shape appears selected by handles, like any other graphic object. You can drag the handles to change its size, or use options from the property bar to customize its shadow, fill style, line, or position in relation to other overlapping objects.

For even more choices, select Shapes from the Insert menu to see the Draw Object Shapes dialog box with a list of shape categories:

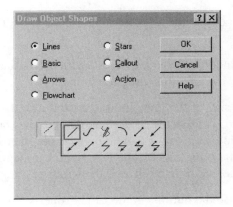

Select the options button for the type of shape you want to create to display choices in the lower area of the dialog box. Click on the shape of your choice, close the dialog box, and then drag to create the selected shape in the size desired.

You can also drag one or more diamond-shaped handles to change its shape. In this example, you can see the original shape from the Action category and how it appears after the diamond-shaped handle was dragged in toward the center:

Drawing Lines

If you just want to add a small unobtrusive graphic element to a page, consider using a horizontal or vertical line. The easiest way to draw a horizontal line is using the QuickLines feature:

1. Start a new line by typing four hyphens or four equal signs.

2. Press ENTER.

WordPerfect 10 replaces the characters with a solid single or double line across the page.

You can also draw a horizontal line by selecting Horizontal Line from the Insert Line menu. To draw a vertical line down the entire page at the horizontal position of the insertion point, select Vertical Line from the Insert Line menu.

Because the lines are graphic elements, you can change their sizes and positions just as you can for graphic boxes:

1. Click on the line with the left mouse button to select it, displaying the handles.

2. To move the line, point to the line so the mouse is shaped like a four-headed arrow, and then drag the mouse.

3. To change the size of the line, point to a handle so the mouse is a two-headed arrow. Drag the center handle on top or bottom to change the height of the line, and drag a handle on a corner to change both the width and height at the same time. If the line is thick enough, drag the center handle on the left or right to change the width of the graphic.

4. You can also use the buttons in the Line Property Bar to set the line style, thickness, and color; change the orientation of the line; and edit the line graphic.

Creating Custom Lines

You can create a custom-sized and formatted line by choosing Insert | Line | Custom Line to display the Create Graphics Line dialog box. Choose to create either a horizontal or vertical line, and then use the Line Style list to choose the line's shape and thickness or to insert multiple lines.

 The Line Style list shows right-angled sample lines, although only a straight line will be inserted. To draw a right angle, you have to coordinate the position of separate vertical and horizontal lines.

You can then use the remaining options in the box to customize the line:

■ Choose from a palette of 256 colors in the Line Color list.

■ Choose a line thickness. The list has ten options ranging from 0.01 to 0.12 inch, and you can enter a custom thickness.

■ Set Space Above Line and Space Below Line to determine the distance of the line from the text above and below it.

■ Enter the Length of the line.

■ Set the line's Horizontal Position in relation to the left and right margins.

■ Set the line's Vertical Position in relation to the top margin. The default Baseline positions the line on the same baseline as the text.

WordPerfect 10 also lets you create your own line style:

1. Click on Line Styles in the dialog box, and then click on Create to open the dialog box in Figure 13-11. (Click on Edit to edit an existing line style.)

2. Give your style a name, so you can later choose it from the Line Style list.

3. Select a color, pattern, and thickness.

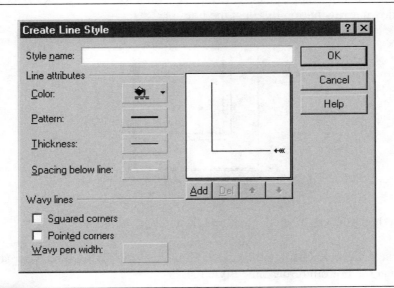

FIGURE 13-11   Creating custom line style

4. Select one of the Wavy Line options and a pen width to create a line that is not straight, like this:

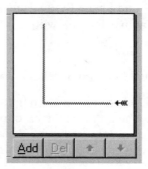

5. To create a multiple-line style, select a distance between lines in the Spacing Below Line list, and then click on Add. Select options for the new line, and then add and format any others.

6. Once you have multiple lines, you have to choose which one you want to edit or change. The current line is indicated by an arrow pointing to it in the preview area. Click on the line you want to edit, or click on the up or down arrow button to select the line.

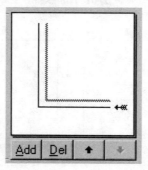

7. When you've finished, click on OK and then Close.

To use your style, display the Create Graphics Line dialog box. Your style will be listed at the bottom of the Line Style list.

Inserting Charts

Numbers can be very boring and difficult to read in a document even when displayed in a table. When you want to show a trend or make a quick point, nothing is better than a chart. WordPerfect 10 lets you create charts directly from the document window—you don't have to start Quattro Pro or Corel Presentations. Here's how:

Integrate IT! *Charting works about the same in WordPerfect 10, Quattro Pro 9, and Corel Presentations 10. You can move charts, and the information you need to create them, between applications.*

1. Select Chart from the Insert menu to see a sample chart and table of information, as shown in Figure 13-12. Notice that the X-axis labels are listed in the row marked "Labels" and the name for each series in the column marked "Legend." The color next to each legend entry shows the color that the chart bar or line will appear in.

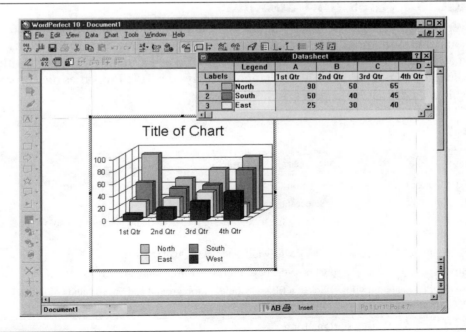

FIGURE 13-12 Default chart and data

2. To enter your own information into the chart, delete the sample data by clicking on the empty box above the word "Labels" to select all of the data, and then pressing DEL.

3. In the box that appears, click on Both to delete both the data and formats from the chart. Click on OK.

4. Type the information that you want to chart.

Corel Presentations creates the chart as you enter the information.

To return to WordPerfect 10, just click outside of the chart. You can now change the size, position, borders, and fill using the property bar, QuickMenu, or Edit Box tools. To change the design of the chart, double-click on it.

There are a lot of options to choose from to customize the chart. We'll be looking at these in detail in the Quattro Pro 9 section of this book because many of the techniques are the same. For now, we'll summarize some of the most typical options.

Adding Titles and Subtitles

Even though you may be describing the chart in the text of your document, you should add a title or subtitle to make its purpose immediately clear to the reader. To add a title, select Title from the Chart menu. To add a subtitle, choose Subtitle from the Chart menu. Corel Presentations displays the Title Properties dialog box. Table 13-2 describes the pages of this dialog box.

Page	Description
Title Options	Position the text on the left, center, or right of the chart
Title Font	Select the font, size, and color of the text
Text Fill	Select a fill style, pattern, foreground and background colors, and fill method
Text Outline	Choose the width and line style of the text
Box Type	Choose the type of the box surrounding the text
Box Fill (appears only if a box type is selected.)	Select a fill style, pattern, foreground and background colors, and fill method for the box

TABLE 13-2   Setting options for text

Enter the title or subtitle in the text box. If you deselect the Display Chart Title box, the title or subtitle does not appear—use this option if you want to remove the title but leave the text available.

Customizing Charts

By default, Corel Presentations creates a bar chart. You can change the type of the chart in two ways, by using the Gallery and Layout/Type options from the Chart menu.

The Gallery lists 12 general categories of charts that you can create. When you select a category, two or more different styles of the type appear in preview boxes. Click on the style that you want to use, and then click on OK.

For more control over the chart type, use these steps:

1. Select Layout/Type from the Chart menu to display the dialog box in Figure 13-13.

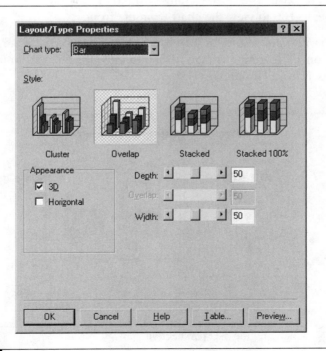

FIGURE 13-13   Selecting a chart category, type, and other options

2. Choose a category from the Chart Type list. As with the Gallery, two or more styles of the type appear in the preview area.

3. Click on the style you want.

4. Select or deselect the 3D checkbox to select either a 3-D or 2-D chart.

5. Click on Horizontal for a horizontal chart; clear the box for a vertical chart.

The other options that appear in this dialog box will depend on the type of chart you select. Choose from the options, and click on Preview to minimize the dialog box so you can see how the chart will appear. In the box that does appear, click on OK if you want to accept the chart as it is. Click on Back to reopen the dialog box or on Cancel to return the chart to its previous settings.

If you do create a 3-D chart, you can further customize it by selecting Perspective from the Chart menu to see the dialog box shown in Figure 13-14.

- Use the *Horizontal* text box or the horizontal scroll bar to rotate the chart around its base. The settings range from 0 to look directly at the chart from its side, to 100 to view the chart from the front.

- Use the *Vertical* setting or the vertical scroll bar to rotate the chart from top to bottom. The settings range from 0 to view the chart from the top, to 100 to view it from "ground level."

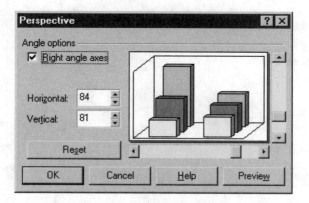

FIGURE 13-14   Changing the 3-D perspective

- Select the *Right Angle Axes* checkbox to make the X axis and Y axis perpendicular to each other.

- Click on *Reset* to return the chart to the default settings.

You can change the settings for any part of the chart by double-clicking on the part, which opens a dialog box of options for just that part. For example, double-click on the Y-axis lines to see the Primary Y Axis Properties dialog box. In this box you can change the spacing, appearance, and position of axis labels, as well as the scale of the measurements along the axis. Double-click on a series bar to change its shape, color, and spacing. Double-click on a grid line to change its shape and color, and to set the spacing between lines. Double-click on a title or subtitle to change its color, font, size, fill, or the border surrounding it.

Using the Equation Editors

Mathematical and scientific equations require special characters and formats. You can access special characters using the Insert Characters command, and you can create subscripts and superscripts using the Font dialog box and the Advance command from the Typesetting menu. But even with these features, creating complex equations could be difficult.

WordPerfect 10 doesn't want anything to be difficult for you, so they've given you the Equation Editor. This is a special set of tools for formatting equations of all types. Through these tools you have easy access to special characters and formats that would be difficult to access any other way.

> **NOTE** *The Equation Editor formats equations for you—it does not do the math. That you have to do yourself.*

Selecting an Equation Editor

WordPerfect 10 doesn't just offer one Equation Editor—it offers you two. The WordPerfect 5.1 to 7 Equation Editor is the same one used in previous versions of WordPerfect 10. The WordPerfect 10 Equation Editor is new.

To select the Equation Editor you want to use, follow these steps:

1. Select Settings from the Tools menu.

2. Click on Environment.

3. Click on the Graphics tab to see the dialog box in Figure 13-15.

4. In the Default Equation Editor section, click on the option button for the editor you want to use. To select an editor each time you want to create an equation, click on the checkbox below the Default Equation Editor section.

5. Click on OK, and then close the Settings dialog box.

To start the Equation Editor, choose Equation from the Insert menu. If you chose to indicate the editor each time, a box will appear listing the two editors. Make your choice, and then click on OK.

WordPerfect 10 Equation Editor

If you select this option, you'll see the window shown in Figure 13-16. You interact with the Equation Editor using the menus and the toolbar, creating the equation in the entry window. The small dotted rectangle in the entry window is called a *slot*. You enter all text and symbols in slots, which expand to fit what you enter.

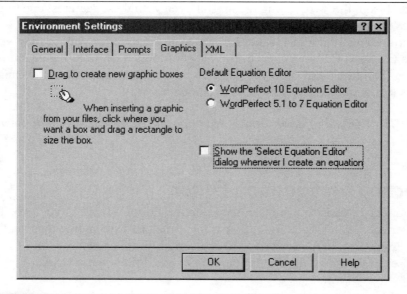

FIGURE 13-15   Selecting an equation editor

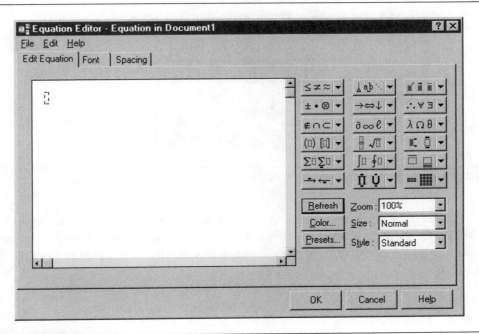

FIGURE 13-16 WordPerfect 10 Equation Editor

Type letters, numbers, and most punctuation marks from the keyboard. You select other special characters and equation graphics and formats from the toolbar. Clicking on a toolbar button displays a list of options—click on the option you want to insert into the equation. Figure 13-17 shows the functions of the toolbar buttons.

The buttons on the top three rows of the toolbar insert symbols. Clicking one inserts the symbol into the active slot in the equation. The buttons on the bottom three rows of the toolbar insert templates. A template is one or more slots, often combined with an equation character, such as a radical or fraction line. You can nest as many templates as you want, such as adding a superscript template to the numerator of a division operation, or to the slot under a radical.

The nested slots represent various levels in the equation. The Equation Editor displays an insertion point where the next character typed or inserted will appear. You'll also see a horizontal line under the section of the equation at that level.

The Equation Editor applies built-in styles to the parts of your equation. For example, variables and lowercase Greek characters will be in italic; matrices and vectors will be in bold. The editor also adds spacing where required, such as on

13

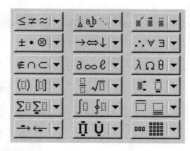

| FIGURE 13-17 | Equation toolbar functions |

both sides of an equal sign. Pressing the SPACEBAR while in the editor, however, has no effect except when you apply the text style. To add spaces yourself between characters when using other styles, you have to select a space character from the toolbar.

Let's go step by step through the process of creating this simple equation. We'll also look at the concept of equation levels.

$$X = \frac{\sqrt{Y}}{2_{-z}}$$

1. Type **X=**. The Equation Editor inserts a space between the X and the equal sign. It displays the X in italic, the default format for variables.

2. Click on the Fraction and Radical button in the toolbar to see following options:

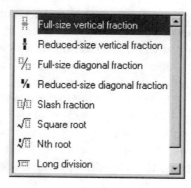

3. Select Full-Size Vertical Fraction. You'll see this template with two slots. The insertion point is in the top slot, so you are ready to insert the radical:

$$X = \frac{\square}{\square}$$

4. Click on the Fraction and Radicals button again, and select Square Root. The radical appears with a slot underneath.

5. Type **Y** in the slot.

6. Now look carefully at the template, shown enlarged here:

$$X = \frac{\sqrt{Y}}{\square}$$

7. The insertion point is immediately following the letter Y and below the radical. The underline appears just under the letter Y, showing that the next character you type or insert will also be under the radical.

8. Press the RIGHT ARROW key. The insertion point now becomes the full height of the radical, and the underline is the full length of the radical. This means that the next character will not be under the radical, but above the division.

9. Press the RIGHT ARROW key again. Now the insertion point is the full size of the fraction, showing that the next character will be to the right of the fraction.

10. Press the DOWN ARROW key, or click in the slot under the fraction.

11. Type **2**. Next enter a subscript template.

12. Click on the Subscripts and Superscripts button to see these options:

13

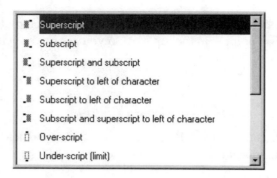

13. Select Subscript. A slot appears in the subscript position.

14. Type **-Z**.

15. Select Exit and Return to Document from the File menu.

The Equation Editor closes, and the equation appears in the document in a graphic box. Click outside of the box to display the equation. You can now change the position and size of the box, or its border or fill, as you would any graphic. To edit the equation itself, double-click on it to open the Equation Editor.

Equation Editor Options

When you are creating or editing an equation, you can use some special techniques, options, and styles.

For example, to make a small change to the position of a character or symbol, select it, hold down the CTRL key, and press an arrow key for the direction you want to move. This is called *nudging*.

You can also change the style that the editor applied to a character using the Font tab, shown in Figure 13-18. For example, if you want subscript characters to be larger than the default size, increase the percentage next to the Subscript style. The Spacing tab of the Equation Editor lets you customize the default spacing between characters.

TIP   *The Greek and Symbol styles must use a font that contains Greek and symbol characters.*

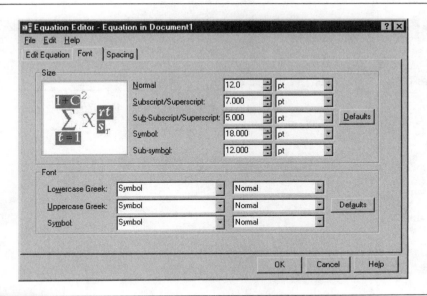

FIGURE 13-18   Changing the font and style of characters

WordPerfect 5.1 to 7 Equation Editor

If you select this option, you'll see the window shown in Figure 13-19. You interact with the Equation Editor using the menus, toolbar, and property bar. The functions of the property bar are shown in Table 13-3.

Button	Function
Save As	Saves the equation in a separate file from the document
Equation Font	Displays a font dialog box for changing the font and point size of the displayed characters
Insert Equation File	Recalls an equation from disk into the Equation Editor window
Symbols	Inserts special characters and symbols
Redisplay	Updates the Display pane
Zoom Equation Display	Displays the Zoom dialog box to select a display magnification
Close	Closes the Equation Editor and inserts the equation into the document

TABLE 13-3   Equation property bar

13

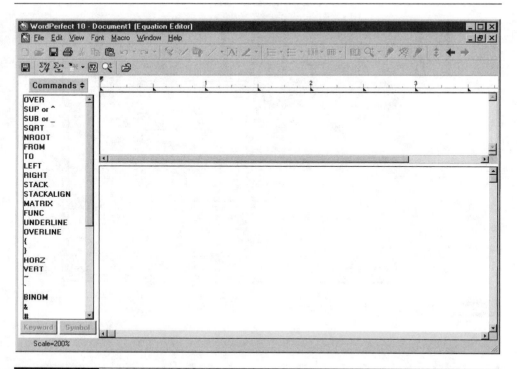

FIGURE 13-19   WordPerfect 5.1 to 7 Equation Editor

You use three panes to create and display your equations. The Editing pane is the large empty box near the top of the window, just below the Equation Editor toolbar. You use this part of the window to type the text and numbers you want in the equation, and to insert formatting commands and codes for special characters. Everything in this pane appears as plain, unformatted text.

Below the Editing pane is the Display pane. This is where WordPerfect 10 will display the formatted equation, showing the special characters and symbols in the proper spacing and size. The image in the Display pane does not update automatically as you enter the equation in the Editing pane. To see how the equation will appear in the document, click on the Redisplay button in the toolbar. WordPerfect 10 displays an error message if your formatting instructions are not complete.

Along the left of the window is the Equation palette. It is here that you select the commands, codes, functions, and symbols that tell WordPerfect 10 how to format the equation in the Display pane. The Equation palette has eight sections that you access from the pull-down list now labeled "Commands." Pull down the list to display a set of characters or commands, and then double-click on the one you want to insert into the Editing pane. Here are the sections and what they do:

- *Commands* lets you select from the most common formats and symbols.
- *Large* displays popular mathematics symbols.
- *Symbols* includes many miscellaneous symbols.
- *Greek* offers Greek characters.
- *Arrows* lists various arrows, triangles, squares, and circles.
- *Sets* includes relational operators and set symbols.
- *Other* includes diacritical marks and ellipses.
- *Function* includes symbols for mathematical functions.

Some of your choices can be inserted into the Editing pane as keywords or symbols—they always appear as formatted symbols in the Display pane. To choose how you want WordPerfect 10 to insert items, click on either the Keyword or Symbol button under the Equation palette. You can usually also type the commands yourself, such as typing **sub** to create a subscript. You can also enter *variables*—characters or words that represent unknown values.

Here's a simple illustration using the Equation Editor:

1. In the Editing pane, type **X~=~** and then click on Redisplay. The tilde character (~) tells WordPerfect 10 to insert a space (you can use the grave accent [`] to insert a quarter space), so the equation will appear as shown here:

$$\overline{X} \ =$$

2. If the Commands palette is not shown, switch to that set.

3. Double-click on SQRT, the square root command.

4. Type **Y OVER 2 SUB {–Z}**. This will place the letter *Y* on a line over 2, and add a subscript –Z to the 2.

5. Click on Redisplay to see the completed equation, as shown here:

13

$$X = \frac{\sqrt{Y}}{2_{-z}}$$

6. Click on the Close button in the property bar and return to the document, inserting the equation into a graphic box using the equation box style.

7. You can now change the size and position of the box, add a caption, or customize the border and fill. Double-click on the equation if you want to edit it in the Equation Editor.

Try It Out

You covered a lot of material in this chapter, so take some time to practice using graphics in documents. As an example, we'll spruce up the columnar document we created in Chapter 10 by adding a graphic within the columns and using TextArt to create an eye-catching banner.

We'll be using the document Tae Kwon Do Columns that we created in Chapter 10's Try It Out section. If you do not have that document, take any WordPerfect document and format it in two equal-sized columns. Refer to Figure 10-22 to see what the document looked like.

You'll see in this section that working with graphics is more of an art than a science. While you can use dialog boxes to specify exact sizes and positions, it is more intuitive to drag graphics to set their position and size. By dragging, you can see the effect of the graphic on the text and make any adjustments that are needed.

1. Open the document Tae Kwon Do Columns.

2. Place the insertion point at the start of the next to the last paragraph in the right-hand column.

3. Select Graphics from the Insert menu and click on ClipArt.

4. Locate a graphic that you feel would look nice with the document and click Insert.

5. Resize the graphic so it is about half as wide as the column.

6. Pull down the Wrap list in the Picture property bar and select Neither Side. The Contour options, by the way, would adjust the text to the shape of the graphic, as shown here:

When an army of over 250,000 Japanese invaded Korea in 1592, the country was not prepared to defend itself. Throughout the next centuries, Korea faced other invasions. Yet, the spirit of the Korean people prevailed. Many of the Koreans who fled their homeland carried Tae Kyon to other countries. There, the martial art was refined. After the war, when Korea was liberated, interest in the native martial art increased and in 1955 the name *Tae Kwon Do* was formally accepted.

8. Click on the Border Style button in the Picture property bar and select one of the borders.

9. If necessary, adjust the position of the graphic so it does not come between the text of a paragraph.

The document contains a small table at the end of the right-hand column. Inserting the graphic may have divided the table between two pages. While nothing is wrong with that, it is better if the entire table were on one page to make it easier to read. Before making any adjustments, however, let's create the TextArt banner. Inserting the banner may correct the table problem automatically.

10. Select the text of the headline. TextArt will use the selection for its text.

11. Select Graphics from the Insert menu and click TextArt.

12. Use TextArt options to create a pleasing banner for the document.

13. Drag the TextArt graphic so it is centered at the top of the page.

14. Pull down the Wrap list in the Picture property bar and select Neither Side.

15. With the TextArt graphic still selected, pull down the Border Style button in the Picture property bar and select one of the borders.

13

16. Now check the position of the graphic. Inserting the TextArt may have moved the graphic elsewhere in the document.

17. Drag the graphic so it is at the bottom of the right-hand column and centered within the column.

18. If necessary, enlarge or reduce the graphic so it does not divide a paragraph between pages.

Figure 13-20 shows how the document might appear.

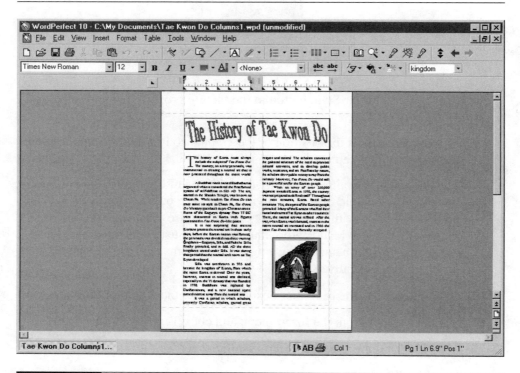

FIGURE 13-20 Completed document

Chapter 14

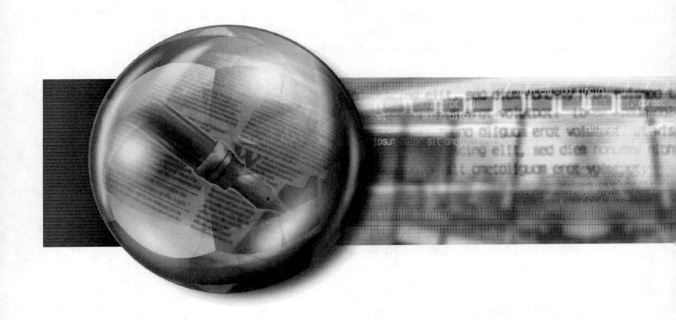

Sharing Information

WordPerfect 10 lets you share information between it and other parts of WordPerfect Office 2002, and even with other Windows applications. Sharing information lets you create compound documents without having to retype information. A *compound document* is one that includes information from more than one application. For example, suppose you created a spreadsheet in Quattro Pro 10, an organization chart in Corel Presentations 10, and a drawing in Windows Paint. You can add all of these items to your WordPerfect 10 document to create a professional-looking document. For instance, you don't need to retype the spreadsheet into a WordPerfect 10 table—you can just cut and paste it into WordPerfect 10, or even open it directly in a document as a table.

Sharing information also lets you send a WordPerfect 10 form document, or name and address information in a Quattro Pro 10 or other spreadsheet, to a mailing list that you've created in Paradox 10. In fact, you can even link the database or spreadsheet with WordPerfect 10 so your document always has the most up-to-date information.

In Chapter 22 you will learn how to use cells from a Quattro Pro 10 spreadsheet in a WordPerfect 10 document. In this chapter, you will learn how to use WordPerfect 10 information with other applications, and how to import and link database and spreadsheet information. You will also learn how to open documents into WordPerfect 10 that have been created with other programs, and how to save your WordPerfect 10 documents in other formats.

Saving Files

While it is difficult to imagine why, not everyone uses WordPerfect 10 as their word processing program. If you have to share your files with these unfortunates, you can make it easier on them by saving your files in a format their program understands.

You should first save your document normally, in Corel WordPerfect 10's own format. Then follow these steps:

1. Select Save As from the File menu.

2. Pull down the File Type list. You'll see a list of formats that Corel WordPerfect 10 can save your documents in.

3. Scroll the list, and click on the format that you want to use.

4. Enter a filename, and then click on Save.

In addition to all previous WordPerfect 10 formats, you can select from the formats shown in Table 14-1. Notice that you can also save your document in a spreadsheet format, such as Quattro Pro 10, Excel, and Lotus 1-2-3. When you choose Quattro Pro 10, however, only the tables in your document are saved. Each table becomes a page in the Quattro Pro 10 workbook, labeled Table A, Table B, and so on.

| NOTE | *You may have to install some of the file formats individually; they are not all provided by the default installation option.* |

The next time you save the document, WordPerfect 10 displays a Save Format dialog box asking you to confirm the format. You can choose to save it in WordPerfect 10 format or in the original type, or click on Other to display the Save As dialog box.

Application/Format	Version
AmiPro	1.2 to 3.0
ANSI Windows	Text, generic word processing, and delimited text
ASCII DOS	Text, generic word processing, and delimited text
EDGAR	
DIF	Spreadsheet and Navy
DisplayWrite	4 to 5
Excel	4.0
IBM DCA	FFT and RFT
Kermit	
Lotus 1-2-3	1.0, 4.0 for Windows, 3.0 and 3.1 for DOS
MS Word	1 to 2000 for Windows, 4 to 5.5 for DOS
OfficeWriter	6 to 6.2
Professional Write	1 to 2.2
Quattro Pro 9 for Windows	1.0, 5.0, and 6.0
RTF	
UNICODE Text	
Volkswriter	4
Windows Write	
WordStar	3.3 to 7, 2000 1 to 3
XyWrite	3.55 to 4

TABLE 14-1   File Format

14

Opening Documents

In WordPerfect 10, one of the quickest ways to use a file that you created with another program is simply to open it. You can open documents created in all of the formats that you can save them in, as well as these additional ones:

- Borland Sprint
- IA5
- QuickFinder Log
- SGML
- WordPerfect for the Macintosh and Far East
- WP Works
- XML

While the Open dialog box has a File Type list, it only contains the All Files (*.*) option, the text file format, and the default formats used by WordPerfect 10. You don't see the other formats because in most cases you don't have to select a format when you open a file. WordPerfect 10 automatically determines the type of file and does what it must to open it and display it on the screen. If it can't determine the file type, the Convert File Format dialog box appears. You can then scroll through the Convert File Format From list and select the format.

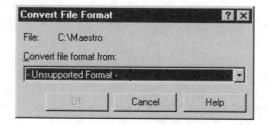

ASCII and ANSI text files, by the way, can be opened using two methods. These text files have a carriage return and linefeed code at the end of each line. These are the codes, abbreviated CR/LF, that tell the computer to move the insertion point to the start of the next line. You can choose to open the document normally, which converts each CR/LF code to a hard carriage return, HRt; or you can select to convert each CR/LF to a soft carriage return, the SRt code. Selecting the SRt option lets you format the document as a series of paragraphs, but you lose the original line breaks.

When you open a spreadsheet or database file, WordPerfect 10 displays a special dialog box. Refer to "Using Databases and Spreadsheets," later in this chapter, for more information about opening spreadsheets and database files in WordPerfect 10.

Sharing Problem Documents

You may have a document in a format that WordPerfect 10 cannot open, or you may be using a program whose format WordPerfect 10 cannot save in. All is not lost. Try to find an intermediate format that both programs can accept. Most programs, for example, have the option to save in ASCII text format. While you will lose your formatting by saving as ASCII text, at least you won't have to retype everything.

Sharing Information Through the Clipboard

If you do not want to use an entire document file from or in another application, you can cut/copy and paste information from one program to the other.

For example, suppose you want to copy some information from a Microsoft Word for Windows document to WordPerfect 10. Follow these steps:

1. Open WordPerfect 10 and the document you want to insert the information into.

2. Open Word for Windows and the document containing the information.

3. Cut or copy the information in the Word for Windows document.

4. Switch to WordPerfect 10.

5. Click on the Paste button in the toolbar, or select Paste from the Edit menu.

You can also paste information from a DOS application. When you run a DOS program in Windows, it appears in a DOS window with this toolbar:

To copy information from the DOS-application window, follow these steps:

1. Click on the Mark button in the DOS window toolbar.

2. Drag the mouse over the text you want to copy.

3. Click on the Copy button in the DOS window toolbar.

4. Switch to WordPerfect 10, and place the insertion point where you want to insert the text.

5. Click on the Paste button in the WordPerfect 10 toolbar.

You can also use the Clipboard to copy information within the DOS application itself. Mark and copy the text in the DOS window, place the cursor where you want the text to appear, and then click on the Paste button in the DOS window toolbar.

Creating Organization Charts

You can easily create organization charts in Corel Presentations 10, but you do have to enter the information and create the structure showing the chain of command. A quicker way to create an organization chart in Corel Presentations 10 is to type the chain of command as a WordPerfect 10 outline.

1. Start WordPerfect 10.

2. Select Outline/Bullets & Numbering from the Insert menu.

3. Click on the Numbers tab, if it is not displayed.

4. Click on the second option in the second row—the Paragraph Numbers only (no styles) format, and then click on OK.

5. Enter the name of the top executive as paragraph number 1, and the immediate subordinate as paragraphs 2, 3, and so on.

6. Enter other levels as indented paragraphs, using TAB to move down a level and SHIFT-TAB to move up.

```
1.Allison Wing
2.Jerry Beebe
      a.Kate Jackson
      b.F. F. Majors
3.Steve Austin
4.William Kildair
      a.Ben Casey
      b.Horace Rumpole
```

7. Save the document.

8. Open or switch to Corel Presentations 10.

9. Display the slide where you want to add the organization chart.

10. Select Organization Chart from the Insert menu, drag to draw the chart, select a chart type from the box that appears, and click on OK.

11. Choose Import Outline from the Chart menu.

12. Select the file containing the organization chart, and then click on Insert.

Corel Presentations 10 forms the organization chart using the text and structure of the outline, as shown in Figure 14-1.

Embedding and Linking Information

Windows lets you insert information from other applications using two general techniques, *embedding* and *linking*.

When you embed information into an application, such as WordPerfect 10, you are actually placing a complete copy of it in the document. You won't be able to edit or format the information using WordPerfect 10 commands because it is treated as one solid object. If you double-click on the object, however, WordPerfect 10 performs these steps:

1. Starts the application that you used to create the object.

2. Transfers a copy of the information from WordPerfect 10 to the application so you can edit the object in that application.

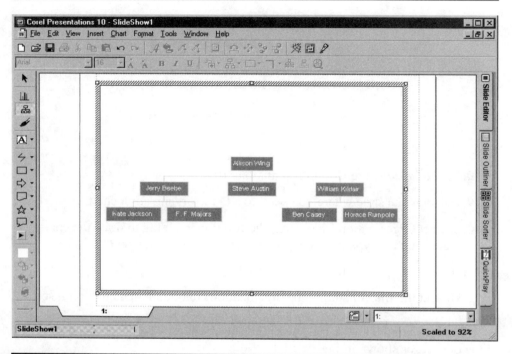

FIGURE 14-1   Corel Presentations organization chart using a Corel WordPerfect outline

When you edit and close the application, the edited version appears in WordPerfect 10. However, there is no actual connection between the object's file on the disk and the copy of the object in the document. If you edit the object separately by opening it directly into the application, the copy of it in WordPerfect 10 is not affected.

When you insert information using a link, however, there is a connection. When you double-click on the object in WordPerfect 10, it:

1. Starts the application.

2. Opens the original file on the disk in which the object is stored.

When you save the edited copy of the object, it is updated in WordPerfect 10 as well. But because there is a link, you can also open the object directly with the application to edit it. The updated version automatically appears in WordPerfect 10.

You can embed and link information in several ways. One method is to use the Paste Special dialog box from the WordPerfect 10 Edit menu. You'll learn how to do that when we discuss using a Quattro Pro 10 spreadsheet in WordPerfect 10 in Chapter 22.

You can also embed and link information using the Object command from the Insert menu. To create and insert an embedded object, select Object from the Insert menu, and click on Create New to see the options in Figure 14-2. The Object Type list contains all of the applications that are registered in Windows as usable as the source of an embedded object.

Select the application that you want to create the object, and then click on OK. Windows starts that application so that you can create the object.

If you have already created the object, such as a drawing in Paint, click on the Create From File option in the Insert Object dialog box. Enter the path and name of the file, or use the Browse button to select it. To embed the object into the document, click on OK. To link the object, click on the Link checkbox and then on OK.

Multimedia Documents

By adding sound and video to a document, you can create an onscreen presentation, a document that comes alive to the reader. While sound and video clips can create very large document files, they can also be very effective. We'll look at some of the techniques that you can use.

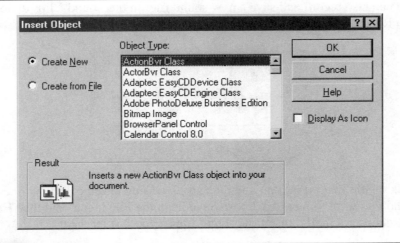

FIGURE 14-2   Embedding a new object

NOTE *You can access some sound and movie files using the Corel Scrapbook*

Inserting a Sound Clip

You can insert or record a sound clip for special effects or just as an annotation that can be played back at some later time. WordPerfect 10 can use sound files in either the WAV or MIDI format, and you can even record WAV sound directly into the document.

To insert an existing sound file, follow these steps:

1. Select Sound from the Insert menu to see the Sound Clips dialog box.

2. Click on Insert to see the Insert Sound Clip into Document dialog box.

3. Enter a name that you want to identify with the clip, and then enter the path and name of the file, or use the Browse button to locate it. Once you choose a file, you can then select Link To File on Disk to create a link to the original file or Store in Document to place a copy of the sound in the document.

4. Click on OK. WordPerfect 10 inserts a Sound Clip icon in the left margin.

5. To play the sound, click on the icon.

You can also record and save a new sound file. In the Sound Clips dialog box, click on Record to display the Windows Sound Recorder dialog box:

Click on the Record button, and then speak or sing into the microphone or play the sound you want to record. Choose Save from the File menu, and then Exit the Sound Recorder. Finally, insert the sound file as you just learned.

To play or delete any sound clip in the document, or edit its description, select Sound from the Insert menu to display the Sound Clips dialog box. Figure 14-3 shows the dialog box with inserted files. To play a sound, click on its name in the list box, and then click on the Play button. There are also buttons to stop, rewind, and fast-forward the clip. The Length indicator shows how long the clip is; the Position indicator shows how far into the clip the sound you are hearing is located.

If you want to access these same features later without redisplaying the dialog box, click on the Transcribe button. The dialog box will close, and you'll see a feature bar (shown in the following illustration) under the ruler. Click on the Sound Clip icon to hear the sound, and then use the feature bar buttons to replay, rewind, or fast-forward it. Click on Close to remove the feature bar.

FIGURE 14-3   Select and play sound clips

Other Multimedia Files

To insert a sound, video, or other multimedia object into the document, select Object from the Insert menu, and then double-click on the Media Clip option. WordPerfect 10 displays the options shown in Figure 14-4. Click on Insert Clip to see the options shown here:

Click on Video for Windows to insert a video clip, Sound or MIDI Sequencer to insert a sound clip, or CD Audio to insert a track from an audio CD in your CD drive. Depending on what you inserted, you'll see either an icon representing the object, or a window displaying the object, such as a video clip. Double-click on the icon or window, or click on the play button to display it.

Using Databases and Spreadsheets

So far you've learned several ways to insert spreadsheet information into a document—you can cut and paste it through the Clipboard, or you can embed or link it using the Object command from the Insert menu.

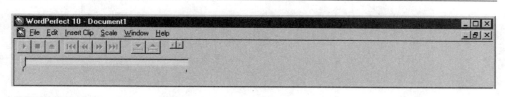

FIGURE 14-4   Media Clip feature bar

Integrate IT!	*In Chapter 22 you will learn even more about using Quattro Pro 10 information in a WordPerfect 10 document.*

You can also use information from a spreadsheet or database by importing it, or by creating a link through a process known as *Dynamic Data Exchange (DDE)*. When you import the information, you are placing a copy of it into the WordPerfect 10 document. When you create a DDE link, the information appears in your document, and you can format and edit it, but it is also linked with the original file on the disk. Changing the file changes the information in WordPerfect 10 as well. This differs from the link you learned about previously, which is called an *OLE link* (from Object Linking and Embedding). With an OLE link you cannot edit or format the information in WordPerfect 10.

Using the import or DDE link technique, you have the choice of how you want to insert the spreadsheet or database information—as a WordPerfect 10 table, into tabular columns, or as a WordPerfect 10 merge file with merge codes. Inserting the information into either a table or merge file lets you then use the information as a data file for a merge operation. So, for example, you can send form letters to clients listed in a Paradox 10 database or a Quattro Pro 10 worksheet.

TIP	*Import or link a spreadsheet or database to use it as a data file for a merge.*

Follow these steps to import or link a spreadsheet or database file:

1. Select Spreadsheet/Database from the Insert menu.

2. Click on Import to import the information, or click on Create Link to link it. WordPerfect 10 displays either the Import Data or Create Data Link dialog box. Figure 14-5 shows the Import Data dialog box. The Create Data Link box is identical except for the name in the title bar, and the text box label Import As is replaced by Link As.

NOTE	*WordPerfect 10 displays this same dialog box when you use the Open command to open a spreadsheet or database file.*

1. Pull down the Data Type list, and choose Spreadsheet if you want to use a spreadsheet file; or choose from these database options: Clipper, dBase, FoxPro, Paradox, ODBC, ODBC (SQL), ASCII Delimited Text, and ANSI Delimited Text.

14

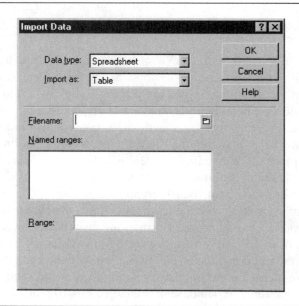

FIGURE 14-5 Import Data dialog box

2. Pull down the Import As or Link As list, and choose how you want to insert the information: Table, Text (as tabular column), or as a Merge Data File.

3. Enter the path and name of the spreadsheet or database file in the Filename text box, or use the Browse icon to search for the file on your disk.

The procedure differs for spreadsheet and database files, so let's look at each separately.

Using a Spreadsheet

If you are inserting information from a spreadsheet file, follow these steps:

1. Click in the Named Ranges box. WordPerfect 10 displays all of the named worksheet ranges, as well as the notation <spreadsheet> that represents the entire worksheet. The Range box shows the range of cells that contain data.

If you named a spreadsheet that has information on more than one worksheet page in the file, you'll see a notation for each page:

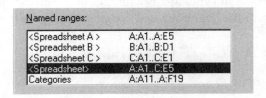

Named ranges:	
<Spreadsheet A >	A:A1..A:E5
<Spreadsheet B >	B:A1..B:D1
<Spreadsheet C >	C:A1..C:E1
<Spreadsheet>	A:A1..C:E5
Categories	A:A11..A:F19

NOTE *If nothing appears in the Named Ranges box, click on the Range text box and press* ENTER.

2. Click on the page you want to insert, or select <spreadsheet> to insert the entire worksheet file, or enter a specific range of cells in the Range text box.

3. Click on OK.

If you insert a workbook with multiple pages as tables, each appears in a separate table. If you insert the workbook as a merge file, the pages are combined into one large merge file.

Using a Database

When you insert a database file, the options in the Named Ranges list are replaced by the Fields list. After you specify the database file and click in the Fields box, WordPerfect 10 lists all of the database field names.

Deselect the checkboxes for the fields that you do not want to insert, and select Use Field Names as Headings to place the field names as the rows in the table. Click on OK to insert the information.

Updating Links

When you import the information, it appears just like any other WordPerfect 10 text. When you link it, however, WordPerfect 10 indicates that it is indeed linked.

This is an important reminder that you should update the information to retrieve the most current version of the data.

When you insert the information as a merge file, you'll see the Link and the Link End indicators at the beginning and end of the merge information:

```
Link: C:\WINDOWS\Desktop\TableImport.qpw
VOLENDFIELD
CATEGORYENDFIELD
TITLEENDFIELD
STOCKENDFIELD
PRICEENDFIELD
ENDRECORD

E11ENDFIELD
EntertainmentENDFIELD
Great Classical ComposersENDFIELD
132ENDFIELD
23ENDFIELD
ENDRECORD

Link End: C:\WINDOWS\Desktop\TableImport.qpw
```

When you insert the information in a table or as tabular columns, WordPerfect 10 displays link icons before and after the information:

VOL	CATEGORY	TITLE	STOCK	PRICE
E11	Entertainment	Great Classical Composers	132	23
H32	History	Austrian Arms and Armor	43	40
T42	Travel	Great European Cathedrals	3	14
T35	Travel	Tibetan Adventures	5	36

If you do not want the icons displayed, select Spreadsheet/Database from the Insert menu, click on Options, and deselect the Show Icons checkbox.

When you want to ensure that the document contains the most up-to-date information, select Spreadsheet/Database from the Insert menu, and click on Update. A dialog box appears asking you to confirm that you want to update all of the linked objects in the document—select Yes or No. If you edited or formatted the information in WordPerfect 10, however, your changes will be replaced by the data and formats in the linked file, just as if you were linking the information for the first time. To have all of your linked files update automatically when you open the document, select Spreadsheet/Database from the Insert menu, click on Options, and select the Update When Document Opens checkbox.

To change the name of the file being linked and its format, select Edit Link from the Spreadsheet/Database submenu.

Try It Out

Now to try out sharing, we'll create a WordPerfect table and save it in several formats—as a database and as a spreadsheet. We'll then import the saved file back into WordPerfect. If you have a database and spreadsheet created by another program, such as Paradox or Excel, you can import that file instead.

1. Start WordPerfect and create the following small table.

VOL	CATEGORY	TITLE	STOCK	PRICE
E11	Entertainment	Great Classical Composers	132	23
H32	History	Austrian Arms and Armor	43	40
T42	Travel	Great European Cathedrals	3	14
T35	Travel	Tibetan Adventures	5	36

2. Choose Save As from the File menu.

3. Pull down the File Type list and select Quattro Pro 6.0 for Windows.

4. Enter **Import Table** as the file name and click Save.

5. Choose Save As from the File menu.

6. Pull down the File Type list and select ASCII (DOS) Delimited Text.

7. Enter **Import Database** as the file name and click Save.

8. Close the document.

9. Select Insert | Spreadsheet/Database | Import.

10. Click the Browse button, select Import Table, and click Select.

14

11. Click in the Range text box and press Enter.

12. Choose the first option in the Named Ranges box and click OK.

13. Follow the same procedure again but select Merge Data File from the Import As list. You'll now have the same information in two formats—as a table and as a data file for merging.

14. Select Insert | Spreadsheet/Database | Create Link.

15. Choose ASCII Delimited Text from the Data type list.

16. Choose Table from the Link As list.

17. Click the Browse button, select Import Database, and click Select.

18. Enable the checkbox labeled First Record Contains Fieldnames.

19. Click OK.

Now compare the format and appearance of the two tables and the merge data file.

Part 3

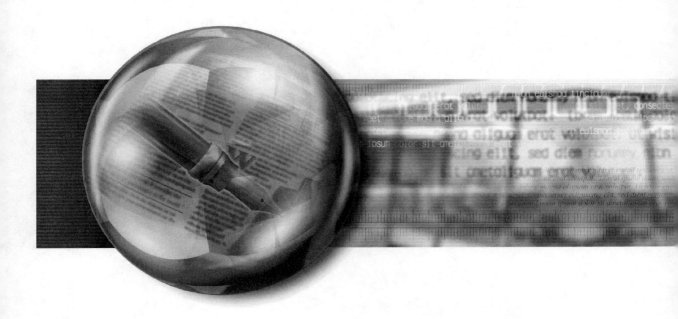

Quattro Pro 10

Chapter 15

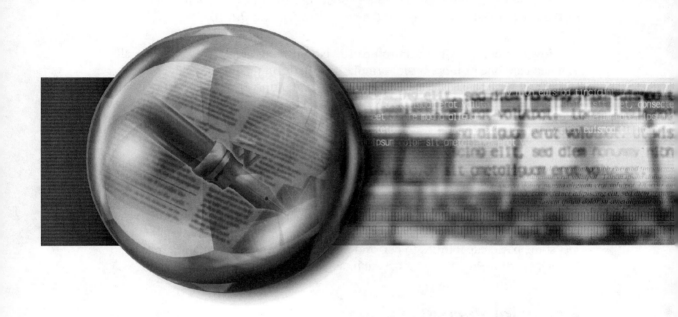

Introducing Quattro Pro 10

Quattro Pro 10 lets you work with information in table format—neatly arranged rows and columns of numbers or text. Formatting capabilities let you design professional-looking tables—combining grid lines, colors, shadings, and special effects for maximum impact. Because the table is computerized, however, you can also perform mathematical and even complex statistical analysis quickly and easily. Don't let the words "mathematical" and "statistical" scare you off. You don't have to know anything about statistics or even much about mathematics to take advantage of the powers of Quattro Pro 10.

How difficult is using Quattro Pro 10? Not difficult at all. In most cases, all you need are one or more basic formulas that perform math using values in the table. You have to know when to add, subtract, multiply, and divide—not do the math yourself. Quattro Pro 10 does the actual math for you. In fact, in many cases, you can just click on a button or select options from a list, and Quattro Pro 10 builds the formula for you.

What's It Used For?

Since you can easily create a table in WordPerfect 10, you may be wondering why you need a separate program such as Quattro Pro 10. WordPerfect 10 gives you just some basic capabilities to perform math and organize information in table format. Quattro Pro 10 specializes in it, as you'll see.

Financial Records

Use Quattro Pro 10 to create financial records and documents of all types. Produce budgets, reports, income statements, balance sheets, sales forecasts, projections, and most of the records that you need to maintain your business, household, or organization. Quattro Pro 10 makes it easy to create professional-looking printouts that will impress your stockholders, bankers, and accountant—perhaps even the IRS.

But Quattro Pro 10 is for more than good looks. It can help ensure that your numbers are accurate, even if you have to make last-minute changes. Suppose that after creating the quarterly budget, you realize that you've entered the wrong numbers in certain areas. If you created the budget on paper, you'd have to change the numbers, then recalculate, and change all of the gross and net profit figures. Not so with Quattro Pro 10. Just correct the figures, and Quattro Pro 10 uses the simple formulas that you've entered to make the recalculations for you.

Business Forms

Use Quattro Pro 10 to create business forms of all types, including invoices, statements, schedules, planners, and professional time and billing logs. Forms are often difficult to create in word processing programs, but they're a snap in Quattro Pro 10.

And don't imagine that we are talking about only blank forms. By adding simple formulas, ones that Quattro Pro 10 can even create for you, you can complete the forms on the screen. For example, how about a sales tool for computing loan or lease information that automatically calculates the customer's maximum purchase amount, total interest, and other statistics to help close that deal? With QuattroPro, all you have to do is fill in a few items and then fax, e-mail, or print and mail it to your customer.

Charts and Maps

Use Quattro Pro 10 to create eye-catching charts and maps directly from information that you've already entered. There is no need to retype the numbers. Just tell Quattro Pro 10 which part of your table contains the numbers you want to chart and where the chart should appear, and the program does the rest. If you want, you can choose the chart type and customize its design; otherwise, just sit back and let Quattro Pro 10 do the work.

When your spreadsheet contains geographic information, such as sales per state or country, then create a map. You'll see at a glance where your strong sales areas are and where you need to concentrate your efforts. You can even overlay maps with major highways, major cities, and capitals.

For even greater impact, you can combine charts and graphs into a slideshow using Corel Presentations. Hook up your PC—even a laptop—to a projector, and you have a complete onscreen presentation for board or sales meetings.

 You can share all of your spreadsheets, graphs, and maps with Corel WordPerfect to create compound documents.

15

Databases

Use Quattro Pro 10 to create databases for recording, finding, and analyzing information. Keep records of clients, employees, products, members, or any other item that you need to track and report.

A database is like an electronic version of an index card file or folders in your filing cabinet. With Quattro Pro 10, you create the database in table format. Each row of the table represents another item in the database, as shown in Figure 15-1. You can print reports, locate specific information when you want it, perform statistical analysis on your information, and even print graphs.

 You can use your Quattro Pro 10 database to create form letters in Corel WordPerfect, or transfer it to a database program such as Paradox or Microsoft Access. You can also move data in the other direction, importing information from a database program into Quattro Pro 10 to analyze or chart it.

Solving Problems

The real jewel in the crown of Quattro Pro 10, however, is its ability to solve what's known as "What If?" problems. What if costs increase by 5 percent? What if employees are given a raise? What if sales go down? What if inventory is increased?

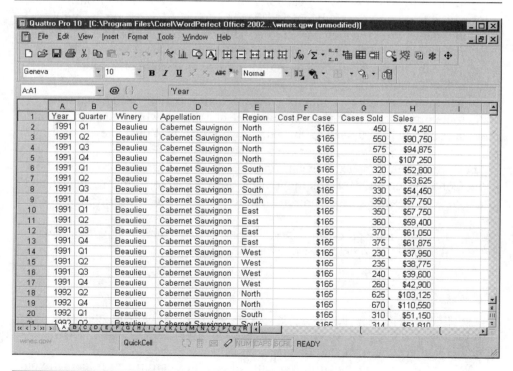

FIGURE 15-1 Using Quattro Pro to record and analyze data

Since Quattro Pro 10 can automatically recalculate the values in an entire table when you change even a single number, you can see how that change affects the entire table. Just change a value or two, and then analyze the results.

Quattro Pro 10 even has special features for those tougher problems. You can have it solve a problem by automatically changing values itself—for example, to find the optimum combination of factors that give you the results you want. A feature called Scenario Manager even saves different combinations of results so you can switch back and forth between them as you attempt to make a decision.

Starting Quattro Pro 10

Starting Quattro Pro 10 is as easy as pointing and clicking:

1. Click on the Start button in the Windows taskbar and point to Programs.

2. Point to WordPerfect Office 2002.

3. Click on Quattro Pro 10.

In a few moments the Quattro Pro 10 screen will appear with a blank notebook, as shown in Figure 15-2.

Notebook Concept

Before looking at the details of the Quattro Pro 10 screen, you should understand the concept of the notebook.

A *notebook* is a collection of sheets, just like a notebook you'd carry to class or to a meeting. Each sheet is made up of columns and rows of cells which hold numbers, text, and formulas that make up the forms, financial reports, or databases that you create. Spreadsheets can also contain charts and graphs that illustrate the values on the same sheet or elsewhere in the notebook. At the very end of the notebook is a special sheet called the *objects page*. This sheet stores copies of all of the charts and graphs in the notebook, as well as custom dialog boxes and maps. You can have as many as 18,278 sheets plus the objects page.

What's the benefit of a notebook? With a notebook, you don't need a separate file for every spreadsheet you want to create. Your budget, for example, may include several related spreadsheets. Rather than store each one separately on your disk, you can create them on different sheets in the same notebook. When you save

15

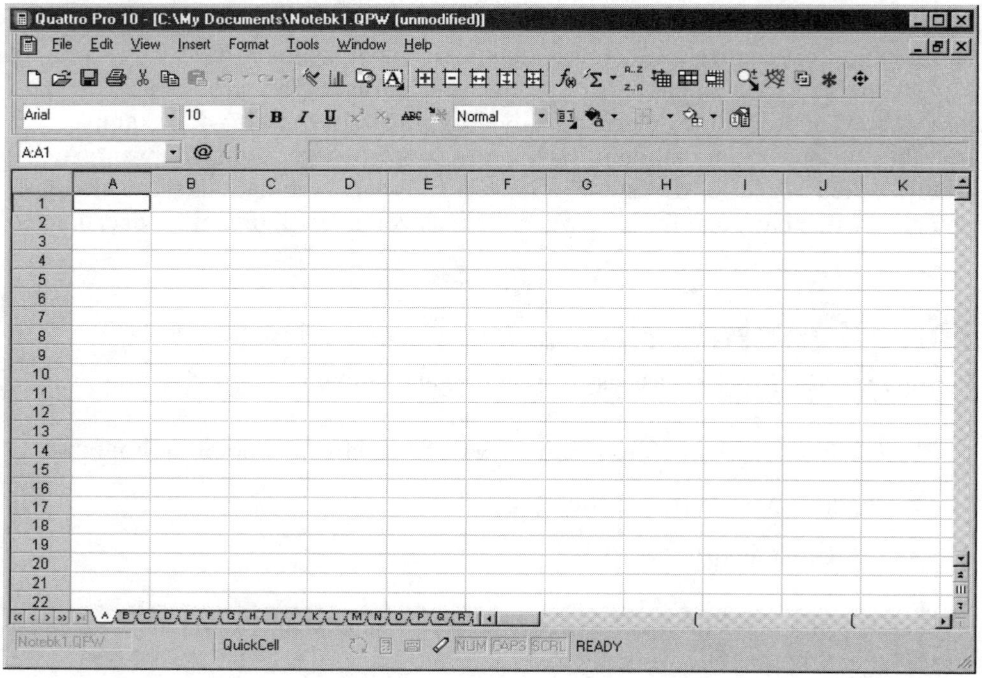

FIGURE 15-2 The Corel Quattro Pro screen

the notebook, Quattro Pro 10 saves all of its spreadsheets, and charts in one file on your disk. Then you can simply open one file to access all of the spreadsheets. If you need to transport the notebook from the office to home, just copy the one file to a floppy disk or to a Windows briefcase to synchronize the notebook between your home and office.

In addition, all of the sheets in a notebook can share common information. A sheet can refer to values in another sheet, so changing a number on one sheet might have an impact on other sheets, even on the entire notebook.

While it is best to use a notebook to store related information, there are other possibilities. You can enter totally unrelated spreadsheets in the same notebook. In fact, you can have more than one report, form, database, or other item on a sheet. If you think of the spreadsheet as a very large piece of paper, you can imagine dividing it up into sections to store more than one table. Quattro Pro 10 won't know the difference.

The Quattro Pro 10 Screen

The Quattro Pro 10 screen, shown labeled in Figure 15-3, is full of useful items, most of which are standard Corel WordPerfect Suite features.

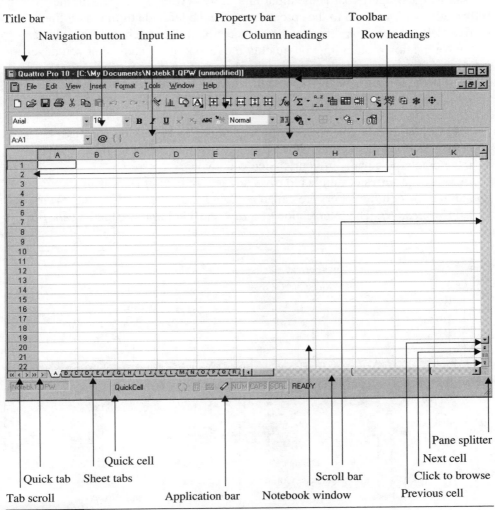

FIGURE 15-3   Parts of the Corel Quattro Pro screen

At the very top of the screen are the title bar, the menu bar, the Notebook toolbar, and the property bar. As expected, pointing to a button or bar area displays a QuickTip, so you can be sure you are choosing the correct command for the job you want to perform. Figure 15-4 shows the buttons in the Notebook toolbar, and Figure 15-5 shows the parts of the property bar. You'll learn more about these buttons later.

Below the property bar is the input line. Here is where you can edit the information that you add to the spreadsheet. On the left side of the input line is the Active Cell Address box that shows your location in the notebook. This also acts as the Navigation tool letting you quickly move to a block name that you have given to a particular section of the notebook.

Below the input line is the Notebook window, where the sheets of the notebook appear. If necessary, you can open more than one notebook at a time, as you'll learn in Chapter 18.

The first notebook you open during a Quattro Pro 10 session is called NOTEBK1.QPW; the second, NOTEBK2.QPW; and so on. Of course, you can give the notebook a name of your choice when you save it.

A *sheet* is a series of numbered rows and lettered columns. The blocks containing the column letters are called *column headers,* the row numbers are called *row headers.* The intersection of a row and a column is called a *cell.* For

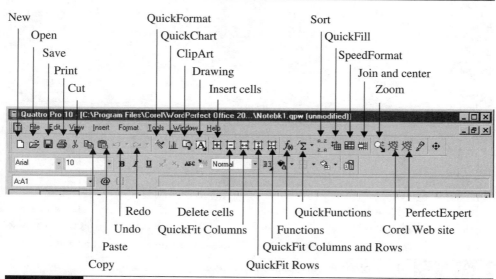

FIGURE 15-4   Notebook toolbar

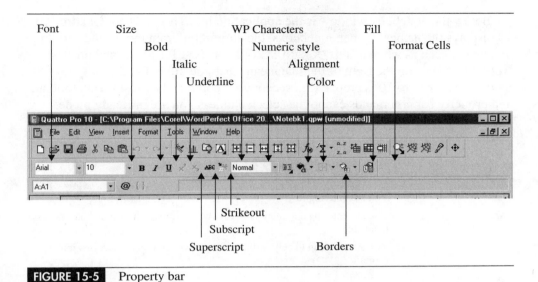

FIGURE 15-5   Property bar

example, the cell in the top-left corner is called *cell A1* because it is in column A and row 1—the column letter always precedes the row number. The cell to its right is cell B1, and the cell below A1 is A2.

Even though you can't see much of the sheet on the screen, sheets are very large. You can setup Quattro Pro 10 to have 18,278 sheets, 18,278 columns, and 1,000,000 rows, for a total of 334,085,284,000,000 cells in all.

> **TIP**   *To change the number of sheets, rows, and columns, select Settings from the Tools menu, and click on Compatibility. Change the settings in the Notebook Sizes section of the dialog box.*

The cell selected at the current time is called the *active* cell. This is the cell that will be affected by what you type or by the commands that you select. You can always tell the active cell because:

- ■ It is surrounded by the *selector,* a dark rectangle.

- ■ You'll see its *cell reference*—the row and column number it represents, as well as its sheet in the Navigation button—on the left side of the input line.

- ■ Its row and column headers will appear to be pressed down.

15

Below the Notebook window is the application bar. This is where Quattro Pro 10 displays the names of open notebooks, the current program mode, and certain indicators, such as when CAPS LOCK, NUM LOCK, or INSERT are turned on. The word "READY" on the right of the line means that you are in Ready mode—Quattro Pro 10 is prepared to accept your commands. Most menu, toolbar, and property bar commands cannot be selected unless you are in Ready mode. There are more then two dozen status and mode indicators, including these that you'll see most often:

Mode	Meaning
Label	You are entering text.
Value	You are entering a numeric value, a date or time, or a formula that results in a value.
Point	You are pointing to cells with the mouse to insert their addresses into a formula.

In addition to the mode, the application bar/status line also contains these items:

Item	Meaning
QuickCell	You can insert a cell into this section of the application bar, and watch it recalculate as you work in the notebook. This saves you the trouble of scrolling back to the cell itself to see its contents.
Circular Reference	This icon becomes bold when a formula refers to itself or to another formula that refers to it.
Calculator icon	An icon of a calculator flashes when formulas need to be recalculated. Click on the icon to recalculate the sheet.
Macro	This icon becomes bold when you are recording a macro.
Typeover	When this button appears pressed down, new characters you type when editing in a cell replace existing characters. When not down, new characters are inserted. Click to toggle on and off.
Num Lock	Indicates the status of the NUM LOCK key on your keyboard. The button appears pressed down when NUM LOCK is on.
Caps	Indicates the status of the CAPS LOCK key on your keyboard.
Scroll	Indicates the status of the SCROLL LOCK key on your keyboard.
Calc-As-You-Go	Quattro Pro displays the sum, average, count, maximum, and minimum values of the selected range of cells.
Function help	When you are entering a function, the function syntax appears on the right of the application bar.

The *sheet tabs* let you change sheets of the notebook. The notebook sheets are named like columns from A to ZZZ, followed by the objects page. Just click on the tab for the sheet that you want to display. After completing a table on the first sheet, for example, click on the next sheet tab—B—to start another spreadsheet. If necessary, you can delete sheets and change their order.

NOTE	*Use the tab name when you want to reference a cell on another sheet. For example, F:A1 represents cell A1 on sheet F of the notebook. The syntax is always Sheet:Coordinates.*

The *tab scroll* lets you scroll through the sheet tabs. This is useful when you're not sure which sheet you want to view. It works like a scroll bar. Click on > to scroll the tab view forward and < to scroll the tab view back. Click on >> to scroll a new set of sheets forward and << to move a set of sheets backward. Note that these buttons do not activate the next sheet, they simply allow the user to scroll through the tabs.

Use the *QuickTab* to quickly move from the sheet you are looking at to the end of the notebook, and vice versa. Click on the QuickTab to see the objects page; click on it again to move back to the previous sheet you were viewing.

TIP	*You can also move back and forth between the objects page and a sheet by choosing Objects Page from the View menu to see the objects page. Choose Draft View or Page from the View menu to return to the sheet.*

The scroll bars, which are standard Windows controls, move you around the sheet. Use the vertical scroll bar to move up and down, the horizontal scroll bar to move side to side. Remember, the Notebook window is a virtual window of the spreadsheet. While you see only a few rows and columns, the Quattro Pro 10 sheet is really very large, so use the scroll bars to display other sections of the sheet.

As you drag the scroll box within the bar, Quattro Pro 10 displays a row or column indicator. When you drag the horizontal scroll box, it shows the letter of the column that will be at the far left when you release the mouse. When you drag the vertical scroll box, it shows the number of the row that will be at the top of the screen.

At the lower-right corner of the Notebook Window—right where the scroll bars meet—is the *pane splitter*. This lets you divide the Notebook into two or more separate panes, or sections. You can view different parts of the Notebook in each panel, or even different tables or charts that share the same sheet.

15

Changing Toolbars

Like other WordPerfect Office 2002 applications, Quattro Pro 10 includes a number of toolbars that you can use to perform common functions. To choose one, right-click on the displayed toolbar to see a QuickMenu of other available toolbars. The toolbars already displayed are indicated with a check mark. Check or uncheck the bars to determine which are displayed.

You can also select toolbars by choosing Toolbars from the View menu, and then selecting the toolbars you want displayed.

Moving Around the Spreadsheet

To create a spreadsheet, you'll have to move from cell to cell to enter or edit information or to see the results of your actions. Using the mouse, click in the cell that you want to enter information into, edit, or format. Use the scroll bars if necessary to bring the cell into view.

Using the keyboard, move around the spreadsheet using the keystrokes shown in Table 15-1. Pressing ENTER does not move the insertion point from cell to cell, as you will soon learn.

To move to a specific cell, pull down the Edit menu, and select Go To to see the dialog box shown in Figure 15-6. Type the cell reference, including the sheet letter if it is not on the current sheet, and click on OK.

You can also use the Go To box to move to a recently edited cell, another sheet, or to a type of object. The Last Edited section shows the cells you recently changed, along with their current and last values. The Other section lets you select groups of cells based on their content, such as all cells containing formulas or comments.

Selecting Cells

To perform an action on a cell, you must select it. To select a single cell, just click on it. This makes it the active cell and selects it at the same time. When you make a cell active, whatever is in the cell also appears in the input line.

There are many actions that you'll want to perform on more than one cell. Groups of selected cells are called *blocks*. To select a block of cells, point to a cell in one corner of the block, hold down the mouse button, and drag to the opposite corner. As you drag the mouse, the cells in the block become highlighted, with a black background. The first cell you selected, however, is just surrounded by a

Keystroke	Direction
LEFT ARROW	One cell left
RIGHT ARROW	One cell right
UP ARROW	One row up
DOWN ARROW	One row down
CTRL-PGDN	Next sheet
CTRL-PGUP	Previous sheet
PGUP	One screen up
PGDN	One screen down
HOME	To cell A1
CTRL-HOME	Cell A1 of the first sheet
END-HOME	To the lower-right nonblank corner
END-CTRL-HOME	To the last nonblank cell in the notebook
END-ARROW	To the next nonblank cell in the direction of the arrow
TAB	One cell right
SHIFT-TAB	One cell left
CTRL-LEFT ARROW	One screen left
CTRL-RIGHT ARROW	One screen right

TABLE 15-1   Keystrokes for moving in a spreadsheet

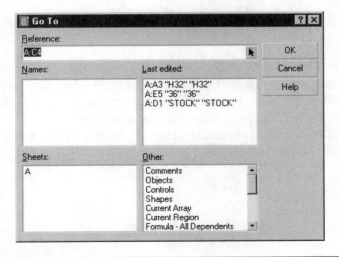

FIGURE 15-6   Using the Go To command to move to a specific cell, sheet, or type of cell

border, called the *selector,* letting you know that it was the starting point of the block. To move the selection to other cells in the block, hold down the CTRL key and click on the cell you want to make active.

 To select cells the mouse pointer must appear as a large arrow. If the mouse pointer appears as a four-pointed arrow, then dragging moves the cell. See Chapter 17 for more details on dragging cells

To select an entire row, point to its row header so the mouse pointer appears as a right-pointing arrow, and then click. To select an entire column, point to the column header so the mouse pointer appears as a down-pointing arrow, and then click. Drag over row headers with the right-pointing arrow, or over column headers with the down-pointing arrow, to select adjacent rows or columns.

Notice that an empty shaded cell is in the very upper-leftmost corner of the spreadsheet. This is the Select All button—click on it to select the entire sheet.

Using basic Windows techniques, you can also select cells, rows, and columns that are not adjacent to each other. Hold down the CTRL key, and click on the cells, rows, or columns that you want to select. With the CTRL key pressed, Quattro Pro 10 does not deselect sections already highlighted when you click elsewhere.

Many Quattro Pro 10 functions refer to a block even though they also act upon a single selected cell. So throughout this part of the book, we'll use the term "block" to refer to any number of selected cells, rows, and columns. When an instruction says to select a block, it means select any number of cells that you want to work with, even if it's only a single cell.

Using the Browse By Button

You can use the Other list in the Go To box to quickly select all cells by their contents. Another way to do this is by using the Browse By button—the button between Previous Cell and Next Cell under the scroll bar.

Right-click on the button to display a list of choices, shown next, and click on the type of cell you want to select.

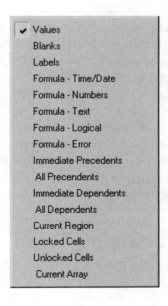

Designating Block References

You reference a single cell by its row and column coordinates. To refer to a block, designate the starting and ending cell references of the group. If the cells are all in one row or column, just use the two end cells in the format A1 . . . A8. In this example, the block A1 . . . A8 includes eight cells—A1, A2, A3, A4, A5, A6, A7, and A8.

If the cells are in more than one row or column, reference any two cells in opposite corners. For example, the reference A1 . . . B5 includes the ten cells A1 through A5, and B1 through B5 as shown here:

15

When you type a block reference, you can type a single period between the cells. Quattro Pro 10 inserts the second period when you accept the entry. In addition, you can use any opposite cells. Traditionally, block references use the cell in the upper-left and lower-right corners, or the first and last cells if they are all in a row or column. You can actually enter the cells in any order, such as the lower-left and upper-right corners of a block, as in A5.C1. When you accept the entry, Quattro Pro 10 rewrites the reference in the traditional way for you.

A block reference can also include noncontiguous cells, that is, cells that are not next to each other. Reference single cells by separating them with commas, as in A2,B4,C10. Include both types of references using the format A1.A10,C3,D5, which refers to the cells in the range A1 through A10, as well as cells C3 and D5.

Pointing to Cells in Dialog Boxes

Many dialog boxes perform a function on a block of cells. In some cases you can select the block of cells before opening the dialog box, and the block reference will appear automatically. If the block is incorrect, or you did not select it beforehand, you can change the reference by typing the block coordinates.

In most cases there will also be a Point Mode button, as shown here:

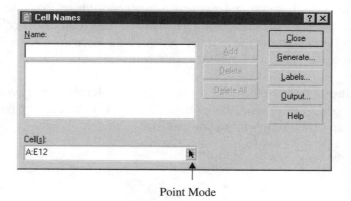

Point Mode

You use Point mode to temporarily leave the dialog box to select the block of cells, rather than type in their references. Here's how:

1. Click in the text box where you want to insert a range of cells.

2. Click on the Point mode button. Quattro Pro 10 reduces the dialog box to two lines—the title bar and a line showing the range the box will act upon—and moves it up so you can see the spreadsheet cells.

3. Drag over the cells that you want to reference, or click on a single cell to reference it. To point to a block on another sheet, click on the sheet tab, and then drag over the cells. As you select the cell, the block reference appears in the range indicator.

4. When the range is correct, release the mouse button, and then click on the Maximize button in the dialog box's title bar to redisplay it.

If the cells you want to reference are not contiguous, enter a comma after clicking or dragging on one cell or block, and then click or drag on the next cell or block. The reference cells will be separated by commas in the dialog box.

TIP   *If you can see the start of the block in the background of the dialog box, just point to it, and hold down the mouse button. (You may have to first select any reference already in the text box.) Quattro Pro 10 automatically minimizes the dialog box and then redisplays it when you release the mouse button.*

Selecting 3-D Blocks

A *3-D block* is a block of cells selected on more than one consecutive notebook sheet. For example, suppose you have the budgets for the last four years on separate sheets of the notebook, with one year per sheet occupying the same area on each sheet. You can apply the same formats to every sheet at one time by selecting them as one block—a 3-D block.

To select a 3-D block, start by selecting the cell or cells on the first sheet you want to include. Then hold down the SHIFT key while you click on the tab for the last sheet you want to include. Quattro Pro 10 displays a black line under the tabs indicating that the 3-D block extends across those sheets. While the line appears under the tabs, perform the function that you want to apply to the selected group.

15

NOTE   *You cannot use this type of 3-D block to enter text into all of the cells, although you can use it with QuickFill. See Chapter 16 for more information.*

The 3-D block is temporary; it remains in force only until you click on another cell. You can create a more permanent 3-D block by using a group, as you'll learn in Chapter 18.

Object Inspector

Everything in Quattro Pro 10 is called an *object*. To change an object's properties (one or more of its characteristics), point to it, click the right mouse button, and choose the Properties option at the bottom of the QuickMenu. You'll see a dialog box with several sheets, each representing a classification of properties that you can change.

Click on the tab for the properties you want to set, and make your selections. When you close the dialog box, your selections are applied.

- To set the properties for a cell or selected group of cells, click on the Set Attributes button on the property bar, or right-click on the block and choose Selection Properties from the QuickMenu.

- To set the properties of the entire sheet, just right-click on the sheet tab, and select Sheet Properties from the QuickMenu.

- To set properties for the entire notebook, restore the notebook so it appears in its own window, then right-click on the title bar, or choose Notebook Properties from the Format menu.

- To customize Quattro Pro 10 itself, right-click on the Quattro Pro 10 title bar, and choose Settings from the QuickMenu, or choose Settings from the Tools menu.

You'll learn about properties later, in Chapter 17.

Changing the View

When you start Quattro Pro 10, it displays the notebook in Draft view and at 100 percent magnification. Draft view means that you won't see the page margins on screen, and the sheet isn't divided into pages. The default magnification means that text and graphics appear the same size onscreen as they will be when printed.

To see how the spreadsheet will be paginated, select Page from the View menu. In Page view, the spreadsheet is divided into pages, just as it will be when printed, and you'll see margin guidelines, page break lines, headers, and footers. You can even change the margins by dragging the guidelines and insert headers and footers by right-clicking in the top or bottom margin area. Return to Draft view by selecting Draft from the View menu.

TIP	*Choose Page Breaks from the View menu to see and work with page breaks but not margins, headers, and footers.*

If your spreadsheet is large, then you may spend a lot of time scrolling to see certain sections. One way to avoid scrolling is to reduce the displayed magnification. You'll be able to see more cells on the screen, although they will be smaller and may be difficult to read. You can also enlarge the magnification to make cells appear larger—although you will see fewer of them.

To quickly change magnification, pull down the Zoom list in the toolbar, and select the magnification desired. You can also choose to zoom the selected cells so they fill the screen and to display a dialog box for using a custom magnification.

The setting applies only to the current sheet, not to other sheets in the notebook. For example, Figure 15-7 shows a spreadsheet in Page view and at 50 percent magnification. The dashed lines are the margin guidelines, and the solid line represents a page break.

You have more control over changing magnification using the Zoom dialog box. Select Other from the Zoom list, or select Zoom from the View menu to see the dialog box shown in Figure 15-8. Click on the desired magnification, or click on Custom and enter another setting. Click on Notebook to set the view for every sheet in the notebook.

Getting Help

The Help system in Quattro Pro 10 works just about the same as it does in WordPerfect. The Help Topics dialog box contains the Contents, Index, and Find tabs. You can also use PerfectExpert to help you create spreadsheets, and access the Corel Web site to go directly to Corel over the Internet.

15

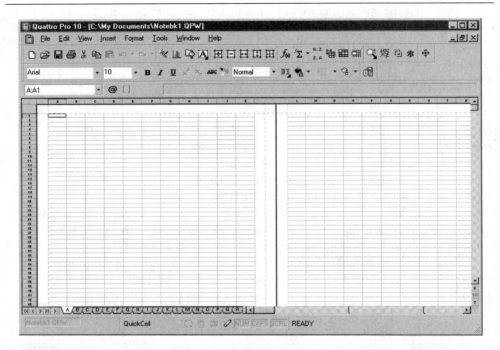

FIGURE 15-7   Worksheet in Page view at 50% magnification

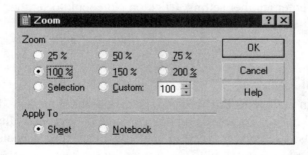

FIGURE 15-8   Using Zoom to enlarge or reduce the display

Try It Out

To get a feel for using Quattro Pro, let's start a new worksheet using one of WordPerfect's templates.

1. Select File | New From Project.

2. Click on the listing Budget, Cash, and then click Create.

3. If a message appears asking if you want to disable macros, click Yes.

4. Look at the sheet tabs. The first three have been given names rather than just letters.

5. Click on the tab Order Form to open it.

6. Click on the tab Cash Budget to return to that sheet.

7. Pull down the Navigation list.

8. Scroll the list and select Order Form!Print Area. A section of the Order Form tab appears.

9. Click on the tab Cash Budget again.

10. Select Page from the View menu.

11. Select Draft View from the View menu.

12. Select File | Close, and click No if a box asks if you want to save the changes.

Chapter 16

Creating a Spreadsheet

535

Creating a spreadsheet is easy if you follow a few basic steps. Most spreadsheets contain titles, labels, and values. The *titles,* normally at the top of the spreadsheet page, explain the purpose of the spreadsheet, just like a title on a report. *Labels* are text that explains what the numbers in the other cells represent. These are usually column and row headings, but text can appear anywhere in a spreadsheet. *Values* are numbers, formulas, or functions that display information or calculate results.

Basic Principles

To enter information into a cell, make the cell active by clicking on it or moving to it using the keyboard, and then type. When you start typing, the insertion point will appear in the cell, whatever you type will appear in the input line, and you'll see four additional boxes, as shown here:

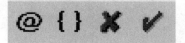

Clicking on the box with the @ sign lists Quattro Pro 10's built-in functions; clicking on the box with the braces lists macros. The box with the X is called the *Cancel box.* Click on this box, or press the ESC key if you want to start again. The box with the check mark is called the *Enter box.* Click on this box, or press the ENTER key to accept your entry and enter it into the cell. You can also accept your entry and move to another cell at the same time by pressing an arrow key, TAB, or SHIFT-TAB. Pressing ENTER accepts the entry and moves the cell selector in the direction chosen by selecting Settings from the Tools menu.

Before you cancel or accept the entry, you can edit it by pressing the BACKSPACE or DEL key, or by moving the insertion point with the arrow keys. Edit the contents just as you would using a word processing program.

The basic procedure for entering information into a cell is as follows:

1. Click in the cell to make it active.

2. Type the information you want in the cell.

3. Click on the Enter box—the box with the check mark—or press ENTER.

When you are entering or editing information in a cell, most of the toolbar and menu commands are inactive but you can use the property bar to format the cell. The word "Ready" in the application bar is replaced by the word "Label" or "Value" depending on the kind of information you are typing. If you are editing the contents of the cell, its original contents appear in the application bar until you accept the new entry. To use the features of the menu and toolbar again, you must accept or cancel the entry to return to Ready mode.

Entering Text

Quattro Pro 10 treats text differently from numbers and distinguishes the two by the first character that you type. This difference is important because Quattro Pro 10 can perform math operations only on numbers, and it aligns text and numbers differently in the cells.

NOTE *Quattro Pro 10 includes QuickCorrect, so common mistakes are corrected automatically.*

If you start a cell entry with a letter, Quattro Pro 10 assumes you are typing text and displays the word "Label" on the right end of the status line. When you click on the Enter box or press ENTER, the text starts on the left side of the cell, the default format for text.

To fill a cell with repeating characters, start with the backslash. Typing *, for example, fills the cell with asterisks; entering \12 repeats the characters "12" across the cell.

NOTE *You will learn how to format the text in a cell in Chapter 17.*

Using QuickType

Sometimes you want to repeat a label in a column, or use a similar word or phrase. For example, you may have a spreadsheet that includes the text "Rentals" and later want to enter the same label further down the column. Fortunately, Quattro Pro 10 uses a feature called *QuickType*.

16

	A
1	Rentals
2	Sales
3	Leases
4	Total Income
5	
6	Salaries
7	Utilities
8	Rentals

When you type a label, Quattro Pro 10 looks through the column for other labels beginning with the same characters and displays the closest match, as shown above, where Quattro Pro 10 has supplied the "entals" after "R" is typed. To accept the entry, press ENTER. To reject the QuickType suggestion, just keep typing—Quattro Pro 10 will continue to look for matching entries using the additional characters that you type. To edit the suggested entry, press the LEFT ARROW or RIGHT ARROW keys, edit the entry, and then press ENTER.

Aligning Text in Cells

You can change the alignment of information in a cell by using the property bar or by starting your entry with a special formatting character.

The Alignment list in the property bar is quick and convenient, but you need to select the alignment before you start typing or after you accept the entry. To choose or change alignment, follow these steps:

1. Click in the cell that you want to format.

2. Pull down the Alignment list of the property bar to see these options:

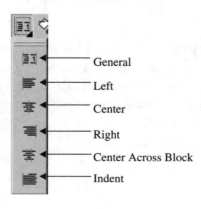

- General
- Left
- Center
- Right
- Center Across Block
- Indent

3. Select the alignment desired.

NOTE *You'll learn about the Center Across Block option later.*

You can also change alignment using a special formatting character as the first character of the entry. To center a label in the cell, start it with the caret (^) symbol, as in ^Net. When you accept the entry, the caret in the cell disappears, and Quattro Pro 10 centers the text. To align text on the right of the cell, start with a single quotation mark (').

If you actually want to start the label with a caret or quotation mark, as in "Swifty" Lazar, enter it as '"Swifty" Lazar. Quattro Pro 10 uses the apostrophe to align the entry on the left, inserting the opening quotation mark rather than using it as an alignment command.

The apostrophe is also useful when you want to insert labels that contain all numeric characters, such as year labels. It tells Quattro Pro 10 that you are entering a label (for example, the year 1999), to align it on the left, and not to use it in a formula if you accidentally include it as a reference.

You do not have to use the apostrophe, however, when entering social security and phone numbers. If you just type a phone number, such as 555-1234, Quattro Pro 10 displays the word "Value" in the status line, as it does when you enter numbers, but it displays the entry exactly as you enter it. It does not subtract 1234 from 555, as it would if this were a math operation.

Remember that the apostrophe and caret characters will not appear in the cell unless you are editing it, but they will appear on the input line when the cell is active. This is an important concept to understand. What you see in the cell is the result of what is in the input line. The input line shows the actual contents stored in the spreadsheet. If the cell contains ^Title, the cell displays the word "Title" centered. This concept is even more important when you are working with formulas and functions.

Centering Across Cells

16

A title often looks better centered across the page, and it is no different with Quattro Pro 10. Rather than trying to center a title by placing it in a column, use the Join and Center feature. This automatically centers text across the group of cells that you select.

Start by entering the text in the leftmost cell of the block. For example, if you want to center a title across the page, use the following steps:

1. Enter the title in cell A1.

2. Select the cells in which you want the title to be centered. In this case, cells A1 to H1.

3. Click on the Join and Center Cells button on the toolbar. You can also pull down the Alignment button on the property bar and select the Center Across Block option. The selected cells will be joined into one cell, and the text will be centered:

   It is best to wait until you have finished adjusting the width of columns before centering text across a block. If you center first and then change column width, the text may no longer appear centered.

Wide Text Entries

If you type more characters than will fit in the cell, Quattro Pro 10 runs them into adjacent blank cells. If an adjacent cell has an entry of its own, however, Quattro Pro 10 displays only as many characters as will fit. Don't worry; the full entry is actually stored in the spreadsheet, and it will appear in the input line when the cell is active. Again, the input line shows the real contents of the spreadsheet; the cell shows only what can be displayed.

   To display the full entry, you have to widen the cell or reduce the font size.

Entering Numbers

To enter a number into a cell, start the entry with a number, a plus sign, or a minus sign. Quattro Pro 10 displays the word "Value" on the status line to indicate that it recognizes your entry as numeric. When you accept the entry, Quattro Pro 10 aligns it on the right side of the cell. You can later change its alignment using the property bar.

TIP	*You can use a dollar sign for currency, and commas to separate thousands when typing numbers.*

By default, numbers appear without *trailing zeros,* zeros that come at the end of a number following the decimal point. If you enter **12.10**, for example, Quattro Pro 10 will display 12.1. If you enter **12.00**, Quattro Pro 10 will display 12.

If you type more characters than can fit in the cell, Quattro Pro 10 displays the number in exponential format. It does not run long numbers into adjacent cells as it does text. To display the number, you have to widen the column width, reduce the font being used, or change its format.

Editing Cell Contents

Once you accept an entry, typing something else in the same cell erases its current contents. This is convenient if you enter the wrong number, for example, and want to quickly correct your mistake. Just move back to the same cell, and type the new entry. This is not convenient, however, if you don't want to erase the entire entry—but only want to edit a long line of text or a complex formula.

You can edit the contents of a cell either in the input line or in the cell itself. To edit in the input line, make the cell active, and then click on the input line. The insertion point appears where you click. To edit in the cell, double-click on it, or make it active and then press F2.

In either case, the contents of the cell appear in the application bar, and you can delete and insert text and numbers, just as you would in a word processing program. Once you are editing a cell, you can switch between the input line and the cell by clicking where you want to work. Before accepting the changes, refer to the application bar if you forget what was originally in the cell.

While editing, use the LEFT ARROW and RIGHT ARROW to move the insertion point in the cell. Press TAB to move to the end of the entry, SHIFT-TAB to move to the start of the entry. Press ENTER to stop editing, or accept or cancel your entry as usual. If you change your mind about editing the entry, just press ESC or click on the Cancel box to retain the cell's original contents.

16

Entering Formulas

The real power of a spreadsheet comes from its ability to recalculate values as you change the contents of cells. This is achieved by using formulas whenever possible. A *formula* is a mathematical operation that uses any combination of cell references and actual values. You can use a formula to simply perform math, such as entering **+106/3** to display the result of the calculation, but the most important use of formulas is to reference other cells.

> **TIP** *With Quattro Pro 10's Fit-As-You-Go feature, if the formula results are too large to fit in the cell, the column width automatically adjusts to display the full value.*

You should start every formula with a plus or equal sign, especially if it begins with a cell reference, or it could be mistaken for a date. This tells Quattro Pro 10 that you want it to calculate and display results. Quattro Pro 10 changes the starting equal sign to a plus sign when you accept the entry.

For example, if you enter **40 * .33**, Quattro Pro 10 performs the math and displays the result—you do not need to start it with a plus or equal sign. If you type **5+C3**, it adds 5 to the value in cell C3. If you type **12/3** (to mean 12 divided by 3), however, Quattro Pro 10 assumes you're entering December 3. Similarly, if you enter **B5+4**, it simply displays your entry as a label—you must type it as **+B5+4**.

> **TIP** *It is a common beginner's mistake to forget the plus sign. If you type a formula and the formula, rather than the result, appears in the cell, you forgot the plus sign.*

When you want to refer to the value in some other cell, just enter its cell reference. For example, the formula to subtract whatever is in cell A1 from what is in cell A2 is **+A2-A1**. When you enter the formula, Quattro Pro 10 calculates the math and displays the result in the cell. If you later change the value in either cell A1 or A2, Quattro Pro 10 recalculates the value and displays the new result. Quattro Pro 10 does not perform the calculation until you accept the change in the cell.

Even though you see the *results* of the formula in the cell, the spreadsheet actually contains the formula. When you make the cell active, you'll see the results of the calculation in the cell but the formula itself in the input line.

To make it even easier to tell that a cell contains a formula, Quattro Pro 10 displays the formula marker in the cell's lower left corner:

Formula Marker

And, when you point to a cell with a formula, the formula appears on a QuickTip, like this:

473.5421

@PMT(67000, 0.07/12,25*12)

As a rule of thumb, use cell references wherever you can in a spreadsheet—wherever you are performing math using the contents of other cells. For example, suppose you have the spreadsheet shown in Figure 16-1. The gross pay can be calculated using the values themselves, as in +40*15.65. But if you change either the pay rate or the number of hours worked, you will need to reenter the value itself and retype the formula with the new value. If you use the cell references, +D5*D4, you only need to change the value; Quattro Pro 10 recalculates the formula for you.

TIP
If you need to use the same value in more than one cell, enter it once, and reference its cell number elsewhere, as in +B2.

You can also reference a cell on another page of the spreadsheet using the format *Tab:ColumnRow,* as illustrated by the cell reference on the left of the input line. For example, B:A1 refers to cell A1 on page B of the notebook. To refer to a cell in another notebook, use the syntax *[Notebook_name]Cell.*

Integrate IT!
You can add your Quattro Pro 10 spreadsheet to a WordPerfect 10 document with a link. Using a link ensures that the WordPerfect 10 document is updated whenever the Quattro Pro 10 spreadsheet is recalculated.

16

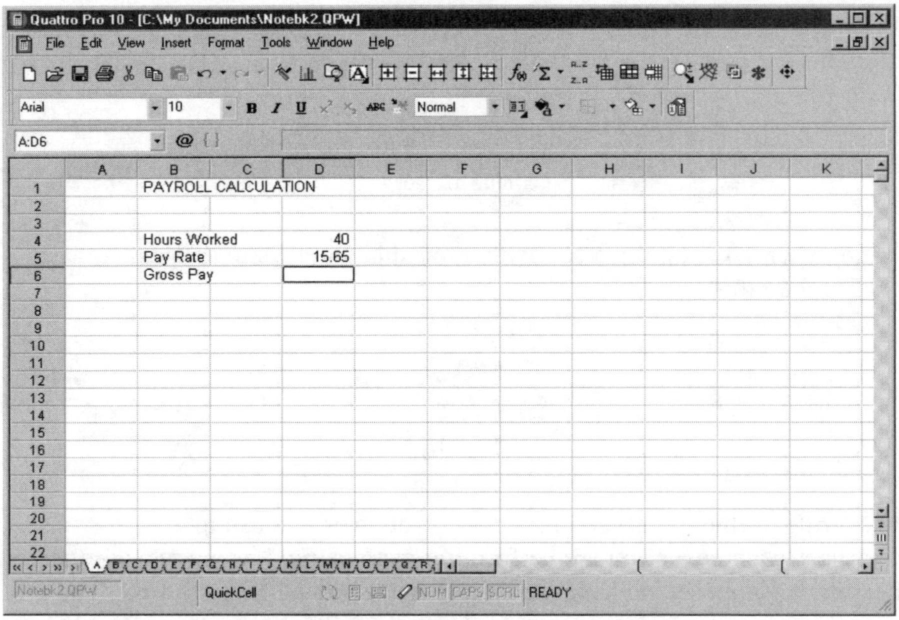

FIGURE 16-1   Spreadsheet for calculating gross pay

Precedence of Operators

When typing formulas, remember "My Dear Aunt Sally," a memory helper for Multiplication-Division-Addition-Subtraction. Quattro Pro 10, and almost every similar program, does not perform math in the exact order of operators from left to right. Instead, it scans the entire formula, giving precedence to certain operators over others. "My Dear Aunt Sally" means that multiplication and division are performed first (whatever order they are in) and then addition and subtraction.

The most common example of this is computing an average. If you enter the formula **+100+100+100/3** (using the values or their cell references), Quattro Pro 10 displays the result as 233.3333. It first divides 100 by 3 and then adds 100 twice.

To perform the calculation correctly, use parentheses to force Quattro Pro 10 to follow a different order, such as **(100+100+100)/3**. Notice that you can start a formula with an opening parenthesis without using a plus sign. Quattro Pro 10 assumes that entries starting with the open parenthesis character "(" are values.

Table 16-1 lists the operators by their order of precedence.

Operator	Function
^	Power of
-, +	Used to denote negative or positive
*, /	Multiplication and division
+, -	Addition and subtraction
>=	Greater than or equal to
<=	Less than or equal to
<, >	Less than, greater than
=, <>	Equal, not equal
#NOT#	Logical NOT operation
#AND#, #OR#	Logical AND, logical OR operations
&	String concatenation

TABLE 16-1   Operators by their order of precedence

Automatic Parentheses Matching

TIP   *Save time by not typing the parenthesis that comes at the very end of a formula. When you accept the entry, Quattro Pro 10 adds it for you.*

You can use more than one level of parentheses, if needed, with complex formulas. You must, however, have a closing parenthesis for every opening parenthesis. To help you out, Quattro Pro 10 has a parenthesis-matching feature. As you enter a formula, parentheses will appear in black when they are unmatched. When you type a closing parenthesis, the pair will change color.

Before accepting complex formulas, scan for black, unmatched parentheses. If you find any, check your formula carefully. You either need to add or to delete a parenthesis to have matching pairs while still performing the math in the order desired.

Pointing to Reference Cells

Making sure you have the correct cell reference is important, so rather than type the entry into a formula, you can point to it. This places the reference to the cell in the input line. To point to a cell, just click in it. To point to a block, drag over the cells.

16

For example, create the simple spreadsheet shown in Figure 16-1. To calculate the employee's gross pay, you need to multiply the number of hours in cell D4 times the pay rate in cell D5. You could do this by typing the formula +D4*D5. Instead of typing the cell references, however, point to them using these steps:

1. Click in cell D6 to make it active.

2. Press the + key to enter Value mode.

3. Click in cell D4. Quattro Pro 10 inserts the cell reference into the active cell so it appears as +D4.

4. Press the * key to enter the multiplication operator.

5. Click in cell D5 to enter its reference into the formula.

6. Press ENTER to accept the entry.

You can also use this technique to reference a cell or block of cells in another page of the notebook. When you want to point to the cell, click on the tab of the page where it is located, and then select the block. As soon as you enter the next operator, or accept or cancel the entry, Quattro Pro 10 switches back to the original page.

> **NOTE** *To select noncontiguous blocks, separate each with a comma in the input line.*

Editing Formulas

You edit formulas the same way you'd edit any cell—double-click on the cell, and either select it and press F2, or select it and click in the input line.

When you edit a formula that contains cell references, however, each referenced cell is enclosed in a blue frame. The frame shows you the values that are represented by the formulas.

To change a reference, either edit the cell address as you would any other text, or use Point mode:

1. Select the address of the cell in the formula.

2. Click on the cell you want to use as its replacement.

Quattro Pro 10 inserts the address of the cell in place of the selected address in the formula.

Formatting Numbers

The default format displays numbers without trailing zeros. You can easily change the format of numbers by pulling down the Number Format list in the property bar to see the options shown here:

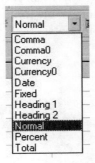

Select from the style list either before you start typing in the cell or after you've accepted the entry. The date and heading styles are not used for numbers, but here's how the number 1234.50 appears in each of the numeric styles:

	A	B	C
1			
2	Normal		1234.5
3	Comma		1,235.50
4	Comma0		1,235
5	Currency		$1,234.50
6	Currency0		$1,235
7	Fixed		1234.50
8	Percent		123450.00%
9	Total		1234.5
10			

The Total style does not change how the numbers appear, but inserts a double line on the top of the cell. Choose a number format first, and then click on the Total style to add a line to it.

Both Comma0 and Currency0 display no decimal places. The Fixed style uses a set number of decimals that you can designate using the Block Properties.

16

If adding the dollar sign, commas, or decimal places of a style causes the cell contents to be wider than the column, the Fit-As-You-Go feature automatically widens the column for you.

Entering Dates

In addition to text and values, a cell can contain a date or a time. Dates and times are treated as values because Quattro Pro 10 can perform calculations on them, such as figuring the number of days between two dates. To be used in calculations, the date or time must be entered in one of the formats that Quattro Pro 10 recognizes.

Enter the date in any of these formats:

DD-MMM-YY	11-Nov-01
DD-MMM	11-Nov
MMM-YY	Nov-01
MM/DD/YY	11/16/01
MM/DD	11/16

The last two formats are accepted as the default Long International and Short International date formats of Quattro Pro 10. You can change these settings to accept other formats by changing the Application Properties.

If you do not enter the year, as in 11/16, Quattro Pro 10 assumes the current year and adds it to the date using all four digits. If you enter two digits for the year, however, it tries to anticipate the turn of the century. Entering a year from 00 to 29 will be accepted as 2000 to 2029. Years after that (30-99) will be inserted as 1930 to 1999.

Enter times in either of these formats:

HH:MM:SS AM/PM	04:12:30 AM
HH:MM AM/PM	04:30 AM

You can also select a Long International and Short International time format using the Application Properties. If you do not enter PM, or enter time in 24-hour format, Quattro Pro 10 assumes times are AM.

When you accept a date or time entry, Quattro Pro 10 displays the date or time in the cell but shows a serial number that represents the date or time in the input line. The serial numbers for dates range from -109,571 for January 1, 1600, to 474,816 for December 31, 3199. December 30, 1899, is represented by serial

number 0. The serial number for a time is a decimal between 0.000 for the stroke
of midnight and 0.99999 for one second before midnight the next day.

Quattro Pro 10 uses the serial numbers to perform math operations. To
calculate the number of days between two dates, for example, just subtract the cell
reference of the first date from the last date, such as +B6-B3. The number that
appears is the difference between their serial numbers.

 You can use Block Properties to force a cell to only accept date formats.

Instant Row and Column Totals

So many spreadsheets contain the totals of rows and columns, that Quattro Pro 10
has made calculating totals automatic. Look at the spreadsheet in Figure 16-2, for
example.

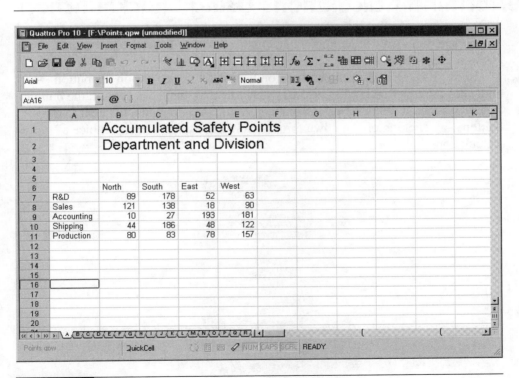

FIGURE 16-2   Adding instant totals

To instantly add row totals, enter the label **Total** or **Totals** in cell F6 and then click elsewhere. Quattro Pro instantly inserts the row totals in cells F7 to F11, like this:

Total
382
367
411
400
398

Similarly, enter the label **Total** or **Totals** in cell A12 and then click elsewhere to instantly insert the column totals.

Performing Calculations Using QuickFunction

There are a number of formulas that are used so often, such as calculating the total or average of a series of numbers, that Quattro Pro 10 makes them available in one easy-to-use list.

Look at the QuickFunction button on the toolbar. The icon on the button indicates the function it will perform when you click on it. By default, the button calculates the total of a series of numbers. If you pull down the list next to the button—by clicking on the down arrow—you'll see the following choice of calculations:

Click on the one you want to perform.

Here's how to use QuickFunction:

If the values you want to use for the calculation, such as a total or average, are contiguous—that is, in a row or column with no blank cells among them—click in the blank cell below the last value in the column or to the right of the last value in the row. Then click on the QuickFunction button to perform the calculation indicated, or pull down the list and choose the one you want to perform. Quattro Pro 10 calculates and displays the results.

When the cells are not contiguous, select the cells first, including the blank cell below or to the right of the series, and then select from the list. The result appears in the blank cell.

Quattro Pro 10 uses a built-in function to perform the math, such as @SUM to calculate a total or @AVG for the average, that you'll see in the input line. The function uses a range reference, citing the first and last cells in the group, such as @SUM(A1 . . . A12).

NOTE   *All functions begin with the @ sign.*

Always check the range reference, especially if you did not select the cells first, to confirm that the correct cells have been included. If the range is incorrect, edit it or point to the range using these steps:

1. Make the cell containing the function active.

2. Click in the input line.

3. Drag over the range reference in the input line that you want to replace. You do not have to delete the range, as long as you leave it selected.

4. Drag over the range in the spreadsheet.

5. Accept the entry.

You can calculate the totals or average, for example, for several rows and columns of numbers at one time. The selection in Figure 16-3, for instance, calculates the averages for the rows and for the columns, as well as an overall average in cell F12, when you use the Average option from the QuickFunction list

16

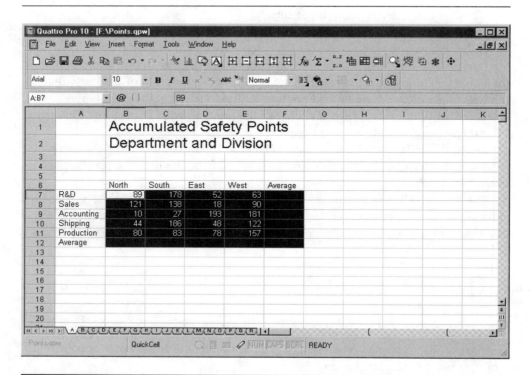

FIGURE 16-3   Selecting cells to total rows and columns and create a grand total in one step

Quick Math

In Chapter 2 you learned that PerfectExpert can guide you through many application tasks. One PerfectExpert feature in Quattro Pro 10 is Quick Math. Using Quick Math, you can perform calculations on rows and columns of numbers, insert formulas, and even perform math on two sets of numbers.

To use this feature, select Help | PerfectExpert and click on Do Simple Math in the Perfect Expert panel. There are five choices:

- *Calculating in Cells* gives you help information on performing math operations in cells.

- *Creating Formulas* opens the Formula Composer that you'll learn about in Chapter 19.

- *Quick Math* lets you select a range of cells and choose the math operation to perform on them.

- *More Quick Math* helps you perform more sophisticated operations, such as finding a fraction, a percentage, a square root, or raising a number to a power.

- *2-Column Quick Math* lets you perform basic math operations on values in two columns.

Using Calc-As-You-Go

If you are interested in the total, average, or other statistic about a range of cells, but don't necessarily want to add it to the spreadsheet, then use Calc-As-You-Go.

When you select a range of cells and release the mouse button, Quattro Pro 10 displays information on the right of the application bar, as shown here:

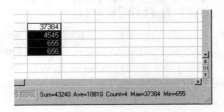

In addition to the total (Sum) and average (Ave) of the cells, Count displays the number of cells containing numeric values, Max shows the largest value in the range, and Min shows the smallest. Calc-As-You-Go ignores blank cells and cells with labels. If you want a blank cell included in the statistics, enter a zero in it.

Using QuickCell

Once you start referencing cells in formulas, you may want to see the effects of your work on a specific cell. For example, suppose you have a spreadsheet that calculates an estimate for a proposal. As you add or change values in the spreadsheet, you want to see how the total estimate is affected.

This is not a problem if the cell is displayed onscreen; but with larger spreadsheets, the cell might be scrolled out of view. Rather than scroll back and forth between the cell and the area in which you are working, insert the cell into the QuickCell box in the application bar:

16

Now, as you work, you'll see the contents of that cell displayed in the application bar, even if the cell itself does not appear onscreen:

To add the cell to the status line, click on the cell, and then click on QuickCell in the application bar.

To remove the cell from the QuickCell, click on an empty cell, and then click on the QuickCell.

Entering Data with QuickFill

In many instances, row and column labels are a series of sequential entries, such as the months of the year or incrementing numbers. These types of entries are so common that Quattro Pro 10 gives you QuickFill, a way of entering a sequence without typing the entire series yourself. This works as follows:

1. Enter the first one or two values of the series. These are called the *seed values.*

2. Select the seed values and the remaining cells in the row, column, or block that you want to fill with the remaining sequence.

3. Click on the QuickFill button, and Quattro Pro 10 completes the range for you.

 You can also right-click on selected cells and and choose QuickFill from the QuickMenu that appears.

Let's try it:

1. Type **Jan** in cell A1.

2. Click on the Enter button.

3. Drag over cells A1 to L1, and then click on QuickFill. Quattro Pro 10 automatically completes the series, inserting the month labels "Feb" to "Dec."

Table 16-2 shows the single seed values that Quattro Pro 10 recognizes.

When the values you want are not consecutive, enter the first two or three of the series. For example, to number rows with even numbers, enter **2** in one row, and enter **4** in the next row. QuickFill completes the sequence of even numbers in the selected cells.

When QuickFill does not complete the series, or when you don't want to drag across a large number of cells, use the Fill option in the Edit menu. Here's how:

1. Click in the cells that you want to fill.

2. Pull down the Edit menu, point to Fill, and click on Fill Series. The dialog box shown in Figure 16-4 appears.

3. The reference for the current active cell or selected range of cells is in the Cells box. If the range is incorrect, enter a new range, or use Point mode to select it, and click on the Maximize button in the Data Fill title bar.

Seed Values	Sequence
1st	2nd, 3rd, 4th, 5th . . .
Qtr 1	Qtr 2, Qtr 3, Qtr 4, Qtr 1 . . .
1st quarter	2nd quarter, 3rd quarter . . .
Jan	Feb, Mar . . .
January	February, March . . .
Mon	Tue, Wed, Thu . . .
Monday	Tuesday, Wednesday . . .
Week 1	Week 2, Week 3 . . .
Jan 97	Feb 97, Mar 97, Apr 97 . . .
100 days	101 days, 102 days, 103 days . . .
1,3,5	7, 9, 11, 13 . . .
11/16/99	11/17/99, 11/18/99 . . .

TABLE 16-2   Seed values for QuickFill

16

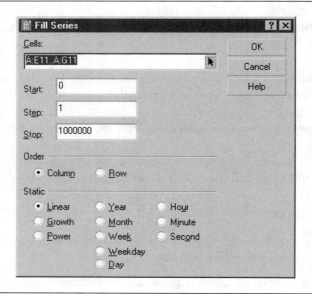

FIGURE 16-4 Data Fill dialog box

4. Once the range is set to the cells you want to fill, enter the starting value that you want to place in the first cell. The starting value can be a number, date, or time.

5. Enter a step value that you want to increment the series by. A step value of 2, for example, displays every other number, date, or time, depending on the series.

6. Enter a stop value. Quattro Pro 10 stops the series when it reaches the last cell in the range or the stop value, whichever is reached first. If you enter a date as the start value, enter a stop value of at least 50,000. Remember that Quattro Pro 10 converts dates to serial numbers, so you need an ending serial number certain to be larger than the last date in the series.

7. Choose if you want them to be filled by column or by row. Filling by column, for example, adds the series down the cells, filling out the first column and then continuing in the column to the right until the range is filled. Using row fill completes the series in the cells across the first row, then the second row, and so forth.

8. Choose the type of series that you want to complete. If the values are numbers, Linear increases it by the step value, Growth multiplies the step value by the previous value, and Power uses the step value as an exponent.

9. If the start value is a date or time, choose one of the date series options. QuickFill uses your starting date to determine the initial value and increment by the series. For example, if you enter **11/16/99** and choose a Month series, QuickFill inserts only the months, starting with November. If you choose Day, QuickFill inserts a series of days.

10. Click on OK.

If none of the series options suits your needs, you can create and save your own custom QuickFill lists. A *list* is a series of values that you can have QuickFill insert for you. For example, suppose your company uses two-letter state abbreviations for column headings. You can create a QuickFill list to access the abbreviations when you need them. To create a list, use these steps:

1. Click on any empty cell.

2. Click on the QuickFill button. You can also right-click on the cell and choose QuickFill from the QuickMenu, or choose Define QuickFill from the Edit Fill menu. The box that appears lists the built-in series that Quattro Pro 10 uses for QuickFill.

3. Click on the Create button to display the dialog box shown in Figure 16-5.

4. Type a series name that you will later use for a QuickFill operation.

5. In the Series Type section, choose List. Choosing Formula lets you enter formulas as the series elements. Choosing the Repeating option starts the list over again each time every element has been inserted once.

6. In the Series Elements text box, type the first item in the series, and then click on Add.

7. Insert the other items in the list the same way. Each item will be added to the bottom of the list. If you want to insert an item elsewhere in the list, click on the list where you want to add it, type the new item, and then click on Insert. Use the Delete button to remove an item from the list, and use Modify to change an element.

16

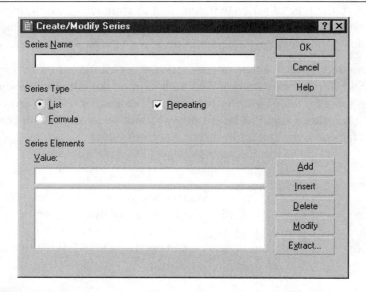

FIGURE 16-5 Dialog box for creating your own QuickFill series

8. If you've already typed the values in a spreadsheet, you do not have to type them again. Click on Extract. In the dialog box that appears, enter or point to the range that contains the value. If you want the extracted range to replace the values in the list, click on Override Existing Values. When you click on OK, the items from the spreadsheet are inserted into the list. Extract is useful because you can enter the values in a spreadsheet and then sort them before adding them to the list.

9. Click on OK to close the Create/Modify Series dialog box. Then click on OK to close the QuickFill dialog box.

When you want to use your list for a QuickFill operation, follow these steps:

1. Select the cells you want to fill.

2. Choose QuickFill from the QuickMenu, or choose Define Fill Series from the Data menu.

3. Pull down the Series list, and click on the name of your custom list.

4. Click on OK.

Inserting a Comment

When you want to make a note to yourself or another user, you can add a comment directly to a cell. The comment appears onscreen as a QuickTip when you point to the cell, so it is useful to explain the type of information that should be inserted, or how a formula was calculated. Here's how:

1. Click on the cell that you want to add a comment to.

2. Select Insert Comment from the Insert menu, or right-click and choose Insert Comment from the QuickMenu menu. You will see a yellow text box next to the cell.

3. Type the text of the comment.

4. Click outside of the box.

Quattro Pro 10 displays a small triangle in the top-right corner of the cell indicating that it contains a comment. When you point to the cell, the comment appears as a QuickTip.

To edit the comment, right-click on the cell and choose Edit Comment from the QuickMenu, or choose Comment from the Insert menu. To delete a comment, right-click on the cell, and choose Delete Comment from the QuickMenu.

Changing Column Width and Row Height

If your entry is too wide for the cell, widen the column so you can see the full text or number. You can also reduce column width to display more columns on the screen and on the printed page. Reducing column width is useful for columns that have short entries—just a character or two—where space is being wasted.

 To quickly change the width of a column so it is as wide as the widest entry, click in the column letter to select the column, and then click on the QuickFit Columns button in the toolbar. You can also double-click on the right boundary of the column header. Quattro Pro 10 widens or reduces the column as necessary. To make the column as wide as a specific cell contents, click in that cell and then on the QuickFit Columns button.

You can also change the width of a column by dragging. Point to the line to the right of the column letter—the line between the column and the column to its right. The mouse pointer changes to a double-headed arrow. Hold down the left mouse button, and drag the pointer until the column is the size you want.

16

To resize several columns to the same width, select the columns by dragging over their column letters, and then change the size of any one of the selected columns. When you release the mouse button, all of the selected columns will be the same size as the changed column.

> **NOTE** *Column width and row height also can be set by use of properties, as explained in Chapter 17.*

You can also adjust the height of rows by clicking or dragging. Select the row or rows you want to adjust to the largest height, and then click the QuickFit Rows button. As an alternative, point to the line under the row letter so the mouse pointer appears as a two-headed arrow, and then drag. Resize several rows by selecting them first.

Finally, you can adjust the column width and row height at the same time by clicking the QuickFit Columns and Rows button on the toolbar

Printing Spreadsheets

You'll probably want a hard copy of your spreadsheet for reference or distribution. To print the spreadsheet, just click on the Print button on the toolbar. Quattro Pro 10 prints your spreadsheet, using all of the default print settings.

For more control over the printing process, use this technique:

1. Select Print from the File menu to see the dialog box shown in Figure 16-6.

2. Make sure that the Current Sheet button is selected.

3. Click on the Print button. This prints the entire contents of the spreadsheet.

Previewing Before Printing

If you want to see how your printout will look, select Print Preview from the File menu, or click on the Print Preview button if you've already opened the Spreadsheet Print dialog box, to see a screen, as in Figure 16-7. Quattro Pro 10 reduces the image so you can see an entire printed page at one time.

To enlarge the image so it is easier to read, move the mouse pointer over the representation of the page so it appears like a magnifying lens. Now each time you click the left mouse button, the magnification is doubled—from 100 percent to 200 percent, then to 400 percent, up to 1600 percent.

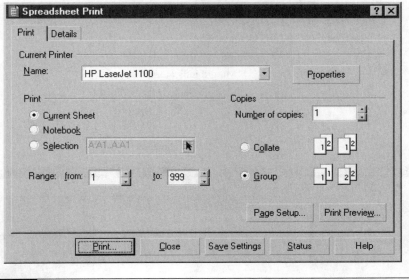

FIGURE 16-6   Print dialog box

Each time you click the right mouse button, the image is reduced to the previous magnification back down to 100 percent.

Use the Print Preview toolbar to adjust the image and select options, as shown in Figure 16-7. When you are satisfied with the print preview, click on the Print button to print the spreadsheet as it is displayed, or close the Print Preview window to change the print range or return to the spreadsheet.

Saving Your Spreadsheet

Soon after you begin entering information into your spreadsheet, you should save the spreadsheet on your disk. You wouldn't want to lose any of your work if your computer suddenly were to act up. When you are ready to save your spreadsheet, follow these steps:

1. Click on the Save button. If this is the first time you've saved the notebook, you'll see the Save File dialog box.

2. Type a document name in the Name text box.

16

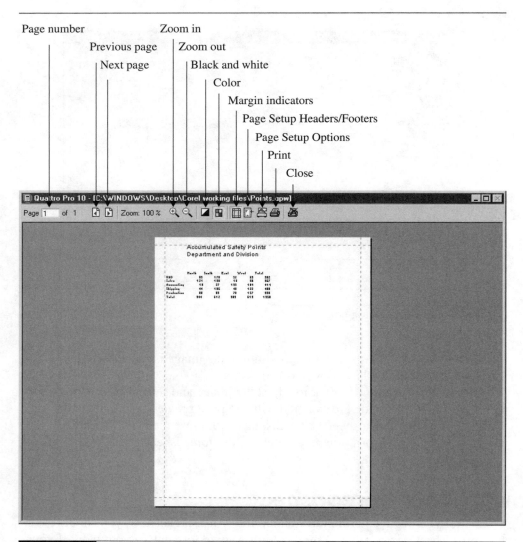

Page number

Previous page

Next page

Zoom in

Zoom out

Black and white

Color

Margin indicators

Page Setup Headers/Footers

Page Setup Options

Print

Close

FIGURE 16-7   Previewing your spreadsheet before printing

3. Click on Save. Quattro Pro 10 saves documents with the QPW extension.

Once you save a notebook the first time, you'll need to save it again if you make changes to it. When you click on Save, Quattro Pro 10 saves it immediately under the same name without displaying a dialog box. If you want to save the edited copy under a new name, select Save As from the File menu and then save the file as if it were being saved for the first time.

Closing Notebooks

To close the notebook, click on the notebook's Close button, or select Close from the File menu. If you did not save the notebook since you last changed it, a dialog box appears giving you the chance to do so. Closing the notebook does not exit Quattro Pro 10, so you can start a new notebook or open an existing one.

Opening Notebooks

There are several ways that you can open an existing notebook. To quickly open one of the last notebooks you worked with, use either of these methods:

- Pull down the File menu, and click on the notebook's name in the list.

- Select New from Project from the File menu, click on the Work On tab, then double-click on the file you want to open.

To open a notebook not listed on the File menu or in the New dialog box, use these steps:

1. Click on the Open button, or choose Open from the File menu to display the Open File dialog box.

2. Select the file, changing folders or drives if necessary. If notebooks are not listed, pull down the File Type list, and choose All Files (*.*) or one of the other options to list files of a specific type.

3. Click on Open.

16

File Formats

Quattro Pro 10 lets you save spreadsheets in formats other than its own, and it allows you to open files created by other spreadsheet and database programs. This means that you can share files with others who do not have Quattro Pro 10, and that you can use other programs to analyze and work with your Quattro Pro 10 information.

Use the Open command to retrieve data from a Paradox database to analyze it using Quattro Pro 10 or to open an HTML document created with WordPerfect 10's Internet Publisher.

To open a file in another format, pull down the File Type list in the Open dialog box, and choose the type of file you wish to open. Then locate and select the file using the Look In list. To save a file in another format, pull down the Save As Type list in the Save As dialog box, and click on the file type. Quattro Pro 10 can open and save files in these formats:

Quattro Pro versions for Windows and DOS	Text
Microsoft Excel	DIF
Lotus 1-2-3	SYLK
Paradox	CSV
DBASE	HTML

 QuattroPro can also open files in the Quicken Interchange Format.

Starting a New Notebook

To start a new notebook, click on the New button, or select New from the File menu to display a new blank notebook onscreen.

You can also use the New from Template command from the File menu to start a new notebook or to load a completely formatted notebook already designed for a specific purpose, such as tracking accounts receivable, computing your net worth, or printing a purchase order. Follow these steps:

1. Select New from Project from the File menu. You'll see the dialog box shown in Figure 16-8.

2. To start a new blank notebook, select [Quattro Pro 10 Notebook] on the Create New page, and then click on OK.

3. To load a formatted notebook, select one of the projects from the Create New page, and then click on OK.

When the project opens, add the information required, and then save and print it.

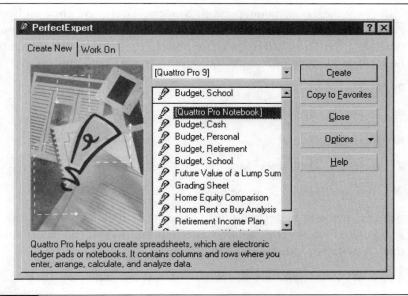

FIGURE 16-8   Using a template to create a professional spreadsheet

While each project is different, there are certain common elements in the PerfectExpert box:

- There are cells designed for data entry, where you need to enter your own information without replacing built-in formulas and functions. If these cells are not highlighted, making them easy to identify, click on the Turn Highlight On/Off button.

- Click on the Insert Sample Data button to fill the data entry cells with sample information so you can see how the template is used.

- When you are ready to enter your own information, click on the Remove Sample Data button.

Using Budget Expert

An *Expert* is a series of dialog boxes that leads you, step-by-step, through a complete task. The Budget Expert helps you create a formatted budget document—all you have to enter are the numbers. To start the Expert, follow these steps:

1. Pull down the Tools menu, point to Numeric Tools, and click on Budget. Now select options in a series of dialog boxes, clicking on the button labeled "Next Step" after you've completed each dialog box. In the first box, select the type of budget you want to create. Your choices are:

   - Home - Actual
   - Home - Actual vs Plan
   - Business - Actual
   - Business - Actual vs Plan
   - Business Income Statement

2. Select the type of budget you want to create, and then click on Next. The second box lists several sample sources of funds. You can delete sources that are not appropriate and add your own.

3. To add a source, type it in the New Item text box, and then click on Add.

4. To delete a source, click on it in the list, and then click on Delete.

5. When you are satisfied with the list, click on Next. The next dialog box lists sample items where your money goes. Add or delete items, and then click on Next.

6. You now need to select the period for the budget, the starting date, and the duration. Click on the desired period: Monthly, Quarterly, or Yearly.

7. Select a starting date. The options that appear depend on the period. If you selected Monthly, you can choose a starting month and year. If you selected Quarterly, you can choose a starting quarter and year. If you selected Yearly, you can select only a starting year.

8. Select the duration of the budget: the number of months, quarters, or years.

9. Click on Next.

10. Select summation options: Quarter-to-date or Year-to-date.

11. Click on Next.

12. In the next dialog box, enter a spreadsheet title and subtitle. Then click on Next.

13. Choose whether to insert the budget in a new notebook or the current one. Then click on Next.

14. Depending on the selected period, you can now choose to change pages each month, quarter, or year. You can also choose to display the spreadsheet in color or in monochrome for output to a laser printer.

15. Click on Finish, and Quattro Pro 10 does the rest.

NOTE *In Chapter 21, you'll learn how to use other Experts to save time.*

Try It Out

Now it is your turn to create a notebook. In this section, we'll create a basic spreadsheet, but we'll use quite a few Quattro Pro features, including QuickFill to complete a series and QuickFunction to perform math. Start with a new blank notebook, and then follow these steps.

1. Enter **Mon** in cell B2 and then press ENTER.

2. Drag over cells B2 to F2, and click on the QuickFill button in the toolbar. QuickFill will complete the days of the week, from Mon to Fri.

3. Enter the following information into the spreadsheet:

	A	B	C	D	E	F
1						
2		Mon	Tue	Wed	Thu	Fri
3	Wing	85	70	72	58	62
4	Beebe	83	60	7	18	18
5	Chesin	42	28	97	45	53
6	Udel	10	11	55	58	64
7	Paul	32	20	15	97	14
8						
9						
10						

4. Click in cell G2, type Totals, and press ENTER.

16

5. Click in cell A8, type Totals, and press ENTER. The totals appear as shown here:

	A	B	C	D	E	F	G
1							
2		Mon	Tue	Wed	Thu	Fri	Totals
3	Wing	85	70	72	58	62	347
4	Beebe	83	60	7	18	18	186
5	Chesin	42	28	97	45	53	265
6	Udel	10	11	55	58	64	198
7	Paul	32	20	15	97	14	178
8	Totals	252	189	246	276	211	1174
9							
10							

6. Click in cell B9.

7. Type @AVG and then press the RIGHT ARROW key. The insertion point should be following the opening parenthesis of the function:

```
      252
@AVG(
```

8. Drag over cells B3 to B7 and then press the ENTER key. Quattro Pro completes the formula so it is @AVG(B3..B7).

9. Drag over cells B9 to F9 and click the QuickFill button.

10. Click in cell H3.

11. Type @AVG and then press the RIGHT ARROW key.

12. Drag over cells B3 to F3 and then press the ENTER key. Quattro Pro completes the formula so it is @AVG(B3..F3).

13. Drag over cells H3 to H7 and click the QuickFill button.

14. Click in cell H9.

15. Type @AVG and then press the RIGHT ARROW key.

16. Drag over cells B3 to F7 and then press the ENTER key. Quattro Pro completes the formula so it is @AVG(B3..F7).

17. Right-click on cell H9 and select Insert Comment from the QuickMenu.

18. Type **Average for the week**, and then click elsewhere in the spreadsheet.

19. Right-click on cell G8 and select Insert Comment from the QuickMenu.

20. Type **Total for the week**, and then click elsewhere in the spreadsheet.

Enter the word Average in cells H2 and A9.

The final spreadsheet, with one of the comments being displayed, is shown in Figure 16-9.

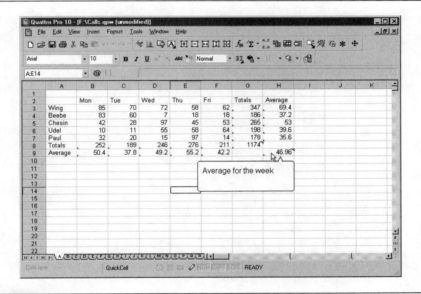

FIGURE 16-9   Completed spreadsheet

16

Chapter 17

Editing and Formatting Spreadsheets

It is as easy to edit your spreadsheet—even make major changes to it—as it is to create it. You can insert and delete information, change its appearance and format, and move and copy information until the spreadsheet is perfect.

Erasing Information from Cells

Sometimes you'll want to erase all of the information from a cell rather than just edit it. You have two choices: clearing and deleting. Although these have similar effects, they are in some ways quite different. *Clearing* removes the contents from a cell, row, or column but leaves the cells in the spreadsheet. *Deleting* actually removes the cells from the spreadsheet, moving any remaining cells up or over to take the place of the deleted cells. If you clear row 5, for example, the row itself remains empty in the spreadsheet. If you delete row 5, then row 6 moves up to take its place, and it becomes the new row 5.

Clearing Cells

Choose clearing when you do not want to change the position of other information in the sheet. You can clear everything from a cell, just the characters, or just the format. Here's how:

1. Select the block you want to clear.

2. Pull down the Edit menu, point to Clear, and select one of these options:

   ■ *Cells* clears all characters and formats from a cell, returning all of the default properties.

   ■ *Values* clears just the displayed contents, leaving formats such as alignment and shading. If you later enter information in the cell, it automatically takes on the formats stored there.

   ■ *Format* leaves the contents in the cell but returns the cell to thedefault formats.

   ■ *Delete Comments* clears just the comment from the cell.

 Pressing DEL *also clears the contents. So to erase the contents of the entire sheet, click on the Select All button (or choose Select All from the Edit menu), and then press* DEL.

Deleting Cells

When you delete cells, you are actually removing them from the spreadsheet. If you delete rows or columns, the remaining ones are renumbered. If you just delete a block of cells, other cells in the row or column shift into their position.

To delete a block, select it, and then use any of these techniques:

■ Click the Delete button in the toolbar.

■ Choose Delete Cells from the Edit menu.

■ Right-click on the selection, and choose Delete or Delete Cells from the QuickMenu.

To delete entire rows or columns, select the ones you want to remove by clicking on or dragging over their headers. When you choose Delete, Quattro Pro 10 removes them immediately. When you delete a cell or block of cells, Quattro Pro 10 first displays the dialog box shown in Figure 17-1, which asks how much you want to delete. When this box is displayed, use these steps to ensure that the correct cells are deleted:

1. If the block reference is incorrect, enter or point to the proper reference.

2. Select the Dimension that you want to delete: Columns, Rows, or Sheets.

3. Select a Span option: Entire or Partial.

4. Click on OK.

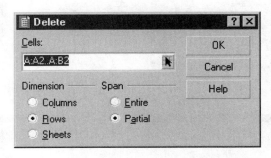

FIGURE 17-1   Deleting cells

17

When Entire is selected in Span, Quattro Pro 10 deletes the entire column, row, or sheet (based on the Dimension setting) in which the selected cells are located. If you select cell C5 and choose Entire and Rows, all of row 5 is deleted, not just the single cell.

To remove just the selected cells, not their entire row or column, click on Partial. Your choice in the Dimension section determines which cells will take the place of the deleted ones. If you choose Rows, for example, the cells below the deleted cells move up. If you select Columns, the cells to the right of the deleted cells move over. Perhaps the best way to visualize this is to look at Figure 17-2. On the left side of the figure is the original block of cells showing the ones to be deleted. In the center is the same block of cells after Columns was chosen in the Delete dialog box. On the right is the same block after Rows was chosen.

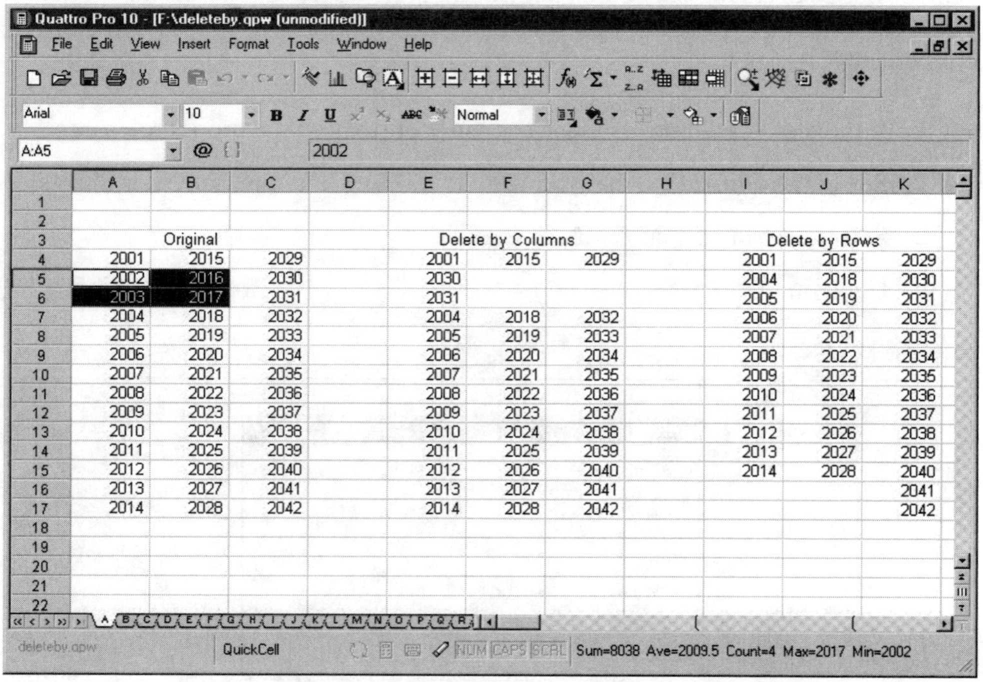

FIGURE 17-2   The different effects of deleting by rows and columns

When you select Partial, only the selected cells are deleted. Existing cells will move up or over, and they will no longer appear in the same row or column they were in originally. If the contents relate to a label, then the label may no longer be in the same row or column. Thus, make certain of the effect you want to achieve.

 To delete the entire sheet, right-click on its tab, and choose Delete Sheet from the QuickMenu.

Inserting Blocks

No matter how well you plan, you may have to insert cells into the spreadsheet. When you insert cells, existing ones shift down or to the right to make room. You insert using either the Insert button in the toolbar or the Insert Cells option from the QuickMenu.

To insert an entire row, follow these steps:

1. Click on the number of the row that you want to shift down. For example, to insert a new row number 5, click on the row 5 header.

2. Click on the Insert button in the toolbar. A new row is inserted, causing the original rows to be renumbered.

3. To insert an entire column, click on the letter of the column that you want to shift to the right, and then click on the Insert button.

4. To insert several rows or columns at one time, select the desired number of rows or columns before clicking on Insert. To insert two rows, for instance, drag to select two entire rows. To insert four columns, drag to select four columns.

You can also insert a cell or block of cells into the spreadsheet, rather than entire rows or columns. As with deleting, you can choose to perform the operation by row or by column. If you insert cells by row, then cells below move down to make room. If you insert cells by column, cells to the right move over. Here's how to insert a block of cells:

1. Select the cells that currently occupy the space where you want the inserted cells to appear. These cells will move to make room for the inserted block.

17

For example, if you want to insert cells in positions A1 and B1, select cells A1 and B1.

2. Click on the Insert button in the toolbar to display the Insert dialog box.

3. Click on Partial in the Span section. (Selecting Entire inserts entire rows or columns.)

4. Choose Rows or Columns in the Dimension section. Choose Columns if you want the existing cells to move to the right to make room; choose Rows if you want the existing cells to move down.

5. Click on OK.

To insert an entire blank sheet, right-click on the tab of the sheet you want to follow the new one, and then choose Insert Sheet from the QuickMenu and click OK in the box that appears. Quattro Pro 10 will insert a new sheet, adjusting the tab letters as needed.

 Change the name on the sheet tab by double-clicking on the tab or by right-clicking on it and choosing Edit Sheet Name from the QuickMenu. Type the name you want, and then press ENTER.

Moving and Copying Information

The capability to move and copy information from one location to another is as useful in Quattro Pro 10 as it is in WordPerfect. You may need to move information when you've entered it in the wrong location, or when you want to copy it to avoid having to reenter it elsewhere. Copying information is especially useful when you need similar formulas in several locations, even when the cell references are not exactly the same.

Before moving or copying information, however, you need to decide how you are going to do it, because Quattro Pro 10 gives you three choices: drag and drop, the Clipboard, and the Copy Cells command.

Using Drag and Drop

Drag and drop works about the same as in all the other Corel Suite applications. You can drag and drop a single cell or a block of selected cells, as long as they are contiguous—that is, the cells must be next to each other and selected as one group.

The advantage of drag and drop over other methods is that you can see where you are placing the information. Here is how it works:

1. Start by selecting the block of cells that you want to move.

2. Point to an edge of the selected block until the pointer appears as a four-headed arrow.

3. Press and hold down the mouse button so the selection is surrounded by a colored outline.

4. Drag the mouse; a colored outline will move along with it.

5. When the outline is in the desired location, release the mouse button. Quattro Pro 10 moves both the contents and format of the cell, so the original cell will be returned to its default format.

NOTE   *Depending on the speed of your system, it may take a little time for the colored outline to appear as you drag.*

To copy a block using drag and drop, hold down the CTRL key when you drag and drop. Technically, you have to hold down the CTRL key only when you release the mouse button, not the entire time. Just make sure that the plus sign appears before you release the button. If it does not, move the mouse slightly, but make sure the colored outline remains where you want it.

To drag and drop an entire sheet, drag the sheet tab. As you drag, an outline of the tab will move with the mouse pointer. Release the mouse button when the tab is where you want the sheet. Hold down the CTRL key to copy the sheet rather than move it—a plus sign will accompany the outline of the tab when copying.

NOTE   *If you did not rename the sheet, Quattro Pro 10 places the moved sheet in alphabetical order; it does not move the original sheet letter to the new position.*

You can also move a sheet with the Move Sheets option from the Edit menu. In the dialog box that appears, enter the number of the sheet you want to move and the number of the sheet you want to move it ahead of, and then click on OK.

17

Using the Clipboard

Moving and copying blocks with the Clipboard are standard Windows techniques—use any of these options:

- Cut, Copy, and Paste buttons in the toolbar
- Cut, Copy, and Paste options from the Edit menu
- Cut, Copy, and Paste from the QuickMenu
- CTRL-X (Cut), CTRL-C (Copy), and CTRL-V (Paste) key combinations

The Clipboard gives you several advantages over drag and drop. Once the information is in the Clipboard, for example, you can paste it as many times as you want. You can paste the same information in several locations after cutting or copying it just once. With drag and drop, you'd have to select the information each time.

You can also select and then cut or copy noncontiguous cells. Hold down the CTRL key while you select the cells, and paste them in a new location. Drag and drop won't allow that. Use the following steps for this operation:

1. Select the block you want to move.
2. Choose Cut using any of the methods just described.
3. Click where you want to place the block. If you are moving a block of cells, click where you want the upper-left corner of the block to begin.
4. Choose Paste.

Copy information the same way but use the Copy command instead of Cut.

Using Paste Special

When you copy using drag and drop or the Clipboard, Quattro Pro 10 copies everything in the block, including the contents and formats, called *properties*. You have more control over what gets pasted using the Paste Special command. When you are ready to paste your copied cells, complete the following steps:

1. Select Paste Special from the Edit menu to see the dialog box shown in Figure 17-3.

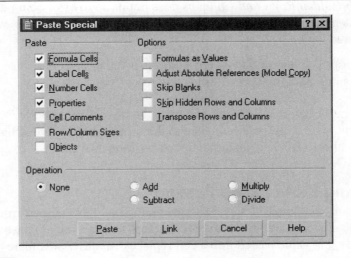

FIGURE 17-3   Paste Special dialog box

2. In the Paste section, select the type of cells in the Clipboard you want to paste.

3. Deselect the appropriate checkboxes if you do not want to paste formulas, labels, or numbers. Deselect the Properties box if you do not want to include the formats with the pasted cells. Select Cell Comments if you want to include comments that are attached to the cells. Choose Row/Column Sizes to duplicate the row height and column width from the selected cell. Choose Objects to insert objects from the select cells.

The following settings in the Options section determine how objects are pasted:

■ *Formulas as Values* pastes the *results* of formulas, not the formulas themselves.

■ *Move Absolute Reference (Model Copy)* changes absolute references to the appropriate address.

■ *Skip Blanks* does not overwrite the existing contents of a cell by pasting a blank cell into it.

17

- *Skip Hidden Rows and Columns* does not paste rows or columns that are hidden in the copied range of cells. This is a useful command when pasting filtered data.

- *Transpose Rows and Columns* rearranges the pasted cells, placing copied rows into columns and columns into rows.

When you've selected your options from the box, click on Paste. You can also click on Link, which inserts a reference to the original cells; if you change a value in the original cells, it changes in the linked position as well.

Performing Math When Pasting

The Operation section of the Paste Special dialog box lets you perform math using the values you copied and the contents of the cells where you are pasting.

Normally, the value pasted into a cell replaces whatever was there originally. But suppose you want to add the copied value to the contents of a cell, or perform another mathematical operation?

Select the cells where you want to paste the information, choose Paste Special from the Edit menu, and then choose the operation you want to perform. Choosing Subtract, for example, subtracts the value in the Clipboard from the contents of the cell, displaying the result.

Using the Copy Cells Command

The Copy Cells command from the Edit menu is yet another way to copy cells. However, this command lets you use block names, and you can control which properties of a block are copied.

| NOTE | *You'll learn about naming blocks in Chapter 18.* |

Select the block that you want to copy, and choose Copy Cells from the Edit menu to see the dialog box shown in Figure 17-4. If the reference in the From box is incorrect, enter it manually, or use Point mode to select the block.

In the To box, enter or point to the location where you want to copy the block. You need only select the upper-left corner.

The Model Copy option lets you select which elements of the block to copy. When the option is not selected, Quattro Pro 10 copies everything—contents, formats, formulas, properties, objects, and the row and column sizes. If you want

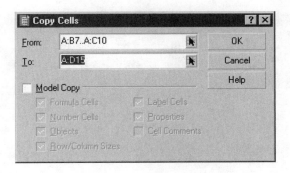

FIGURE 17-4   Copy Cells dialog box

to copy only certain elements, click on the Model Copy option, then remove the checks from the elements you do not want to move. For example, deselecting Formula Cells does not copy any cells that contain formulas.

NOTE   *When Model Copy is turned on, absolute references are also adjusted.*

Moving and Copying Formulas

You can use any of the techniques described above to move formulas from one cell to another. When you move a cell containing a formula, the same formula is placed in the pasted cell. When you copy a formula, however, it is copied using a relative reference. This means that the cell references in the formula are adjusted to use corresponding cells in the new location.

As an example, look at the spreadsheet in Figure 17-5. This spreadsheet needs a number of formulas. The income and expenses in each column must be totaled, and then expenses must be subtracted from income to calculate the net profit in the quarter columns. Because of the way Quattro Pro 10 copies formulas, you only need to enter them once—in the first column—and then copy them across the rows.

Create the spreadsheet in Figure 17-5, using the following steps. (Use QuickFill to repeat the Rent and Insurance figures across the row in the Expenses section.)

1. In cell B7, choose SUM from the QuickFunction list to add the total. Notice that the input line shows @SUM(B5..B6).

17

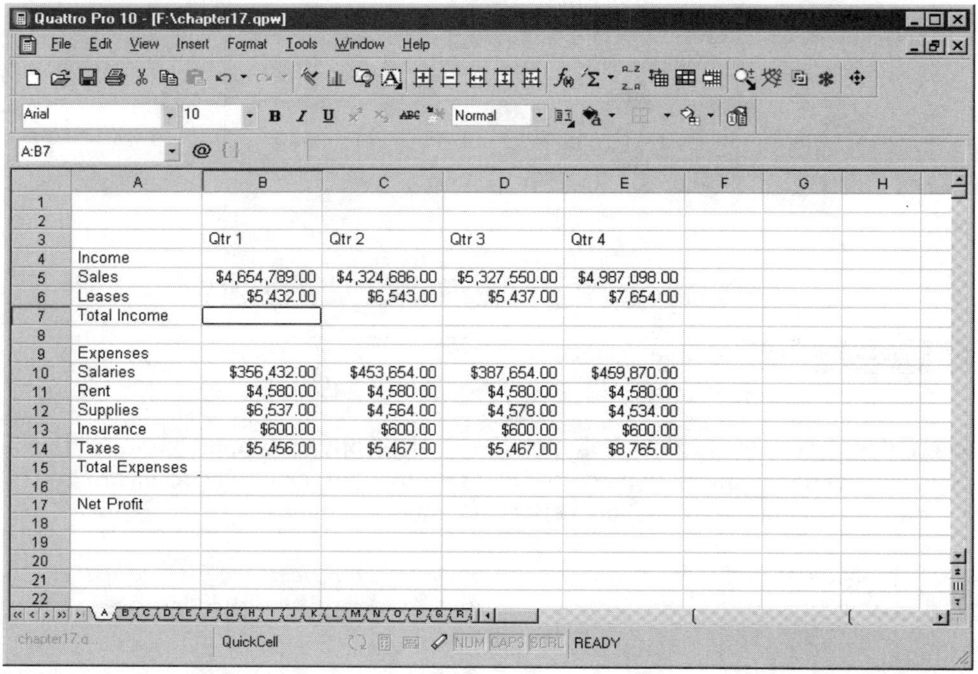

FIGURE 17-5 Spreadsheet to use with copied formulas

2. Click on cell B7, and drag over to select up to cell E7.

3. Point to the selection, press the right mouse button, and click on QuickFill from the QuickMenu. (You could also click on the QuickFill button in the toolbar.) Quattro Pro 10 copies the formula across the selected cells.

4. Point to cell C7, and look at the formula in the QuickTip: @SUM(C5..C6). Quattro Pro 10 did not copy the exact formula, which totals values in column B, but adjusted it to total the values in the cells above it in column C. The formulas in the remaining cells have been adjusted as well.

5. In a sense, Quattro Pro 10 sees the formula in cell B7 as saying, "Total the values in the two cells above." So when it copies the formula, the cell references automatically change to reflect the two cells above the formula (each formula really says the same thing).

6. Continue this process.

7. Enter the total in cell B15, and copy it across the row to cell E15.

8. In cell B17, enter the formula **+B7-B15** to compute net income.

9. Copy the formula across the row to cell E17.

You've completed the spreadsheet with twelve formulas by entering only three.

Cell Reference Checker

As you just learned, relative references make it easy to complete a spreadsheet, but they can create problems. For example, you could copy a formula to a location where the relative reference has no meaning, such as copying a Sum formula to a location where there are no values to total.

Fortunately, Quattro Pro 10 can help with the *Cell Reference Checker*. When you copy a formula, Quattro Pro 10 checks to determine if the newly referenced cells contain the appropriate types of values. If they do not, it indicates the range of cells affected and displays the Cell Reference Checker dialog box with a brief description of the problem, as shown here:

	Qtr 1	Qtr 2	Qtr 3	Qtr 4		
Income						
Sales	$4,654					
Leases	$5,				Close	
Total Income	$4,660					$0.00
					Help	
Expenses						
Salaries	$356		The pasted formula is using a BLANK cell.	Detail >>		
Rent	$4					
Supplies	$6					
Insurance	$600.00	$600.00	$600.00	$600.00		
Taxes	$5,456.00	$5,467.00	$5,467.00	$8,765.00		
Total Expenses	$373,605.00	$468,865.00	$402,879.00	$478,349.00		
Net Profit	$4,286,616.00	$3,862,364.00	$4,930,108.00	$4,516,403.00		

Cell Reference Checker   [Fix It]   [Undo Fix]

If you click on the Fix It button, the program displays the correction it will make by showing the cells that will be referenced in the formula. In this example, the Cell Reference Checker is indicating that it will use the same cells referenced in the original formula:

17

	Qtr 1	Qtr 2	Qtr 3	Qtr 4		
Income						
Sales	$4,654,789.00	$4,324,686.00	$5,327,550.00	$4,987,098.00		
Leases	$5,432.00	$6,543.00	$5,437.00	$7,654.00		
Total Income	$4,660,221.00	$4,331,229.00	$5,332,987.00	$4,994,752.00		*********
Expenses						
Salaries	$356,432					
Rent	$4,580					
Supplies	$6,537					
Insurance	$600					
Taxes	$5,456					
Total Expenses	$373,605					
Net Profit	$4,286,616.00	$3,862,364.00	$4,930,108.00	$4,516,403.00		

Cell Reference Checker [?] [X]

Fix It   Undo Fix   Close

The pasted formula is using a BLANK cell.   Help

Detail >>

You can also click on Details to see the original formula and the formula that will be inserted by the Cell Reference Checker. Click on Close if you agree with the correction; click on Undo Fix if you don't.

Copying Values of Formulas

In most cases, you'll enter formulas in such a way that they will recalculate if referenced cells change. Sometimes, however, you may want to copy the results of formulas to other cells without changing the values in the new location. You can paste formulas as values using the Paste Special dialog box or by following these steps:

1. Select the block that contains the formulas.

2. Select Convert to Values from the Edit menu. A dialog box is displayed with two boxes, From and To.

3. In the To box, enter or point to the destination where you want to copy the values.

4. Click on OK.

 CAUTION *By default, the From and To boxes contain the coordinates of the selected block. If you leave the To block unchanged, the formulas are replaced by their values.*

Absolute References

In most cases, you'll want Quattro Pro 10 to adjust cell references when you copy a formula, but not always. There are times when you'll want to copy a cell reference exactly as it appears. This is called an *absolute reference*.

For example, look at the spreadsheet in Figure 17-6. The spreadsheet will calculate costs based on the labor charges in cell B3. In several cells, we need a formula that multiplies the hours in row 7 times the labor cost to calculate the labor charges. We can do this easily by entering a formula such as **+B7*B3** in cell B8. But if we copy the formula across the row, Quattro Pro 10 will use a *relative reference*. Only the original formula will reference cell B3. Here's why: The formula in B8 means "multiply the value one cell above times the value in the cell five rows up." This same relationship will be applied where the formula is copied. So when it is copied to cell C8, for example, it will be copied as +C7*C3— multiplying the labor amount (one cell up) times the value in cell C3—which is wrong.

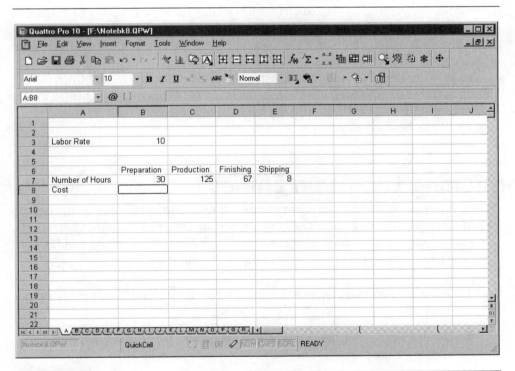

FIGURE 17-6   Copying formulas without a relative reference

17

When you want a reference to a cell to remain constant no matter where it is copied, use an absolute reference. To create an absolute reference, place a dollar sign ($) in front of each part of the reference that you want to remain constant. In this case, enter the formula as **+B7*B3**. This tells Quattro Pro 10 not to change the reference to column B and row 3.

Create the spreadsheet, enter the absolute reference, and use QuickFill to copy the formula across the row. The reference to cell B7 is adjusted because it is not absolute, but the reference to cell B3 remains constant.

Depending on your spreadsheet, the $ symbol is not always needed before both parts of the reference. For example, $C5 tells Quattro Pro 10 to always reference a cell in column C, but to change the row number relative to the location.

Using Model Copy to Adjust Absolute References

There is one problem, however, with absolute references. Suppose you want to copy the entire block of cells illustrated earlier to another location on the spreadsheet so you can use two different labor charges. If you copy cells A3 to E8, the formulas in the new location still reference cell B3 because of the absolute reference. This is not what you want. You really want the formulas to reference the new location, but again using an absolute reference to it.

To perform this copy, use the Adjust Absolute References (Model Copy) option in the Paste Special dialog box or the Copy Cells dialog box. Quattro Pro 10 copies the block of cells, modifying the absolute reference but leaving it absolute to its new location.

Formatting Long Text Entries

When you type a long text entry, characters run over into blank cells on the right. When there aren't enough blank cells to display the entire entry, some of it won't show onscreen or print with the spreadsheet. The Reformat command divides a long entry into more than one row, as in the following steps:

1. Select the cell that contains the long entry—only that cell, not the ones that it spreads into.

2. Choose Text Reformat from the Format menu. A dialog box appears asking for the block where you want to place the text.

3. Enter the block, or use Point mode to select it.

4. Click on OK.

The block must start with the active cell at the upper-left corner, and it must be large enough to hold all of the text. Pick sufficient cells, in as many rows and columns as needed. For instance, suppose you have a note that spans three columns. Your block can be three or four rows and one column wide, or two rows and two columns wide. Both blocks would be sufficient to hold the text.

Keep in mind, however, that Quattro Pro 10 reserves a little space before the first character in a cell and after the last. Some long entries may require a slightly larger block than you imagine. An entry that completely fills three columns, for example, would require a block four cells high.

 Using Cell Properties, you can also wrap a long entry so it fits entirely within a cell.

Transposing Columns and Rows

Once you set up your spreadsheet, you may find it more convenient if your rows and columns were switched, or *transposed*. For instance, you may find that you have more columns than rows, and that the spreadsheet would look better if the row labels were used for the columns instead. That way, perhaps, you could fit the entire spreadsheet on one page, rather than have some columns print on a second sheet.

Before transposing rows and columns, however, find an empty place in the notebook large enough to store the transposed block (a block that contained information would be overwritten with the transposed cells). Remember that the rows and columns will be reversed, so make sure there are enough empty rows to store the original columns and enough empty columns to store the original rows.

You can transpose a copied block using the Paste Special dialog box, or by following these steps:

1. Select the block that you want to transpose.

2. Pull down the Tools menu.

3. Point to Numeric Tools, and click on Transpose. A dialog box appears with two boxes, From and To.

17

4. In the To box, enter or point to the destination where you want to copy the values.

5. Click on OK.

 Cell references are not adjusted when you transpose cells, so avoid transposing cells with formulas or functions.

Formatting Your Spreadsheet

Not only must your spreadsheet be accurate, but it should look good. It should be easy and pleasant to read—formatted to enhance the material, not distract from it. By formatting a spreadsheet, you can change the typeface and size of characters, add lines and shading to cells, and change the way and position that text appears in the cell.

You can format cells before or after you enter contents into them. You can also format text as you enter or edit it. In fact, you can even apply formats to cells and later add information to them. Your entries will automatically assume the applied formats.

 Formatting blank cells that you never use, such as entire rows or columns, needlessly increases the size of your files.

There are two ways to format cells—using the property bar or setting cell properties. Setting cell properties may take a little longer than the other method, but it gives you the most options and enables you to set multiple formats at one time.

Remember, you must be in Ready mode to apply most formats to blocks. Except for character formats, you cannot format while you are entering or editing information in a cell.

 Character formats, such as typeface and size, bold and italic, can be applied to individual characters in a cell.

Formatting with the Property Bar

The property bar contains a number of buttons and pull-down lists for formatting cells.

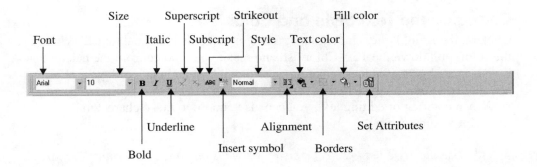

Some buttons are dimmed in Ready mode.

If you are in Ready mode, your selections from the bar affect all of the text in the cell or block of selected cells. When you click on the Bold button, for example, all of the text becomes bold. When you make a cell active, by the way, the buttons appear pressed down to indicate the formats that have been applied to the entire cell.

If you're entering information into a cell or editing a cell, you can use the property bar to format specific characters, just as you format text in WordPerfect 10.

Changing the Font and Text Size

To change the font or size of characters, make your selection from the Font and Size lists in the property bar.

If you are in Ready mode, your choice is applied to the entire cell. If you are entering or editing the information in a cell, your choices are applied to new characters that you type or to characters that you've selected.

Quattro Pro 10 also offers RealTime Preview. In Ready mode, point to an item in the Font or Size list to see how it affects the entire cell. If you are entering or editing text in a cell, this instant preview affects only text that's selected at the time.

When you make a cell active, by the way, the list boxes indicate the font and font size of the first character in the cell. To see the font or size applied to other characters in the cell, double-click on the cell to enter Edit mode, and then select the characters that you are interested in changing.

17

Changing the Text Style and Color

Click on the Bold, Italic, Underline, or Strikeout buttons to format text. To change the color, pull down the Text Color list, and make your choice from the palette that is displayed. Again, if you are entering or editing information in a cell, your choices are applied to new characters that you type or to characters that you've selected.

When entering or editing text, you can also choose to make characters subscript or superscript.

> **NOTE** *Use the Style list to select a style. A style is one or more formats that are applied at one time. Two built-in text styles are Heading 1 and Heading 2. Heading 1 is 18-point Arial bold; Heading 2 is 12-point Arial bold. You can create your own styles and add them to the list.*

Changing Cell Grid Lines and Fill Color

In Ready mode, you can also use the property bar to specify the type of lines around the cell or block of selected cells.

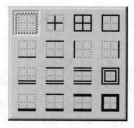

The icon on the Border button shows the lines that will be applied when you click on the button. To choose a different line, pull down the list next to the button to display these options. You can select various combinations of single and double lines, as well as outside borders and inside borders. The outside border choice adds the line to the outside of a selected range of cells. The inside border choice adds lines inside the selected range. Point to a choice for an instant preview of its effects, then click on the border to apply it. Your choice will also be placed on the face of the button as the new default.

To add a fill pattern to a cell or selected block of cells, pull down the Fill Color list, and make your choice from the palette that appears. To select a custom color, click on the More button in the palette to see additional color choices.

Inserting Special Characters

When you are entering or editing information in a cell, you can insert special symbols and other characters just as you learned for WordPerfect 10.

Select Symbol from the Insert menu, or click on the Insert Symbol button in the property bar, to see the Symbols dialog box. Pull down the Character Set list box, and select the character set. Click on the character that you want to insert, and then click on the Insert and Close button.

Quattro Pro 10 inserts the character at the position of the insertion point, in a size and style that matches the surrounding text. If you want to insert a number of characters, leave the dialog box on the screen, and move back and forth between your document and the dialog box. Drag the dialog box out of the way and then double-click on the character you want to insert, or choose the character and then click on Insert.

 See "Using Special Characters and Symbols" in Chapter 7 for additional information on this dialog box.

SpeedFormats

As you will soon learn, you can apply a number of different formats to an entry, such as the font and size, grid lines, and cell shading. Assigning each of the formats yourself develops your creativity but can be time consuming. The SpeedFormat command lets you completely format an entire block of cells, even the entire spreadsheet, by choosing from a list of designs. You can even create and save your own custom SpeedFormat so you can apply it again later with a few clicks of the mouse. Here's how:

1. Select the block that you want to format.

2. Click on the SpeedFormat button in the toolbar to display the dialog box shown in Figure 17-7. The Formats list box on the left contains the names of all of Quattro Pro 10's built-in designs. When you click on a design in the list, a sample spreadsheet using that style appears in the Example box.

3. Choose which aspects of the design will be applied to the cells. In the Include section, deselect the items that you do not want applied. For example, to accept all of the formats except the shading, click on the Shading option to deselect its checkbox.

17

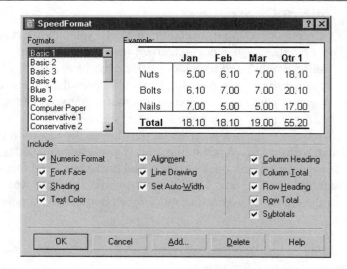

FIGURE 17-7   Applying an entire design to the spreadsheet with SpeedFormat

4. The items on the right of the Include section determine if special styles are applied to those parts of the spreadsheet. Deselect any element that you do not want formatted. If you deselect Column Heading, for example, the column headings will not be formatted differently from the body of the cells. As you choose options in the Include section, the example illustrates the results.

5. Click on OK to apply the format to the selected cells.

Creating Custom Formats

Once you've designed a spreadsheet, you can add the design to the SpeedFormat list. The next time you want to apply that combination of formats, you can select it from the list just as easily as you can select those built in by Quattro Pro 10. Use the following steps:

1. Start by selecting the block of cells that contain the design.

2. Click on the SpeedFormat button and then on Add.

3. In the dialog box that appears, type a name for the format and then confirm—or reenter or point to—the block of cells.

4. Click on OK. Your new format will be added to the list.

Copying Formats

Once you've gone to the trouble of selecting a combination of formats that you like for one cell, you do not have to make the selections all over again for some other cell. Just apply the same combination using QuickFormat.

 Click on the cell containing the formats you want to copy, then click on the QuickFormat button in the Standard toolbar. The shape of the mouse pointer changes to a paint roller. Then click on or drag over the cells you want to format. Quattro Pro 10 leaves QuickFormat on after you release the mouse so you can apply the same formats to other sections of text. To turn off the feature, click on the QuickFormat button again.

Formatting with Properties

Every format and style that you can apply is a property. Instead of using a variety of bars and menus to apply formats one at a time, you can select multiple formats in the Active Cells dialog box. You can also set the properties for a sheet or for the entire notebook, and even to customize Quattro Pro 10 itself.

Active Cell Properties for Cells

The Active Cells dialog box, shown in Figure 17-8, is used for formatting cells, rows, and columns. To display the box, use any of these techniques:

■ Choose Selection Properties from the Format menu.

■ Click on the Set Attributes button in the property bar (in Ready mode).

■ Right-click on the selected block, and choose Selection Properties from the QuickMenu.

■ Press F12

The coordinates of the block that will be affected are shown on the title bar. If that is not the block you want to format, close the dialog box, and start over by selecting the desired block. You cannot change the reference while the dialog box is open.

> **NOTE** *When you are entering or editing within a cell, clicking on Set Attributes displays the Text Font dialog box for changing the font, size, style, and color of text.*

Let's take a look at the properties that you can set.

Cell Font   Use the Cell Font tab to select the typeface, size, style, and color of the characters. The styles are Bold, Italic, Underline, and Strikeout. Use Strikeout to indicate information that you want to delete.

You can also select an accounting underline style that uses a single or double underline. With an accounting style, the underline extends the full width of the cell, not just under the characters within the cell.

Numeric Format   As you can see in Figure 17-8, the Numeric Format tab gives you more choices than the Style list in the property bar. When you choose some

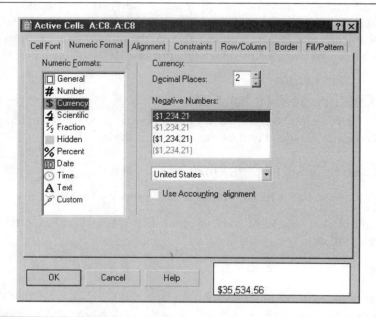

FIGURE 17-8   Using cell properties to format cells

items in the list, additional choices appear to the right. For example, clicking on Currency gives you the option of selecting the number of decimal places and the country, so Quattro Pro 10 can use the correct currency format.

The Hidden format prevents the contents from appearing in the cell, onscreen, and when printed. Values in the cell will still be used in formulas that reference it, the cell still appears in the Input Line, and you can still edit the cell to change its contents. The information in the cell reappears when you are in Edit mode but disappears again when you accept the entry.

Alignment   The alignment section on the property bar gives you choices for horizontal alignment—the position of text in relation to the right and left sides of the cell. Using the Alignment page in the Active Cells dialog box, you can also choose vertical alignment and choose to rotate text and to wrap a wide text entry so it fits within the cell borders.

The default vertical alignment is bottom. If you increase the row height or use a smaller font, you'll see that the characters appear nearer the bottom of the cell. Vertical Alignment lets you place the text in the center or near the top of the cell.

Long text entries run over into blank cells on the right. The Wrap Text option increases the row height and divides the long entry so it fits entirely within the cell. This differs from Reformatting Text, which divides the entry into more than one cell. The Join Cells option combines the selected cells into one.

Text orientation determines whether the characters appear across the cell (the default setting) or up and down, increasing the row height if needed. You can also select to rotate text a specific number of degrees, as shown here:

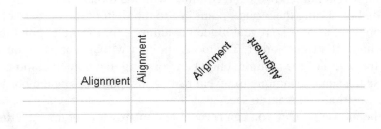

Constraints   The Constraints tab lets you protect a cell from being changed and allows you to specify the type of entry that will be accepted.

By default, all cells are set to be protected. To implement the protection, you need to turn it on using the Active Sheet dialog box (which you'll learn about next). In the Constraints tab, however, you designate whether or not you want the cells to be protected when page protection is turned on.

You can also specify if any type of information can be inserted into the cell, or if you just want labels or dates. General is the default setting. If you select Labels Only, whatever you type in the cell is treated as text. Numbers, formulas, dates, and functions appear just as you type them, aligned on the left and treated as text. If you select Dates Only, Quattro Pro 10 displays an error message if you do not enter a valid date into the cell.

Row/Column   These properties let you set the row height and column width to an exact measurement in points, inches, or centimeters. They are more exact than dragging the row with the mouse, but you may have to experiment to get the height correct for your text.

You can also choose to temporarily hide rows or columns that you do not want to appear onscreen or to print with the spreadsheet. This feature is useful when you've added some information for limited distribution, or notes and messages to yourself. The format is similar to the hidden numeric format, except that it affects entire rows and columns, not individual cells or blocks of cells. When hidden, values in the cells are still used to calculate formulas, but you cannot edit the contents until you reveal them.

To hide a row or column, click in any cell within it, and then display the Row/Column page of the Active Cells dialog box. Select Hide in the Row Options or Column Options section, depending on what you want to hide. When you close the dialog box, the rows or columns will no longer appear, but the remaining rows and columns will retain their original numbers and letters. If you hide row 5, for example, your visible rows will be numbered 1, 2, 3, 4, 6, 7, 8, and so on.

You can reveal hidden rows and columns with the mouse or using the Active Cells dialog box. Using the mouse, point just to the right of the border before the column you want to see. To reveal hidden column C, for example, point just to the right of column B's right border. The mouse pointer will appear as if you are changing the width of the column, but when you drag, the hidden column will appear. Use the same technique to reveal rows—just point below the border line before the row that you want to see.

With the mouse pointer you can reveal only one row or column at a time, and you have to resize the row or column as needed. To reveal more than one row or column, and to have it appear in its original width, use the QuickMenu or the Active Cells dialog box. Select a block that contains the hidden area. To redisplay row 5, for instance, select cells in rows 4 and 6. To use the QuickMenu, right-click on the selected rows or columns and choose Reveal. You can also display the Row/Column page, and then click on Reveal in the Row Options or Column Options section.

Border   One way to make a block of cells really stand out is to add custom borders and fill. The Border page of the dialog box is shown in Figure 17-9.

Use this dialog box to select the location, type, and colors of lines. Start by choosing where you want to place lines. The options in the Segment Selection list provide quick preset locations, such as outline, verticals, and horizontals. The All and Inside options are only available when you have first selected a block of more than one cell. The All button inserts lines around every cell in the selected block. The Outline button inserts lines only around the outside of the block. The Inside button inserts lines only on the inside.

You can add or delete lines, and change their size and color using the Custom Segments and Border Properties section. To specify the individual segments, click on the location in the illustration in the Custom Segments section that represents where you want to place the lines. Click on an arrow buttons to indicate a line in that position. When you select a segment, the arrow button appears pressed down and the arrow opposite it will be bold. This indicates that the line type and color that you choose from the Border Properties section will be applied to that line.

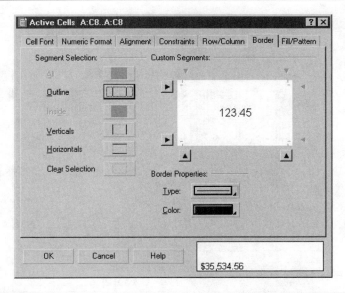

FIGURE 17-9   Choosing a border style and color

17

Next, choose the border type and color. Choose the no line option (the line with an X through it) from the Type list to remove lines from a cell; choose the blank option in the top-left corner of the Border Type list to cancel your selections. You can choose a color and line type for each individual line if you want. To give the block a shadow box look, for example, add a thin line to the top and left side, and add a thick line to the bottom and right.

Fill/Pattern   Use the Fill/Pattern page, shown in Figure 17-10, to add a color, shade of gray, blend of colors, or pattern that fills the selected block.

First choose the pattern that you want to apply—select the solid pattern on the left of the first row to add a solid color. Next, choose the pattern color from the Pattern Color list and the background color from Background Color list.

Active Sheet Properties

The Active Sheet dialog box controls the overall look of the sheet, rather than selected cells. To display the Active Sheet dialog box, shown in Figure 17-11, choose Sheet Properties from the Format menu, or right-click on the sheet tab and

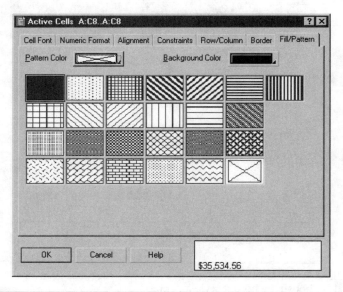

FIGURE 17-10   Adding a fill color or pattern to cells

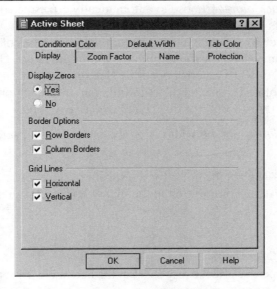

FIGURE 17-11   Using Sheet Properties to format the entire sheet

select Sheet Properties from the QuickMenu. Here's a recap of the option in this dialog box:

- *Display*—Display or hide zeros when entered or when they are the result of a calculation; display or hide row and column borders; display or hide the nonprintable grid lines without affecting borders you added yourself.

- *Zoom Factor*—Select a default magnification for the entire sheet, without affecting other sheets.

- *Name*—This is one of the most useful of the properties. Rather than stick with tabs A, B, C, and so on, you can name them for the type of spreadsheet that appears on the sheet—such as "Budget" or "Amortization."

- *Protection*—Turn on cell and object locking. Only cells with the Cell Property set for locking in the Constraints tab will be affected. By default, all of the cells are set for protection, so if you turn this on, you will not be able to enter or edit information until you turn it off again.

17

- *Conditional Color*—Choose to automatically color the contents of a cell based on its value or error condition. The options are shown in Figure 17-12. Enter a minimum and maximum value and the color that will appear when an entry is below the minimum, within the range, above the maximum, or when an error occurs. Click on each option you want, and choose a color. To turn on the coloring, you must click on the Enable box. This property is useful for displaying negative numbers in a special color.

- *Default Width*—Set the width of every column in characters, inches, or centimeters.

- *Tab Color*—Select the color for the sheet tab. To choose a color, deselect the Use System Color option in the dialog box, and then pick a color from the list.

Notebook Properties

The Notebook Properties affect every sheet in the notebook. To set these properties, choose Notebook Properties from the Format menu. You can also right-click on the notebook title. To display the notebook title bar, however, click on the restore button on the right of the menu bar to display the notebook in its own window.

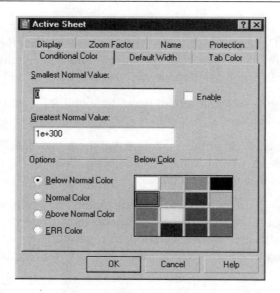

FIGURE 17-12   Using Conditional Color to color cells based on their contents

Here are the Notebook Properties:

■ *Display*—Chooses whether to display the scroll bars and sheet tabs, and whether to display or hide objects or just to show their outline.

■ *Zoom Factor*—Selects the default magnification for every sheet.

■ *Recalc Settings*—Determines how and when Quattro Pro 10 will recalculate your spreadsheet. The Mode section has three options. Background recalculates as you work, Automatic waits until you stop working, and Manual lets you recalculate by pressing F9. You can also select a calculation order. Natural first calculates formulas that are referenced by other formulas; Column-wise calculates all formulas in column A, then column B, and so on; Row-wise calculates all formulas in row 1, then row 2, and so on. If you have a lot of formulas and functions in your spreadsheet—and a slow computer—Background and Automatic recalculation may slow down your system's response. If you select Manual, however, remember to recalculate the spreadsheet before relying on any of its numbers. The # of Iterations option determines the number of times Quattro Pro 10 recalculates your spreadsheet when circular references are used. A circular reference occurs when formulas refer to each other. You can choose a number of iterations between 1 and 255. The Audit Error option will display the cell reference where a calculation problem first started.

■ *NBPalette*—Determines the palette of colors that you can select from when setting other properties that relate to color, such as text color.

■ *Macro Library*—Allows the storage of macros in a special file, called the Macro Library, rather than in your notebook. The library will be available for every notebook. Select Yes, and Quattro Pro 10 automatically searches the macro library when a macro you are running is not in the active notebook.

■ *Password Level*—Uses a password to protect a notebook. Refer to "Protecting Your Spreadsheet" later in this chapter.

■ *System*—Converts a notebook into a system notebook—a special notebook that you can hide but keep open even when all other notebooks are closed. The system notebook becomes a convenient location to store macros and other objects that you want available at all times. To convert a notebook into a system notebook, choose Yes for this property, and then hide the notebook with the Window Hide command.

17

- *Summary*—Stores a title, subject, the author's name, keywords, and comments about the notebook for later reference.

- *Statistics*—Displays the notebook's name and path, when it was created and last saved, who saved it, and the revision number.

Application Properties

When you want to customize the way Quattro Pro 10 works, set Application Properties. Right-click on the Quattro Pro 10 title bar, and choose Settings from the QuickMenu.

Here's a review:

- *Display*—Displays the input line, formula markers, file history, scroll indicators, shortcut keys, comment markers, Quick Tips, and Real-Time Preview.

- *International*—Selects the format of currency, punctuation, dates, times, country, and whether negative values are displayed with a minus sign or in parentheses.

- *Macro*—Chooses which elements of the screen appear while a macro runs. By default, all menus, dialog boxes, and other elements used to record the macro are suppressed so they do not appear as the macro performs its steps. You can choose to suppress just panels (menus and dialog boxes) or windows. Suppressing everything allows macros to run faster and without distracting elements appearing onscreen. You also use this tab to choose which element of the screen is made active when you press the slash key (/) and what macro runs automatically when you start Quattro Pro 10.

- *File Options*—Selects the default directory used for the Save and Open dialog boxes, and a notebook that opens each time you open Quattro Pro 10. You can choose to automatically save your work at a specified interval, and to display the complete path with the filename in the title bar. You can also choose to use enhanced file dialog boxes.

- *General*—Customizes some of the ways that Quattro Pro 10 operates. You can turn off the Undo feature, use the key combinations from Quattro Pro 10 for DOS, and choose the direction to move the cell selector when you press ENTER. The Mathematical Formula Entry option lets you start formulas without first entering the plus sign. If you choose this option, however, entering a phone number or social security number will be seen as a formula. The number 555-1234, for example, will appear as -679. You can also turn off Fit-As-You-Go, Calc-As-You-Go, QuickType, and the Cell Reference Checker. The Cell Drag And Drop Delay Time option sets the interval at which drag-and-drop mode is activated when pointing at cells with the mouse.

■ *Compatibility*—Determines some of the general ways that Quattro Pro 10 operates to make it more compatible with other versions of Quattro Pro or with Microsoft Excel. You can also select a custom set of options. Settings include the default file type to save to and to filter for in the Open file dialog box. You can choose the syntax of 3-D block references (the choices are A . . . B:A1 . . . B2 or A:A1 . . . B:B2) and to use letter or numbers on the sheet tabs, and you can set the default number of sheets in new notebooks. You can also set the default number of columns and rows in the notebook.

NOTE	*You can also set the application properties by choosing Settings from the Tools menu.*

Customizing Menus and Toolbars

In addition to changing the appearance of your spreadsheet on the screen, you can customize the look of Quattro Pro itself. You can adjust the appearance of the menu bar, toolbar, property bar, and application bar, and you can even customize the appearance of individual buttons. You can also save various combinations of bars and buttons by creating custom workspaces.

The general procedure for customizing a menu or toolbar is:

1. Right-click on the item you want to customize.

2. Point to Customize on the QuickMenu.

3. Select an option to customize.

If you right-click on a menu name, you can choose from these three options:

■ Menu Item

■ Main Menu

■ Workspace

17

If you right-click on a toolbar button you can choose these options:

- ■ Toolbar Item
- ■ Notebook Toolbar (or whatever toolbar or property bar you are pointing to)
- ■ Workspace

 The Menu Item and Toolbar Item options do not appear if you right-click on a blank area of the menu bar or toolbar.

Selecting a Customize option displays a submenu of choices. For example, for individual items, such as a menu item or toolbar item, you can select from these options:

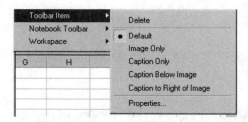

The choices for customizing a toolbar, rather than a specific item within the toolbar, are shown here:

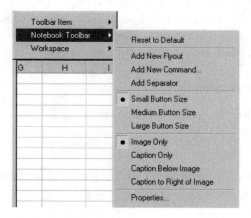

The Add New Flyout command, by the way, inserts a new button that offers a list, similar to the Zoom button. You can then add commands to the button to access them from the toolbar. When you are working with a menu, the option is Add New Menu.

The Properties item on the QuickMenu opens the Options dialog box with the Customization option is selected. (You can also open this dialog box by selecting Customize on the Tools menu.) If you chose Properties from the Main Menu or Toolbar QuickMenu option, the Toolbar page is displayed. If you chose Properties from the Menu Item or Toolbar Item QuickMenu option, the Commands page is displayed.

The Toolbar page of the Options dialog box is shown in Figure 17-13.

In the large list box, select the toolbars you want to display. To change the appearance of the toolbar, select it in the list box and then set the size and border style of buttons, and their default appearance. The remaining options depend on the selected bar. For toolbars other than the application bar, you can select to show the bar title when the bar is floating on the page. For the application bar, you can select the number of lines it contains and its position on the page—either at the top or bottom of the screen.

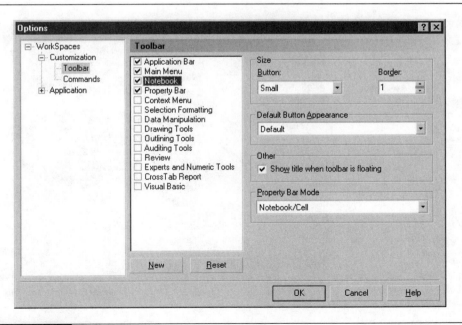

FIGURE 17-13   Selecting and setting toolbar options

The Commands page of the Options dialog, shown in Figure 17-14, lets you add and delete toolbar buttons, customize the QuickTip that appears when you point to the button, assign a shortcut key to perform the function, and edit the actual appearance of the button's icon.

The Currently Available On list on the General tab shows on which toolbars or properties bars the button is found.

To add a button to a toolbar or property bar, follow these steps:

1. Click on Toolbars under Customization, and select the checkbox for the toolbar or property bar to which you want to insert the button. For the property bar, also select the mode that you wish to customize. This displays the bar on the screen.

2. Click Commands under Customization, and click the General tab if it is not already selected.

3. Click to pull down the command list and select the category of the command you want to add.

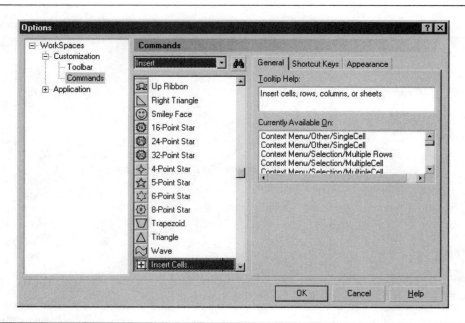

FIGURE 17-14   Customizing bars and buttons

4. Click on the command in the large list box.

5. Drag the command to the position you want to place it on the property bar.

 Remove a button by opening the Options dialog box and dragging the button off of the toolbar or property bar.

Protecting Your Notebook

The Password level setting in the Active Notebook Properties dialog box lets you determine the extent to which your notebook is protected. The options are:

- *None*

- *Low* requires a password to display cell formulas

- *Medium* requires a password to open the notebook unhidden

- *High* requires a password to open the notebook

- *Edit With Controls Only* requires the user to edit the notebook using advanced form controls

 To quickly save and protect a notebook, select the Password Protect checkbox in the Save File dialog box. When you click on Save, a box appears for you to enter the password. This applies High-level security to the notebook.

To specify a password, select an option other than None and then click OK. In the box that appears, type the desired password and click OK. Reenter the password to confirm it and click OK again.

If you later want to turn off password protection, open the notebook, and display the Active Notebook Properties dialog box. Click Disable Password, enter your password and then click OK. Use the Change Password button if you need to change the password assigned to the notebook.

Formatting with Styles

The SpeedFormat dialog box is handy when you want to create a style for an entire spreadsheet. Often, however, you'll want a style for a section or element of a spreadsheet, such as a heading, grand total, or note. A style is merely a collection of properties saved under one name. You can apply all of the properties in the collection by selecting the style name.

Quattro Pro 10 already comes with the Heading 1 and Heading 2 styles. You can modify these styles and create your own so they are available in the Style list of the property bar.

The easiest way to create a style is to first apply all of the formats to a cell and use the cell as a pattern. The following steps show this process:

1. Click in the cell, and then choose Define Styles from the Format menu to see the dialog box shown in Figure 17-15.

2. Type a name for the style, and then click on the Merge button.

3. In the dialog box that appears, click on Cell.

4. If the cell reference in the Select Cell box is incorrect, point to or type the cell reference.

5. Click on OK

The formats applied to the cell will be used to create the new style.

To create a style from scratch, type a name for it in the Styles dialog box, and then select options from the dialog boxes that appear when you click on the Alignment, Format, Protection, Line Drawing, Shading, Font, or Text Color button. To apply the selected options, make sure the checkbox next to the button is selected. You can also choose to use the style as the default for all new notebooks.

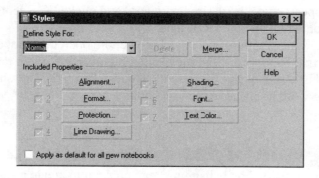

FIGURE 17-15   Creating your own styles

You can delete any style except the Normal style. You can also copy styles to other notebooks. To delete a style, select Styles from the Format menu, click on the style name in the list, and then click on Delete.

To apply your style, pull down the Style list on the property bar, and click on the style name.

Creating Numeric Formats

Quattro Pro 10 offers a variety of numeric formats, but you still might have your special requirements. You can create your own custom formats for numbers, dates, and times, so they can be easily selected from the list.

You can also designate conditional formats to change the way the value is displayed, or to perform a math operation on the value, based on its contents.

To create a format, follow these steps.

1. Select the cells that you want to format.

2. Right-click on the cells, and choose Selection Properties from the QuickMenu.

3. Click on the Numeric Format tab, if necessary.

4. Click on Custom in the Numeric Formats list. A list box labeled "Custom" is displayed.

5. Click Add to display the Add Format dialog box, shown in Figure 17-16.

NOTE *To base a new format on an existing custom one, select it in the list, and then click on Add. Use the Edit button to modify an existing custom format.*

1. Type a name for the format.

2. Delete any existing conditions that you do not want included in the style. Select it in the list box on top of the dialog box and click Delete.

3. Create a condition in which to apply the format.

4. Specify formats to use when the condition is true.

17

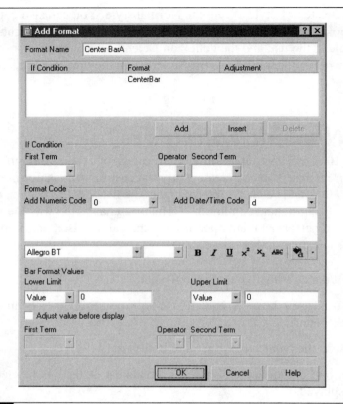

FIGURE 17-16   Creating a custom numeric format

5. Enter any format codes from the two list boxes in the Format Codes section. You use the codes to specify how the value appears in the cell. The first list contains codes for text and numeric entries, the second list for date and time entries. The meanings of some of the codes are shown in Table 17-1.

6. Specify any adjustment to make to the value.

7. Click Add.

With conditional formats, certain formats will be applied when a condition is met, such as when the cell contains a certain value. To establish a condition, start by using the options in the If Condition section of the Add Format dialog box.

Symbol	Action
0	Placeholder for any digit (displays a 0 if empty)
9	Displays a digit in that location
,	Uses a thousands separator
.	Decimal point separator
E- or e-	Uses scientific notation, with minus sign before negative exponents
E+ or e+	Uses scientific notation, with minus or plus sign
?//M	Converts decimals into a fraction in which the denominator will be no larger than the maximum value that you specify.
?//	Converts decimals into a fraction in which the denominator will always be the value that you specify.
?//R	Converts decimals into a fraction in which the denominator will be rounded to the maximum value that you specify.
#	Fills the cell with the character that you specify.
_	Skips a space for a character you specify.
l	Specify a character to display and a character to skip a space for.
Left Bar	Converts a value into a graphic bar on the left of the cell.
Center Bar	Converts a value into a graphic bar in the center of the cell.
Right Bar	Converts a value into a graphic bar on the right of the cell.
d or D	Shows the day of the month in one- or two-digit numbers
dd or DD	Shows the day of the month in two digits, as in 05
1wday, 1Wday, 1WDAY	Shows the day of the week abbreviated to the number of characters that you specify, all lowercase, initial capitalized, or all uppercase
weekday, Weekday, WEEKDAY	Shows the complete day of the week all lowercase, initial capitalized, or all uppercase
m, M, or Mo	Shows the month in one or two digits (1–12)
mm, MM, or Mmo	Shows the month in two digits
mon, Mon, MON	Shows the month as a three-character abbreviation, all lowercase, initial capitalized, or all uppercase
month, Month, MONTH	Shows the complete name of the month all lowercase, initial capitalized, or all uppercase
1mon, 1Mon, 1MON	Shows the month abbreviated to the number of characters that you specify, all lowercase, initial capitalized, or all uppercase
yy or YY	Shows the year in two digits

TABLE 17-1   Codes for creating numeric formats

17

Symbol	Action
yyyy or YYYY	Shows the year in four digits
h or H	Shows the hour in one or two digits using 24-hour format. Follow by ampm or AMPM for 12-hour format
hh or HH	Shows the hour in two digits; include ampm or AMPM for 12-hour format
Mi	Shows the minutes in one or two digits
Mmi	Shows the minutes in two digits
s or S	Shows the seconds in one or two digits
ss or SS	Shows the minutes in two digits
A, a, AM	Uses 12-hour format displaying either AM or PM
*	When the entry is shorter than the column width, fills the remainder of the cell to the right of the last character with asterisks
"	Displays the characters enclosed in single quotation marks; use when you want to display a character that is also used as a format code (quotation marks are not needed for characters not used as codes)
\	Performs the same function as quotation marks but only for the single character following the backslash

TABLE 17-1   Codes for creating numeric formats *(continued)*

In the First Term list, choose Value, This Cell, or Other Cell. For example, if you want to create a condition that compares the cell with another, choose This Cell. If you select Value, you can enter a specific value to look for, or if you choose Other Cell, you can enter or point to another cell to use for the condition.

Next, select an operator such as equal to or greater than.

Then choose Value, This Cell, or Other Cell from the Second Term list, and complete the condition. In this example, the condition determined that the value in the selected cell is greater than cell A10:

Choose a format for the cell when it meets the condition, including font, font size, and other attributes, then click Add to add the condition. You can continue to add conditions to test for other values. Quattro Pro 10 applies the conditions in the order they are listed, with new conditions added to the top of the list. To insert a condition in another position, select the condition you want to follow it, and click Insert. Use the Delete button to delete a selected condition from the list.

You can also choose to change the value in the selected cell or another cell in the spreadsheet when a condition is true. Enable the checkbox labeled "Adjust Value Before Display." Then specify the change to make by choosing from the options in that section of the dialog box, just as you learned for creating conditions. The only difference is that the operators are not comparisons but mathematical—letting you add, subtract, multiply, or divide values.

The Bar Format Values let you adjust when bar formats are displayed. There are three bar formats available in the Add Numeric Code list: Left Bar, Center Bar, and Right Bar. Each format displays a color rectangle in the cell, in the specified position, whose width indicates the cell value. The smaller the value, the narrower the bar. When you create a bar format, you can specify the lower and upper values that will be represented by bars. The cell will appear blank when you enter a value below the lower limit or above the higher limit.

Your custom format will be added to the Custom Formats list and will be available for that notebook or any notebook that is open at the same time. To apply a custom format, display the Cell Properties dialog box, click on Custom in the Numeric Format tab, and then choose the format from the Custom Formats list.

Try It Out

Now it is your turn to try out your QuattroPro editing and formatting skills. Just follow these steps.

1. Open the Calls notebook that you created in Chapter 16. If you did not save the notebook, see Figure 16-10 to create it.

2. Select cells H2 to H9.

3. Hold down the CTRL key and select cells A9 to G9.

4. Press DEL. The values displayed in the cells are removed, but the comment marker still appears in cell H9. To remove the comment, you have to use the Clear feature.

17

Right-click on the selected area and choose Clear from the QuickMenu. The comment is now removed from the cell.

Now suppose that several values were mistakenly not added to the information in row 3, for Wing. Rather than manually make the correction to each of the cells, we'll use the Paste Special feature to make the calculations for us.

5. Click cell B10.

6. Enter these values in cells B10 to F10. These represent the adjustments we want to make to the cells in row 3: adding 5 to cell B3, 2 to cell C3, and so on.

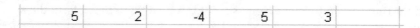

5	2	-4	5	3	

7. Select cells B10 to F10 and click the Cut button in the toolbar.

8. Click in cell B3.

9. Select Paste Special from the File menu.

10. Click Add and then Paste. The values are added and the totals recalculated.

Now let's transpose some of the cells in the table to use a bar format that graphically shows a pattern over the week.

11. Select cells A2 to F7, click on the Copy button in the toolbar.

12. Click in cell A12.

13. Select Paste Special from the File menu.

14. Click Transpose Rows and Columns, and then Paste. The resulting pasted cells appear like this:

	Wing	Beebe	Chesin	Udel	Paul	
Mon	90	83	42	10	32	
Tue	72	60	28	11	20	
Wed	68	7	97	55	15	
Thu	63	18	45	58	97	
Fri	65	18	53	64	14	

15. Select cells B13 to F17.

16. Right-click on the selected area and choose Selection Properties from the QuickMenu.

17. Click the Numeric Format tab.

18. Select Custom in the Numeric Formats list.

19. Select Center Bar in the Custom list and then click OK. As shown here, you can now look down the column and see the pattern for each person. It is clear from the example, that the values for Wing tend to decrease through the week, while those for Udel increase.

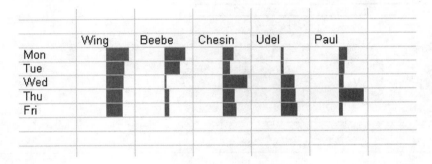

20. Drag over row numbers 1 to 3 to select all three rows.

21. Right-click on the selected rows and choose Insert Cells from the QuickMenu. Three new rows are inserted at the top of the spreadsheet.

22. Now add and format the text shown in Figure 17-17, and choose options from the SpeedFormat dialog box to customize sections of the spreadsheet. In Figure 17-17, for example, the Basic 3 style was applied to cells A5 through G11, and the Sculpted 1 style to cells A15 to G21. In both cases, the Numeric Format option was disabled in the Include section to retain the original numeric formats.

   Use the Save As command from the File menu to save the spreadsheet under a new name.

17

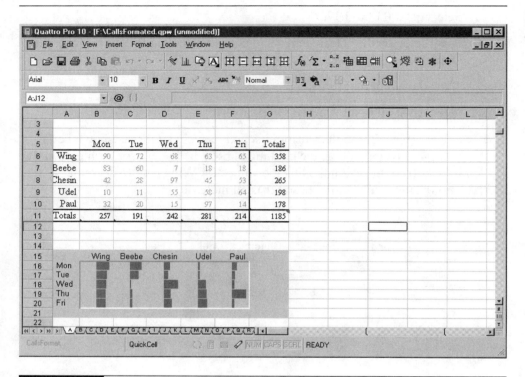

FIGURE 17-17 Completed spreadsheet

Chapter 18

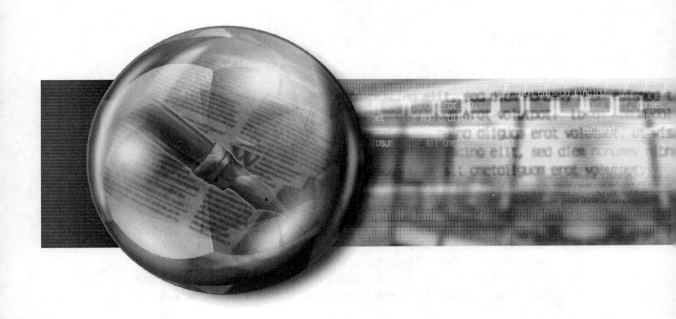

Working with Blocks, Windows, and Notebooks

///////////////

Sometimes you need to make sweeping changes to a spreadsheet or take actions that affect entire groups of cells, multiple sheets, or the whole notebook. With Quattro Pro 10 you don't have to repeat your work on individual cells or sheets. In this chapter, you will learn how to use names to quickly refer to sections of your spreadsheet, set up your sheets for printing, create groups of sheets, and use other timesaving techniques.

Cell Names

Point mode makes referring to cells and ranges of cells easier than typing coordinates, but it can be inconvenient when you need to scroll to a distant area of the spreadsheet or refer to the same cell or range frequently. You can try to remember the references of cells that you use often, but who can keep all of those numbers in their head?

The solution to this common problem is using *cell names*—giving an easy-to-remember name to a cell or group of cells. When you need to refer to the cells in a formula or dialog box, just use the name. You can even display a list of your cell names to make them easier to recall.

Not only are names easier to remember than coordinates, they make more sense. After creating a large spreadsheet, you may forget what the formula +G4–H5 means, but not the formula +Gross–Expenses. The names show you what your formula represents and make it easier to track down spreadsheet errors. Quattro Pro 10 won't necessarily know, for example, if you enter the wrong coordinates in a formula, but it will warn you if you use a name that hasn't been defined.

To name a group of cells, follow these steps:

1. Select the group of cells you want to name. Remember, you can also name a single selected cell.

2. Choose Name from the Insert menu, and click on Name Cells to see the Cell Names dialog box listing any existing cell names.

3. In the Name text box, type a name for the cell or group of cells that is not already assigned.

4. Click on Add, and then close the dialog box.

A cell name can be up to 63 characters long, including numbers, letters, spaces, and most punctuation marks. You can't use the operator characters (+, _, *, /, ^, =, <, >, #, or &) because they are reserved for formulas; you also cannot use the dollar sign and the opening and closing parentheses. Don't use any numbers or names that are cell coordinates, such as A1. Cell names are not case sensitive, but they always appear uppercase in the input line.

You can have as many cell names as you need in a spreadsheet, and their ranges can overlap. The same cells can be in more than one name. In fact, the same set of cells can have more than one name.

 When you click in a cell that has its own name, or select a range of cells that are named, the name appears in place of the coordinates in the Navigation button.

Using Cell Names

When you want to use a cell name in a formula or dialog box, just enter its name where you would otherwise type coordinates or use Point mode.

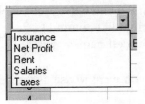

To see a list of cell names when you are in the input line, press the F3 key, or pull down the list box next to the cell address on the left of the input line. The F3 key, however, works this way only when you are ready to enter a cell coordinate, such as after a plus sign, an operator, or an opening parenthesis. Otherwise, pressing F3 opens the File Save dialog box. Click on the cell name in the pull-down list to insert it into the formula, or double-click on it in the Cell Name dialog box that opened when you pressed F3.

 When you are not entering or editing information in a cell, use the pull-down list in the input line to quickly move to or select a cell or group of cells. Pull down the list, and then click on the name representing the cells you want to move to or select.

18

Changing a Cell Name

To rename a cell, you must first delete the name and then start over by redefining the same cell. Delete a name by selecting it in the Cell Names dialog box and clicking on Delete. (Click on Delete All to remove all of the names from the spreadsheet.)

Deleting a cell name does not affect formulas. Quattro Pro 10 automatically replaces the names with their references wherever the name appears in a formula. However, it does not automatically replace the coordinates when you give a name to a referenced cell or group of cells.

It is easier to change the reference that a name represents. Display the Cell Names dialog box, and click on the name you want to reassign. Enter the cell coordinates in the Cell(s) text box, and then click on Add. The name now refers to the new cell.

Creating Cell Names from Labels

It is common to have a number of cells that correspond to a series of labels, as shown in Figure 18-1. You can automatically assign the labels as the names for their corresponding values. In the example, each label in column C would become the name for the value to its right in column D.

Here's how to use labels as cell names:

1. Select the labels that you want to use as the cell names. They must be labels, not values.

2. Point to Name in the Insert menu, and click on Name Cells.

3. Click the Labels button to display the dialog box shown here:

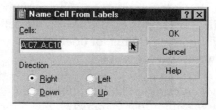

4. Select the position of the cells you want to name in relation to the labels. In the example, you'd select Right.

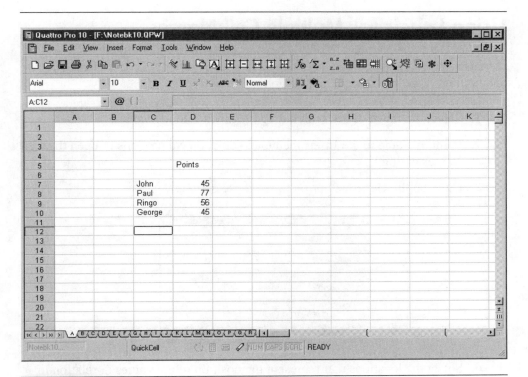

FIGURE 18-1 Assigning labels as cell names

5. Click OK. Each of the labels will now be listed as cell names.

6. Close the Cell Names dialog box.

If you later change the text of a label, the cell name does not change automatically. You must still use the old label as the name. To change the name, you must delete it and assign a new one.

If error messages appear when you use one of the names, check the label carefully for extra spaces before or after your label text. For instance, you may accidentally enter a blank space after a label when you're typing it in the cell. You may not notice the space in the cell, but Quattro Pro 10 will include the space in the cell name. If you later leave out the space when typing the cell name, Quattro Pro 10 will display a message indicating that the cell name does not exist.

18

Using Labels for Multiple Cell Names

The Labels button can be used only when naming single cells immediately next to the label. You can also assign label names to a range of cells, or to combine a row and column label into one cell name. Follow these steps:

1. Select the range of cells, including the labels and the values.

2. Point to Name in the Insert menu, and click on Name Cells to open the Cell Names dialog box.

3. Click on the Generate button to see these options:

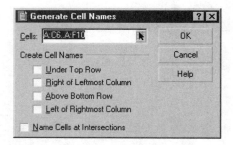

4. Select the locations that represent the position of the values in relation to the labels.

5. Click on OK to close the Generate Cell Names dialog box, and then close the Cell Names dialog box.

The most important step in this procedure is selecting the correct location options. For example, to use a label as the name for a group of cells in the row to its right, click on Right of Leftmost Column. To use a column header as a label for cells below it, click on Under Top Row.

You can also combine a row and column heading to reference a single cell. For example, suppose you have a value in the row labeled "Wages" and in the column labeled "Qtr 1". Select the range, choose both Under Top Row and Right of Leftmost Column, and click on Name Cells at Intersections. The value at the intersection of those labels will now be named "Qtr1_Wages".

Displaying a Cell Name Table

The address list on the input bar and the F3 key make it easy to list your cell names. As a more visual reminder, you can display a table directly on your spreadsheet listing the cell names and their coordinates. To do so, follow these steps:

1. Display the Cell Names dialog box, and click on the Output button.

2. Select the top-left cell where you want the name table to appear on your spreadsheet. Quattro Pro 10 overwrites existing information when it displays the table, so make sure enough blank cells are below and in the column to the right to display all of the names and their references.

3. Click on OK, and then close the dialog box to display the table. The cell names will be in the first column, sorted alphabetically.

If you add, rename, or delete cell names, Quattro Pro 10 does not update the table automatically. Create the table again in the same location to replace it.

Page Setup

The default print settings are fine if you're printing a draft copy of a small spreadsheet. When you're printing a spreadsheet for distribution, however, you may want to adjust the page size and margins, or add other elements such as headers and footers. A *header* is text that prints on the top of each page; a *footer* prints on the bottom of each page. You can enter your own text into the header and footer, and choose built-in elements such as the date, page number, or filename.

You can adjust the margins, and add headers and footers, directly in the spreadsheet in Page view. Those, and other page options, are also accessible in the Page Setup dialog box.

> **TIP** *If you want to print a copy of the spreadsheet for reference showing formulas, choose Formulas from the View menu. Choose Comments from the View menu to print comments.*

Using Page View

To display your spreadsheet in Page view, select Page from the View menu. In Page view, you'll see the margin guidelines as well as elements such as headers and footers.

To change the margins, point to a guideline so the mouse appears as a two-directional arrow, and drag.

> **NOTE** *You can also set margins by dragging margin lines in Print Preview mode.*

To enter a header directly into the spreadsheet, right-click in any margin area—the area outside of the guidelines—to see the options shown here:

Select Create Header from the QuickMenu to display a header area between the margin and the spreadsheet, indicated by another guideline, and the header/footer property bar:

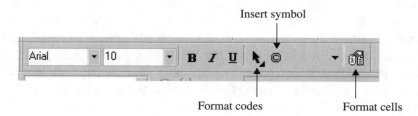

Type your header, using the Insert Symbol button in the property bar to insert special characters, and the property bar lists and Format Cells button to format characters. To later edit the header, double-click on the header area to place the insertion point there.

> **NOTE** *Use the same technique to create a footer, but choose Create Footer from the QuickMenu.*

You can also select special codes, explained in Table 18-1, from the Format Codes list in the property bar, or by typing the codes directly into the header preceded by the # symbol. For example, enter **Page #p of #P** to display Page 1 of 4, or **File #f printed on #d** for the notebook name and date it was printed. You can use any combination of the codes in the header, footer, or both.

The vertical bar (|), usually entered with SHIFT-\, works like a tab. Enter one to center text and two to align text on the right. To center the notebook name and its full path, for instance, enter |#F.

| TIP | *To remove a header or footer, right-click in the margin area, and select Remove Header or Remove Footer.* |

Using the Page Setup Dialog Box

You can set even more page options using the Spreadsheet Page Setup dialog box shown in Figure 18-2. To display the box, select Page Setup from the File menu, or right-click in the margin area and choose Page Setup from the QuickMenu.

Code	Function
		Centers or right-aligns text
N	Prints the remainder of the header or footer on a second line
F	Inserts the name of the notebook
F	Inserts the name and path of the notebook
P	Inserts the page number
p+*n*	Inserts the current page number plus a number *n*
P	Inserts the number of pages being printed
P+*n*	Inserts the number of pages plus a number *n*
D	Inserts the current date in the Short International format as set in the Application properties
D	Inserts the current date in the Long International format as set in the Application properties
Ds	Inserts the current date in the Windows Short Date format
Ds	Inserts the current date in the Windows Long Date format
T	Inserts the current time in the Short International format as set in the Application properties
T	Inserts the current time in the Long International format as set in the Application properties
Ts	Inserts the current time in the Windows Short Time format
Ts	Inserts the current time in the Windows Long Time format

TABLE 18-1   Codes for creating headers and footers

18

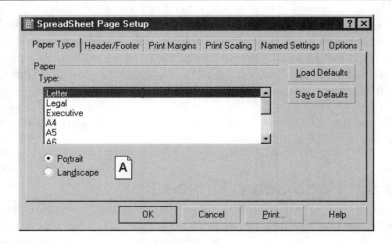

FIGURE 18-2   Spreadsheet Page Setup dialog box

In the Paper Type page, select the paper size and orientation. Your choices depend on the printer you have installed in Windows. Use landscape orientation when you want to print more columns on a page.

To add a header or footer, click on the Header/Footer tab. Click on the Create checkbox in the Header or Footer section, and then enter the text that you want to appear on your printout. Use the Font button to change the font and size of the text, and use the codes shown in Table 18-1 to enter page numbers and other elements. Use the Header and Footer height settings to control the distance between the header and the first row, and between the footer and the last row. The exact position of the first row, then, is the sum of the top margin and header settings.

Setting Margins

The margin settings contribute to determining the number of rows and columns that fit on the page. Click on Print Margins in the Spreadsheet Page Setup dialog box, and then enter the top, bottom, left, and right margins. As you highlight a measurement, a line darkens in the drawing that indicates the page, and an arrow points to the line, showing you the margin you are setting.

The top margin determines the distance between the top of the paper and the header; the bottom margin determines the distance between the bottom of the page and the footer. Enter your settings in the same unit of measurement that is displayed, inches or centimeters.

Many laser printers cannot print very close to the edge of the page and need at least a quarter-inch margin. If you get a printer error, or some text does not print properly, increase the margins.

When your spreadsheet is more than one page long, Quattro Pro 10 inserts soft page breaks to divide it into pages. If you are using continuous paper or want to fill as much of the page as possible and let your printer change pages, deselect Break Pages in the Margins tab. This will also turn off all headers and footers.

Printing Large Spreadsheets   Quattro Pro 10 prints a large spreadsheet by printing as many columns as can fit on the first page, and all of the rows in those columns on consecutive pages. It then goes back to the first row and begins printing the next series of columns.

If you want your pages divided differently, add hard page breaks where you want one page to end and another to begin. To insert a hard page break, click in the row where you want the break to occur, choose Page Break from the Insert menu and select Create.

In Page view and Page Break View, you can also change page breaks relative to rows and columns by dragging the page break lines. These are the solid slides that represent the ends of the pages. Drag a horizontal page break line, for example, to adjust the number of rows on the page. Drag a vertical page break line to adjust the number of columns.

Changing the Print Scale

By adjusting the font size, margins, column width, and row height, you can determine how much of a spreadsheet prints on a page. You can also reduce or enlarge the entire printout without changing any other formats. Reducing the print size fits more cells on each page but makes it more difficult to read. If you've already adjusted margins and other settings and still need to fit an extra row or column on the page, try reducing the scale slightly.

To change the scale, use the Print Scaling option in the Page Setup dialog box. In the Scale To box, enter a setting less than 100 to reduce the printout, more than 100 to enlarge it. To scale the spreadsheet to fit on a specific number of pages, click the Shrink To option button, and then enter the number of pages wide and high. Quattro Pro 10 will automatically reduce the scale to print the spreadsheet on the designated number of pages.

Scaling affects the size of all characters and graphics, as well as the header and footer margin settings. Other page margins will not be affected.

Page Setup Options

The Options tab of the dialog box lets you further customize your printout. Headings are rows or columns that print on every page. If you have a long spreadsheet, labels in the top row do not print on the top of every page, so readers may have difficulty relating information in the columns. To repeat a row on each page, enter the coordinates of at least one cell in the row in the Top Heading box. To print several rows as a heading, select cells in all of the rows. To repeat a column, enter cells in the columns you want to repeat in the Left Heading box. When you specify the print range, do not include the heading rows or columns. If you do, they will print twice.

The choices in the Print Options group determine what elements of the spreadsheet appear on paper.

- *Cell Formulas* prints the actual formulas in the cells, not their calculated results. This is handy for a backup copy of your spreadsheet; however, headings, grid lines, and row and column borders will not print at the same time, and groups of cells will not be centered.

- *Gridlines* prints the normally nonprinted grid lines. Don't use this option if you've already added your own grid lines using line drawing.

- *Row/Column Borders* prints the row letters and column numbers. This is a good choice if you're printing a reference or backup copy.

- *Center Cells* centers your printout between the left and right margins. Normally, the first column prints at the left margin.

If your print range includes two or more noncontiguous groups of cells, you can determine how they are spaced on the page. The Lines setting in Print Between Selections determines the number of blank lines to place between groups. The Lines setting in the Print Between 3D Sheets group determines the number of lines to print between groups on each page. To start each group of cells on a new page, click on Page Advance.

Saving and Restoring Print Settings

If you change your mind about Print Options or Page Setup settings, you can quickly return to Quattro Pro 10's default values by selecting the Load Defaults button in either dialog box.

Your print and page setup settings only affect the current notebook. If you want to change the default for the current notebook click on the Save Defaults button in either dialog box. Keep in mind that your own settings will now be used when you click on the Load Defaults button.

Saving Named Group Settings

If you use a variety of setups, you can save each as a group and then load the group by name when you need to. The group includes the settings in the Print, and Page Setup dialog boxes. Save your settings under a name using these steps:

1. Display the Page Setup dialog box.

2. Click on Named Settings.

3. In the New Set text box, type a group name, and then click on Add. Click on Update if you want to change an existing group.

4. Click on OK.

5. Save the notebook. Unlike default settings, which are globally available to all notebooks, named groups are stored with the notebook itself.

When you want to use a group, click on the Named Settings tab, select the group you want to use, and then click on Use.

Preventing Titles from Scrolling

As you scroll around a sheet, the row and column labels will scroll out of view. So if you scroll down the page, for example, you will no longer see the labels that identify the purpose of each column. Likewise, as you scroll to the right, you will no longer see the labels that identify the rows. By locking titles into place, you prevent the labels on rows or columns from scrolling out of view, making it easier to enter information into large spreadsheets.

18

To lock titles from scrolling, use these steps:

1. Make sure you are in Draft view, and then select the uppermost cell that you do not want to be locked. For example, to lock row 1 and column A, click in cell B2. To lock just rows 1 and 2, but no columns, click in cell A3.

2. Pull down the View menu, and click on Locked Titles. (Click on the same option again later to unlock the titles.)

A blue line appears indicating the locked rows and columns.

Locking titles prevents them from scrolling, but it does not affect your printout. The locked titles do not print on every page even though they always appear onscreen. To repeat the titles on each page, set the Top Heading and Left Heading sheet options.

Creating Groups

In Chapter 15 you learned how to select a 3-D group of cells by clicking on the page tabs while holding down the SHIFT key. These groups are temporary because they remain in effect only until you take some action on the group, such as applying a format or using QuickFill. If you want to use a group periodically, or add or delete information to multiple pages at one time, then name the group of pages, and turn on Group mode.

For example, suppose you want to enter the same label in a cell in the first ten pages of the notebook. Or perhaps you want to use Point mode to quickly select the same group of cells on several pages. Rather than repeat your actions on each page every time, you can create a group so Quattro Pro 10 will duplicate your actions on every page for you.

Create a group by selecting the pages that you want to include and then giving the group a name. Here's how:

1. Click on the first tab of the sheets that you want to group.

2. Hold down the SHIFT key, and click on the last tab of the sheets you want to include in the group.

3. Pull down the Insert menu, point to Name, and click on Name Group of Sheets to display the Define/Modify Group dialog box shown in Figure 18-3.

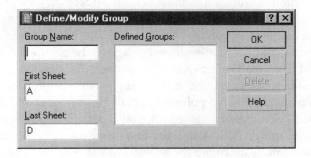

FIGURE 18-3   Creating a group name

4. Type a name for the group using the same rules as you used for naming cell names.

5. Confirm that the correct tabs are shown in the First Sheet and Last Sheet boxes—correct them if necessary.

6. Click on OK to close the dialog box.

When you want to perform an action on a 3-D block of cells in the group, you must first turn on Group mode. Pull down the View menu and click on Group mode, or press ALT-F5. Quattro Pro 10 displays a blue line below all of the tabs in your group to indicate that Group mode is turned on.

Now, formatting and other changes (except entering and deleting) to one cell or group of cells on a sheet in a group are duplicated on every sheet in that group. When you no longer want to act on the 3-D block, turn off Group mode—deselect Group mode on the View menu or press ALT-F5 again. The line under the tabs will disappear, showing that the group function is turned off.

To avoid unwanted effects, text that you type directly in a cell when Group mode is turned on will not be duplicated across the pages. When you want to enter text on every page, turn on Group mode, type the text on any of the pages in the group, hold down the CTRL key, and press ENTER. This is called "drilling down." You must press ENTER; clicking the Enter box in the input line does not drill down the text.

| NOTE | *Use the Clear command or* CTRL-DEL *to delete information from every page.* |

18

When Group mode is turned on, most actions affect every sheet of the group. You have to be careful not to accidentally change something on one page that will affect others. For example, if you select a group of cells and choose Clear or Delete from the Edit menu, all of the cells on every page of the group will be cleared. The Delete command from the Edit or QuickMenu works the same way. To erase information from just one page, use the DEL key, or turn off Group mode first.

The same warning applies to pointing to cells for formulas and functions and in dialog boxes. With Group mode turned on, you'll get a 3-D reference, using the syntax *group-name:range*. So if you point to a range on one sheet to average a row of cells, you will actually calculate the average of the cells from all of the pages in the group. Before pointing to cells, turn Group mode off.

If you want to copy information from one page to all of the pages, you'll also need to turn off Group mode; otherwise, you'll copy a 3-D group rather than just cells from one page. Turn off Group mode, copy the cells, turn on Group mode, and then paste them. The same 2-D block will be pasted to all of the pages.

You can have more than one group in the same notebook, although a sheet cannot be in more than one group. To delete a group, display the Define/Modify Group dialog box, click on the group and then on Delete. To change the pages included in the group, choose its name, and then edit the entries in the First Sheet and/or Last Sheet edit fields in the Define/Modify Group dialog box.

Splitting Windows into Panes

When you need to refer to a section on a large spreadsheet, you can always scroll or use the Go To command. But then you'd have to scroll back to your original location to continue working. Instead of scrolling back and forth, you can divide your screen into two *panes,* either vertically or horizontally, and view two parts of the same spreadsheet at the same time. You can create panes using the pane splitter at the lower-right corner of the window, where the horizontal and vertical scroll bars meet, or by using the Split Window command from the View menu.

To split the screen into two horizontal panes, point to the top portion of the pane splitter so the arrows point left and right. To split into two vertical panes, point to the lower portion so the arrows point up and down. Now drag the mouse into the window. As you drag, a line appears showing the position of the pane. Release the mouse when the line is where you want the panes to appear. As shown in Figure 18-4, both panes have page tabs, tab scrolls, and scroll bars to move about the notebook. The pane splitter appears where the two panes meet.

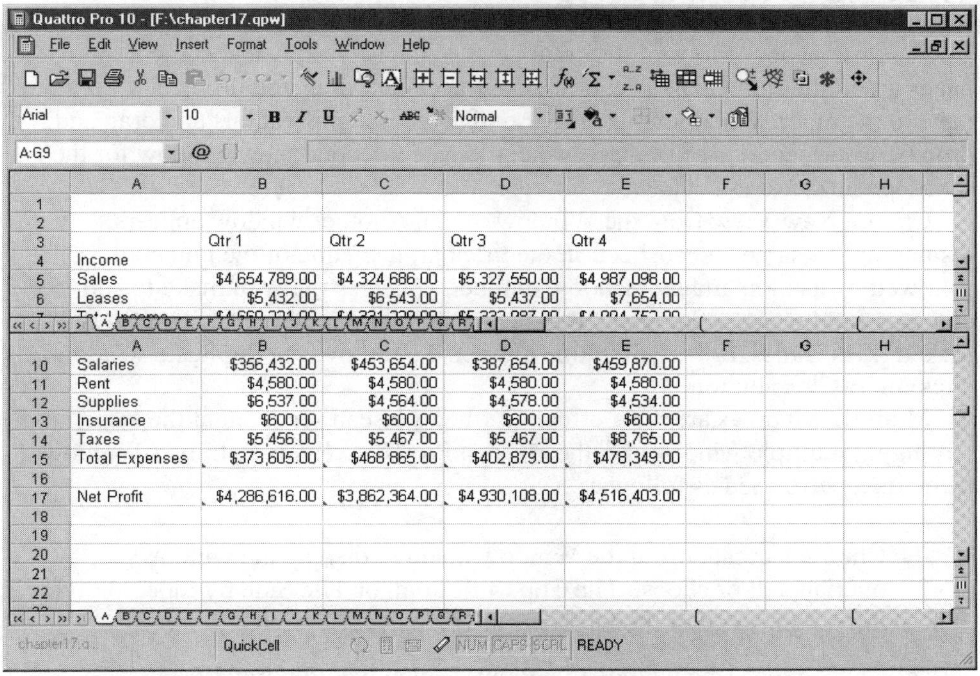

FIGURE 18-4   Spreadsheet divided into panes

Changes you make in one pane are duplicated in the other. By default, the two panes are synchronized. This means that scrolling one pane in the direction of the split scrolls the other as well. For example, scrolling horizontal panes in a horizontal direction and vertical panes in a vertical direction are synchronized.

If you unsynchronize the panes, you can scroll them independently to reveal different parts of the same spreadsheet. To unsynchronize panes, choose Split Window from the View menu, and deselect Synchronized. Click on the same option if you later want to synchronize the panes again.

To move from one pane to another, click in the pane with the mouse, or press the F6 key to move from pane to pane.

To change the size of the panes, drag the pane splitter. Dragging it all the way off the window removes a pane, displaying one view of the spreadsheet.

18

Duplicating Windows

You can use panes to look at different parts of the same spreadsheet, but both panes are in the same magnification, and you cannot drag and drop cells from one pane to the other. When you want to use different magnifications and drag and drop between sections of the spreadsheet, create a second view window for the same spreadsheet.

Choose New View from the Window menu. Another window appears, displaying the same spreadsheet. In the title bar, the name of the notebook is followed by a colon and the window number. Changes that you make to cell contents and format are duplicated in both windows. However, changes to the locked titles, panes, or magnification are not. To remove the duplicate window, click on its Close button.

Multiple windows are most effective when you can see them at the same time. Arranging multiple windows on the Quattro Pro 10 screen is a straight Windows technique, performed as follows:

1. Choose Cascade from the Window menu to display the windows overlapped; or choose Tile Top to Bottom, or Tile Side by Side, to divide the screen so all of the windows are displayed.

2. Change the size and move windows as you would normally.

To select a window when more than one is displayed, click anywhere in the window, or select Window from the menu bar and then click on the window name. Use the Window menu to change windows when they are not arranged onscreen, or when one window is in the background and cannot be seen. Copy and move cells between windows the same as you would within a window, using drag and drop or cut and copy.

All of these techniques also apply to windows from more than one notebook. To work with several notebooks at one time, open each of them, and then arrange the screens as desired, cascading or tiling them with the Window menu.

Try It Out

Using cell names makes it much easier to create a spreadsheet. Not only can the names help you understand formulas, but also you can use the names to quickly move to a specific location in a notebook. In this section, we'll see how easy it is to create names for multiple cells at one time, and then use the names for formulas and navigation. We'll also insert a header and footer into a spreadsheet to improve its printed version.

1. Open the Calls notebook that you created in Chapter 16.

2. Select cells A2 to H9.

3. Select Insert | Name | Name Cells, and click Generate.

4. Select the Under Top Row and the Right of Leftmost Column options.

5. Select Name Cells at Intersections.

6. Click OK and then Close.

7. Pull down the list on the left of the formula bar to see the named cells.

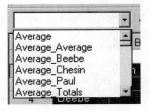

8. Scroll the list and select Totals_Chesin to quickly move to the Totals column in the row for Chesin.

9. Click in cell C15 and enter **+Totals_Wing+Totals_Beebe**. The cell names will appear in the QuickTip for the formula:

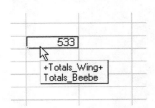

18

10. Click in cell C16 and enter **+Fri_Average** to reference cell F9. Now let's see what happens if you delete the cell names.

11. Select Insert | Name | Name Cells.

12. Click Delete All, then on Yes and Close.

13. Point to cell C15, and notice that the QuickTip shows that the cell names have been replaced by their references.

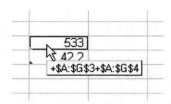

Now let's add a header and footer to the page.

14. Select File | Page Setup, and click the Header/Footer tab.

15. Enable the Create check box in the Header section.

16. Type |**Notebook #f**. The | symbol will center the text on the notebook page.

17. Enable the Create check box in the Footer section.

18. Type |**Created by**, and then your name.

19. Click OK.

20. Select File | Print Preview. The notebook with its header and footer is shown in Figure 18-5.

21. Print a copy of the spreadsheet.

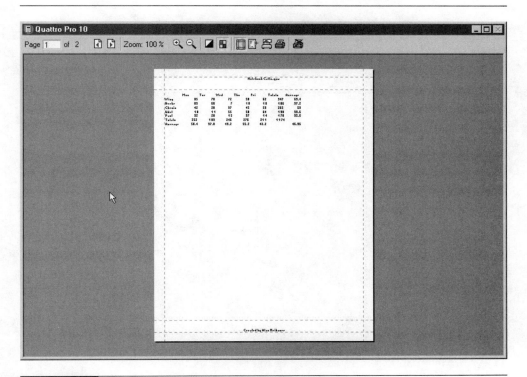

FIGURE 18-5   Notebook with header and footer.

Chapter 19

Working with Functions and Formulas

Y ou use formulas and functions to take advantage of the recalculation and "What If?" capabilities of Quattro Pro 10. In fact, you should use formulas whenever possible, especially when you need to perform a mathematical operation on the values in other cells. To begin with, formulas help ensure that your results are accurate. As long as you use the proper formula, Quattro Pro 10 calculates the correct result. In addition, formulas can save you a great deal of time. The few extra seconds or minutes it takes to enter a formula can save you countless hours manually recalculating and checking your work.

In Chapter 16, you learned how to enter formulas, and you saw how the @SUM function could quickly total a row or column of numbers. In this chapter, you will learn how to enter formulas that perform all types of operations.

Functions

A *function* is a built-in shortcut that you can use to do, in one quick statement, what might take a very complex single formula or even a series of formulas to accomplish. For example, suppose your budget spreadsheet includes a series of daily expenditures. To calculate the average of the expenditures, you could count how many items you have listed (let's suppose 30), and enter a formula such as +(A1+A2+A3+A4+A5 . . . , and so on)/30. That's quite a lot of typing. If you now insert another item into the spreadsheet, you'll have to edit the formula, adding the other cell and increasing the count to 31.

The alternative is to use the built-in function for calculating an average, @AVG. If you want to average the values in cells A1 through A30, all you have to enter is @AVG(A1..A30). The function returns—calculates and displays—the average of the values specified in that range. If you later add a row of information within the range, Quattro Pro 10 automatically adjusts the range reference to include the additional values.

A function can also perform a calculation that you would not otherwise know how to do using a formula alone. As an example, suppose you're looking for a home and want to calculate your monthly mortgage payments. Unless you are an accountant, you probably won't even know where to begin to write a formula to perform the calculation. Fortunately, Quattro Pro 10 has a built-in function for this called @PAYMT. Entering the function @PAYMT(.07/12, 25*12, 56000), for instance, returns the monthly mortgage payment for a loan of $56,000 for 25 years at 7 percent annual interest. Just substitute your own values, or cell references to the values, in place of the numbers.

The result of the @PAYMT function, by the way, appears as a negative number. For a positive result, precede the principal amount with a minus sign, as in -56000.

You don't have to know how the function works, just its syntax—its name and how to enter the information that it needs to calculate its results.

The Structure of Functions

Functions use the general syntax of @NAME(arguments). The @ symbol tells Quattro Pro 10 that a function, not a label, follows. The function name can be entered in either uppercase or lowercase, with no spaces between it and the @ sign. The arguments, in parentheses, are the values, cell references, or special instructions that the function needs to do its work. You can have spaces around arguments, but Quattro Pro 10 removes them when you accept the entry.

Some functions have no arguments. The function @TODAY, for example, displays the current date's serial number, and the function @MEMAVAIL displays the amount of conventional memory available. Just type the function into the cell without any parentheses. When you accept the entry, the result appears in the cell.

In the function @AVG(A1..A30), the argument is the cell range A1..A30. This function needs just one argument: the range of cells that contains the values to average. Many other functions require several arguments, separated from each other by commas. The mortgage payment function, for example, requires three: the rate per period, the number of payments, and the principal amount, in that order. If you insert them in any other order, you'll get incorrect results.

Some functions have optional arguments. These are arguments that you can enter if you need to use them. The mortgage payment function, for example, has two optional arguments. The first represents any future value of the investment; the second indicates if you pay at the beginning or end of the period. The function @PAYMT(.07/12, 25*12, 56000, -20000, 1) uses the optional arguments to calculate the payment on a mortgage that includes a balloon payment of $20,000, with payments at the end of the month.

The Help system and online manual will show you the syntax of functions and how to use optional arguments.

When you leave out the optional arguments, Quattro Pro 10 assumes a default value for them. The defaults for the @PAYMT function, for instance, assume no future value and payments at the beginning of the month. If you use an optional argument, however, you must use all the information that comes before it. You could not, for instance, use the second optional argument without including the first.

19

You can use functions by themselves in the input line or in combination with formulas and other functions. Using a function as an argument for another function is called *nesting*. Here are some examples:

+B3+@AVG(A1..A10)	Here a formula includes a function, adding the value in one cell to the average of a block of cells. Since the formula does not begin with the function, it must start with the + sign.
@PAYMT(B1/12, 1, B2*12, B3)	Arguments can be formulas when their values are calculated. This function returns the amount of the first payment on a loan that goes to pay off principal. It contains formulas to calculate monthly interest from the annual rate in cell B1, and the number of monthly payments from the number of years in cell B2. The loan amount is in cell B3.
@TODAY - @Date(A1)	A formula can include several functions. In this example, two functions are used to determine the number of days between the date in cell A1 and the current date.
@INT(@AVG(A1..A10))	A function can even be used as the argument to another function. Here, the @INT function returns the integer (whole number) portion of the calculated average.

Entering Functions

You type a function directly into the cell or input line as you would any other formula. If you are just using a function, start with the @ symbol; there is no need to enter the + sign. Quattro Pro 10 recognizes the @ sign as a value entry.

Once you start to enter the name of the function, QuickType displays the first function name starting with those letters, along with the opening parenthesis for the arguments. For example, if you type **@p**, QuickType displays @pbday(. If the suggested function is incorrect, continue typing. If you then press the letter *a*, QuickType changes @pbday(to @paymt(. When the function is correct, press the RIGHT ARROW key to begin entering the arguments.

Quattro Pro 10 also displays a Function Hint in the application bar at the bottom of the window: the function name and the name and order of the arguments. The argument names are abbreviated with <> symbols around optional arguments, as in @paymt(rate, nper, pv, <fv>,<type>). This helps you enter the required and optional arguments in the correct order.

As you type in the function, the argument that you should enter at the position of the insertion point appears in a QuickTip above the insertion point and appears uppercase in the application bar. So, for example, after you type the opening parenthesis for the @PAYMT function, the ScreenTip reads Rate, and the application bar displays @paymt(RATE, nper, pv, <fv>,<type>), reminding you to enter the value, cell reference, or formula for the mortgage rate. Once you enter the comma following the rate, the application bar appears as @paymt(rate, NPER, pv, <fv>,<type>), telling you to enter the number of periods. As you move the insertion point within the function, Quattro Pro 10 uppercases the current argument.

> **NOTE** *The parentheses-matching function helps ensure that you match opening and closing parentheses properly. Parentheses appear in black when unmatched.*

Selecting Functions

If you can't remember or don't know the function name, use the Function dialog box. If you are not yet in the input line, press ALT-F3, or right-click in the cell and choose Insert Function from the QuickMenu. If you are entering or editing in the cell already, click on the Function button (@) in the input line. You'll see the dialog box shown in Figure 19-1.

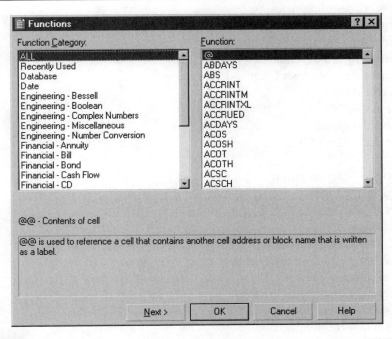

FIGURE 19-1 Displaying the function list to select a function

NOTE	*You can move into the input line and display the entire list at one time by pressing* ALT-F3.

The list on the left of the dialog box shows the categories of functions; the list on the right shows the functions within the selected category. Choose the ALL category to display every function in alphabetic order, or choose Recently Used to see the functions that you've recently entered. Select the category of the function you want, and then double-click on the function, scrolling the list as needed, to insert it into the input line. Quattro Pro 10 will insert the @ symbol, the function name, and the opening parenthesis.

TIP	*Clicking on Next in the Functions dialog box opens Formula Composer to help you with the function. Refer to the section "Formula Composer," later in this chapter.*

The function categories are:

Database
Date
Engineering—Bessel
Engineering—Boolean
Engineering—Complex Numbers
Engineering—Miscellaneous
Engineering—Number Conversion
Financial—Annuity
Financial—Bill
Financial—Bond
Financial—Cash Flow
Financial—CD
Financial—Depreciation
Financial—Stock
Logical
Mathematical
Miscellaneous—Attribute
Miscellaneous—Cell and Table
Miscellaneous—Status
Miscellaneous—Table Lookup
Statistical—Descriptive
Statistical—Inferential
String

Getting Help with Functions

Once you type or insert the name of a function, you can press the F1 key to get help on the function, or you can look it up in the Help system. In the Help Index page, enter **functions, list** and press Enter. Select Quattro Pro Functions List in the box that appears and click Display to see a list of functions.

Click on the alphabetic letter for the function, or scroll the list until it appears. Then click on the function name for detailed information. The Help system will show you the syntax of each function, what the arguments represent, and even samples of their use, as in Figure 19-2.

Formula Composer

Perhaps the best way to enter functions and complex formulas is to use Formula Composer. This is a special dialog box that helps you check your syntax and pinpoint errors in your logic; it also prompts you for arguments. You can use the Formula Composer to create a formula or function, or to troubleshoot one that you've already entered.

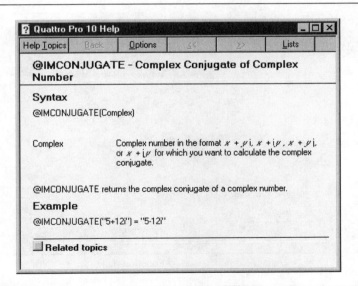

FIGURE 19-2   Using Help for complete information on functions

Click in the cell where you want to enter or edit a formula, and then click on the Formula Composer button to see the dialog box.

The box is shown, labeled with a function already selected, in Figure 19-3. The toolbar buttons, except the standard Cut, Copy, Paste, and Undo buttons, are listed in Table 19-1.

You enter or edit a formula in the Expression text box. To enter a function, either type it in, or click on the Function button and make your choice from the dialog box that appears. As you work on the formula, the results are calculated and displayed in the Cell Value box so you can watch the effect of your formulas to see where a mistake takes place. The Cell Value appears as ERR (error) until you enter a complete function or formula, without any missing or incorrect arguments and with the correct syntax.

The @Function pane explains the function being used, while the Argument pane lists each of the arguments for you to enter. The Outline pane displays a

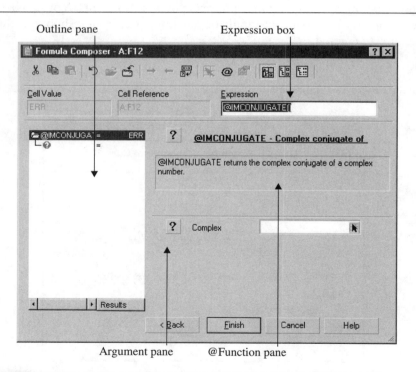

FIGURE 19-3 Formula Composer

Button	Function
Expand the formula	Expands the outline one level
Collapse the formula	Collapses the expression one level
Follow the formula	Displays the referenced cell
Return from the formula	Moves back to the selected cell
Convert to value	Converts an expression into a value
Point	Switches to Point mode
Function	Displays the Function dialog box
Insert a block name	Displays block names
Standard view	Displays all panes
Argument view	Displays just the Outline and Argument panes
Outline view	Displays just the Outline pane

TABLE 19-1   Formula Composer toolbar buttons

breakdown of the formula in sections, showing the value of cell references and calculations.

Use the Outline pane to see how Quattro Pro 10 is performing the calculation. For example, here is what appears in the pane if you incorrectly tried to average values using the formula +100+100+100/3:

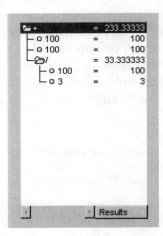

The result of the division is shown as 33.333333, and the values under it, 100 and 3, indicate how the operation was performed. You would know right away that

19

you don't want to divide 100 by 3, so you would know that the structure of the formula is incorrect. Here is the outline when the formula uses parentheses:

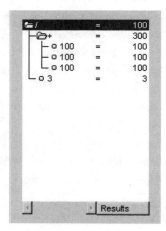

Now you can see that the values are grouped correctly.

You can double-click on the folder icons or click the Collapse and Expand buttons to expand or collapse parts of the outline to concentrate on certain sections of the formula, just as you can expand and collapse an outline. Folder icons to the left of the outline indicate whether expressions have been expanded or collapsed. A small yellow circle means that that part of the expression cannot be expanded. A red question mark indicates that the expression is incorrect. When you select a section of the formula in the Outline pane, it also appears in the Expression box.

Sometimes, just seeing the cell references in the Outline pane is not enough. Because the value of a cell depends on the cells that it references, you often have to trace through the spreadsheet to find the source of a problem.

You can trace a cell's references directly from Formula Composer using the following steps:

1. Click on the cell reference in the Outline pane.

2. Click on the Follow button in the Formula Composer toolbar.

3. Look at the dialog box's title bar; it indicates the cells being referenced.

For example, if cell C6 refers to cell B4, clicking on the Follow button displays A:C6 -> A:B4 in the title bar and shows cell B4 selected in the background. If cell B4 refers to cell A1, then clicking on Follow again displays

A:C6 -> A:B4 -> A1 in the title bar and selects cell A1. Clicking on Back moves back to the original cell.

Perhaps the best way to visualize Formula Composer is to actually use it, so let's calculate a mortgage payment. We'll be entering values directly in the function, although you can enter or point to cell references just as well.

1. Click on cell B5, and click on the Formula Composer button.

2. Click on the Function button to display the Functions dialog box.

3. Choose the Financial—Annuity category.

4. Scroll the list, and double-click on PAYMT. The Formula Composer dialog box appears as shown in Figure 19-4. Each of the required and optional arguments is listed in the Argument pane.

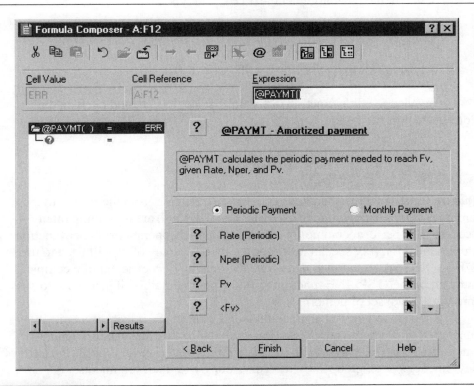

FIGURE 19-4   Formula Composer with PAYMT functions

5. Click on the Monthly Payment option button. This lets you enter annual interest and number of years rather than worry about calculating monthly interest and the number of monthly payments. It also adds the necessary operators into the Expression box, so it appears as @PAYMT(/12,*12,).

6. Click in the Rate (Yearly) argument text box, and type **.06**. Quattro Pro 10 adds the value to the appropriate location in the Expression box; you do not have to worry about positioning the insertion point. If you do not see the Rate (Yearly) argument, scroll the Argument pane.

> **TIP** *For help with a specific argument, click on the Help button before the argument's name. Take a moment to notice the other sections of the dialog box. The Cell Value shows ERR because the function is not yet complete. The Outline pane indicates that section of the function and the values.*

7. Click in the Nper argument text box, and type **30**.

   Click in the Pv argument text box, and type **-50000**. The Cell Value now indicates a valid result, and the breakdown is shown in the outline.

8. Click on OK to display the results in the cell.

If you need to edit a function or formula, select its cell, and click on the Formula Composer button.

Function Reference

Quattro Pro 10 includes hundreds of functions, ranging from the simple to the sublime. Some functions, such as @SUM and @AVG, are used quite often because they perform commonly used mathematical operations. Other functions are designed for very special needs. After all, how many of us will need to use the @IMAGINARY function to determine the imaginary coefficient of a complex number, or the @SPLINE function to find a polynomial fitted piecewise to pass through a given set of points?

If you need to perform an operation, and want to see if there is a built-in function that can help you, use the Function dialog box, or scan through the categories in the Help system. As a quick reference, however, you'll find a list of key functions here, grouped by category, along with their arguments.

Database Functions

You use database functions to help analyze information. You will learn about databases in Chapter 21. All of the functions use the same three arguments: Block, Column, and Criteria. *Block* is the range of cells that contains the database. *Column* is where the data that you want to analyze is located. *Criteria* are cells that indicate conditions that values have to meet to be included in the process. For example, the @DAVG function computes the average of the values in the designated column, using cells meeting the criteria.

Here are the database functions:

@DAVG(Block,Column,Criteria)	Calculates the average of the values
@DCOUNT(Block,Column,Criteria)	Calculates the number of values
@DGET(Block,Column,Criteria)	Returns a value or label from a field
@DMAX(Block,Column,Criteria)	Calculates the maximum value in the column
@DMIN(Block,Column,Criteria)	Calculates the minimum value in the column
@DPRODUCT(Block,Column,Criteria)	Multiplies the values in a field from all records in the database
@DPURECOUNT(Block,Column,Criteria)	Calculates the amount of all number field entries
@DSTD(Block,Column,Criteria)	Calculates the population standard deviation of the values
@DSTDS(Block,Column,Criteria)	Calculates the sample standard deviation of the values
@DSUM(Block,Column,Criteria)	Calculates the sum of the values
@DVAR(Block,Column,Criteria)	Calculates the population variance of the values
@DVARS(Block,Column,Criteria)	Calculates the sample variance of the values

Date Functions

These functions calculate dates, times, and days. The date and time functions can be used in processing accounts. If you enter dates and times in an accepted format, Quattro Pro 10 can use these functions to perform math operations. For example, the function @TODAY−A4 determines how many days have passed since the date in cell A4.

To calculate the difference between two dates, just subtract them, as in +A4−A1, where both references are to cells containing dates. Dates are always converted to a series number, so subtracting them results in the number of days between them.

19

You can also move in the other direction, from a date serial to a formatted date. For example, suppose you want to schedule an appointment 30 days from today. Use the function @ACDAYS(@Today, 30) to insert the date of the appointment in the active cell. To count just business days, use the formula @ABDAYS(@TODAY, 30). Both of these functions, however, will display the serial number of the date. To see the date itself, use the Block properties to change the Numeric Format to Date.

Common arguments used in these functions include a date, time, number of days, years, months, hours, and minutes. Some optional arguments include the following:

- *Holidays* indicates whether a range of dates contains dates that are holidays. Use 0 to indicate no holidays, or enter the date of a holiday in the group.

- *Saturday* signifies if you want to include Saturday as a business day (1) or not (0).

- *Sunday* indicates if you want Sunday to be counted as a business day (1) or not (0).

Here are some useful date and time functions:

@ABDAYS(Date,Days,<Holidays>, <Saturday>,<Sunday>)	Calculates the date in a specific number of business days
@ACDAYS(Date,Days,<Calendar>, <EndMnth>)	Calculates the date in a specific number of calendar days
@AMNTHS(Date,Months,<EndMnth>)	The date in a specific number of months
@BDAYS(StartDate,EndDate, <Holidays>,<Saturday>,<Sunday>)	Calculates the number of business days between two dates
@BUSDAY(Date,<Direction>,<Holidays>, <Saturday>,<Sunday>)	Calculates the closest business date
@CDAYS(StartDate,EndDate, <Calendar>,<February>)	Calculates the number of calendar days between StartDate and EndDate, including EndDate
@DATE(Yr,Mo,Day)	Calculates the serial number for a date
@DATEDIF(StartDate,EndDate, Format)	Calculates the number of years, months, or days between two dates
@DAY(DateTimeNumber)	Calculates the day of the month
@EMNTH(Date)	Calculates the last day of the month

@FBDAY(Date,\<Holidays\>, \<Saturday\>,\<Sunday\>)	Calculates the first business day in the month
@LBDAY(Date,\<Holidays\>, \<Saturday\>,\<Sunday\>)	Calculates the date of the last business day of the month
@MDAYS(Month,Year)	Calculates the number of days in the month
@NBDAY(Date,\<Holidays\>,\<Saturday\>, \<Sunday\>)	Calculates the first business day after a date
@TODAY	Calculates the serial number of the current date
@NENGO(Date)	Converts a date to its Kanji (Japanese) format

Engineering Functions

These functions perform calculations used in engineering applications. They are divided into five categories.

Bessel functions calculate values that satisfy the Bessel equation or the modified Bessel equation, used in physics and engineering applications. Here are the Bessel functions:

@BESSELI(x,n)	Performs the modified Bessel function $In(x)$
@BESSELJ(x,n)	Performs the Bessel function $Jn(x)$
@BESSELK(x,n)	Performs the modified Bessel function $Kn(x)$
@BESSELY(x,n)	Performs the Bessel function $Yn(x)$

Boolean functions deal with logic and bitwise operations. They are useful if you are working with binary or hexadecimal numbers. Some of the useful functions are listed here:

@ADDB(Binary1,\<Binary2\>,\<BitIn\>,*\<Bits\>)*	Adds two binary numbers
@ADDBO(Binary1,Binary2,\<BitIn\>,*\<Bits\>)*	Returns the overflow bit of a binary sum
@ADDH(Hex1,\<Hex2\>,\<BitIn\>,*\<Bits\>)*	Adds two hexadecimal numbers
@ADDHO(Hex1,Hex2,\<BitIn\>,*\<Bits\>)*	Returns the overflow bit of a hexadecimal sum
@INVB(Binary,\<Bits\>)	Returns the inverse of a binary number
@INVH(Hex,\<Bits\>)	Returns the inverse of a hexadecimal number
@ORB(Binary1,\<Binary2\>,\<Bits\>)	Returns the OR results of two binary numbers
@ORH(Hex1,\<Hex2\>,\<Bits\>)	Returns the OR results of two hexadecimal numbers
@SUBB(Binary1,Binary2,\<BitIn\>,*\<Bits\>)*	Returns the difference between two binary numbers

19

@SUBBO(Binary1,Binary2,<BitIn>,*<Bits>*)	Returns the overflow bit of difference between two binary numbers

Complex number functions convert or modify a complex number. A complex number is one whose square is a negative real number. Some complex number functions are as follows:

@IMCOS(Complex)	Returns the cosine of a complex number
@IMDIV(Complex1,Complex2)	Returns the result of dividing one complex number by another complex number
@IMLN(Complex)	Returns the natural logarithm of a complex number
@IMLOG10(Complex)	Returns the base 10 logarithm of a complex number
@IMLOG2(Complex)	Returns the base 2 logarithm of a complex number
@IMPOWER(Complex,Power)	Returns a complex number raised to a power
@IMSQRT(Complex)	Returns the square root of a complex number

Miscellaneous functions serve assorted engineering needs, such as data conversion and returning error codes. Here is a sample:

@CONVERT(*X*,FromUnit,ToUnit)	Returns the value X in FromUnit units, converted to a value in ToUnit units
@GAMMA(*X*)	Calculates the gamma function of the value X
@SPLINE(Known*X*'s, Known*Y*'s, OutputBlock)	Returns a polynomial fitted piecewise to pass through a given set of points

Number conversion functions convert a value from one number system to another. These can be useful if you are working with a programming language or an application that uses ASCII codes or binary, hexadecimal, or octal numbers. Some conversion functions include the following:

@ASCTOHEX(ASCII,<Places>)	Returns the hexadecimal equivalent of an ASCII value
@BINTOHEX(Binary)	Returns the hexadecimal equivalent of a binary number
@BINTONUM(Binary)	Returns the decimal equivalent of a binary number
@BINTOOCT(Binary)	Returns the octal value equivalent of a binary number
@HEXTOASC(Hex)	Returns the ASCII character of a hexadecimal number
@HEXTOBIN(Hex)	Returns the binary equivalent of a hexadecimal number
@NUMTOBIN(Decimal)	Returns the binary equivalent of a decimal number
@OCTTOBIN(Oct)	Returns the binary equivalent of an octal number

| @OCTTOHEX(Oct) | Returns the hexadecimal string equivalent of an octal number |
| @OCTTONUM(Oct) | Returns the decimal equivalent of an octal number |

Financial Functions

These functions perform financial calculations and operations. They are divided into several categories based on their use, and most have a number of arguments.

Annuity functions deal with periodic payments and investments. Arguments typically include interest rates, the number of payment periods, loan amounts, and payment amounts. The functions return one value when given the others.

Some of the less obvious arguments include:

- *n*—The number of payments made

- *Part*—Part of a period passed

- *Residual*—Remaining loan balance at the end of loan term

- *ResOff*—The number of periods after the last periodic payment that residual is to be paid

- *Adv*—The number of advance payments

- *Odd*—The number of periods between the start of the loan and the first payment

- *Simp*—Compound (0) or simple (1) interest

Here's a sample of the annuity functions:

@AMAINT(Principal,Int,Term,*n*, <Part>,<Residual >,<ResOff>, <Adv>,<Odd>,<Simp>)	Calculates the accumulated interest paid on a loan after *n* payments
@AMPMTI(Principal,Int,Term,*n*, <Residual>,<ResOff>,<Adv>, <Odd>,<Simp>)	Calculates the interest portion of a loan payment
@AMRPRN(Principal,Int,Term,*n*, <Part>,<Residual>,<ResOff>, <Adv >,<Odd>,<Simp>)	Calculates the balance remaining after so many loan payments
@CUMPRINC(Rate,Nper,Pv, StartPeriod,EndPeriod,Type)	Calculates the cumulative principal paid on a loan between two periods
@FVAL(Rate,Nper,Pmt,<Pv>, <Type>)	Calculates the future value of an annuity

19

@MTGACC(Int,TtlPer,Principal, Residual,ExtraPrin,<Fper>,<Lper>, <Rper>,<Option>)	Calculates the interest saved, and the new loan term and payoff date, after paying extra monthly principal
@PPAYMT(Rate,Per,Nper,Pv,<Fv>, <Type>)	Calculates the portion of a loan payment that goes to principal

Bill functions calculate values for Treasury bill investments. The arguments typically include the settlement and maturity date of the issue and the investment amount. Other arguments include:

- *Price*—The price per 100 face value

- *Redemption*—The redemption value per 100 face value

- *Calendar*—A number that represents the type of calendar: 0 = 30/360, 1 = actual/actual, 2 = actual/360, and 3 = actual/365

Here are the functions in this category:

@DISC(Settle,Maturity,Price, <Redemption>,<Calendar>)	Returns the discount rate based on the discount price
@INTRATE(Settle,Maturity, Investment,Redemption, <Calendar>)	Returns the simple annualized yield
@PRICEDISC(Settle,Maturity, Discount,<Redemption>, <Calendar>)	Returns the price of a discounted security
@RECEIVED(Settle,Maturity, Investment,Discount,<Calendar>)	Calculates the redemption value of a discounted security
@TBILLEQ(Settle,Maturity, Discount)	Returns the bond equivalent yield for a Treasury bill
@TBILLPRICE(Settle,Maturity, Discount)	Calculates the price per 100 face value of a Treasury bill
@TBILLYIELD(Settle,Maturity, Price)	Calculates the yield of a Treasury bill
@YIELDDISC(Settle,Maturity,Price, <Redemption>,<Calendar>)	Returns the annualized yield for a discounted security

Bond functions deal with corporate and municipal bond investments. The arguments also include the settlement and maturity date, as well as coupon dates and frequency of payments.

The functions include the following:

@ACCRINT(Settle,Maturity,Coupon, <Issue>,<FirstCpn>,<Par >, <Freq>, <Calendar>)	Calculates the accrued interest on a bond
@COUPDAYBS(Settle,Maturity, <Freq>,<Calendar>)	Returns the number of days from the start of a coupon period to the settlement date
@COUPDAYSNC(Settle,Maturity, <Freq >,<Calendar>)	Returns the number of days between the date of settlement and the next coupon date
@PRICE(Settle,Maturity,Coupon,Yield, <Redemption>,<Freq>, <Calendar>)	Calculates the price per 100 face value of a security that pays periodic interest
@YIELD(Settle,Maturity,Issue,Coupon,Price, <Calendar>)	Returns the yield on a security

Cash flow functions perform analysis on income and expenditure data. Here are some cash flow functions:

@FUTV(Intrate,Flows,<<Odd|Periods>>, <Simp>,<Pathdep>, <Filter>,<Start>,<End>)	Returns the future value of a cash flow
@IRR(Guess,Block)	Returns the internal rate of return
@NETPV(Discrate,Flows,<Initial>, <<Odd |Periods>>,<Simp>, <Pathdep>, <Filter>,<Start>,<End>)	Returns the net present value of a cash flow

CD functions perform calculations relating to certificates of deposit. These functions are as follows:

@ACCRINTM(Issue,Settle,Coupon,<Par>, <Calendar>)	Returns the accrued interest for a security that pays interest at maturity
@PRICEMAT(Settle,Maturity,Issue,Coupon, Yield,<Calendar>)	Calculates the price per 100 face value of a security that pays interest at maturity
@YIELDMAT(Settle,Maturity,Issue,Coupon, Price,<Calendar>)	Returns the annual yield of a security that pays interest at maturity

Depreciation functions calculate depreciation of assets over time using a specific method. Arguments include the cost of the item, its salvage value, and its life. They may also include the current period held, or a starting and ending period. The depreciation functions are as follows:

@DB(Cost,Salvage,Life,Period, <Month>)	Returns the depreciation of an asset using the fixed-declining balance method
@DDB(Cost,Salvage,Life,Period)	Returns depreciation using the double-declining method

19

@SLN(Cost,Salvage,Life)	Returns depreciation using the straight-line method
@SYD(Cost,Salvage,Life,Period)	Calculates the sum-of-the-years'-digits' depreciation allowance
@VDB(Cost,Salvage,Life, StartPeriod,EndPeriod,<Factor>, <Switch>)	Returns depreciation allowance using the variable rate method

Stock functions calculate common values when dealing with stocks. The stock functions are as follows:

@DOLLARDE(FracDollar,Denom)	Converts a fractional price into dollars
@DOLLARFR(DecDollar,Denom)	Converts a dollar price into a fractional price
@FEETBL(Tu,Ppu,<StdTbl IVal>, <<MinTbl IVal>>,<<MaxTbl IVal>>, <RndPlcs>)	Returns the fee for a stock transaction, using values established in a fee table
@STKOPT(OptCode,OptPrem,UndStkVal, Date,Load,CmdString)	Calculates the time value and earnings value of a stock option

Logical Functions

These functions deal with logical expressions. They return a true or false value based on a range of cells, filename, or value. These functions are normally used to test the value or contents of a block of cells to determine a course of action.

The most important of the functions is @IF. This function tests the results of an expression, inserting one value into the active cell if the expression is true, another if false. The syntax is @IF(Condition, TrueExpression, FalseExpression).

For example, suppose cell D3 contains the number of days a client's bill has been outstanding. This could have been calculated with an expression such as @TODAY−A4, where A4 is the date the bill should have been paid. To determine an entry based on the number of days, use a function such as @IF(D3>30,"Deadbeat","Valued Customer"). The function says "If the value in cell D3 is greater than 30, then insert the label 'Deadbeat' into the active cell; otherwise, insert the label 'Valued Customer.'"

The condition can be any logical expression that returns a true or false value. It can be a formula or one of the other logical functions. One very typical use of the function is to avoid generating error messages when you attempt to divide a value by 0, an improper mathematical operation. Suppose you need to perform the formula +A1/A2. To avoid generating the error, use a function such as @IF(A2=0,

"NA", +A1/A2). If cell A2 has a value of 0, the formula displays the characters "NA". Otherwise, it performs and displays the calculation.

Here are some other useful logical functions:

@FILEEXISTS(FileName)	The function is true if the file exists; false if not.
@ISBLANK(Cell)	The function is true if the cell is blank.
@ISBLOCK(Block)	This function returns true if the block is a defined name or a valid block address.
@ISNUMBER(X0)	This function returns true if the argument is a numeric value; otherwise, it returns false.

Mathematical Functions

Mathematical functions calculate numeric values. Many of these functions use one or two arguments representing a value or cell reference. Some common mathematical functions, such as Average and Sum, are classified as statistical functions and will be discussed later in this chapter.

There are quite a few mathematical functions, including these:

@ABS(X)	Returns the absolute value of X
@COS(X)	Returns the cosine of angle X
@DEGREES(X)	Returns the number of degrees in X radians
@EVEN(X)	Returns the closest even value of X, rounded away from zero
@GCD(X,Y)	Returns the greatest common divisor of X and Y
@LCM(X,Y)	Returns the least common multiple of X and Y
@LOG(X)	Returns the log base 10 of X
@MOD(X,Y)	Returns the remainder of the division X/Y
@ODD(X)	Returns the closest odd value of X, rounded away from zero
@PI	Returns the value of pi
@RAND	Returns a random number between 0 and 1
@RANDBETWEEN(N,M)	Returns a random number between N and M
@ROMAN(Number,<Form>)	Returns the Arabic numeral corresponding to the Roman numeral in the argument
@ROUND(X,Num)	Rounds the value X to the number of digits specified with Num (up to 15)
@SQRT(X)	Returns the square root of X

Miscellaneous Functions

These are functions that do not fall into other categories, but are quite useful. They are divided into four categories.

Attribute functions return a specific attribute or property of a cell, or of the top-left cell in a block. The Block argument is the cell or block of cells for which you want to find an attribute. The Attribute argument determines which attribute is returned. The function @CELL("type",A1), for example, returns a code representing the type of entry, either *v* (value), *l* (label), or *b* (blank). The Attribute arguments are:

- *"address"*—Cell coordinates

- *"row"*—Row number

- *"col"*—Column notebook pages A through IV

- *"sheet"*—Sheet number

- *"NotebookName"*—Notebook name

- *"NotebookPath"*—Path where the notebook is referenced

- *"TwoDAddress"*—2-D address

- *"ThreeDAddress"*—3-D address

- *"FullAddress"*—Complete address, including notebook name

- *"contents"*—Contents of the cell

- *"type"*—Type of the contents: *b* (blank), *v* (value), or *l* (label)

- *"prefix"*—The alignment character: '(left), ^ (centered), " (right), or \ (repeating)

- *"protect"*—The protected status: 0 (not protected) or 1 (protected)

- *"width"*—Column width

- *"rwidth"*—Block width

- *"format"*—Format

Here's a recap of the Attribute functions:

@CELL(Attribute,Block)	Returns the requested attribute of the cell block
@CELLINDEX(Attribute,Block, Column,Row,<Page>)	Returns the attribute of the cell in the position offset from the block
@CELLPOINTER(Attribute)	Returns the requested attribute of the active cell

Cell and Table functions supply information about a cell or block, such as its block name or the number of rows and columns it contains. These functions include:

@@(Cell)	Returns the contents of the cell—both @ signs are required
@BLOCKNAME(Block)	Returns the name assigned to the cell or block
@CHOOSE(Number,List)	Returns the value in a cell in a list of cells
@COLS(Block)	Returns the number of columns in a block
@COLUMN(<lock>)	Returns the column number for a cell or block
@COUNTBLANK(Block)	Returns the number of blank cells in a block
@FIRSTBLANKPAGE(Block)	Returns the letter of the first unnamed blank page in a notebook
@ROW(<lock>)	Returns the row number for a cell or block
@ROWS(Block)	Returns the number of rows in a block

Status functions return a setting for a command, property, or other element of the Quattro Pro 10 environment. They include the following:

@COMMAND(Command Equivalent)	Returns the current setting of command equivalent
@CURVALUE("menu", "menuitem")	Returns the current setting of a menu item in the Quattro Pro for DOS environment
@MEMAVAIL	Returns the amount of available conventional memory
@MEMEMSAVAIL	Returns the amount of available expanded (EMS) memory
@PROPERTY	Returns the current setting of Property for the requested Object
@VERSION	Returns the version number of Quattro Pro 10

Table Lookup functions search for a value in a block of cells. These are typically used with lookup tables. For example, you can create a table of shipping charges based on the number of items and the designation zone, as shown in Figure 19-5. Use the function @Index(A7..E12,G3,G2) in cell G14 to find the shipping charge for a specific shipment, and insert the charge into an invoice.

19

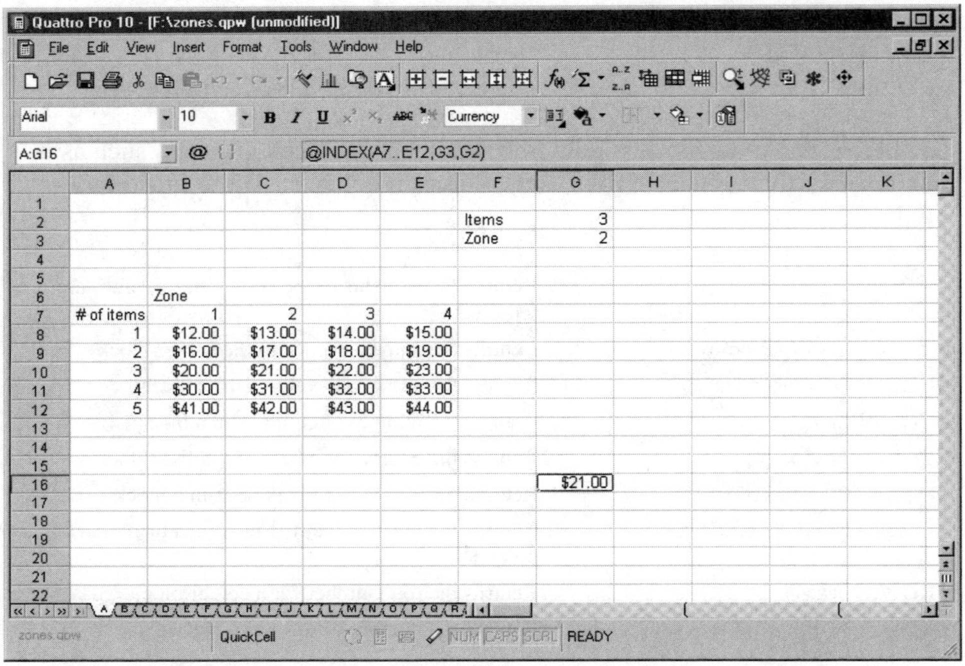

FIGURE 19-5 Using a table to retrieve information

Here is a sampling of the functions:

@HLOOKUP(*X,* Block, Row*)*	Returns the value of the cell in Row number of rows beneath *X* in a block
@INDEX(Block, Column, Row)	Returns the value in the column and row of the specified block
@LOOKUP(Value, LookupVector, ResultVector)	Returns a value in a specified row or column
@VLOOKUP(*X,* Block, Column*)*	Returns the value of the cell in Column number of columns to the right of *X* in a block

Statistical Functions

Statistical functions perform mathematical and analysis operations on a list or group of values. They are divided into two types—Descriptive and Inferential.

Descriptive functions return a value to describe or summarize a group of values. Typical Descriptive functions include the following:

@AVG(List)	Returns the average of a block or list of cells
@COUNT(List)	Counts the number of nonblank cells in a block
@GEOMEAN(List)	Returns the geometric mean of values in a block
@MAX(List)	Returns the largest value in the block
@MEDIAN(List)	Returns the median of values in the block
@MIN(List)	Returns the smallest value in the block
@STD(List)	Returns the population standard deviation of all nonblank values in the block
@SUM(List)	Returns the sum of the values in the block

Inferential functions help you draw conclusions about a group of values. These functions include the following:

@AVEDEV(List)	Calculates the average deviation of the items in a block from their mean
@NORMSDIST(X)	Calculates the standard cumulative normal distribution function
@SUMSQ(List)	Calculates the sum of the squares of the numbers in a block
@ZTEST(Array,X,<S>)	Calculates the two-tailed probability value of a z-test

String Functions

These functions perform tasks on strings of characters or text. Arguments include one or more strings, and the function returns either a string or a numerical value. For example, suppose you have an e-mail address in cell D19 and you want to find the domain—the characters following the @ sign. Use this function:

@RIGHT(D19,@LENGTH(D19)-@FIND("@",D19,1)-1)

The function @FIND("@",D19,1) locates the position of the @ character from the left of the string, starting with position 0. The function @LENGTH(D19) returns the number of characters in the string. The formula @LENGTH(D19)–@FIND("@",D19,1) -1) determines the number of characters following the @ sign, and the @RIGHT function displays them in the cell.

Here are some String functions:

19

@CHAR(Code)	Returns the ANSI character that corresponds to the decimal code
@CLEAN(String)	Returns the string with all nonprintable ASCII codes removed
@CODE(String)	Returns the ANSI code of the first character in the string
@CONCATENATE(List)	Combines all of the strings in the list into one large string
@FIND(SubString,String,StartNumber)	Returns the position of a substring in a given string, starting from a specified position
@LEFT(String,Num)	Returns a given number of characters from the beginning of the string
@LENGTH(String)	Returns the number of characters, including spaces, in a string
@LOWER(String)	Converts a string to all lowercase letters
@MID(String,StartNumber,Num)	Returns a number of characters from the string, starting with the character in the specified position
@RIGHT(String,Num)	Returns a number of characters from the end of the string
@STRING(X,Num)	Converts a numeric value into a string
@TRIM(String)	Removes all leading, trailing, and multiple spaces from a string
@UPPER(String)	Converts a string to all uppercase (capital letters)
@VALUE(String)	Returns the numeric value of a string; results in ERR if the string cannot be converted to a number

Try It Out

Functions are easy to enter and use, but you have to know the correct function for each task you want to perform. In this section, we'll tackle a problem that requires a number of functions.

Imagine that you are the manager of a health club. Clients can pay either annually, quarterly, monthly, or weekly, the rate depending on the number of family members being signed up. A sample rate table appears here:

	A	B	C	D	E	F
7						
8		1	2	3	4	>4
9	Yearly	365	550	565	625	700
10	Quarterly	100	150	165	175	200
11	Monthly	50	60	70	75	95
12	Weekly	15	18	20	25	35
13						

So for example, a family of three paying quarterly would pay $165 in each of the four quarters of the year, for an effective annual rate of $660. The same family would pay only $565 on an annual basis, for a saving of $95.

You want to automate the calculation of the effective annual rate to quickly show members how much they can save by paying on an annual basis, as shown in Figure 19-6.

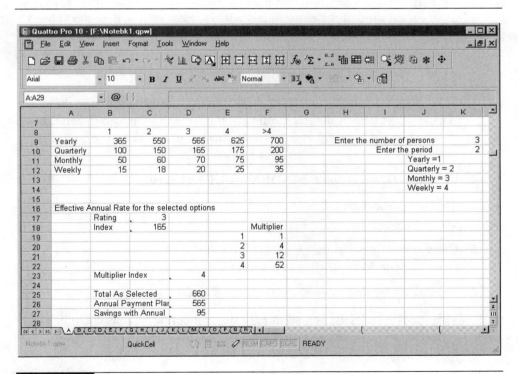

FIGURE 19-6   Notebook to calculate rates

In the spreadsheet, cells A8 to F12 represent the payment table. The user enters the number of persons in cell K9 and the payment method in cell K10. The information in cells E18 to F22 represents the multiplier for the number of periods. For example, if a family selects monthly payments, the payments must be multiplied by 12 to calculate the effective annual rate.

We'll explain the other cells as you create the spreadsheet.

1. Create the spreadsheet by entering the information shown in Figure 19-6, except for the formula cells.

2. Click cell C17 and enter **@IF(K9>4,5,K9).**

   If a family of more than four persons is enrolling, the value in the >4 column of the rate table must be used. This is the fifth column in the rate tables. So no matter how many persons greater than 4 are entered, we have to create an index function that uses the fifth column. This formula, in essence, says that if the entry in cell K9 is greater than 4, then the value 5 will be inserted into cell C17. Otherwise, cell C15 will contain the same entry as cell K9.

3. Click cell C18 and enter **@INDEX(A8..F12,C17,K10).**

   This index function locates the payment in the rate table found in the range A8 to F12. It locates the intersection of the column indicated in cell C17 (the number of persons) and the row indicated in cell K10 (the payment period).

4. Click cell D23 and enter **@INDEX(E18..F22,1,K10).**

   This index function locates the multiplier for calculating the effective annual rate.

5. Click cell D25 and enter **+C18*D23** to calculate the effective annual rate—the periodic rate times the multiplier from cell D23.

6. Click cell D26 and enter **@INDEX(A8..F12,C17,1).**

   This index locates the annual rate for the number of persons entered. The formulas find the intersection of the column indicated in cell C17 (the number of persons) and the first row of the table, which holds the annual rate.

7. Click cell D27 and enter **+D25-D26** to calculate the difference between the actual payments and the annual rate.

Try out the spreadsheet by entering various values in cells K9 and K10. Try a value greater than 4 in cell K10. You'll see that most of the formulas will contain ERR indicating that an error has occurred. This is because the rate table only contains 4 rows of rate information. How would you solve this problem?

The solution is another @IF function. Somewhere on the spreadsheet, say cell E17, enter the function **@IF(K10>4,4,K10).** This tells Quattro Pro that if the value in cell K10 is greater than 4, assume monthly payments. Then edit the formula in cell C18 to be **@INDEX(A8..F12,C17,E17)** and edit the formula in cell D23 to be **@INDEX(E18..F22,1,E17).** These formulas now use the adjusted payment method in cell E17 which accounts for values greater than 4.

Chapter 20

Charts, Maps, and Graphics

When you want your data to have maximum impact, try presenting the information as a graph or map, or emphasizing points with a graphic. You can insert ClipArt and TextArt into a Quattro Pro 10 spreadsheet just as you can with a WordPerfect 10 document. Charts and maps, however, are ideally suited to Quattro Pro 10 because they can visually convey trends and patterns in numeric data. The techniques for charts and maps are similar—if not almost identical—so once you learn how to create one, you can easily create the other. There are some important differences, so read over each section in this chapter carefully. You can also combine charts, maps, and ClipArt into an impressive onscreen slide show using Presentations 10.

 Add TextArt to a spreadsheet by choosing Graphic from the Insert menu and clicking on TextArt. Use the TextArt window just as you learned to do in Chapter 13.

Creating Charts

Before creating a graph for the first time, you should understand a few things that go into one. A graph must have at least one data series. A *data series* is a set of numbers representing the values of something you are measuring or reporting. For example, the graph shown in Figure 20-1 has two series, both of which show dollar amounts in each of four quarters. The first series, represented by the darker color bars, shows revenue in the four quarters. The second series, in the lighter bars, shows expenses. The chart also contains X- and Y-axis labels. The X-axis labels explain what each set of numbers represents, in this case the four quarters of the year. The Y-axis label shows the values being represented.

 When you have more than one series, you can include a legend that explains what each series represents.

You can create a graph either as a floating object or in a separate window. A floating object appears on the spreadsheet, so you can print it on the same sheet as the data that it represents and change its position on the page. When you create a chart in its own windows, you must print it separately from the spreadsheet.

 You can insert charts and maps that you create with Quattro Pro 10 into your WordPerfect 10 documents.

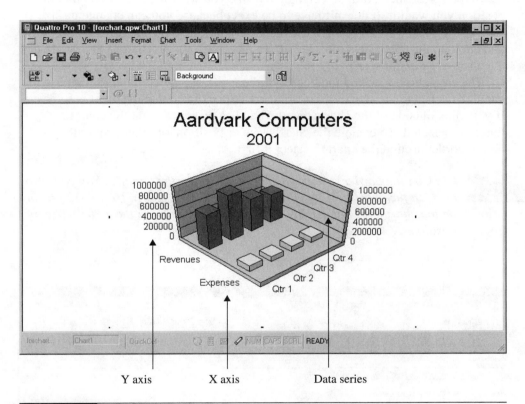

Y axis   X axis   Data series

FIGURE 20-1   The parts of a chart

Floating Objects

You can create a floating chart in two ways—using the QuickChart button in the toolbar or the Chart Expert. The Expert lets you choose the chart type and other options as you create the chart. You don't get those options with the QuickChart tool, although you can edit any chart to change its properties after you create it.

To create a chart, select the block that contains the information you want to chart—including the row and column labels. The column labels will become the X-axis labels, while the row labels will identify each series in the legend. If you use numbers, such as years, for the column labels, enter them as text starting with the apostrophe character. Then click on the QuickChart button in the toolbar. The mouse pointer will change to a crosshair with a miniature chart.

20

In the spreadsheet, drag a rectangle the size you want the chart to be into the position you want it. It doesn't have to be exact because you can change its size and position later. When you release the mouse button, the chart appears. (If you just click on the spreadsheet instead of dragging the mouse, Quattro Pro 10 creates the chart in a default size.)

The small boxes around the border of the graph are called *handles*. You use the handles to change the size of the graph, and they indicate that the chart is selected. If you click outside of the chart area, the handles disappear, and the chart no longer is selected. To change the chart's size or position, or other properties, click on the border around the chart to select it first.

NOTE *Click on the border around the chart to display the handles. You can also click on the chart itself to edit it, as you will soon learn. However, clicking on the chart does not display the handles for changing the chart's size or position.*

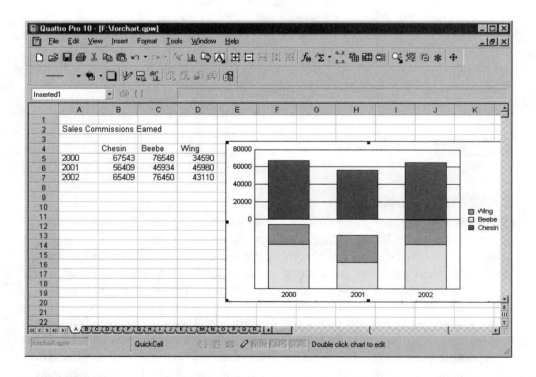

FIGURE 20-2 Sample chart and worksheet

The chart is linked to the spreadsheet cells that you selected to create it. So if you change any of the data used to create the graph, Quattro Pro 10 adjusts the chart automatically. One advantage of the floating chart is that you can place the chart and the spreadsheet side by side on the screen to instantly see the effects of changing values on the chart.

TIP	*To delete a floating chart, select it, and then press* DEL.

Using Chart Expert

You can also create a chart using the Chart Expert. It takes a few extra steps, but you get to select chart options in the process. You can also choose to create a floating chart or to place the chart in its own window. Here's how to use Chart Expert:

1. Select the range of cells that you want to chart.

2. Pull down the Insert menu, and click on Chart. The first Chart Expert box appears, showing the coordinates of the selected block.

3. If you did not select the range first, or if it is incorrect, enter the range, or use Point mode. The box has these other options:

   - *Series As* lets you choose to use rows or columns for the data series. If you choose columns, Quattro Pro plots columns as the series

   - *Reverse series* plots last series first. Use this option if you are creating a 3D chart, for example, and the first series has larger bars that obscure the others. Reversing the plot would place the smaller bars in the foreground.

   - *Place Chart In* gives you the option to insert the chart in the current sheet or in its own window.

   In addition, there is an Advisor's Choice button indicating that Quattro Pro selected the type of chart is feels best suits your data. If you make changes to the chart, you can click Advisor's Choice to restore the suggested format.

4. Click on Next to see the second Expert dialog box shown in Figure 20-3. In this box, choose the category of chart (the general type) you want to create and the specific type of chart. You can also choose to create a 3-D chart and several options, depending on the chart type. Click on Next when done.

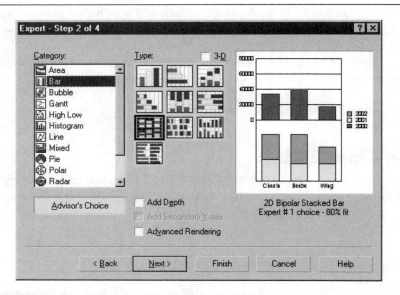

FIGURE 20-3   Selecting a chart type in the Chart Expert dialog box

5. Enter a chart title and subtitle and labels for the X axis and Y axis. You can also enter text for a footnote. Click on Next when done.

6. Choose an overall color scheme, and click on Finish.

7. Click on Finish. If you choose to place it on the current sheet sheet, drag the mouse to indicate the position and size. When you release the mouse button, the chart appears.

Changing Graph Size

You can easily change the size and position of a chart, using the same techniques you use to edit a graphic in WordPerfect 10. To change the size of a floating chart, point to one of the graph handles and drag.

- ■ Drag a handle on the top or bottom border to change the height.

- ■ Drag a handle on the right or left to change the width.

- ■ Drag a handle on a corner to change the height and width at the same time.

To move a graph, use the following steps:

1. Point to the border around the chart so the mouse pointer appears as a four-pointer arrow.

2. Drag the mouse to change the location. The screen scrolls as you drag, and an outline of the graph moves with the pointer.

3. Position the outline where you want the graph to appear and release the mouse button.

NOTE	*You won't be able to resize or move the chart if a box with handles does not surround it. Click outside of the chart to deselect it, and then click on the border around it.*

Creating a Chart in a Window

When you create a chart in its own window, the chart is not on the spreadsheet, and Quattro Pro 10 determines its size. This is a good choice if you don't want the chart and spreadsheet to appear together, and you don't want to use spreadsheet space for the chart.

To create a chart in a window, use Chart Expert and select the Chart Window option in the first Chart Expert dialog box. If you already created the chart as a floating object on the spreadsheet, display it in its own window by right-clicking on the chart (when in Select mode) and selecting Open from the QuickMenu.

A chart in its own window is shown in Figure 20-4.

As with a floating chart, the chart in the window is also linked to the spreadsheet data, and it changes if you edit the values in the associated cells. To see both the chart and spreadsheet onscreen at the same time, however, you must tile the windows and adjust their sizes.

The Chart window appears in the foreground, with the spreadsheet behind. When you want to return to the spreadsheet, pull down the Window menu and click on the spreadsheet name in the list of windows. To redisplay the chart, select its name from the Window menu.

If you close the Chart window by clicking on its Close button, you can open it again only from the Objects page. Icons for every chart and map—floating or in their own windows—are placed on the Objects page that you'll learn about later.

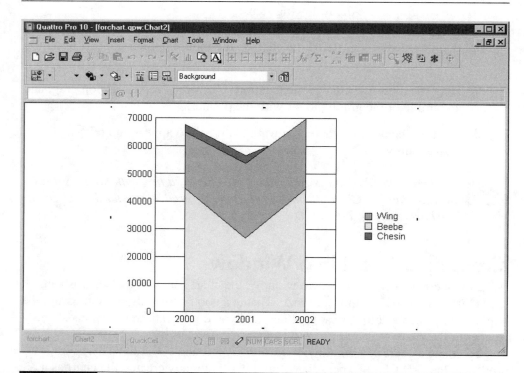

FIGURE 20-4 Chart in its own window

Editing Charts

You can modify a chart at any time, changing its type, titles, appearance, and other properties. If you created a chart in its own window, all of the menu and toolbar tools for editing appear when its window is active.

One way to change some properties of a floating chart is to point to its border (so the mouse pointer appears as a four-pointed arrow) and click, and then use the property bar and QuickMenu. The buttons in the property bar that appear when a chart is selected are shown here:

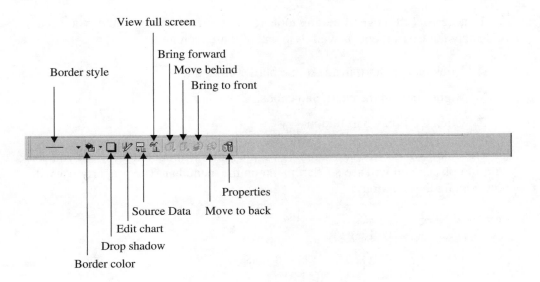

The QuickMenu that appears when you right-click on the chart is shown here:

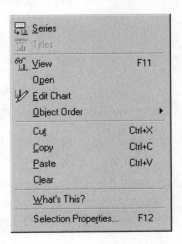

Using the property bar and QuickMenu (in Select mode), you can change the source data. Choose View to display the chart full screen—click the mouse when you have finished.

To access a full range of editing tools to customize a floating chart, you need to display the Chart menu as well. Use one of these techniques:

■ Click on the chart, inside of the border around it.

■ Right-click on the chart, and choose Edit Chart.

■ Click the Edit Chart button.

The chart will now be surrounded by a thick line without handles, and you can edit it in place. You will see a Chart menu on the menu bar. The property bar will now contain these options:

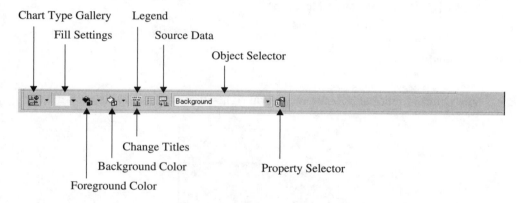

If you right-click on the chart you'll now see these options:

To edit the chart in a separate window, even though it was created as a floating chart, right-click on the chart, and choose Open from the QuickMenu. When you close the separate Chart window you will still see the chart on the spreadsheet page.

TIP   *The Edit Chart and Open options only appear in the QuickMenu when the chart is not already in the Edit mode. If you are already editing the chart, click outside of it, and then right-click on the chart to show the QuickMenu.*

Use the Chart menu and the property bar to edit the chart and add other elements to it. The Chart menu lets you change the appearance and type of the chart. Options are Gallery, Render Chart, Source Data, Titles, Legend Properties, Axes, 3D Options, Lighting Options, Riser Models, Visualize Palette, Background Properties, Text Properties, Export to File, Retrieve Template, and Save Template.

Let's take a look at some of the ways you can customize a chart.

Changing the Chart Type

After you create your chart, you may find that the type you selected does not adequately convey the information that you want to get across. You may also want to experiment by selecting other chart types and subtypes until you find the most effective design. To change the chart type, whether you are editing a floating chart or a chart in a window, pull down the Chart Type Gallery list in the property bar to see the options shown here. Click on the chart type that you want to apply.

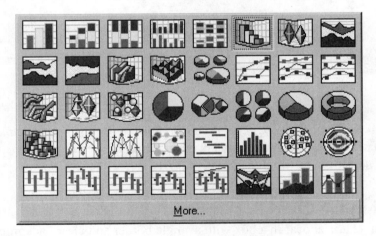

For even more choices, select More from the Gallery list or click on the Chart Type Gallery button in the property bar to open the Chart Type Gallery shown in Figure 20-5. You can also select Gallery from the Chart menu. From this dialog box, select the general and then specific type of chart. Pull down the Color Scheme list to select from background colors and patterns.

Click on the Advisor tab to let Quattro Pro 10 help you choose the best type for your data, as shown in Figure 20-6. Use the Custom tab to select from special designs created by you or choose from the predefined designs provided by Quattro Pro.

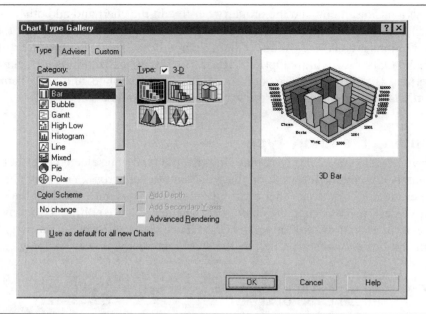

FIGURE 20-5 Chart Gallery dialog box

NOTE	*To save a custom template, create a chart the way you want it and then choose Save Template from the chart menu. In the box that appears, enter a name for the template and click Save.*

Changing the Chart Background

By default, charts appear in a box with a single border and clear background. To select other settings when you are editing the chart, select from the Fill Style, Foreground Color, and Background Color lists in the property bar.

If you are editing the chart in a window, you can also select Background Properties from the Chart menu to select a fill color and style.

TIP	*When you are editing the selected chart, you set the box type and color using the Border Style and Border Color buttons in the property bar.*

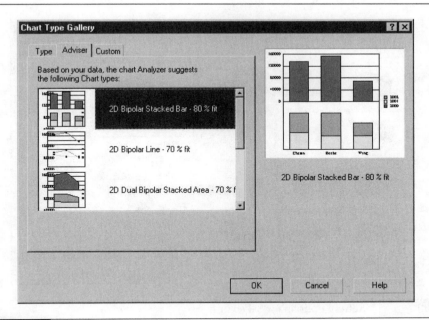

FIGURE 20-6   Using the Advisor to help select the best chart for your data

Changing 3D Options

Charts rendered in 3-D can be quite effective and eye-catching. To customize their appearance, choose 3D Options from the Chart menu and click Advanced Options in the box that appears to see the dialog box shown in Figure 20-7.

The thumbnails on the left of the dialog box show different views from which you can select. Scroll the list of thumbnails to display all of the choices. The option you choose is also shown in the box on the right. To choose from over 60 styles, pull down the list under that box. You can also use these buttons to scroll through the list one at a time or automatically scan forward or backward displaying each item in turn:

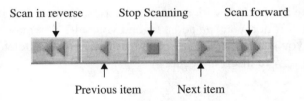

20

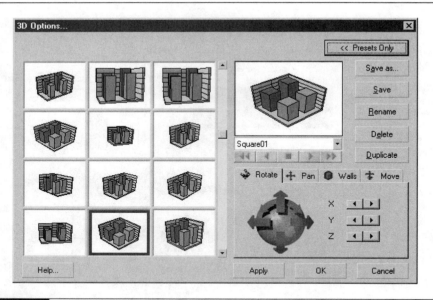

FIGURE 20-7   Setting options for 3-D charts

Use the options in the Rotate, Pan, Walls, and Move tabs to adjust the perspective. Changing rotation changes the perspective as if you were walking around the chart, and viewing it either from left to right or from top to bottom. The Pan settings let you move the chart from left to right, and top to bottom, as well as zoom in and out. Use the Walls options to change the distance between the chart walls and the data series, and to customize the wall thickness. The Move options let you move the chart in relation to its axis.

 Use the buttons along the right of the box to create new preset styles from your choices.

Inserting a Legend

When you create a 2-D chart with at least two series, Quattro Pro 10 normally also includes a legend. If not, you can add a legend yourself. You may have to do this, for example, if you add a series to an existing chart, or if you delete the legend by mistake. Here's how to insert a legend:

1. Select Legend Properties from the Chart menu, or click the Legend button in the property bar, to display a dialog box with three tabs.

2. Use the Format tab to display the legend, choose a position for the legend, select a horizontal or vertical style, and to place the legend inside the chart area itself.

3. Use the Box Style tab to choose the shape of the legend box, the type and color of line around it, and to create a shadow effect.

4. Use the Fill tab to select a color, pattern, or graphic to fill the background of the legend.

5. Click on OK.

You can later move the legend and change its properties.

Changing the Charted Cells

If you realize that you created the chart with the wrong cells, you can change the cells without having to delete the chart and start over. Click on the Source Data button in the property bar. The dialog box is different depending on the chart type selected, but the box allows you to enter or point to the cells to use for your data. You can also choose to reverse the series and plot series as rows or columns.

Choosing Overall Chart Settings

Every element of the chart, including the chart itself, is associated with a series of properties. While you are editing a floating chart (that is, one surrounded by a box with handles), you can change the properties by clicking on the Properties button in the property bar. The dialog box that appears has six tabs:

- *Source Chart* lets you select the chart you want to edit.

- *Border Color* sets the color of the border around the chart.

- *Box Type* lets you select none, thin, medium, or thick border lines, add a drop shadow, or make the chart transparent so you can see the worksheet in its background.

- *Protection* allows you to unlock the chart so it can be edited when the sheet is protected.

- *Object Name* specifies the name of the chart for use in macros.

- *Print* lets you turn on and off Print Control.

Editing Chart Sections

In addition to editing the overall chart, you can customize each of its individual elements, such as an axis, series bar, or section of the pie. You can edit individual sections only when editing the chart in a window—either an in-place window or a separate chart window. If the Chart menu bar is on the screen, you can select and edit individual chart sections.

The trick is to first select only that portion of the chart. Either click on the area you want to edit, such as a title or axis label, or select the item from the Object Selector list. You'll know the part is selected when the handles appear just around it—not around the entire chart or some other section. Once you select a section, choose options from the menu bar, the property bar, or from the QuickMenu that appears when you right-click on the section. Before choosing options, however, make certain that only the desired portion is selected—sometimes it takes a few tries.

The options that appear on the property bar and in the QuickMenu depend on the object you selected. Regardless of the object, however, every property bar contains a Properties button, so you can click on this button to display settings for the selected object.

Properties for wall and background areas, for example, are usually limited to the fill color and pattern, and the shape and size of the border line. The properties for series and axis are more extensive.

Customizing a Series

Setting the properties for a data series controls how the bar, line, area, pie slice, or data points appear on the chart. To change a series, click on any of the bars or lines that represent one of its values, then click on the Properties button on the property bar. You can also change the color and fill properties of just one bar or data point by clicking once to select the series, and then clicking again on the data point you want to format.

The exact options that you can set depend on the type of chart, and whether it is 2-D or 3-D. With 2D bar charts, for instance, you can change the width of the bars, the spacing between them, and the extent that they overlap. In some cases, you can also change the type of just the selected series, so you can show one series with bars and another with lines, for example. For pie charts, you can explode a section and choose the distance it appears from the center. Properties for 3-D bar charts also let you change the shape of the bars, called *risers*, as shown here:

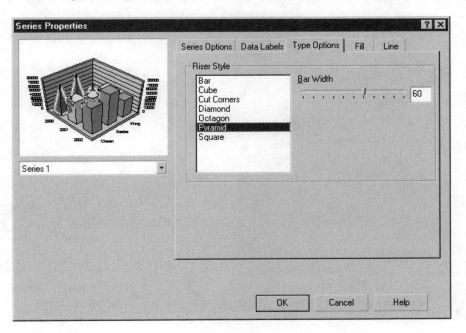

Axis Settings

Select and customize the properties for the Y axis to change the scale, tick marks, and appearance of the line.

The *scale* determines the values that appear along the axis. When Quattro Pro 10 creates a chart, it automatically assigns values to the axis. The uppermost value, at the very top of the Y-axis line, corresponds to the largest value being plotted. The bottom of the scale usually is set at zero, with negative values below the zero line. You may want the scale to rise above the highest value.

For example, suppose you are charting student grades and want the scale to reach 100, even though no student had a perfect score. To change the scale, click on the Y axis so only it is selected, and then click on the Properties button in the property bar (or right-click on it and select Y-Axis Properties from the QuickMenu). Quattro Pro 10 opens the dialog box shown in Figure 20-8. In the Scale tab, enter the highest and lowest values that you want to appear on the axis, and the steps in between. The Minors represents grid lines between the numbered points.

20

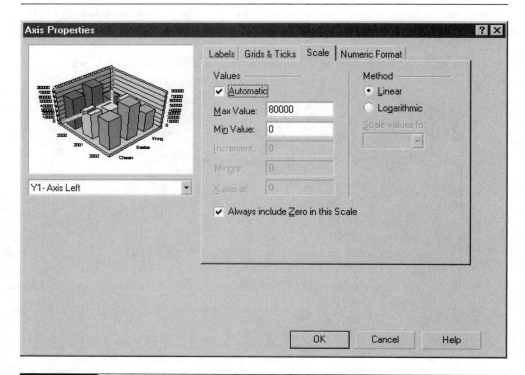

Customizing the Y axis

If you are using large numbers, you may want to take advantage of the Scale Values function. This abbreviates large values and displays their units, such as T for thousands, next to the value. Scale Values can only be used if the Numeric format has been set to Currency or Number.

Printing Charts

When you print your spreadsheet, Quattro Pro 10 also prints any floating charts or maps on the page or in the print block.

If you have a chart selected, or a Chart window is active, Quattro Pro 10 prints only the chart itself.

NOTE *These same techniques apply also to printing maps.*

Creating Maps

When your data is organized by geographic areas, such as states or countries, you can chart it on a map. The map uses colors and patterns to represent the values, which is quite useful in revealing trends and patterns. The map in Figure 20-9, for example, shows membership by state in the United States. By studying the map, you can see where sales need improvement.

 To use mapping, you must perform a custom installation of WordPerfect Office 2002 or you can use Install-As-You-Go, which will allow you to install mapping on the fly without closing Quattro Pro. To trigger the Install-As-You-Go dialog simply select the Mapping command.

Before creating a map, make sure that your spreadsheet is set up using state or country names as the row labels. You can use the state name or the standard postal abbreviations for states. Then follow these steps:

1. Select the cells that contain the data.

2. Choose Graphics from the Insert menu, and click on Map to see the first Map Expert box, shown in Figure 20-10.

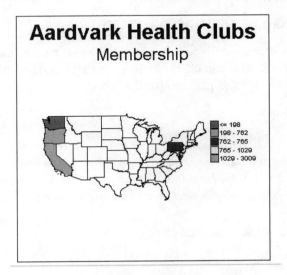

FIGURE 20-9 Quattro Pro map

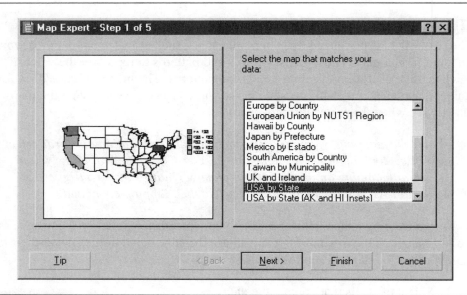

FIGURE 20-10   Map Expert dialog box

3. Select a map to use. Quattro Pro 10 suggests a map based on your data and illustrates it in the pane on the left.

4. Click on Next.

5. Accept or enter the cells representing the region names, and color and pattern ranges. You can chart two different sets of data on a map, using colors for one set and patterns for the other.

6. Click on Next.

 Quattro Pro 10 warns you if you've entered a region that it does not understand and lets you choose a new label. The warning appears, for example, if you used England as a label. In this case, scroll the list of choices, choose Britain, and then click on Replace.

7. Choose a color scheme, and click on Next.

8. Choose an optional overlap map, or have Quattro Pro 10 mark the locations with pin numbers or labels. An overlay could be lines showing major United States highways or a world map showing all of the continents.

9. Click on Next.

10. Enter a title and subtitle, an optional title for the legend, and choose if you want to place the map in the current sheet as a floating object or in a separate window.

11. Click on Finish, and then drag to draw the map areas.

Map Overlays

An *overlay* is an additional map that appears superimposed over the map that you've charted. You can overlay a world map on a map of the United States or Europe, for example, to get a broader view. You can also overlay maps of U.S. highways on maps of the United States, and add major cities or state capitals.

To add an overlay, right-click on the map, and choose Map Data from the QuickMenu. In the Map Data dialog box that appears, click on Add Overlay to see a second dialog box labeled Map Data, shown in Figure 20-11.

Choose the type of overlay you want to add:

- *Region*—Select another map.

- *Static*—Add U.S. highways or a world grid.

- *Pin*—Add names or coordinates of major cities or state or national capitals.

Click on OK to return to the initial Map Data dialog box. To later delete an overlay, select it in the list in the Map Data dialog box, and click on the Delete Overlay button.

Zooming Maps

Quattro Pro 10 inserts an overlay map in a position in relation to its actual coordinates on the globe. If you overlay a map that does not share a common area with the charted map—for example, overlaying Japan on Europe—you may not see it onscreen. To display the overlay, you have to Zoom Out the display to see a larger section of our planet.

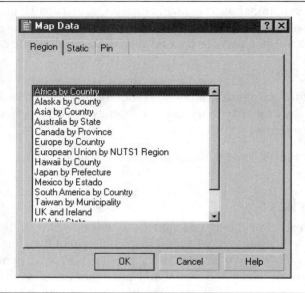

FIGURE 20-11   Adding overlays to enhance a map

While you are editing the map in place (with the thick border around it) or in a window, right-click on the map, and select Zoom Out from the QuickMenu, reducing the magnification until you can see the overlay.

The other Zoom options available in the QuickMenu, and from the Zoom command in the Edit menu, are:

- *Zoom to Normal* returns the map to its default size.

- *Zoom In* enlarges the map.

- *Center* displays the area where the mouse pointer is located in the center of the window.

Creating Your Own Art

You can customize a spreadsheet, chart, or map by adding text boxes, arrows, and other objects that you draw, as shown in Figure 20-12.

To draw basic shapes or a text box, pull down the Shapes list in the toolbar, or select Shape from the Insert menu and choose the shape you want to draw. When

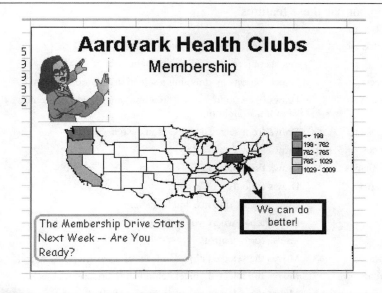

FIGURE 20-12   Customizing a chart or map

you select the shape, you'll see a property bar with buttons for changing the fill style and the foreground and background colors, setting the border style and color, and displaying the object's properties.

Add a piece of clip art using the ClipArt button in the toolbar, or by selecting Graphic from the Insert menu and clicking on ClipArt. You can also select Graphics from the Insert menu, and click on Draw Picture to access the Corel Presentations drawing tools. Create basic shapes by selecting Shapes from the Insert menu, and choosing the type of shape you want to create.

For more drawing options, display the Drawing Tools toolbar, using the following steps:

1. Right-click on the toolbar to display the QuickMenu.

2. Click on Drawing Tools.

The toolbar has these features:

Insert an OLE Object	Opens the Insert Object dialog box.
Select Shapes	Selects objects by clicking on them.
Select Objects	Selects objects by dragging a selection box around them.
Line Objects Tool	Draws lines, solid arrows, arcs, and other shapes; hold down the SHIFT key for a straight line.
Basic Shapes	Draws from selected shapes and designs.
Arrow Shapes	Draws arrows.
Flowchart Shapes	Draws flowchart symbols.
Callout Shapes	Draws callouts with pointers.
Star Shapes	Creates stars, ribbons, and banners.
Text Box	Inserts a box where you enter text.
Controls	Inserts form controls
Bring Forward	Moves the selected object in front of an overlapping object.
Move Behind	Moves the selected object behind an overlapping object.
Bring to Front	Moves the selected object to the top of all objects.
Move to Bottom	Moves the selected object to the back of all objects.

Each of the drawing buttons has a default shape shown on the button. To draw that shape, click on the button, and then drag the mouse where you want the object to appear. You can also pull down the list associated with each button, and choose a specific shape. After creating a text box, type the text that you want in it.

Use the Selection Properties option from the QuickMenu or the Set Properties button in the property bar to change fill patterns, line colors, and other characteristics. You can also use the property bar that appears when you select the object.

Working with Layers

Each new object you draw appears overlaid on top of existing ones, so one object may obscure, or partially obscure, another. To visualize this, imagine the screen as consisting of many layers of clear plastic. Each object you draw is on another layer. You can change the order of layers to move one object in front of or beneath another.

To change the layer of an object, click on it, and then choose one of these buttons from the Drawing Tools toolbar:

- Bring Forward
- Move Behind
- Bring to Front
- Move to Bottom

You can also change the object's order by right-clicking on it, pointing to Object Order in the QuickMenu (or choosing Object Order from the Format menu). Your choices are as follows:

- *Bring Forward* moves the object one layer closer to the top layer.
- *Send Backward* moves the object one layer closer to the bottom layer.
- *Bring to Front* moves the object to the foreground, the top layer.
- *Send to Back* moves the object to the background, the bottom layer.

The Objects Page

The Objects page at the end of the notebook displays an icon for every chart and map that you create. To display the page, select Objects from the View menu, or click on the QuickTab navigation button. Figure 20-13, for example, shows the Objects page with several charts and maps.

When you display the Objects page, the property bar contains these features:

- *Display Full Screen*—Shows the selected object full-screen. Objects page
- *Edit Chart*—Opens the selected chart in a window ready for editing.
- *Create Dialog Box*—Creates a dialog box.

To edit an object, double-click on its icon. Quattro Pro 10 opens it in a separate window, even though you might have created it as a floating chart or map.

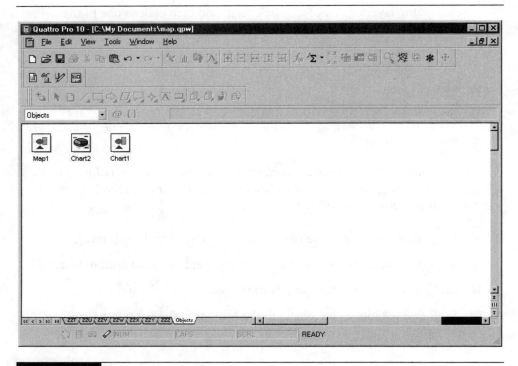

FIGURE 20-13   Objects page

Try It Out

Time to try your own hand at graphs and maps—you'll see how easy it is. In this exercise, we'll create a basic spreadsheet and then create a graphic and a map from the same data. We'll experiment a little with the graphic types and map features to give you a feel for what Quattro Pro can do.

1. Create the spreadsheet shown here.

	A	B	C	D	E	F	G
1		Zone 1	Zone 2	Zone 3	Zone 4	Total	
2	PA	6035	9388	8538	10119	34080	
3	NJ	6676	10981	8380	11474	37511	
4	NY	5710	9512	10273	6058	31553	
5	MA	10529	7014	8862	8774	35179	
6	FL	11908	6667	11723	7747	38045	
7							

2. Select cells A1 to E6.

3. Select Insert | Chart to open the Chart Expert.

4. Select Chart Window and then click Next.

5. Choose Area in the Category list, and select the 3-D checkbox.

6. Click Next.

7. In the Title text box, enter **East Cost Zone Analysis**.

8. Click Next.

9. In the final Expert box, select each of the color schemes to see the effect on the chart—you may have to wait a moment after each selection for the thumbnail of the chart to be redrawn.

10. Click Finish to see the chart shown in Figure 20-14.

11. Click on the Close button in the chart window—not the Close button in the title bar—to return to the spreadsheet. Rather than select cells first to create a map, we'll go through each of the Map Expert dialog boxes to create the map manually.

12. Select Insert | Graphics | Map to begin the Map Expert.

13. Scroll the list of maps and choose USA by State. If you want to include Alaska and Hawaii in the map, select USA by State (AK and HI Inserts).

14. Click Next to display the second Map Expert.

15. Click on the Point mode button to the left of the Region Names text box.

16. Select cells A2 to A6, and then click on the Restore button on the Map Expert title bar.

20

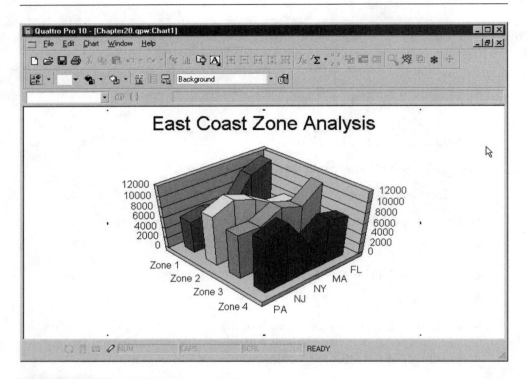

FIGURE 20-14 **FIGURE 20-14**   Completed chart

17. Click on the Point mode button to the left of the Color Data text box.

18. Select cells F2 to F6, and then click on the Restore button on the Map Expert title bar.

19. Click Next to display the third page of the Map Expert in which you select a color scheme.

20. Select each of the color schemes to see the effect on the map, and then click Next.

21. Select US Interstate Highways as an overlay, and then click Next.

22. In the Title text box, enter **East Coast Sales.**

23. In the Legend text box, enter **Thousands**.

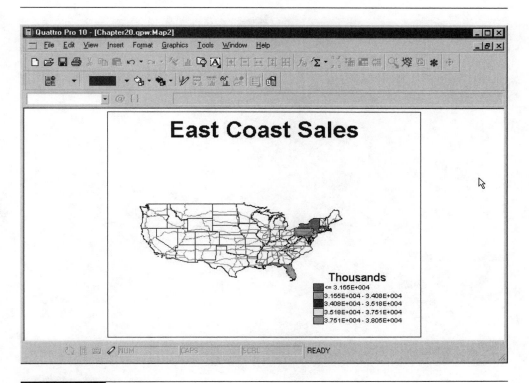

FIGURE 20-15 Completed map

24. Select the Map Window option button, and then click Finish.

25. If the legend obscures the map, click on the legend and drag it down out of the way, as shown in Figure 20-15.

Chapter 21

Analyzing Data

While charts and maps can help you see trends, sometimes you have to analyze data the old-fashioned way. You have to draw conclusions by examining the values in cells and performing statistical operations on them. By analyzing your data, you can make wiser business decisions, and prepare plans and projections. There are hundreds of ways to analyze information and perform statistical analysis with Quattro Pro 10. You can work with information as a database, sort rows to group records, and apply some rather sophisticated analytical techniques. This chapter will survey some of the techniques that you can use.

Working with Databases

A *database* is a place where you store information, an electronic version of a box of 3 x 5 index cards, or even a filing cabinet full of folders and papers. In Quattro Pro 10 you store a database as a series of rows and columns. Each row holds a record, which is a collection of information about one object in the database, such as a client, inventory item, or sales record.

 You can use Quattro Pro to analyze information in databases that you've already created with other programs. See "Analyzing External Data" later in this chapter.

The columns represent the *fields,* each piece of information that makes up a record. The fields for a client record, for example, can include first and last names, address, and phone number. The fields for an inventory record might include the item name and stock number, quantity on hand, and price. Each column is another field, and all of the columns in a row represent the complete record for that item.

Quattro Pro 10 has one other element in a database, the *criteria table*. This enables you to find information quickly based on its content, and to create a subset of your database so you see only the information that you are interested in.

 You can import or link the database into WordPerfect for use as a data file for merging.

Creating a Database

Your first task is to enter the information into the table. A database must be one contiguous block and fit on one sheet. It can be no more than 255 columns. It must have labels in the first row that represent the names of the fields, and each label must be unique. Field names can contain up to 16 characters. They can have spaces between words, but not before or after.

 If you are entering ZIP codes into a database, enter them as text using the apostrophe. Otherwise, leading zeros will not appear with ZIP codes that have them.

Next, assign a block name to the entire database. This isn't mandatory, but it will save time when you need to refer to the database in dialog boxes and functions. Use these steps to assign a block name to the database:

1. Select the database, including the column headings.

2. Pull down the Insert menu, point to Name, and click on Name Cells.

3. Type **Database** as the name, so it will be easy to remember.

4. Click on Add and then Close. Whenever you need to insert the database block, just use the name "Database."

Next, make each of the column labels a field name. Again, this isn't necessary, but it will make it easier to enter criteria to locate specific records. Select the entire database block, pull down the Tools menu, point to Data Tools, and click on Notebook Query to see the Notebook Data Query dialog box. Click on the Field Names button and then on Close. This assigns a block name to each of the labels.

Adding Information to the Database

If you later insert additional rows within the database, Quattro Pro 10 will automatically adjust the block definition. However, if you add information to the blank row following the database, you have to reassign the block name to include the new row as well. It doesn't matter where you add new rows because you can sort them at another time. You'll learn how later.

The best way to add information to the database, however, is to use a database form. This is a dialog box listing the field names, and which lets you navigate through records. You do not have to create the form; Quattro Pro 10 does it for you.

To open the database form, click in any cell within the database, point to Data Tools in the Tools menu and click on Form. Quattro Pro 10 highlights the entire database and displays a box showing its range of cells. Click OK to confirm the range, and to display a data form. A form for a typical database is shown here:

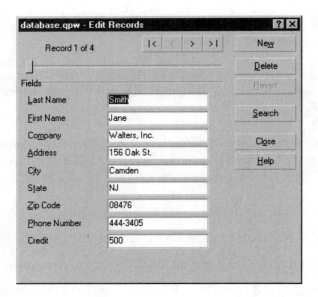

Use the navigation buttons or the slider control on the top of the form to move between records. Click on New to clear the text boxes and enter information for a new row. If you edit information for a record, click on Revert if you change your mind. To accept your changes, move to another record, add a new one, or just close the dialog box. You will not be able to enter information in fields that are calculated.

Searching for Information Using Criteria Tables

Quattro Pro 10 lets you search for information in the database using a method called *query by example*. This means that you type the information you are looking for, as well as any logical conditions, and Quattro Pro 10 searches the database for you.

You have to start by creating a criteria table—a spreadsheet of at least two rows. Create the table anywhere in the notebook, even on the same page as the database if there is room for it on the page. The first row of the criteria table must contain the names of the fields that you want to search in the database. As a shortcut, copy the field names from the first row of the database and paste them into the first row of the criteria table. This ensures that the field names in the criteria table exactly match those in the database.

> **TIP**   *Copy the field names to a row directly below the database. This way, you can take advantage of QuickType to insert values from the rows above.*

You use the other rows in the criteria table to enter the information that you want to search for. For example, Figure 21-1 shows a criteria table to find a record in a database that has the name "Adam" in the First Name column, and "Chesin" in the Last Name column. Searching for values in more than one column of a row is treated as an AND operation. This means that a record must match all of the information in the criteria table row. So, for example, the same search will not locate the record for Adam Smith because only the First Name field would match.

To create an OR operation, enter search information in more than one row. The following criteria table will locate records for Adam Chesin, as well as records for everyone with the last name of Smith, matching one row or the other in the criteria table:

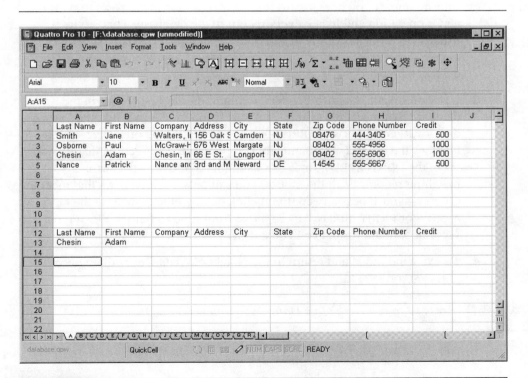

	Last Name	First Name	Company	Address	City	State	Zip Code	Phone Number	Credit
12	Last Name	First Name	Company	Address	City	State	Zip Code	Phone Number	Credit
13	Chesin	Adam							
14	Smith								

FIGURE 21-1   Using a criteria table to locate a name

Searching for Information

Once you define the database and labels, and create a criteria table, you're ready to search. Here's how:

1. Pull down the Tools menu, point to Data Tools, and click on Notebook Query to display the Notebook Data Query dialog box. You'll notice that the coordinates you used to define the field names are still shown in the Database Block text box. Quattro Pro 10 maintains the last settings you used in this box as default values for the notebook. If you wish, you can replace the coordinates with the name "Database" (the results will not change). If you ever want to clear the defaults, click on Reset and then Close.

2. In the Criteria Table text box, enter the coordinates of the criteria table, or use Point mode to insert them. Just make certain that you do not include any blank rows under the last row of the table that contains search information. If you do, Quattro Pro 10 will use the blank rows to perform an Or operation and locate every record in the database. That's why it usually does not save time to select and assign the criteria table a block name. You'd have to redefine the block only if you later add rows to the criteria table.

3. Click on Locate. Quattro Pro 10 will highlight the first record in the database that meets the criteria and enter Find mode. In Find mode you use the UP ARROW or DOWN ARROW key to move from record to record that matches the criteria, automatically skipping over any records that do not. Press the DOWN ARROW once, for example, to move to the second matching record. With the mouse, you can only click on rows that meet the criteria—you'll hear a beep if you click on any other row. Use the LEFT ARROW or RIGHT ARROW key to move from field to field within a record so you can edit and format cell contents as you need.

4. To exit Find mode and return to the Notebook Data Query dialog box, press ESC or ENTER.

| TIP | *Press F7 to repeat the last Data Query operation.* |

Deleting Records

The Delete button in the Notebook Data Query dialog box clears the contents of records that meet the criteria. You will be asked to confirm the deletion, and you can immediately undo it with the Undo button.

As a safeguard, however, perform a Locate first to confirm the records that will be deleted, using these steps:

1. Click on Locate.

2. Press the DOWN ARROW to scroll through the database looking at the selected records.

3. The DOWN ARROW key should select only records that you want to delete. If that's the case, open the Notebook Data Query dialog box again, and then delete the records.

If pressing DOWN ARROW locates a record that you do not want to delete, then try refining the search criteria.

Using Criteria to Pinpoint Information

Searching for specific values is useful, but it has limitations. If you misspell a person's name in the criteria table, for example, it will not be located in the database. By using *wildcards* and *logical operators* in the criteria table, however, you can design searches that pinpoint the exact information you are looking for.

Using Wildcards

Wildcards are special characters that represent one or more characters in text that you are searching for:

?	Represents a single character
*	Represents any number of characters
~	Excludes text from the search, locating records that do not match the value

If you want to find all persons whose last name begins with the letter "N," for example, type **N*** in the Last Name column of the criteria row. This tells Quattro Pro 10 to locate records that start with the letter "N" and have any number of characters following it in that field.

The phrase **c*r** would locate all words that start with "c" and end with "r"—no matter how many characters are between them. On the other hand, entering **c?r** would only locate labels that have one letter between them—"car" but not "caviar."

To locate all clients except those in California, enter **~CA** in the State field. The tilde character must be the first character of the search text.

Logical Conditions

To locate records that fall within a certain range, enter a logical condition in the form of a formula as the search criteria. The condition +Amount Due > 400, for instance, would locate records with a value greater than 400 in the Amount Due field. You can use any of the usual operators:

=	Equal to
<>	Not equal to
>=	Greater than or equal to
>	Greater than
<=	Less than or equal to
<	Less than

> **TIP** *If you did not assign the column labels as field names, use the cell reference of the column label instead.*

You can enter a logical statement in any cell of the criteria table. It does not have to be in the column that it represents. The Amount Due condition, for instance, can be in any column and still locate the proper records.

When you type the formula in the criteria table, however, Quattro Pro will evaluate it and display its results rather than the formula itself. So all you'll see in the cell is a 1 (for true) or 0 (for false). To make criteria tables easier to work with, format the cells by setting their Numeric Format to Text in the Active Cells dialog box. This way you'll see the formulas in the table, as under the Credit label in the criteria table shown here:

	Last Name	First Name	Company	Address	City	State	Zip Code	Phone Number	Credit	
11										
12	Last Name	First Name	Company	Address	City	State	Zip Code	Phone Number	Credit	
13									>500	
14										

Output Blocks

The problem with locating records is that you have to scroll down the database with the DOWN ARROW key to see which records have been located. If you have a large database, you won't get an overall view of the selected records because they are spread out over the entire table.

As an alternative, you can copy all of the located records to an output table. This is a separate table that will contain just the located records. You can then view the selected records as a set, without being distracted by the other rows in the database.

To create an output table, follow these steps:

1. Copy the field names to the location where you want the table to appear. If you leave out any fields, they will not be copied along with the record. So, if you only want to see selected fields in the output table, copy only those field names.

2. Pull down the Tools menu, point to Data tools and click on Notebook Data Query to display the Notebook Data Query dialog box.

3. Enter the coordinates of the row of field names for the output table in the Output Table text box, or use Point mode or an assigned block name.

4. Click on Extract to copy all of the matching records to the output table, or click on Extract Unique to remove any duplicate records when the output table is created.

When you designate the output table coordinates, only include the cells containing labels. If you select blank rows under the cells, Quattro Pro will only copy as many records as there are selected rows.

When you want to merge a form document with selected records from a Quattro Pro 10 database, extract them to a separate block. Then import the block into WordPerfect 10.

Using Database Functions

As you learned in Chapter 18, database functions help you locate and analyze information in a database. All database functions have the same three arguments: Block, Column, and Criteria.

- *Block* is the range of cells that contains the database. Use the block name or coordinates.

- *Column* is where the data is located that you want to analyze, counting from 0. The first column is 0, the second is 1, and so on.

- *Criteria* is the coordinates of the criteria table. If you use the @DAVG function, for instance, only the values in rows meeting the criteria will be averaged. To include all of the rows, create a criteria table using the field names and one blank row under them.

> **NOTE** *You can still use standard functions to calculate sums, averages, and other operations on rows and columns.*

Using QuickFilters to Find and Sort Information

You learned how to use a criteria table to locate specific information, and how to separate it into an output table. Creating and using a criteria table, however, takes quite a few steps. When you want to find specific information, or sort the records in your database, use a QuickFilter instead. If you have a database of student information, for instance, you can use a QuickFilter to list only students with failing grades, or those in the top 10 percent of the class.

To use QuickFilter, click anywhere in the database, pull down the Tools menu, and click on QuickFilter. Quattro Pro will add drop-down arrows to each of the field names:

Clicking on the drop-down arrow displays a menu of options and a list of the values in the column:

To display records that match a value, just click on the value in the list. Using our illustration, for example, you could display only records in Delaware by selecting DE in the pull-down list. When you select a value from the list, the arrow on the list button changes color to remind you that the display is being filtered.

TIP   *Remove all QuickFilters, displaying all records in their original order, by selecting QuickFilter from the Tools menu.*

Select values from other lists to perform an And operation, further limiting the records displayed. Use two lists, for example, to select records meeting two criteria, three lists for records meeting three criteria, and so on.

To remove the filter from a column, pull down the list and choose [Show All]. This removes the filter from the selected column, but not from others. To display all of the records in your database, you must choose [Show All] from every filtered column.

Use the [Sort A-Z] and [Sort Z-A] options in the list to quickly sort the rows of the database. You can sort on more than one field by selecting sort options in multiple lists. Select [Blanks] to display records with no value in the column, or [Non Blanks] to display records with information.

The [Top 10] and [Custom] options give you greater control over selecting records by helping you to analyze the information as well as to limit the records displayed. The [Top 10] option actually lets you select any number of records at the top or bottom in terms of value or percentage, such as the items with the top 5 amounts, the top 20 percent, or the 2 lowest. Selecting Top 10 displays this dialog box:

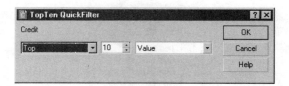

 You can only use the Top 10 option with a column containing numeric values.

From the first list, select if you want to find records in the top or bottom. Use the second list to specify the number of values you want to locate, such as the top 10 or bottom 5. From the last list select if you want to locate items by their value or percentage.

The Custom options let you select records on up to three criteria. You can choose an operator and value for each criteria, and select to perform an And or an Or operation.

Using the Data Sort Feature

When you sort records using a QuickFilter, the sort is always performed from left to right across the database. The leftmost sorted column is sorted first, followed by those to its right. Use the Sort command from the Tools menu to sort the database in any order.

To sort a table, select the block that you want to sort. If you are sorting a database or another spreadsheet that has column labels, it doesn't matter whether you include the row of labels—you can later choose not to include that row with the sort. If you do include the row in the sort, however, the labels will be sorted along with the other information and may end up in some row other than the first.

Next, pull down the Tools menu, and click on Sort to see the dialog box shown in Figure 21-2. The block that you selected will appear in the Cells text box. If it doesn't, enter or point to the coordinates.

You now can specify up to five keys in the Left to Right section. A key is a column that you want to sort by. If you want the records for clients in their name order, for example, enter **Last Name** as the first key, and **First Name** as the second key. If you are sorting a database, enter the field names; otherwise, select

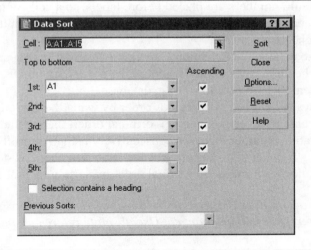

| FIGURE 21-2 | Data Sort dialog box |

the appropriate column from the drop-down provided. Quattro Pro 10 will sort all of the records by the first key, then by the second, and so on.

By default, records are sorted in ascending order. Uncheck the Ascending checkbox to sort in descending order.

The Selection Contains a Heading box determines how Quattro Pro 10 handles the column labels. Chances are this will be set correctly for you. If you selected the label row, for example, the box will be checked so the labels will not be sorted. If you did not select the row, the box will most likely be cleared. Just to be safe, confirm that the option is set the correct way.

Next, click on the Options button to see the dialog box shown here. Choose Top to Bottom to sort the rows in the database, or choose Left to Right to sort the columns. Check Sort Blank Cells First to place blank cells at the start regardless of the sort order.

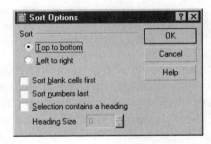

Also by default, numbers are placed before labels, so a cell containing "1" will appear before a cell containing "A." To change the order, click on the Sort Numbers Last checkbox.

You can also change the Selection Contains a Heading setting and designate the number of heading rows in the Heading Size box. Click on OK to accept your settings, and then click on Sort to sort the database.

You can always revert to the previous order by using the Undo command. If you want to be able to revert to the rows' original order, then include an extra column in the table. Number the rows consecutively using AutoFill, or use some other identifying number in consecutive order, such as a client or stock number. You can then quickly return to the original order by sorting on that field.

 Avoid sorting cells that contain relative references to outside the block. The references will be changed. Use absolute references before sorting.

Creating a Cross Tabulation

A *cross tabulation* (CrossTab, for short) analyzes information based on two or more variables. For example, the spreadsheet shown here compares the quarterly sales from four regions. The information for the CrossTab was taken from a database. The values across the top of the CrossTab were extracted from the Quarter column, and the values down the left of the CrossTab from the Regions column. The information analyzed according to the variables Quarter and Region was summarized by another column in the table—the Sales column.

	A	B	C	D	E
1	Year	[All] ▼			
2					
3	Sum of Sales	Quarter			
4	Region	Q1	Q2	Q3	Q4
5	East	569280	581424	604500	611493
6	North	572380	590367	609410	627607
7	South	387832	391859	390742	422599
8	West	384230	392010	397109	414782
9					

The information is further organized by year. As the value in cell B1 indicates, data for all of the years in the database is currently displayed. Pull down the list in cell B1, however, to select specific years from the Year column in the table. Quattro Pro calls this field the *pages*.

Quattro Pro 10 helps you create CrossTabs using one or more variables for the pages, columns, rows, and values to be summarized. Here's how:

1. Click in any cell in the database.

2. Pull down the Tools menu, point to Data Tools, then to CrossTab, and click on Report. Quattro Pro 10 selects the database and display the dialog box shown in Figure 21-3.

The Fields list shows the column headings of the table. The boxes next to the list represent the elements of the CrossTab—the pages, columns, rows, and data fields.

3. Drag a field that you want to use for a page to the Pages box

4. Drag a field that you want to use for a row to the Rows box.

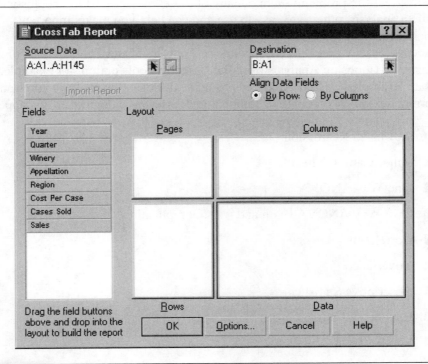

FIGURE 21-3   Creating a CrossTab

5. Drag a field you want to use for a column to the Columns box.

6. Drag a field you want to summarize to the Data box.

7. Add any additional row, column, or data fields. To remove a field from the table, drag it off of the box.

8. Click on OK.

Quattro Pro 10 creates the CrossTab and inserts it into the next empty sheet. You can now add more informative labels, and format the CrossTab for printing or onscreen display.

Analyzing Data

Quattro Pro 10 offers a number of features to help you analyze your spreadsheet and solve real-life problems. While many of these features perform sophisticated statistical analysis, others are easy to use and can help you make important business decisions.

Access these features from the Numeric Tools and Data Tools options of the Tools menu. Choosing Analysis from the Numeric Tools option, for example, starts an Expert that includes the tools listed next. Select the analysis you want to perform, click on Next, and then complete the series of dialog boxes that appears.

- Advanced Regression
- Amortization Schedule
- One-Way ANOVA
- Two-Way ANOVA (with and without replication)
- Correlation
- Covariance
- Descriptive Statistics
- Exponential Smoothing
- Fourier Transformation
- f-Test

- Histogram
- Mortgage Refinancing
- Moving Average
- Random Number
- Rank and Percentile
- Sampling
- t-Test
- z-Test

You can also access these tools by displaying the Experts and Numeric Tools toolbar—right-click on any toolbar, then select Experts and Numeric Tools from the QuickMenu. In addition to statistical, financial, and engineering Experts, the toolbar includes buttons for creating a new chart or map.

In this chapter, we'll explain several especially useful features that do not require an MBA or Ph.D.

Using Solve For

In most cases, you use a formula or function to calculate and display results from the values you already know. Sometimes you have to work in reverse. You know the result you would like to achieve, but not the combination of arguments that will get those results. The mortgage payment function is a good example. If you know the loan rate, number of periods, and amount of principal, then you can calculate the amount of your monthly mortgage payment.

But suppose you already know how much you can afford to spend each month, and you'd like to determine how much of a dream home those monthly payments could obtain. You now have to work backward, a perfect use for the Solve For feature.

To use Solve For, you need a formula that contains a reference to the unknown value. In the @PAYMT function, reference a cell that will contain the principal amount. Solve For automatically changes the value in the referenced cell until the results of a formula reach a value that you specify.

Suppose you know the rate for a 25-year mortgage is 6 percent. You want to find out how much you can borrow to maintain a maximum monthly payment of $1,000. Enter the function **@PAYMT(.06/12,25*12,-A1)**, where A1 is a blank cell.

Pull down the Tools menu, point to Numeric Tools, and click on Solve For to see the dialog box shown here:

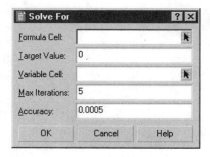

Now use the Solve For dialog box to find the maximum amount you can borrow by following these steps:

1. In the Formula Cell box, enter or point to the coordinates of the formula you want to solve, in this case the cell containing the @PAYMT function.

2. In the Target Value box, enter **1000**, the result that you want to achieve.

3. In the Variable Cell box, enter the cell that Quattro Pro 10 can vary to achieve the results, cell **A1**.

4. Adjust the other options as desired. The Max Iterations option determines how many times Solve For will run through its steps to solve the problem. Accuracy determines how close the result has to be to the target value.

5. Click on OK.

Solve For performs its calculations and displays the result in cell A1.

Optimizer

Solve For is limited because it can only adjust one variable cell. When you have more variables to consider, or have constraints placed on their values, use Optimizer. The spreadsheet shown in Figure 21-4 is a good example. It is our friend the @PAYMT function, but with three cells that can vary: mortgage rate, number of years, and amount of principal. Use Optimizer to find a combination of values that results in a target payment.

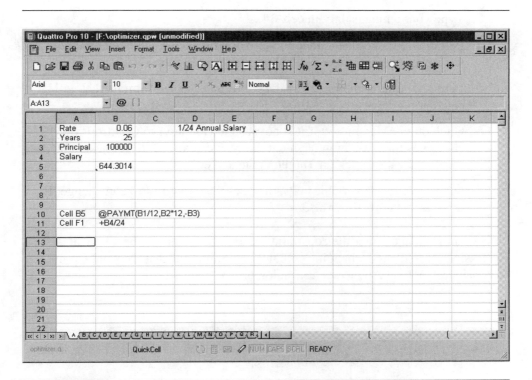

FIGURE 21-4   Spreadsheet to solve a formula based on three variables

In real life, however, we'd have to place some constraints on the values that
Quattro Pro 10 can use. We know that a realistic mortgage rate might be between 6
and 8 percent, and that we need a loan for at least 20 years to minimize our
payments. We're also going to add another constraint: our monthly mortgage
payment cannot be more than 1/24th of our salary. That is, we don't want to spend
more than half of our monthly income on the mortgage. When we tell Quattro Pro
10 our constraints, we cannot include a formula, but we can reference a formula in
a cell. So create the spreadsheet shown in the figure, using these steps:

1. In cell B5, enter the function **@PAYMT(B1/12,B2*12,-B3)**.

2. In cell F1, enter the formula **+B4/24** that you'll use to limit the mortgage
   payment based on salary.

3. Type your annual salary in cell B4.

4. Pull down the Tools menu, point to Numeric Tools, and click on Optimizer to display the Optimizer dialog box shown in Figure 21-5.

5. In the Solution Cell box, enter the coordinates of the formula that will be calculating the result, cell **B5**.

6. Click on the Max button if it is not selected already, so Quattro Pro calculates the maximum payment that you can afford. If you wanted to find a specific value, click on Target Value and enter the amount.

7. Next, specify the variable cells, the ones that Quattro Pro can change. In this case, enter cells **B1..B3**.

You now have to enter the constraints. Each constraint will be a logical expression referencing a changing cell and the limitations that we want Optimizer to consider. Click on Add to see the dialog box in Figure 21-6.

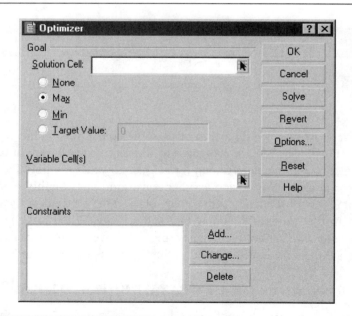

FIGURE 21-5   Optimizer dialog box

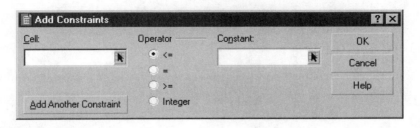

FIGURE 21-6   Adding a constraint to Optimizer

The first constraint is that the rate must be 8 percent or less. Enter **B1** in the Cell column, leave the operator set at <=, and enter **.08** in the Constant box. The expression B1<=.08 means that the values entered in the cell by Optimizer must be less than or equal to 8 percent. Click on Add Another Constraint.

The second constraint is that the rate must be 6 percent or greater. Enter **B1** in the Cell column, click on >=, and enter **.06** in the Constant box. With these two constraints, Quattro Pro 10 will only test rates between 6 and 8 percent. Click on Add Another Constraint.

Now complete the remainder of the constraints, clicking on OK after you complete the last:

Constraint	Cell	Operator	Constant
Number of years less than 30	B2	<=	30
Number of years greater than 19	B2	>=	19
Mortgage payments no more than 1/24 of your salary	B5	<=	F1

When you have finished entering the last constraint, click on Close. The constraints will appear in your Optimizer dialog box, as shown next. If they do not, select the constraint that is incorrect and click on Change. Use Delete to remove a constraint. Now click on Solve. Quattro Pro 10 calculates the maximum value for cell B5 by varying the values in cells B1, B2, and B3, but using the constraints specified. If you do not want to change the spreadsheet to these values, select Undo, or display the Optimizer dialog box and click on Revert.

Optimizer Options

You can customize Optimizer for your specific problem by clicking on Options in the Optimizer dialog box to see the options shown in Figure 21-7. Most of these options perform rather sophisticated operations, and they require an equally sophisticated understanding of data analysis. We'll look at options that are more frequently used.

Reporting   The Optimizer solves your problem, but it does not automatically show you how it arrived at its conclusion. The Reporting option lets you create two types of detailed reports explaining how Optimizer works:

FIGURE 21-7   Optimizer options

- The *Answer Report* lists the coordinates of the solution and variable cells, along with the starting and final values that Optimizer calculated. It also lists the variable gradient, increment, and decrement values.

- The *Detail Report* lists values from the solution and variable cells at each iteration, so you can see how they changed during the process.

To create one or both of the reports, click on Reporting. In the dialog box that appears, enter or point to the range of cells where you want to place one or both of the reports. You can designate an entire block, or just the upper-left corner.

Because the report overwrites any existing contents, make sure there are enough blank cells. The Answer Report needs six columns and at least ten more rows than the total number of solution cells and constraints. The Detail Report uses as many rows as iterations, plus three headings.

When you solve the problem, the reports will appear in the designated blocks.

Saving Optimizer Settings   When you save your spreadsheet, Quattro Pro saves the Optimizer settings along with it. If you use Optimizer to solve several problems, you should save each set so you can quickly retrieve it. Save the set in a blank area of the spreadsheet.

Once you have the settings the way you want them, click on Options in the Optimizer dialog box, and then click on Save Model. In the dialog box that appears, enter or point to a location in the spreadsheet at least three columns wide and six rows deep, and then click on OK. Saved settings appear like this:

```
Solution Cell
+B5          Maximize          0
Variable Cells
@COUNT
Constraints
@COUNT  <=            0.08
@COUNT  >=            0.06
@COUNT  <=              30
@COUNT  >=              19
@COUNT  <=          +F1..F1
```

When you want to use the settings, choose Load Model from the Optimizer Options dialog box, and enter the top-left cell where you saved the settings.

Saving Scenarios

Using formulas and functions makes it easy to solve "What If " problems. Each time you change a value, you can see the results throughout the spreadsheet. But once you change them again, the previous results are gone. Certainly you can use Undo to revert to the last values. But what if you want to see the results of values that you entered before that, or even on a previous day?

A *scenario* is a set of values that you've used to generate results—a snapshot of the spreadsheet with one set of values. By saving a scenario, you can quickly return to it when you want to see its effects. By saving a number of scenarios, you can quickly compare results to help make informed decisions.

For example, suppose you create a presentation for an important client. The spreadsheet contains a series of cost projections based on varying expenses. You can use scenarios to switch between the sets of data, so the client gets a feel for the pros and cons of each plan.

Start by deciding on three things:

1. The range of cells that you want to include in the scenario

2. The cells that will change in value for each scenario, called the changing cells

3. The formulas that reference the changing cells, called the result cells

Using Scenario Expert

The fastest way to create a series of scenarios is to use the Scenario Expert. Start by preparing the spreadsheet so it contains the first set of the values and results that you want to save. This is called the *base scenario*. Then pull down the Tools menu, point to Scenario, and click on New. A series of dialog boxes will appear for you to select options.

In the first dialog box, enter or point to the changing cells—the cells whose values will change with each scenario.

The second dialog box contains text boxes for each of the changing cells, showing the base settings currently in the spreadsheet (Figure 21-8). To create another scenario, change the values in the text boxes, type a name for the scenario, and then click on Add Scenario. Repeat this for each set of values and then click on Next.

The next Expert dialog box lists all of the scenarios. To see the values in the spreadsheet, click on a scenario name and then on Show Scenario. If you want to remove one of the scenarios, click on it and then on Delete.

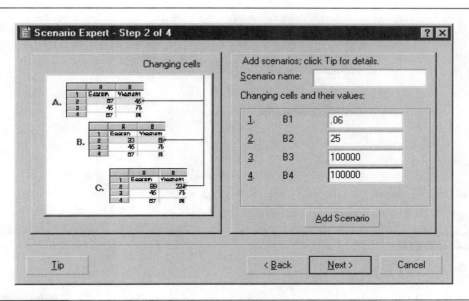

FIGURE 21-8   Using base settings and adding scenarios in Scenario Expert

In the last Expert dialog box, you can create an optional report or just exit. If you create a report, Quattro Pro 10 will create a Scenarios page after the first nonblank sheet. Display the page to see the changing and result cells and their values in each scenario.

Scenario Manager

Scenario Expert saves the scenarios in the Scenario Manager, a dialog box where you select which scenarios to display, and where you can add, delete, and modify scenarios.

Pull down the Tools menu, point to Scenario, and click on Edit to display the dialog box shown in Figure 21-9. You will see a list of scenarios that you created with the Expert—the base and other scenarios. To see a scenario, just click on it in the list. The values from the scenario will be applied to the spreadsheet.

NOTE   *Use the Highlight button to select a color for the formulas and to select changing cells for each scenario.*

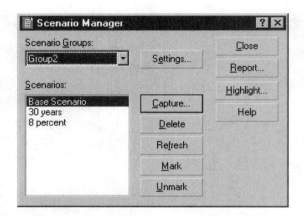

FIGURE 21-9   Scenario Manager

To add a new scenario, exit Scenario Manager, and edit the values in the changing cells. Then display Scenario Manager and click on Capture. Type a name for the scenario and then click on Close. A scenario can also include a change in a result cell formula.

Creating Scenarios Manually

It is just as easy to create scenarios without using the Expert. Prepare the spreadsheet with the base values and then display Scenario Manager by selecting Tools | Scenario | Edit. By default, the scenario will include the entire page of the spreadsheet, keeping track of cells with changing values and formulas that reference them. If you want to track just a specific block of the page, or the entire notebook, then click on the Settings button. In the dialog box that appears, enter or point to the range of cells, or click on Notebook or Sheet to change the capture area. Then close the dialog box to return to Scenario Manager.

Now click on Capture and enter a name for the base scenario—the default is Base Scenario—and then click on OK and close Scenario Manager.

You can now edit the changing cells and capture each of the scenarios. When you capture the first scenario after the base, Quattro Pro 10 will automatically identify the changing and the result cells and show them highlighted. The changing cells will be those that have different values than in the base. The result cells are formulas that reference the changing cells. If the cells are not identified correctly, click on the Find button in Scenario Manager. If this still doesn't identify the cells, do it manually—select the cells and then click on Add.

Scenario Groups

You can have more than one group of scenarios in a notebook. Each set can track a different set of cells or page, and each can have its own base. To create a new group, prepare the spreadsheet the way you want the base scenario to appear. Open Scenario Manager and click on Settings to display the dialog box shown in Figure 21-10.

Click on New and enter a name for the group. Use the Rename button to change the name of an existing group. Close the dialog box.

Use the Scenario Groups list in Scenario Manager to change groups. First, display the page of the spreadsheet that contains the captured cells, and then open Scenario Manager and choose the group that you want to display. The scenarios in the group will be listed.

Deleting Scenarios

You can delete individual scenarios or entire groups. To delete a scenario, select it in the Scenario Manager list and click on Delete. If you delete the base scenario, Quattro Pro 10 will also delete all of the other scenarios that are based on it.

To delete a group, click Settings in Scenario Manager, choose the group in the Scenario Groups list and then click on Delete.

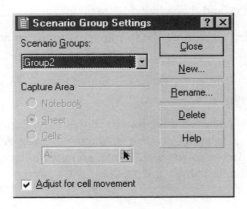

FIGURE 21-10   Adding a group

Creating What-If Tables

One problem with Scenario Manager is that you must choose a scenario each time you want to see the results of changing cells. Wouldn't it be easier if you could just create a table showing the various values in the changing cells and each effect on the result cell? You can do this by creating a What-If table.

There are two types of What-If tables. A one-variable table displays the results of changing one cell on one or two formulas. A two-variable table shows the results of changing two variables on a single formula. As an example, look at Figure 21-11. Both of the tables use the @FVAL function to determine how much an annual investment is worth after a number of years. On the left is a one-variable table that compares the results of saving different annual amounts. The amounts are shown in column B, and the total savings after ten years for each amount is shown in column C. The table on the right compares different amounts and interest rates. The formulas for a one-variable table must reference only one cell, while two-variable formulas reference only two cells.

You can create What-If tables manually or by using the What-If Expert. Let's use the What-If Expert to create the one-variable table shown in the figure.

1. Enter **200** in cell A1, and the formula **@FVAL(6%,10,-A1**) in cell A2.

2. Pull down the Tools menu, point to Numeric Tools, and click on What-If Tables.

3. In the dialog box that appears, click on Expert.

4. In the first Expert, leave the option set at Vary One Cell Against One or More Formulas, and then click on Next.

5. Specify the cell containing the formulas. Enter or point to cell A2, and then click on Next.

6. You can now designate a second formula to track. This example only uses one, so click on Next.

   In this box, you designate the input cell that is referenced in the formula, and a name for it that will appear on the table. Enter **A1** as the input cell, type **Annual Investment** as the name, and then click on Next. The input cell must contain a value.

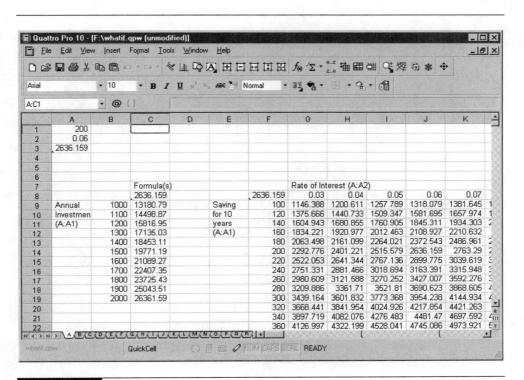

FIGURE 21-11   What-If tables

7. This box lets you select the values that will be used in the input cell. As you can see in Figure 21-12, Quattro Pro 10 suggests some values for you. For this example, increase the savings.

8. Click on Calculate Different Values. Text boxes will appear so you can enter the starting and stopping values, as well as the steps between.

9. Enter **1000** as the Start value, **100** as the Step value, **2000** as the Stop value.

10. Click Rebuild List to see the new values in the list box, and then click on Next.

11. In the last box, enter or point to the block where you want the table to appear, and then click on Make Table.

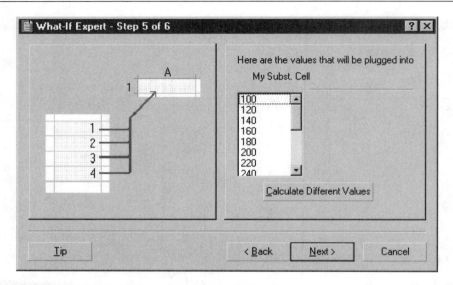

FIGURE 21-12 Quattro Pro's suggested values based on the content of the changing cells

NOTE *The two-variable Expert is the same, except you designate two input cells.*

To create a What-If table manually, you have to start the table by entering the column of values that you want to substitute in a formula. In the cell above and to the right of the first substitute value, enter the formula that you want to calculate, including a reference to a blank input cell. Pull down the Tools menu, point to Numeric Tools, and click on What-If Tables to see the dialog box shown in Figure 21-13. In the What-If Table box, enter or point to the block of cells that contains the substitution values and formula. In the Input Cell box, enter the cell referenced in the formula. Click on Generate to create the table.

To create a two-variable table using the What-If Expert, you need a second changing cell. In Figure 21-11, for example, A1 is the first changing cell, and A2 is the second changing cell. To create the table manually, you need to add a row of substitution values starting above and to the right of the substitution column. Enter the formula into the top-left cell of the table, making sure that it refers to two blank input cells. In the What-If dialog box, click on Two Free Variables. Indicate the Data Table and the Column Input and Row Input cells, and then click on Generate.

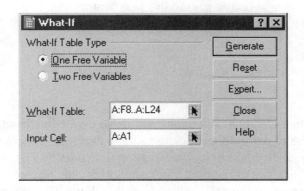

FIGURE 21-13 What-If dialog box

If you later change a formula used for the table, click on Generate to recalculate the results.

Analyzing External Data

Quattro Pro 10 includes a number of tools for working with data that was created with other programs. The External Data option from the Insert menu, for example, lets you query, link, and import information from database files.

You might also have data that you've saved as a text file. Importing a text file into Quattro Pro 10 could be difficult because you have to specify how the text in the file should be divided into rows and columns.

QuickColumns is a fast solution to importing text files. Pull down the Tools menu, point to Data Tools, and click on QuickColumns to see the Expert dialog box shown here:

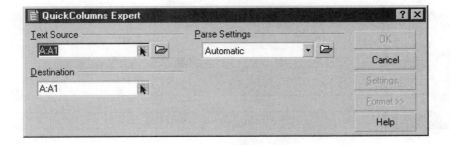

Click on the browse button next to the Text Source box, and select the file containing the data you want to import. Specify the range to place the data in the Destination box.

NOTE *You'll learn about the Parse Settings list later.*

When you click OK, QuickColumns will try to divide the data based on its spacing or the use of delimiting characters, but to check the spacing, click on the Format button to see the additional information illustrated in Figure 21-14.

The spreadsheet area of the dialog box shows how the text will be divided into columns and the numeric format applied to each column. Column width is

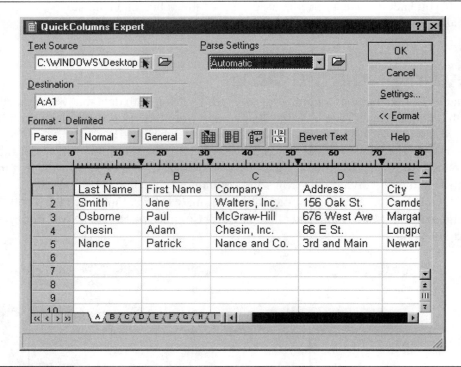

FIGURE 21-14   Advanced options for importing a text file

indicated in character positions along the ruler, with column boundaries marked by a triangle. The lists and buttons above the spreadsheet serve these functions:

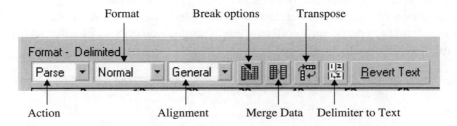

- To select how a row is treated, click on its row header, then choose an option from the Action list: Parse, Skip, or Label.

- To change the format or alignment, click on the column header of the data you want to change, and then choose options from the Format and Alignment lists.

- To insert a row, column, or new spreadsheet between the data, click the Break Options button and select from the dialog box that appears.

- To change the width of columns, drag the column boundary in the preview pane.

- To combine the contents of cells into one cell, select the cells in the row and click on the Merge Data button.

- To transpose rows and columns, select the information and then click on the Transpose button.

- To combine the contents of cells into one cell, but have them delimited so they appear in separate columns in the spreadsheet, select the cells and click the Delimiter to Text button.

- Restore the text to its original layout by clicking on the Revert Text

Dividing text into spreadsheet columns is called parsing. The Parse Settings option determines a set of rules that tells QuickColumns how to parse the information. When set to Automatic, QuckColumns determines the best arrangement for you. You can also choose Delimited Auto or Fixed Width Auto from the Parse Settings list. Delimited Auto assumes that some character, such as a tab or comma, separates information. Fixed With Auto assumes that the text can be divided into columns based on its spacing.

You can create your own rules for parsing by clicking on the Settings button to open the dialog box shown in Figure 21-15.

Select options from the General, and then indicate if you are setting rules for delimited or fixed width parsing. If you choose Delimited, choose the characters that represent the end of each cell, row, and sheet. If you choose Fixed Width you can then select from these options:

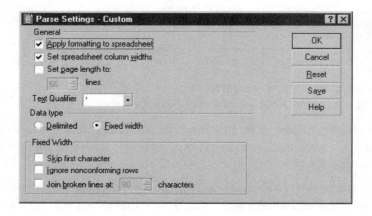

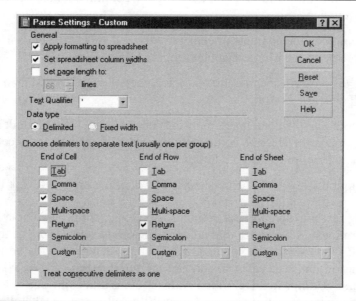

FIGURE 21-15   Creating custom parse settings

When you're done, click Save to open the Save QuickColumns Settings dialog box. Enter a filename for the settings file and the click on Save.

When you want to use your custom settings file to parse information, open the QuickColumns dialog box and click on the browse button next to the Parse Setting list to open the Load QuickColumns Settings dialog box. Select the file that you saved and click Open.

Try It Out

You learned quite a bit of material in this chapter, so we'll highlight a few of the techniques that you can use to analyze information. In this section, we'll create a sample database and look at it in several ways.

1. Create the database shown in Figure 21-16. The formula in cell E2 is **+D2/C2**. The formula in cell F2 is **+D2*I1**. Copy the formulas down the columns.

   Now use QuickFilter to see just the records for the salesperson named Wing, and then locate which of Wing's years are included in the top five in the database.

2. Select QuickFilter from the Tools menu.

3. Pull down the Salesperson list and select Wing.

4. Pull down the Sales list and select Top Ten.

5. In the Top Ten QuickFilter box, change the second setting from 10 to 5, and click OK. Three records will be shown, indicating that Wing had three of the top five sales figures.

	A	B	C	D	E	F	G	H	I	
1	Year	Salesperson	Calls	Sales	Average Per	Commissions		Rate	0.15	
2	2000	Wing	118	$278,480	$2,360	$41,772.00				
4	2001	Wing	109	$276,910	$2,540	$41,536.50				
6	2002	Wing	171	$259,652	$1,518	$38,947.80				

6. Select Show All from the Salesperson and Sales lists to display all of the records.

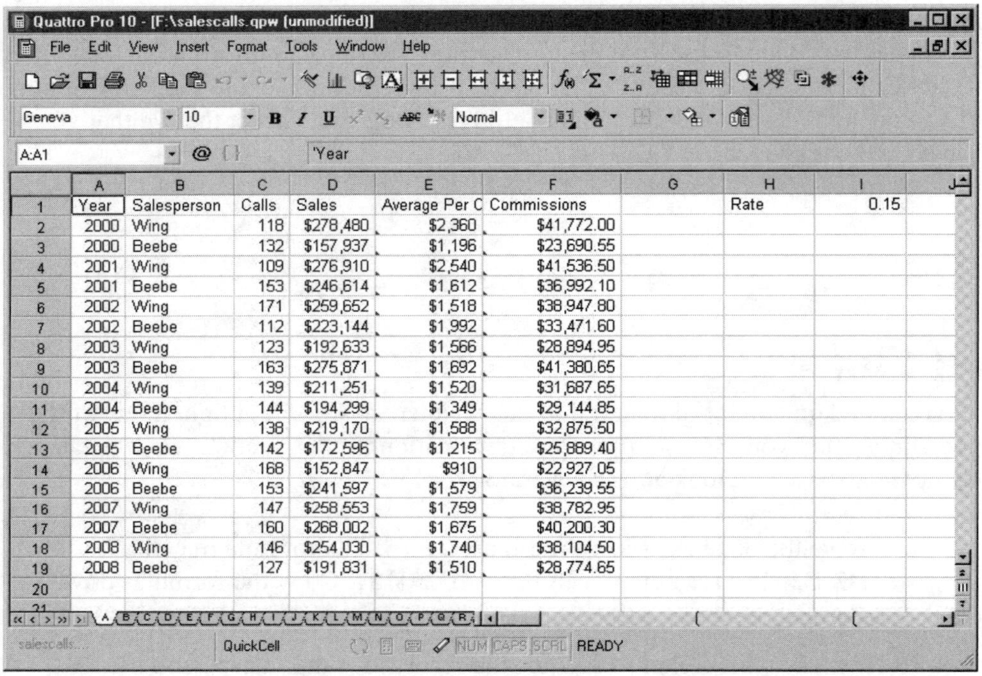

FIGURE 21-16 Database for project

Next, let's create a separate table containing just the records for Beebe.

7. Select QuickFilter from the Tools menu.

8. Select cells A1 to F1, copy them, and paste them to cell A23.

9. Paste them again in cell A27.

10. Enter Beebe in cell B24.

11. Select Tools | Date Tools | Notebook Query.

12. In the Database Cells box enter **A1..F19**.

13. In the Criteria Table box enter **A23..F24**.

14. In the Output Cells box enter **A27..F47**.

15. Click Extract to see the separate table:

	Year	Salesperson	Calls	Sales	Average Per C	Commissions		
22								
23	Year	Salesperson	Calls	Sales	Average Per C	Commissions		
24		Beebe						
25								
26								
27	Year	Salesperson	Calls	Sales	Average Per C	Commissions		
28	2000	Beebe	132	$157,937	$1,196	$23,690.55		
29	2001	Beebe	153	$246,614	$1,612	$36,992.10		
30	2002	Beebe	112	$223,144	$1,992	$33,471.60		
31	2003	Beebe	163	$275,871	$1,692	$41,380.65		
32	2004	Beebe	144	$194,299	$1,349	$29,144.85		
33	2005	Beebe	142	$172,596	$1,215	$25,889.40		
34	2006	Beebe	153	$241,597	$1,579	$36,239.55		
35	2007	Beebe	160	$268,002	$1,675	$40,200.30		
36	2008	Beebe	127	$191,831	$1,510	$28,774.65		
37								
38								

Next, build a scenario to see the effects of changing commissions to 10% and 18%.

16. Select Tools | Scenario | New.

17. In the Changing Cells enter I1, and click Next.

18. As Scenario name, enter **10 percent**.

19. In the changing cell text box enter **0.1**.

20. Click Add Scenario.

21. As Scenario name, enter **18 percent**.

22. In the change cell text box enter **0.18**.

23. Click Add Scenario and then click Next and Exit.

24. Select Tools | Scenario | Edit. You'll see a dialog box listing the three scenarios.

25. Click 10 percent in the Scenarios list. The worksheet in the background behind the dialog box changes to reflect the new scenario, as shown in Figure 21-17.

26. Click 18 percent in the Scenarios list.

27. Click Base Scenario in the Scenarios list and then click Close.

28. Select cells A1 to F19 and then select Tools | Data Tools | CrossTab | Report.

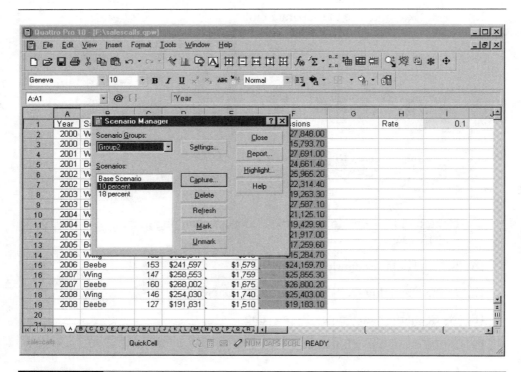

FIGURE 21-17   New scenario

29. Drag Salesperson into the Rows box.

30. Drag Year into the Columns.

31. Drag Sales into the Data box. It appears as Sum of Sales.

32. Drag Commissions into the Data box.

33. Click OK to see the CrossTab report shown here:

	A	B	C	D	E	F	G	H	I	
1			Year							
2	Salesperson	Data	2000	2001	2002	2003	2004	2005	2006	
3		Sum of Sales	157937	246614	223144	275871	194299	172596	241597	
4	Beebe	Sum of Commissions	23690.55	36992.1	33471.6	41380.65	29144.85	25889.4	36239.55	4
5		Sum of Sales	278480	276910	259652	192633	211251	219170	152847	2
6	Wing	Sum of Commissions	41772	41536.5	38947.8	28894.95	31687.65	32875.5	22927.05	38
7										

Chapter 22

Streamlining Your Work

737

You have a wide range of tools and Experts to make your work easier with Quattro Pro 10. But there is still more. By recording macros, you can quickly repeat a series of keystrokes and menu selections whenever you need to. You can build libraries of macros to carry out common tasks, and you can write macros that perform sophisticated functions. By linking macros with the keyboard, you run them without using a menu or dialog box, and you can even create a button to run a macro with a single click.

Another way to increase your productivity is to share your Quattro Pro 10 spreadsheets, charts, and maps with WordPerfect 10 and Corel Presentations 10. Use the formatting capabilities of these programs to display or publish your data and graphics with maximum impact.

Macros

A macro serves the same function in Quattro Pro 10 as it does in WordPerfect 10 and any other computer application. It lets you save a series of keystrokes and commands and then replay the entire series at any time. Recording a macro in Quattro Pro 10, however, is a little different than in WordPerfect 10 because of the nature of the program.

 Use PerfectScript from the WordPerfect 10 Accessories menu to create a macro so you can run it from the taskbar.

You can record and play two types of macros in Quattro Pro 10. PerfectScript macros are compatible with the macro language used by other WordPerfect Office 2000 applications and by the PerfectScript accessory. The macros are stored on your disk as individual files, and you can edit them using an editor of your choice, even WordPerfect 10. Quattro Pro 10 macros are compatible with previous versions of Quattro Pro for Windows. They are stored directly in a spreadsheet, and you can edit them as you would any labels in the spreadsheet. These are the easiest macros to create and troubleshoot because all the work is done in one application. You can even take advantage of macros that you or others have written for previous versions of Quattro Pro.

Recording a Macro

You don't have to do any preparation before recording a PerfectScript macro because it is stored on your disk. But before creating a Quattro Pro 10 macro, locate a blank area in the spreadsheet in which to store the macro. It should be one column wide, with at least as many blank cells as the steps that you want to record. To play it safe, make sure that the remainder of the column is empty and that you won't need any of those cells for the task you'll be recording. You might consider recording all of the macros you want to use for the notebook on sheet IV, which you probably won't be using for anything else, and which you can reach with the QuickTab button. Using one column for each macro allows you to record 1,000,000 macros before you have to worry about space.

To record a macro, follow these steps:

1. Pull down the Tools menu, point to Macro, and click on Record to display the dialog box in Figure 22-1. Your first choice is to choose to record either a Quattro Pro 10 or PerfectScript macro. If you select a PerfectScript macro, the box changes so you can indicate the macro name and location where you want to save it.

2. To record a Quattro Pro 10 macro, designate in the Location text box where in your notebook you want the macro recorded. Enter the coordinates or use Point mode to indicate the first empty cell that you've identified for the macro location. If you gave a block name to the cell, select the name from the Macros/Named Cells list. Designate only a single cell. If you designate a block of cells, Quattro Pro 10 records commands only until the block is filled. By specifying a single cell, it continues recording commands until the column ends or you stop recording the macro.

3. Click on OK to close the dialog box. Quattro Pro 10 displays an icon of a recording tape in the application bar as a reminder that you are recording a macro.

4. Perform the tasks that you want to record in the macro. You'll even see the commands appear if the macro block is onscreen.

5. When you have finished recording the macro, pull down the Tools menu, point to Macro, and click on Record again.

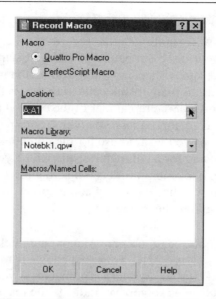

FIGURE 22-1   Selecting the type of macro you want to record

6. Give your macro a name so you can replay it easily. Click in the first cell in which the macro is stored, pull down the Insert menu, point to Name, click on Name Cells. Enter the macro name, and then click Add and then Close.

To play a macro, just follow these steps:

1. Select Macro from the Tools menu, and click on Play.

2. In the dialog box that appears, double-click on the macro name.

If you need to stop a macro while it is running, press CTRL-BREAK, and then click on OK in the message box that appears. Quattro Pro 10 will sound a beep and display an error message if it cannot follow the macro instruction. You usually get errors not with recorded macros, but from ones that you edit or write.

NOTE   *You can play a macro even if you did not give it a name. In the Location text box of the Play Macro dialog box, simply enter the coordinates of the first instruction in the macro, and then click on OK.*

Relative and Absolute Addresses

By default, macros are recorded using *absolute addresses*. This means that if you click on cell A:A1 when recording the macro, the macro always selects cell A:A1 when you run it. There's nothing wrong with that if that's what you want. But suppose you want to record a macro that inserts a series of labels at a different location each time you play the macro?

To accomplish that, you must change to *relative addresses*. Here's how:

1. Pull down the Tools menu, point to Macro, and click on Options to see this dialog box.

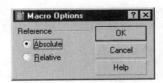

2. Click on Relative and then on OK.

Now each cell selection command you record will select a cell relative to whatever is the active cell at that time. So suppose you start recording when you're in cell A1, and your first action is to click in cell B2. When you run the macro, it will start by selecting the cell one column over and one row down from the current active cell.

This all means that you have to plan your macro well and think about what you want it to do and where. Consider starting by selecting the cell you will first want to use when you record the macro. Then as your first recorded step, click on that same cell, even though it is already active. This ensures that your macro starts at some known location.

If you are using an absolute address, the macro starts in that cell no matter what cell is active when you begin. If you use relative addresses, the macro always begins in whatever cell is active at the time—just select it before running the macro.

NOTE *If you select a cell at the start of the macro but perform any action on it except selecting another cell, the command to select the first cell will not be recorded in the macro.*

Let's record a small macro so you can get the feel for it. The macro will enter a series of row and column labels starting in the cell next to the active cell, and insert a row of formulas. Follow these steps:

1. Click in A1.

2. Select Tools | Macro | Options | Relative | OK.

3. Select Tools | Macro | Record to display the Record Macro dialog box.

4. In the Location box, enter **B:A1** to save the macro in the first column of sheet B. (You can also point to the cell by clicking on the sheet B tab and then on cell A1.)

5. Click on OK. You can now record the macro.

6. Click in cell B1, type **Qtr 1**, and press ENTER.

7. Drag over cells B1 to E1, and then click on the QuickFill button to complete the series.

8. Click in Cell A2, and type **Income**.

9. Click in Cell A3, and type **Expenses**.

10. Click in cell B4, type **+B2-B3**, and press ENTER.

11. Drag over cells B4 to E4, and click on QuickFill to copy the formulas.

12. To stop recording, select Tools | Macro | Record.

> **NOTE** *The Absolute and Relative macro record options do not affect the way Quattro Pro 10 copies formulas.*

Naming Your Macro

To name the macro, you assign a block name to the first cell of the macro instructions. Let's name the macro we just recorded.

1. Go to sheet B to see the instructions of the macro, as shown in Figure 22-2. The instructions of the macro are listed in the block you selected in the Quattro Pro 10 macro language.

2. Click on cell A1.

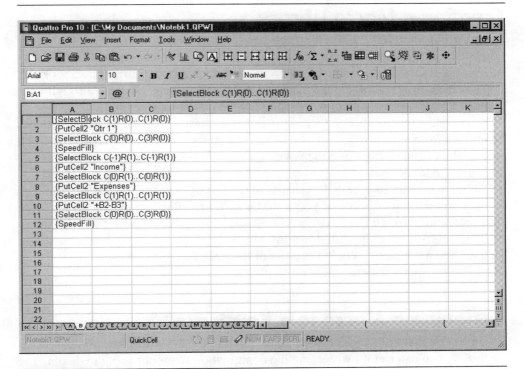

FIGURE 22-2   Recorded macro instructions

3. Select Insert I Name I Name Cells.

4. Type **Budget** as the block name.

5. Click on Add.

6. Click on Close.

Running Your Macro

Now run the macro. Click on any cell in sheet A, select Tools I Macro I Play.
Double-click on Budget in the macro list. The labels and formulas will be inserted
starting in the cell next to the active cell on the sheet.

Creating a Macro Library

A *macro library* is a notebook in which you can store macros. You open the notebook and leave it in the background as you work with other notebooks. When you play a macro, Quattro Pro 10 will first search for it in the current notebook. If it is not there, it will look for the macro in the macro library. You can also tell Quattro Pro 10 to find it there when you play the macro to save time.

To create a macro library, record the macros in a spreadsheet. Select Notebook Properties from the Format menu to display the Active Notebook dialog box. Click on the Macro Library tab, and then click on Yes. Close the Properties dialog box, and save the notebook.

When you want to access the macros in the library, open the notebook. It must be open to access its macros. If you want Quattro Pro 10 to run the macro without first searching through the active notebook, pull down the Tools menu, point to Macro, and click on Play. Pull down the Macro Library List dialog box, and click on the library file name. You'll see a list of the macros and cell names. Double-click on the macro you want to run.

Assigning a Macro to a Keystroke

If you have a macro that you run often, assign it to a CTRL-SHIFT key combination. That way, you can run it by pressing the combination without having to display the Macro dialog box. When you name the macro, name it with a backslash (\) followed by one letter (a to z), such as \c. Then to run the macro, press CTRL-SHIFT and the letter.

Assigning a Macro to a Button

One problem with using a keystroke to run a macro is that you have to remember the keystroke. As an alternative, you can assign the macro to a button on the spreadsheet. Just click on the button to play the macro.

First, create the button.

1. Display the spreadsheet where you want the button to appear.

2. Select Form Control from the Insert menu, and click on Push Button. You can also choose to insert a checkbox or radio button to perform the macro in the same way.

3. Either click where you want a default-sized button to appear, or drag to create a button of any size. When you release the mouse, the button appears selected with handles.

You can always change the size of the button later by dragging the handles. To move a button, use drag and drop.

If you click elsewhere in the spreadsheet, the handles disappear. Until you assign a process to the button, you can click on it with the left mouse button to select it so the handles appear. Once you assign a process to the button, right-click on it to select it. If you click the left mouse button, Quattro Pro 10 performs whatever function the button has been assigned.

Once you create the button, you must associate the macro with it, using these steps:

1. Right-click on the button, and choose Selection Properties from the QuickMenu; then click on the Macro tab to see the dialog box shown in Figure 22-3.

2. In the Enter Macro text box on the Macro page of the dialog box, type the command **{Branch macroname}**, substituting the name of your macro for *macroname*. You must enclose the command in braces.

3. Click on the Label Text page of the Button Properties dialog box, and enter what you want to appear on the button's face.

4. Click OK.

You can also link the button to an URL address on the Web or open a custom dialog box. Select Link to URL on the Macro page of the dialog box, and enter the URL address. To browse the Web to select a site, click on the Web Browse button in the toolbar.

The other button properties let you change the border color and button box style, protect the button from change, and give it an object name so you can refer to the button itself in macros.

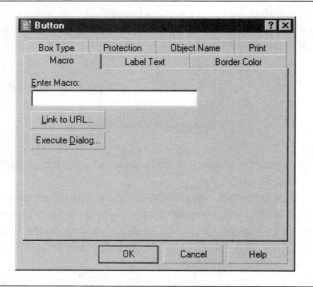

FIGURE 22-3   Button properties

> **TIP**   *You'll learn about the other controls that you can add later in this chapter.*

Running Macros Automatically

Sometimes you want to run a macro every time you start Quattro Pro 10 or when you open or close a specific notebook. You may want to open your Macro Library file, for example, or insert a standard heading on the initial sheet. You can designate both an *autoload file* and a *startup macro*. An autoload file is opened whenever you start Quattro Pro 10. A startup macro is played when you start Quattro Pro 10.

You create both features in the Application Properties dialog box. Select Settings from the Tools menu, and then click on the Macro section under Application. Enter the macro's cell name in the Start-up Macro text box. Also use this dialog box to determine which elements are suppressed as the macro runs.

You may also have a macro that you want to run whenever you open or close a specific notebook. Perhaps you want to display a certain area of the spreadsheet when you open the notebook or want to print the spreadsheet when you close the notebook. These are called *notebook startup macros* and *notebook exit macros*.

To create a notebook startup macro, just give it the name _NBSTARTMACRO. Name an exit macro _NBEXITMACRO. When Quattro Pro 10 starts, it looks for a macro named _NBSTARTMACRO. If it finds one in the spreadsheet, it plays the macro. When you exit Quattro Pro 10, it runs the macro called _NBEXITMACRO.

The Macro Language

Macros follow their own rules of syntax. Each macro command may be followed by one or more arguments, and the entire instruction is enclosed in braces. For example, the command {ESC} has no arguments because it simply equals the task of pressing the ESC key. The command to select a cell, SelectBlock, has one argument: the coordinates to select. A relative address is shown as {SelectBlock C(1)R(0) . . . C(1)R(0)}. This means to select a block starting one column to the right of the current cell in the same row. The 0 in the cell reference means to use the current row. Movement to the right and down is shown in positive numbers, movement to the left and up in negative numbers. An absolute address appears as {SelectBlock A:D6 . . . D6}. The command to select an entire row uses only the sheet and row number, as in {SelectBlock A:1} to select row 1 on sheet A. The command {SelectBlock C:H} selects the entire column H on sheet C.

Multiple arguments must be separated by commas, as in the command {BlockInsert.Rows A:1,Entire}. The first argument (A:1) specifies where to insert the row; the second argument indicates an entire, not a partial, row. Notice that the command name itself includes a period. The BlockInsert command is used generically to insert many different objects. The syntax is {BlockInsert.Object block, entire|partial}, using commands such as BlockInsert.Columns and BlockInsert.Pages.

Macro commands do not simply mimic keystrokes. If you use the arrow keys to select a cell, for example, you won't see instructions for each arrow that you press. Quattro Pro 10 records the results of your keystrokes, not individual actions. If you press the UP ARROW and RIGHT ARROW keys to select cell B3 using absolute addressing, the command simply appears as {SelectBlock A:B3..B3}.

Dialog Boxes Commands

It is likely that you'll be recording macros that select options from dialog boxes, such as opening or printing a file. The command to open a file is simply {FileOpen filename}, as in {FileOpen C:\Corel\Office10\Corel Quattro10\Notebk1.qpw}.

When a dialog box contains multiple options, there is usually a different command for each option, often starting with the name of the dialog box. All Print macros, for example, begin with the word "Print," followed by a period and then the command that it performs. Use {Print.DoPrint}, for example, to print the current spreadsheet using all of the default values.

Other commands are used to set the print options before actually printing. This macro, for example, prints three copies of a block:

{Print.Block "A:A1..H4"}
{Print.Copies "3"}
{Print.DoPrint}

The first command sets the print block. The name shows that it involves the Print function and the Block option. The second command designates three copies using the Print function and the Copies option. The final command initiates printing.

Writing Macros

Macro instructions are stored as text in the spreadsheet, so you can edit a macro by changing, deleting, or inserting commands just as you edit spreadsheet labels. You can also copy instructions from one macro to another, even if they are on different sheets or in different notebooks.

One way to insert additional commands into a macro is to record them as a new macro in another location in the spreadsheet, and then cut and paste them where you want them inserted. Do not try to record additional instructions directly into the macro—new instructions could overwrite existing ones—unless you record them in the first blank cell after the macro's last command.

You can also edit and write macros by typing the macro commands yourself. In order to write macro commands, however, you need to know the Quattro Pro 10 macro language, and a little about the way computer programs work.

To write a macro, just start in any blank cell in an area of a spreadsheet that you won't need for anything else. Type the commands, making sure to enclose them in braces. At the end of the macro, make sure there is a blank cell, or enter the command {Quit} or {Return}. If there is anything else immediately after the macro, Quattro Pro 10 will try to run it as a macro command and will generate an error. When you've finished, give a cell name to the first instruction, and then save the spreadsheet.

You can test a macro quickly by clicking on the first cell, selecting Macro from the Tools menu, clicking on Play, and then on OK. The coordinates of the active cell will be in the Location text box of the Play Macro dialog box.

Copying Commands

If you are not certain of a command's syntax, you can look up the command in the macros help feature. To look up a command, press SHIFT-F3 to see a dialog box listing the categories of macro commands.

The categories are as follows:

- Keyboard Macro Commands

- Screen Macro Commands

- Interactive Macro Commands

- Program Flow Macro Commands

- Cell Macro Commands

- Command Equivalents

- OLE and DDE Macro Commands

- UI Building Macro Commands

- Object Macro Commands

- Analysis Tools Macro Commands

- Miscellaneous Macro Commands

Select the category of the command you want to use. If you see a further listing of categories, choose one to see a list of commands in the category. Click on the command you want to learn about to see a description of its syntax and several examples of its use. In most cases, the syntax for the macro command is shown at the top of the dialog box. To place the command into your macro, select and copy the line showing the complete syntax, then paste it into your macro on the spreadsheet. You can then delete any optional arguments that you do not need, and insert your own data into the sample arguments you want to retain.

Use the following steps to write a macro that inserts your name on the top of the current spreadsheet:

1. Click on sheet tab C and then in cell A1.

2. Type **{SelectBlock A1..A1}**, and then press the DOWN ARROW to select cell A2. Notice that the sheet name has been left off the range reference in

order to make the macro move to cell A1 of the current sheet. In a sense, this command is absolute to the cell reference but relative to the sheet.

3. Type **{BlockInsert.Rows A1..A1,Entire}**, and then press the DOWN ARROW. This command inserts a row into the spreadsheet.

4. Type **{PutCell "Your Name"}**, and press the DOWN ARROW key.

5. Type **{SelectBlock A1..H1}**, and press the DOWN ARROW key.

6. Type **{SetProperty "Alignment.Horizontal",Center across block}**. This command centers the label in the active cell across the selected block.

7. Type **{Quit}**, and then press ENTER. The completed macro is shown in Figure 22-4.

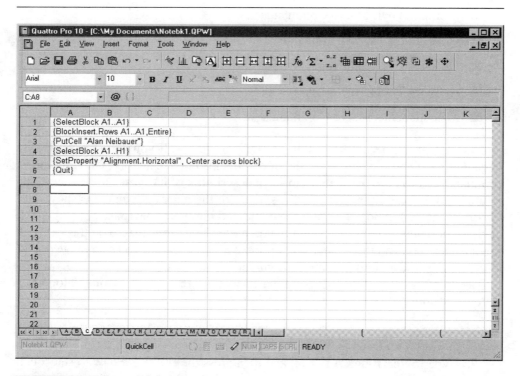

FIGURE 22-4   Completed macro

8. Select cell A1, the first cell of the macro.

9. Pull down the Insert menu, point to Name, and click on Name Cells.

10. Type **\b** as the cell name, and then click on Add and then on OK.

To run the macro, just press CTRL-SHIFT-B. Try it now. Click on sheet tab D, and type something in cell A1. Press CTRL-SHIFT-B to run the macro. You can also select Macro from the Tools menu, click on Play, and then double-click on the macro name.

> **TIP** *To quickly go to your macro, click on the Navigate button in the input line, and click on the macro name.*

Fundamental Macro Commands

There are hundreds of macros. As with functions, many of them are for rather sophisticated purposes. In this chapter, however, we will review a basic set of commands that also illustrate some principles of programming.

Entering Information into Cells

There are several commands for inserting information into cells. The simplest is PutCell, which uses the syntax {PutCell*Data*,[*Date*(0|1)]}. To insert a numeric value in a cell, enter the value as the argument, as in {PutCell 764.76}. Enclose labels, formulas, functions, and dates in quotation marks.

The optional argument is needed only when you insert a date. Use 1 to store the value as a date, or 0 to insert it as a label. The command {PutCell"11/16/45",1}, for example, inserts the date into the active cell as a date.

You can also use a related command, {PutCell2*Data*}, which has only one argument. You must start all numeric values with a plus sign, as in {PutCell2 +345}, and dates are always inserted as dates, not labels.

To enter the same information in multiple cells, use the PutBlock and PutBlock2 commands, using the syntax

{PutCell*Data*,[*Block*],[*Date*(0|1)]}

and

{PutCell2*Data*,[*Block*]}

If you do not specify the optional block, the contents are inserted into the active cell or selected block. Designate noncontiguous blocks in parentheses.

Controlling the Flow of Commands

Macros that you record are always *linear*. This means that all of the instructions are performed in the exact order in which they appear in the macro. When you write a macro, however, you can control the order in which commands are performed, repeating or skipping over them as you want.

These types of macros, more than any others, require a basic understanding of program logic, the type of logic applied to programming languages such as C or Basic. If you are familiar with a programming language, you will find the concepts discussed in this chapter familiar. If you are new to programming, you will get a good starting lesson.

Using Subroutines   A *subroutine* is a series of macro instructions that you can perform when needed. For example, suppose you need to perform a series of tasks several times in the same macro. Rather than repeat the same lines each time, write them once in a separate location on the spreadsheet and give the series of instructions its own name.

Now whenever you need to perform those tasks, you call the routine by enclosing the name in braces, as in {Do_This_Routine}. The macro performs the commands in the subroutine until it reaches a blank cell, a value, or the command {Return}, after which it goes back and follows the instructions where it left off in the original macro.

By creating a library of subroutines, you can write complex macros more easily and quickly. In fact, some macros may contain little more than subroutine calls to other macros.

Moving To Other Instructions   One other way to perform another macro, or set of commands in the running macro itself, is to use the Branch command. Unlike a subroutine, however, the Branch command does not return to the original location when the command ends.

You use the Branch command to leave one macro and perform another, or to move to another location in the same macro that you've given a cell name. The syntax is {Branch macro}. The command is most commonly used in conjunction with the If command.

Making Decisions   One advantage of writing a macro is that you can have it make decisions for you—for example, skipping over some instructions that you may not want it to perform, or moving to other instructions only under certain conditions.

For example, suppose you only want to print your spreadsheet if the value in a cell reaches a certain level. Use the If command to test the value in the cell, and print the spreadsheet based on that value. The syntax is {If *Condition*} {DoWhenTrue} {DoWhenFalse}. *Condition* is a logical expression. Look at this example:

    {If due>500}{Branch Overdue_Notice}
    {Branch GoodClient}

When the value in the cell named "due" is over 500, the macro branches to the macro named "Overdue_Notice" and performs its instructions. When the amount is not over 500, the macro branches to the GoodClient subroutine.

In a strict sense, the If macro command does not work like an If . . . Else statement in most programming languages. In these languages, the command specified in the (DoWhenFalse) part of the If statement is only performed when the condition is false. With Quattro Pro 10, if you do not use the Branch or Quit command, the macro performs both statements when the condition is true. Look at this example:

    {If due>500}{PutCell "Deadbeat"}
    {PutCell "Good Client"}

If the condition is true, Quattro Pro 10 performs the command and inserts "Deadbeat" into the cell. However, it then continues with the macro, immediately placing "Good Client" in the same cell. It does not skip over the command just because the condition is true.

If this is the last command in the macro, you can always write it like this:

    {If due>500}{Putcell "Deadbeat"}{Quit}
    {PutCell "Good Client"}

Then the macro will not run the last statement when the condition is true.

Keep in mind that you can use multiple Branch statements to perform multiple tests. For example, suppose you are checking student grades to determine what values to enter in a cell. Use a macro such as this:

```
{If grade>=90}{Branch a_student}
{If grade>=80}{Branch b_student}
{If grade>=70}{Branch c_student}
{Branch Failing}
```

The macro now tests for three conditions, and if none of them are true, it performs the macro named Failing.

Even though you are branching elsewhere to the macro, or to another macro, you can still return to the statement following the false statement. Give a cell name to the command after the false statement, and then branch back to that when you are ready. For example, look at this logic:

```
{If grade>=90}{Branch a_student}
{If grade>=80}{Branch b_student}
{If grade>=70}{Branch c_student}
{PutCell2 "You are failing, sorry"}
{PutCell "The End"}
```

Now assume that you've assigned the cell name Continue to the cell with the command {PutCell "The End"}. When a student has a grade of 90 or more, the macro branches to this macro named a_student:

```
{SelectBlock A1}
{PutCell2 "You are very smart. You got an A."}
{SelectBlock A2}
{Branch Continue}
```

The last command branches back to the original macro and continues after the final test of the If command.

Repeating Commands   In addition to making decisions with the If command, let's say you want a macro to repeat a series of instructions with the For macro. The syntax is:

```
{For CounterLoc,Start#,Stop#,Step#,StartLoc}
```

Here's the purpose of each argument:

- CounterLoc is a cell that Quattro Pro 10 will use to keep track of the number of repetitions. The value in the cell will change with each repetition of the loop, so Quattro Pro 10 will know when the maximum value has been reached.

■ Start# is the initial value that Quattro Pro 10 places in the CounterLoc cell.

■ Stop# sets the maximum value of CounterLoc. When the number in CounterLoc exceeds this value, the repetition ends.

■ Step# determines how Quattro Pro 10 increments the value in CounterLoc. When set at 1, for example, the value in CounterLoc is incremented by 1 with each repetition.

For example, the following command runs the subroutine Repeat_This ten times:

{For A1,1,10,1,Repeat_This}

It places the value 1 in cell A1 and then performs the subroutine starting at the cell named Repeat_This. It then increments the value in cell A1 by 1—the Step value—and runs the macro again. It repeats this process until the value in cell A1 is greater than 10.

Interactive Macros   Although Quattro Pro 10 has hundreds of macro commands, sometimes you just don't know exactly what you want a macro to do. You might want to insert different text each time the macro runs, or set a dialog box in some specific way. In these instances you want an interactive macro—one that pauses to give you a chance to enter text or select options from a dialog box.

When you want a macro to open a dialog box and then pause so you can select options from the box, use a command in the form {DialogBox}. The command {Print}, for example, displays the dialog box on the screen. Once you choose an option from the box and select Print or Close, the macro continues at the next instruction.

To pause a macro so you can enter text, use the GetLabel command with this syntax:

{GetLabel Prompt,Location}

The Prompt argument is a string up to 70 characters long that tells you what type of information to enter. It can be text, such as "Enter your telephone number" or a reference to a cell containing the text you want to appear as the prompt. To reference a cell, enter it as a formula, such as +D3. The Location argument is the cell where the information should be placed.

When Quattro Pro 10 encounters the GetLabel command, it pauses the macro and displays your prompt in the Enter a Label dialog box. Type the text you want to enter, up to 160 characters, and then click on OK, or press ENTER.

For example, the following command displays a message on the screen and accepts an entry into cell A1:

{GetLabel "Enter your name", +A1}

The GetNumber command works the same way but accepts a numeric value. The syntax is {GetNumber Prompt,Location}. You can enter a number or a formula that returns a numeric value.

Adding Controls

You learned earlier in this chapter how to add a button to quickly run a macro. A button is just one type of *control* that you can add to spreadsheet to let you perform some tasks quickly. You add other controls in much the same way, by choosing Form Control from the Insert menu and selecting from the following list:

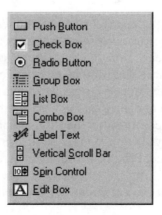

Then click in the spreadsheet where you want the control to appear, or drag to create the control in the desired size. Once inserted, you can select the control, and drag it to another position or use the handles to change its size. To specify how the control works, right-click on it, and choose the Properties option from the dialog box that appears.

TIP   *Once you assign a process to a control, select it by right-clicking on it.*

For example, a list box lets you choose an item from a list by clicking on it. In Quattro Pro, you add items to the list by selecting them from a range of cells. The cells can be from any sheet in the notebook. You also designate where your selection from the list appears, called the *designation block*. Click on the first item on the list to insert the number 0 in the designation block, click on the second item to insert the number 1, and so on.

NOTE	*A Combo box works the same way, but you must pull down the list to display it. A Spin Control lets you insert a number by increasing or decreasing a value in a control.*

Here's how to create and use a list box:

1. Start by entering the items that you want to add to the list down a column somewhere in the notebook.

2. Display the area of the spreadsheet where you want to place the list box.

3. Select Control from the Insert menu, and click on List Box.

4. Click where you want the list box to appear.

5. Right-click on the list box control, and choose List Box Properties from the QuickMenu to see the options in Figure 22-5.

6. Click on the Source Block tab if that page of the dialog box is not already displayed.

7. Select the cells containing the items to add to the box. Just click on the sheet in the background of the dialog box. If the list is on another sheet, click on its tab, and then select the cells.

8. Click on the Destination Block tab of the dialog box.

9. Click on the cell where you want to place your selection from the list box.

10. Click on the Box Type tab of the dialog box.

11. Choose the type of border around the box—none, thin, medium, or thick—and whether to add a drop shadow.

12. Click on OK.

13. Click away from the list box to deselect it.

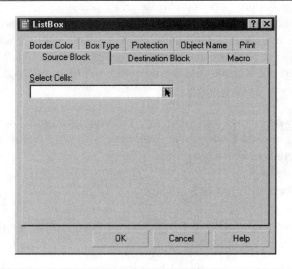

FIGURE 22-5   Setting properties for a list box

When you want to choose an item from the list, just click on it. The number representing your selection will appear in the destination block.

To change any of the properties of the control, right-click on it, and choose List Properties from the QuickMenu.

> **TIP** *Any changes you make to the contents of the source block cells are automatically made in the list as well.*

Using Custom Dialog Boxes

In Chapter 11 you learned how to create dialog boxes that you can access in a WordPerfect macro. You can also create and use dialog boxes in a Quattro Pro macro. While the basic principles are the same with both programs, the programs used to create the dialog boxes differ.

To create a dialog box in Quattro Pro, choose Dialog Designer from the Tools Macro menu. A new dialog box appears, with OK and Cancel buttons, along with the Dialog Designer property bar, shown in Figure 22-6.

Add controls to the box by selecting from the Insert menu or from the Controls button on the left of the toolbar. Choose the control you want to insert and then click or drag where you want the control to appear. The options in the Insert menu are shown here—the choices from the Controls button on the toolbar are basically the same, just listed in a different order.

22

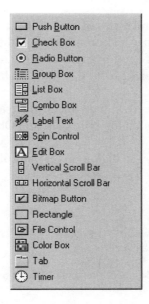

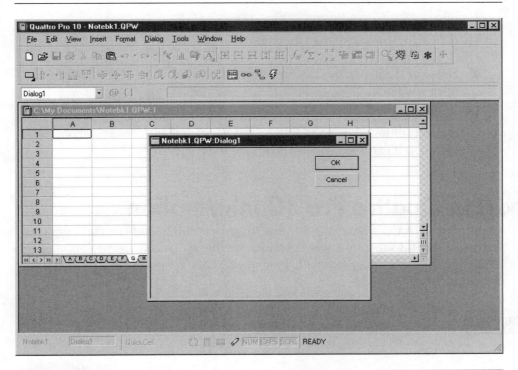

FIGURE 22-6   Creating a dialog box in Quattro Pro

Define the function and properties of the control by right-clicking on the control and choosing the Properties command from the shortcut menu. You can also set properties for the box itself by right-clicking on the form background and choosing options from the QuickMenu. Close the dialog box when you're done designing it.

Your dialog boxes are stored on the Objects page along with charts, maps, and clip art. To make changes to a dialog box, go to the Objects page, and double-click on the dialog box icon.

When you want to display the dialog box as part of a macro, use the DoDialog command, as in this example:

{SelectBlock A1..A1}			
{BlockInsert.Rows A1..A1;Entire}			
{PutCell "Alan Neibauer"}			
{SelectBlock A:A1..A:H1}			
{Setproperty "Alignment.Horizontal";Center across block}			
{DoDialog "Dialog1",A10)			
{Quit}			

The DoDialog command has two required arguments:

- Name of the dialog box, along with the notebook name if it is not in the open notebook.

- The address of a cell where you want to place a value indicating how the dialog is closed. The value will be 1 if the dialog was closed with an OK button; 0 if canceled.

Sharing Quattro Pro 10 Information

Quattro Pro 10 has a wide range of formatting capabilities, and you can enter text into cells, but it is far from a word processing program. When you need more than a few lines of explanatory text with your spreadsheet, consider sharing it with WordPerfect 10.

 Share a spreadsheet with WordPerfect 10 so you do not have to retype the information into a WordPerfect 10 table.

The quickest way to use a spreadsheet with WordPerfect 10 is to cut and paste. Select the range of cells in Quattro Pro 10, switch to your WordPerfect 10 document, and then click on Paste. The spreadsheet will be inserted into the document as a WordPerfect 10 table. You can now use WordPerfect 10's table commands to format the information and work with rows and columns.

When selecting cells in Quattro Pro 10, keep in mind the page margins and width of your document. In Quattro Pro 10, spreadsheets wider than a page just run over into additional columns. If you paste a wide table into WordPerfect 10, however, the columns scroll off the edge of the page, as shown in Figure 22-7. Before printing the document, reduce the column size or font so the spreadsheet fits on the page. The information is there; it just doesn't fit on the page.

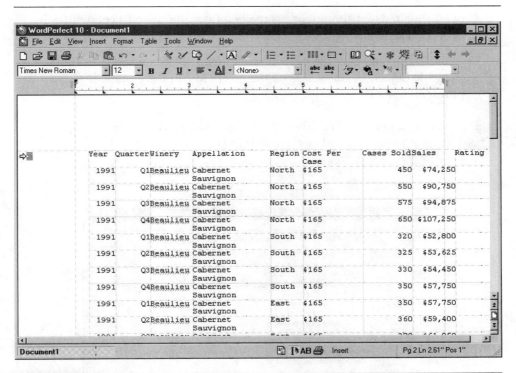

FIGURE 22-7   Wide spreadsheets scroll off the screen when pasted into Corel WordPerfect

Using Paste Special

For more choices in sharing a spreadsheet, select Paste Special from the Edit menu. You'll have several options, shown in Figure 22-8, including buttons to Paste and Paste Link. Let's look at the Paste options first.

You have a number of ways to paste the table:

■ Quattro Pro 10 Notebook inserts the spreadsheet as one object that you cannot edit in WordPerfect 10.

■ Rich Text Format inserts the spreadsheet as a WordPerfect 10 table, but using the text formats that it has in Quattro Pro 10.

■ Quattro Pro Format also inserts the spreadsheet as a WordPerfect 10 table, but with the same grid lines and text formats as in Quattro Pro 10.

■ Unformatted text simply inserts the text from the spreadsheet, with cell contents separated by tabs.

■ The Picture and Device Independent Bitmap options insert the cells as a graphic object. Double-click on the object to edit the graphic in Corel Presentations 10.

 Pasting a Quattro Pro 10 chart or map always inserts it as an object. Double-click on the object to edit it in Quattro Pro 10.

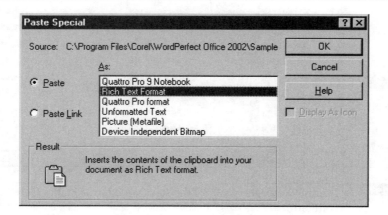

FIGURE 22-8   Paste Special dialog box

If you elect to paste the spreadsheet as a Quattro Pro 10 Notebook, the cells are inserted as one object, surrounded by handles:

Year	Quarter	Winery	Appellation	Region	Cost Per Case
1991	Q1	Beaulieu	Cabernet Sauvignon	North	$165
1991	Q2	Beaulieu	Cabernet Sauvignon	North	$165
1991	Q3	Beaulieu	Cabernet Sauvignon	North	$165
1991	Q4	Beaulieu	Cabernet Sauvignon	North	$165
1991	Q1	Beaulieu	Cabernet Sauvignon	South	$165
1991	Q2	Beaulieu	Cabernet Sauvignon	South	$165
1991	Q3	Beaulieu	Cabernet Sauvignon	South	$165
1991	Q4	Beaulieu	Cabernet Sauvignon	South	$165
1991	Q1	Beaulieu	Cabernet Sauvignon	East	$165
1991	Q2	Beaulieu	Cabernet Sauvignon	East	$165
1991	Q3	Beaulieu	Cabernet Sauvignon	East	$165
1991	Q4	Beaulieu	Cabernet Sauvignon	East	$165

This is an *embedded object*. This means that along with the object, Windows also stores the name of the program used to create it—Quattro Pro 10. You can't edit or format the information as an object in WordPerfect 10, but if you double-click on Object, Windows opens Quattro Pro 10 and transmits the data from the object to it.

Quattro Pro 10 is opened, for in-place editing. You'll see a miniature version of the Quattro Pro 10 spreadsheet right on the WordPerfect 10 window. However, WordPerfect 10's menus and toolbars are replaced by those of Quattro Pro 10. This way, you can edit the spreadsheet data while seeing the document in which it will be printed. If you pull down a menu item, you'll see the Quattro Pro 10 menu options, not WordPerfect 10's. Nevertheless, the spreadsheet window appears within the WordPerfect 10 document window.

Keep in mind that there is no link between the object in WordPerfect 10 and the actual Quattro Pro 10 file from which the data was copied. What's in WordPerfect 10 is a copy of the data linked to Quattro Pro 10 as its program of origination. If you change the information in the original disk file, the data in WordPerfect 10 does not change.

If you click on the Paste Link option in the Paste Special dialog box, you can choose from the first four options discussed previously. However, pasting the spreadsheet in this way inserts it as an object with an OLE (Object Linking and Embedding) link. Now there is a link between the object in WordPerfect 10 and the Quattro Pro 10 file from which it was obtained. If you change the information in the file, it changes in WordPerfect 10 as well.

When you double-click on the object, Windows opens Quattro Pro 10 and the associated file, not in place but in a Quattro Pro 10 window. When you edit and save the spreadsheet, the changes are also shown in the WordPerfect 10 document.

 If you want to copy the WordPerfect 10 document to another computer, you must also copy the original source file.

Try It Out

With hundreds of macro commands available, it is possible to create complete automated applications from within Quattro Pro. As an example, we'll create a macro that automates the process of calculating mortgage payments. The macro will ask a user to input information and then automatically print a copy of the mortgage data and payment amount. We'll create a button linked to the macro, so the user only has to click the button to begin the process.

An application such as this can be used in a real estate office, and similar applications can be developed for almost any business.

This macro introduces some new macro commands.

The GetLabel command displays a box in which the user enters information, as shown here:

The syntax of the command is {GetLabel Prompt, cell}. The prompt appears in the box telling the user the type of information they have to enter. The information they enter is then inserted into the specified cell. The prompt can be either text enclosed in quotation marks, or the location or name of a cell containing the text, as in these examples:

{ GetLabel "Please enter your name", G1}
{ GetLabel myprompt, C1}
{ GetLabel +F1, C1}.

In these examples, the text you want to use for the prompt is in a cell named myprompt or located in cell F1.

The GetNumber command is similar to GetLabel, except the information entered must be numeric.

The macro will also include these commands:

- Print.Block sets the area of a spreadsheet that will be printed.

- Print.Area Selection tells Quattro Pro to limit the printout to the selected block.

- Print.DoPrint begins printing.

Now let's create the macro.

1. Start a new notebook and click on the sheet B tab. We'll create the macro in this sheet but place the button that launches the macro in sheet A. This way, the user will not see any of the commands or other cells that are needed for the report, just the printout itself.

2. Enter the macro commands and text labels shown in Figure 22-9. The {;} command in cell A1 lets us insert a comment or message into a macro that will not be executed as a Quattro Pro instruction.

3. In cell F10, enter the function **@IF(F1>1,F1/100,F1).**

   While we will prompt the user to enter the mortgage rate as a decimal (as in .07), there is always a possibility that the user will enter a non-decimal number (as in 7). This command converts the non-decimal number into a decimal which is required by the @PAYMT function. Notice that we use the command in cell A4 to import the rate into cell F1. This allows us to test and convert the value to place it into cell F10.

4. In cell F12, enter the function **@PAYMT(F10/12,F11*12,-F9)**. This function calculates the mortgage payment.

5. Click cell A1.

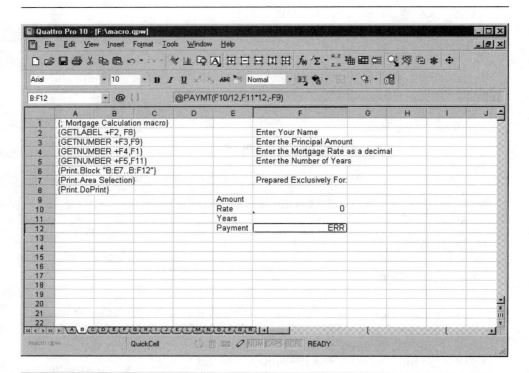

FIGURE 22-9   Macro to automate mortgage calculations

6. Select Insert | Name | Name Cells.

7. Type **MortgageMacro** as the macro name and click Add, and then Close.

   Next, add a button to sheet A and link the button to the macro.

8. Click the sheet A tab.

9. Select Insert | Form Control | Push Button.

10. Drag the mouse to create a button about five columns wide and six rows high.

11. Right-click on the button and select Selection Properties from the QuickMenu.

12. In the Macro tab of the Button dialog box, enter **{Branch MortgageMacro}**.

13. In the Label Text tab of the dialog box, type **Click to Calculate Mortgage Payments**. The final button appears something like this:

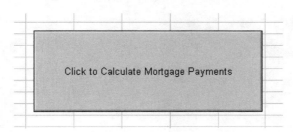

Click to Calculate Mortgage Payments

To run the macro, just click on the button. A series of four prompts appear asking you to enter your name, amount of the mortgage, mortgage rate, and the length of the loan in years. The macro will then print out the report using cells E7 to F12 on sheet B.

Part 4

Corel
Presentations 10

Chapter 23

Using Corel
Presentations 10

Corel Presentations 10 is a remarkable program that lets you create anything from a simple cover page for a report to a complete multimedia slide presentation. What makes it even more remarkable is that it's easy—you don't need a background in art or design, and you don't have to spend hours in front of your computer screen to create special effects.

Certainly the program gets its name because you can use it to create a presentation. You can design a series of slides to show on a monitor, to display on a large screen using a projector, or to convert to actual 35mm photographic slides or overhead transparencies. If you design the presentation for computer display, you can also add sound effects and create special effects for the transitions from one slide to the next.

You can also use Corel Presentations 10 when your goals are not that grand. You can create one or more slides to use for report covers, handouts for meetings, and even for organization or data charts.

Corel Presentations 10 Basics

Before starting Corel Presentations 10, let's review some basic concepts that will help you along the way. Corel Presentations 10 lets you create one or more slides. They are called *slides* even if you do not plan to convert them to photographic slides or show them on the screen. So if you use Corel Presentations 10 to design a report cover, for example, you are still creating a "slide."

> **NOTE** *You can also create just a drawing and save it as a WPG graphic file.*

Every slide consists of three separate layers. The bottom layer is, appropriately, called the *background*. The background contains designs and colors that make up the general appearance of the slide. Imagine going to the store and purchasing colored paper to draw on—the color on the paper is the background. With Corel Presentations 10, you can select from a list of professionally designed background designs, modify them, or create your own.

> **NOTE** *You can also create pictures that are not slides and that do not have layers.*

Over the background is the *layout layer*. This determines the general position and type of contents for each slide. The contents are represented by placeholders—boxes that appear onscreen suggesting the type of items that should be on the slide. If you do not add any text to a placeholder, it does not appear onscreen when you show the presentation, and it does not print with the slide. Corel Presentations 10 comes with templates for seven general layouts, listed in Table 23-1.

NOTE   *You can change the position and size of the placeholders, delete them, or add your own elements to a slide. You can also create your own layouts*

The top layer is called the *slide layer*. This is where you enter the text, drawings, clip art, or other items that you want to appear on the slide.

With Corel Presentations 10 you can work on your slides in three views:

- ■ *Slide Editor* lets you create or edit the slide contents or background, one slide at a time.

- ■ *Slide Outliner* displays the organization of a presentation as a text outline, using titles, subtitles, and bullet lists as the outline levels.

- ■ *Slide Sorter* displays thumbnails of the slides for changing their order.

One of the first choices you should make when creating a presentation is the master category. The master determines the overall look of the slides, offering options best suited for the type of presentation intended, such as using 35mm slides, a formal business presentation, or displaying in color or in printed copies. The category determines basic design elements, such as the color choices and

Slide Template	Placeholders
Title	Title, subtitle
Bulleted List	Title, subtitle, bullet list
Text	Title, subtitle, text box
Organization Chart	Title, subtitle, organization chart box
Data Chart	Title, subtitle, chart box
Combination	Title, subtitle, bullet list, and chart box
Blank	No placeholders

TABLE 23-1   Default Slide Layouts

aspect ratio, for the type of media. You would use Color, for example, if you plan to display the presentation on a color monitor or if you have a color printer. You might also select Color if you have a black and white printer but are using a background design that translates well into shades of gray. Select the Printout category for simple backgrounds that print well on a monochrome printer, or choose 35mm if you plan to convert the slides to photographic slides.

Starting a Presentation

You can start a new presentation using a template and then just fill in the information that you want to get across. Or you can design your presentation from scratch, selecting from professional-looking backgrounds.

Follow these steps to create a presentation:

1. Click on Start in the taskbar, point to WordPerfect Office 2002, and click on Corel Presentations 10. You'll see the Perfect Expert dialog box. You can choose to open a presentation template to use as the basis for your own work or to open one of your existing presentations using the Work On tab.

2. Click on [Corel Presentations Slide Show] in the Create New page and then on Create. The Startup Master Gallery window appears, as shown in Figure 23-1.

Your first choice should be to select a master slide background to set the overall look of the presentation. You can change the master background at any time, and you can choose a different background for individual slides.

1. Pull down the Category list to see the categories available. When you select a category, several sample backgrounds appear.

2. Look at all of the background designs, scrolling the list if necessary.

3. Click on the design you want, and then click on OK to apply the choice to your presentation.

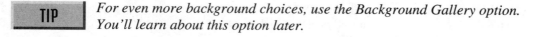

TIP   *For even more background choices, use the Background Gallery option. You'll learn about this option later.*

The Corel Presentations 10 window appears with a blank title slide, as shown in Figure 23-2.

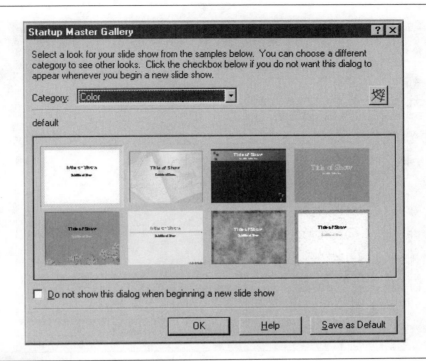

23

FIGURE 23-1   Startup Master Gallery

The Corel Presentations 10 Window

Look at the Corel Presentations 10 window shown in Figure 23-2. Under the menu
bar are the toolbar and a property bar. In addition to the first nine standard toolbar
buttons, the toolbar contains the buttons shown here:

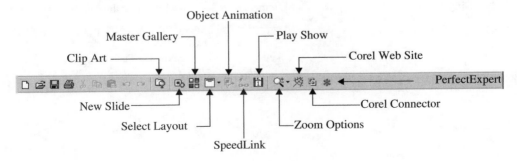

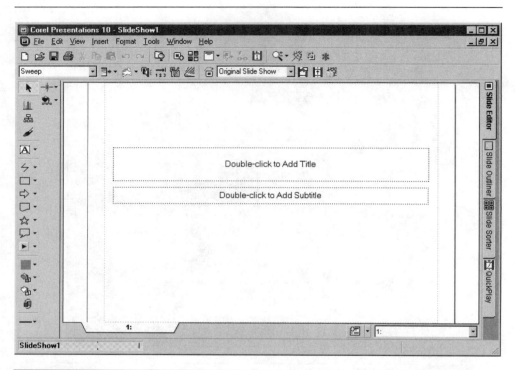

FIGURE 23-2 Corel Presentations

The default property bar contains these items:

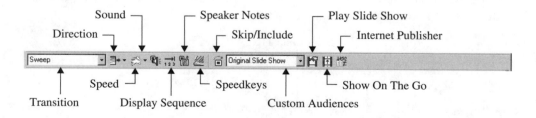

Along the right of the screen are tabs for changing the view and for running the show. At the bottom of the screen is the application bar. Along the left of the screen is the Tool palette that you use to create and format charts and objects.

Corel Presentations 10 starts with a blank title slide. Below the slide is a tab. A tab appears for each slide you add so you can change slides quickly. To the right of the tab is the New Slide list and then the Slide list:

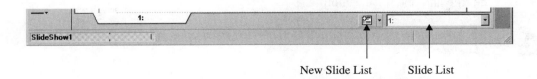

New Slide List   Slide List

Use the New Slide list to add a slide to the presentation and the Slide list to change slides, as well as to see the slide title.

Corel Presentations 10 generally offers many of the same features as Corel WordPerfect and other applications. So if you are familiar with one application, you'll feel at home here. In addition to the common buttons in the toolbar and power bar, here are some of the common features:

- Select Insert | Date/Time to insert the date as text or a code, or to select or create a date format.

- Select Insert |Graphics to insert clip art and create TextArt graphics.

- Click the Scrapbook button on the toolbar to insert a graphic from the Scrapbook.

- Select Insert | Shapes to draw shapes.

- When you are editing a placeholder that contains text, choose to use Spell Check, Thesaurus, Grammatik, Dictionary, or QuickCorrect from the Tools menu.

- Select Tools | Settings to customize the way Corel Presentations 10 works. The Settings box offers these options: Display, Environment, Files, and Customize to change toolbars, property bars, tool palettes, keyboards, and menus.

- Use the File menu to access file management options.

- Play and record macros using the Tools menu.

Working with Placeholders

Now look at the template. The Title template contains just two placeholders, one for the title and one for the subtitle.

 You can use the Clipboard to paste text from other applications into slides.

To insert contents into a placeholder, double-click on it. For example, double-click on the Title placeholder to enter and format text into the title.

A placeholder is similar to a graphic box in WordPerfect 10. Click on the placeholder to display handles around it and then perform any of these functions:

- Drag the box to change its position.

- Drag a handle to change its size.

- Press DEL to delete the box.

- Select to cut, copy, and paste the box.

While a placeholder does not appear with the slide if you do not use it, you may want to delete unused placeholders from the slide. This makes it easier to select other objects to add, without accidentally selecting the empty placeholder. To delete the placeholder, click on it, and press DEL. If you later want to restore the original placeholders, select Format | Re-Apply Layout. However, this procedure also returns anything you've moved or resized to their default settings, so use this option with caution.

 To change the layout of a slide, pull down the Select Layout list in the tool bar, and click on the layout you want to apply to the slide.

Now let's create our first slide:

1. Double-click on the title placeholder. The box is surrounded by heavy lines, and the insertion point appears in the middle, the default justification for titles and subtitles.

2. Type the text of the title: **Educational Technology**. Do not press ENTER unless you want to add a second line to the title.

3. Double-click on the Subtitle placeholder.

4. Type **Planning for the Future** as the subtitle text.

 The font, size, and justification of the text depends on the Master Gallery you selected. You can use the arrow keys to navigate from one text object to another while in text edit mode.

Formatting Text

To edit the text, double-click on the placeholder; then add, delete, or change the text as needed. When you are entering or editing text, the property bar includes these items:

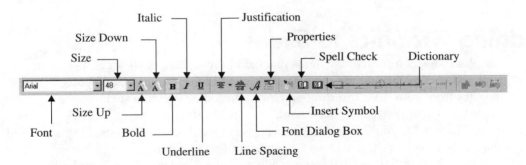

For other formatting options, select from the Format menu or the QuickMenu that appears when you right-click on the text. You can select line, paragraph, and justification formats similar to those for text in WordPerfect 10.

To change the appearance of text, select Font from the Format menu or QuickMenu to see the Font Properties dialog box. Use the Font, Fill, and Outline pages in this dialog box to change the style, color, and size of text; add a fill pattern or color; and select the type and color of the outline around the characters.

You can also change the font color and background using these buttons in the Tool palette:

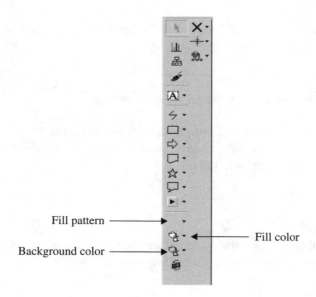

Fill pattern ——————————————→

————————— Fill color

Background color ——————————→

Adding Graphics to Slides

The placeholders represent the items that Corel Presentations 10 suggests should be included. You can use the drawing tools to add other elements, and you can add graphics from your disk. Inserting graphics into a slide is similar to adding a graphic to a WordPerfect 10 document.

In Chapter 24, you'll learn how to work with graphics of all types. In this chapter, however, we'll introduce the concept of adding clip art.

Just as in WordPerfect 10, you can add graphics from the Corel Scrapbook or from a file on disk. To use an image from the Scrapbook, click on the Scrapbook button on the toolbar, or select Insert | Graphics | ClipArt to see the Scrapbook. Scroll the Scrapbook to locate the image, drag it onto the slide, and then close the Scrapbook window.

To insert another type of graphic, select Insert | Graphics | From File to see the Insert File dialog box. Go to the folder containing the graphic, and then double-click on the image you want to insert, or click on it and then on the Insert button.

The graphic appears in the slide surrounded by eight handles. Change the position and size of the graphic by dragging it or its handles. When you drag a handle to change its size, an outline of the graphic appears so you can see the resulting size. You can also drag a handle all of the way to the other side to flip the

23

image vertically or horizontally. Later you'll learn other ways to edit and change graphics.

Adding a Slide

You are now ready to add another slide. Add a slide by selecting its template from the New Slide list at the bottom of the window or by clicking on the New Slide button in the toolbar and choosing from the dialog box that appears. Next, enter a *bulleted list slide.* A bullet slide is just like a bullet list in WordPerfect 10, with major bullet items and minor ones indented to their right.

> **TIP** *The dialog box that appears when you click on the New Slide button in the toolbar also lets you select the number of slides to insert.*

When you add a slide, Corel Presentations 10 inserts it following the current slide. So if you are working on the last slide of the presentation, the new slide is inserted at the end. To insert a slide elsewhere, click on the tab of the slide that you want to precede the new slide, and then add the slide. You can add a slide in any of Corel Presentations 10 views. You can also change the order of slides in Outliner and Slide Sorter views.

> **Integrate IT!** *You can create a bullet chart directly from a WordPerfect 10 outline.*

1. Click on the down arrow next to the Add Slide button to see the types of slides you can add. If you click on the button itself, Corel Presentations 10 adds the type of slide indicated on the button.

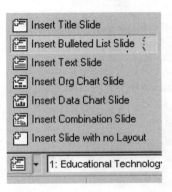

2. Select Insert Bulleted List Slide. Corel Presentations 10 displays the new slide with the Bullet Chart layout, including a title, subtitle, and bullet chart placeholder.

3. Double-click on the Title placeholder, and type **Benefits of Technology**.

4. Double-click on the Subtitle placeholder, and type **Academic Achievement**.

5. Double-click on the bullet list placeholder. The first bullet appears at the left margin of the box, followed by the insertion point.

6. Type **Improved Test Scores,** and then press ENTER to insert the next bullet.

7. Press TAB to indent the insertion point and to insert a second-level bullet.

8. Type **National achievement tests, such as SAT**, and then press ENTER. The program inserts another bullet at the same level. Use TAB to enter entries at subordinate levels and SHIFT-TAB to move back to a higher level.

9. Complete the bullet chart shown in Figure 23-3.

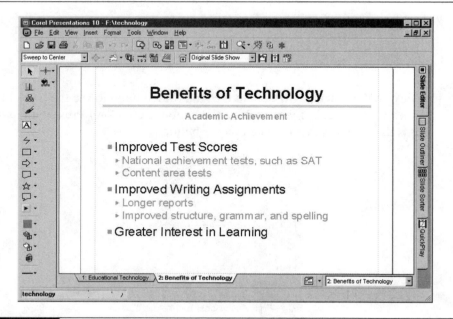

FIGURE 23-3   Completed bullet chart

If you need to edit a bullet chart, double-click on it. You can also click on it and choose Edit Text from the Edit menu or QuickMenu. To add a new bullet item at the end of the chart, place the insertion point at the end of the last line, and press ENTER. Use TAB or SHIFT-TAB to change the position of the item.

To insert an item within the chart, place the insertion point at the start of a line, following the bullet, and press ENTER. Use this technique, for example, to insert a new item at the top of the list.

You can add a bullet chart to a slide even if it does not have a bullet chart placeholder. Suppose, for example, that you create a title slide and then decide that you want it to have a bullet list. Follow these steps:

1. Select Insert | Bulleted List, or pull down the Text Object Tools button in the Tool palette and click on the Bulleted List icon.

2. Drag to create a rectangle the size you want the chart, or just click to create one that fills the slide.

The Bulleted List placeholder appears when you release the mouse.

Importing a WordPerfect 10 Outline

If you've already typed an outline in WordPerfect 10 using the Paragraph Numbers feature, you can import it into a bullet chart. The bullet levels correspond to the document's indentation levels. Here's how:

1. Create a bulleted list chart, and then double-click on the chart placeholder.

2. Select Insert | File.

3. Select the file that you want to use for the chart.

4. Click on Insert.

Creating a Text Slide

A *text slide* is similar to a bullet slide in that it has three placeholders. The Bulleted List placeholder, however, is replaced with a text box. Double-click on the box to place the insertion point there, and then type and format the text. When you press ENTER, Corel Presentations 10 inserts a carriage return to start a new line.

To add text to any slide, pull down the Text Object Tools button in the Tool palette, and click on the Text Box or Text Line icon.

Creating an Organization Chart

An *organization chart* shows the chain of command within an organization. To create one manually, you must draw boxes and lines and try to keep everything in the proper order. Or, you can let Corel Presentations 10 do it for you:

1. Pull down the New Slide list.

2. Select Insert Org Chart Slide. Corel Presentations 10 displays the new slide with three placeholders: title, subtitle, and the organization chart.

3. Add the title and subtitle, and then double-click on the Organization Chart placeholder to display a default chart as shown in Figure 23-4.

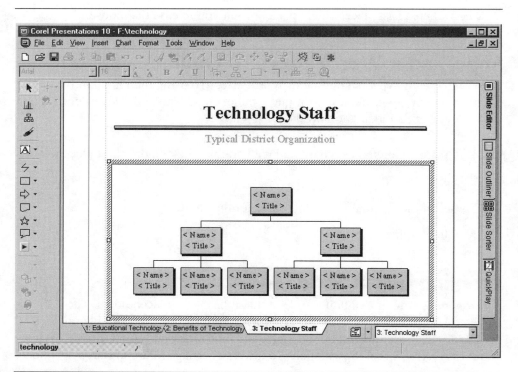

FIGURE 23-4   Organization chart

4. Double-click the Name placeholder in the top box.

5. Type the name of the person for that top position.

6. Press TAB to move to the Title placeholder.

7. Type the title.

8. Continue entering names and titles in the same way.

9. Delete the boxes you don't need by clicking on a box and pressing the DEL key.

The default organization chart includes a basic set of positions. You can add other positions as required by your organization's structure. Here are the positions that you can insert:

■ A *staff* position comes directly off of another position, as the assistant position in the following example. The position is not in the chain of command.

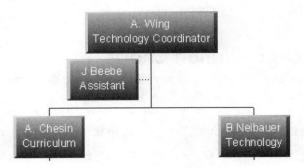

■ A *subordinate* is under another position in the chain of command.

■ A *manager* is above another position.

■ A *coworker* is a position of equal authority, neither under nor below the next box in the chain of command. The only limitation is that you cannot insert a coworker position in the box at the top.

TIP   *To change the structure of the chart, click on a box, and select Format |
Branch Structure. Choose a design in the dialog box that appears, and*

then click on Close. You can use the same dialog box to change the branch's orientation.

To add a position, use these steps:

1. Click the box that you want to add the position to.

2. Pull down the Insert menu, and click on the position you want to add. The dialog box that appears depends on the position.

3. Enter the number of positions you want to add. When you add a coworker, you can also choose to insert the box to the left or right of the current box.

4. Click OK.

5. Double-click the Name and Title placeholders, and type the names and titles.

TIP	*Use the buttons in the property bar that appears when you are editing an organization chart to insert any number of subordinates and to customize the appearance of the chart.*

Inserting Organization Charts

You can add an organization chart to any slide, even one that does not have a placeholder for it.

1. Click on the Organization Chart button in the Tool palette, or select Insert | Organization Chart.

2. Drag to create a rectangle the size you want the chart to be, or just click to create one that fills the slide. A box appears showing formats of organization charts, as in Figure 23-5.

3. Click on the type of chart you want to insert.

4. Click on OK.

	You can use a WordPerfect 10 outline to add titles and positions to an organization chart. Refer to Chapter 13.

23

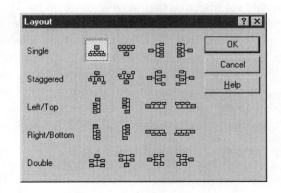

FIGURE 23-5   Selecting the type of chart to insert

Creating Data Charts

A *data chart* is a chart or graph, exactly like the charts and graphs you can add to WordPerfect 10 and Quattro Pro 10. In fact, you use almost the same techniques for working with charts—changing their type, customizing chart elements, adding legends, and so on.

Integrate IT!   *Use the Clipboard to insert Corel Presentations 10 charts into WordPerfect 10 or Quattro Pro 10.*

To create a data chart, either select the Insert Data Chart Slide from the Add Slide list, or choose Insert | Data Chart to place a placeholder for it on another slide. To use the template, follow these steps:

1. Pull down the Add Slide list.

2. Select Insert Data Chart Slide. Corel Presentations 10 displays the new slide with the data chart slide template. It has three placeholders: title, subtitle, and data chart.

NOTE   *A Combination template has four placeholders: title, subtitle, bullet chart on the left, and data chart on the right.*

3. Add the title and subtitle, and then double-click on the Data Chart placeholder to see the Data Chart Gallery. The gallery includes a list box of chart types and preview areas showing styles of the selected type. There are two checkboxes: Use Sample Data and 3-D. Select the Use Sample Data when you want a default chart and datasheet to appear. This may be useful when you are not sure about the chart design, because you can change the data in the sample chart to see the effect on the chart itself. Use the 3-D box to determine if the chart is 2D or 3D.

4. Click on the category of chart you want to create.

5. Click on the style of the chart.

6. Click on OK. If you used the default setting to use sample data, you'll see a chart with sample information in the Datasheet window, as shown in Figure 23-6.

7. Enter your own information into the datasheet.

8. Select options from the menu bar or toolbar, and then click outside of the chart area.

| TIP | *Refer to Chapters 13 for more information on charts.* |

To add a chart to a slide that does not have a chart placeholder, click on the Chart button in the Tool palette, or select Insert | Data Chart. Click on the slide or drag to create a rectangle that will be the chart area.

Inserting Blank Slides

As you've seen, you can insert bullets, data, and organization charts into a slide even when it does not have placeholders for the objects. So if you want, you can start with a blank slide and then add all of your own elements.

To add a blank slide, choose Insert Slide with No Layout from the Add Slide list. You can then add charts using the Insert menu, and text and other elements, as you will learn in Chapter 24.

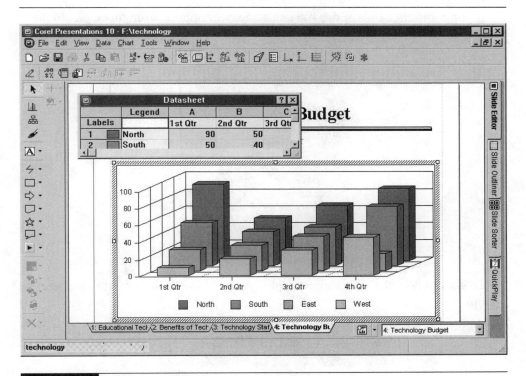

FIGURE 23-6   Default sample chart

Playing a Slide Show

To display a slide show of your work, with each slide displayed full screen, select
the slide that you want to start with, and then click the QuickPlay tab to the right
of the slide or click on the Play Slide Show button in the toolbar. The first slide in
your presentation appears. To move from slide to slide, use these techniques:

- Click the left mouse button, or press the SPACEBAR or RIGHT ARROW to
  display the next slide.
- Press the LEFT ARROW key to display the previous side.
- Press ESC to stop the slide show.

If you right-click on a slide, you can also select options from this QuickMenu:

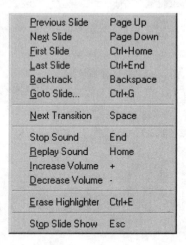

To control how the slides appear, select View | Play Slide Show to see these options:

The Beginning Slide box is set at the number of the current slide. Use the Beginning Slide box to change the starting slide number, or type the number of the slide in the text box and then click on Play. You'll learn all about playing slide shows in Chapter 24.

Saving a Slide Show

Before doing too much work on your slides, you should save them to your disk. Corel Presentations 10 uses the same file management dialog boxes as other Corel WordPerfect Office 2002 applications. To save the presentation that you've been creating through this chapter, use these steps:

1. Click on the Save button in the toolbar, or select File | Save.

2. In the Name box, type a name for your presentation.

3. Click on OK. Corel Presentations 10 saves your work with the default extension SHW.

Now save the slide show you've been working on in this chapter, using the name Technology.

Printing a Presentation

You need to print copies of your slides if you created them to be included in a report or as handouts. To print your slides, click on the Print button in the toolbar or select File | Print to see the dialog box with all of your printing options. To print the entire presentation, just click on the Print button.

The dialog box offers a number of options that should be familiar from working with other WordPerfect Office 2002 applications, such as the number of copies, collating choices, and the Layout and Advanced pages of the dialog box. There are also some new options that are only in Corel Presentations 10.

Click on Preview on the Print page of the dialog box to see how the slides will appear on paper. The slides appear full-screen, so click the right mouse button to move forward from slide-to-slide, click the left mouse button to move backward. Press the ESC key to end the preview, or just navigate past the first or last slide.

You use the Print option buttons in the dialog box to determine what gets printed. When set at the default Full Document, all of the slides will be printed. You can also choose from these options:

- Current view
- Selected objects
- Slides
- Handouts
- Speaker notes
- Audience notes

On the Advanced page of the dialog box, the Adjust Image to Print Black and White option prints color slides in black and white. Deselect this option if you have a color printer and you want color copies. When you print a color slide on a noncolor printer, the colors are converted to shades of gray. If your printer can reproduce the shades so they appear clear and the text and graphics are readable, then you may want to deselect this option as well. Leave this option selected, however, if you want to speed the printing process, if your printer does not handle shades well, or if you want to copy the pages on a copy machine that does not adequately reproduce shades or colors.

The Print background option determines if the slide background prints. Again, print the background only when your printer is color-capable or can adequately print shades of gray.

There are also options to print the slide title and the slide number along with the slide and to print slides upside down.

On the Layout page of the dialog box, you can choose to scale the printed page. Use the Two-Sided Printing options to print your slides as a booklet on both sides of the paper.

Printing Notes and Handouts

In addition to printing the slides themselves, you can print handouts, speaker notes, and audience notes.

Handouts have thumbnails of several slides on each page, as shown in the Print Preview in Figure 23-7. The audience can refer to them during your presentation and take them home as a reference. To print handouts, follow these steps:

1. Click on the Print button in the toolbar, or select File | Print.

2. Click on the Main tab of the Print dialog box.

3. Select Handouts in the Print Range section.

4. Select the number of slides per page.

5. Click on Print.

NOTE *The Audience Notes option on the Print tab of the dialog box is similar to handouts, but it prints a series of lines below each slide so the audience can take notes as you talk.*

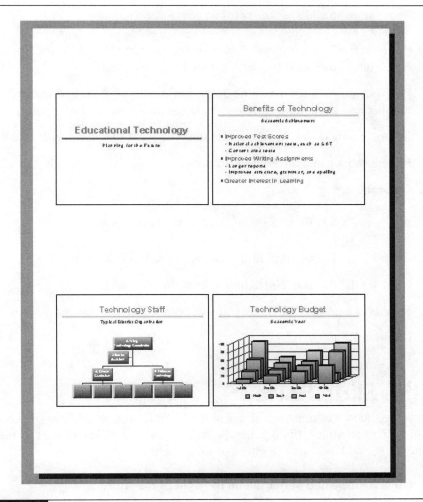

FIGURE 23-7   Handouts, with four slides on each page

Speaker Notes

It would be nice if you could memorize an entire presentation, but it's all too easy to lose track. To help you, you can print speaker notes. These are thumbnail sketches of each slide along with your own script, reminders, or notes. Before printing speaker notes, however, you must create them.

Use these steps to add speaker notes to your slides:

1. Click on the Speaker Notes button on the property bar to see the Speaker Notes tab of the Slide Properties dialog box.

2. Pull down the Slides list at the bottom of the dialog box, and select the number and title of the slide you want to add a note to.

3. In the large text box, type the note that you want to appear with the slide.

4. Repeat steps 2 and 3 for all of the slides.

5. Close the dialog box.

When you are ready to print the notes, follow these steps:

1. Click on the Print button in the toolbar, or select File | Print.

2. Click on the Speaker Notes option button.

3. Specify the number of slides you want printed on each page.

4. Click on Print.

Using the Slide Sorter

So far, we've been working with slides in the Slide Editor, which lets you create and edit individual slides. For a general overview of your slides, change to the Slide Sorter view. To do so, use either of these techniques:

■ Click on the Slide Sorter tab on the right of the slide.

■ Select View | Slide Sorter.

The Slide Sorter window, shown in Figure 23-8, displays thumbnail sketches of your slides. To change the order of a slide, just drag it to a new position. As you drag, a vertical bar appears indicating the new position. Release the mouse when the position is correct. To move several slides at the same time, select them all. To choose slides that are not consecutive, hold down the CTRL key, and click on each slide. To select consecutive slides, click on the first in the series, and then hold down the SHIFT key and click on the last in the series.

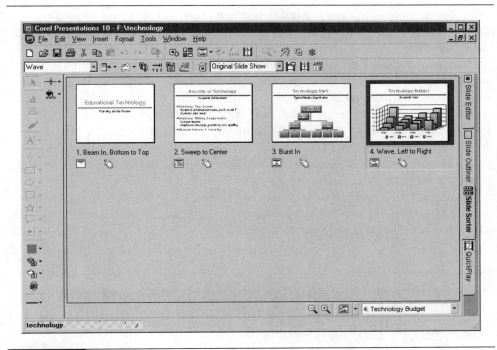

FIGURE 23-8   Slide Sorter

Below each slide thumbnail is the type of transition and its direction, as well as an icon representing the type of slide. If the slide is set to be displayed with a mouse click or key press, you'll see a mouse icon. A clock appears if the slide is set to change automatically.

To add a slide, select a template from the Add Slide list. The slide is inserted after the currently selected slide.

> **TIP**   *Use the buttons next to the Add Slide list to change the magnification of the display.*

Using the Outliner

While the Slide Sorter is useful for viewing your slides graphically, you cannot read much of the information on the slides. When you want to look at the contents of the presentation, change to the Outliner. The Outliner displays the titles, subtitles, and other text from each slide in outline format. This makes it easy to see the structure of your presentation without being distracted by graphics and backgrounds.

You can also use the Outliner to add slides to the presentation, even to create an entire presentation of bullet lists, text, and titles (but not graphics or charts) by typing an outline. The outline is converted into a series of slides when you change views. To change the order of slides, drag the slide icon up or down. As you drag, a red line appears where the slide will be inserted—release the mouse button when the line is in the correct position.

To change to the Slide Outliner view, either click on the Slide Outliner tab, or select View | Slide Outliner.

A typical Outliner window is shown in Figure 23-9. Each slide in the chart is marked by the Slide icon. The name of the text placeholders are shown on the left, with the text in the placeholders on the right.

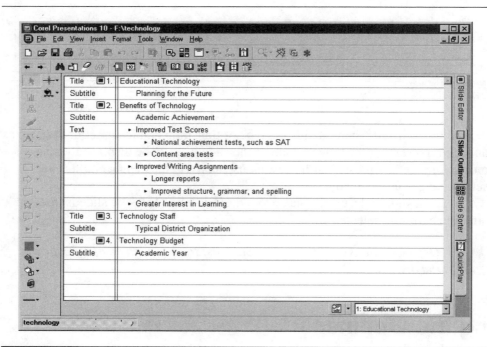

FIGURE 23-9   Outliner

To add a slide to the presentation in Outliner view, use these steps:

1. Place the insertion point at the end of the slide above where you want the new slide to appear.

2. Pull down the Add Slide list, and choose the type of slide you want to add.

3. Type the title for the slide, and press ENTER.

4. Type an optional subtitle.

5. Press ENTER, and add other text that you want on the slide.

| Integrate IT! | *Use a WordPerfect 10 outline to create a slide presentation. Select File | Insert, select the file that you want to use for the chart, and click on Insert.* |

Editing Slides

You have complete control over the appearance and format of your slides. In addition to the toolbar and property bar formatting options, you can edit and format slides by setting properties and by changing the master background.

Changing the Master Background

After you create your slide show, it is not too late to select a different master background. Just click on the Master Gallery button in the property bar, or select Master Gallery from the Format menu, and select another master. Your selection is applied to all of the slides in the presentation.

You can have two separate backgrounds and switch between them. One uses the style you selected from the master background choices, the other is blank.

| TIP | *You can select from additional backgrounds to apply as the master using the Slide Appearance command. See the section "Changing a Slide's Background and Template," later in this chapter.* |

You can also add your own elements to the master background so it is used for all of the slides in the current presentation. For example, suppose you want your company logo to appear on every slide. Choose a master that you like and that has room for the logo. Then follow these steps:

1. Select Edit | Background Layer. A slide appears with only the background and two tabs—Background and Blank. Choose the tab for where you want to add your logo—either to the background or blank tab.

2. Insert your logo using the ClipArt option from the toolbar, or add any other elements that you want in every slide.

3. Select Edit | Slide Layer.

Changing a Slide's Background and Template

While the master background is used as the default for all slides, you can apply a different background to an individual slide or a group of selected slides. You can select the slide or slides that you want to format first either before or after displaying the dialog box. Here's how:

1. In Slide Editor, click on the tab for the slide that you want to change. In Slide Sorter, click on the slide, or hold down the CTRL key and click on each of the slides you want to format. Use the typical Windows method to select a group of slides by clicking on the first slide, and then holding down the SHIFT key and clicking on the last slide.

2. Right-slick on the slide and choose Appearance from the Quickmenu, or choose Format | Background Gallery, to see the Slide Properties dialog box shown in Figure 23-10. The background category is set at <Within slide show>, so you'll see thumbnail sketches of the current backgrounds being used in the presentation.

NOTE	*You'll learn about the other options in this dialog box in Chapter 24.*

1. Look at the slide number in the slide list at the bottom of the dialog box. If the slide is not the one you want to format, choose the slide from the list. The list is dimmed when you select multiple slides from Slide Sorter view.

2. To change the slide's template, click on one of the samples in the Background section.

3. To change a background, pull down the Category list, and select from the choices. Thumbnail sketches of the category appear in the dialog box.

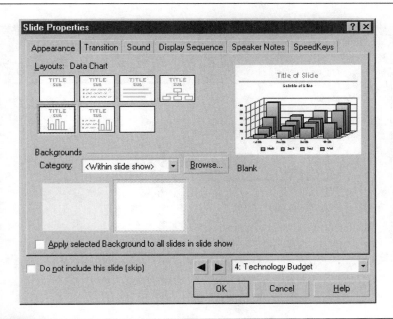

FIGURE 23-10   Changing the slide's appearance

4. Click on the background that you want to apply.

5. To use the background as the master for the entire presentation, click on Apply Selected Background to All Slides in Slide Show.

6. Click on OK.

Customizing Template Layouts

You know that each template has two or more placeholders in specific positions on the slide. The text in the title and subtitle placeholders uses a default format, font, and font size. While you can change the position of a placeholder and format the text within it, you can also change the default values for all slides using the template. This presents a consistent look throughout your presentation, so you don't have to worry about making the same changes to each slide individually.

1. Select Edit | Layout Layer to display the screen shown in Figure 23-11. A slide appears, showing the placeholders.

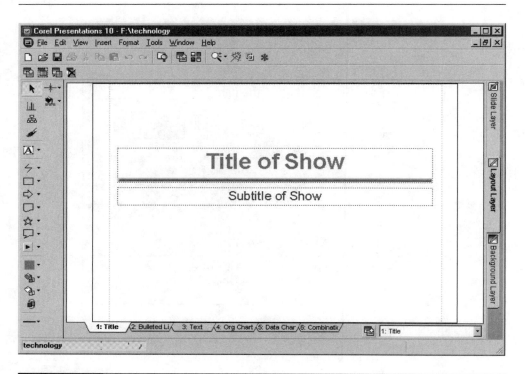

FIGURE 23-11   Changing the layout layer

2. Click on the tab for the type of template you want to change.

3. Change the size or position, or format the font in the placeholder. You can also add any text or graphics that you want to appear on each slide of that type.

4. Select Edit | Slide Layer, or click on the Slide Layer tab.

Your changes are automatically applied to all existing and new slides that use the template.

 While the Layout Layer is displayed, click on the Background Layer tab to change the background.

Changing Object Properties

In addition to changing the individual formats to text, you can customize all of the properties applied to slide objects, such as titles, subtitles, and charts.

 Click to select the object, and then click on the Object Properties button in the property bar. The icon on the button and the name of the button in the QuickTip depend on the object. When you select a subtitle, for example, the icon appears to point to a subtitle in the button, and the QuickTip is Subtitle Properties. The options that appear also depend on the object. Figure 23-12, for example, shows the properties for a title.

Use the pages of the dialog box to customize the objects. If you click on Apply to All, the formats are applied to every slide using the current layout. So if you change the title properties when viewing a bulleted list slide, all bulleted list slides are affected. Click on OK to apply the changes just to the current slide.

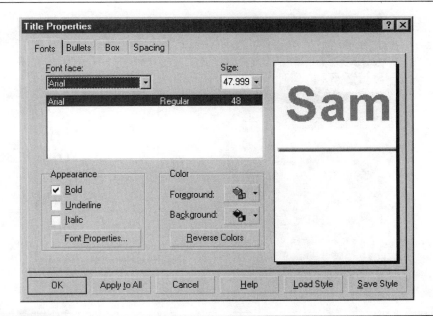

FIGURE 23-12   Changing object properties

Customizing Bullet Charts

Bulleted lists contain several elements that you can modify—the appearance and spacing of the text and bullets, and the box around the chart. While you can format selected text using the toolbar and property bar, it is best to be consistent. By setting Bulleted List Properties, you ensure that the style of the levels is consistent throughout the entire presentation.

To set properties, click on any bulleted list or placeholder and then on the Object Properties button in the property bar.

Use the Fonts page to format the text at each level. Select the level you want to change, and then choose options from the Font Face, Font Style, and Size lists. Choose an appearance and foreground and background colors, select to reverse the colors, or click on Font Properties to see the options in Figure 23-13 for customizing the fill style and outline.

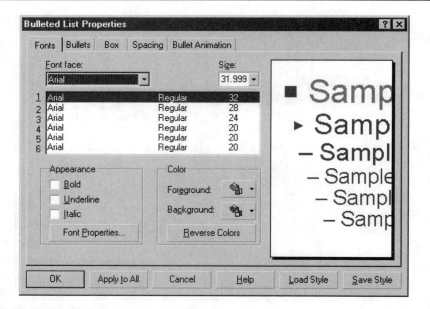

FIGURE 23-13   Changing font properties for bullets

Changing Bullet Style and Justification

Use the Bullets tab in the dialog box, shown in Figure 23-14, to customize the type of bullet used for each level. The Bullet Set list contains several choices that apply styles to every bullet level. To change the style of individual levels, use these steps:

1. Click on the level that you want to change.

2. Pull down the Justification list (it says Auto), and select a justification—Left, Center, Right, or Auto.

3. Pull down the Bullet list, and choose the character to use for the bullet. To choose a special character from the Corel WordPerfect Characters box, select Other from the Bullet list (even if it is already shown the list). In the Symbols dialog box, choose the character set and the character, and then click on the Insert and Close button. This box works just as it does in Corel WordPerfect.

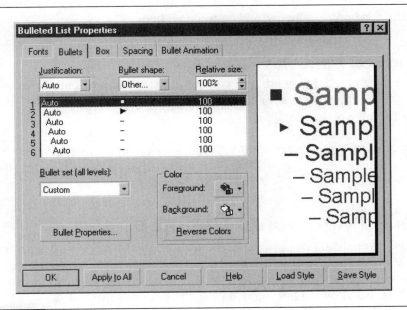

FIGURE 23-14   Customizing bullet styles

4. Choose a relative size for the bullet. By default, the bullets are the same size as the text. You can choose a relative size from 50 to 150 percent of the text size.

5. Select a color for the bullet.

6. Repeat the steps for each level bullet you want to customize.

7. Click on Apply or Apply to All.

To remove a bullet from a level, click on the level, and choose None from the Bullet list.

 Use the Save Style and Load Style buttons to save your custom bullet formats. You are actually creating a style as you would in WordPerfect 10.

Adjusting Bullet Spacing

The options on the Spacing page of the dialog box control the spacing between items. You can set the spacing between main and subordinate items, between consecutive subordinate items, and between all lines.

Setting Box Attributes

The Box page of the dialog box lets you add a box around the bullet chart, with a custom shape, color, pattern, or color fill. Click on the Box tab, and then choose options from the dialog box.

 You'll learn about the Bullet Animation page of the dialog box in Chapter 24.

Using the Page Setup Dialog Box

The Page Setup dialog box provides a number of other ways to customize your slides. Many of these options are similar to those found in WordPerfect 10.

Use the Page Setup page of the dialog box to select the page size and orientation and to set the left, right, top, and bottom margins.

Use the Fill page to select a color and background other than that of the master. You can also choose to use a picture, texture, pattern, or gradient fill. If you choose a picture, you can select the way it is repeated on the slide.

Creating a Presentation with Projects

So far, we've been concentrating on the format of slides, letting you decide on the contents. While you want your slides to look good, the most important part of your presentation is the message within them.

If you need help organizing your thoughts, start a presentation using a project. The project creates an outline for you, showing the type of information that should be included in common types of presentations. Here's how to use it:

1. From within Corel Presentations 10, choose File | New From Project, or close your open presentation.

2. In the dialog box that appears, click on the Create New tab.

3. Instead of selecting [Corel Presentation Slide Show], double-click on one of the projects that you want to use. The Slide Editor appears showing the first of the slides, along with the Corel PerfectExpert panel of options.

4. Click on the Slide Outliner tab.

5. Replace the text in the outline with your own.

6. Edit and format the presentation as desired, adding your own slides where needed.

Try It Out

In this chapter, you created a small slide presentation. The presentation includes the slides shown in Figure 23-7. In this section, we'll add some slides to the presentation and customize their appearance.

1. Open the slide show Technology that you created in this chapter. If you did not create the slides, or save the show, create it now using Figure 23-7 as a guide.

2. To add a new slide to the end of the presentation, click on the tab for slide 4.

3. Pull down the New Slide list and select Insert Text Slide.

4. Double-click on the title placeholder and type **Curriculum Areas**.

5. Click on the Subtitle placeholder to select it and press DEL.

6. Double-click on the Add Text placeholder and enter the following:

> **Now, let's take a look at the various curriculum areas that will directly benefit from computer technology in the classroom.**

7. Pull down the New Slide list and select Insert Text Slide.

8. Double-click on the title placeholder and type **Liberal Arts**.

9. Click on the Subtitle placeholder to select it and press Del.

10. Click on the Add Text placeholder and press Del.

11. Select Insert | Bulleted List.

12. Drag the mouse to create a rectangle half the width of the screen starting on the left, as shown here:

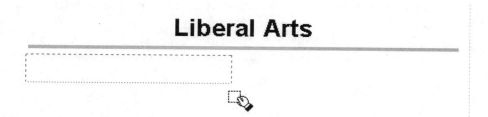

13. Enter the following text:

> **English**
> History
> Sociology
> Political Science

14. Select Insert | Bulleted List.

15. Drag the mouse to create a rectangle half the width of the screen to the right of the previous box.

16. Enter the text and adjust the spacing and position of the boxes, as shown in Figure 23-15.

17. Select Edit | Background Layer.

18. Select Insert | Text Line.

19. Click near the top of the slide.

20. Enter **Educational Consultants, Inc.**

21. Select Edit | Slide Layer. Your company name now appears at the top of each slide. To change its position or size, select Edit | Background Layer, make your changes, and then select Edit | Slide Layer.

22. If needed, adjust the position of any titles or other placeholders.

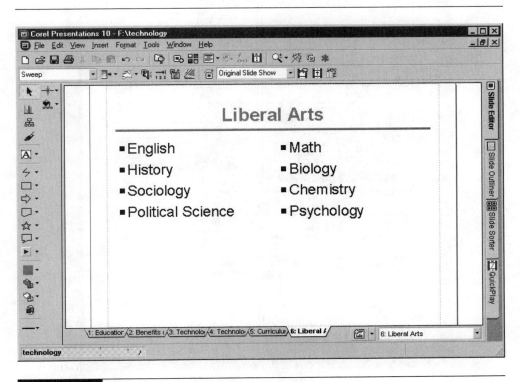

FIGURE 23-15   Two bulleted list boxes

23. Select File | Save.

24. Select File | Print.

25. Select the Handouts option button and enter 6 in the Number of slides per page box.

26. Click Preview. The preview appears in Figure 23-16.

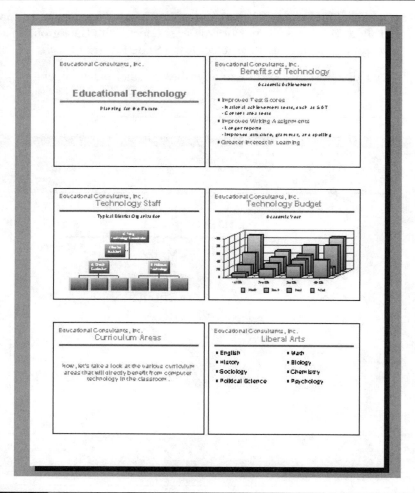

FIGURE 23-16   Completed presentation

Chapter 24

Working with Corel
Presentations 10
Graphics

809

In Chapter 23, you learned how to insert clip art and other graphic images into a presentation. Part of the power of Corel Presentations 10 is that you can customize graphics and even create your own drawings. In this chapter, you will learn how to work with and customize two types of graphics: vector and bitmap.

Working with Vector Graphics

Clip art and WPG images are vector graphics, which means that they are made up of a series of individual lines and curves. Putting three lines together, for example, creates a triangle—four lines, a rectangle. You can make changes to the entire graphic, such as altering its size or rotating it, and you can edit the individual lines and curves within it.

There are two ways to work with a graphic. You can click or right-click on the graphic to select it and to apply certain formats, such as changing its size and rotation. You can also double-click on it, or select Edit Points from the QuickMenu to access the individual segments that make up the graphic. If you want to rotate the entire graphic, for example, you right-click on it, and choose Rotate from the QuickMenu. If you want to rotate one of the objects within the graphic, you have to double-click on the graphic to enter the Edit mode, and then right-click on the segment you want to rotate.

Vector images have a transparent background, which means that you'll be able to see the background of the slide under portions of the graphic that do not have any fill or color themselves. To select a graphic, click on a filled portion of it or a line, not on the background of the slide that shows through. If you want to display the QuickMenu, right-click on a filled portion.

NOTE *If the entire graphic is not selected when you click on it, choose the Selection tool in the toolbar, drag around the entire graphic, then right-click and select Group from the QuickMenu.*

When you select a graphic, Corel Presentations 10 will display this property bar:

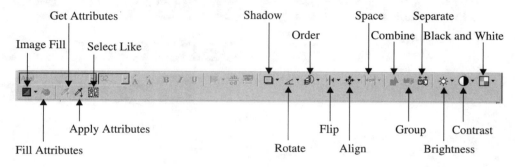

At the bottom of the tool palette along the left of the screen are buttons for setting the fill color or pattern, changing the foreground and background colors, and reversing the colors. Set the attributes of the object by right-clicking on it and choosing Object Properties from the QuickMenu.

Setting View Options

Before learning how to work with graphics, consider four options on the View menu that can be very useful: Auto Select, Ruler, Crosshair, and Grid/Guides/Snap.

The *Auto Select* option in the View menu is selected by default. This means that after you create an object, it appears selected with handles so you can immediately work with it. If you turn off this option, you have to select the object after you create it.

By selecting *Ruler* from the View menu, you display a horizontal ruler along the top of the window and a vertical ruler down the left side. Use the rulers to position objects in precise locations. You can also use the rulers to position guidelines. A *guideline* is a horizontal line across the screen or a vertical line down the screen that you can place at a position along the ruler. Set and use the guidelines for aligning objects. To create a guideline, use these steps:

1. Select View | Ruler to display the rules.

2. To create a horizontal guideline, click anywhere in the horizontal ruler, and then drag the mouse down into the window.

3. As you drag, a horizontal line appears across the screen at the mouse pointer.

4. Using the measurements on the vertical ruler as a guide, drag until the line is in the position you want it, and then release the mouse button.

Create a vertical guideline the same way, but click and drag from the vertical ruler. Change the guide position by dragging it.

You can create as many horizontal and vertical guidelines as you need. To remove a specific guideline, point to it so the cursor appears as a two-headed arrow. Then, either drag the line off of the screen, or right-click on it and choose Delete Guide from the QuickMenu.

TIP	*If the Delete Guide option does not appear in the QuickMenu, right-click on a section of the guide, not over a placeholder.*

If you select *Crosshair* from the View menu, horizontal and vertical lines appear with the intersection following the movement of the mouse pointer. As you drag the mouse, the crosshairs move with it. The crosshairs are useful for judging the position of objects in relation to others on the screen, and in relation to guidelines. Use the crosshair, for example, to place the mouse at a specific position relative to both the horizontal and vertical rulers.

A grid is a pattern of evenly spaced dots superimposed on the screen. By displaying the grid, you can use the pattern to align objects. The *Grid/Guides/Snap* option has six choices:

- *Display Grid* displays the grid pattern. Click on the option to turn off the grid.

- *Snap to Grid* forces all objects that you move or draw to align on a grid line.

- *Display Guides* centers a horizontal and vertical guideline on the screen.

- *Snap to Guides* forces all objects that you move or draw to align on a guideline.

- *Clear Guides* removes the guidelines from the screen.

- *Grid/Guides/Snap Options* lets you change the spacing of the grid pattern and guidelines.

Changing a Graphic's Size and Position

You already know how to use the mouse to change the size and position of an image by dragging. You can also change its size and position using dialog boxes. The boxes let you change the size by entering a specific ratio, such as 50 percent, and by aligning the box with a side or the exact center.

To change the size, use these steps:

1. Click on the graphic to select it and display the handles.

2. Point to a handle so the mouse pointer appears as a two-headed arrow, and then right-click. If you clicked on a corner handle, you'll see the Size dialog box. If you clicked on a middle handle you'll see the Stretch dialog box. Both boxes have the same options, only their titles differ.

3. In the Multiplier box, enter the amount to reduce or enlarge the box. For example, enter **1.2** to enlarge it 20 percent or **0.8** to reduce it 20 percent.

4. Select the Around Center option to change the size of the box while leaving its center position in the same location. Without this checked, the upper-right corner of the graphic is the anchor position.

5. Select Size (or Stretch) a Copy of the Object(s) when you want to create a copy of the graphic in the new size, leaving the original as it is.

6. Click on OK.

To adjust the position of the graphic, right-click on the graphic and point to Align in the QuickMenu, or click the Align button in the property bar. Your choices are:

- *Left* moves the graphic to the left of the slide in its current vertical position.

- *Right* moves the graphic to the right of the slide in its current vertical position.

- *Top* moves the graphic to the top of the slide in its current horizontal position.

- *Bottom* moves the graphic to the bottom of the slide in its current horizontal position.

- *Center Left/Right* centers the graphic between the left and right.

- *Center Top/Bottom* centers the graphic between the top and bottom.

- *Center Both* places the slide in the exact center of the slide.

Rotating a Graphic

Another way to customize a graphic is to rotate it. Sometimes you can rotate a graphic that doesn't seem to fit, so that it no longer interferes with text. But most often, you rotate a graphic to add a special effect, or to have it appear as if it is pointing in another direction. With Corel Presentations 10, you can both rotate a graphic and skew it. *Skewing* changes just one axis of the image, while keeping the other stationary. Let's see how this works:

1. Right-click on Graphic and select Rotate from the QuickMenu, or select Manual Rotation from the Rotate list in the property bar. The graphic will

be surrounded by eight special handles that control rotation, and by a center point:

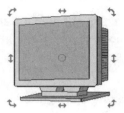

2. Drag a handle in the corner to rotate the entire image.

3. Drag one of the center handles on the top, bottom, left, or right to skew the graphic. When you drag, only that side of the image moves with the mouse:

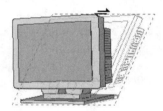

4. Drag the center point to change the pivot point of the rotation.

5. Click the mouse when you have finished.

You can also rotate the object a specific number of degrees using the Rotate button in the property bar. Click on the button to display a list of rotation degrees:

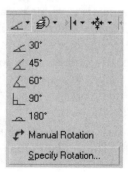

This feature uses real-time preview, so pointing to an option shows how the graphic will appear at that rotation.

You can also select to manually rotate the graphic using handles, or to display a dialog box to enter a specific rotation amount.

> **TIP** *To flip the image, click on the Flip button in the property bar, and choose Flip Left/Right or Flip Top/Bottom. You can also right-click on the object and choose Flip options from the QuickMenu.*

Changing the Object's Appearance

In addition to rotating the graphic, you can use the property bar and Graphics menu to change the appearance in other ways. The Shadow button in the property bar, for example, lets you add a shadow to the graphic itself. Use the Line Width and Line Color button to change the lines that create the vectors or to remove the lines altogether.

> **TIP** *To remove an applied shadow, select the option in the center of the list of shadow choices.*

Use the Selected Object Viewer command in the View menu to display the graphic in a separate window, so you can visualize how it appears without the other slide information. Figure 24-1, for example, shows a graphic with a shadow and outline pattern, with the Selected Object Viewer displayed.

To create even more visual effects, use the Brightness, Contrast, and Black and White buttons in the toolbar, or the Image Tools command on the Tools menu. Click on the Image Fill button in the property bar so you can choose to display the image with these effects:

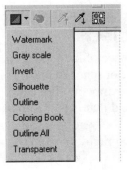

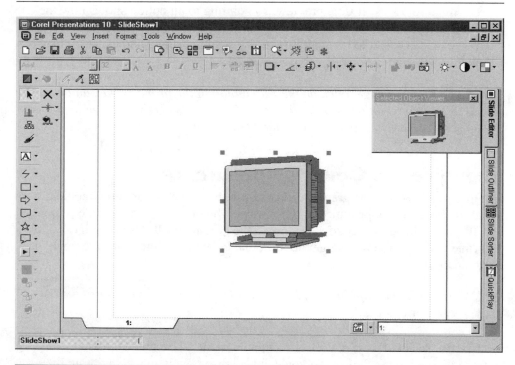

FIGURE 24-1   Vector graphic with shadow and pattern

You can also select Object Properties from the QuickMenu, to see the dialog box shown in Figure 24-2. Use the Outline and Shadow pages of the dialog box to change the appearance of the graphic. You'll learn about the SpeedLink and Object Animation pages in the next chapter.

Editing Graphic Objects

While a vector graphic is composed of individual lines, groups of lines are collected into objects, such as a rectangle or other shapes. You can customize the objects themselves, as well as the entire drawing. For example, the graphic shown next contains a bear and a background that is made up of several different objects. By selecting only the object that is the bear, you can change its fill pattern or color without affecting the rest of the graphic.

You can edit an object in two ways: by using Edit mode or by separating the picture into a series of separate objects. Edit mode also lets you change the individual lines that make up each object, so let's look at it first.

TIP   *Use the Selected Object Viewer to help edit vector graphics. Sometimes it is difficult to see which object is selected onscreen. Displaying the viewer shows exactly which object is selected.*

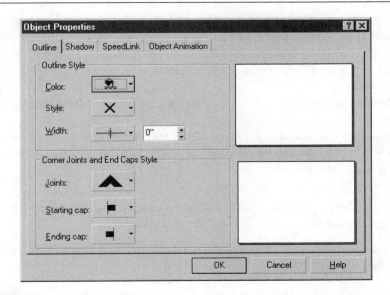

FIGURE 24-2   Setting the object properties

To enter Edit mode, either double-click on the image, or right-click on it and select Edit from the QuickMenu. You'll know you are in Edit mode when the graphic is surrounded by a thick line with *white* handles. You can now select and edit the individual objects that make up the image. Click on the part of the graphic that you want to edit to display handles around that part. You can then move, resize, or delete that part of the artwork. For example, here is the graphic with one of its objects moved to another position:

The choices in the QuickMenu and property bar affect just the selected objects. For example, choose Rotate from the QuickMenu to see rotation handles appear around only the selected object, or choose an Align option to change its position.

To make even more changes, use the Object Properties dialog box. Select the object that you want to edit, right-click, and then choose Object Properties from the QuickMenu.

To change the fill pattern or color of a clip art graphic, follow these steps:

TIP	*You can select and apply fill patterns and colors directly to drawing objects that you create yourself. Just select the object and choose Options from the tool palette.*

1. When the graphic is not selected, choose the fill pattern, foreground, and background colors desired from the tool palette.

2. Double-click on the graphic, and select the portion to which you want to apply the settings.

3. Click the Apply Attributes button on the property bar:

To copy the attributes from an object so you can apply them to another, use the Get Attributes button. This button works like the QuickFormat button in WordPerfect 10, in that it copies formats applied to a selected object. When you click the button you'll see this box:

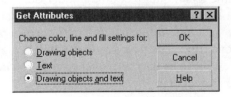

You can choose to copy the attributes of drawing objects, text, or both. To apply those same formats to another object, click on the object and then on the Apply Attributes button.

Separating Graphic Segments

While you can edit the individual parts of a graphic in Edit mode, the entire graphic is still treated as one object outside of that mode. As long as you do not double-click on it and select a specific object segment, for example, you can rotate and drag the entire graphic as one unit.

If you wish, however, you can separate the graphic into its objects so each one is a separate entity on the slide. Follow these steps:

1. Make sure you are not in Edit mode—click outside of the graphic so it is not selected.

2. Right-click on the graphic, and choose Separate Objects from the QuickMenu.

3. Click away from the object to deselect it.

4. You can now select the individual objects to change size, position, color, or rotation. As far as Corel Presentations 10 is concerned, each object is a separate graphic.

If you later want to work with the entire graphic again as a unit, you have to regroup it. Here's how:

1. Select all of the individual objects. Either drag the mouse to draw a selection box around them, or hold down the CTRL key and click on them.

2. Right-click on the selected objects, and choose Group from the QuickMenu.

You can use the same technique to combine individual elements of a graphic. The bear in the graphic shown previously, for example, is actually two parts – the body and the head. By selecting both parts and grouping them together, you can edit the entire bear at one time. The new group is actually a group within the graphic, and you can tell if this is the case when you see an edit box within the overall graphic box, as shown here:

Working with Layers

Just as a slide is composed of several layers, so is a graphic. Two or more objects can overlap, with one in the foreground partially (or totally) obscuring the others in the background. You can also change the position of an object in relation to others, moving an object from the foreground to the background, even moving, in several steps, through multiple overlapping objects.

To change the position of one object in relation to another, use these steps:

1. Click in the object.

2. Click on the Order button on the property bar, and choose one of these options:

■ *To Front* moves the object to the foreground, on top of all others.

■ *To Back* moves the object to the background, behind all others.

■ *Forward One* moves the object one level up.

■ *Back One* moves the object one level down.

In Edit mode, you can also right-click on the object and choose To Back or To Front in the QuickMenu.

| TIP | *You can use the Order commands to layer separate graphic objects as well.* |

Moving Segment Points

You already know that each object in a vector graphic consists of a series of lines. The intersection of two lines is called a *point*. If you drag the point, then you change the size and position of the lines on either side.

1. In Edit mode, right-click on the object that you want to edit, and select Edit Points from the QuickMenu. The points that make up the object appear as shown here:

2. Drag one of the points to a new position; when you point to a point, the cursor appears as a crosshair. To create the effect you want, you may have to drag a series of points.

3. If you right-click on a point, a QuickMenu appears with these options:

   - *Delete* deletes the selected point.

   - *Add* inserts a new point after the selected one.

   - *Close* closes the object by connecting the first and last point.

   - *Open* opens the object by removing the segment between the selected point and the next point.

   - *To Curve* creates a Bezier curve at the selected point(s).

   - *To Line* replace the curve with lines at the selected point(s)

   - *Smooth* rounds the curve at the selected point(s)

   - *Symmetrical* evens out the length of the direction lines at the selected point(s)

Creating Your Own Drawing

You can create your own vector artwork as stand-alone graphics or to supplement a bulleted list, clip art graphic, data chart, or organization chart.

Each object that you draw is treated independently, and you can apply all of the same techniques to it as you've learned previously—choosing colors and patterns, setting object properties, rotating objects, and editing points. If you create a picture by drawing and positioning several objects, however, you may want to group them so you can move and resize them as one unit. You can also add an object to a graphic and group them. To group graphic objects, select them using the CTRL key, right-click on them, and choose Group from the QuickMenu.

Using the Tool Palette

The Tool palette offers a number of tools with which to add some of your own custom artwork to a slide. You can use the tools to draw objects directly on the slide, such as adding a text box or an arrow pointing to another object.

The Select Tool

 You use the Select tool to return to Select mode after drawing an object. Select mode means that clicking on an object selects it. This cancels the function of the previously used tool.

Text Object Tools

Use the Text Object tools to insert text into the drawing. There are four tools, as shown here:

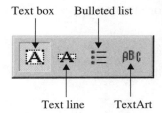

Use the Text Box tool to enter multiple lines of text, and use the Text Line tool to enter just a single line. Use the Bulleted List tool to insert a list of bulleted lines, and use the TextArt tool to create special effects.

For example, to add lines of text to a drawing, use these steps:

1. Pull down the Text Objects list, click on the Text Box tool, and then drag in the window to create a box the width you want the text. When you release the mouse button, a box appears with the insertion point inside.

2. Type the text. When the insertion point reaches the right side of the box, it wraps to the next line.

3. Click outside of the box when you have finished.

The background of a text box is transparent, so it becomes the same color as the background. Presentations does this so you can place text on other subjects, such as buttons, callouts, and flowchart symbols.

NOTE   *If you use the Text Line tool, just click where you want the line of text to begin, and then type.*

You can edit the text and the box just as you would a graphic box:

1. Drag the box to change its position.

2. Drag a corner handle to change its size.

3. Drag a side handle to add space between the text and the right side of the box.

4. Rotate the text in the box by choosing Rotate from the QuickMenu.

5. Change the position using the Align option in the QuickMenu.

6. Change the size ratio by right-clicking on the handle.

Use the property bar to format the text just as you would any text on a slide.

Drawing Lines

The Line Object tool offers these choices:

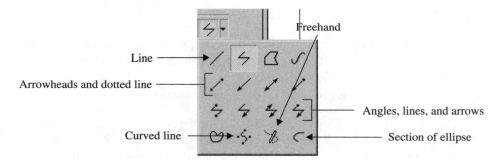

Select the object you want to create, and then drag to draw it. It's that simple. As with all graphics, when you release the mouse button, the line appears surrounded by handles—drag one of the handles to change the shape of the line. To move the line, point to it so the mouse pointer appears as a four-pointed arrow, and then drag.

You should also notice a smaller extra handle on one end of the line. Use this handle to position the graphic at a specific starting position. Point to the handle so the mouse pointer appears as an arrow and then drag.

| TIP | *Select Show Pointed Position from the View menu to display the exact pointer position on the right side of the status bar.* |

Drawing Basic Shapes

The Basic Objects tool lets you create rectangles, circles, arrows, and other objects. Click on the tool to select from the following options:

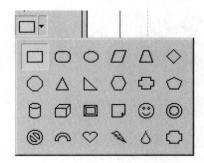

Click on the tool you want, and then drag to draw the object. When you've finished, you can change its size, position, or color, add a shadow, or edit it like other graphic boxes.

To add text inside one of the shapes, insert a text box or text line within it.

Drawing Arrows

The Arrow Shapes tool offers these choices:

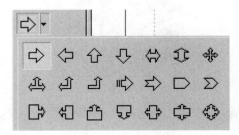

Select the object you want to create, and then drag to draw it. The arrow will have one or more diamond-shaped handles, like those shown in the following illustration. Drag one of those handles to adjust the shape or proportions as shown.

Drawing Flowchart Shapes

The Flowchart Shapes tool lets you create flowcharts that represent a series of steps. Pull down the list to select from the following options:

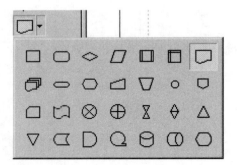

Drawing Star Shapes

The Star Shapes tool lets you create stars and banners. Pull down the list to select from the following options:

Drawing Callouts

A callout is a box with a pointer. The Callouts Shapes list offers these options:

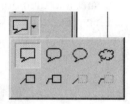

Drawing Action Shapes

Action shapes are buttons with icons that represent various tasks, such as playing a sound or launching your Web browser. The Action Shapes list offers these options:

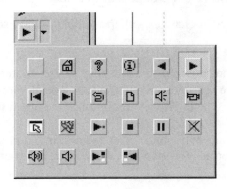

To actually perform the action when clicking on the button, however, you have to assign it a SpeedLink, as you'll learn in Chapter 25.

Customizing Objects

The Tools menu and property bar give you a number of ways to customize your object even further. Experiment with the options by selecting one or more objects and seeing the effects that each option applies.

For example, the Space Evenly button on the property bar spreads out selected objects so they are spaced evenly between the left and right or top and bottom of the slide.

In the Tools menu, take advantage of these features:

- *Trace Text* converts each character in selected text into a vector drawing.

- *Trace Bitmap* converts a bitmap drawing to a vector image.

- *Convert to Bitmap* converts the selected vector image to a bitmap.

- *Resample Bitmap* optimizes the display of a bitmap onscreen by adjusting the resolution after you resize it.

- *Image Tools* displays options to change the brightness, contrast, and black and white settings of the object.

- *Blend* creates a blended object.

- *Quick3D* creates 3D characters from a selected text box.

- *QuickWarp* forms selected text into a shape, similar to TextArt.

- *Contour Text* forms text around a graphic object.

- *Convert to Polygon* changes a shape into a polygon so it can be edited by points.

Most of these options are intuitive and easy to use. If an option in the menu is dimmed, then you have not selected any objects. You'll know how these options work when you first try them. However, contoured text and blending require some explanation.

While the QuickWarp command forms the text into a preset format, the Contour Text option forms it around any shape you can create with drawing tools, as shown here:

Here is how to use it:

1. Drag the text so it is next to the object.

2. Select both the object and the text.

3. Choose Contour Text from the Tools menu to see the Contour Text dialog box.

4. Pull down the Position list, and choose where you want the text to appear around the graphic.

5. The Display Text Only option makes the object transparent. Leave this selected if you just used the object to create the shape for the text, and you really do not want it shown. Deselect the checkbox if you want both the object and the text to appear.

6. Click on OK.

The Blend command creates a series of smaller objects. Select two or more objects, and then choose Blend from the Tools menu. In the dialog box that appears, select the number of objects to create, and then click on OK. You can then delete any duplicates that you do not want. The following illustration shows two examples of blending. On the left is the arrow and text object immediately after they were blended. On the right, the duplicate copies of the text were deleted.

 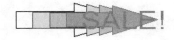

Saving Your Drawing

Your drawing will be saved along with the slide presentation. You can also save the drawing as a separate graphic file for use later in a presentation or with any other document. Select the drawing object you want to save, and then click on the Save button. Choose Selected Items from the box that appears, and then click on OK.

By default, the For Type box is set at WordPerfect 6.0 Graphics so you can save the drawing as a WordPerfect graphic file. You can also select from other graphic formats, such as PCX, JPEG, and GIF. For example, if you want to share the drawing with a friend who has a Macintosh computer, select MacPaint Bitmap. Enter a filename, and then click on OK.

Creating a Presentation Drawing

You can also create a new vector drawing outside of a slide presentation, in a separate drawing window. To create a new drawing, select the [Presentations Drawing] when starting Corel Presentations 10 or after selecting New from Project from the File menu. The Drawing window appears as in Figure 24-3.

You have most of the same drawing options from the toolbar and the Graphics property bar but with a few extra features:

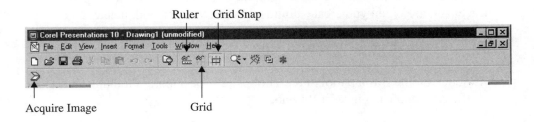

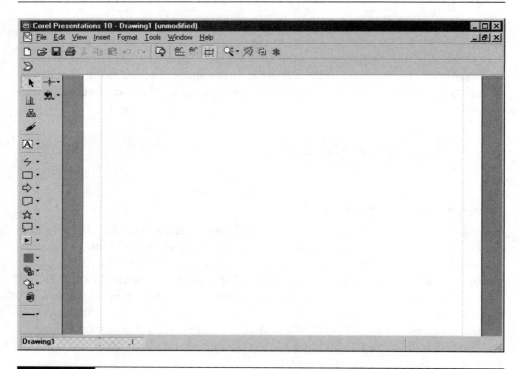

FIGURE 24-3   Drawing window

In fact, when you draw and select an object, the Graphics property bar will be the same one you used from within a slide.

Creating Bitmaps

Corel Presentations 10 also lets you create a bitmap graphic. Unlike a vector drawing that consists of lines, a bitmap graphic is a series of individual pixels, or picture elements. When you create a bitmap image, you can add, delete, and modify each of the individual pixels.

To start a bitmap image, use these steps:

1. Click on the Bitmap tool in the Tool palette, or point to Graphics in the Insert menu and click on Bitmap.

2. Click in the window to create a full-page bitmap area, or drag to create a bitmap of a selected size. Corel Presentations 10 will display the Bitmap Editor window with its own toolbars (see Figure 24-4).

You can now create the bitmap drawing (as you will learn next in the section "Using the Bitmap Editor"). When you have finished, pull down the File menu or right-click to display the QuickMenu, and select Close Bitmap Editor, or click on the Close Bitmap button on the toolbar.

The bitmap will appear in the slide in a graphic box, just like a vector image, so you can use the handles and other tools to change the size and position of the graphic, or to rotate or skew it. If you want to edit the graphic itself, however, double-click on it to display the Bitmap Editor.

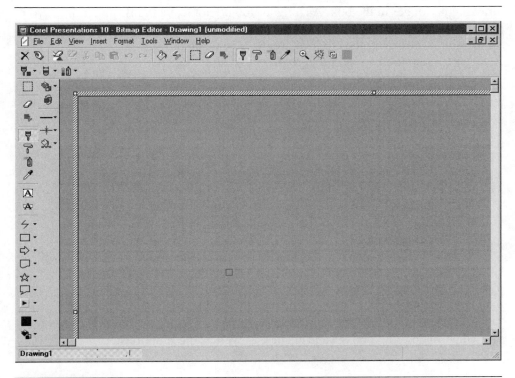

FIGURE 24-4   Bitmap Editor

Double-click on an inserted bitmap, such as those found in the Graphics\Pictures folder, to edit it in the Bitmap Editor.

Using the Bitmap Editor

The Bitmap Editor has the tools you need to create and edit bitmap images. In addition to the toolbar and property bar, you can select tools from the menus. You will learn how to use these tools throughout this chapter.

 If you do not like working with pixels, create the drawing as a vector graphic and then convert it to a bitmap drawing.

Before you start drawing the picture, you can change the size of the drawing area by dragging one of the handles. After you start drawing, however, dragging the handles to make the box smaller crops the area—cutting out the part of the drawing no longer in the box. As long as you do not leave the Bitmap Editor, you can restore the deleted area by making the box larger. If you close and then return to the editor, however, the cropped area will be deleted.

The Bitmap toolbar and property bar have these options:

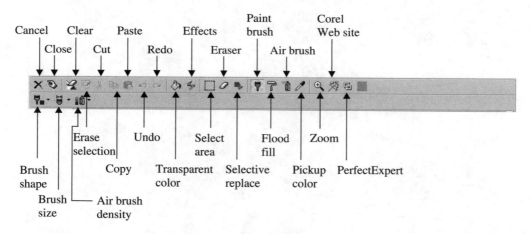

The Bitmap Tool palette has many of the same options available for vector drawings, such as text boxes and shapes, as well as these options:

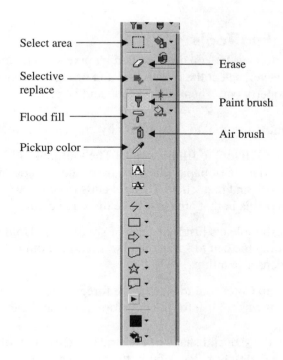

Select area

Selective
replace

Flood fill

Pickup color

Erase

Paint brush

Air brush

24

Using the Eraser

There are a number of eraser tools to delete or change pixels. Make sure you select the correct tool for the function you want to perform:

 The Eraser tool deletes (erases) pixels. When you select the tool, the mouse changes to a small square. Drag the mouse over the area that you want to erase.

 The Selective Replace tool erases just the foreground color, replacing the pixels with the background color.

 The Erase Selection tool deletes the currently selected area of the drawing.

 The Clear tool deletes the entire drawing.

 TIP *Click on the Clear button on the toolbar to erase the entire contents of the image. Click on the Erase button to delete the selected object.*

Using the Painting Tools

Several tools in the toolbar let you draw by adding pixels to the drawing. Before using the tools, however, select the foreground and background colors and a fill pattern from the property bar. Then select a tool, and be creative.

1. Use the Paint Brush tool to draw pixels by dragging the mouse.

2. Use the Flood Fill tool to fill in an area. The tool looks like a paint roller with a small triangle of paint. Place the tip of the triangle in the area that you want to fill, and then click. The tool adds the color to all of the consecutive pixels in that area that have the same color.

3. The Air Brush tool acts just like a can of spray paint. Hold down the mouse button and drag the can to spray the pixels onto the drawing. Drag the tool slowly for denser painting.

4. Use the Pickup Color tool to change the foreground color. Point it to the color that you want to use for the new foreground and then click.

You can change the size and shape of the Brush and Spray tools using either the property bar or a dialog box. By default, the brush shape is square, 11 pixels wide. The air brush has a density of 15 pixels. Change the size and shape, for example, if you don't like how your artwork appears. To do this with the property bar, follow these steps:

1. Pull down the Brush Shape list in the property bar, and choose a shape for the brush. The options are Circle, Square, Diamond, Horizontal Line, Vertical Line, Forward Slash, and Backward Slash.

2. Pull down the Brush Width list, and select a width.

3. Pull down the Air Brush Density list, and choose the density of the spray.

You can also change all three settings from a dialog box using these steps:

1. Click on More in the Brush Width or Air Brush Density lists, or select Brush from the Format menu to see the Brush Attributes dialog box.

2. Pull down the Shape list, and choose a new shape.

3. Set the brush width in pixels.

4. Set the density of the air brush.

5. Click on OK.

Editing Pixels

Because a bitmap is pixel-oriented, Corel Presentations 10 gives you a way to work on each individual pixel. This means you can edit the graphic at its smallest level, each dot that makes up a line or other shape.

You work with pixels in a special Zoom mode with three panes, as shown in Figure 24-5. In the upper left of the window is a pane containing a picture of the entire bitmap drawing area. The small rectangle within the pane represents the area that is enlarged on the right so you can see and work with the individual pixels. The pane in the lower left shows that area full size. That pane also has a rectangle indicating the enlarged area.

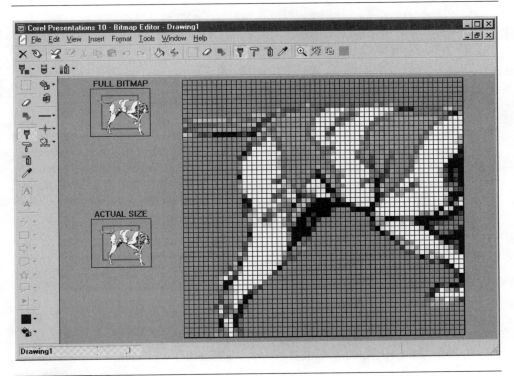

FIGURE 24-5   Zoom display of bitmap

You can display the Zoom panes using any of these techniques:

- Click on the Zoom button in the toolbar.
- Select Zoom from the View menu.
- Right-click and select Zoom from the QuickMenu.

Here is how to work with pixels:

1. Enter Zoom mode using either of the techniques described.

2. To change the area of the drawing that is enlarged, drag one of the rectangles in the two smaller panes. Drag the rectangle to the area of the picture that you want to edit, and then release the mouse.

3. Select the pattern and foreground and background colors that you want to apply.

4. Click the mouse or drag it to change the color of the pixels.

5. When you have finished, select Zoom again.

Creating Special Effects with Bitmaps

You can apply a special effect to the entire bitmap drawing to create some unusual and appealing designs. The effects apply a pattern, adjust the colors, or modify the appearance of pixels. When you are satisfied with the content of your drawing, save it before applying an effect. You may not be able to restore your original design after choosing several effects. If you save the design first, you can always insert the original bitmap into a slide and double-click on it to edit it.

When you are ready to add a special effect, use these steps:

1. If you want to apply the effect to a specific area, choose the Select tool, and then drag on the drawing. You can drag over an area that you want to apply the effect to, or drag over an area that you want to protect from the effect.

2. Click on the Effects button on the toolbar, or select Special Effects from the Tools menu or QuickMenu to see the dialog box shown in Figure 24-6.

3. Scroll the Effects list, and choose the effect that you want.

24

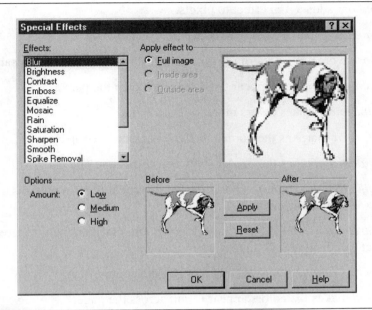

FIGURE 24-6   Special Effects dialog box

4. If you selected an area prior to displaying the dialog box, select an option in the Apply Effect To area—the Full Image, Inside Area, or Outside Area.

5. Some effects offer additional choices in the Options section. Set or select options as desired.

6. Click on the Apply button to see the effect of your choice in the After preview area. Compare it with the Before preview. If you change your mind, click on Reset, or click on Cancel.

7. When you are satisfied with your choice, click on OK.

Here is a list of the effects:

■ *Blur* blurs the borders between color and objects.

■ *Brightness* darkens or lightens the drawing.

■ *Contrast* changes the contrast between colors.

- *Emboss* adds a 3-D effect to pixels.

- *Equalize* evens the contrast between objects.

- *Mosaic* creates a pattern of squares of different colors, like mosaic tiles.

- *Rain* makes colors appear to be running down the page.

- *Saturation* makes colors more, or less, vivid.

- *Sharpen* sharpens the borders between colors and objects.

- *Smooth* smoothes the borders between colors and objects.

- *Spike Removal* removes horizontal and vertical lines in patterns, leaving pixels at the intersection.

- *Stereogram* converts the image to a random black and white stereogram that can display 3-D images when stared at.

- *Trace Contours* removes all colors by the contour lines.

- *Wind* makes the colors appear to run across the page.

When you close the Bitmap Editor, the graphic appears selected in the slide. When a bitmap is selected, the property bar contains many of the same features available for working with vector graphics, as well as these:

- Resample Bitmap
- Trace
- Edit

Try It Out

You can do a lot with graphics in a slide show, even if you are not very artistically inclined. In this chapter, we'll add some graphics to a slide and customize it in a variety of ways. We'll be using the Technology slide show we created in Chapter 23. If you don't have that slide show available, just follow these instructions but insert the graphic into a blank slide in a new presentation.

1. Open the Technology slide show.

2. Display the first slide in Slide Editor, if is not already onscreen.

3. Click the ClipArt button in the toolbar.

4. Scroll the list of graphics and choose a graphic that you feel illustrates technology. For this example, we're using the graphic g0186364.wpg, shown here:

5. Click Insert and then Close.

6. Move and resize the graphic, if needed, so it appears centered under the slide's subtitle.

7. Select the graphic, pull down the Rotation list in the property bar and select 30 degrees.

8. Pull down the Shadow list and select the second option from the left in the top row.

9. Click on the rectangle button in the tool pallete. (If a rectangle does not appear on the Basic Shapes button, pull down the Basic Shapes list in the tool pallete and select the rectangle shape.)

10. Drag the mouse to draw a rectangle around the graphic. When you release the mouse, the rectangle may obscure the graphic.

11. Right-click on the selected rectangle and choose Object Properties from the QuickMenu.

12. On the Fill tab of the Object Properties dialog box, click the button with the X—it represents no fill pattern.

13. Click OK.

14. Make sure the rectangle is still selected, pull down the Line Color list in the tool pallete, and choose a color for the line.

15. Pull down the Line Width list in the tool pallete and select a thicker line style. The completed graphic might appear as shown here:

16. Save the presentation.

17. Select the graphic.

18. Pull down the Black and White list in the toolbar and point to each of the options, watching the effect on the graphic.

19. Pull down the Image Fill list and point to each of the options.

Figure 24-7 illustrates four of the possible effects.

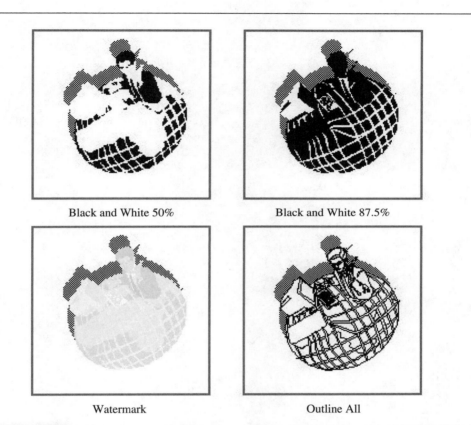

Black and White 50%   Black and White 87.5%

Watermark   Outline All

FIGURE 24-7   Sample graphic effects.

Chapter 25

Creating Slide Shows

One of the most effective ways to display Corel Presentations 10 slides is as a slide show. By using a large monitor or a video projection system, your slides become an instant multimedia presentation. You can add special effects, such as animation and transitions between slides, sound, and music. You can even link a slide to the Internet to jump to a Web page.

By publishing your entire presentation to the Internet, you can make it accessible to the world. Web surfers can download your presentation to their own computers with a click of the mouse, and they can use a page frame to select slides from a table of contents.

In this chapter, you will learn how to create a slide show, adding effects and features that create professional presentations.

Slide Transitions

When you display a slide show, you click the mouse or press the SPACEBAR to move from slide to slide. The next slide immediately replaces the previous one, just as if you had changed slides in a slide projector. By adding a transition, you can create a special effect that happens as one slide replaces the other.

You've probably seen a television show or movie in which one scene slowly fades out as the next fades in. A *fade* is just one of over 50 transitions that you can select for your slides. Other transitions make it appear as if a slide flies in from the side or appears slowly from a mosaic or other pattern. Because most transitions let you select which direction the slide appears from, there are more than 150 different combinations. Just don't overdo it. Adding too many transition effects can make the presentation difficult on the eye and can distract from the content of your slides.

You can add a transition using either the property bar or a dialog box. The property bar includes lists for the transition, direction, and speed:

To add a transition effect, use these steps.

1. In Slide Editor view, display the slide you want to add the transition to. In Slide Sorter view, click on the slide, or select several slides to apply the same transition to them.

2. Pull down the Transition list in the property bar. When you point to one of the transitions, an actual moving sample of it appears next to the list.

3. Click on the transition you want to apply.

4. Pull down the Direction list in the property bar. The options depend on the transition; in some cases the list may be empty. For example, if you select the Sweep transition, your choices are Top to Bottom, Bottom to Top, Left to Right, and Right to Left. Other transitions include these sets of choices:

   ■ Clockwise or Counter Clockwise

   ■ Right and Down, Left and Down, Left and Up, or Right and Up

   ■ Horizontal or Vertical

5. Choose a direction.

6. Pull down the Speed list in the property bar.

7. Select Fast, Medium, or Slow.

You can also apply a transition using the Slide Properties dialog box from any view. Select Layout Gallery from the Format menu, and then click on the Transition tab to see the dialog box shown in Figure 25-1. Use the Slide list at the bottom of the dialog box to select the slide you want to format. Remember, the list will be dimmed if you selected a group of slides in Slide Sorter view. Then, choose the transition from the Effect list and a direction and speed. Repeat these steps for each slide you want to add a transition to.

To use a transition for every slide in the show, click on the Apply to All Slides in Slide Show checkbox.

| TIP | *Click on the Do Not Include the Slide (Skip) checkbox when you do not want to show the current slide during playback. You can also click on the Skip Slide button in the property bar.* |

When you view your slide show in Slide Sorter view, the type of transition and its direction are listed under the slide's thumbnail. In both Slide Editor and Slide Sorter views, the transition, direction, and speed are indicated in the property bar. The name of the transition appears in the Transition box, and icons representing the direction and speed appear on the face of the Direction and Speed buttons.

| TIP | *Choose None in the Transition list to remove the effect from a slide.* |

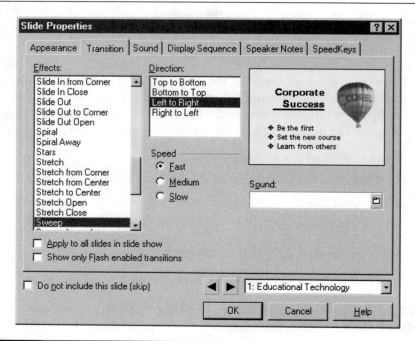

FIGURE 25-1   Transition options

Advancing Slides

The default setting leaves a slide on the screen until you advance it manually by clicking the mouse or by pressing the spacebar. Rather than manually advancing slides, however, you can set a time delay which determines how many seconds each slide appears. By using a time delay, you can leave your slide show playing as you do other things.

You set advance options in the Display Sequence page of the Slide Properties dialog box, shown in Figure 25-2. Open the dialog box by clicking on the Display Sequence button in the property bar, or by clicking on the Display Sequence tab whenever the Slide Properties box is onscreen. Use the Slide list to select the slide you want to format, and then click on the After a Delay Of option button in the Display Next Slide section. Enter the number of seconds, or use the up and down arrows to increment or decrement the time. Use the Apply to All Slides in Slide Show checkbox to apply the delay to every slide, or repeat the procedure for other slides using the Slide list.

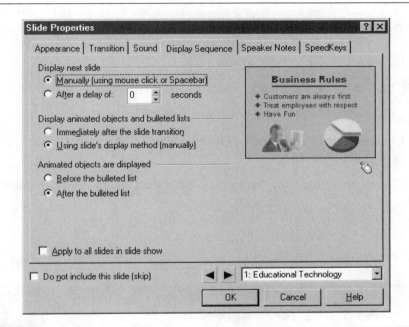

FIGURE 25-2   Display Sequence options

Animating Bullets

A slide transition determines how a slide appears on the screen. You can also create some special effects to determine how a bullet chart appears. There are two types of effects that you can apply to bullet charts: animate in place and animate across the screen. When you animate in place, the options are the same as for transitions, except the bulleted items appear using the effect from within the slide. When you select to animate across the screen, the bullets appear from outside of the viewing area, flying into the screen.

After the title and subtitle appear, the bullet chart list is added to the display using the selected effect. By using one transition for the slide itself, and another for the bullet chart list, you can add a lot of movement to the slide display.

You can also choose to cascade the individual items in the bullet chart. With a cascade, each item appears by itself, rather than the entire list at one time, which is quite effective when you want to explain or describe each item separately. In fact, you can even have the program dim the bulleted items already shown to highlight just the current point.

You apply all of these techniques using the Bulleted List Properties dialog box, shown in Figure 25-3. Here's how to use it:

1. Display the slide in Slide Editor view.

2. Click on the bulleted list to select it.

3. Click on the Object Animation button on the property bar.

4. Click on either the Animate Objects in Place or Animate Objects Across Screen option button.

5. Choose an option from the Effects list to see a sample in the preview pane.

6. Select a direction and a speed.

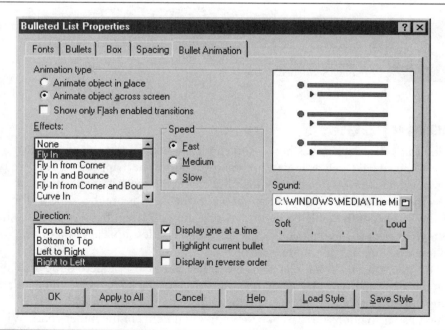

FIGURE 25-3   Animating bullets

7. To cascade the items, click on the Display One at a Time checkbox. If you select this option, you can also choose to display the bullets in reverse order.

8. To dim each previously displayed bullet item, click on the Highlight Current Bullet checkbox.

9. To play a sound file as the items are displayed, enter its path and name in the Sound box, or use the Browse button to locate it, and drag the slider below the box to choose its volume. The volume slider does not appear until you enter or select a sound file.

10. To apply the effect to all bulleted list slides, click on Apply to All; otherwise, click on OK.

11. When you are using manual advance, click the mouse when you are ready for the bulleted list to appear. If you are using a time delay, however, Corel Presentations 10 begins the transition automatically before the next slide is displayed.

Animating Objects

You can also add an animation to one or more graphic objects in a slide, such as clip art, and even to text boxes. With animation, graphics bounce onto the screen or fade into view. You can select an animation for every object, so when combined with the slide transition and cascading bullets, the entire presentation can be animated.

Follow these steps to animate a graphic object:

1. Display the slide in Slide Editor view.

2. Click on the object that you want to animate.

3. Select the Object Animation button in the property bar.

4. Choose the Animate Objects in Place option if you want the object to be animated from its position on the slide, or choose the Animate Objects Across Screen option to have the object move into position from the edge of the slide.

5. Choose an option from the Effects list to see a sample in the preview pane.

6. Select a direction and a speed.

7. If you already have an effect assigned to an object on the screen, you can choose the sequence that the current slide appears in. Pull down the Object Display Sequence list, and click on the number for the current object.

8. To play a sound file as the items are displayed, enter its path and name in the Sound box, or use the Browse button to locate it, and drag the slider below the box to choose its volume.

9. Click on OK.

 You cannot animate a title or subtitle in a slide placeholder. To create the same effect, replace the placeholder with a graphic text box and apply a transition or animation to it.

Animating Text

When you apply an animation to a text box, all of the text in the box enters the screen at one time. You can also animate each character individually as a special effect. Use these steps:

1. Select the text object.

2. Choose Macro from the Tools menu and click on Play.

3. Double-click on the macro Textanim.

In the dialog box that appears, select an effect and a speed, then click on OK. This macro works on text that you enter using the text tool in the tool palette, not with titles and subtitles. It converts the text to individual vector graphic objects and then applies the animation.

Advancing Animated Objects

Using the default settings, you have to click the mouse to begin each object transition or animation. If you want the items to appear automatically, choose options for the slide in the Display Sequence page of the Slide Properties dialog box, which you saw previously in this chapter.

You can, for example, have all of the objects appear automatically in sequence, or only after you click to display the first one. Here are the options you can select from:

- *Immediately after Slide Transition* starts to display the first object as soon as the slide appears—you do not have to click the mouse.

- *Using the Slide's Display Method (Manually)* shows the objects using whatever method you chose for the slide—either manually or delayed.

- *Before the Bulleted List* displays the objects before any bulleted list on the slide.

- *After the Bulleted List* displays the objects after the bulleted list.

Enhancing Slides with Sounds

Recorded music, sound effects, and narration make a slide show more entertaining and effective, adding another dimension to a purely visual presentation. You can insert a sound clip, a track from an audio CD, and your own narration into a slide.

There are two ways to insert sounds into a slide. You can add the sound as an object that plays automatically when the slide appears or as a SpeedLink that you have to click on or press a keystroke to play. You can insert three types of sound objects on a slide: WAV, MIDI, and tracks from an audio CD. You can add as many sounds as you want associated with SpeedLinks, and, if your system supports it, up to three sound objects that play simultaneously.

| NOTE | *WordPerfect Office 2002 comes with a selection of sound files that you can insert. They are in the WAV and MIDI formats in the Sounds subdirectory. Most of the filenames are self-explanatory.* |

To insert an existing sound clip or CD track, follow these steps:

1. Click on the Sound button in the property bar, or click on the Sound tab when the Slide Properties dialog box is onscreen, to see the dialog box in Figure 25-4.

   Use the Slide list to select the slide you want to add the sound to, or click on the Apply to All Slides in Slide Show checkbox.

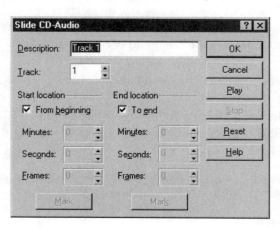

FIGURE 25-4   Slide Properties dialog box for sounds.

2. Click on the Browse button next to the WAV or MIDI boxes, and select the sound file you want to play. Click on the CD icon to display the dialog box shown here, and select the track you want to play.

3. Repeat the steps, if desired, to add one or more of the other types of sound files to the slide.

4. For each type of sound you add, you'll see a slider and additional options, as shown here. Adjust the volume, and choose to save the sound with the presentation, or to loop the sound to play repeatedly. Saving the sound with the slide, which is not available for a CD track, ensures that the sound is available whenever you play the slide show.

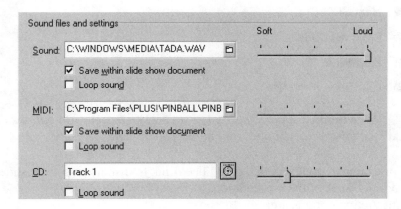

5. Repeat the procedure to add sounds to other slides.

6. Click on OK.

The sounds play when the slide appears.

You can record your own narration or sounds, and add them to the slide. Click on Record from the Sound dialog box to display the Sound Recorder application. Record and save the file, and then add it to the slide as just described.

Creating a SpeedLink

A *SpeedLink* is an object on the slide that you click on to perform an action. Use a SpeedLink to play a sound file, launch your Web browser and jump to a Web site, open another application, or move to another slide in the show.

For example, suppose you have one or more slides in the show that you might not want to display, depending on the audience. You can add a SpeedLink to the slide before these. When you choose not to display the slides, just click on the link to skip over them.

You can add a SpeedLink to any graphic object in the slide layer. When you point to a link, the mouse pointer appears as a hand—just click to perform the action. A link can perform two general categories of functions: a Go To event or an Action. A Go To event lets you display a slide. It can be linked to a specific slide number or to any of these options:

- Next Slide

- Previous Slide

- First Slide

- Last Slide

 SpeedLinks are particularly effective when assigned to buttons created with the Action Shapes tool in the Tool palette.

For example, you can click on a SpeedLink to display a specific slide or to return to the start of the presentation.

The Action options are:

- Play Sound

- Stop Sound

- Quit Show

- Launch Program

- Browse Internet

 You can use a SpeedLink to launch another WordPerfect Office 2002 application.

To add a SpeedLink, follow these steps:

1. Display the slide in Slide Editor view.

2. Click on the object that you want to use for the link.

3. Click on the SpeedLink button in the toolbar to see the dialog box in Figure 25-5.

4. Select either the Go To or Action option button, and then choose the specific event or action.

5. If you choose to play a sound, click on the Sound button to display the Sound dialog box, and then select any combination of Sound, MIDI, or CD tracks just as you previously learned. If you choose to launch a program, select the program file. For the Internet browser action, enter the URL of the Web site.

6. In the ActionLink Name text box, type a name for the link.

7. If you do not want the object to appear onscreen during the presentation or when printed, select the Invisible While Playing or Printing Slides

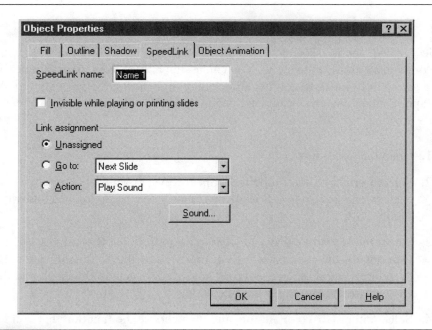

FIGURE 25-5   Creating a SpeedLink

checkbox. Use this when you want to perform an action but not take up screen space with the link. To find the link when showing the slides, move the mouse until the pointer changes to a hand.

8. Click on OK.

Editing and Viewing Links

After you create SpeedLinks, you can edit or delete them, or just display a list of the links in your presentation. Pull down the Tools menu, and click on SpeedLink List to see the SpeedLink List dialog box. Use the arrow keys to display the slide that has the link you are interested in. To change a link, or to delete it, click on the link name and then on Edit to display the ActionLink dialog box. To delete a link, click on the Unassigned option button. To change the link, just choose other options from the box, and then click on OK.

Using SpeedKeys

While a SpeedLink is associated with an object, a SpeedKey is associated with a slide or even an entire slide show. You can assign a SpeedKey, for example, to play a sound or to move to another slide at any time during the presentation. As with SpeedLinks, you can assign an SpeedKey to a Go To or an Action event. Here's how:

1. Open the slide show.

2. Select Format | Slide Properties | SpeedKeys, or right-click on the slide background and choose SpeedKeys. You'll see the dialog box shown in Figure 25-6.

3. Select the keystroke that you want to press from the Keystrokes list. The list contains the characters A to Z, followed by the 12 function keys. Below those are several system-assigned keystrokes, such as Escape to end the slide show and Home for the first slide.

4. Select either Go To or Action, and then choose the function that you want the link to perform. You cannot change the function of a system-assigned keystroke.

5. Click on OK.

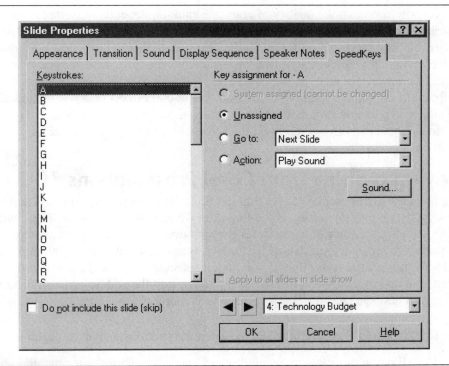

FIGURE 25-6   Creating a Speedkey

    To remove a SpeedKey, choose the keystroke in the SpeedKey dialog box, and then click on the Unassigned option button.

Playing a Slide Show

You can run your slide show in two ways—from within Corel Presentations 10 or directly from the Windows desktop.

- Run the slide show from Corel Presentations 10 when you are still working on it and may want to make changes as you go along.

- Run the show from Windows on machines that do not have Corel Presentations 10 installed or when you want a stand-alone application.

Keep in mind that the quality of your presentation depends to some extent on your hardware. Watching a slide show on a small laptop monitor or a low-resolution desktop monitor is not the best way to view your work. For greater impact, hook up your computer to a large-screen television or, better yet, to a projection device for an even larger screen.

In addition to the transition, animation, and sound effects that you've added to the slides, you can use the mouse as a pointing and highlighting tool. By dragging the mouse, you can draw directly on the screen, emphasizing major points.

Playing a Show from Corel Presentations 10

To play a show from within Corel Presentations 10, open the presentation and then click on the QuickPlay tab or on the Play Show button on the toolbar. There will be some delay between slides as Corel Presentations 10 displays them, but you can also select to create a QuickShow file, which is a separate disk file containing the slides. It runs a little faster than if you do not select to create a QuickShow file, but it can take up large amounts of disk space. If you edit the slides, you also have to generate a new QuickShow file to reflect the changes.

1. Start Corel Presentations 10, and open the slide show that you want to play.

2. Pull down the View menu, and select Play Slide Show to see the dialog box in Figure 25-7.

3. The presentation is set to start with whatever slide is selected in the current view. To start with a different slide, enter the slide number in the Beginning Slide text box.

4. Select a color and width for the highlighter. Choose a color that can be seen over the slide background and a width that supports the type of highlighting you want to do. Use a smaller width, for example, if you want to write on the screen without taking up a great deal of space. Use a larger width to highlight an area with a line or circle.

5. To save a QuickShow version of the presentation, click on the Create QuickShow button.

6. To run the show continuously, click on the Repeat Slide Show Until You Press 'Esc' checkbox.

7. To use the QuickShow file, click on Use QuickShow.

FIGURE 25-7   Playing a slide show

8. Click on Play.

9. If you are using manual advance, click on the left mouse button or press the SPACEBAR to move from slide to slide, to display animated bullets and objects, or to click on SpeedLinks.

10. Drag the mouse to draw in the screen with the highlighter. Your highlighting disappears when you change slides.

11. Press ESC if you want to end the presentation before the last slide.

 If you edit the slides, you have to re-create the QuickShow file.

Running the Show from Windows

Once you perfect your slide show, why go through the trouble of starting Corel Presentations 10 just to show it? By creating a Show on the Go, or runtime, version of the show, you can display it on a computer that doesn't have the Corel Presentations 10 program, which is ideal if you are on the road.

Integrate IT! *Save your slides as a WordPerfect 10 document—select Send To from the File menu, and click on WordPerfect 10.*

The runtime version is a special version of your presentation. The runtime file is a stand-alone version of your slide show that can be played on any computer even if Corel Presentations is not installed. The runtime file works with Windows

95, 98, 2000, ME, and NT. You can choose to create a runtime version that can run with any Windows display, or with one having the same resolution and color options as your machine.

To create a runtime version of your presentation, follow these steps:

1. Open the presentation that you want to play.

2. Click on the Show on the Go button on the property bar, or select Show on the Go from the File menu. A dialog box appears reporting the name of the file and the type of show that will be created.

3. Click on Change. A dialog box appears where you can select the drive to place the show and the option to e-mail the show. The runtime version requires only one file. If you plan to transport the show to another computer, select the floppy disk drive or other removable drive, so you don't have to copy the file yourself. Chances are, however, that the file will not fit on a floppy disk.

4. Select the drive, and then click on Next. A dialog box appears where you select to run the show on any Windows display, or only on a display matching the current setup. If you choose Any Windows Display, you can show the slides on a display at 640 x 480 resolution with 256 colors.

5. Make a choice from the box, and click on Finish to see the first Show on the Go dialog box.

6. Click on Create.

Try It Out

It is now time to practice adding transitions and other effects to your own slide presentation. We'll use the Technology presentation that we modified in Chapter 24. If you do not have that presentation, create a new slide show with at least six slides. We'll be adding a different transition effect to each slide, and some other animations, so you can see some of the possible effects available. In your own slide shows, limit the special effects so they do not interfere with the presentation itself.

1. Open the Technology slide show.

2. Click on the Slide Sorter tab, or choose Slide Sorter from the View menu.

3. Click on the first slide if it is not already selected.

4. Pull down the Transition list in the Property Bar and select Beam In.

5. Pull down the Direction list and select Bottom to Top.

6. Pull down the Speed list and select Medium.

7. Click on the second slide.

8. Pull down the Transition list and select Sweep to Center.

9. Now on your own, add the Burst In transition to slide 3; add the Weave transition to slide 4; add the Dissolve transition to slide 5; and add the Sweep transition to slide 6. The slides and their effects are shown in Figure 25-8.

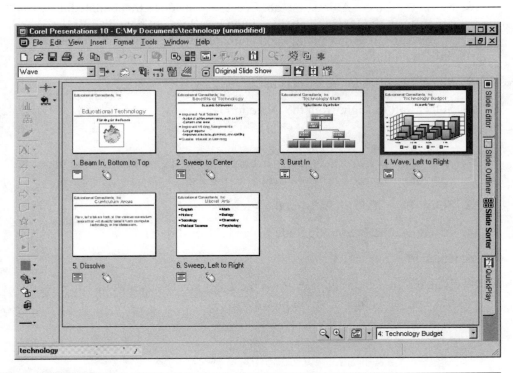

| FIGURE 25-8 | Effects added to slides |

10. Click on slide 2 and then on the Slide Editor tab.

11. Right-click on the bulleted list and choose Bulleted List Properties from the QuickMenu.

12. Click the Bullet Animation tab.

13. Choose Fly In from the Effects list.

14. Select the Display one at a time checkbox.

15. Click OK.

16. Click the tab for slide 6.

17. Right-click on the bulleted list on the left and choose Bulleted List Properties from the QuickMenu.

18. Select the Object Animation tab. Because you added this bulleted list as an object from the Insert menu, the dialog box does not contain a Bullet Animation tab. You can only add animation to the entire list, not the individual lines of the list as you could to slide 2.

19. Select Fly In from the Effects list.

20. Select Left to Right from the Direction list.

21. Click OK.

22. Now on your own, add the Fly In animation to the bulleted list on the right, choosing Right to Left from the Direction list.

23. Select Play Slide Show from the View menu.

24. Pull down the Beginning Slide list and select slide 1.

25. Click Play.

26. Watch as the slides appear. Press the Enter key to advance the slides and the animated objects within the slides.

Index

A

Abbreviations, using to speed typing, 175-177

Absolute addresses, 741

Absolute references, 585-586

Absolute tab, 237

Accessories (WordPerfect Office 2002), 6-8

Action Shapes list (Presentations Tool palette), 827

Activate Hypertext Links, 388

Active cell, 521

Active Cell Address box, 520

Active cell properties, 593-598

Active Cells dialog box, 593-598
    Alignment, 595
    Border, 597-598
    Cell Font, 594
    Constraints, 595-596
    Fill/Pattern, 598
    Numeric Format, 594-595
    Row/Column, 596

Active Sheet dialog box, 598-600

Active sheet properties, 598-600

Add Format dialog box, 610

Add New Form dialog box, 291

Address Book (CorelCENTRAL), 8-17
    publishing, 86-87
    searching for addresses, 15-17
    sorting addresses, 14-15
    using as a data file, 416
    using filters when searching, 15-17

Address information, templates for, 273

Adobe Acrobat Reader, 22

Advanced Find dialog box, 43

Agendas, in shared calendar, 112-113

Air Brush tool (Presentations), 834

Alarm
    setting in day planner, 96-97
    using Quick Alarm for, 97-98

Align and Distribute dialog box, 454

Aligning graphic objects, 454-455

Aligning text between margins, 227-228

Aligning text in cells, 538-539

Aligning text on the right, 228-229

H

T

INTERNATIONAL CONTACT INFORMATION

AUSTRALIA
McGraw-Hill Book Company Australia Pty. Ltd.
TEL +61-2-9417-9899
FAX +61-2-9417-5687
http://www.mcgraw-hill.com.au
books-it_sydney@mcgraw-hill.com

CANADA
McGraw-Hill Ryerson Ltd.
TEL +905-430-5000
FAX +905-430-5020
http://www.mcgrawhill.ca

**GREECE, MIDDLE EAST,
NORTHERN AFRICA**
McGraw-Hill Hellas
TEL +30-1-656-0990-3-4
FAX +30-1-654-5525

MEXICO (Also serving Latin America)
McGraw-Hill Interamericana Editores S.A. de C.V.
TEL +525-117-1583
FAX +525-117-1589
http://www.mcgraw-hill.com.mx
fernando_castellanos@mcgraw-hill.com

SINGAPORE (Serving Asia)
McGraw-Hill Book Company
TEL +65-863-1580
FAX +65-862-3354
http://www.mcgraw-hill.com.sg
mghasia@mcgraw-hill.com

SOUTH AFRICA
McGraw-Hill South Africa
TEL +27-11-622-7512
FAX +27-11-622-9045
robyn_swanepoel@mcgraw-hill.com

**UNITED KINGDOM & EUROPE
(Excluding Southern Europe)**
McGraw-Hill Education Europe
TEL +44-1-628-502500
FAX +44-1-628-770224
http://www.mcgraw-hill.co.uk
computing_neurope@mcgraw-hill.com

ALL OTHER INQUIRIES Contact:
Osborne/McGraw-Hill
TEL +1-510-549-6600
FAX +1-510-883-7600
http://www.osborne.com
omg_international@mcgraw-hill.com